MARRIAGE AND THE FAMILY

Diversity and Strengths

MARRIAGE AND THE FAMILY
Diversity and Strengths

SECOND EDITION

David H. Olson
University of Minnesota

John DeFrain
University of Nebraska

Mayfield Publishing Company
Mountain View, California
London • Toronto

This book about families
is dedicated to our families

Copyright © 1997, 1994 by Mayfield Publishing Company

Library of Congress Cataloging-in-Publication Data

Olson, David H.
   Marriage and the family : diversity and strengths / David H. Olson, John DeFrain. —2nd ed.
      p.   cm.
   Includes bibliographical references and index.
   ISBN 1-55934-656-6
      1. Family—United States—Psychological aspects.   2. Marriage—United States—Psychological aspects.   3. Circumplex Model of Marital and Family Systems.   4. Family assessment—United States.
   I. DeFrain, John D.   II. Title.
   HQ536.046   1996
   306.8'0973—dc20   96-9872
                                                                            CIP

Manufactured in the United States of America
10 9 8 7 6 5 4 3 2

Mayfield Publishing Company
1280 Villa Street
Mountain View, CA 94041

Sponsoring editor, Franklin C. Graham; developmental editor, Kathleen Engelberg; production editor, Lynn Rabin Bauer; manuscript editor, Beverley DeWitt; text designers, Gary Head and Jeanne M. Schreiber; cover designer, Jeanne M. Schreiber; cover image, Karen Barbour; art editor, Bettina Borer; photo researcher, Brian Pecko; illustrators, Joan Carol and Mark. H. Schultz; manufacturing manager, Randy Hurst. The text was set in 10/12 Janson Text by York Graphic Services and printed on 45# Somerset Matte by R. R. Donnelley & Sons.

Brief Contents

Contents

PART II Developing Intimate Relationships 113

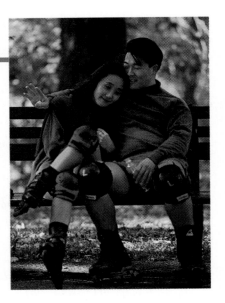

PART III   Dynamics of Intimate Relationships   221

PART IV Stages of Marriage and Family Life 347

PART V   Challenges and Opportunities   441

RESOURCES

Preface

Our colleague and friend, the late Dr. David R. Mace, once said, "Nothing in the world could make human life happier than to greatly increase the number of strong families." Our goal in writing *Marriage and the Family: Diversity and Strengths*, Second Edition, is to provide students with knowledge about families and relationships that will help them move toward Mace's goal.

Three distinctive themes have guided our efforts in writing this book. First, we stress that the growing *diversity* of families in our society is a positive, enriching trend. Second, we express our belief that certain family *strengths* help families maintain themselves and weather the inevitable storms of life. And third, we emphasize the concept that families are *systems* of relationships, functioning both within themselves and with other systems beyond themselves, such as society at large.

Our intent, further, is to make the concepts and ideas presented in this book useful and meaningful enough to students that they will want to apply them to their own lives. We hope to help students integrate intellectual ideas and personal experience, thereby enriching both. Numerous features of the book, ranging from personal stories related by real people to student activities at the ends of chapters, are designed to help students see the relevance of the material to their lives. And although the text deals with complex ideas and materials, it is written in a style accessible both to students new to the field of family studies and to the more experienced reader.

Diversity and Strengths

Family diversity is a key theme in this book. Wherever possible, we consider how concepts, research, and theories about the family apply to families of diverse ethnic and cultural backgrounds. We also focus on the diversity in structure that characterizes families today, looking at the many different forms that "family" can take. Diversity in sexual orientation—gay and lesbian relationships and families in our society—is a third type of diversity we explore. The theme of diversity is introduced in Chapter 1, "Perspectives on Intimate Relationships," and discussed in detail in Chapter 2, "Cultural Diversity: Family Strengths and Challenges." As a prominent characteristic of our society and the world, family diversity is integrated into discussions throughout the book.

Family strengths is another key theme in this book. The family strengths perspective is based on the premise that if you approach families from a "problem" perspective, you will find problems. If you look for strengths, you will find strengths. Growing numbers of family educators and family therapists are using this approach today, helping families recognize their own strengths and use them as a foundation for positive growth. In Chapter 1, we identify a number of strengths that have been found to be present in healthy families all over the world. Throughout the book, we show how these strengths help families provide healthy settings for the growth of individual family members, face challenges, and solve problems.

Although diversity and strengths are integrated throughout the book, three chapters focus especially on these themes: Chapter 2 highlights the family strengths of diverse ethnic and cultural groups; Chapter 14, "Family Stress and Coping," examines how families can use their strengths to manage crisis and stress; and Chapter 18, "Strengthening Families in the Future," looks at how families and societies can work together to build healthier societies in the future.

Family Systems, the Family Circumplex Model, and Family Strengths

We present many theories of family in this book, but we focus especially on family systems theory. Recognizing that the family unit is a system of interdependent parts, we look at how families maintain themselves and yet change, how family members can be separate and yet connected, and how communication facilitates the processes of change and growth. We focus on communication and conflict resolution skills as essential tools for creating healthy intimate relationships. We also look at how families can learn to function well within the larger systems of community and society.

The Family Circumplex Model, an assessment tool developed by David Olson and colleagues, is based on concepts from family systems theory. Focusing on the three dimensions of cohesion, flexibility, and communication, the Family Circumplex Model has been used in hundreds of studies to help researchers understand and evaluate families. The model is introduced in Chapter 3, "Understanding Relationships in Marriage and Family," and studies that have used the model as a theoretical base are reported throughout the text. An ongoing family case study project is described in *The Resource Book* to help instructors show students how the Family Circumplex Model is applied.

The family strengths perspective, developed by Nick Stinnett, John DeFrain, and many colleagues across the country, is also used throughout the text as a model for understanding and evaluating families. It identifies and focuses on six key qualities of healthy families: commitment, appreciation and affection, positive communication, time together, spiritual well-being, and the ability to cope with stress and crisis. The research driving this model has involved thousands of family members in the United States and around the world. In this book, we show how the family strengths perspective and the Family Circumplex Model, two independently derived models of healthy families, fit together and enhance each other in the study of how families succeed. The integration of concepts from the two models and from family systems theory throughout the book gives *Marriage and the Family* an unusually high degree of thematic coherence and unity.

Changes to the Second Edition

A good textbook is like a healthy family: It grows and changes in positive directions over the years. Although the first edition of *Marriage and the Family: Diversity and Strengths* was published just three years ago, this second edition incorporates a number of improvements, many of them based on the suggestions of students and instructors. Changes include the following:

- The field of family science continues to grow explosively. This edition of *Marriage and the Family* includes the newest research and latest statistics available. Cutting-edge literature has been included from such sources as the *Journal of Marriage and the Family, Family Relations, Journal of Family Psychology, Child Development, Family Process*, and *Journal of Marital and Family Therapy*. We used several family science, psychology, sociology, and humanities databases to locate new journal articles, books, and other resources. Treatment of many topics has been substantially updated and revised; for example, material from 20 new sources has been included in our revision of Chapter 14, "Family Stress and Coping."

- Family systems theory is more thoroughly and clearly described in Chapter 1, and the relationships among systems theory, the Family Circumplex Model, and the family strengths perspective have been clarified. We hope that students will see how interrelated approaches can provide coherence and richness to family studies.

- More than 60 new "personal stories" have been included in this edition to bridge the gap between concept and "real life." The voices of real people are heard as they describe their family relationships, their struggles and achievements, their disappointments and hopes. These stories, drawn from the authors' files, illustrate family dynamics in a variety of situations, settings, and life stages. They touch on such issues as single parenting, sexual intimacy, family violence, managing money, dividing chores, expressing difficult emotions, adjusting to the death of a family member, and many more. One of our goals in including these stories is to help students realize how much they share with families everywhere.

- New material on diversity and family strengths has been added to this edition and integrated throughout. Chapter 18 in particular now offers current views on these topics, ranging from personal strategies for strengthening relationships to statements by the United Nations in support of the International Year of the Family.

- Several changes in organization have helped make the book clearer and more focused. As mentioned earlier, the discussion of family systems theory in Chapter 1 has been greatly expanded and clarified. Material on the family strengths perspective has been moved to Chapter 1 from later chapters to provide a more effective introduction to this model. The Family Circumplex Model is introduced in Chapter 3, and its use is clearly explained. For interested students, the Family Circumplex Scales are given in Resource Section A (formerly Resource Section F) to show exactly how a practitioner applies the model.

Material in the chapters in Part II, "Developing Intimate Relationships," has been rearranged to reflect a more realistic grouping of topics. Chapter 4, which formerly covered friendship, singlehood, and cohabitation, now covers friendship, love, and intimacy—the emotional, affective aspects of relationships. Chapter 5, formerly covering love and intimacy, now covers singlehood, dating, and mate selection. The contents of Chapter 7 (dating and mate selection) have been incorporated into Chapter 5. Chapter 6, on sexual intimacy, remains the same. Thus, Part II now has three chapters rather than four. The topic of cohabitation, formerly in Chapter 4, now appears in Chapter 11, "Cohabitation, Marriage, and Early Married Life," reflecting the virtual institutionalization of this living pattern in our society as a new "stage" of family life.

Material on pregnancy and childbirth (Chapter 13 in the first edition) now appears as Resource Section D. Like other topics included in the Resource Section (such as sexual anatomy and response, contraception, abortion, and sexually transmissible diseases), the topics of pregnancy and childbirth are certainly important for students to understand but are not the main thrust of this book. We hope that students will get good use out of all the materials in the Resource Section.

In sum, then, the second edition of *Marriage and the Family* has 18 rather than 20 chapters and 7 rather than 6 individual resource sections.

- The visual appeal of *Marriage and the Family* has been greatly enhanced in this edition. Full color throughout, fresh photographs, and a revised design make the second edition a book that students will find attractive and enjoyable to use.

Content and Organization

This textbook has been written for students who are interested in learning more about themselves, their family, and their close relationships. Each chapter provides a comprehensive and up-to-date look at salient issues. Each chapter contains a chapter outline, a chapter summary, activities, and suggested readings. Most chapters contain a list of key terms.

An awareness of how the textbook is organized is a prerequisite to using it successfully. Due to the growing complexity of the marriage and family field, the three chapters in Part I, "Introduction," emphasize the critical themes of diversity and strengths and their centrality to the subject of marriage and family. Chapter 1 presents "Perspectives on Intimate Relationships," including the realities of marriage and family life today; defining marriage and family; trends in marriage and the family; conceptual frameworks for studying marriage and the family; and family science as an emerging field. Chapter 2, "Cultural Diversity: Family Strengths and Challenges," discusses the nature of cultural diversity; family strengths, stereotypes, and challenges in various ethnic and cultural groups; and issues in cross-cultural family studies. In Chapter 3, "Understanding Relationships in Marriage and Family," the focus is on cohesion, flexibility, and communication. The Family Circumplex Model is described as a tool for understanding families.

Part II, "Developing Intimate Relationships," provides a foundation for understanding how individuals pair up and move toward intimate and committed relationships. Chapter 4, "Friendship, Love, and Intimacy" explores the differences between friends and lovers; how people move from intimate experiences to intimate relationships; and intimacy games people play. Chapter 5, "Singlehood, Dating, and Mate Selection," looks at the pros and cons of being single, and then explores how people select a mate. In Chapter 6, "Sexual Intimacy," the focus is on sex and society; American sexual behavior as uncovered by various surveys; sex education; premarital sexual behavior; marital and extramarital sexual behavior; and how couples can move toward sexual health.

In Part III we emphasize the "Dynamics of Intimate Relationships." Chapter 7 is a discussion of "Gender Roles and Power in the Family," beginning with traditional and contemporary views of gender roles; continuing on to theories of gender-role development and change; and ending with a discussion of power in families. In Chapter 8 the subject is "Communication and Intimacy," beginning with perspectives on communication; using communication to develop and maintain intimacy; and types of talk. Chapter 9, "Conflict and Conflict Resolution," outlines the hierarchy of conflict in intimate relationships; notes the relationship between intimacy and conflict; and shows ways to resolve conflict successfully. Chapter 10, "Managing Economic Resources," discusses the stresses related to family financial issues; why finances cause family problems; family income and expenses; the process of family financial resource management; and uses and abuses of credit in our society.

In Part IV, "Stages of Marriage and Family Life," we look in Chapter 11 at "Cohabitation, Marriage, and Early Married Life." The chapter begins with a discussion of cohabitation as a possible way of preparing for marriage, followed by a formula for successful marriage; reasons for marrying; parental perspective and influence on marriage; preparing for marriage; using the Family Circumplex Model in premarital counseling; and the wedding and early years of marriage. Chapter 12, "Parenthood," begins with a discussion of the challenge of parenthood; continues on to look at parenting and the Family Circumplex Model; and ends with a discussion of various important issues in parenting. Chapter 13, "Midlife and Older Couples," discusses family life in the middle years, including sexuality, middle-aged marriage, empty or spacious nests, the sandwich generation, and grandparenthood; the discussion of family life in the later years focuses on definitions of old age, conventional wisdom about aging, retirement, family dynamics and the aging couple, and losing a spouse.

In Part V the focus is on "Challenges and Opportunities." Chapter 14, "Family Stress and Coping," looks at cultural perspectives on family stress; the curvilinear nature of stress; stressors families face; family stress theory; family coping strategies; the biopsychosocial approach and family problems; medical care and the family; and the family's influence on health behaviors. Chapter 15, "Family Problems, Domestic Violence, and Alcohol Abuse," begins with a discussion of family problems and family systems theory and continues with physical abuse and neglect of children; sexual abuse of children; sibling and child-to-parent abuse; and alcohol problems in families. Chapter 16, "Divorce and Adjustment," discusses trends in divorce; how to understand divorce; and how people adjust to divorce. Chapter 17, "Single-Parent Families and Stepfamilies," looks at the changing picture of the family; single-parent families from a strengths perspective; and stepfamilies from a strengths perspective. Chapter 18, the concluding chapter of the text, is entitled "Strengthening Families in the Future." We discuss the future of families from a global perspective and present some thoughts about the future of our own individual families. The chapter then focuses on personal strategies to strengthen marriage and family relationships, and ends with recommendations for making every year an International Year of the Family, and how we can work together in our communities and the community of nations to help families succeed in life's most important task: creating healthy, satisfying human relationships.

The goal of a marriage or of a family must be more than simply to survive; it must be to thrive. Couples and families must be proactive rather than reactive in dealing with ongoing relationship issues. Strong relationships, strong marriages, and strong families require time, energy, and commitment. The rewards of these investments include an enhanced and healthy emotional and physical life for every family member. Finally, strong families also provide the foundation for a strong and caring society.

Ancillary Materials

This textbook is accompanied by an attitude assessment inventory called AWARE and a 10-segment custom video. The teaching package also includes *The Resource Book: Teaching with Marriage and the Family*, a computerized test bank using Chariot software for Windows and Macintosh, and a student *Study Guide*. New to this edition is a two-hour custom videotape with segments keyed to important issues in the book. Topics presented include gender roles, contraception, STDs, and communication. Contact your Mayfield sales representative for more details.

AWARE (AWareness of Attitudes and Relationship Expectations) is an attitude inventory that can be administered the first day or week of class. As an attitude scale, AWARE explores 13 content areas with 10 items per category (a total of 130 items). Student answer sheets are computer scored; each student receives a 13-page scored summary evaluating her or his attitudes. Instructors receive a general report containing results for the entire class. Each student's AWARE report is personal and private, designed to allow the student to compare his or her responses on the attitude scale with information presented in the textbook in class. Guidelines and procedures for integrating the AWARE Inventory into the course are provided in *The Resource Book*, along with a chart illustrating how AWARE correlates with and reinforces specific text chapters.

For each chapter of the textbook, *The Resource Book* includes a chapter outline, learning objectives, a summary, key terms for most chapters, lecture notes, activities, and suggested readings. *The Resource Book* contains guidelines for using the AWARE Inventory in the course, descriptions of and suggestions for using the videotapes with specific textbook topics and chapters, strategies for using Family Quads in class, and instructions for the Family Case Study assignment. The test bank with answer key, included in *The Resource Book*, contains about 1,550 items, including multiple-choice, true/false, short answer, and essay questions. Hundreds of the items included have been classroom tested. *The Resource Book* also includes 63 transparency masters.

The *Study Guide to Accompany Marriage and the Family: Diversity and Strengths* has been written by Dr. Jeanne Kohl of the University of Washington. It includes review materials to help students master the concepts in each chapter of the textbook, prepare for examinations with practice tests, assess their personal attitudes and beliefs, and apply their knowledge to real-life situations. To further the assessment and application objectives, each chapter of the *Study Guide* concludes with a Personal Involvement Assessment and a Knowledge in Action exercise. The Personal Involvement Assessment gives students the opportunity to examine in some depth one of the important issues discussed in the textbook (for example, stereotyping, attitudes about money, accepting criticism). Knowledge in Action exercises highlight key research studies on important topics. Each exercise is designed to encourage students to apply what they have learned to real-life situations involving others. Projects include content analyses, interviews, and surveys.

Acknowledgments

We wish to thank the following people for their thoughtful reviews of the manuscript: Esther Devall, New Mexico State University; Genie H. Dyer, Baylor University; Preston M. Dyer, Baylor University; Gerald E. Harris, University of Houston; Eugene W. Jacobs, Greenville Technical College; Ed Long, Central Michigan University; Nilufer Medora, California State University at Long Beach; Gail Overbey, Southeast Missouri State University; Kay Pasley, University of North Carolina at Greensboro; Shulamit Ritblatt, San Diego State University; and Kenrick S. Thompson, Northern Michigan University.

About the Authors

David H. Olson, Ph.D., is professor of family social science at the University of Minnesota, where he has been for more than 20 years. He is founder and president of Life Innovations; a past president of the National Council on Family Relations (NCFR); a past president of the Upper Midwest Association for Marriage and Family Therapists (UMAMFT); a fellow and clinical member of the American Association for Marital and Family Therapy (AAMFT); and a fellow of the American Psychological Association (APA). Olson is also a member of the editorial boards of six family journals. He has received numerous awards, including the Distinguished Contribution to Family Therapy Research Award from both AAMFT and the American Family Therapy Association (AFTA). Olson has written or edited more than 20 books, including *Families: What Makes Them Work, Circumplex Model, Power in Families, Treating Relationships*, and 10 volumes of the *Inventory of Marriage and Family Literature*. He has published more than 100 articles with the theme of bridging family research, theory, and practice. Olson and his colleagues at the University of Minnesota have developed the Circumplex model of Marital and Family Systems and a variety of couple and family assessment tools, including PREPARE, ENRICH, FACES, PAIR, and AWARE. He is happily married to Karen Olson, who has provided companionship and support throughout this and numerous other projects. They have three terrific children (Hans, Amy, and Chris) and four wonderful grandchildren (Adrienne, Evan, Chelsea, and Alex). Olson has been blessed with a fun-loving and caring family that continues to sustain and support him.

John DeFrain, Ph.D., is a professor of family science at the University of Nebraska-Lincoln and has focused his professional and personal energy for the past 25 years in better understanding how families learn to live happily together. He received his doctorate from the University of Wisconsin-Madison in 1975 and has been on the faculty of UNL for more than 20 years. He has experience as a newspaper reporter and preschool and kindergarten teacher; has codirected a graduate training program in marriage and family therapy; was cofounder of the National Symposium on Building Family Strengths; and has been a consultant to courts, universities, churches, agencies, and individual families on marriage, parenting, grief, divorce, and child custody issues. DeFrain has co-authored three dozen professional articles on family issues and 15 books, including *Secrets of Strong Families, Sudden Infant Death: Enduring the Loss, Stillborn: The Invisible Death, On Our Own: A Single Parent's Survival Guide, Parents in Contemporary America: A Sympathetic View*, and *Good Families*. He and his wife and best friend, Nikki DeFrain, M.S., are the parents of three daughters: Amie, 27, Alyssa, 20, and Erica, 18. Nikki was especially important in the development and writing of this textbook, offering support in innumerable areas of the project and expertise in her own areas of study: life-span human development in a family context and, especially, older people. The DeFrains are very interested in the understanding of family strengths and challenges from a global perspective, have conducted Fulbright-sponsored research in the South Pacific, and recently led 22 students in a semester-abroad study tour of Europe.

MARRIAGE AND THE FAMILY

Diversity and Strengths

PART I

Introduction

Perspectives on Intimate Relationships

Family life is a microcosm of life itself. It can bring both great joy and excruciating pain. A healthy family can be a valuable resource during difficult times. Conversely, an unhealthy or dysfunctional family can create problems for family members that will persist from one generation to the next.

The family is perhaps society's oldest and most resilient institution. From the beginning of human life, people have grouped themselves into families to find emotional, physical, and communal support. Although in recent years social commentators have predicted the demise of the family, it not only survives but continues to change and evolve. Family structures may vary around the world, but the value of "family" endures.

Family life, even in successful families, is not always easy. This is perhaps because human beings are much like porcupines—we find it necessary to sleep close together to keep warm, but our prickliness also makes living at close quarters perilous. Families can provide intimacy and closeness, but with them come disagreement and conflict.

"We sure have our ups and downs in our family," Rachel, a 22-year-old college student in Ohio noted. "But I think we're a good family. Scratch that, I think we're a great family. We bicker sometimes and Dad's so conservative, but when you're in trouble, the family is always there to help.

"It was terrible when Mom and Dad divorced. I was 12 at the time and I hated Dad for 3 years. But today I can see things a bit differently. Maybe it's better they're apart. They were staying together the last several years just for us kids, and that wasn't working out for anybody very well. They went to counseling for a long time, but in the end they separated.

"It's a lot better today. I even get along with Dad pretty well. He's been a great help for me. I wouldn't be here at the U without him.

"Sometimes I don't let my family know how much I really care for all of them, but I do. I plan to get married some day, and I'll probably have a child or maybe two. And my family will not really change through all of it. It will only get bigger. We'll still look at the world differently, and I suppose Mom will always be there trying to smooth things out between us. We'll just go on and on and on.

"Because we're Family!"

If you had a happy family life when you were growing up, you should feel fortunate. Such an experience provides an important foundation and model for developing a happy family of your own. If you grew up in a troubled family, the task of building a strong family of your own will be more difficult. But the task is possible. Countless individuals have transcended the family they grew up in and created healthy, new families for themselves and their loved ones.

This book provides a realistic portrayal of marriage and the family today. Its purpose is to help individuals become more aware of important personal and relationship issues and to give people the tools to develop and maintain satisfying intimate relationships.

Realities of Marriage and Family Life

Most human beings search for intimate experiences and relationships throughout their lives. Although most individuals are able to create some type of intimate relationship, they often have difficulty maintaining and increasing their levels of intimacy over time. As a result, many people experience marital problems, and many marriages end in divorce.

Marriage and the Family Are Changing

Statistics on divorce, domestic violence, and alcohol and other drug abuse, as well as stories of families in crisis, paint a negative picture of the American family. These snapshots of troubled families may be newsworthy, but they are not new. For decades, many respected social scientists have predicted that marriage and the family would not survive. For example, in 1927, psychologist John B. Watson predicted, "In 50 years, unless there is some change, the tribal custom of marriage will no longer exist." He believed marriage would disappear because family standards had broken down. In 1937, Pitirim Sorokin, a respected Harvard sociologist, wrote, "The family as a sacred union of husband and wife, of parents and children, will continue to disintegrate." Ten years later, Carl Zimmerman, also a Harvard sociologist, noted, "There is little left now, within the family itself or the moral code, to hold the family together" (Bernard, 1970, p. 42).

Another commentator wrote, "The last 50 years have apparently changed the marriage relation from a permanent and lifelong state to a union existing for the pleasure of the parties. The change thus swiftly wrought is so revolutionary, involving the very foundations of human society, that we must believe it to be the result not of any temporary conditions." The only surprising thing about this statement is that it was made in 1887 and referred to changes in marriage between 1837 and 1887 (Reiss & Lee, 1988, p. 309).

Although some professionals emphasize the decline of the family, others see it as being in a state of transition. As Ernest Burgess stated in 1953, "Certainly marriage and the family in the U.S. are in the process of rapid change. But is it change for the worse? Perhaps it may be for the better" (Bernard, 1970, p. 43). In a similar vein, David and Vera Mace, pioneers in the marriage and family enrichment movement in Great Britain and the United States, argued that "marriage has not failed—it is simply in transition" (Mace & Mace, 1980, p. 260). Skolnick and Skolnick (1977), in their classic study *Family in Transition*, clearly illustrated the dramatic changes in family life over the centuries. In fact, one of the salient characteristics of the family is its ability to adapt to changing times and new challenges.

What are today's families like? Current trends include later marriage, fewer children, more divorce, more single-parent families and stepfamilies, more working mothers, greater need for day care, more child abuse, more spouse abuse, and less connection to kin networks.

One of the strengths of the family as an institution is its ability to adapt to changing social, economic, and political conditions. American families today reflect various current trends in our society. High divorce and remarriage rates, for example, have led to more families like this one, in which one or both partners bring children from a previous marriage and then have another child together.

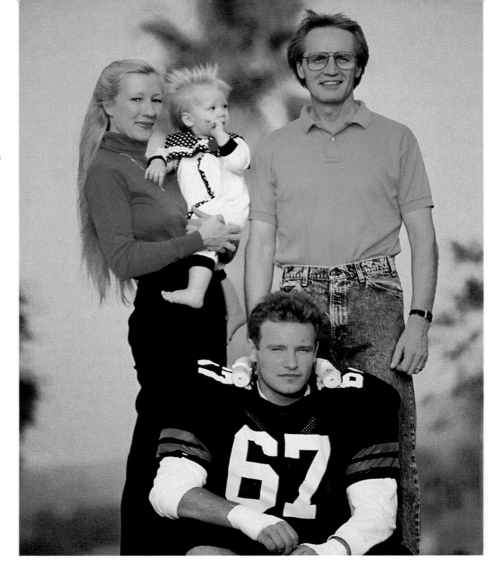

Pessimists and optimists disagree about how to interpret these trends and what to do about them. The pessimists see recent changes as an indication that marriage and family are in serious trouble and are declining in their significance to society. They believe we need to return to a more traditional value system to curtail these negative trends. The optimists, on the other hand, see recent changes as a reflection of the flexibility of marriage and family and the ability of these institutions to adapt to the increasing stresses of modern life. They believe the family will survive and thrive.

In fact, marriage and the family *do* continue to survive, despite all the predictions of their imminent collapse. Moreover, marriage remains the most popular voluntary institution in our society, with more than 90% of the population marrying at least once (Glick, 1989).

For a look at how family patterns in the United States have evolved over the course of our history, see Box 1.1.

BOX 1.1

Family Types over Time

Families don't exist in isolation; they are embedded in a particular society, a particular culture, a particular historical period. Thus, they evolve over time and reflect the beliefs and values of the larger society. Family patterns in turn influence how individuals and their family systems operate.

William Doherty, of the University of Minnesota, has developed a useful framework for understanding changing family patterns (Doherty, 1992). The four family types he identifies are the institutional family, the psychological family, the pluralistic family, and the intentional family. Each type represents a cultural ideal of family life in the United States in a broadly defined historical period. (There is some overlap between time periods as the new type emerges and the earlier type recedes.) Characteristics of the four types follow.

Institutional Family: Pre-1925

This family type is organized around economic production, with the father as the authority. The kinship network is strong, and the family has many community connections.

- *Marriage:* Functional partnership.
- *Important aspects:* Family loyalty, family tradition, and solidarity.
- *Chief value:* Responsibility.

Psychological Family: 1925–1975

This family type is more nuclear, more mobile, less tied to kin networks, and less connected to the broader community than the institutional family.

- *Marriage:* Friendship, love, and attraction.
- *Important aspects:* Personal satisfaction of family members.
- *Chief value:* Satisfaction.

Pluralistic Family: 1975–1990

This family type encompasses a diversity of family structures, including single-parent families, stepfamilies, and never-married families. Gender equality and personal freedom are increasingly important themes. Women become more independent as they work outside the home and see marriage as less necessary. Other variations include dual-career families and gay-male and lesbian families. There is no broad cultural consensus on the ideal type of family structure.

- *Marriage:* Changing forms.
- *Important aspects:* Diversity and tolerance.
- *Chief value:* Flexibility.

Intentional Families: 1990 and into the Future

Families of the future will combine elements of the psychological and pluralistic family types. Couple and family relationships will be more intentional, and interest in maintaining quality relationships will grow.

- *Marriage:* Changing forms.
- *Important aspects:* Equality and diversity.
- *Chief value:* Flexibility and responsibility.

Why Do So Many Marriages End in Divorce?

Although marriage is popular, it is not necessarily lasting. Based on current trends, more than 50% of all recent U.S. marriages are likely to end in divorce (U.S. Bureau of the Census, 1995). And even though 50% survive, the quality of some of those marriages may be very poor. Many marriages last in which one partner is unhappy; typically, it is the wife who is more unhappy than the husband. A Gallup poll (1989) found that 40% of married individuals had considered leaving their partners, 20% said they were dissatisfied with their marriage about half the time, and 28% had already been divorced at least once. Why are there so many divorces and unhappy marriages in our society? First, many people go into marriage with unrealistic expectations about it. Second, many marry the wrong person for the wrong reasons. Third, marriage is a very difficult type of relationship, even if one chooses a partner wisely.

In intact marriages, intimacy and quality often decline over time. Couples face many challenges together, including disagreements over money, difficulties communicating, questions regarding past friendships with members of the other sex, the complexities of blending two family systems together and dealing with in-laws, sexual relations, the question of whether to have children, and decisions about how to divide household tasks. Even newlywed couples face serious problems during the first year of marriage. A study of several hundred newlywed couples found that 63% had serious problems related to their finances, 51% had serious doubts about their marriage lasting, 49% had significant marital problems, 45% were not satisfied with their sexual relationship, 42% found marriage harder than they had expected, and 35% stated that their partner was often critical of them (Arond & Pauker, 1987).

Many couples cannot handle the major stressors in married life. They simply are not mature enough, sufficiently committed to the relationship, or creative enough in their problem-solving abilities. We discuss these issues and challenges in detail in later chapters of this book.

Defining Marriage and Family

Few people today live in the so-called traditional family, with Dad at work and Mom at home with the kids. Only about 25% of all families in the United States match this model. In addition to the diversity of types of family structure, families may vary in cultural or ethnic background, income, size, and longevity. Today, there are many possible family structures, not one "right" way for a family to be organized.

What Is a Family?

"Family" can be defined in many ways. One dictionary offers four definitions:

> **1.** A fundamental social group in society consisting of a man and woman and their offspring. **2.** A group of persons sharing a common ancestry. **3.** Lineage, esp. distinguished lineage. **4.** All the members of a household under one roof. (*American Heritage Dictionary*, 2nd College Ed., 1985)

BOX 1.2

Some Definitions of Family

A family is any two or more related people living in a household.

> U.S. BUREAU OF THE CENSUS, 1995

Family is a group of people who love and care for each other.

> ASSOCIATED PRESS, RANDOM SAMPLE OF 1,200 PEOPLE

A family is defined as two or more persons who share resources, share responsibility for decisions, share values and goals, and have a commitment to one another over time.

> AMERICAN ASSOCIATION OF FAMILY AND CONSUMER SCIENCES

Families provide emotional, physical, and economic mutual aid to their members. Ideally such families are characterized by intimacy, intensity, continuity, and commitment among their members.

> FAMILY SERVICE OF AMERICA (*definition provided by a network of 300 families*)

The definition of a family "should not rest on fictitious legal distinctions or genetic history" but instead should be based on the functional and psychological qualities of the relationship: the "exclusivity and longevity" of relationship; the "level of emotional and financial commitment"; the "reliance placed upon one another for daily family services"; and how the couple (members) "conducted their everyday lives and held themselves out to society."

> NEW YORK STATE SUPREME COURT

A family is . . . cohabiting groups of some duration composed of persons in intimate relations based on biology, law, custom or choice and usually economically interdependent.

> FAMILY POLICY IN THE 1980s: CONTROVERSY AND CONSENSUS by Joan Aldous and Wilfried Dumon, published in the *Journal of Marriage and the Family*, November 1990

Any definition of family should be broad enough to encompass a range of family structures, dynamics, and functions. Our definition of **family** is two or more people who are committed to each other and who share intimacy, resources, decisions, and values. This definition is inclusive rather than exclusive and allows for diversity in family structure, family values, and ethnic groups.

Other definitions of family are given in Box 1.2, including the definition used by the U.S. Bureau of the Census: any two or more related people living in a household. Although these definitions vary, they tend to emphasize emotional connections, commitment, and the sharing of resources between people. In many cases, the importance of family increases when individuals need emotional support. In Robert Frost's (1946) words, "Home is the place where, when you have to go there, they have to take you in."

"I get pretty fed up with people putting down single parents," said Clinton, a 23-year-old college student from a small town in North Carolina. "Sometimes the way people talk, it's as if a family with only one parent isn't even a family at all.

"Well, I come from a family. A really strong family. My mom worked two jobs to keep us fed and clothed. She's a great person and [chuckling] tough as nails. She didn't take any stuff from any of us boys. There were six kids in our home—four boys and two girls—when I was growing up.

"Dad's an alcoholic. He beat Mom bad when I was 14 or 15, and she took us and left. It's good she did. Somebody might have gotten killed. Maybe Dad [smiling]. I was just getting big enough to put up a good fight.

"Mom yelled at us and loved us and kept us in order. I'm the first ever in our family to be graduating from college, and three of the other kids are in college right now, too. They'll make it for sure, and we'll all be able to take care of Mom when she gets old. She's had a real hard life and deserves our support after what she's done for us.

"One kid, Andrew, he got in trouble as a teenager and spent some time in a detention center. He got in with a bad group, and Mom couldn't stop him. But I'm going back home when I graduate, and I'll be working in a family-service agency. I'll be able to help other families like ours, and I'll be able to keep on Andrew's case till he gets his life straightened out also."

What Is Marriage?

Marriage is by nature a multifaceted institution. We define **marriage** as the emotional and legal commitment of two people to share emotional and physical intimacy, various tasks, and economic resources. Although people typically think of marriage as between individuals of two different sexes, same-sex couples are also interested in marriage. The definition of marriage used in this text can be applied to same-sex couples, except that there is no legal commitment. At the time this book went to press, marriage licenses for same-sex relationships were not issued by any state in the United States. However, several states (including Hawaii) are considering bills that would make same-sex marriages legal.

The following nine characteristics of marriage were identified by Carlfred Broderick (1984). A former president of the National Council on Family Relations, Broderick found these characteristics to be common across income levels, educational levels, and ethnic groups in the United States:

- Marriage is a demographic event. Each marriage creates a social unit in society.

- Marriage is the joining of two family and social networks. When individuals marry, they marry not only each other but their partner's family and friends. Friends of both partners may be affected; only those friends liked by both partners tend to remain friends of the couple.

- Marriage is a legal contract between the couple and the state. Each state specifies the rights and responsibilities of the partners.

- Marriage is an economic union. A married couple usually becomes a single financial unit for most purposes. As a group, married couples are probably society's most important financial decision makers—buying, selling, borrowing, and sharing resources as one.

Table 1.1 Five Key Changes in Marriage and the Family		
	1960	**1993**
Percentage of childbirths outside of marriage	5	28
Percentage of teenage mothers who are unmarried	15	64
Divorced individuals per 1,000 married individuals	35	130
Percentage of children living with only one parent	9	30
Percentage of adult life spent with spouse and children	62	43

Source: Update of data from "American Family Dilemmas" (p. 15) by D. Blankenhorn. In *Rebuilding the Nest*, edited by D. Blankenhorn, S. Bayne, and J. B. Elshtain, 1990, Milwaukee: Families International, Inc. Copyright 1990 by Family Service America. Adapted by permission.

- Marriage is the most common form of adult cohabitation. Few people choose to live alone. Marriage is by far the most popular living arrangement for adults.

- Marriage is the context of most human sexual activity. Most couples rate this aspect of their marriage positively, especially in the early years.

- Marriage is a reproductive unit. Most married couples become parents and see parenting as an important goal and value in their lives.

- Marriage is a unit that socializes children (although children can also be raised by single parents, extended families, grandparents, and other caregivers).

- Marriage is an opportunity to develop an intimate, sharing relationship. Although many marriages fail, many others provide a supportive context in which people develop and maintain intimacy.

Trends in Marriage and the Family: Change and Continuity

The emergence of a greater variety of family structures has been prompted primarily by high rates of divorce and remarriage. It is also occurring because of the growing number of women who have chosen to have children without being married. Table 1.1 shows changes in five key aspects of marriage and family life between 1960 and 1993. These changes include a dramatic increase in the percentage of childbirths outside of marriage, in the percentage of unmarried teenage mothers, in the number of divorced people, and in the percentage of children living with a single parent. Conversely, the percentage of adult life spent with a spouse and children has decreased dramatically since 1960 (Blankenhorn, 1990).

Figure 1.1 Family Structure in the United States. *Source:* U.S. Bureau of the Census (1995, p. 242).

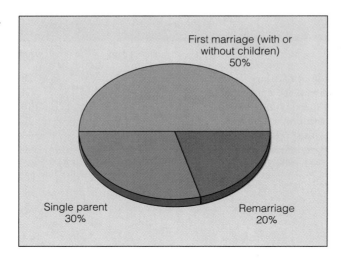

Additional statistics reflect the change in types of family structures. Fifty percent of U.S. families are currently headed by couples in their first marriage, 30% are single-parent families, and 20% are headed by remarried couples (Figure 1.1).

Family structure is also becoming more complex through remarriage, which creates new kinship relationships. New family terminology is needed to describe these complex relationships, but as yet, little progress has been made in clarifying or adequately defining these new structures. Even less has been done in describing the complexity of family dynamics in these new relationships.

Trends in Family Structure

The following trends illustrate the changes in family dynamics in the latter part of the 20th century in the United States:

- Single-parent families with children under the age of 18 are increasing dramatically. In the 1970s, only 12% of children lived in a single-parent home. In 1980 this number had increased to 22%, and in 1990, to 28%. By 1994, the rate was 30% (U.S. Bureau of the Census, 1994, p. 63). The percentage of children raised by a single parent varies by the ethnic group of the mother. In 1993, the rate was 25% for Whites, 35% for Latinos, and 63% for African Americans (U.S. Bureau of the Census, 1994, p. 62). Social scientists predict that 60% of children who are 2 years old today will have lived in a single-parent household by the time they are 18 years of age.

- The number of **stepfamilies**—families in which one or both of the partners have children from a previous marriage—is growing. Rising divorce and remarriage rates are the primary reason for this increase in the number of stepfamilies. About 75% of those who divorce eventually marry again.

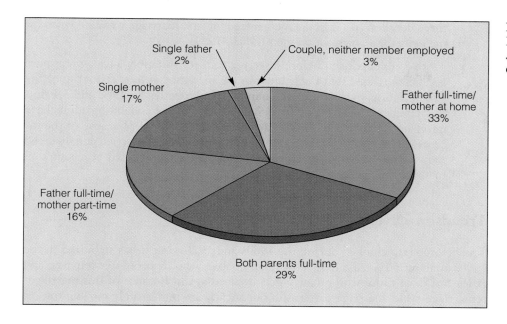

Figure 1.2 Employment Patterns of Families. *Source:* U.S. Bureau of the Census (1995, p. 246).

Today, about 20% of all U.S. families are stepfamilies. The percentage will probably increase to about 25% by the year 2000.

- Families are having considerably fewer children, except for certain ethnic groups. In 1970, more than 50% of 40-year-old women had three or more children; by 1994 the number had dropped to less than 30%. In 1989, couples with no children or with one child represented one third of all families. Currently, the average number of children per family in the United States is 1.7.

- In many families, both partners work. In the 1950s in more than 70% of families, the father worked and the mother stayed at home. Today, only about 33% of U.S. families are characterized by this pattern (Figure 1.2). In nearly 30% of U.S. families, both parents work full-time. In many others (16%), the father works full-time and the mother works part-time.

Trends in Marriage

As mentioned earlier, marriage continues to be one of the most popular voluntary institutions; more than 90% of all American adults marry at least once (Glick, 1989). Although this figure has not changed significantly since the 1960s, the following trends have occurred:

- More individuals delay marriage until their late 20s. Currently, the median age for first marriage is 25.5 years for men and 23.7 years for women, the oldest in American history. Age at marriage has been on the increase for three decades. In 1960, the median age for first marriage was 22.8 years for men and 20.3 years for women (Glick, 1989).

- More couples cohabit before marriage, and cohabitation is becoming more acceptable. The rate of cohabitation has increased at least sixfold since the 1960s, with about 2.5 million couples living together in 1988 and 3.5 million couples cohabiting in 1993. More than 50% of cohabiting adults have never been married (U.S. Bureau of the Census, 1994). Because of the increased rate of cohabitation among both previously unmarried and divorced individuals over the past 5 years, cohabitation has gained acceptance in many segments of our society.

Trends in Divorce and Remarriage

The divorce rate climbed during the 1960s and 1970s, but it has stabilized in the 1990s at about 50%. About 75% of those couples who divorce later remarry, and at least 50% of those who remarry get divorced again. Because of this marriage-remarriage cycle, marriage patterns in our society are increasingly moving toward what anthropologist Margaret Mead originally described as serial monogamy.

Only 54% of those who marry each year are doing so for the first time. In 23% of marriages, both the bride and the groom have been married before, and in the remaining 23%, it is the first marriage for one partner and a remarriage for the other person (U.S. Bureau of the Census, 1994, p. 102).

After divorce, men tend to remarry more quickly and more often than do women. The majority of younger divorced men and women, however, do remarry. According to one survey, 72% of recently divorced women remarried (Glick, 1989), but the rate of remarriage decreased as the number of children increased. About 81% of divorced women with no children remarried, 73% of women with one or two children remarried, and only 57% of women with three or more children remarried. In other words, the more children a woman has, the less likely she is to remarry. Box 1.3 provides some statistics on marriage and divorce trends.

Continuity in Marriage and the Family

Although we tend to focus on how marriage and the family have changed, in many ways these institutions have remained the same over several decades and continue to provide stability in our lives. For example, most people in the United States want to marry, and most couples who do so see marriage as a lifelong commitment and do not plan to divorce. Many couples want to have an egalitarian marital relationship, but equality does not mean that they will share exactly the same roles around the house. Rather, equality means that they work together to accomplish the many tasks and responsibilities required by family life on a regular basis.

Most couples who marry want to have children. Parenthood is an important goal for many couples, a fact that becomes more evident when a couple is not able to have a child. Most parents want their children to have a good education and to be at least as successful as they, the parents, are in society. In fact, most parents would like their children to do better than they have in all aspects of life.

B O X   1 . 3

The Statistics of Marriage and Divorce

- About 90% of all Americans marry at some time in their lives.

- In 1995, there were 2,354,000 marriages and 1,187,000 divorces.

- People marrying today have a 50–55% chance of divorcing (Glick, 1989).

- The median age for first marriage is 25.5 for men and 23.7 for women.

- The median duration of marriage is 7 years.

- The average age of remarriage for men is 37 years and for women, 33.6.

- First marriages for both the bride and groom account for only 54% of the marriages each year.

- Most divorces involve children, and more than 1 million children are affected by divorce each year in the United States.

- Most divorced individuals eventually remarry. For younger divorced individuals, this remarriage occurs within 5 years of the divorce.

Source: U.S. Bureau of the Census (1995), unless otherwise indicated.

Most family members also have a commitment to each other, although they might not always get along. They have an emotional connection to their immediate and extended family network and feel it is appropriate to call on them in time of need. This family network is an important support system, although it is often taken for granted until a crisis arises. In other words, the family is an interdependent system of people who are emotionally connected to each other.

Most families also have a value system that includes spiritual beliefs that provide the foundation for their attitudes and behaviors. These values become even more important to couples after they have children or in times of crisis. There is an ongoing commitment and connection between parents and their children, even after divorce. This is particularly true if the parents are given joint custody of their children. Most people also feel that the family is the most effective and efficient way of socializing children.

In summary, marriage and family provide significant continuity in our society. Unfortunately, emphasis on marriage and family problems often overshadows the stability and continuity these intimate relationships offer us in our daily lives.

Conceptual Frameworks for Studying Marriage and the Family

A **conceptual framework** is a set of interconnected ideas, concepts, and assumptions that helps organize thinking from a particular perspective. A **theory** contains general principles that are composed of interrelated concepts and **hypotheses** (presumed relationships between variables). A **research study** is designed to test one or more specific hypotheses.

Most family professionals maintain that there are many ways of looking at families; they therefore use ideas and principles from several conceptual frameworks to help them understand what is happening in a family. This open-minded approach to learning and to life is often termed an "eclectic" approach, and most family researchers, family life educators, and family therapists subscribe to it.

However, professionals with an eclectic approach can sometimes be too open and accepting of contradictory ideas. This text encourages the reader to begin developing a personal set of principles and concepts that will help in understanding family life. For most family scientists, this pursuit of understanding is a lifelong task, and many find that their theoretical perspectives change with time.

Some family scientists maintain that human beings and families are unique and that it is therefore difficult to construct a broad conceptual framework that applies to all families. This view has been labeled **idiographic,** meaning that it focuses on the individual or the unique. Professionals who lean in this direction are more interested in individual case studies and tend to have a clinical focus. On the other end of the theory spectrum is the **nomothetic** orientation. This approach focuses on developing a theory that works for a great number of cases. Researchers using this approach believe that it is important to try to develop a broader understanding of families and to work toward a general family theory. Each of these approaches has some value and usefulness, because every family *is* unique and yet has much in common with other families.

This text focuses on five conceptual frameworks that are currently considered valuable to family professionals. They are family systems theory (or the family systems framework), the family strengths framework, the family development framework, the symbolic interaction framework, and the feminist framework. The most popular of these perspectives is family systems theory, which focuses on the family as an ongoing system of interconnected members. (Because it is a broad and comprehensive set of principles, this perspective is referred to more often as a theory than as a conceptual framework.) The family strengths framework is becoming more accepted because it highlights the positive aspects of couples and families, rather than their problems. The family development framework looks at how the family changes over time. The symbolic interaction framework has historically been valuable to family professionals because it examines how family members learn roles and rules in our society. The feminist framework is increasingly important to the family field because it emphasizes the value of a woman's perspective on family life and society.

Family Systems Theory

According to **family systems theory** (or the **family systems framework**), everything that happens to any family member has an impact on everyone else in the family because family members are interconnected and operate as a group, or **family system.** This approach to describing the family as a system has become very popular in both theory and practice, particularly with therapists working with families who have problems.

Family therapist Carl Whitaker (1979) has commented that in a metaphorical sense "there are no individuals in the world—only fragments of families." In other words, individual human beings are inextricably tied to their families. How people think and behave is deeply influenced by family background, and people are best understood by understanding their families. From a family therapist's standpoint, an individual can most effectively change if his or her family also changes. If a family is in trouble, both parents and children need to become involved in the therapy.

Some people believe that a family systems approach has been a natural part of many cultures for thousands of years. Carolyn Attneave (1982), a psychology professor and Native American, believes that Native Americans have used family systems concepts and even broader approaches to healing for a long time. When an individual has a problem, not only the family but also the whole community is often involved in finding a solution. This idea is epitomized in the popular statement "It takes a whole village to raise a child." A family simply cannot do it all by themselves. Troubled families often live in troubled communities, and if individuals are to be well, the community must find a way to create health for all its members.

The family systems theory grew out of general systems theory, a conceptual framework developed in the 1960s by Ludwig von Bertalanffy (1968). **General systems theory** is a broad-based model, used in a variety of fields; it is a set of principles and concepts that can be applied to all types of systems, living and nonliving. The dictionary defines a **system** as a set or arrangement of things so related or connected as to form a unity or organic whole, and as a whole made of interacting parts.

Therapists working with troubled individuals over the years discovered through trial-and-error that working with the individual alone simply was not enough. A disturbed child might calm down and show evidence of increasing health when in a treatment center under the guidance of committed and sensitive professionals, but the same child was likely to revert to severely disturbed behavior when placed back with the family members who have an impact on the child's life.

When a child has problems, there are often problems in the family system. For example, some family therapists believe that if there is a disturbed child in a two-parent family, there is a high probability of a troubled marriage at the root of the child's difficulties. Treating the child alone and ignoring the marriage relationship would be like replacing the motor in an automobile when the gas tank is empty. The family systems framework helps therapists get to the root cause of the problem, rather than simply treating symptoms.

Proponents of the family systems theory have expanded on ideas and terminology developed by general systems theorists, and family therapists use these ideas in their practice. Several concepts from systems theory have particular application to family systems; we discuss these concepts next.

Wholeness General systems theory includes **wholeness,** the concept that the whole is more than the sum of its parts. From a family systems perspective, the whole family is more than the total of all its individual members. You cannot know the family simply by knowing each person as an individual because you cannot predict how they will interact as a group (Day, Gilbert, Settles, & Burr, 1995; Goldenberg & Goldenberg, 1991). For example, Carla, a student living in an apartment, has a certain identity related to her life at the college she attends and in the city in which she lives. An observer could study her very carefully and come to a reasonably good understanding of what she is like, at least in the college environment in which she is living. But when Carla goes home to visit her family for a holiday break, she becomes a different person in many ways during that time. She is transformed into a daughter, a granddaughter, a big sister, a little sister; she is part of her family in many more ways than she is while attending college away from home.

Each family member regularly emerges from the family to go to work, to school, or to activities with friends. Every member becomes a slightly different person outside the family and is a unique individual within the family. But when family members return from work, school, and other activities, they merge to some degree to become a whole family, and a unique entity is created by this fusion.

Just as a good cook takes individual herbs, spices, and vegetables and combines them to create a wonderful, zesty sauce, likewise, the whole family system is something more than the sum of its parts. In the case of a strong family, the whole family system can be argued to be something *greater* than the sum of its parts.

Interdependence of Parts   Another concept of general systems theory is **interdependence of parts:** The parts or elements of a system are interconnected in such a way that if one part is changed, other parts are automatically affected (Burr, Day, & Bahr, 1993; Day et al., 1995). Visualize for a moment a mobile, an artistic creation suspended in mid-air, made up of many carefully balanced elements. Each element in the mobile is weighted and placed in such a way as to create not only a pleasurable artistic effect but also a delicate system that can be easily set in motion. A slight ripple of wind or a soft touch is enough to set the mobile spinning. A stronger onslaught might knock it out of balance. Healthy families, in a sense, are like a mobile: Each member fits into the whole in a unique way and adds to the beauty of the whole. If one individual changes—for better or worse—the total creation is affected. Consider how one event changed the family in the following story.

> Julia was a single parent living with her two young children, Camille and Katy. Their life together was a hectic but satisfying round of school, work, family visits, and activities with friends. Last year Julia was involved in an auto accident and was seriously injured. She could neither work nor care for her children. The family's delicate balance was upset until Julia's mother, Eloise, her brother, Tim, her sister, Allison, and her best friend at work, Sheryl, all stepped in to help create a new sense of family balance.
>
> These four adults spent countless hours at the hospital, reassuring Julia and listening to her express her uncertainty and pain. They also worked out some new arrangements to make up for her absence. Camille and Katy temporarily moved in with Eloise. She took care of them, prepared their meals, made sure they had clean clothes for school, and took over many details of their lives. Tim, who lived nearby, drove Camille and Katy to and from school and took care of them afterwards. Allison, who still lived at home, got them to bed at night and took them on outings on the weekends. Camille and Katy took on some new responsibilities themselves, like walking the dog and doing their homework without prompting. Sheryl kept things going at the office by taking on several of Julia's responsibilities herself.
>
> After an initial period of confusion and difficulty, all these individuals became familiar with their new roles and proud of their new skills. Julia was hospitalized for several weeks and had physical therapy for several months,

but eventually she regained her strength and her courage. When she returned home, the whole family celebrated. In the months that followed, she established a new balance with her children, assimilating the experiences they had all had since the accident. It was a different balance than before but one that evolved naturally out of the circumstances.

Julia's family will probably never return to the way things were before the accident because families rarely go back. But as Julia's case shows, the nuclear family, with the help of extended family members, is capable of establishing a more integrated family system.

Balance of Openness to Change and Resistance to Change   Systems exhibit both stability and the capacity to change, depending on the circumstances. A strong family is like a flower in the wind; by being flexible and bending with the breeze, it endures. General systems theorists use the term **open system,** or **morphogenic system,** when referring to a system that is open to growth and change. A **closed system,** or **morphostatic system,** is one that has the capacity to maintain the status quo, thus avoiding change (Becvar & Becvar, 1993; Burr et al., 1993; Day et al., 1995). The key is figuring when to bend under pressure and when to stand firm, for both strategies are useful.

In their work with families with problems, family therapists have been quick to discover that many families are highly resistant to change, even though they need to adapt to solve the problems they face. Families are likely to want to maintain the status quo out of habit, lack of insight, or fear of something new. Jay Haley, a pioneer family therapist, argued that "when one person indicates a change in relation to another, the other will act upon the first so as to diminish and modify the change" (1972, p. 189).

As an example of a morphostatic system, consider the following story:

Ken and Katherine have been married for 15 years. Ken is an alcoholic, though he manages to hold on to his job as a floor supervisor at a printing plant. Ken has been having an extramarital affair with Winona, a co-worker at the plant, for 6 months. When Katherine discovers the affair, she tells Ken she is leaving him. He responds by begging for forgiveness and promising to give up the relationship with Winona. He wants to avoid divorce for a number of reasons: embarrassment at work, shame in his extended family, and financial consequences. Besides, although the thrill is gone from the marriage, he and Katherine have a long history together, and she is a good mother to their three children.

Katherine is skeptical about Ken's promises. She tells him that she wants him to give up drinking as well. He says he can control his drinking and just drink "socially." He doesn't really need to go "cold turkey," he argues. Katherine remains skeptical; she has heard such arguments many times before.

In spite of her skepticism, however, Katherine decides to forgive Ken, as she has before, and to stay. She genuinely loves him, even though she hates his drinking and, now, his seeing other women. And he provides a good income for her and the children. Katherine also fears being on her own, both socially and financially. She dreads the thought of going back into the work-

Many cultures embrace a form of family and community life that reflects what theorists think of as family systems. Among many Native American tribes, for example, significant life events are marked with community-wide ceremonies, and individual problems are considered problems that can only be solved within the context of the group.

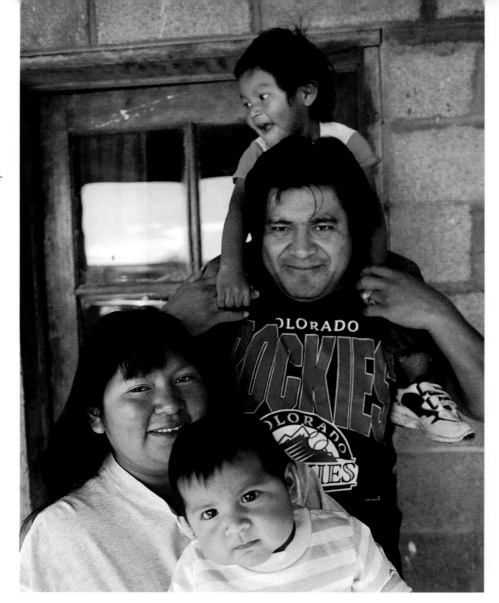

place after so many years at home. Whatever she has now, she feels, is better than what she would have as a divorced mother of three.

By failing to deal openly and effectively with their relationship problems, Katherine and Ken are beginning a free fall into despair. They are an example of a morphostatic family system, unable or unwilling to change. A morphogenic system, one open to growth and change, might have been able to prevent such a scenario.

The family systems framework assumes that systems operate on a continuum from extreme morphostasis to extreme morphogenesis. In a healthy system, there is a balance between these extremes. The family needs to be open to change, but not to the point of being rootless or chaotic. Conversely, the family needs to be centered and stable, but not to the point of being rigid.

Balance of Separateness and Connectedness   Couples and families need to find a balance between their separateness as individuals and connectedness as a system. The dynamics that help systems maintain this separateness-connectedness balance are the opposing forces of centrifugal and centripetal interactions. **Centripetal interactions** pull family members together and increase family closeness; **centrifugal interactions** tend to push family members apart, thereby increasing separateness (Stierlin, 1972).

Family therapists have found that a family crisis can spark both centripetal and centrifugal interactions. Faced with a death, one family may pull together and come out stronger as a result of the loss. Another family, faced with the same type of loss, may find itself torn apart by the events. The first family resolves to hold on to each other, communicate about how they are feeling, and help each other. These centripetal interactions strengthen the bonds of love and concern. The members of the second family are afraid, cannot talk with one another, and attempt to deal with the death as individuals. They separate completely from the family and look for comfort outside it, or they bury themselves in personal despair, refusing to talk with anyone.

Family therapists agree that a healthy balance of separateness and connectedness works best for families in crisis. In the face of death, family members can draw on each other's strengths and skills for comfort and at the same time seek out positive people in the community who can be growth-enhancing for the family as a whole. If family members choose to go their separate ways as a result of the crisis, the likelihood of a positive outcome for the family as a whole lessens considerably.

Feedback Within the System   Another basic principle from general systems theory is that communication in the system is essential. No matter how hard one might try, one simply cannot *not* communicate (Becvar & Becvar, 1993). Even if we completely withdraw from our family, we are communicating an important message: that the family is not a safe, healthy, or happy place to live.

Systems provide information to their components on how the various parts of the system are functioning. Family systems function successfully when important information is regularly exchanged among the members. General systems theorists talk about information feedback loops, which can be either positive or negative (Burr et al., 1993; Goldenberg & Goldenberg, 1991). **Positive feedback** in families is intended to create change, whereas **negative feedback** is designed to minimize change and keep things the same. Feedback can be either from family members or from outside the family. Positive and negative do not connote value judgments or indicate whether the change was good or bad, but rather whether change occurred in the system or not. For example, Sandy suggests that the members of her family exchange jobs around the house so that everyone can better understand what the various jobs entail, and for variety. If Sandy's family members accept this idea and change their routine, then Sandy's feedback to the system is considered positive; if not, it is considered negative.

In sum, balance and openness are key concepts in the family systems framework. Families under stress sometimes pull inward and desperately try to prevent new information or people from coming into the system, even if these additions could be helpful. Perhaps these families are simply in a state of emotional shock and are incapable of thinking openly and creatively for a while. It is in every family's long-term best interest to find a dynamic balance between the need to maintain stability and the need to adapt successfully to change. They also must find a

Figure 1.3 An Ecological Approach to Human Systems

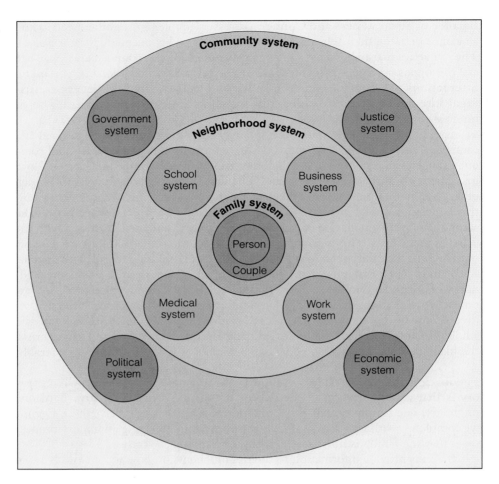

balance between the need to solve problems among themselves and to seek help outside the family when appropriate.

Multiple Levels   One of the most basic assumptions of general systems theory is that systems are embedded within other systems. Whenever attention is focused on a given system, there is usually a **suprasystem** (a large system) and a **subsystem** (a smaller system) that are interrelated. In a couple, the suprasystem is the family and the subsystem consists of the two individuals. In a family, the suprasystem is the extended family and the subsystem is the couple or any other dyadic (two-person) unit, such as parent and child. Any system can be the focus of interest. That system is both embedded in other larger systems and made up of smaller systems.

Systems are both connected to and separated from other systems by **boundaries.** The notion of a boundary also implies a hierarchy of interconnected systems, each system larger than the one before it (Burr et al., 1993; Day et al., 1995; Goldenberg & Goldenberg, 1991).

Different tools and techniques are used to help focus on different system levels. A biologist might use a very powerful electron microscope to study DNA in a cell or a less powerful microscope to study the cell as a whole. Observational approaches might suffice when studying an entire animal or plant. By the same token, an astronomer could use a telescope to get information about the planets and stars, but might want to rely on a radio telescope or an orbiting satellite for more detailed information.

Human systems have many different levels that can be characterized in many different ways. These levels can be pictured as a set of concentric circles. For example, the smallest circle in the center would be the individual; this circle would be encircled by the couple, a dyad or two-person human system; around this system would be the family circle; around the family would be the local neighborhood, including shops, schools, businesses, and so on; then the village or town or city; the nation; the continent; and the world. **Ecology** is the study of how all the organisms in a system relate to one another. Thinking about human systems in this way is to take an ecological approach. General systems theory assumes that all the concentric circles are connected to one another and that the people in each of the circles influence the people in the other circles—creating a human ecosystem (Figure 1.3). An individual family influences how the total community functions, and vice versa. Strong families help build strong communities, and strong communities support strong families. When trying to understand an individual family system, we need to consider the various system levels it influences and that influence it. Helping a family through a crisis can be a very different experience for a family therapist depending on whether the family is living in a middle-class suburban neighborhood, an inner city area, or a poverty-stricken rural environment. Families do not function in a vacuum; they are part of larger systems.

The Family Strengths Framework

The **family strengths framework** focuses on how families succeed rather than on why they fail. This perspective arose from the notion that strong families can serve as models for other families wanting to succeed. One advantage of the family strengths framework is that it tends to change the nature of what one finds in families. Simply stated, if one studies only family problems, one finds only family problems. Similarly, if researchers and therapists are interested in family strengths, they have to look for them. When these strengths are identified, they can be the foundation for continued growth and change in a family.

Family therapists and other counselors are finding the family strengths framework helpful in treating family problems. Many professionals have found that just solving problems is not enough. They need a model of healthy family development as a goal for troubled families to work toward. Identifying a family's strengths also boosts morale among family members.

> "In our child abuse treatment and prevention program here in Lincoln, we focus on the strengths of our families," Romney, a family therapist, explained. "This may surprise you, but it works really well. Sure, we also are aware that these families have lots and lots of problems. But we always try to remember their important strengths. A family I'm working with now is a good example: a mom and dad and three kids under age 7. Though they don't have much

The family strengths framework focuses on the positive qualities of families. Apparent in this family are such strengths as warmth, caring, appreciation, affection, trust, commitment, and enjoyment of each other's company.

money and the little boy has severe health problems, they've got a lot going for them: They are resilient and can cope with a lot of difficulties; they are resourceful and creative; they love each other and are committed to their family. We use these strengths as a foundation to build on. We focus on their strengths and use these strengths to meet the challenges head on.

"And it works. Instead of always looking at the problems, we accentuate the positive, and this gives the family a sense of optimism and courage. As a counselor I find myself being more optimistic about how much the family can accomplish with my help."

Perhaps the most extensive series of studies of family strengths has been done by Nick Stinnett and his colleagues (DeFrain & Stinnett, 1992; Stinnett, Sanders, & DeFrain, 1981; Stinnett, Stinnett, DeFrain, & DeFrain, 1997, in press). In over 20 years of study, the researchers have collected data on more than 16,000 families in every state of the United States and more than 25 countries around the world. Stinnett and his colleagues propose that six major qualities are commonly present in strong families, especially in Western industrial societies and in more developed countries (Box 1.4). These qualities are

- Commitment

- Appreciation and affection

- Positive communication

- Time together

- Spiritual well-being

- Ability to cope with stress

B O X   1 . 4

Qualities of Strong Families

Commitment
Trust
Honesty
Dependability
Faithfulness

Appreciation and Affection
Caring for each other
Friendship
Respect for individuality
Playfulness
Humor

Positive Communication
Sharing feelings
Giving compliments
Avoiding blame
Being able to compromise
Agreeing to disagree

Time Together
Quality time in great quantity
Good things take time
Enjoying each other's company
Simple good times
Sharing fun times

Spiritual Well-Being
Hope
Faith
Compassion
Shared ethical values
Oneness with humankind

Ability to Cope with Stress
Adaptability
Seeing crises as challenges and
    opportunities
Growing through crises together
Openness to change
Resilience

Sources: Adapted from Stinnett & DeFrain (1985, p. 14); Olson, McCubbin, et al. (1989, p. 52).

All these family strengths are interrelated, overlap to some degree, and interact. Appreciation and affection for one another make family members more likely to spend time together, and time together is enhanced by positive communication. Communication enhances commitment, and commitment leads to spending more time together. A feeling of spiritual well-being gives people the confidence to weather a crisis, and the ability to cope with crisis makes family members appreciate each other more. Family strengths are thus interconnected like a large, complex puzzle. Let's look at each strength in more detail.

Commitment   Members of strong families generally show a strong **commitment** to one another, investing time and energy in family activities and not letting their work or other priorities take too much time away from family interaction. "My wife and kids are the most important part of my life," one father said in describing commitment. Another noted that "what we have as a family is a treasure." Commitment does not mean, however, that family members stifle each other. "We give each other the freedom and encouragement to pursue individual goals," one wife noted. "Yet either of us would cut out activities or goals that threatened our time together."

Commitment includes sexual fidelity. Some of the people contacted by the researchers admitted to having engaged in an extramarital affair earlier in the marriage. Some believed the affair precipitated a crisis that in the final analysis led to a stronger marriage. But marriages can change for the better without a crisis of such major proportions. "Being faithful to each other sexually is just a part of being honest with each other," one young woman noted. Honesty, indeed, is the best policy.

Appreciation and Affection   People in strong families care deeply for one another, and they let the others know this regularly. Many people don't express **appreciation and affection** in their families, reasoning, "She cooked dinner every evening, but it never occurred to me to thank her for it. She doesn't thank me for going to work every day." Such an attitude is unfortunate, because expressing affection and giving and receiving sincere thanks in families foster a positive atmosphere and help people get along better. A pat on the back, a smile, or a hug builds a bond of caring. One member of a strong family explained it this way, "He makes me feel good about me and about us as a couple. Very few days go by without him saying something positive."

One strong family developed an excellent technique for keeping the home a positive place. If a family member feels the need to criticize another member, the criticizer must maintain a ratio of ten positive strokes to one critical statement. "We criticize each other on occasion in our family," the father explained, "but we try to criticize with kindness. And we try to make sure that we express appreciation for something positive the person does at least ten times for each negative thing we say." Positive feelings tend to snowball. If Mom feels good about herself, she will be more likely to say kind things to Dad. And when Dad feels good, he is likely to be especially nice to the children.

People in dysfunctional families more often focus on the negative. Family therapist Herbert Otto calls these people "energy vampires," people who gain energy by feeding off the self-esteem and good feelings of others. They believe that by putting other people down they can build themselves up. The approach usually backfires, however, often producing only countercriticism in return.

Researchers have found that sexual behavior in strong marriages is often a form of appreciation for each other. "Foreplay does not begin at 10:30 P.M. on Saturday night," one husband explained. "It begins when I take out the garbage on Wednesday morning, when I cook dinner on Friday night, and when I help Jeannie solve a problem at her work on Saturday afternoon." Sex is a natural way to express warm feelings for the partner. Another person reported, "The times when sex was best have been times when we've felt especially close and in tune with each other, when we'd solved a problem or when we were working on a project together."

Positive Communication   When people are asked to list the qualities they consider essential to a strong family, most list **positive communication.** Yet many families don't spend much time talking to one another. Although successful families are often task-oriented, identifying problems and discussing how to solve them, family members also spend time talking with and listening to one another just to stay connected.

In strong families, some of the most important talk occurs when no one is working at communication. Open-ended, rambling conversations can reveal important information. How does your teenager feel about sex? Or grades? Or her future? When parents and children get comfortable with each other, important issues arise.

Communication does not always produce agreement in strong families. Family members have differences and conflicts, but they speak directly and honestly about them without blaming each other. They try to resolve their differences but may agree to disagree. Dysfunctional families, on the other hand, are either overly critical and hostile in their communication with each other or deny problems and avoid verbal conflict. Although verbal hostilities are not productive, neither is avoidance of problems.

Studies of communication in healthy families have found it to have several important aspects. Members of strong families are extremely good at listening. "I'd much rather listen to other people talk," one father explained. Family members are also adept at asking questions, and they do not try to read one another's minds. Members of strong families understand that people's views of the world change. The only way to avoid mind-reading is to check out positions regularly and to ask questions.

Humor is an important part of healthy family communication. Strong families like to laugh. A study of 304 mothers, fathers, and teenagers makes it quite clear that humor is a valuable source of family strength. Wuerffel, DeFrain, and Stinnett (1990) reviewed the scientific literature on humor and found that humor can be used in many different positive and negative ways. Humor can reduce daily tension, facilitate conversations, express feelings of warmth and affection, lessen anxiety, point out mistakes made by others, and entertain. It can also help put others at ease, and help maintain a positive outlook on life.

The study found positive correlations between the uses of humor in families and how strong the families were based on their responses to a family strengths inventory. The stronger the family, the more likely they were to use humor to maintain a positive outlook on life, for entertainment, to reduce tension, to express warmth, to put others at ease, to facilitate conversations, to lessen anxiety, and to help cope with difficult situations. But the stronger families in the study reported negative effects when humor was used to put down other family members. Putdowns and sarcasm were used less often by the stronger families.

The study concluded that families benefit from humor that points out the incongruous aspects of life—the inconsistent, bizarre, silly, illogical things that happen to people every day. Families, however, do not benefit from humor that places someone in a superior position or from sarcasm aimed at demeaning a family member. Sarcasm is often an attempt to mask anger; it is rarely used out of love.

Time Together   "What do you think makes a happy family?" a researcher asked 1,500 schoolchildren. Few replied that money or cars or fancy homes or television sets made a happy family. The most frequent response? A family is happy because they do things together and spend **time together.** Although the response seems simple enough, family therapists see many couples and families who haven't figured this out. "I don't have a lot of time with my family," many people like to say, "but I try to make it quality time."

Happy memories exemplify "quality time": "I remember stories Mom and Dad told me when they tucked me into bed." "Going with Dad to work on the farm. I felt so important." Another said, "Singing together—we had an old piano, and I learned to play, and we would all sing corny old songs." Yet another responded, "Vacation. We would go fifty miles to the lake and rent a cabin, and Dad would swim with us."

Strong families spend time together. Whether it's a bedtime story or a picnic, the family activities that become the happiest memories are usually simple ones.

These happy memories share common threads. First, happiness often centers on activities together as a family. Second, pleasurable time together often centers on simple activities that don't cost a lot of money. Strong families identified these popular family activities: meals together; house and yard chores; and outdoor recreation, including camping, playing catch and other yard games, canoeing, hiking, and picnicking.

Spiritual Well-Being Perhaps the most controversial finding of the family strengths researchers is the importance of religion or spirituality in strong families. Some families call this **spiritual well-being.** Others talk about faith in God, hope, or optimism about life. Some say they feel a oneness with the world. Others talk about their families in almost religious terms, describing the love they feel for one another as sacred. Others express these kinds of feelings in terms of ethical values and commitment to important causes.

Spiritual well-being can be the caring center within each individual that promotes sharing, love, and compassion. Spiritual well-being is the feeling or force that helps people transcend themselves. "I feel my family is a part of all the families of the world," said one respondent. Another important aspect of membership in a religious or spiritual group is the caring, supportive community it provides. When illness strikes, a baby is born, or an accident occurs, friends in the group are often quick to help each other (Stinnett, Stinnett, DeFrain, & DeFrain, 1997, in press).

Ability to Cope with Stress Strong families are not immune to stress and crisis, but they are not as crisis-prone as dysfunctional families tend to be. Rather, they possess the **ability to cope with stress** effectively. Strong families are often creative at preventing troubles before they occur. Some stressors in life are inevitable, however. The best a family can do is to meet the challenge as efficiently as possible, minimizing its damage and looking for any growth opportunities in the process.

What are the most difficult family crises for strong families? Serious illness or surgery was cited as the toughest by 23% of adult respondents. A death in the family was next in order of frequency; 21% saw that as their most difficult crisis in the 5-year period preceding the study. Marital problems were the third most common form of crises the strong families faced. The majority of these marital crises involved adult children, in-laws, or brothers and sisters. A child's unwanted pregnancy, delinquency, or poor adjustment in school was also occasionally listed (Stinnett, Stinnett, DeFrain, & DeFrain, 1997, in press).

Fully 96% of the strong families said they were successful in meeting these crises. Among the strategies strong families use for weathering crises is pulling together. Each person, even a very young child, has a part to play in easing the burdens of the others. Finally, strong families seek help if they cannot solve the problem themselves. Although this may surprise some people, members of strong families do get counseling in an attempt to learn better ways of coping with crisis. Truly troubled families often do not have the strength to admit they have troubles and to seek advice (Stinnett, Stinnett, DeFrain, & DeFrain, 1997, in press).

The Family Development Framework

Family development as a conceptual framework was originally designed to describe and explain the process of change in couples and families (Rodgers & White, 1993). Researchers and clinicians working from a **family development framework** are primarily interested in how family members deal with various roles and developmental tasks within the family unit as they move through various stages of the family life cycle. Table 1.2 (p. 30) lists those roles and tasks and provides a good indication of why the process of development in a family is both stressful and challenging. The family development framework assumes that the more efficient a family is at completing these tasks, the more successful the development of the various family members will be.

Evelyn Duvall, a major founder (with Reuben Hill) of the family development approach, has described some of the advantages of this framework (Duvall & Miller, 1985). For one thing, it places the focus on development and change in individuals and the family over time. It also encourages attention to process. The family is viewed not as a static and unchanging group but as a dynamic system.

There is some controversy about the number of stages needed to describe the family life cycle. Duvall originally identified 8 stages; other family science professionals have identified 4–24 stages (Rodgers & White, 1993). The sequence of stages is clearest and easiest to apply when there is only one child in the family. The number of stages and the complexity of overlapping stages increase when there is more than one child or when the couple gets divorced and one or both partners remarry.

The family development framework has been very useful in describing family tasks. However, its static approach and its focus on stages of the family life cycle have resulted in a failure to tap into the complexity of today's family systems.

Table 1.2 Family Life Cycle Stages and Family Developmental Tasks		
STAGE OF THE FAMILY LIFE CYCLE	**POSITIONS IN THE FAMILY**	**FAMILY DEVELOPMENTAL TASKS**
1. Married couple	Wife	Establishing a mutually satisfying marriage
	Husband	Adjusting to pregnancy
		Fitting into the kin network
2. Childbearing	Wife/mother	Having and adjusting to an infant
	Husband/father	Establishing a satisfying home for parents and infants(s)
	Infants	
3. Preschool	Wife/mother	Adapting to needs of preschool children
	Husband/father	
	Daughter/sister	Coping with energy depletion and lack of privacy as parents
	Son/brother	
4. School	Wife/mother	Fitting into the community
	Husband/father	Encouraging children's educational achievements
	Daughter/sister	
	Son/brother	
5. Teenage	Wife/mother	Balancing freedom with responsibility
	Husband/father	
	Daughter/sister	Establishing postparental interests
	Son/brother	
6. Launching	Wife/mother/grandmother	Launching youth into adulthood
	Husband/father/grandfather	Maintaining a supportive home base
	Daughter/sister/aunt	
	Son/brother/uncle	
7. Middle-aged parents	Wife/mother/grandmother	Refocusing on marriage relationship
	Husband/father/grandfather	Maintaining kin ties with older and younger generations
8. Aging family members	Widow/widower	Coping with death and living alone
	Wife/mother/grandmother	Selling the family home
	Husband/father/grandfather	Adjusting to retirement

Source: Adapted from "Stages and Family Developmental Tasks" in *Marriage and Family Development* (6th ed.) by Evelyn Millis Duvall & Brent C. Miller. Copyright © 1985 by Harper & Row Publishers, Inc. Adapted by permission of HarperCollins Publishing, Inc.

The Symbolic Interaction Framework

As the name indicates, the **symbolic interaction framework** focuses on symbols, which are based on shared meanings, and interactions, which are based on verbal and nonverbal communication. This framework helps explain how we learn through communicating with each other about various roles in our society. The family is seen as a unit of interacting personalities, which Ernest Burgess (Burgess & Wallin, 1943) described as the way to explain the importance of family interaction in creating an ongoing group.

A **role** is the expected behavior of a person or group in a given social category, such as husband, wife, supervisor, or teacher. Every family member plays a variety of roles at different times. For example, a man can be a parent, spouse, manager at work, and coach of a baseball team. A woman can be a parent, spouse, manager at work, and chairperson of a fundraising committee. A young girl can be a daughter, student, and musician.

Roles are learned in society by **role taking,** the process whereby people learn how to play roles correctly by practicing and getting feedback from others. **Role making** involves creating new roles or revising existing roles. For example, as a couple's relationship changes from husband-led to a more equalitarian relationship, they need to change the way they interact with each other.

Some of the assumptions of symbolic interaction can help clarify the value of this framework for understanding family behavior (LaRossa & Reitzes, 1993). One assumption is that meaning arises in the process of interaction between people. Shared meaning helps people understand each other and learn how to play various roles. Another important concept is **definition of the situation,** developed by William Thomas: Each person subjectively interprets a given situation, and different people will interpret an interaction or situation in different ways. This helps explain why there are often different perceptions of a marriage; there can be "his" marriage and "her" marriage, as described by Jessie Bernard (1970).

Another assumption is that people learn about themselves and develop a self-concept based on their interaction with others. An early theorist, Charles Cooley (1864–1929), developed the concept of the **looking-glass self,** the idea that you learn about yourself based on the feedback you receive from others who are reacting to your behavior. In other words, your feelings about yourself are derived from how others react to you. Another important theorist was George Mead (1863–1931), who described how the self-concept emerges in childhood. The child plays out a certain role, which helps him or her learn to take the role of the generalized other—to understand and even predict the feelings of another person. This ability can be valuable in any situation because it enables a person to understand another's feelings.

The Feminist Framework

Central to the **feminist framework** is the notion that women are exploited, devalued, and oppressed and that society should commit to empowering women and changing their oppressed condition (Osmond & Thorne, 1993; Walker & Thompson, 1984). Although the roots of the feminist movement were evident in earlier years, a wave of feminist activity began with the publication of Betty Friedan's best-selling book *The Feminine Mystique* (1963). Friedan argued that women need a more active voice in decisions that affect them and society. More recently, Friedan (1985) has proposed ways to free women from the burden of guilt they often feel because they are unable to adequately balance motherhood and a career outside the home.

Although the women's rights movement has a long history in the United States, Betty Friedan's *The Feminine Mystique* triggered the wave of feminist sentiment and awareness that continues today. Friedan gave voice to the dissatisfaction felt by a generation of women whose role in life was confined to that of homemaker.

Feminist theories have a common interest in understanding the subordination of women with the goal of changing it (Osmond & Thorne, 1993). Feminists assume that women's experiences are central, not less important than those of men, and that gender must be explicitly used as a central focus. **Gender** is defined as the learned behaviors and characteristics associated with being male or female in a particular culture. Feminist theories examine gender differences and how gender-based distinctions legitimize power differences between men and women.

Feminists have also challenged the definition of family that is based on traditional roles. They see the family as a dynamic, changing, and open system that does not restrict roles and opportunities. They have criticized the "structural/functional framework," which prescribed the roles of males and females. Parsons and Bales (1955) assumed that the family was most functional if the male played the **instrumental role,** being in charge of tasks, and the wife played the **expressive role,** being nurturing. Feminists maintain that both men and women can play both roles. This perspective provides more flexibility within a couple, because both members can play roles based on their unique skills and interests.

Even though some men today are offended and threatened by feminist thinking, feminism may have certain benefits for both men and women in family relationships. It encourages men to express their feelings, to share wage-earning responsibilities, and to focus less on their careers and more on their children. For men, the pressure of being the only person bringing home money is reduced when both partners are working outside the home. At the same time, working outside the home helps women to enjoy an identity separate from their role within the family. It also provides them with independent economic security. Sharing the responsibility for childrearing allows men to participate in their children's development and women to pursue professional and personal interests. When work and power are shared, both partners have more opportunity to develop their full potential.

Many feminists propose that women act in anticipation of future problems by making specific job and career plans. Social and economic realities dictate that the "homemaker" option is no longer available for many women. As difficult as it is, most woman will need to build both a career and a family at the same time.

Women's and men's roles continue to converge in American society, and distinctions between male and female activities are blurring. As this convergence continues, women and men will find more ways to work together. Betty Friedan (1985) has argued that the feminist frontier now is the family and that "the problem is how to juggle work, love, home, and children."

Family Science: An Emerging Profession

Family science is growing rapidly, as a profession and as a social science. In recent years, research on the family has improved in both quality and quantity. Family researchers use many of the same methods as other social scientists, but they tailor these methods to their own interests and purposes. This section describes several research methods, including questionnaires, interviews, case studies, and observational approaches.

Table 1.3 Disciplines Contributing to Family Science

DISCIPLINE	TOPICS IN FAMILY SCIENCE
Anthropology	Cross-cultural studies; kinship; diversity in families
Biology	Conception and reproduction; growth, development, and aging
Child development	Development of infant and child; interpersonal skills
Economics	Family finances; consumer behavior
Education	Family life education; marriage preparation
English	Families in literature (present and past)
History	Historical perspectives on the family throughout time
Human ecology	Ecosystem perspective on family, nutrition, housing, clothing
Law	Marriage and divorce laws; child custody laws
Medicine	Families and health
Psychiatry	Family therapy
Psychology	Family psychology; assessment of couples and families
Social work	Treating problem families; family policy
Sociology	Marriage and divorce statistics; sociological theories about families

A Knowledge Explosion

Family science is a multidisciplinary field; that is, many disciplines contribute to the understanding of families (Table 1.3). During the past 20 years, this science has emerged as a genuine discipline unto itself. Its primary goal is to achieve a better understanding of families so that the quality of family life may be enhanced. Professionals whose main interests are research, theory, and programs for families tend to call themselves family scientists. Those who develop educational programs for families sometimes call themselves family life educators. Those who work clinically with troubled families are called marriage and family therapists.

Family scientists have backgrounds in a wide variety of disciplines: human development, family science programs, human ecology, home economics, social work, nursing, educational psychology, psychology, sociology, psychiatry, and anthropology. Family scientists may be researchers, professors, teachers, family life educators, family therapists, ministers, nurses, social workers, or attorneys. Box 1.5 (p. 34) describes how you can do family research yourself.

Research Methods

The whole of science is nothing more than a refinement of everyday thinking.
—ALBERT EINSTEIN *in* National Geographic, *1983*

Research is often the principal way that new ideas and facts are discovered. The word *research* is derived from words meaning "to seek out, to search again." Sci-

Family Science Research: Past and Present

Research on families has a long history that has expanded rapidly in recent years. In the 1960s, Reuben Hill and Joan Aldous began their pioneering work at the University of Minnesota in developing a database for marriage and family research going back to 1900. The first reference work they published, *The International Bibliography of Research in Marriage and the Family*, contained 12,610 research articles that had been published between 1900 and 1964. Volumes 3–12, representing research done between 1975 and 1987, were compiled by David Olson and colleagues at the University of Minnesota. Volume 12 alone lists 2,636 articles written by 3,156 authors and published in 750 journals (Olson & DeRubeis, 1987). Today, this series of reference works is called the *Inventory of Marriage and Family Literature (IMFL)* and is published by the National Council on Family Relations (NCFR), the predominant national and international organization of family scientists and family life

educators. Students can use these *IMFL* reference books at their local university library to identify research studies and locate relevant articles.

The data from all the volumes of the *IMFL* are also contained in an integrated computerized **family database.** The current family database contains more than 90,000 research articles on families that have been published in English language journals (Touliatos, 1993). Students or researchers can access this family database through the Bibliographic Retrieval Systems (BRS) database, a national database available at most large libraries. It is possible to do a computer search of published research on hundreds of family topics and obtain references and abstracts with little cost or effort using this system. An undergraduate student thus has access to much of the same information available to academic researchers and can even learn how to conduct his or her own research using a personal computer.

ence, in the final analysis, is an examination of events or information in an attempt to make new discoveries.

It has been argued that the family is the most difficult institution in human society to study. The reason for this is that families tend to be closed to outsiders; they often "put their best foot forward." To study important issues and to solve family problems, researchers and practitioners have to get below the surface and deal with both the positive and negative aspects of family life.

Family researchers have a creative mix of tools and techniques for learning more about family realities, using both "insider" and "outsider" perspectives. An **insider perspective** is provided by family members when they describe how they see their relationships. An **outsider perspective** is provided by researchers or therapists observing and describing the activity from their point of view. Methods that tap the insider perspective are questionnaires, interviews, and case studies. Outsider perspectives are obtained by observational approaches. Family researchers often use only one method in a particular study, but there are advantages to a multimethod approach that uses both insider and outsider perspectives.

Research methods also have to be suitable for the population being studied. Written questions, for example, are inappropriate for people whose culture is predominantly oral. For more on adapting to cultural differences, when conducting research, see Box 1.6.

Research Methods in Cross-Cultural Studies

Research involving families in cultures outside the United States offers challenges and opportunities for American family researchers. John DeFrain traveled to the South Pacific to study the strengths and challenges of South Pacific families. Upon arrival in Fiji, two things became exceedingly clear very quickly.

First, the South Pacific is a huge geographic area with lots of water, little land, and few people. Fiji has only about 715,000 people, but they are scattered over about 80 islands. Travel from island to island can be very expensive, time-consuming, and sometimes dangerous.

Second, everything about the culture in Fiji is different. Nothing is familiar or easy. It was tempting to focus on the differences—in the language, the food, the landscape, the sports, and the family customs—which were at times overwhelming and disorienting.

It soon became apparent that the approaches used in U.S. family research would not work in Fiji. Questionnaires were a failure, but it then became apparent that the families have a strong oral tradition of story telling. So people were asked to talk about important stories in their families. Many of the stories were about holidays, birthdays, and other occasions when families got together. Individuals also told stories about family strife and pain: about beatings, extramarital affairs, attempted murder of family members, and drug abuse. These stories made clear the importance of family during difficult times.

When the barriers of the initial differences in other cultures are overcome, similarities tend to emerge. Use of methods appropriate to the culture reveals cross-cultural commonalities.

Questionnaires   Perhaps the most common method of studying families is the questionnaire. The researcher carefully prepares a series of questions based on a review of previous reasearch on the topic. Fixed-response questions are questions to which an individual picks his or her response from a selection of possible responses; open-ended questions are those to which the individual responds in his or her own words. A questionnaire might contain either or both types of questions.

Developing a questionnaire is a challenge. What questions one asks and the manner in which the questions are phrased can greatly influence the results of a study. Questions should be pilot-tested with a small sample of families to see whether they are clear and precise. The process of developing **validity** in a survey instrument—ensuring that the instrument measures what it is intended to measure—often takes researchers several months or even a number of years, depending on the complexity of the problem they are studying.

After the questionnaire is deemed satisfactory by the research team, it is distributed to a sufficiently large sample of family members. The size of the sample is determined by a number of factors, including how much money the research team has to spend on the project, how important the topic is to the researchers, and how difficult it is to find a group of families who are willing to participate in the study.

In the past, it was quite common for family research to consist simply of studies of what mothers thought was going on in their families. Fathers and children were often ignored. It was assumed that one individual could speak for the family as a whole. Often the reason for this approach was that studies of multiple family members were much more time-consuming, expensive, and difficult to analyze. Today most researchers recognize that fathers, mothers, and children often differ in their perceptions of what is going on in a family and that a good study demands information and perceptions gathered from multiple family members (LeMasters & DeFrain, 1989).

Interviews   The interview—whether face-to-face or by telephone—is another method used in family research. Some investigators believe that interview data are more valid than data from questionnaires because the researcher can ask follow-up questions and get more information. On the other hand, some research has found that people are more honest on questionnaires. Interviews tend to cost more in terms of time and money, and fewer people are reached with interviews than with questionnaires. Variation from one interviewer to another may also be a problem because it can taint the results. Questionnaires, of course, are standardized. Perhaps the best approach is to use both questionnaires and interviews. The results can then be compared with each other to provide **cross-validation.**

Case Studies   Some of the most emotionally gripping research findings have come from family therapists working with troubled families using the case study method. A **case study** is an approach in which a particular family is described in detail to illustrate some specific ideas, concepts, or principles about families. In this approach, the painful complexities of family dynamics are recorded in narrative form and analyzed by the researcher. Great care is taken to protect the privacy and anonymity of the family members, in part by concealing their names and disguising any identifying family characteristics.

The major problem with case studies is that the families described are probably not representative of all American families. For example, if a researcher were to analyze the case of a stepfamily in treatment at a counseling agency, the researcher might conclude that stepfamilies have numerous problems. This conclusion would be biased, however, because it was based on a family that had come for help. If the researcher were to question stepfamilies by randomly telephoning people in the community, the result would be a more **representative sample**—that is, a random selection—of stepfamilies and probably a more positive description of interactions in this type of family.

Observational Approaches   Social psychologists who study families and family therapists who deal with problem families tend to work by observing family interactions in natural settings like the home. Observational approaches, which tap the outsider perspective, have both strengths and limitations. One strength is that the researcher does not have to rely on family members' self-reports of their own behavior. One major limitation is that having a stranger present influences family members' behavior, making it less natural. Researchers also need to consider whether families who volunteer for such studies differ in some ways from families who refuse researchers' requests. These are important issues in any research study, but they are more problematic in observational studies.

Sometimes a family is brought into a research laboratory for a study. Often the laboratory is set up like a living room or a dining room, and the family is asked to perform a particular task together, such as playing a game. The researchers videotape the interaction and later study the video to analyze and evaluate the family members' communication styles. Many families are not willing to participate in such studies, of course, and those who do may act differently than they do behind closed doors. But in spite of all the difficulties with observational research, there have been many creative observational family studies.

Historical and Multicultural Studies   Studies of families in earlier generations are often useful and interesting to us today. As historians point out, we cannot know where we are going in the future unless we know where we have been. Historical research, which often relies on diaries and historical statistics about families, can help us understand families in the past.

Feminists argue that much of what has been presented as family history in the past has focused on the lives of men ("his-story") and has neglected the lives of women ("her-story"). The history of the family, in many cultures traditionally the domain of women, has not sparked a great deal of interest from historians (who have for the most part been men). But in recent decades, a resurgent feminist history movement has begun to look at the past from women's perspectives.

Similarly, multicultural studies of families can contribute rich insights into family life and family interactions. The United States has innumerable family cultures: African American, Caucasian, Latino, Italian American, Chicago suburban, inner-city Boston, gay-male, lesbian, middle-class, upper-class, rural, urban, and so forth. Family life is different in each of these cultures. A family in the commuter culture of Los Angeles, for example, lives a life quite different from that of a family in rural Iowa. Diversity in families is discussed in greater detail in Chapter 2.

Research Designs

Researchers are often interested in how particular families grow and change over time. Three types of research design that take the passage of time into consideration are longitudinal studies, cross-sectional studies, and cross-sectional cohort studies.

Longitudinal Studies   In a longitudinal study, a family is interviewed or observed several times over a period of months or years. This obviously takes a fair amount of time, effort, and money. For those reasons, only a small proportion of family research is longitudinal. The results of such projects, however, are often well worth the effort because they provide valuable information about long-term processes, such as the effect of the birth of a child on a marriage.

One longitudinal study focused on couples who took a premarital inventory called PREPARE 3 months before marriage and were followed up 3 years after marriage (Larsen & Olson, 1989). PREPARE is a 125-item questionnaire that focuses on 12 important areas of a couple's relationship, including communication, conflict resolution, role relationships, and sexual intimacy. Couples who were separated or divorced at the 3-year follow-up were compared with couples who remained happily married. The scores on the PREPARE inventory were found to predict with about 80–85% accuracy which couples later divorced and which were happily married. The findings indicate that problems experienced by couples before marriage can lead to more serious problems after marriage. This study also demonstrates the predictive validity of PREPARE and the value of longitudinal research.

Cross-Sectional Studies   A cross-sectional study selects couples or families at various stages of the family life cycle and compares the differences between the various stages. For example, four stages of the life cycle could be compared by selecting a group of newlywed couples, couples with young children, couples with adolescents, and older couples whose children had left home. This approach can help describe the similarities and differences between couples and families at these four stages.

The advantage of the cross-sectional design is efficiency: Data can be collected from all four groups at about the same time and then immediately compared. A disadvantage to this type of study is that it is not possible to know if identified similarities and differences are due only to the stage of the life cycle or whether they are also influenced by or due only to that characteristics of these specific families. This question could only be answered by a longitudinal study that follows the same families over time. Another problem with a cross-sectional study is that it is impossible to know the effect of the historical context for each group.

Cross-Sectional Cohort Studies   Because of the problems in both longitudinal and cross-sectional studies, researchers have designed a shortcut known as the cross-sectional cohort approach. Using this approach, researchers do not follow a group of families for many years; instead, they study various families at different stages of the family life cycle for shorter periods. They might, for example, study one family with a 10-year-old, another with a 12-year-old, a third with a 14-year-old, and a fourth with a 16-year-old. If they followed these families for 5 years, they would see changes from age 10 to 15, 12 to 17, 14 to 19, and 16 to 21. The result would be a view of an 11-year period (age 10 to age 21), achieved in only 5 years of research.

A Final Word About Research

No single study can provide definitive answers to important questions in family science. In fact, each study almost invariably raises new questions that are complex and difficult to answer. The advancement of scientific knowledge is a slow and painstaking process. People researching a particular topic in family science have to examine data from many related studies on the topic.

Sometimes studies produce findings that conflict with the results of other studies. These differences may occur because researchers have asked their questions in slightly different ways, because they used different research methods, or because they studied different populations or types of families. For example, a sample of families drawn from the Midwest may look at gender role issues in families somewhat differently from a sample of families drawn from Latino families living in California. Likewise, two-parent traditional American families may have a different way of looking at certain issues than do single-parent families.

Although studies may have different results, good studies tend to complement each other. When dozens of researchers from various parts of the United States look at a problem from many different theoretical approaches, using different research methods and different statistical analyses, a fairly comprehensive picture emerges. When the findings are similar in spite of all the differences in sample, method, and analysis, the results are more conclusive and help to build a more valid theory about families.

Summary

- The family today is not in danger of extinction, but it is changing. There is greater diversity in American families, in terms of family structure and ethnicity, than ever before.

- More than half of people marrying today will probably divorce at some time in their lives, often because they go into marriage with unrealistic expectations, marry the wrong person, marry for the wrong reasons, or have few skills to deal with the many challenges of marriage.

- A family is two or more people who are committed to each other and who share intimacy, resources, decisions, and values. Marriage is the emotional and legal commitment of two people to share emotional and physical intimacy, various tasks, and economic resources.

- Some of the major trends in family structure, marriage, divorce, and remarriage are the following: There are both more families headed by single women and more stepfamilies today than there were in the 1950s and 1960s; families are smaller today; women are more likely to work outside the home after marriage; both men and women are marrying at a later age; cohabitation before marriage has increased sixfold; the divorce rate increased but has now stabilized at about 50%; and about 75% of those who divorce later remarry.

- The conceptual frameworks from which researchers, theoreticians, and clinicians look at families include family systems theory (also called the family systems framework), which focuses on the family as a system of interdependent elements; the family strengths framework, which examines the characteristics of healthy families and what helps them maintain the quality of their family life; the family development framework, which views how families change across the stages of the family life cycle; the symbolic interaction framework, which looks at the internal perceptions of family members and how they learn roles and rules; and the feminist framework, which focuses on the world as women see it and on women's empowerment as a way of improving close relationships.

- Family researchers use a variety of tools and techniques in their work, including questionnaires; interviews; case studies; observation; historical and multicultural studies; longitudinal, cross-sectional, and cross-sectional cohort studies; and statistical analyses with computers.

Key Terms

family

marriage

stepfamily

conceptual framework

theory

hypothesis

research study

idiographic

nomothetic

family systems theory
(or framework)

family system

general systems theory

system

wholeness

interdependence of
parts

open system

morphogenic system

closed system

morphostatic system

centripetal interaction

centrifugal interaction

positive feedback

negative feedback

suprasystem

subsystem

boundaries

ecology

family strengths
framework

commitment

appreciation and
affection

positive communication

time together

spiritual well-being

ability to cope with
stress

family development
framework

symbolic interaction
framework

role

role taking

role making

definition of the
situation

looking-glass self

feminist framework

gender

instrumental role

expressive role

family science

family database

insider perspective

outsider perspective

validity

cross-validation

case study

representative sample

Activities

1. Form small groups of six to eight people. Write down your own definition of family, and then list the members of your family. Share what you have written with others in your group and compare how your ideas are similar and/or different.

2. Are human beings *really* all that different from each other? The answer is yes and no. In this exercise, sit down and talk with a person from another country, another social class, another sexual orientation, or another cultural/ethnic group. Make a list of the *similarities* and the *differences* between your families (attitudes, beliefs, behaviors, customs, and so forth). How many of the differences can be attributed to the different cultures your families come from, and how many of these differences are simply differences between two unique families?

3. Sit down with a grandparent, a great-grandparent, or another older person you would like to get to know better. Ask about family life in "the old days," both positive and negative aspects. Some interesting areas to explore might be growing up in a family, "women's place" in the world 50 or more years ago, gender roles, the Great Depression of the 1930s, World War II, major family crises this individual experienced, religion, and philosophies of child-rearing.

Suggested Readings

Booth, A. (Ed.). (1991). *Contemporary families: Looking forward, looking back.* Minneapolis, MN: National Council on Family Relations. *Most up-to-date guide to recent family science research available.*

LeMasters, E. E., and DeFrain, J. (1989). *Parents in contemporary America: A sympathetic view.* Belmont, CA: Wadsworth. *The social and psychological aspects of parenthood.*

Stinnett, N., Stinnett, N., DeFrain, J., and DeFrain, N. (1997, in press). *Good families.* New York: Doubleday. *Explanation of the family strengths conceptual framework emphasizing six qualities, based on studies with more than 16,000 family members.*

CHAPTER 2

Cultural Diversity: Family Strengths and Challenges

America is a meeting place of many cultures. Each cultural group that has come to America has surrendered some of its past in an effort to build a new life in a new land. But America is not so much a "melting pot," in which each of these distinct cultures meld together, as it is a salad bowl, in which each of the ingredients retains its distinct flavor. The United States can also be likened to a symphony and its various cultural groups to instruments. Each instrument has its distinct part to play—its distinct contribution—but all must work together to produce beautiful music.

One Midwest teacher we know appreciates the diverse instruments in the symphony of his life a great deal:

"I have friends from so many different cultures and ethnic groups that it makes my life really interesting. One woman I know is part–Lakota Indian and part–African American. Her perspective on life in the United States is fascinating. She likes to tease me: 'White boy, you just don't get it!' she says. Sometimes, I think she's right. My experience still is pretty narrow, but I'm learning.

"Another friend is part–Polynesian from the South Pacific and part–White American. She grew up with her mom, the Polynesian, and identifies culturally more with her than with her father from the United States. Then there's my friend Edie, who is a lesbian. She and her friend Tasha are working with a medical doctor right now so they can have a baby together via artificial insemination.

"My friend Paul is a Czech American from a small farm town in South Dakota. He drives a diesel truck and keeps me attuned to the male blue-collar world he lives in. Xia Wen is a friend from China. She's working on her doctorate in computer science. Ali comes from Istanbul in Turkey and is married to my friend Mary, who comes from a suburban Milwaukee family. My buddy Frank is a refugee from ethnic strife in Romania. Our family friend Enid is an Indian/African mix from Tobago in the Caribbean. She married Edward, a Kiwi from New Zealand. Mark, an all-American boy from Chicago, is never home because he's always wandering the world. He just recently got married in Israel to a Jewish woman from France.

"The news on television has a personal impact on me almost every evening because I have friends from so many different backgrounds. How boring my life would be if the only people I hung out with were chubby middle-aged White guys like me."

One's cultural identity is an important aspect of being human. **Cultural identity** evolves from the shared beliefs, values, and attitudes of a group of people. It includes standards of behavior and the ways in which beliefs, values, and attitudes are transmitted to the younger generation. Cultural identity also includes the ways in which kinship relationships and marital and sexual relationships are structured. The vast array of cultural identities in the United States includes Anglo American, Italian American, African American, and Asian American—to name just a few.

Cultural identity transcends **ethnic identity,** or ethnicity, which refers to the geographic origin of a minority group within a country or culture, and **race,** which is commonly used to refer to the physical characteristics of a particular group of people. Most cultures contain subgroups called **co-cultures,** distinct cultural or social groups living within the dominant culture but also having membership in another culture, such as gay men and lesbians.

This chapter describes the nature of cultural diversity in the United States and examines family strengths in a variety of ethnic and cultural groups. It discusses the challenges ethnic families face in the United States and concludes with an examination of some of the issues family researchers explore, such as ethnocentrism and racism.

The Nature of Cultural Diversity

The United States today is one of the most culturally diverse nations in the world. Although the dominant culture of the United States is Anglo American, this country is home to many other ethnic and cultural groups. The major ethnic **minority groups** that are usually distinguished in the United States are African Americans (or Blacks), Latinos (or Hispanics), Asian Americans, and Native Americans. When discussing ethnic and other minority groups, however, it is important to remember that tremendous diversity exists among the people who are commonly grouped together.

This section focuses on the mythology of race and the problems that arise in classifying people into particular ethnic and cultural groups. It also explores a variety of terms that help describe the range of marital, family, and kinship relationships among various cultural groups in the United States.

A Changing Picture: Demographic Trends in the United States

White Americans represent about 75% of the U.S. population; African Americans are the largest minority, representing about 12% of the population. The second largest minority group is Latinos, who make up about 9% of the total population. Latinos are very diverse and include Mexican Americans, Puerto Rican Americans, and Cuban Americans as well as smaller numbers of individuals from Central or South American and Caribbean backgrounds. Asian Americans, who number more than 11 million people, include Japanese Americans, Chinese Americans, Vietnamese, Laotians, Cambodians, Koreans, Filipinos, Native Hawaiians, and Samoans, as well as other Pacific Islanders. Native Americans, including Alaska Natives, number about 2.2 million; however, most embrace a tribal identity, such as Navaho, Hopi, or Sioux, rather than identifying themselves as Native Americans.

Although a majority (75%) of Americans are White, the rate of growth of this group between 1980 and 1995 was only about 12%. The second largest ethnic group in the United States is African Americans, who represent about 11.4% of the population; their rate of growth was about 24%. The number of Latinos increased 83% in the 1980–1995 period, and the group represents about 9% of the population. Native Americans, the smallest segment of the population at 1%, grew 56% in the same period. The ethnic group that grew the most between 1980 and 1995 was Asian Americans, with an increase of 161%; they represent about 3.4%

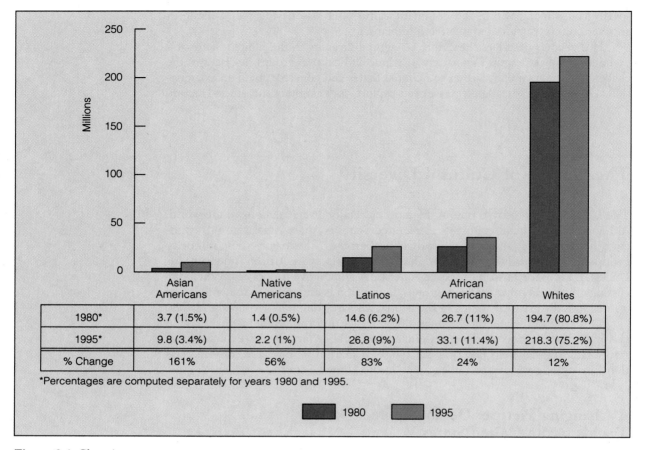

	Asian Americans	Native Americans	Latinos	African Americans	Whites
1980*	3.7 (1.5%)	1.4 (0.5%)	14.6 (6.2%)	26.7 (11%)	194.7 (80.8%)
1995*	9.8 (3.4%)	2.2 (1%)	26.8 (9%)	33.1 (11.4%)	218.3 (75.2%)
% Change	161%	56%	83%	24%	12%

*Percentages are computed separately for years 1980 and 1995.

■ 1980   ■ 1995

Figure 2.1 Changing Ethnic Composition in the United States, 1980–1995. *Source:* U.S. Bureau of the Census (1995, p. 14).

of the U.S. population. Figure 2.1 shows the growth of various ethnic groups during the 1980–1995 period.

Not only are Asian Americans the fastest growing ethnic group, but they also have the highest median household income among Whites, African Americans, Latinos, and Native Americans (Figure 2.2). Greater percentages of African Americans, Latinos, and Native Americans live below the poverty line than do Asian Americans or Whites. Figure 2.2 summarizes data on income level, percentage living in poverty, level of education, and percentage of married couples for these five ethnic groups.

The Mythology of Race

Anthropologist Ashley Montagu argued in his book *Man's Most Dangerous Myth: The Fallacy of Race* (1964) that similarities among ethnic groups are far greater than differences among them (Box 2.1, p. 48). Montagu continued that "the term 'race' itself, as it is generally applied to man, is scientifically without justification, and

Figure 2.2 Characteristics of Families from Various Ethnic Groups, 1995. *Source:* U.S. Bureau of the Census (1995, p. 212).

that as commonly used, the term corresponds to nothing in reality" (p. 351). In a similar vein, anthropologist Conrad Phillip Kottak pointed out that "American racial classification isn't based on biology but is an arbitrary creation of American culture" (1989, p. 45).

From a strictly scientific perspective, so-called racial characteristics do not exist (Root, 1992). Skin color, for example, can be defined only on a continuum, just as the colors black and white exist on a continuum with gray in the middle and no clear-cut distinctions in between. Classifying people into racial groups becomes rather arbitrary. For example, consider the child of an Irish American mother and a Japanese American father. The child may have a skin color like her mother's and

There Are More Things That Link Us Than Set Us Apart

Kristine M. Holmgren

Syl Jones

We are female and male, black and white, rural and sub-urban. We grew up in segregated sections of large cities. The differences between us are obvious. Because of them, we may not always see the world the same way, or share the same point of view. . . .

Twelve days ago, a jury in Los Angeles found O. J. Simpson not guilty of the murders of his ex-wife and her friend Ron Goldman. Like some of you, we were both surprised at the verdict. . . .

Although the verdict allows Simpson to walk away from his jail cell, he will forever be branded as a wife-battering drug abuser. But we are not going to let the evil that surrounded O. J. Simpson, the trial, and the attendant media circus turn us against each other. We still believe it is possible to live in separate worlds, have different views, and find common ground. . . .

Simpson's triumph came at great cost to everyone. The two families who grieve over their murdered loved ones feel no sense of justice. Likewise, it is also wrong to stew in a vat of anger and insult an entire race by implying that group-think took over the jury. . . .

We think it is time to get on with the difficult work ahead in racial and gender matters.

- We deplore the mistreatment of women and believe that the increasing violence against women around the world must be addressed.

- We agree that racial injustice is endemic, and we stand against it with others in our communities.

- We see the wealthy being well-served by the courts of our nation while the poor suffer, and we abhor the corruption of a system that encourages such unequal justice.

Despite our different skin colors, the values we share are as similar as the color of our blood. We will hold out for peace.

Kristine M. Holmgren of Northfield, Minnesota, is a writer and Presbyterian pastor. Syl Jones of Excelsior, Minnesota, is a playwright, journalist, and communication consultant.

Source: "There Are More Things That Link Us Than Set Us Apart" by S. Jones and K. M. Holmgren, October 15, 1995, Minneapolis–St. Paul *Star Tribune*, p. 3. Copyright 1995 by the Minneapolis–St. Paul *Star Tribune*. Reprinted by permission.

A home wedding ceremony. A successful intercultural marriage can be an important mechanism for helping to bring cultural groups together. Fortunately, the elements that are identified as core family strengths are common to all cultures.

the eyes of her father. Genetically and aesthetically, she is an expression of both her father's and her mother's characteristics.

For this reason, the term *race* will not be used again in this book. Rather, the terms *ethnic group* and *cultural group* will be used to identify social groups formed by people who share somewhat similar religious, linguistic, ancestral, or physical characteristics. Due to the great diversity within these groups, however, even calling them ethnic or cultural groups can be misleading. Jews, for example, are often classified as an ethnic group, but doing so stretches the imagination considerably, for a number of reasons: (1) Individual Jews hold a wide variety of religious views, from very conservative to very liberal—some are Orthodox believers, others are atheists; (2) Jews speak a variety of languages, and many Jews today cannot speak Hebrew, the language of tradition; (3) Jews spring from a wide variety of ancestors because people around the world have converted to Judaism over the centuries; and (4) Jews exhibit a variety of physical characteristics, ranging from very dark skinned, black-haired African Jews to light-skinned, blue-eyed, blond European Jews. From a cultural viewpoint, a nomadic Ethiopian Jew tending his sheep has much more in common with other Africans than he does with a Jewish dentist in suburban Chicago.

Perhaps the key issue in determining membership in an ethnic or cultural group is whether the individual *believes* he or she is a member of that group.

Ethnic identity is more a social construction than a biological fact. The children in this family are of mixed Anglo and Asian heritage; their ethnic identity depends not on their physical characteristics but on the tradition within which they are being raised.

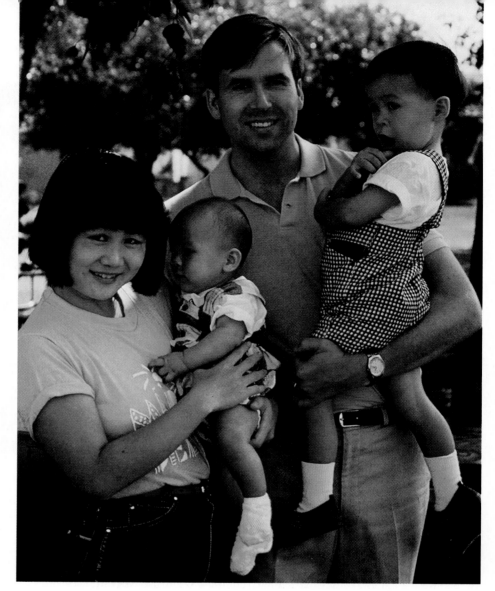

Human beings are diverse. Classifications cannot be based solely on religious views, language, ancestry, or physical characteristics.

Kin Relationships Across Cultures: Concepts and Terms

Most of us learn about kinship early in our lives, with little or no theoretical explanations. We learn, for example, about brothers and sisters and about aunts, uncles, and cousins; but we identify them as people, not based on kinship principles. We know who Uncle Jack and Aunt Libby are long before we understand the concepts of "mother's brother" or "father's sister."

All cultures recognize **kinship,** the relatedness of certain individuals within a group, and have norms and expectations that structure and govern kin behavior.

The diversity of these norms is wide-ranging. These kinship concepts describe kinds of kinship groups and the norms that govern marital forms, family structure and organization, inheritance, authority, and residence.

Kinship groups range from nuclear families to various forms of extended families and may even include symbolic relationships. The **nuclear family**—the smallest, most elementary kinship unit—usually consists of two parents and their dependent children. Even in societies in which the nuclear family is embedded within a larger group, it is recognized as a distinct entity. The nuclear family is a **conjugal family system,** one that emphasizes the relationships formed through marriage. Typically, a conjugal system includes only two generations and is relatively transitory, dissolving when the parents die or the children grow up and leave. Because nuclear families are comparatively small and short-lived, they are less likely to develop strong traditions. Many family functions are better performed by composite family groups constituting **consanguineal family systems,** those that emphasize blood ties more than marital ties.

In consanguineal systems, married couples and their children are embedded in a larger kin group of three or more generations related by blood. Consanguineal systems can include extended families or families resulting from plural marriages. An **extended family** consists of a nuclear family and those people related to its members by blood ties, such as aunts, uncles, cousins, and grandparents. A **plural marriage,** or **polygamy,** is a marriage in which a man has more than one wife—**polygyny**—or, more rarely, a marriage in which a woman has more than one husband—**polyandry.** In **monogamy,** a man or woman has only one mate. Although people from monogamous societies often perceive potential hazards in plural marriages, family patterns appear to operate smoothly in groups in which plural marriages are the norm.

A third kind of kinship group is a **pseudo-kin group,** in which relationships resembling kinship ties develop among unrelated individuals. Relationships within these groups range in intensity, from close friendships to godparent-godchild connections to individuals living together and caring for each other without any legal or blood relationship.

"I don't really have a biological family anymore," a 35-year-old woman explained. "I have a real family, though. I call it my psychological family. You see, my father was an alcoholic and died in an automobile accident. My mother was mentally ill and died several years ago in an institution. I didn't have any brothers or sisters, but when I was in high school a family in the parish knew how bad our family was doing and kind of took me in like a lost lamb.

"They've been my real family since then. I celebrate all the holidays with them, and Alf, the father, calls me the daughter his wife, Nancy, never gave him. Nancy returns the joke, calling me the daughter Alf was incapable of giving her. So I've got a dad and mom and two big brothers. It's a very special family to live in, and they're always there for me in a pinch."

Cultural norms influence family structure, but they also influence concepts of **lineage,** or lines of descent; of who holds authority in a family; and of where newly married couples should reside. Lineage is important in determining membership in a particular kinship group, patterns of inheritance, and kinship obligations or responsibilities. In some societies, descent is traced through sex;

matrilineal societies trace descent through females, and **patrilineal societies** trace descent through males.

In a matrilineal society, for example, a man inherits group membership through his mother, and lines of descent through his sister(s) are also important. Although a man may live with his wife or wives, he perceives the households of his mother and sisters as his true home. In a patrilineal society, a man's sister will be in his descent group but her children will not; they belong to their father's descent group. **Bilateral descent** is common in many Western societies, with children tied equally to relatives of both the mother and the father. In this "family tree" approach to descent, in which ancestors and descendants multiply geometrically, true descent kinship groups are not formed unless limited by generation or to particular ancestors and descendants.

Norms for lines of descent may or may not be linked to lines of authority within a kin group. If females exercise the authority in a kin group, it is considered to be a **matriarchal group.** If males are dominant and exercise the authority, it is considered a **patriarchal group.** Note that these terms emphasize femaleness and maleness, rather than motherhood and fatherhood. In a patriarchal group, for example, the grandfather is likely to wield more authority than the father of a nuclear family. But the criterion of gender always supersedes that of age in matriarchal and patriarchal kin groups.

In **equalitarian groups,** such as those found in the United States, the ideals of democracy suggest that the rights and perspectives of each sex and each generation be respected. A given family's structure and interactions may lean toward the patriarchal or matriarchal, but the norms of the group would most likely be considered equalitarian.

Norms of residence for newly married couples can also be categorized by a society's emphasis on biological sex. In a **matrilocal society,** the norm is that newly married couples live with or near the wife's kin, especially her mother's kin group. Newly married couples in **patrilocal societies** are expected to live with or near the husband's kin, usually his father's kin group. In a **neolocal society,** norms encourage newly married couples to establish a separate, autonomous residence, independent of either partner's kin group.

Although a society may have norms regarding marital and family organization and interaction, diversity is generally also evident within that society's families and kin groups. Understanding the concept of kin relationships, however, enables observers to describe the structure and dynamics of a broad range of kinship groups in ways that foster comparison and analysis.

Family Strengths, Stereotypes, and Challenges in Various Ethnic and Cultural Groups

It has been hypothesized that strong families, whatever their ethnic identification or country of origin, share three major clusters of qualities: cohesion, flexibility, and communication. These three broad clusters encompass the six qualities of strong families identified by the family strengths framework, as described in Chapter 1. **Family cohesion** includes commitment and time together. Commitment to the family includes trust, honesty, dependability, and faithfulness. Time together means spending a considerable amount of quality time together, sharing activities, feelings, and ideas, and enjoying each other's company.

Family flexibility includes the ability to deal with stress and having helpful spiritual beliefs. Coping abilities include using personal and family resources; helping each other; seeing crises as challenges, not denying them; and growing together by working through crises. Spiritual well-being includes happiness, optimism, hope, faith, and a set of shared ethical values that guide family members through life's challenges.

Family communication focuses on positive communication and on appreciating and having affection for family members. Positive communication includes open, straightforward discussion, being cooperative rather than competitive, and sharing feelings with one another. Appreciation and affection include kindness, caring for each other, respect for individuality, and a feeling of security.

More than 500 successful families from five American ethnic groups—Native Americans, Hmong refugees, African Americans, Mexican Americans, and Caucasians—were studied by Douglas Abbott and William Meredith (1988). They focused on the three clusters, cohesion, flexibility, and communication. They also used the family strengths scale developed earlier by David Olson, Andrea Larsen, and Hamilton McCubbin (Olson, McCubbin, et al., 1989).

The family strengths scale revealed more similarities than differences across the five groups. In fact, there were significant similarities among all the groups, with correlations in the range of .60–.85, except between the Hmong and the Native Americans and between the Hmong and the Caucasians. All five groups agreed that strong families (1) use effective communication and listening skills; (2) are trusting and trustworthy; (3) are affirming and supportive; and (4) teach a sense of right and wrong behavior. Other common strengths were teaching respect for others, spending time doing things together, and feeling a sense of shared responsibility. Table 2.1 (p. 54) details the responses from the various ethnic groups.

In summary, Abbott and Meredith noted that the most striking finding was the consensus among all five ethnic groups on the traits they considered most important to healthy family functioning. The researchers concluded that strong families are those that are high in family cohesion, family flexibility, and family communication. These traits of strong families, according to Abbott and Meredith, "extend beyond ethnic boundaries" (1988, p. 146).

In describing successful families, we have emphasized family system characteristics, but it is also important to consider the sociocultural context in which families live. Figure 2.3 (p. 55) includes the family system characteristics of cohesion, flexibility, and communication and also illustrates the connection of the extended family system, the social system, and the belief system.

The **extended family system,** which includes relatives, kin, and other family members connected to the family system, is a particularly important resource for families of color (McAdoo, 1993). The **social system** is an important resource for families because it includes economic resources and educational and related opportunities. Families of color are often at a disadvantage in the social system because they are likely to be of middle or lower socioeconomic status. Because of their lack of both education and economic resources, and as a result of discrimination against them in various settings, the social system is often more a liability

Table 2.1 Family Strengths in Various Ethnic Groups

FAMILY TRAIT	ETHNIC GROUP					
	Caucasian N = 210	African American N = 103	Mexican American N = 105	Hmong N = 80	Native American N = 57	CHI SQUARE[a]
Communicates and listens	88%	67%	86%	81%	60%	36.2**
Trusting and trustworthy	87	69	88	73	51	46.7**
Is affirming and supportive	86	70	82	75	81	13.2*
Teaches a sense of right and wrong	85	77	78	76	61	16.6*
Teaches respect for others	73	58	85	41	74	48.0**
Shares leisure time	67	41	51	41	23	47.4**
Is responsible for family welfare	65	52	51	43	53	15.5*
Has a sense of play and humor	58	55	35	18	37	47.9*
Respects privacy of family members	57	57	72	56	39	17.9*
Shares religious beliefs	56	30	32	15	32	50.9**
Has two parents living at home	46	39	63	24	30	34.6**
Values family traditions	41	38	45	73	35	29.9**
Seeks help with problems	40	36	36	41	23	N.S.
Encourages individuality	38	27	26	14	17	22.0*
Financial security	36	51	42	35	40	N.S.
Has a base of parental rules	34	41	28	41	18	N.S.
Respects elders	34	35	66	54	79	60.4**
Shares similar values	32	27	30	38	21	N.S.
Allows for negotiation of family rules	31	14	20	20	35	17.5*
Values a college education	29	28	45	64	23	42.3**
Prays together	26	36	34	39	28	N.S.

Note: Traits reported in this table had to be considered important by at least two thirds of the parents in at least two ethnic groups.
[a]Chi square is a statistic that compares the frequencies or percentages in two or more groups to determine if their differences are significantly greater than the differences expected by chance. In the Chi Square column, * indicates $p < .01$, ** indicates $p < .001$, and N.S. indicates nonsignificant differences between rankings.
Source: "Characteristics of Strong Families: Perceptions of Ethnic Parents" by D. A. Abbott and W. H. Meredith, 1988, *Home Economics Research Journal, 17* (2), p. 144. Copyright 1988 by American Home Economics Association. Reprinted by permission.

than an asset to families of color. The **belief system** of families includes spiritual beliefs and a certainty that family members on their own and as a unit can deal with the challenges that confront them. Families of color often have a solid belief system that helps them maintain a strong and successful family.

The sections that follow identify some of the stereotypes, strengths, and challenges of several ethnic and cultural groups in our society. The text emphasizes each group's strengths; summary figures present the stereotypes and challenges, as well as review the strengths.

Unfortunately, most of what people know about ethnic and cultural groups other than their own is based on **stereotypes**—standardized, oversimplified views. When a person from one group describes people from another, the description is often a stereotype. **Prejudice,** which literally means prejudging, is also closely linked with stereotyping; both attitudes reinforce each other. As a society we need to move beyond stereotypes and focus on each group's strengths and challenges. Recognizing others' strengths helps reduce prejudice.

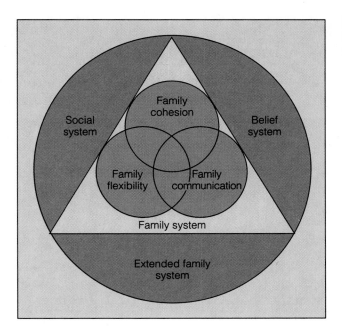

Figure 2.3 Sociocultural Context and Family System Characteristics

Strengths of White Families

Much of the early research on family strengths focused on White families and resulted in the family strengths framework of Nick Stinnett and John DeFrain (1985) (which was introduced in Chapter 1). In a study of 1,000 couples and families throughout the family life cycle, David Olson and his colleagues identified strengths that helped families at each stage maintain high levels of marital and family satisfaction (Olson, McCubbin, et al., 1989). Because these strengths were described in detail in Chapter 1, they will simply be summarized here:

- *Commitment to family.* Strong White families are very committed to one another and are able to give all family members the freedom and support they need to achieve their individual goals.

- *Time together.* White families that remain strong throughout the family life cycle find ways to spend time together and enjoy each other.

- *Ability to cope with stress.* Although all families encounter marital and family stress, strong families see stress as a challenge and deal directly with issues as they occur.

- *Spiritual well-being.* Strong White families have spiritual beliefs and values, including religious beliefs, that help them deal with ongoing life issues.

- *Positive communication.* One of the most important characteristics of healthy White families is that they feel good about their communication with one another.

- *Appreciation and affection.* Sharing the positive feelings they have about one another helps keep relationships positive in strong White families.

Figure 2.4 Stereotypes, Strengths, and Challenges of African American Families

Stereotypes	Strengths	Challenges
• Low income; on welfare • Low intelligence • Criminal • Lack of education • Athletic • Entertainers • Religious • Promiscuous	• Strong kinship bonds • Strong work orientation • Flexibility in family roles • Strong motivation to achieve • Strong religious orientation • Caring parenting	• Being judged as a financial risk • Feeling powerless • Building self-esteem • High risk of young men being killed • Discrimination/racism • Lack of education • Violence against each other • Lack of male role models

Strengths of African American Families

A number of family researchers have been interested in African American family strengths for more than two decades (Boyd-Franklin, 1989; McAdoo, 1993; Willie, 1988). The picture they have developed of healthy African American families is similar to the picture of healthy White families. One of the earliest studies was by Marie Peters (1981), who reviewed her own work and that of other African American family investigators and identified six strengths of African American families (Figure 2.4):

- *Strong kinship bonds.* The extended family is very important to many African American families, and African Americans tend to take relatives into their households.

- *Strong work orientation.* Dual-job households are common among strong African American families.

- *Flexibility in family roles.* Role flexibility serves as an effective coping mechanism in healthy African American families. Because it has been necessary for many mothers to work outside the home, Black mothers tend to have more power in the family. The typical strong African American family is not matriarchal or patriarchal but is egalitarian in style. African American families have a longer tradition of egalitarian marriages than White families; compared with African American couples, White couples as a group are relative newcomers to the dual-job arena (McAdoo, 1993).

- *Strong motivation to achieve.* African American parents commonly believe education is important, and many would like to see their children go to college.

- *Strong religious orientation.* African American churches provide emotional, spiritual, and intellectual satisfaction to African American families. Church

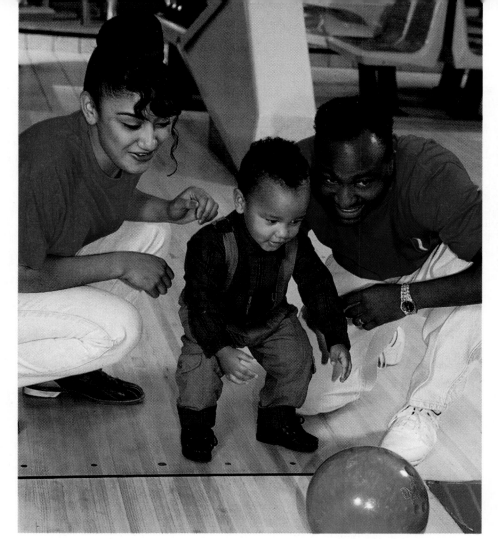

Caring parenting has been identified as a particular strength of African American families. When parents take the time to share recreational activities with their children, as this couple is doing, they make an investment in both the emotional development of the children and the future stability of the family.

work provides meaning and purpose for many African Americans. Dr. Martin Luther King, Jr., for example, achieved "greatness . . . through the leadership developed and cultivated in the African American church" (Azubike, 1987, p. 99).

- *Caring parenting.* Researchers have studied rates of corporal punishment (slapping and spanking) across all income levels of African American and White families. Murray Straus, a nationally known family researcher who has focused on violence in families, reports that 78% of White parents hit their 4-year-old children in a given year, compared with 70% of parents of color (1994). In families having 16-year-old adolescents, 48% of White parents hit their teenagers, compared with 39% of parents of color. When facing economic stress and social disadvantage, African American parents are apparently better than Whites at staying cool. This is especially noteworthy in light of the fact that African American parents, being members of a minority group, must also contend with racism.

B O X   2 . 2

Kwanzaa Holidays Celebrate
Black Principles, Unity

In many homes in our community, from December 26 through the new year, African American families and individuals practice a unique, non-heroic observation called Kwanzaa.

The word *Kwanzaa* is from the Kiswahili language, which is noteworthy because Kiswahili is a non-ethnic trading language used throughout Africa and not tribal specific. Kwanzaa is derived from the expression "matudnad ya Kwanzaa," which means "first harvest" or "first fruits," and the ritual/observance bears similarity to community celebrations which follow the harvest in many African cultures.

Kwanzaa was initiated in this country by Malauna Ron Karenga, a small group of African American adults, and seven children in Los Angeles, in 1966. Karenga is widely respected as a scholar, social activist, critical thinker, founder of "US" (United Slaves) and the "Soul Patrol," and as the originator of the "Nguzo Saba," which literally translated means "seven foundations" or "seven principles" of blackness, on which Kwanzaa is based and which form the bedrock of "Kawaida," the black value system.

Regrettably, when explaining what Kwanzaa is, it is often most helpful to explain what Kwanzaa is not. Kwanzaa is not—and should not be considered—a "black Christmas." The emphasis in Kwanzaa is earth-based—not mystical, commercially exploitative, or based on people traveling through the clouds. Kwanzaa stresses our African roots; it seeks to narrow and deny the differences between black people throughout the world and to demonstrate and define our historical and cultural unity, while facilitating its acceptance.

Kwanzaa is primarily a practice of gathering and celebration among black people, and its reinforcing gestures (often called rituals) are practiced or observed during the seven-day period from December 26 to January 1. It was created to strengthen our collective self-concept as black people, honor our past, critically evaluate our present, and commit ourselves to a fuller, more productive future. While Kwanzaa does involve gifts for children and one another (preferably items we have created or cultural and educational gifts), again, the primary force or focus of Kwanzaa revolves around children and the Nguzo Saba, or seven principles, with each day of the Kwanzaa observance dedicated to one of the principles.

The Nguzo Saba are as follows:

1. *Umoha (unity):* To strive for and maintain unity in the family, community, nation, and race.

2. *Kujichagulia (self-determination):* To define ourselves, name ourselves, create for ourselves, and speak for ourselves.

3. *Ujima (collective work and responsibility):* To build and maintain our community together and make our sisters' and brothers' problems our problems—to be solved together.

4. *Ujamaa (cooperative economics):* To build and maintain our own stores and other businesses and to profit from them together.

5. *Nia (purpose):* To make our collective vocation the building and developing of our community, to restore our people to their traditional greatness.

6. *Kuumba (creativity):* To do always as much as we can, in order to leave our community more beautiful and beneficial than we inherited it.

7. *Imani (faith):* To believe with all our heart in our people, our parents, our teachers, our leaders, and the righteousness and victory of our collective struggle.

Again, Kwanzaa is primarily intended for children, the hope of our future, and is not a mere seven-day observation but a model to live by for African Americans. Happy Kwanzaa!

Researchers at Howard University (Gary, Beatty, & Berry, 1986) studied 50 strong African American families in Washington, D.C., and found that the strengths these families exhibited were very similar to the strengths reported in a study of strong families who were predominantly White (Stinnett, Sanders, & De-Frain, 1981). Looking at various studies of African American and White family strengths, one might conclude that if there are differences between healthy families in these two groups, they are that religious values and kinship ties are somewhat more important in African American families than in White families.

In the past few years, many African Americans have begun celebrating their heritage in an observance called Kwanzaa. Meaning "first harvest" in Kiswahili, Kwanzaa is a seven-day celebration from December 26 to January 1. See Box 2.2 for more information on this celebration.

Strengths of Latino Families

As mentioned earlier, Latinos encompass people from numerous Spanish-speaking cultures. About two thirds are Mexican Americans, but even within this group there is diversity:

> Scholars Mario Garcia and Rodolfo Alvarez suggest that people of Mexican descent in the United States constitute several rather than a single demographic group (Shorris, 1992, pp. 95–100). Two such reference groups are Mexican Americans and Chicanos/Chicanas. The Mexican American group comprises people who immigrated to border states, such as California and Texas, following World War II. People who consider themselves Mexican Americans are generally older and more conservative than those who identify themselves as Chicanos or Chicanas, who are younger and more militant.
>
> Chicanos and Chicanas came of age in the 1960s and gained some attention in the 1970s. They perceived Mexican immigrants who wanted to assimilate with the predominant Anglo culture as sellouts. To distinguish themselves from the Mexican American group, Chicanos and Chicanas adopted specific patterns of behaving, including their own code words. (Brydon & Scott, 1997, p. 262)

Although this kind of diversity is real, there are still cultural commonalities that allow us to refer, in general terms, to the Latino population of the United States. (*Hispanic* is the term most often used in studies and statistics, including those published by the U.S. government, for Latino populations.) But always keep in mind that commonalities are broad and general; every individual and every family is unique in its own ways.

Countless Latinos in the United States have managed to preserve a strong family system in spite of the difficult challenges they face. Latinos place a high priority on the family as a source of identity and support. Family includes the immediate family unit (*la casa*), the extended family (*la familia*), and godparents (*los compadres*). In Latino culture, the well-being of the entire family system is given priority over individual goals. Box 2.3 (p. 60) highlights common stereotypes of Latino Americans. Rather than focusing on such stereotypes, however, this chapter emphasizes family strengths.

BOX 2.3

Getting Beyond Latino Myths

According to the stereotype, Latino Americans are a monolithic interest group. Among other myths about Latinos are that they prefer liberal immigration policies, favor the Spanish language over English, and tend to vote in political blocs. A [1992] study [has] shatter[ed] those beliefs and should help Americans move beyond wholesale descriptions of population groups based on race and ethnicity.

The Latino National Political Survey discovered that Latinos share a driving commitment to be part of American society. That dedication often eclipses ethnic loyalties among the three largest groups, Mexican Americans, Puerto Ricans, and Cuban Americans.

Yet for decades the media and the federal government have generalized from the most visible part of the Latino population. The resulting stereotypes alienated Latinos from the mainstream.

The Census Bureau, for example, has tried to classify Latinos by color. In 1940, Latinos were categorized as "black" or a "racial" nonwhite group. In 1950 and 1960, the Census used the category of "white persons of Spanish surname." In 1970, the classification was changed to "white persons of Spanish surname and

Spanish mother tongue." Then, in 1980, the expansive "nonwhite Hispanic" [was introduced]. Because the Census uses "white" and "black" to classify residents, it has shuttled Latinos back and forth between the two extremes. In each case, the principle behind the label is the perceived presence or absence of color.

In reality, the mirror that Latinos hold up to America reflects many opportunities to move beyond a system of racial distinctions. Latinos often prefer to juggle two languages, or two cultures or national heritages, even if the resulting syntheses seem messy or dangerous. To those conditioned to tidy ethnic compartments, Latino ambiguity is indeed threatening. A people who violate boundaries of race, language, and culture upset myths of a nation-state based on borders and exclusion.

But in a nation increasingly transformed by global restructuring, and collapse of some mythic categories that once defined its identity, Latinos may be the vanguard. Their seemingly discordant virtues—ethnic identities and faith in America—can be a source of celebration and strength. Latinos can help America move closer to a future in which all its citizens will be accomplices in a multiracial kinship and culture.

Source: "Getting Beyond Latino Myths," editorial, December 26, 1992, Minneapolis *Star Tribune*, p. 10A.
Copyright 1992 by the Minneapolis *Star Tribune*. Reprinted by permission.

In one extensive overview of the strengths of Latino families, William Vega (1995) identified the six most important characteristics, which are very similar to those that have been identified for families from other cultures in the United States (Figure 2.5):

- *Familism.* The family is a major priority; it is highly valued. There is a strong emotional commitment to the family.

- *High family cohesion.* Strong Latino families have very high cohesion, although cohesion decreases across generations somewhat among Latino families living in the United States.

- *High family flexibility.* There is considerable flexibility in roles in Latino families, in contrast to the stereotyped view in which the male is seen as dominant.

- *Supportive kin network system.* The large kin network system of most Latino families is very important as a supportive resource and is a strong tradition.

Stereotypes	Strengths	Challenges
• Lack of education • Large families • Migrant workers • Macho males/machismo • Superstitious • Religious • Illegal aliens • Alcohol abuse • Women in traditional gender roles	• Familism • High family cohesion • High family flexibility • Supportive kin network system • Equalitarian decision making • Strong ethnic identity	• Remaining family centered • Maintaining traditions • Gaining financial resources • Overcoming the language barrier • Overcoming economic discrimination • Handling relocation issues • Increasing education • Acculturation across generations

Figure 2.5 Stereotypes, Strengths, and Challenges of Latino Families

- *Equalitarian decision making.* More and more, families share roles more equally; decision making is equalitarian.

- *Strong ethnic identity.* The importance of the Latino culture and values binds families together and helps give them a strong ethnic identity.

Many Latino families are going through transitions similar to those that Anglo (non-Latino White) families have experienced through the generations. Alfredo Mirandé (1977, 1979) outlined how social scientists' views of Chicano (Mexican American) families have evolved over the years. Historically, social scientists have tended to disagree on the nature of these families. After reviewing research on Mexican American families, Mirandé (1979) concluded that the dominant pattern of decision making and action is not male dominated and authoritarian but equalitarian—that is, power is shared among relative equals. Most husbands and wives share not only in decision making but in the performance of household tasks and child care. Although many have assumed clear gender-role segregation, Mirandé found this pattern to be the exception rather than the rule.

Two of the strengths of Mexican American families parallel the strengths of Anglo families. Using an assessment scale called FACES (Family Adaptability and Cohesion Evaluation Scales), William Vega and colleagues (1986) studied cohesion (togetherness) and adaptability (flexibility) in a group of low-income Mexican American parents and a group of middle-income Anglo parents. The researchers expected to find differences between the two groups, based not so much on culture but on social class. In short, they assumed money helps family life run a bit more smoothly. They were surprised to find that even though the Mexican American families had the additional challenges that come with low income, their group scored no differently on cohesion and adaptability than the middle-income Anglos.

Another study focused on immigrant Puerto Rican families in New York City. Lloyd Rogler and Rosemary Santana Cooney (1984) interviewed 100 intergenerational families, each consisting of an older married couple in the parent generation and a younger married couple in the child generation. As expected, ethnic

Contrary to some common stereotypes, research indicates that both decision making and household chores tend to be shared in Latino families. By cooking dinner together, this husband and wife not only create an enjoyable family time but model an equalitarian relationship for their children.

identity—identification with Puerto Rican rather than American culture—was stronger in the parent generation, but it remained relatively strong in the children's generation. Those who had arrived in New York City from Puerto Rico at a younger age were more likely to have a less exclusively Puerto Rican identity. Younger people appeared to be more adaptable and more readily influenced by the host society. They were more willing to take on a dual identity—saying, in effect, "I am both Puerto Rican and American."

Conflicts between generations are a common family problem in many ethnic and cultural groups. The case of a Chicana student whose extended family found her struggle for a graduate school education and personal success threatening illustrates this point (Box 2.4). But the case also shows the transitions many Chicano families are undergoing—and the strengths they possess. Because of the support of her Chicano husband and her mother, this young woman was able to overcome hostility and lack of support from other family members.

Strengths of Asian American Families

Families with roots in Asia are another very resilient group in this country. Although Asian Americans have faced prejudice and discrimination throughout their history in the United States, they have fared better than other ethnic minorities economically and have managed to preserve their family ties, traditions, and val-

Cultural Conflicts for a Female Chicana College Student

I am a Chicana graduate student who wants to complete a Ph.D. in family studies so I can teach at the college level and help the family field be more inclusive and up-to-date regarding Chicano families. Fortunately, the choices I've made are not in conflict with my family of procreation.

It was very difficult for my family of origin initially to understand why I wanted or needed to go to school for so long. Since my grandparents and parents struggled just to provide for adequate housing, food, and clothing, they find it difficult to see why education is so important. They were also somewhat threatened by the fact that I wanted to study families because I might learn too much.

Another conflict was regarding my interest in my own development versus their emphasis on the whole family. They felt I was focusing too much on myself and not giving back enough to the family. Also, they felt this was making me more competitive and less cooperative, which is a quality valued highly. Another issue is the use of the Spanish language and whether I would use both Spanish and English in my home. Since we decided to raise our children using English only, some family members viewed that choice as rejecting our heritage. Also, as my years of college education increased, my relatives tended to distance themselves more from me.

Fortunately, my husband, who is also Chicano, is totally supportive and is a house husband for our two small children. He takes care of the children, and I am the primary wage earner. This is not the traditional family model for most Chicanos, and so it does challenge some of our other family members and kin.

While I was not initially aware of the importance of my mother's support, I have lately become even more appreciative of her encouraging words. I have finally been giving her more credit for her support. She also served as a positive role model since she began working full time when I was young. She also has strongly encouraged me to work outside the home and even to try to seek a career.

In general, I have made it because I am determined to have a professional career and have the strong support of my husband and my mother. My other relatives are less understanding and supportive since they question my goals and values. In spite of it all, education is necessary for me to help advance myself and my family.

Source: Unpublished manuscript by Julie Palacio, 1992, former graduate student in Family Social Science, University of Minnesota, St. Paul, MN. Reprinted by permission.

ues (McLeod, 1986; Schwartz, Raine, & Robins, 1987). A period of disruption occurred in the 1940s, when Japanese Americans—even those born in this country—were confined to what were essentially prison camps. After Pearl Harbor, fear of further attacks by Japan led the U.S. government to resettle Japanese American families in these camps until the war ended. Four decades later, the federal government agreed to modestly recompense surviving family members for the ill-treatment they suffered.

Although Asian Americans probably do not face the same level of discrimination that African Americans face in the workplace, a report by the Commission on Civil Rights was forced to conclude that "anti-Asian activity in the form of violence, vandalism, harassment and intimidation continues to occur across the nation" (Schwartz et al., 1987). Even today there is a degree of discrimination against Asian Americans, fueled by fear of competition from the powerhouse economies in East Asia. Many Asian immigrants come to this country because hard work in their homeland did not produce much economic progress. In this country, working hard

A tradition of hard work, discipline, high regard for education, and commitment to the family has translated into a valuable and important strength for many Asian American families. This graduate honors his family with his achievement, but he has probably also enjoyed their whole-hearted support and encouragement as he worked toward it.

Figure 2.6 Stereotypes, Strengths, and Challenges of Asian American Families

Stereotypes	Strengths	Challenges
• Submissive women • High intelligence • Obedient children • Competitive • Hard working • Unemotional	• Strong family orientation • Filial piety • High value on education • Well-disciplined children • Extended family support • Family loyalty	• High expectations for self • Loss of ties with kin • Emotional vulnerability • Stigma against seeking help • Distrust of those outside the group • Excessive focus on work

often provides greater rewards. This energy can be somewhat intimidating to those who have been in this country longer and have "settled in" to a comfortable life.

Many Asian Americans share a cultural heritage that values discipline, family commitment, hard work, and education. Young people reared in such an environment become challenging competitors in a society such as ours, which values competition and individual initiative.

Asian American families are very diverse, but they all share many of the same strengths. Following are the six major strengths of these families, which are summarized in Figure 2.6:

- *Strong family orientation.* Both the nuclear and the extended family are very important historically and today.

BOX   2 . 5

A Life History Approach to Understanding Families from Southeast Asia

To better capture the family dynamics in families that came to the United States from Vietnam, Cambodia, and Laos, Daniel Detzner used the life history approach. The question: How does forced relocation to another culture change family structure, dynamics, and rituals? The life history approach was considered relevant to the study of Asian elders because storytelling and sharing of oral traditions were part of the culture. Elders were also held in high esteem as advisors and wise people.

In field-testing the questions, Detzner found denial of any family conflict or even disagreement. This is understandable because the traditional teachings of Confucius and Buddha describe conflict as shameful. Reworking the questions to ask about family rules and the consequences when rules were broken revealed more than 200 cases of conflict. Then, in-depth, semi-structured interviews were done with the oldest generation in each household, using a translator. These interviews were then coded into a computer system for analysis.

The surprising finding was that despite the reluctance of those interviewed to discuss conflict directly, the indirect approach revealed conflict in almost every life history case, across the cultural groups and at every stage of the family life cycle. So conflict was seen as normative and was rather frequent, even though as an issue it was avoided and even denied. A related finding was that the elders felt their traditional power was disappearing and they were no longer respected by the younger generation, many of whom were rebelling against traditional practices.

Source: From "Life Histories: Conflict in Southeast Asia Refugee Families" by D. F. Detzner. In *Qualitative Methods in Family Research*, pp. 85–102, edited by J. Gilgun, K. Kaly, and G. Handel, 1992, Newbury Park, CA: Sage. Copyright © 1992 by J. Gilgun and D. F. Detzner. Adapted by permission of the publisher.

- *Filial piety.* The great respect that Asian American families have for their elders is noteworthy. It helps explain the high level of mutual support each generation receives from the other generations.

- *High value on education.* Asian American families emphasize the importance of education, from nursery school through college.

- *Well-disciplined children.* Traditionally, children are expected to be quiet, well behaved, and somewhat passive.

- *Extended family support.* Financial and emotional support is provided by the extended family when the nuclear family needs it.

- *Family loyalty.* Family members support each other and protect privacy.

Recent immigrants from Southeast Asia (Vietnam, Cambodia, and Laos) have had a more difficult time adjusting to American culture than earlier immigrants from Japan, China, and Korea did. Although many recent arrivals were farmers from rural areas, these immigrants often find themselves in poor inner-city neighborhoods, where their traditional values are challenged. This has made the adjustment to American culture difficult. To better understand the acculturation process of these families, one researcher used a method called the life history approach, in which elders told their stories rather than responded to questionnaires (Detzner, 1992). The findings are described in Box 2.5.

Figure 2.7 Stereotypes, Strengths, and Challenges of Native American Families

Stereotypes	Strengths	Challenges
• Lazy • Unmotivated • Irresponsible • Passive • Nonexpressive • Easily influenced by alcohol	• Extended family system • Traditional beliefs • High family cohesion • Respect for elders • Bilingual language skills • Tribal support system	• Conflicting values of tribe and U.S. society • Maintaining family traditions • Staying cohesive and connected • Lack of role models • Improving education

Strengths of Native American Families

There are approximately 1.5 million Native American families in the United States, representing roughly 400 tribes. About half live on reservations (Carson, Dail, Greeley, & Kenote, 1990). The tremendous degree of diversity among tribes contributes to the difficulty researchers have in studying Native American families. This has led one investigator to conclude, "What we know, then, about Indian families is fragmented, anecdotal, descriptive, and often overpowered by poor understanding of the particular cultures being studied" (Stauss, 1986, p. 345).

The six major strengths of Native American families are as follows (Figure 2.7):

- *Extended family system.* The extended family is very strong in Native American families.

- *Traditional beliefs.* The belief system of Native American tribes includes harmony with nature and the value of contentment.

- *High family cohesion.* The connectedness of the family is important. The family is broadly defined to include the nuclear family, the extended family, and the tribal community.

- *Respect for elders.* Elders are the most respected individuals in traditional Native American tribes, and the family reinforces this attitude.

- *Bilingual language skills.* Most Native Americans work hard to maintain their native language, but this is becoming more difficult because the children attend school off the reservation and have access to an increasing amount of television and other mass media.

- *Tribal support system.* Many Native Americans rely on their tribal support system for all types of problems. Only when that is inadequate do they turn to outside support.

Native American families have many strengths but society tends to focus on their problems as they try to strike a balance between maintaining their culture and fitting in to contemporary society.

Although Native American families are characterized by diversity (Stauss, 1986), some investigators have asserted that the family remains the basic unit of the Native American community and that the Native American family can be characterized as having traditional beliefs, practices, and languages and a unique history and lifestyle. Native American families find support from the strengths of both individual family members and the clan or tribal group to which they belong (R. Lewis, 1981).

Studies have found that many Native American tribes emphasize mutual dependence among tribal members, responsibility, respect for others, courage, optimism, and contentment. This contentment comes from identification with the cosmos (feeling one with the world), a spiritual orientation to life, and traditional religious practices. Living in harmony with nature and with other human beings is of utmost importance, nature being a powerful learning tool for family members and the tribe (R. Lewis, 1981; J. S. Olson & Wilson, 1984).

The extended family is still a source of strength for many Native Americans, but this is changing as more family members leave the reservation to seek opportunities elsewhere. Native American youths may have a wider array of people to whom they are attached than non–Native Americans. In times of crisis, support from both the extended family and the tribal community helps people survive (Robbins, 1987). Nuclear families are important, but the tribal community also acts as a safety net, assuming a great deal of responsibility for the welfare of its individual members. Many fathers actively care for their own children along with the mothers and serve as father substitutes for children whose fathers have died or deserted the family (Staples & Mirandé, 1980; Carson et al., 1990).

How an individual behaves, in both positive and negative ways, reflects upon the individual's family and tribe (Carson et al., 1990). The group is in part collectively liable for the transgressions of its individual members, so the group provides a collective conscience and consciousness that emphasize individual responsibility. Respect for elders is common among Native American tribes, and grandparents often hold a unique position, helping to pass on cultural values and beliefs to their grandchildren and educating the young about the physical, social, and spiritual world. Social shame (i.e., embarrassment) is a common tool for disciplining children. In general, physical punishment is not encouraged or condoned. Parents usually praise their children only for special accomplishments. The young are not socialized to expect praise, and it is not given out lightly (Burgess, 1980).

A number of tribes stress marriages based not only on an attraction between two people but on the consensus of their relatives and the tribal community (Medicine, 1981). This approach to marriage recognizes the fact that an individual marries not only another individual but also that person's family and cultural community. Research suggests that these officially sanctioned marriages are more stable than those not recognized by the couple's family members or the tribe (Stauss, 1986).

The bilingual childrearing seen in some tribes and families is also identified as a strength of Native American families (Carson et al., 1990). Although most Native Americans learn English for survival in a White-dominant culture, they often find strength in sharing their own common language. The family strengths and culturally adaptive patterns of Native Americans deserve more extensive study in the years ahead (Carson et al., 1990).

Challenges for Ethnic Families

Ethnic families in the United States have many challenges. Among them are intercultural marriage, the issue of assimilation, and relationships between men and women and between parents and children. Ethnic families do not experience the "advantages of being in the majority" that Whites in the predominant culture do (Box 2.6).

Marriage Outside the Group

In many countries throughout the world, marriage is seen primarily as an agreement between two families. An alliance through marriage between two successful families can enhance the power, prestige, and well-being of all the members of both families. In this sense, one marries not just an individual but also that person's family.

Because individuality is stressed in American culture, the importance of a good "fit" between families is often overlooked, and individuals who wish to marry of-

The Advantages of Being in the Majority

If you're a member of the predominant culture in any society, there are innumerable benefits that accrue to you. You receive these benefits every day of your life regardless of whether you worked for them—and, thus, "deserve" them—or whether you didn't do anything at all. They are yours—a birthright, like being born into a wealthy family.

If you're a member of the majority culture, you take these benefits for granted. In fact, you hardly ever think about them. One of the few times they come to mind is when members of a minority culture point out that they don't have the same benefits but would like to have them. When this happens, the response of the majority culture member is relatively predictable. No matter where you are living in the world, the majority culture member is likely to (1) feel a bit guilty and ashamed and want to share these advantages with the minority culture; (2) deny that this is the case and refuse to listen; or (3) get outright angry and defensive.

We're not just targeting American culture here; we believe this is a cross-cultural phenomenon. Many countries throughout the world have a dominant culture. The dominant culture does not necessarily have the most members in the society, but does hold most of the power. (In South Africa, for example, Blacks outnumber Whites by a vast majority, but power has traditionally rested in White hands.)

As one cynic observed, the group that has the most guns dictates which language people speak in the society. Basically, the dominant culture creates rules, customs, and agencies that best serve the needs of the dominant culture. Some people might argue that this is only natural: if there are more of your particular group, or if your particular group is in command, you will almost without thinking create a world good for your group.

The problem with this thinking, of course, is that most societies in the world are not composed of only one culture, but a collection of diverse cultures. To fa-vor one culture over another is simply unfair. Minority cultures—that is, those who do not hold the most power—rarely ask that the majority culture change completely to accommodate them. Rather, members of minority cultures generally tend to ask for a more level playing field, in addition to respect, sensitivity, and con-sideration—the basic rights that members of the ma-jority culture also demand. Only when minority cultures feel pushed up against the wall do they demand a rev-olution, and this usually happens when the dominant culture has turned a deaf ear on their feelings.

What, in essence, are we talking about here? If you're a member of the majority culture:

- People speak the same language you speak.

- The educational system is patterned on your ways of thinking and honors your history, your beliefs, and your values.

- The job market is more open to you because you are the "right" color, gender, religion, sexual orientation, political affiliation, or social class, and you don't have a disability that makes the majority culture uncom-fortable.

- People will not discriminate in renting an apartment to you or selling you a house in their neighborhood.

- The laws, the police, and the courts all are sensitive to your cultural values and will be likely to deal with you in a relatively open-minded fashion.

- Religious and spiritual values of the culture are ideals that you can agree and live with.

- Music, literature, movies, and art teach values with which you are in harmony.

The list of advantages accruing to those in the ma-jority culture is almost endless. What advantages can you add to this list?

ten purposely ignore advice from family members. Sometimes that advice is based on ignorance of the proposed marriage partner's personal strengths and/or on prej-udice toward the cultural group from which the proposed partner comes. The greater the differences between the two families, the more likely the chance for conflict.

As our society becomes more ethnically diverse, there is more marriage across ethnic groups, which in turn increases ethnic diversity. Asian Americans have the highest rate of **intercultural marriage**—marriage between people from two different cultural or ethnic groups—of all U.S. groups. The rate of intercultural marriage is 34% among Japanese Americans, 31% among Korean Americans, and 16% among Chinese Americans. African Americans and Latinos have the lowest rates of intercultural marriage, at 2% and 12%, respectively (S. M. Lee & Yamanaka, 1990).

Family therapists have questioned whether some young people "fall in love" with someone from another cultural group as a way of rebelling against their parents. Such a strategy may work in the short run, but it is a weak foundation upon which to build a long-term relationship. Movie director Spike Lee points out in his film *Jungle Fever* that some intercultural couples may be attracted to each other because of the mystery represented by the other group. In the movie, the lead male character says that his affair with a White woman was a matter of simple curiosity: "You were curious about Black. . . . I was curious about White." After the movie was completed, the actress who played the female lead told an interviewer that "within the cast there were some very, very different points of view about whether or not interracial love was acceptable or healthy" (Kroll, 1991, pp. 44–45).

When same-culture and intercultural marriages are compared statistically, intercultural couples are somewhat more likely to divorce. Lack of support from parents and other family members probably contributes to this higher divorce rate. This is not to say that intercultural marriages cannot succeed, but couples in such marriages need the support of their family and friends.

Black-White Marriages

As suggested above, Black-White relationships and marriages are not common among Americans; in 1995, out of a total of 56 million married couples in the United States, only about 296,000 consisted of one Black partner and one White partner (U.S. Bureau of the Census, 1995). One study found that Black-White couples experienced more negative reactions and discrimination than either African American couples or European American couples.

To gather information about Black-White couples, Paul Rosenblatt, Terri Karis, and Richard Powell (1995) conducted a study of 21 multiracial couples (*multiracial* was the term the couples preferred). All of the couples were interviewed by Terri Karis, a White woman, and Richard Powell, a Black man, who are themselves a couple. In 16 of the 21 couples in the study, the man was African American; in the other 5 couples, the woman was African American. This percentage is similar to the national sample. Nineteen of the 21 couples were married, and most were between the ages of 20 and 50. The couples were generally well educated.

Most of these multiracial couples said they became interested in each other because they were so alike in values and interests. Similar findings were reported in a 1993 study of 29 Black-White couples (Kouri & Lasswell, 1993). Most of these couples said they had much in common and felt like "soul mates."

Most of the multiracial couples in the Rosenblatt, Karis, and Powell study experienced opposition from the family of the White partner. Fathers and other kin are often more opposed than mothers. These families typically will not discuss with other family members or friends that their White daughter is involved with a Black man. The White partner often grows distant from family members who are not supportive of the relationship.

Rosenblatt, Karis, and Powell identified six principal objections to the multiracial relationship that family members of the White partner made. First, they worried about disapproval by other family members, friends, and society in general. Second, they expressed concern about the safety and well-being of their adult child. Third, they pointed to the alleged clannishness of African Americans. Fourth, they worried about problems the children of the couple might have. Fifth, they expressed concern about the likelihood of a poor economic future. And sixth, they foresaw other problems that were often not specified. The White partners' reaction to the parents' opposition was often complicated; some said their feelings were a "blend of pain, anger, frustration, desperation, [and] determination" (p. 81).

The African American family was often more accepting of the multiracial relationship than the White family (Kouri & Lasswell, 1993). The mother was generally more accepting than the father and other kin. About half of the Black families did have some objections. These objections included concerns that their child was marrying outside the group, perhaps marrying "down" in terms of education or status, or "sleeping with the enemy."

All the multiracial couples hoped that they would not experience racism. They hoped others would see them as any other couple and not relate to them on the basis of racial stereotypes. One person said, "I want the larger society to know that interracial relationships or not, people are people. All races of people require the same thing . . . we all need love and affection" (Rosenblatt et al., 1955, p. 278). Another person felt that "interracial couples . . . aren't good or bad because of being interracial. . . . It is what that relationship becomes that determines its goodness or badness, but it has nothing to do with the complexion of the people" (p. 281). And a third person suggested that the biggest difference between partners in a Black-White marriage was not their race but their gender—something that most couples have to deal with, no matter what their skin color (p. 294–5).

Assimilation, Acculturation, or Segregation

People in the "out" group, people with little power, and newcomers to any society face a difficult set of choices: Should they swiftly reject their former life and the culture from which they came? Should they downplay their ethnic origins in an effort to fit the mainstream view? Or should they build their own ethnic enclave and try to create a safe microworld that reflects their cultural heritage? These questions are extremely difficult to answer, and minority-group members often disagree on how to proceed. Some families are torn apart by controversies of this nature.

There are three important processes that help explain what happens when a cultural group from another country encounters the dominant culture of the country to which they have moved. **Assimilation** is the process in which old cultural traits and values are relinquished and replaced by those of the dominant culture. **Acculturation** is the process whereby cultural traits and values from one ethnic group become intermeshed with those of the dominant culture. **Segregation** is the process in which an ethnic group isolates itself or is forced into isolation within the dominant culture. All three of these processes can occur in an interactive way as a family adapts to living in another culture.

Members of the majority culture whose families have been in the United States for two, three, or more generations sometimes do not understand why immigrants are hesitant about assimilation—adopting the values of the dominant culture. But it is clear that immigrants are in a difficult psychological position. They see the strengths of American culture, especially its abundance of economic resources, and are attracted by those strengths. But they also see the weaknesses of American culture—materialism, competitiveness, wasteful exploitation of the natural world, a fast-paced and often impersonal existence. Immigrants are in some ways in a better position to see America's strengths and weaknesses than are Americans, for they have another culture with which they can compare this one.

Relationships Between Men and Women

There tends to be a great deal of friction between women and men around the world. On the one hand, males and females would like to love each other. On the other hand, different socialization processes and biological inheritances produce misunderstanding and anger. Women in developed countries, due to greater education and more employment opportunities outside the home, tend to have more options. If they are dissatisfied with their marriage and can support themselves, they are not as likely to stay in the marriage. Women in rural areas and in developing countries have fewer options, even though they may be just as unhappy as their divorcing urban counterparts. As a result, divorce rates tend to be higher in industrialized, urban-oriented societies around the world and lower in less developed, agrarian societies. But the lower divorce rates in the more rural societies do not necessarily indicate happier marriages.

Relationships Between Parents and Children

Children often develop into adults much like their own parents. In the process of growing up, however, a great deal of conflict between children and parents can occur. The younger generation strives to create a relatively independent life, and the older generation tries to maintain control of their children. These struggles are played out in most cultures around the world. Family power structures in various cultures around the world seem to change gradually over time as societies move from an agricultural orientation to industrialization. In an agriculturally oriented family, the father, who is responsible for making sure the farm runs smoothly, has more control over his children. In the city, the father's influence lessens, and the influence of others (peers, school) increases. Rural societies generally emphasize respect for the authority of the dominant males. In more modern societies, the rights of the individual receive more weight because the family is more likely to succeed if all its members become well educated and find good jobs.

When a family moves from one culture to another, parent-child relationships can be especially strained, as the youngsters struggle to fit into the new culture and inevitably begin to forget the past.

Nicole, a 35-year-old woman who married an American and emigrated to the United States from France, explains why it is important for their children, born in France but being raised in the United States, to be able to speak not only English but her native language as well: "Of course, they need to know English. They're going to end up being Americans. That's obvious. We aren't going back to France to live, only to visit.

"It's hard for them. They speak English in school and in the neighborhood, but in the home we speak French. They get confused sometimes and mix languages. Sometimes the neighbor kids tease them about it. It's especially difficult for Jared, our son, but Emily is doing great. I think they'll both catch on and see why it's important in the long run.

"I want them to appreciate their roots, to remember the wonderful civilization they come from. And, most important, I want them to know me, their mother. I live in the United States but probably always will be French deep down, because that's where I grew up. I can't help it. That's home. The language of emotion, the language of love is your native language. How can I show my true emotions, my true love for my children if they cannot understand my French? How can they really know me?"

It will be a delicate balancing act for the family to maintain connections to both French and American cultures, but the benefits of such an accomplishment can far outweigh the difficulties.

Issues in Cross-Cultural Family Studies

Cross-cultural family studies tend to focus on two interrelated questions: First, how are families in the United States different from those in other parts of the world? Second, how are they similar? At first glance, people are often struck by the obvious differences between family cultures. Clothing styles, food preferences, religious beliefs, housing, music, education—all these aspects of culture vary from one society to another. When visiting a new culture, people often look for the differences between it and their own culture but eventually also begin to see the similarities. When learning about another culture, then, the key is to emphasize similarities rather than differences.

Cross-cultural family studies focus on how particular cultural contexts influence a wide variety of issues: family values and behaviors, courtship patterns and weddings, marital and parent-child communication, power and gender roles, work and the family, ethical and religious values, childrearing patterns, sexuality, the role of grandparents and the extended family, and the role people outside the immediate family play in helping families in crisis.

Ethnocentrism

We are all ethnocentric to some extent; we see others through unique lenses that are shaped by our own culture. **Ethnocentrism** is the assumption that one's own culture is the standard by which other cultures should be judged. Our ethnocentricity influences the extent to which we judge other people, families, and cultures to be similar or different from us. Tolerance of the traditions and values of other cultural and ethnic groups is the first step in transcending our overconcern with human differences. Understanding other ways of looking at life and the world around us can lead to genuine appreciation among people of different backgrounds.

Related to the issue of ethnocentrism is the matter of what anthropologists have called perspective. When one looks at a society from the outside, or **etic perspective,** one views it externally, describing its characteristics in isolation rather than as they relate to the structure of the society as a whole. On the other hand, when one looks at a society from the inside, or **emic perspective,** one analyzes behaviors in terms of the internal structural elements of the society. The etic perspective tends to focus on and exaggerate differences, whereas the emic perspective makes it easier to see similarities between cultures.

Family researchers attempt to combine these two perspectives, recognizing the differences between cultures but also trying to identify similarities. Researchers from one culture can never completely discard their personal lenses. They can, however, try to become more open to new ideas and behaviors by submerging themselves in another culture, even learning that culture's language and living within that culture.

Racism

Racism is closely related to ethnocentrism and may even be a by-product of it. All the various "isms" tend to distance human beings from each other by accentuating differences and ignoring fundamental similarities, which in turn leads to tension and conflict. **Racism** develops when the most powerful group in a society creates an elaborate mythology (a set of beliefs that grossly distort reality) about a minority group. These prejudices often endure because of the need to feel superior to someone else.

Racist myths focus on a wide variety of issues. The minority group may be said to lack intelligence, eat strange foods, play weird music, be extremely violent and dangerous, or take dreaded drugs. The men of the minority group are often reputed to be sex starved, lusting after the women of the majority group. These fears are powerful and can increase prejudice and discrimination against minority-group members.

In sheer numbers, a minority group may actually outnumber the majority. For example, African Americans outnumber Whites in many counties in the South, in Washington, D.C., and in South Africa.

Because minority-group members are often the victims of prejudice and discrimination, they may develop prejudices against the "other" group. Unfortunately, this reduces both groups to the charge of stereotyping. In effect, "We have met the enemy, and they are us."

The movie *Do the Right Thing*, directed by Spike Lee, revealed the absurdity—and the reality—of ethnic hatred and violence in the United States. In the movie, escalating arguments among ethnic groups led to violence that foreshadowed the real-life Los Angeles riot of 1992.

Spike Lee does a fine job of portraying hatred in his film *Do the Right Thing*, which focuses on three groups who have experienced discrimination. In the climactic scene, an argument among African Americans, Korean Americans, and Italian Americans ends in a neighborhood riot. The scene is both stunningly funny in the grotesqueness of the combatants as they display their prejudices—and also terrifying in its potential for being realized. Lee helps us see ourselves, and the picture is not appealing. It is hard to deny that a great deal of progress has been made in improving the rights of various minorities in the United States. But one does not have to look far to see examples of the dark undercurrent of bigotry that still stains the fabric of American society.

Appreciating Diversity

Understanding American families with their wide-ranging cultural variations is challenging. Trying to understand families around the world is probably even more difficult; both the closed nature of family life and the greater degree of cultural variations worldwide make it so. It would be useful to learn to appreciate diversity when it comes to families from other ethnic and cultural groups.

One way to increase our appreciation of diversity is to seek out opportunities to talk with people who have ethnic backgrounds different from our own. Sharing feelings about one's cultural heritage with someone from another ethnic group can be a mutually rewarding experience. Each person can learn more about the other and about another culture.

Summary

- Kin relationships—the structure of marital and family relationships—vary considerably across ethnic and cultural groups.

- Although there is a great deal of diversity both within and across cultural and ethnic groups, there are also common family strengths. Strong families share the traits of cohesion, flexibility, and communication.

- The family strengths of African American families include strong kinship bonds, strong work orientation, flexibility in family roles, strong motivation to achieve, strong religious orientation, and caring parenting.

- The family strengths of Latino families include familism, high family cohesion, high family flexibility, supportive kin network system, equalitarian decision making, and strong ethnic identity.

- The family strengths of Asian American families include strong family orientation, filial piety, high value on education, well-disciplined children, extended family support, and family loyalty.

- The family strengths of Native American families include a strong extended family system, traditional beliefs, high family cohesion, respect for elders, bilingual language skills, and a tribal support system.

- Intercultural marriage creates problems for families, but it can also be the source of considerable learning and personal growth.

- The issues of assimilation, acculturation, and segregation must be faced by any new ethnic or cultural group.

- Male-female relationships and parent-child struggles are common issues in families from a variety of ethnic groups.

- Cross-cultural family studies tend to focus on two broad, interrelated questions: How are families in various ethnic groups different? How are they similar?

- Such studies can be hindered by ethnocentrism and racism.

Key Terms

cultural identity
ethnic identity
race
co-culture
minority group
kinship
nuclear family
conjugal family system

consanguineal family system
extended family
plural marriage
polygamy
polygyny
polyandry
monogamy

pseudo-kin group
lineage
matrilineal society
patrilineal society
bilateral descent
matriarchal group
patriarchal group
equalitarian group

matrilocal society	social system	segregation
patrilocal society	belief system	cross-cultural family study
neolocal society	stereotype	ethnocentrism
family cohesion	prejudice	etic perspective
family flexibility	intercultural marriage	emic perspective
family communication	assimilation	racism
extended family system	acculturation	

Activities

1. Make a list of strengths you recognize in your family. How do they compare with the strengths identified by family researchers?

2. For a week, observe and collect examples of racism in American society. Jot down in a notebook all the examples you find of prejudice and discrimination. Share these examples with others in a small-group discussion.

3. Racial and ethnic jokes are one of the most effective ways we pass our prejudices from one generation to the next. Discuss how you feel about this type of humor and what effect it has in society.

Suggested Readings

Billingsley, A. (1992). *Climbing Jacob's ladder: The enduring legacy of African-American families.* New York: Simon & Schuster. *Argument by a professor of family studies at the University of Maryland, College Park, that African American families are amazingly "strong, enduring, adaptive, and highly resilient."*

Bornstein, M. H. (Ed.). (1991). *Cultural approaches to parenting.* Hillsdale, NJ: Lawrence Erlbaum Assoc. *Childrearing practices in a wide variety of cultures in the United States and around the world.*

Bozett, F. W., & Hanson, S. M. H. (1991). *Fatherhood and families in cultural context.* New York: Springer. *Fatherhood from historical and cross-cultural perspectives, social class and fatherhood, religion and fatherhood, rural and urban influences on fatherhood, the future of fatherhood, and more.*

CHAPTER 3

Understanding Relationships in Marriage and Family

The relationships we experience growing up in our families stay with us all our lives. These relationships strongly influence the kinds of families we create as adults. We all carry parts of our families—both their strengths and their weaknesses—into our adult lives and relationships. Therefore, the better we understand our original family relationships and those of our partner, the more successful we will be in establishing the kind of family we want. It is also useful to understand how couple and family relationships change over time and why some relationships are capable of surviving the most terrible storms in life and other relationships fail.

How can individuals begin to understand their families of origin and build successful relationships in their adult lives? Sometimes the depth and complexity of family relationships make it seem difficult, if not impossible, to understand and change them. But when many theorists and researchers, such as those introduced in Chapter 1, find common ground in talking about marriage and families, there is good reason for optimism. The information and knowledge they produce can benefit every type of intimate and family relationship.

Among the basic qualities that these scholars agree make relationships, marriages, and families strong are cohesion (togetherness), flexibility (the ability to change), and communication. This chapter describes how these basic dimensions are prominent components of family systems theory, the family strengths framework, and the family development framework, as well as other theories and frameworks.

We also look first at how the three basic qualities of cohesion, flexibility, and communication are integrated into the Family Circumplex Model, which some prefer to call a relationship map. The Family Circumplex Model is a useful tool for applying concepts derived from theories to the dynamics of real, everyday family life. It has been said that there is nothing more practical than a good theory. It could also be said that nothing makes a theory more practical than the means to apply it, and that is the strength of the Family Circumplex Model.

"We came from such very different families. It took a long time for us to really realize all the implications of that," said Yolanda, a 29-year-old emergency room nurse living in Cincinnati. "Tommy's family was small and rich and stable. Or, at least, that's how I saw them when we got married."

"And your family was big and poor and fun," said Tommy, an electrical engineer. "Or so I thought."

What drew them together—fascination with their different backgrounds—threatened to break them up in the early years of marriage. "I liked the fact that his parents were quiet and reserved," Yolanda explained. "My family's so loud and rowdy."

"Yeah, her family did turn out to be too loud for my taste," Tommy agreed. "But before we got married, I thought it was fun. They were always together, always laughing. It seemed like a party going on all the time—constant confusion, along with a lot of drinking by her parents. I liked it because my parents are so uptight and work oriented and critical.

"But after a while Yolanda's family really wore me down," Tommy went on. "They wanted us to participate in all their family gatherings, every week. Yolanda and I both began to see that her father was an alcoholic. I didn't want to see them that often, but Yolanda didn't want to hurt their feelings."

"Tommy's family wanted to see us too, but I had a hard time getting to feel comfortable with them," Yolanda noted. "The house seemed to echo with every sentence anyone said. I felt awkward."

The crisis came in the second year of their marriage. Yolanda's father lost his job because of his drinking and wanted Yolanda and Tommy to bail him out financially. Yolanda and Tommy spent long hours talking about what kind of relationships they wanted to have with their extended families and what kind of relationship they wanted to have with each other. Eventually they agreed on ways to set boundaries for themselves, as well as ways to adopt the best from both families of origin without also taking the worst: "We want to build a family that has good times together but can do it without alcohol," Yolanda said. "A family that likes to laugh a lot and not be critical or judgmental of each other. We also want to make a good living, so we can buy some things and travel a little and give our kids a good education. These are our goals. We're committed to reaching them."

"Yes, we are," Tommy agreed, smiling at his wife.

Three Basic Qualities: Cohesion, Flexibility, and Communication

Family Systems Theory

As you recall from Chapter 1, the key idea identified in family systems theory is that every family member and his or her behaviors are interconnected with those of every other family member. The theory stresses that each family, as a system, needs to find a balance between separateness and connectedness. This may seem obvious, until you stop and think about the depth and breadth of this core idea about systems. Think about an automobile engine. A typical engine is made up of hundreds of parts, each ideally molded and shaped as an individual component. Yet once the engine is started, every part must function effectively in coordination with all the others. Otherwise, the engine will quickly fail, even break or fly apart.

So it is with the family: Family members are individuals and must develop their individuality, but they must also be able to function together. Centripetal interactions, such as a family hike on Saturday or the preparation of a meal together, require coordination of everyone's movements and functions. The hike or dinner preparation can pull the family together and increase their sense of closeness. Centrifugal interactions, such as an unsettled argument over where to take the hike or who is going to make the salad, can push family members apart if the disagreements are serious. One focus of family systems theory is family cohesion—how well the family holds together and balances the forces that propel it smoothly forward or act to pull it apart.

Every couple and family also experiences periods of stability and periods of change. Families need to find a healthy balance between these two opposing forces, as noted in Chapter 1. A morphostatic system, as the name implies, resists change and seeks to maintain the status quo. A morphogenic system is open to change. This is the dimension of flexibility, the ability of a family system to change over time and yet to remain stable enough to offer comfort, security, and continuity to family members.

Communication, the process by which family members share information about personal needs, wants, and values, is another important feature of a family in family systems theory. Negative feedback is communication intended to minimize change and keep the family the same. Positive feedback is communication intended to maximize change. If Talia, a 24-year-old graduate student, talks with her family about cutting down on the number of Christmas presents they exchange, and the other members agree with her and change the tradition, the feedback to the system is considered positive. If they don't want to change and reject her idea, the feedback to the system is considered negative, and things stay as they are.

Family systems theory recognizes that there are forces and events in most families that promote both separateness and connectedness, both change and stability. The theory is interested in the interdependence that characterizes the system itself, as well as in different kinds of family structures and how well each functions. Regardless of variations in structure or specific features, however, certain family functions and dynamics must work for a family or a relationship to be strong and healthy.

The Family Strengths Framework

The family strengths framework is based on the cumulating findings of studies of thousands of families throughout the United States. As outlined in Chapter 1, the six major strengths identified by Stinnett, Stinnett, DeFrain, and DeFrain (1997, in press) as key to making a family strong and healthy are commitment, appreciation and affection, positive communication, time together, spiritual well-being, and the ability to cope with stress.

Although the family strengths framework describes six characteristics, the underlying dimensions can be identified as cohesion, flexibility, and communication. Both commitment and spending time together are aspects of the dimension of cohesion; spiritual well-being and the ability to cope with stress relate to the dimension of flexibility; and appreciation and affection and positive communication are related to the communication dimension. These three dynamic characteristics are what make families strong and help them maintain their relationships over the life span.

The Family Development Framework

The focus of the family development framework is change over the family life cycle. Every family experiences changes we think of as transitional—adjustment to a new marriage, the arrival of a baby, the departure of a young adult for college or work, the death of an elderly parent. Other changes are unexpected—the loss of a job, a serious illness, divorce. Whether normative or not, each change brings a challenge, a time of increased stress, as the family attempts to regain its balance. The family development framework asks the question, How flexible, how adaptable, is this family? Can they adapt to change and establish a new balance? Or are they unable to find ways to continue as a family? Flexibility is the quality that strong families need in order to adapt to change.

Other Family Theories and Frameworks

There are other theorists and researchers who may not identify themselves as proponents of one of these frameworks but who nonetheless use and rely on the concepts of cohesion, flexibility, and communication in their work. For example, David Reiss (1981) developed a useful model for focusing on problem solving. The dimension he called coordination is quite similar to cohesion, and his concept of closure is similar to flexibility. Another example is the W. R. Beavers System Model (Beavers & Hampson, 1990). It is this model that discusses the related concepts of centripetal and centrifugal forces that act on families to bind them together or split them apart.

Table 3.1 (p. 84) lists a number of family theories in which the characteristics of successful families fit naturally into one or more of the three categories of cohesion, flexibility, and communication. Without question, then, these three concepts are important to our understanding of intimate, committed relationships, especially marriage and family relationships.

The Family Circumplex Model: A Tool for Understanding Families

How can we represent in a clear and compelling way the dynamics of relationships within marriage and families? The Family Circumplex Model is one especially useful model for this purpose. Developed by David Olson and his colleagues at the University of Minnesota, especially Douglas Sprenkle and Candyce Russell, who worked on the original model, the **Family Circumplex Model** is a tool with which we can identify and map family relationships. It serves to identify the key characteristics of any given relationship in terms of cohesion, flexibility, and communication. For the theorist, researcher, or interested lay person, the model offers a way of mapping and understanding family relationships. It can also be applied by therapists, counselors, and family members themselves who are interested in changing the dynamics within a family experiencing difficulties.

The Family Circumplex Model is built primarily on principles and concepts from family systems theory, but it also has features in common with other frameworks. As a graphic model, it clearly represents the dimensions of cohesion and flexibility; the third dimension, communication, serves a facilitating function. It is through communication that family members identify and work out their concerns about cohesiveness—issues of spending time together versus having enough separateness to retain a sense of oneself—and flexibility—issues of adapting to the demands of change versus minimizing such demands if they threaten the stability of the relationship. Communication thus helps families move between the extremes of cohesion and flexibility to find a balance that works for them. If a couple or family has good communication

Table 3.1 Major Family Theorists and the Concepts of Cohesion, Flexibility, and Communication

THEORIST	COHESION	FLEXIBILITY	COMMUNICATION	OTHER

Barnhill (1979)	Mutuality
	Clear parent-child
	  boundaries
	Individuation
		Flexibility versus
		  rigidity
		Clear roles
			Clear communications	

Beavers and
  Hampson (1990)
	Centripetal/Centrifugal
	Closeness
	Parent coalition
	Autonomy
		Adaptability
		Egalitarian power
		Goal-directed
		  negotiation
		Ability to resolve
		  conflict
			Clarity of expression
			Range of feelings
			Openness to others
			Empathic
			Understanding	

Billingsley (1986)	Strong family ties			Strong religious
				  orientation
				Educational
				  aspirations/
				  achievements

Curran (1983)	Togetherness Respect and trust Shared leisure Privacy valued Shared mealtime	Shared responsibility Family rituals	Communication Affirmation of each other	Religious love Humor/play

Epstein, Bishop,
  Ryan, Miller,
  and Keitner
  (1993)
	Affective
	  involvement
		Behavior
		  control
			Communication	

Kantor and Lehr (1975)	Affect	Power		

Krysan, Moore,
  and Zill (1990)
	Commitment to family
	Time together
	Encouragement of
	  individuals
		Ability to adapt
		Clear roles
			Communication
			Expressing
			  appreciation
				Religious
				  orientation
				Social
				  connectedness

J. M. Lewis (1989)	Strong marriage
	Family closeness
	Encouragement of
	  autonomy
		Shared power
		Good at problem
		  solving
		Openness to change
			Express feelings
			Good communication
				Positive values

Olson, McCubbin,
  et al. (1989)
	Strong marriage
	High family cohesion
		Good family flexibility
		Effective coping with
		  stress and crisis
			Positive couple
			  and family
			  communication	

Reiss (1981)	Coordination	Closure		

Stinnett, Stinnett,
  DeFrain, and DeFrain
  (1997, in press)
	Commitment
	Time together
		Ability to cope with
		  stress and crisis
		Spiritual well-being
			Communication
			Appreciation and
			  affection	

skills, they are more likely to be able to maintain their cohesive structure, adapt to change, and work out whatever problems confront them (Olson, 1993).

There are several advantages to using the Family Circumplex Model to understand marital and family life. First, the model provides a common descriptive language for talking about real couples and real families—a language that the expert and the lay person can use to talk with each other. One of the reasons the model was developed was that a plethora of terms was being used to describe family dynamics. Some of those terms and concepts are shown in Table 3.1.

A second reason for using the Family Circumplex Model is that it draws on concepts and ideas from each of the three major frameworks we have discussed—family systems, family strengths, and family development. It offers a means of bringing together and applying all three frameworks to the examination of real families and their interactions. It grounds theory in examples of relationships based on intimacy and commitment.

Third, the Family Circumplex Model is highly predictive of how a relationship or a family will change as time passes or as stresses and challenges appear. Seeing where a couple or a family is on the relationship map gives us information about their present dynamics and what they need to do if they want to change. It provides a means to visualize where one is and where one might wish to be.

Finally, the Family Circumplex Model turns concepts into working themes with which we can observe and measure family dynamics. Just where is a given family on the relationship map? Is this family a rigid, inflexible, suffocating environment for its members? Is it an unpredictable, unsafe, chaotic place to be? Or is it flexible and nurturing? Can family members communicate what their problems are and express what kind of family they would like to become? What changes must they make to move toward that ideal or maintain the aspects they wish not to lose as they change others?

Before we examine some concrete illustrations of family types as they would be identified within the Family Circumplex Model, let's look at the model itself in some detail to see how it helps us understand the major dimensions of family dynamics.

Cohesion

Cohesion is defined as a feeling of emotional closeness with another person. The Family Circumplex Model distinguishes four levels of cohesion (togetherness) in couple and family relationships: disengaged, connected, cohesive, and enmeshed (Figure 3.1). The extreme low level of cohesion is called *disengaged*, and the extreme high level, *enmeshed*. Although being disengaged or enmeshed is appropriate at times, relationships become problematic when they are stuck at one of these extremes. The two middle levels of cohesion—*connected* and *cohesive* types of relationships—seem to be the most functional across the life cycle, in part because they balance separateness and togetherness. Connected and cohesive relationships are both classified as balanced family systems.

Balance Between Separateness and Togetherness   Balance between separateness and togetherness is the essence of family cohesion. Family members need to

Figure 3.1 Four Levels of Family Cohesion: Balancing Separateness and Togetherness

DISENGAGED System	**Separateness** vs Togetherness	Unbalanced
CONNECTED System	**Separateness** vs Togetherness	Balanced
COHESIVE System	Separateness vs **Togetherness**	Balanced
ENMESHED System	Separateness vs **Togetherness**	Unbalanced

Table 3.2 Levels of Family Cohesion

CHARACTERISTIC	DISENGAGED (UNBALANCED)	CONNECTED (BALANCED)	COHESIVE (BALANCED)	ENMESHED (UNBALANCED)
Separateness-Togetherness	High separateness	More separateness than togetherness	More togetherness than separateness	Very high togetherness
I–We balance	Primarily I	More I than We	More We than I	Primarily We
Closeness	Little closeness	Low to moderate closeness	Moderate to high closeness	Very high closeness
Loyalty	Lack of loyalty	Some loyalty	Considerable loyalty	High loyalty
Activities	Mainly separate	More separate than shared	More shared than separate	Mainly shared
Dependence-Independence	High independence	More independence than dependence	More dependence than independence	High dependence

balance between being intimate with and feeling close to other family members and being independent from the family so that they can develop as individuals. The concept of balance involves having both autonomy and intimacy—and the ability to move back and forth between the two. Establishing a dynamic balance between the two requires shifting back and forth on a weekly, daily, or even hourly basis.

Table 3.2 defines the four levels of family cohesion, from low to high. There is a balance between separateness and togetherness at both the connected and the cohesive levels of cohesion. At the *connected* level, there is more emphasis on the individual and less on the relationship. Levels of closeness are often low to moderate in a connected family system, with lower levels of loyalty. There is often more independence than dependence and more separateness than togetherness. At the *cohesive* level, there is more emphasis on togetherness and less on separateness. There is some loyalty to the relationship, and there is often more dependence than independence.

Disengaged relationships (those with a low level of cohesion) emphasize the individual. There is often very little closeness, a lack of loyalty, high independence, and high separateness. *Enmeshed* relationships emphasize togetherness: very high levels of closeness, loyalty, and dependence on one another. Enmeshed relationships are often typical of couples in love. When this level of intimacy occurs between a parent and a child (for example, an enmeshed father-daughter relationship or an enmeshed mother-son relationship), the relationship often becomes problematic.

Kahlil Gibran describes a balance between separateness and togetherness in his poem "On Marriage":

> *Love one another, but make not a bond of love:*
> *Let it rather be a moving sea between the shores of your souls.*
> *Fill each other's cup, but drink not from the same cup.*
> *Give one another of your bread, but eat not from the same loaf.*
> *Sing and dance together and be joyous,*
> > *but let each one of you be alone,*
> *Even as the strings of a lute are alone*
> > *though they quiver with the same music.*
> *Give your hearts, but not into each*
> > *other's keeping.*
> *For only the hand of Life can contain your hearts.*
> *And stand together yet not too near together:*
> *For the pillars of the temple stand apart,*
> *And the oak tree and the cypress grow*
> > *not in each other's shadow.*
> *But let there be spaces in your togetherness,*
> *And let the winds of the heavens dance between you.* (1923/1976, pp. 16–17)

The relationship Gibran describes is an ideal. In the real world of loving relationships, few find this perfect balance with their partners. It is a useful goal, but one that is difficult to maintain for long. It is also important to note that in intimate relationships, people can experience and even enjoy, at least for a short time, both extremes on the togetherness-separateness continuum. Couples can remain in love with each other while also enjoying being apart for periods of time.

Extreme Togetherness and Extreme Separateness   Too much togetherness can lead to relationship fusion, or enmeshment. People "in love" often feel they need each other. Although this feels good for a while, soon the enmeshment begins to prickle. After too much togetherness, lovers can get on each other's nerves.

Especially in the early stages of a relationship, couples enjoy being totally together. When a couple is just "falling in love," being away from the other person for very long literally hurts. Each one aches and pines and feels pent-up emotion in the expectation of seeing the other again. Couples in this type of situation are enmeshed; being together so totally can be very exciting for a time. To expect to be totally sheltered from the storms of life by a loved one is a nice fantasy—but it *is* a fantasy. Judy Altura has expressed it poetically:

Within every family, each member must find a balance between autonomy and intimacy. If they are like other families, these five people will experience periods of greater and lesser separateness and togetherness over the course of their lives.

Togetherness Poem

We do everything together.
I am here to meet all your needs and expectations.
And you are here to meet mine.
We had to meet, and it was beautiful.
I can't imagine it turning out any other way. (1974, p. 20)

Two of the most common reasons that an enmeshed relationship becomes troublesome are jealousy and personification. People feel jealous when they fear they might lose their partner to another person. Tied closely to jealousy is **personification,** the notion that everything one's partner does is a personal reflection on oneself. A person who personifies his or her partner's actions will try to control the other's behavior. This may work in the short run, but it can destroy intimacy in the long run.

Enmeshment is problematic both for the people in the relationship and for the relationship itself because it romanticizes the relationship and puts impossible expectations upon the partners. It also tends to stifle individual development. One way to improve an enmeshed relationship is for each person to invest more time developing individual interests and abilities.

In the 1970s, one cultural theme in American society was "doing your own thing." Young people were dubbed "the me generation." This overfocus on self was problematic for relationships. "Doing your own thing" can lead to a disengaged relationship, where there is very little emotional closeness. The ideal of extreme separateness is expressed in this prayer by psychotherapist Fritz Perls:

Gestalt Prayer

I do my thing, and you do your thing.
I am not in this world to live up to your expectations.
And you are not in this world to live up to mine.
You are you and I am I.
And if by chance we meet, it's beautiful.
If not, it can't be helped. (1969, p. 4)

Successful couples tend to be those who have figured out how to balance effectively between "I" and "We." They maintain both their own individuality and their intimacy as a couple.

Flexibility

The second major dimension of the Family Circumplex Model is flexibility, the amount of change that occurs in leadership, role relationships, and relationship rules. (Flexibility was called adaptability in earlier versions of the model, but that term was dropped because of its similarity with the term adaptation.) Like cohesion, flexibility has four levels, ranging from low to high. Those levels are rigid, structured, flexible, and chaotic (Figure 3.2, p. 90). The extreme types of family systems—the *rigid* and the *chaotic*—can work well in the short run, but they have difficulty adapting over time. Conversely, the balanced types—the *structured* and the *flexible*—are more able to adapt to change over the family life cycle.

Balance Between Stability and Change   The essence of family flexibility is to balance stability and change. Families need a basic foundation that gives them stability, but they also need to be open to change when necessary. Change is particularly important when families are under stress and need to adapt in a crisis (Olson, 1993).

The Family Circumplex Model deals with both first order change and second order change. **First order change** is the amount of change that occurs within any given family system. On the Circumplex Model, first order change is measured by the flexibility dimension. Families who are rigid are lowest on first order change, and chaotic families are highest. However, because either too much or too little change is problematic, there is a curvilinear relationship between first order change and effective family functioning. Families who are unbalanced on flexibility (either rigid or chaotic) are less functional than families who are balanced (structured or flexible) on the flexibility dimension.

Second order change is change from one system type to another. It is change "in the system itself" and can only be assessed over time. When families are under stress, they often change their system type completely from one level to another to better manage the stress. Second order change has a linear relationship with effective family functioning because the greater the second order change, the better. Balanced family types are higher on second order change than unbalanced

Figure 3.2 Four Levels of Family Flexibility: Balancing Stability and Change

RIGID System	Stability vs Change	Unbalanced
STRUCTURED System	Stability vs Change	Balanced
FLEXIBLE System	Stability vs **Change**	Balanced
CHAOTIC System	Stability vs **Change**	Unbalanced

Table 3.3 Levels of Family Flexibility

CHARACTERISTIC	RIGID (UNBALANCED)	STRUCTURED (BALANCED)	FLEXIBLE (BALANCED)	CHAOTIC (UNBALANCED)
Leadership	Authoritarian	Sometimes shared	Often shared	Lack of leadership
Discipline	Strict discipline	Somewhat democratic	Democratic	Lenient discipline
Negotiation	Limited discussion	Organized discussion	Open discussion	Endless discussion
Roles	Roles very stable	Roles stable	Role sharing	Dramatic role shifts
Rules	Rules very clear, stable	Rules clear and stable	Rules clear, flexible	Rules unclear, changing
Change	Very little change	Some change	Moderate change	Considerable change

types because they can change their system to another type to adapt to a crisis situation. In some cases, this might mean moving from a balanced (e.g., flexibly connected) to an unbalanced (e.g., chaotically enmeshed) type for a short time but usually becoming a balanced type again after the crisis has passed.

The two balanced levels of change are called *structured* and *flexible*. Of the two, structured relationships have more moderate levels of change, with leadership that is sometimes shared. Discipline is often democratic, and the roles are stable. In flexible relationships, there is more change. Often both the relationship between the couple and the relationships among family members are more democratic, and there is also more role sharing between the couple, as shown in Table 3.3.

The two extremes of change are described as *rigid*, to indicate a very low degree of change, and *chaotic*, an extremely high degree. Both extremes are unbalanced and problematic because families are often stuck at these extreme positions.

In rigid relationships, the leadership is often authoritarian. As a result, the discipline is strict, and the roles are very stable. In chaotic relationships, there is too much change, often because there is a lack of leadership. Discipline is erratic and inconsistent, partly because there are often dramatic shifts in family roles.

Extreme Stability and Extreme Change   Families by nature tend to resist change; they are basically rigid (Haley, 1959). Most families function primarily to maintain the status quo: "When an organism indicates a change in relation to another, the other will act upon the first so as to diminish and modify the change" (Haley, 1959, p. 281).

In short, when one partner tries to make changes in a relationship, the other partner's first reaction is often to defend against the change or at least to slow it down until he or she can better understand what is happening. People often fear that the change will bring more harm than good. The family, which is maintenance oriented and conservative in its approach to change, often creates even more problems for itself. As Lyman Wynne sees it, "Families that rigidly try to maintain homeostasis [the status quo] through successive developmental phases are highly disturbed and atypical. Enduring success in maintaining family homeostasis perhaps should be regarded as a distinctive feature of disorder in families" (1958, p. 89).

Extreme stability is seen in rigid families, those in which there is little room for change. The family rules are always the same, even though the game of life outside the family continuously changes. This rigidity can be seen in such relatively trivial matters as the schedule for family meals. Family members do not permit one another to make even the slightest changes although they might help one or more members. The rigidity may also be evidenced by resistance to changes in roles within the family. For example, a mother wants to find work outside the home but the father opposes it, or a son wants to become a musician but his parents are not supportive.

On the other extreme of change are chaotic families. These families are almost completely without structure, rules, and roles. No one knows what to expect. For example:

> A young former prostitute described the family she grew up in as very chaotic, saying, "It was like a sieve. Anybody could come into it, and anybody could leave, and anybody could fall through the gaps. The family wasn't safe or reliable for anybody at all." The young woman related that her mother divorced her father and then invited another man to move in with her. This newcomer raped the young woman when she was 11 years old. When she told her mother what had happened, her mother refused to believe her and decided to let the man stay. She also decided that the 11-year-old daughter was a divisive influence on the family and chose the new lover and her younger son over her daughter. She left the daughter to fend for herself on the street, and the girl was soon involved in drugs and prostitution.

A chaotic family operates on the premise that "nothing is constant in life but change." It is difficult to go through life without some change—and individuals and relationships often do better if they are open to some change over time. However, constant change is problematic for most people.

Table 3.4 Levels of Family Communication			
Characteristic	**Poor**	**Good**	**Very Good**
Listening skills	Poor listening skills	Appear to listen, but feedback is limited	Give feedback, indicating good listening skills
Speaking skills	Often speak for others	Speak for self more than for others	Speak mainly for self rather than for others
Self-disclosure	Low sharing of feelings	Moderate sharing of feelings	High sharing of feelings
Clarity	Inconsistent messages	Clear messages	Very clear messages
Staying on topic	Seldom stay on topic	Often stay on topic	Mainly stay on topic
Respect and regard	Low to moderate	Moderate to high	High

Communication

Family communication is the third dimension in the Family Circumplex Model and is considered a facilitating dimension because it aids movement on the other two dimensions. Communication is not graphically illustrated in the Circumplex Model, but it should always be considered when looking at a family system.

The following six dimensions are considered in the assessment of family communication: listening skills, speaking skills, self-disclosure, clarity, staying on topic, and respect and regard (Table 3.4). *Listening skills* involve empathy, understanding feelings, and giving feedback. *Speaking skills* include speaking for oneself and using "I" statements rather than speaking for others. *Self-disclosure* includes sharing personal feelings and ideas openly. *Clarity* involves whether messages are clear and whether double messages are given. *Staying on topic* is important because many interpersonal exchanges wander and end up far from the original topic. Last, *respect and regard* reflect the good intentions of family members and keep communication positive.

Communication is the grease that smoothes the many frictions in couples and families. Family communication is linear: The better the communication skills, the stronger the family. In contrast, with family cohesion and family flexibility, either too much or too little is problematic.

Good communication helps couples and families stay balanced on cohesion and flexibility. Conversely, couples and families who are unbalanced (at the extremes) on cohesion and/or flexibility tend to have problematic communication.

The Circumplex Model As a Relationship Map

Representing the Family Circumplex Model as a relationship map makes it possible to identify 16 types of couple and family relationships (Figure 3.3). The logic is quite simple: The dimensions of cohesion and flexibility are broken down into four levels each, and 4 × 4 = 16. A marriage or family relationship can be classified as one of these 16 types based on how the family functions. This relationship map graphically represents how family and couple relationships operate.

The 16 types of family relationships can be clustered into three general types

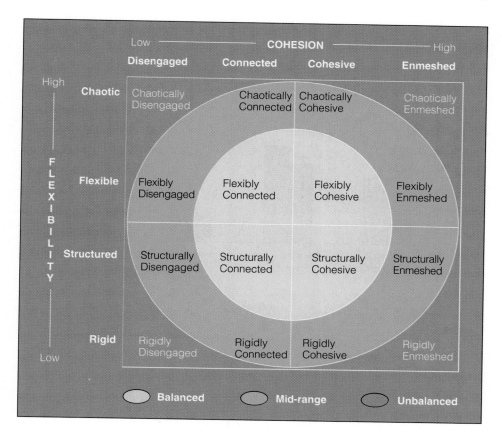

Figure 3.3 Family Circumplex Model: A Relationship Map

of family systems: balanced families, mid-range families, and unbalanced families. **Balanced families** are those that fit into the four central categories (yellow section) on the relationship map in Figure 3.3. Balanced families are labeled flexibly connected, flexibly cohesive, structurally connected, and structurally cohesive. **Mid-range families** (orange section) are extreme on one dimension (e.g., cohesion) but balanced on the other (e.g., flexibility). **Unbalanced families** (red section) are those that score at extreme levels on both dimensions. In the Activities section at the end of this chapter, you will have the opportunity to classify your own family using the Family Circumplex scales.

Balanced Versus Unbalanced Relationships   One of the values of the Family Circumplex Model is that hypotheses can be derived from it and can then be tested to validate or invalidate it. A few of the most important hypotheses that have been developed and tested in numerous studies are discussed in the rest of this chapter.

One hypothesis is that *balanced* (two central levels of cohesion and flexibility) *couple and family systems generally function more adequately across the family life cycle than unbalanced types* (two extremes on cohesion and flexibility). Families balanced on cohesion allow their members to be both independent from and connected to the family. Families balanced on flexibility maintain some stability but are also open

Figure 3.4 Degree of Balance in Problem and Healthy Families

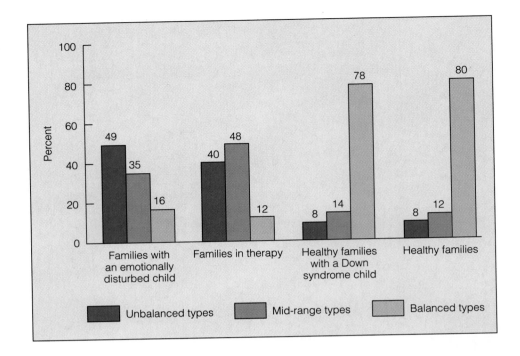

to change. Although balanced family types are located in the central area of the model, they can experience the extremes of the dimensions when necessary to deal with a situation, but they do not typically function at those extremes for long.

Conversely, couples and families with problems are more typically found at the extremes of the dimensions; they are unbalanced types. Problem families often experience too much separateness (disengaged type) or too much togetherness (enmeshed type) on cohesion. On flexibility, problem families tend to have too much stability (rigid type) or too much change (chaotic type).

There is considerable support for another hypothesis derived from the Family Circumplex Model: that *balanced family types are healthier and more functional than unbalanced family types* (Olson, 1993). One systematic study that found strong support for this hypothesis is by Volker Thomas (Thomas & Olson, 1993). Thomas tested four groups of families with an adolescent, videotaping each family while they discussed some family topics. The four samples included 35 families with an emotionally disturbed child, 25 families in family therapy for a variety of problems, 62 healthy families with a Down syndrome child, and 60 other healthy families.

The findings strongly supported the hypothesis (Figure 3.4). As hypothesized, only 16% of the families with an emotionally disturbed child and 12% of the families in therapy were balanced types, whereas about 78–80% of the healthy families were balanced types. Conversely, almost half (49%) of the families with an emotionally disturbed child and 40% of the families in therapy were unbalanced. Only 8% of the healthy families were unbalanced.

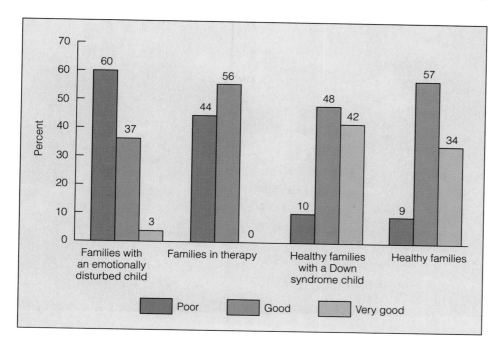

Figure 3.5 Communication Skills in Problem and Healthy Families

Communication in Balanced Relationships   Another hypothesis based on the Family Circumplex Model is that *balanced families have more positive communication skills than unbalanced families.* Communication can be measured at both the marital and the family level. Strong support for this hypothesis was found in the previously described study by Thomas and Olson (1993). Based on videotaped family interactions during problem solving, researchers rated the quality of communication using the characteristics listening skills, speaking skills, self-disclosure, clarity, staying on topic, and respect and regard (Figure 3.5). As hypothesized, problem families had poor communication (60% of those with an emotionally disturbed child and 44% of those in therapy), whereas communication was poor in only about 10% of the healthy families. Conversely, about 90% of the healthy families had good to very good communication. Only 0–3% of the problem families had very good communication.

Using data from a national survey of 1,000 families, Olson and colleagues (1989) investigated parent-adolescent communication and family functioning. In "non-problem" families, data from the parents supported the hypothesis that balanced families have better communication skills, but this hypothesis was not supported by data from the adolescents. Future research is needed to test this hypothesis at both the marital and family level with both healthy and problem families.

A different study comparing balanced and unbalanced families found clear support for the hypothesis that balanced families have more positive communication skills (Rodick, Henggler, & Hanson, 1985). Based on observational measures of

Good communication is important in all human relationships and essential in healthy families. Parents with the ability to listen to their children in a nonjudgmental way, as this mother is doing, not only provide needed emotional support but strengthen family relationships. Families that are balanced on the Circumplex Model are characterized by more open, positive, and supportive communication.

mother-adolescent interaction, mothers in the balanced group had significantly higher rates of supportive communication, explicit information, and positive affect than did mothers in unbalanced types of families, where the majority of the problem mother-adolescent dyads were chaotically enmeshed.

Dynamic Balance and Skiing: An Analogy The difference between a balanced family system and an unbalanced family system is like the difference between a professional skier and a novice skier (Walsh & Olson, 1989). In general, to stay balanced, both skiers and families need to make small, subtle changes or adjustments over time. Without these small adjustments, they may lose their balance, and it will take a major adjustment to regain that balance.

In terms of cohesion, both families and skiers need to balance separateness and togetherness. In balanced families, members are able to move in a somewhat fluid manner between separateness and togetherness; members in unbalanced systems tend to be stuck at one extreme or the other and have a difficult time shifting between these two aspects of life. Similarly, a professional skier keeps both legs somewhat separated but working together, whereas the novice skier often frantically shifts from one leg to the other.

In terms of flexibility, both families and skiers need to balance stability and change. In balanced families, people retain some basic stability while also being able to change. However, in unbalanced systems there is often too much rigidity or too much change, both of which lead to an unstable system. Like balanced families, professional skiers flex their legs to absorb the shock of bumpy terrain while keeping their upper body straight to provide stability. Novice skiers, on the other hand, often become more rigid on a difficult run, leading to instability and ultimately to a fall.

In terms of communication, balanced families use good communication to maintain their balance, whereas poor communication often keeps families out of balance. A professional skier is very much "in touch" with all aspects of the hill, the snow conditions, and the structure of the terrain. Conversely, a novice skier often misreads conditions and misses cues about the terrain.

Another important characteristic shared by balanced families and professional skiers is that they tend to become more cohesive and flexible under stress. Conversely, unbalanced families tend to become either too enmeshed or too separated and, like novice skiers, often also too rigid. Like skiers, families need to become more flexible and cohesive to cope with life's bumpy terrain.

"I like the skiing analogy," said Jean, a 30-year-old mother living in Madison, Wisconsin. "It describes what happened to Jerry and me over the first 10 years of marriage. We were so close at first that we drove each other crazy. Jerry would follow me around clothing stores like a puppy. I think he thought I wanted him to be with me, but he was bored and I liked being on my own shopping."

"Yeah, it took me a while to get the message she was happier without me there," Jerry added. "She was being polite. You see, my parents got divorced a few years before I met Jean and I wanted to do anything I could to keep us together."

"Meanwhile," Jean continued, "I think I drove Jerry crazy because I was so rigid in the way I did things in life. Jerry loves to travel. His father was in the Army, and they lived all over the world when he was growing up."

"And Jean's idea of a big vacation is to go to Oak Lake, 30 miles from town. Every year. Year after year. It took me several years to convince her that the world is bigger than Greater Cedar Bend."

This young couple wobbled down the slope of marriage for several years before they understood each other well enough to make the minor adjustments in course that demonstrate an expert-level performance in a marital relationship.

Accounting for Cultural and Ethnic Diversity   To make the Family Circumplex Model relevant to families with different ethnic and cultural backgrounds, a hypothesis was developed to reflect diversity. The hypothesis states that *if normative family expectations support behavioral extremes on one or both of the dimensions, the family will function well—as long as all its members are satisfied with these expectations.* In this way, the family serves as its own norm base. This approach, however, necessitates measuring each family member's family satisfaction.

Families in our culture vary greatly in the extent to which they encourage their members to develop in ways that differ from the family's values. Although parents prefer their children to develop values and ideas similar to theirs, most let their children become somewhat autonomous and differentiated from the family system. Many families, however, have normative expectations that strongly emphasize emotional and physical family togetherness and high levels of consensus and loyalty, often at the expense of individual development.

Some ethnic groups in this country (including Slovak, Puerto Rican, and Italian American) and religious groups such as the Amish and the Mormons have high expectations about family togetherness (enmeshed family type) coupled with low flexibility (rigid family type) (Woehrer, 1989). These expectations are also common, but less predominant, in many other American families. Many of these families could be described as rigidly enmeshed, but as long as the family members are willing to go along with the expectations, these families will probably not have problems. When the children reach adolescence and want more independence from the family, however, the potential for problems may grow.

Movies As Illustrations of Family Circumplex Types

Movies often provide excellent examples of Family Circumplex types. Because they tend to be more dynamically and dramatically interesting, the unbalanced family types are depicted more often than the balanced types. Movies may also illustrate how families change in response to a stressor or over time as people age. Taking a close look at some movie families can offer a vivid and immediate picture of family types that written descriptions fail to convey.

What About Bob?: A Rigidly Connected Family

The Marvin family is headed by a prominent psychiatrist, Dr. Leo Marvin (played by Richard Dreyfuss), author of a popular book called *Baby Steps*. His family includes his wife Fay (played by Julie Hagerty), a teenage daughter, Anna, and a 9-year-old son, Sigmund. Leo is very self-confident and maintains strong control over his family. Fay is a warm and caring homemaker who tries to support her husband; both children are rather distant from their father. As a family the Marvins operate as a rigidly connected system because the father is so controlling and there is a low level of emotional closeness in the family. Their communication is rather poor, mainly because the father controls the information conveyed and does not let others have much say.

The family experiences a great deal of change when Bob Wiley (played by Bill Murray) becomes a patient of Dr. Marvin. Helped in one session by ideas from Marvin's book, *Baby Steps*, Bob becomes very dependent on Dr. Marvin and follows him to the family's vacation home. About the same time, "Good Morning America" contacts Dr. Marvin and arranges to interview him at his lake home. Bob becomes involved in the production because he wants to share how helpful Dr. Marvin's counsel was. During the filming of the interview, Bob is very articulate; Dr. Marvin, on the other hand, becomes so flustered and frustrated that he is often speechless.

After the "Good Morning" show the family system changes. Bob encourages the family to express their feelings and have fun together. He helps the son, Siggy, learn to dive in the lake, something the boy's father had failed to do. The family becomes more flexibly cohesive, with good communication skills. The father loses his total control over his family, and they enjoy the more flexible style of operating that Bob encourages. Dr. Marvin becomes increasingly frustrated and disengaged from his family, which leads him to become depressed. Eventually he is hospitalized. But, in the end, the family changes and becomes more balanced, with good communication, as a result of Bob's becoming part of the family.

Ordinary People: **A Rigidly Disengaged Family**

The other extreme of the cohesion dimension is the disengaged family in the movie *Ordinary People*. This pleasant suburban family—a mother (played by Mary Tyler Moore), a father (played by Donald Sutherland), and one son—is also very rigid. This family is outwardly pleasant, maintaining a good appearance to outsiders, but passively controlling.

The rigidity is borne in part out of the family's need to survive the loss of the first-born son in a boating accident, just a few months before the story begins. Buck was the star of the family: handsome, charming, an excellent student, a star athlete. His death has left an emptiness in the mother, to which she reacts with rigidity and disengagement. The rest of the family becomes rigid and disengaged in response. In this family, emotions are controlled, roles are strictly defined, and there are strict (but unspoken) rules about what feelings can be discussed. The surviving son, who has attempted suicide because he feels guilty about the boating accident, cannot talk about his feelings with the family because of the implicit rules forbidding such intimate self-disclosure.

The disengagement in this family is painfully apparent. Distance is carefully maintained to prevent any further grief. The son and the father try to make contact with the mother, but they fail. Near the end of the movie, the mother wakes up in the middle of the night and discovers that her husband is not at her side. She goes downstairs and finds him sitting in the dark, crying softly to himself. He says he doesn't think he knows her anymore—the woman she has become—and he is not sure he loves her anymore. Without a word, she goes upstairs and begins to pack her suitcase. There is a brief moment when she gasps, and nearly cries. But she regains control, finishes her packing—and leaves.

The rigidity in this family affects the degree of emotional closeness among family members. It maintains emotional disengagement and keeps feelings of grief and guilt over the loss of the oldest son from surfacing. In this family, the mother keeps her son and husband at arm's length—emotionally stiff-arming them. Although both husband and son attempt to break through this rigidity, they finally give up in despair because they cannot connect with her emotionally.

Shoot the Moon: **A Chaotically Disengaged Family**

The family in *Shoot the Moon* is falling apart due to a divorce. The father (played by Albert Finney) is having a secret affair, but his oldest daughter is suspicious and listens in on an extension to a call he makes to his lover from home. His wife (played by Diane Keaton) has suspected for some time that her husband might be having an affair but has not confronted him. His excuses about "working late" finally wear thin, however, and she does confront him; a dish-breaking fight ensues. He suggests that he leave; she says she packed his bag last night. This couple has been disengaged for a long time, and now their estrangement intensifies. When the father finally moves out, the chaos in the family system takes over.

To try to escape her pain, the mother sleeps late, buries her head under the pillow, and moans. Before, this woman was never tired and always had time for her four daughters. The oldest daughter, Julie, takes over her mother's role. In a scene typical of the family chaos, Julie is simultaneously trying to make breakfast, phoning to schedule a doctor's appointment for a sister who has sprained her foot, and yelling to her sisters to come downstairs to breakfast—which is burning. The sisters yell back that they don't want her breakfast (that she worked so hard to prepare). She yells back that she doesn't need this, throws the frying pan of scrambled eggs into the sink, and heads out the door to the school bus.

Dad—trying both to overcome his guilt and to spend some time with his daughters—is waiting in his car at the end of the driveway to take the children to school. His daughter-turned-parent sees him, walks around his car, and gets onto the school bus without saying a word to him. As the bus pulls out, Julie can be seen looking through the window, crying.

Before the separation, the father had been disengaged from his daughters for some time. The mother had been close to her daughters, but now she too has become disengaged from them due to her depression and inability to function. The oldest daughter, despite taking over some of the parenting roles, still wants a mother and a father to care for her and to be in charge. All the rules and roles are up for grabs in this family.

Dynamic Changes in Family Relationships

Relationships change as time passes. The type of relationship a family has may change as its members grow older, when the children become adolescents, and when they move out of the home. These changes can affect everyone in the family. Some generalizations can be made about how relationships change as time passes:

- An intimate relationship can balance between too much togetherness and too much separateness.

- An intimate relationship can balance between too much change and too much stability.

- Staying too long at either extreme on the cohesion and/or the flexibility dimension can destroy an intimate relationship.

- Too much togetherness can lead to feeling smothered.

- Too much separateness can lead to feeling alone.

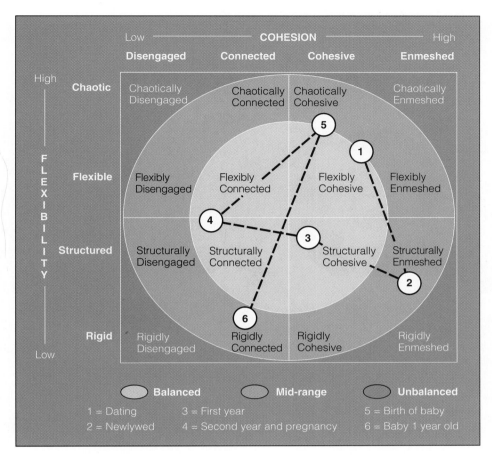

Figure 3.6 Changes in Early Marriage

- Too much change leads to unpredictability and chaos.
- Too little change leads to high predictability and rigidity. It also leads to people controlling each other, which is a barrier to intimacy.

Changes in Early Marriage

Another important hypothesis derived from the Family Circumplex Model is that *couples and families change their levels of cohesion and flexibility to adapt to the developmental changes, needs, and preferences of family members.* This means that couples and families will change their type of family system as developmental changes occur. For example, when a couple has a child, the couple system usually changes to adapt to the new family member.

Even in the early years of marriage, cohesion and flexibility can change relatively dramatically. Figure 3.6 shows the changes one young couple goes through

The birth of a baby creates a tremendous upheaval in a couple's relationship. Although life becomes more hectic, a healthy family can thrive and temporarily enjoy a state of chaotic cohesion. Before too long, however, a new balance must be reached.

in a period of only 5 years. As a dating couple, Norm and Rachel begin their relationship as *flexibly cohesive*. They feel close (cohesive) and have a flexible style in terms of leadership and decision making.

After marriage, the structurally enmeshed style best describes the newlywed couple's relationship. They are structured because they are still getting organized in terms of their roles and leadership. Being in love and enjoying spending maximum time together helps to keep them enmeshed. By the end of their first year of marriage, the so-called honeymoon effect has worn off and they become structurally cohesive. The excitement with each other is not as great as it once was (which is typical), their togetherness has dropped into the more balanced range, and flexibility has increased somewhat. Their relationship now is a balanced one because both cohesion and flexibility are at balanced levels. As the second year of their marriage ends, Rachel becomes pregnant. Pregnancy means change for any couple, and Norm and Rachel's flexibility increases. Their togetherness decreases some as Norm becomes more involved in his work and Rachel becomes more involved in both work and pregnancy. Remaining in the balanced area of the model, they are now flexibly connected.

Another year passes. Baby Evan has arrived, and Norm and Rachel are forced to adapt to this new member of their family. Although life is hectic, the family continues to thrive and is happy being chaotically cohesive. The birth of a baby is a momentous time in any couple's relationship. Change is inevitably high. Having a totally dependent and demanding infant has changed the lives of this young mother and young father and put many pressures on their relationship. Their life is in relative turmoil: They are up a couple of times each night to feed the baby, Rachel has quit her job, they can't go out with friends the way they used to, they're short on money, there are 15 to 25 diapers to change each day. But they are so busy that they don't have time to think about how chaotic their life has become. Evan's presence has increased the sense of bonding between the couple, and they feel united in their goal of rearing a happy, healthy child.

Five years have passed since we first met this young couple in their dating period. The baby is a year old. Life has stabilized, and they are functioning as a rigidly connected family. They are experiencing very few changes now. Rachel is home caring for and enjoying Evan. Norm also spends some time with him. They have successfully scaled down on spending. They are enjoying the stability, especially in comparison with the chaos they experienced when Evan was born. Their cohesion scores have also dropped off somewhat. Rachel is more involved with the baby than Norm is. Although he is aware of the demands his work places on him, he cannot control them to the extent he would like.

In summary, this couple has changed over time and has experienced various types of family systems. These changes are rather common and even predictable. The partners' chances for satisfaction increase if their relationship dynamics change as a way of coping with stress. In fact, this couple would have had more problems if they had resisted changing their relationship system to deal with the new demands put on them as a couple and a family.

Family Cohesion Across the Family Life Cycle

Support for the hypothesis from the Family Circumplex Model that *couples and families change their levels of cohesion across the life cycle* was found in a study of 1,000 non-problem families (Olson, McCubbin, et al., 1989). These families were divided into four stages: young couples, families with young children, families with teenagers, and older couples. Because these were non-problem families, most of the respondents' scores fell into the two balanced levels of cohesion (i.e., connected and cohesive). Figure 3.7 (p. 104) summarizes the percentage of families at each level.

As expected, a high percentage (71%) of young couples without children felt cohesive, with only 29% feeling connected. Among families with young children, the percentage feeling cohesive dropped a few points. Among families with teenagers, however, there was a reversal: A majority (60%) of families felt connected rather than cohesive (40%). Not only should this reversal be expected, but it is also appropriate for that stage of the life cycle. It enables the teenagers to develop autonomy and independence. Older couples whose children had left home showed a shift back to an almost equal balance between the number who felt connected and those who felt cohesive.

A related finding was that the adolescents saw their family as significantly lower

Figure 3.7 Family Cohesion Across Four Stages of the Family Life cycle. *Source:* Data from *Families: What Makes Them Work?* (2nd ed.) by D. H. Olson, H. I. McCubbin, H. Barnes, A. Larsen, M. Muxen, and M. Wilson, 1989. Los Angeles: Sage Publications. Reprinted by permission of the publisher.

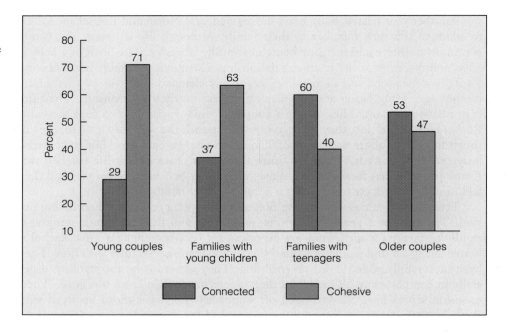

in cohesion than did their mothers and fathers (Olson, McCubbin, et al., 1989). This is consistent with the interpretation that adolescents seek to differentiate themselves from the family. To accomplish this task, they often must become less cohesive with their parents. They say, in effect, "I don't need a lot of togetherness with Mom and Dad, so we really don't have a very close family."

At this stage, parents also have mixed emotions about how cohesive a relationship they wish to have with their adolescents. As one father explained, "Just two months ago I was feeling quietly perturbed that my daughter didn't go out with any other kids at all. She just hung around the house looking bored. I thought she should be running around a bit. But now, only two months later, she has turned sixteen. She's got her driver's license, and we never see her. She's always driving around. I miss her a lot. There's got to be some happy medium in between somewhere!"

Family Flexibility Across the Family Life Cycle

It is also hypothesized from the Family Circumplex Model that *couples and families change their level of flexibility across the life cycle to deal with developmental issues.* As changes occur over the life cycle, families need to adapt to meet the challenges presented by changing family and individual needs. Flexibility is change in the couple's and/or family's leadership, role relationships, and relationship rules (Olson, McCubbin, et al., 1989).

The question is, Can the family change when it is appropriate or necessary? For example, a grandfather dies, leaving his blind wife alone. The family decides

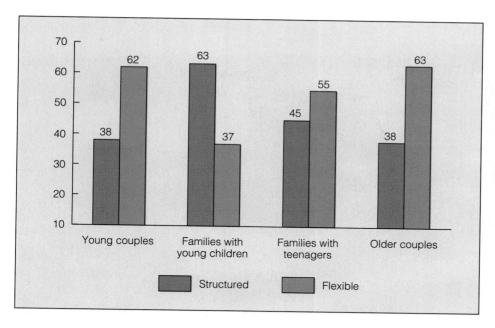

Figure 3.8 Family Flexibility Across Four Stages of the Family Life cycle. *Source:* Data from *Families: What Makes Them Work?* (2nd ed.) by D. H. Olson, H. I. McCubbin, H. Barnes, A. Larsen, M. Muxen, and M. Wilson, 1989. Los Angeles: Sage Publications. Reprinted by permission of the publisher.

it would be unfair to put grandma in a nursing home simply because she needs some help getting around the house and caring for herself. The members of the family decide to take her into their home, where she will live in the spare bedroom. Will the family be able to make the many adaptations necessary to accommodate a new household member?

The study of 1,000 families (Olson, McCubbin, et al., 1989) also explored family flexibility across the four stages of the life cycle. In general, these non-problem families fell into the balanced area of the Circumplex Model and were classified as either structured or flexible. Figure 3.8 summarizes the study's results. Of young couples without children, almost two thirds (62%) were flexible; the other third (38%) were structured. When children arrived, however, this pattern reversed; about two thirds (63%) of the families were structured, and about one third (37%) were flexible.

Another shift in flexibility occurred among families who had teenagers. As is appropriate, these families shifted toward greater flexibility. This style enables the family to change their roles and loosen their rules so that their teenagers can have more freedom. After the teenagers had left home, almost two thirds of the older couples (63%) had a more flexible style of relating to each other; this was almost identical to the finding for young couples without children.

Another interesting family dynamic is the difference between adolescents' and parents' descriptions of family flexibility. When teenagers' descriptions of their family's flexibility were compared with those of their parents, teenagers tended to see their families as more structured—and at times rigid—than did their parents (Olson, McCubbin, et al., 1989). These parent/adolescent differences are consis-

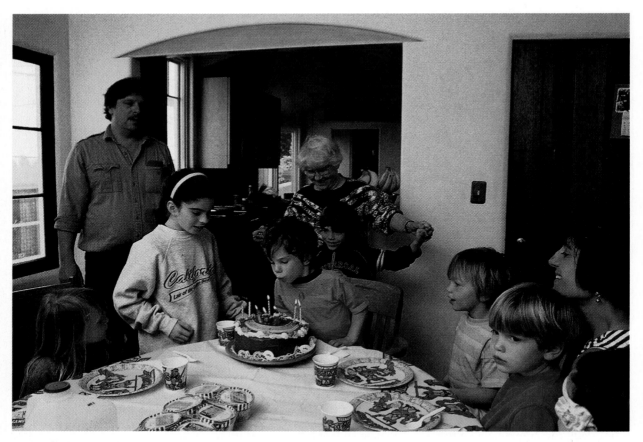

Family members of all ages have to be flexible in order to meet individual needs and the inevitable challenges that life brings. This family has found a satisfying way to include an elderly member in family activities.

tent with what was found regarding family cohesion. Because adolescents are seeking greater freedom, they tend to view the restrictions in their family as problematic and, therefore, tend to see more rigidity than their parents do. This difference in perception can create conflict in the relationship, but it is an inevitable part of family development for these differences between generations to emerge as adolescents seek more freedom and autonomy.

This cross-sectional study provided snapshots of different families at four stages of the life cycle and found significant differences in family cohesion and flexibility at the four stages. Because the study was not longitudinal (i.e., it did not follow the same families across the various stages of the cycle), caution must be exercised in applying its findings. There is a good probability, however, that a longitudinal study would produce similar findings because the results are predictable and are supported by other studies.

"You know, we've had kids, kids, kids in our lives for 26 years now," said Al, a middle-aged father living in Cornwall, New York, to his wife, Sharon. "I think it's about time the nest emptied." It wasn't that he didn't like his two youngest children, ages 19 and 17, still living at home. It was simply that their needs for autonomy were great and their ability to be on their own was rapidly growing. "I think they'll be ready to take off in not too long a time," he remarked.

"They've felt that way for the past 3 years," Sharon replied. She knew the two girls better than he did simply because she was around them more, but she didn't rub this fact in. "I think we might let them try out their wings this summer. Why don't we see if they could get jobs at your brother's lodge in Canada?" With this conversation, the family began to move toward a new stage of the family life cycle.

Summary

- The three basic qualities of cohesion, flexibility, and communication have been identified as qualities that make families strong. These three are features of family systems theory, the family strengths framework, the family development framework, and other theories and frameworks.

- The Family Circumplex Model is a tool for understanding couple and family relationships. It is based on family systems theory and is structured on the three dimensions of cohesion, flexibility, and communication.

- Cohesion focuses on the dynamic balance between the extremes of separateness and togetherness in both couple and family relationships. Balancing these two extremes entails experiencing both autonomy and intimacy, but not remaining stuck at either extreme for long periods.

- Flexibility focuses on the dynamic balance between stability and change. The most functional couples and family systems have both characteristics, and they are able to move back and forth between them. Families with problems over time tend to become stuck at one of the extremes, either too much stability (rigid) or too much change (chaotic).

- Communication is a facilitating dimension that can help create change in the levels of cohesion and flexibility when change is necessary.

- The Circumplex Model describes 3 general types of family systems—balanced, mid-range, and unbalanced—and 16 specific types within those 3.

- Balanced family types are the flexibly connected, the structurally connected, the flexibly cohesive, and the structurally cohesive. Unbalanced types are the chaotically disengaged, the rigidly disengaged, the chaotically enmeshed, and the rigidly enmeshed.

- The Family Circumplex Model is a dynamic model that assumes relationships change over time. More specifically, it assumes that couples and families change over the family life cycle and that this change is most evident when families face a major stressor.

Table 3.5 Family Circumplex Scales

COHESION							
DISENGAGED (UNBALANCED)		**CONNECTED** (BALANCED)		**COHESIVE** (BALANCED)		**ENMESHED** (UNBALANCED)	
SCORE							
1	2	3	4	5	6	7	8
Separateness/ Togetherness — High separateness		More separateness than togetherness		More togetherness than separateness		Very high togetherness	
I–We balance — Primarily I		More I than We		More We than I		Primarily We	
Closeness — Little closeness		Low to moderate closeness		Moderate to high closeness		Very high closeness	
Loyalty — Lack of loyalty		Some loyalty		Considerable loyalty		High loyalty	
Activities — Mainly separate		More separate than shared		More shared than separate		Mainly shared	
Dependence/ Independence — High independence		More independence than dependence		More dependence than independence		High dependence	

FLEXIBILITY							
RIGID (UNBALANCED)		**STRUCTURED** (BALANCED)		**FLEXIBLE** (BALANCED)		**CHAOTIC** (UNBALANCED)	
SCORE							
1	2	3	4	5	6	7	8
Leadership — Authoritarian		Sometimes shared		Often shared		Lack of leadership	
Discipline — Strict discipline		Somewhat democratic		Democratic		Lenient discipline	
Negotiation — Limited discussion		Organized discussion		Open discussion		Endless discussion	
Roles — Roles very stable		Roles stable		Role sharing		Dramatic role shifts	
Rules — Unchanging rules		Few rule changes		Some rule changes		Frequent rule changes	
Change — Very little change		Some change		Moderate change		Considerable change	

COMMUNICATION						
POOR		**GOOD**		**VERY GOOD**	
SCORE					
1	2	3	4	5	6
Listening skills — Poor listening skills		Appear to listen, but feedback is limited		Give feedback, indicating good listening skills	
Speaking skills — Often speak for others		Speak for self more than for others		Speak mainly for self rather than for others	
Self-disclosure — Low sharing of feelings		Moderate sharing of feelings		High sharing of feelings	
Clarity — Inconsistent messages		Clear messages		Very clear messages	
Staying on topic — Seldom stay on topic		Often stay on topic		Mainly stay on topic	
Respect and regard — Low to moderate		Moderate to high		High	

Key Terms

Family Circumplex Model

personification

first order change

second order change

balanced families

mid-range families

unbalanced families

Activities

1. Use the Family Circumplex scales (Table 3.5) to describe your family of origin. Select a time period when you were all together (e.g., when you were in high school). Make a list of the people you are including in your family. Then do the following:

   a. Review the six categories shown in the scales (Table 3.5) for assessing cohesion, flexibility, and communication.

   b. On a separate piece of paper, rate your family on a scale of 1–8 for each of the categories in the three dimensions.

   c. To determine a total score for each dimension, review the scores and select a number that represents the best average score. Record the score below.

Cohesion	**Flexibility**	**Communication**
Score: _____	Score: _____	Score: _____
Level: _____	Level: _____	Level: _____

   d. Now, plot the scores for cohesion and flexibility onto the Family Circumplex Model (Figure 3.9, p. 110) and identify the type of family system in which you grew up.

   e. After plotting your scores onto the model, consider the following questions:

   • What is/was it like to live in your type of family (e.g., flexibly connected, rigidly enmeshed, etc.)?

   • In what ways related to cohesion and flexibility is/was your family satisfying and in what ways is/was it frustrating?

   • How did your family change on cohesion and flexibility as you were growing up?

   • In what ways did communication affect your family's dynamics?

2. If you are dating someone, are engaged, or are married, both you and your partner should answer the questions on the Family Circumplex scales twice: first, in terms of your families of origin (same as Activity 1) and second, in terms of your couple relationship. Compare your partner's description of your couple relationship with yours, and discuss the similarities and differences. Then compare each of your families of origin with your couple relationship.

   (For more details on using the Family Circumplex scales, see Resource Section A.)

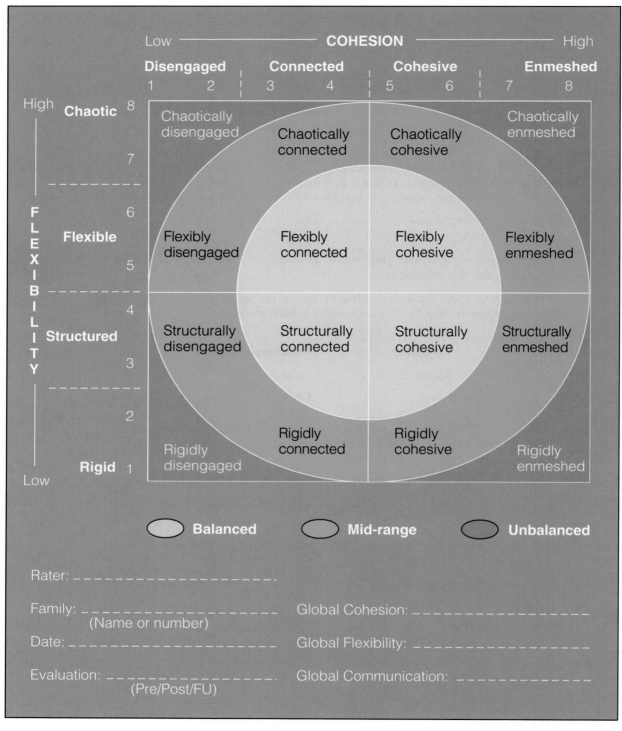

Figure 3.9 Family Circumplex Model

Suggested Readings

Olson, D. H., McCubbin, H., Barnes, H., Larsen, A., Muxen, M., and Wilson, M. (1989). *Families: What makes them work* (2nd ed.). Beverly Hills, CA: Sage Publications. *Describes a nationwide study, conducted at the University of Minnesota, of 1,000 intact families at all stages of the life cycle, ranging from newlyweds to retired couples. Focuses on different types of families, the stresses they encounter, the internal and external resources that help them cope, and the factors that produce marital and family satisfaction across the family life cycle.*

Olson, D. H., Russell, C. S., & Sprenkle, D. H. (1989). *Circumplex Model: Clinical assessment and treatment intervention with families.* New York: Haworth Press. *Use of the Family Circumplex Model to assess and treat family problems.*

PART II

Developing Intimate Relationships

Friendship, Love, and Intimacy

Love and friendship bind society together, providing both emotional support and a buffer against stress that preserve our physical and psychological health. Love is clearly much more than friendship, and thus we treat love relationships more seriously. However, the strongest love relationships have roots in friendship: Satisfying and stable love relationships come from shared interests and values. When friends fall in love, they are adding passion to the emotional intimacy we call friendship.

Love is different things to different people. Definitions of love are almost endless (Box 4.1). No other topic demands so much attention and generates so much confusion in our society. We cannot turn on the radio or TV, or drive down the street, or converse with a friend for long without being confronted with words about love, thoughts of love, acts of love, scenes of love, or advertisements using love. Despite the ubiquitous nature of love, it remains a mystery to many. It is often regarded as a strange force that can overpower us and at times take control over our lives: People speak of being "under love's spell" or "swept away" with passion.

Intimacy, too, is mysterious. In healthy human relationships, love and intimacy are inextricably interwoven. Intimacy is the goal of most love relationships, yet because it requires revealing vulnerabilities, it can be a frightening prospect for some.

This chapter explores various ways of defining love and the related concept of intimacy. It also identifies a number of constructive and destructive "games" people play in their intimate relationships. Its aim is to help you understand love and intimacy and learn how to enhance your own intimate experiences and relationships.

Friends Versus Lovers

Research comparing love and friendship indicates that they are alike in many ways, but that crucial differences make love both more rewarding and more volatile than friendship. After conducting several studies, Keith E. Davis and his colleague Michael J. Todd came to this conclusion:

> Typical love relationships will differ from even very good friendships by having higher levels of fascination, exclusiveness and sexual desire, a greater depth of caring about the other individual (which would be manifest in a willingness to give the utmost when needed), and a greater potential for enjoyment and other positive emotions. Love relationships will also have, however, a greater potential for distress, ambivalence, conflict, and mutual criticism. (Davis, 1985, p. 30)

Love, in short, runs deeper and stronger than friendship. And because the stakes are so high with love, the possibility of interpersonal difficulties increases, and we jealously guard this important relationship.

B O X   4 . 1

On Love

In love the paradox occurs that two beings become one yet remain two.

—ERICH FROMM, *psychiatrist*

Love doesn't just sit there, like a stone, it has to be made, like bread; remade all the time, made new.

—URSULA K. LE GUIN, *writer*

Being in love isn't ever really loving, it's just wanting. And it isn't any good. It's all aching and misery.

—JAMES LEO HERLIHY, *writer*

Love is the history of a woman's life; it is an episode in man's.

—MADAME DE STAËL, *writer*

He who knows nothing, loves nothing . . .
But he who understands also loves, notices, sees . . .
The more knowledge inherent in a thing, the
   greater the love.

—PARACELSUS, *philosopher*

The trouble with some women is that they get all excited about nothing—and then marry him.

—CHER, *actor*

When the satisfaction or the security of another person becomes as significant to one as is one's own security, then the state of love exists.

—HARRY STACK SULLIVAN, *psychiatrist*

Chains do not hold a marriage together. It is threads, hundreds of tiny threads which sew people together through the years. This is what makes a marriage last—more than passion or even sex!

—SIMONE SIGNORET, *actor*

Love is a state of perpetual anesthesia.

—H. L. MENCKEN, *journalist*

My brother refers to my husband, in his presence, as "Joan's husband." Marriage is the classic betrayal.

—JOAN DIDION, *writer*

The Fabric of Friendship

Davis and Todd began their research by developing a hypothetical model of friendship and love (Davis, 1985). In their original profile of friendship, they first assumed that two individuals participate in a reciprocal relationship as equals. The fabric of friendship included eight important elements:

- *Enjoyment.* Friends enjoy each other's company most of the time, although disagreements and friction occasionally occur.

- *Acceptance.* Friends accept each other for who they are and don't try to change the other person.

- *Trust.* Friends assume that they will act in each other's best interest. "Even when he's hassling me, I know it's for my own good." "She would never intentionally hurt me, except in a fit of extreme anger."

Love has much in common with friendship, but it is more intense and passionate. Like the young man and woman on the left, couples in love tend to be fascinated with each other, spending long moments gazing unself-consciously into each other's eyes. Like the couple on the right, they also tend to have interests in common and enjoy just being together.

- *Respect.* Friends respect each other; they assume the other has good judgment in making choices in life.

- *Mutual assistance.* Friends help and support each other; they can count on each other in times of need.

- *Confiding.* Friends share life experiences and feelings with each other.

- *Understanding.* Friends know each other's values and understand what is important to each other. "I know what makes her tick."

- *Spontaneity.* Friends feel free to be "real" around each other. They don't feel they have to play a role or hold back their true feelings.

The Tapestry of Love

Davis and Todd assumed at the outset of their studies that romantic relationships would have the same characteristics as friendship, but that they would also have additional, unique characteristics. The unique characteristics were grouped in two

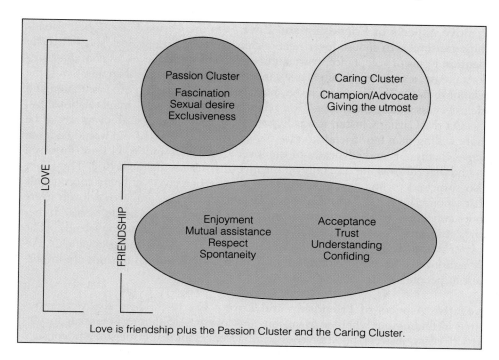

Figure 4.1 Love and Friendship. *Source:* "Near and Dear: Love and Friendship Compared" by K. E. Davis, 1985, *Psychology Today* (February), p. 24. Copyright 1985 by Sussex Publishers, Inc. Reprinted by permission from *Psychology Today* magazine.

broad categories: the Passion Cluster and the Caring Cluster. The model of friendship and love that Davis and Todd developed is shown in Figure 4.1.

The **Passion Cluster** includes three related characteristics: fascination, sexual desire, and exclusiveness. Fascination is a preoccupation with the other person—a tendency to think about, look at, want to talk to, and want to be with that person. Sexual desire is the lovers' desire to touch each other and to make love, even though they may not engage in sexual intercourse for religious, moral, or practical reasons. Exclusiveness is giving the partner priority over other relationships in one's life.

The **Caring Cluster** contains two components: being an advocate for one's partner and giving the utmost. Being a champion and an advocate means defending and supporting each other, even during difficult times. Giving the utmost is easy for people in love; sometimes they give to the point of self-sacrifice.

Contrasting Friends and Lovers

Davis and Todd found that love is friendship with a few added components, but they were surprised by a few other findings. In their survey of 242 friends, spouses, and lovers (two thirds students, one third community members), the researchers discovered specific similarities and differences between friends and lovers.

Positive Aspects of Friendship and Love On the Caring Cluster, best friendships are similar to spouse/lover relationships in several ways: Both show virtually identical levels of acceptance, trust, and respect and similar levels of confiding, understanding, spontaneity, mutual assistance, and satisfaction and happiness with the relationship. On the Passion Cluster, however, there is much more fascination and exclusiveness among the spouse/lover relationships than in best-friend relationships.

On the Caring Cluster, it was hypothesized that spouses and lovers would be more willing than best friends to give the utmost when needed and would be more active champions and advocates of the loved one. Davis and Todd were surprised to find that this was the case only on the give-the-utmost characteristic. They were also surprised to find that best friendships were perceived as being more stable than spouse/lover relationships. Spouses and, especially, unmarried lovers were more concerned that their relationships might break up. As a single woman in her early 30s put it, "Lovers come and go, but I can always count on my friends." The loss of friends and, especially, loved ones can lead to illness and even suicide. Although love is much more than friendship, both kinds of relationships are important in people's lives.

Negative Aspects of Friendship and Love The researchers also were interested in finding out whether friendship and love have different potentials for destructiveness, distress, possessiveness, ambivalence, mutual criticism, and conflict. They hypothesized that clear-cut differences should be apparent because love relationships are more charged with fascination and exclusiveness than friendships.

When people enter a love relationship, they usually commit to one individual and give up other, similar love relationships. Being a spouse or a lover also means close coordination of activities with the loved one and giving the loved one's interests priority over relationships with others. This strong commitment can lead to such questions as, "Am I giving up too much?" "Did I do the right thing by committing to her?"

Davis and Todd found that because the stakes are so high, love relationships can easily become breeding grounds for ambivalent feelings and conflict. They also found that spouses and lovers were significantly less accepting of each other than were friends. Spouses and lovers had a greater desire to change each other; they were also more willing to criticize their partners than their friends.

Friendship into Love It appears that the strongest love relationships have roots in friendship. Lillian B. Rubin (1985) argues that satisfying and stable relationships come from shared interests and values, and "that's what love is about." According to Susan S. Hendrick (cited in B. Jacob, 1986), the signs of the end of a beautiful friendship and the beginning of love are that you are suddenly aware of your friend's wonderful smile, great body, or cute freckles; you get dressed up when you know you're going to see each other; you feel excited at the thought of meeting; and you begin to feel shy and less spontaneous when you're together.

Similarly, psychologist Robert Sternberg (1986) believes that when friends fall in love, they are simply adding passion to the emotional intimacy we call friendship. The temptation is to let oneself be swept away by romance, but Hendrick (cited in Jacob, 1986) argues that individuals should use some uncommon sense. This includes letting things develop slowly, being honest with the other person

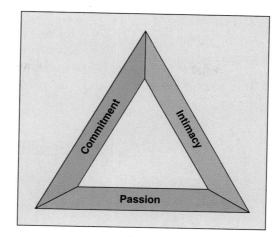

Figure 4.2 The Love Triangle. *Source: The Psychology of Love* (p. 37) edited by R. Sternberg and M. Barnes, 1988, New Haven, CT: Yale University Press. Copyright 1988 by Yale University Press. Reprinted by permission.

and with oneself, and keeping an open mind and a sense of humor. It is important to remember that it is easier to "fall in love" than to "stay in love."

> "I'm so happy we were friends for a long time before we became lovers," Josh, a graduate student, related. "Passion is really great, but it clutters up a relationship a great deal. You don't know what you have underneath the passion if it drains away. But the friendship shines on and on, through good times and bad times." Josh explained that he had met Jessica while doing laundry one afternoon in Berkeley. He was dressed pretty shabbily, and so was she.
>
> "I didn't really think of Jessica in a genuinely sexual way until several months after I got to know her. She was just always that good friend down the hallway in the apartment building who I could talk to about anything. Sometimes she would counsel me on my girlfriends, and then one day I looked at her and thought, 'Wow, she ought to be my girlfriend!'"

The Love Triangle

Although "love triangle" usually brings to mind a relationship in which one person has two lovers, another sort of love triangle was developed by Sternberg (Sternberg & Barnes, 1988). The three dimensions of the triangle are commitment (the cognitive component), intimacy (the emotional component), and passion (the motivational component) (Figure 4.2).

A relationship can start off with intimacy (friendship) and develop into love. A relationship can also start off only with passion and later develop the other two components. A relationship (such as an arranged marriage) can also begin simply with commitment to each other for economic reasons or for reasons dictated by the couple's families; even this type of relationship can later develop intimacy and passion and bloom into love (Sternberg & Barnes, 1988; Trotter, 1986).

Figure 4.3 Eight Types of Love Relationships.
Source: The Psychology of Love (p. 51) edited by R. Sternberg and M. Barnes, 1988, New Haven, CT: Yale University Press. Copyright 1988 by Yale University Press. Reprinted by permission.

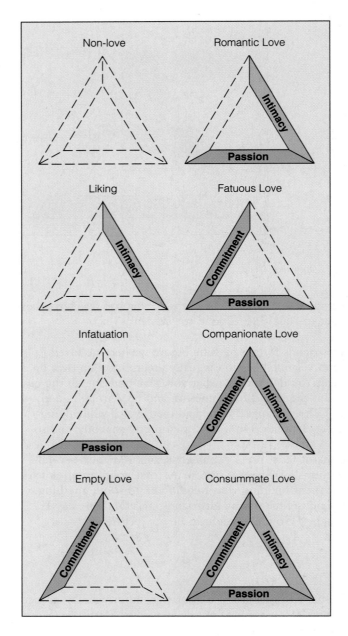

Commitment is a cognitive attachment to another person. It also develops over time, beginning slowly and increasing at a faster rate if the relationship is positive. If the relationship fails, commitment disappears. People express commitment when they move their relationship to a more advanced stage (from dating to engagement, from engagement to marriage), by being faithful, or by staying in the relationship during difficult times.

Intimacy involves sharing feelings and providing emotional support. It usually includes high levels of self-disclosure, the sharing of personal information not ordinarily revealed because of the risk involved. Intimacy gradually increases as closeness grows and deepens as a relationship matures. Few couples are likely to share everything with each other. People need some private space, a bit of their world that is closed to everyone else. But in a mature intimate relationship, most areas are open for discussion and sharing. By opening up, by earning each other's trust and becoming vulnerable to each other, people can build a strong emotional bond of intimacy. The paradox is that by expressing feelings of weakness and vulnerability, individuals can gain support and strength from trusted loved ones.

Passion is usually expressed by touching, kissing, and being affectionate, which is linked to physiological arousal; it is also expressed through sexual interactions. Due to its intensity, passion develops quickly but can also fade quickly. Passion is like an addiction; when it ends, a person can experience withdrawal symptoms such as irritability and depression.

Combining the three dimensions of love in various ways, Sternberg identified eight types of love relationships: non-love, liking, infatuation, empty love, romantic love, fatuous love, companionate love, and consummate love (Figure 4.3). **Non-love** occurs when there is no commitment, intimacy, or passion. **Liking** begins when there is just intimacy, but no passion or commitment. When there is just passion, **infatuation** occurs. **Empty love** involves commitment, but no passion or intimacy. **Romantic love** has both intimacy and passion, but it is lacking in commitment. **Fatuous love** occurs when a person is committed based on passion, but has not had the time to develop true intimacy. (For example, two people fall in love and, after seeing each other only on weekends for 2 months, get married.) **Companionate love** is more characteristic of couples who have been married for years. These couples have both commitment and intimacy, but they lack the passion they had when they were first married. Finally, **consummate love** is complete love, containing all three dimensions. It is the goal of most couples.

Most people have experienced several of these types of love and can recognize that each of them feels rather different. Even within one relationship, it is possible to experience two or more types of love over time. A couple, for example, may start out as close friends (liking) and then two years later become sexually involved (romantic love); a year later they may decide to live together (consummate love). However, three months later he has an affair; she finds out about it and moves out, ending the relationship (non-love).

Three Perspectives on Love

In his classic book *The Art of Loving*, Erich Fromm (1956) described several important myths about love. He believes that too many people think love is simple, whereas he maintains that finding the right person is difficult, requiring work and practice. Fromm believes that "falling in love" is very different from "being in love," which involves facing the realities of living together. He also suggests that "being a loving person is the best way to be loved."

Love can also be seen as an addiction. In *Love and Addiction*, Stanton Peele (1985) suggests that, unfortunately, many people "in love" are addicted to love much as people are addicted to alcohol, tobacco, or other drugs. As with other

Many different needs, interactions, and experiences have been given the name "love." In the movie *Fatal Attraction*, Glenn Close and Michael Douglas create a chilling portrait of love as a dangerous addiction.

addictions, people seek stability and comfort in the addiction and suffer withdrawal when it is not available. Infatuation generates a good deal of adrenaline in the body, causing a high that people learn to seek. When not involved in "the hunt," people can have a sensation of "crashing," similar to the feeling people experience when other drugs wear off. The search for this high is one explanation for why some people have dozens or even hundreds of different sexual partners during their lifetime.

Peele developed several criteria for determining whether one has a mature love relationship or an addictive love relationship. He believes that if you can honestly answer "yes" to these questions, then you have a mature love relationship:

- Do you each value yourself?
- Are you both better people as a result of this relationship?
- Do you both have serious interests outside the relationship?
- Is the relationship not the totality of your life?
- Are neither of you possessive or jealous of your partner?
- Are you best friends?

Another perspective on love—"tough love"—was espoused by James Dobson (1983) in his book, *Love Must Be Tough*. He believes that loving toughness can help

couples and families overcome serious problems and develop stronger relationships. He maintains that in couple conflict, one person is often more independent
than the other; the dependent person panics if the other suggests he or she is unhappy or otherwise starts to withdraw from the relationship. Rather than pursue
the partner, Dobson suggests, the more dependent person should also pull back
from the relationship and be "tough" by demonstrating independence and putting
some realistic demands on the relationship. The tough love concept has also been
suggested for parents who are having little success dealing with troubled adolescents in more traditional ways.

Exploring Intimacy: From Experience to Relationship

Like love, intimacy is also an elusive concept. The word generally brings to mind
images of physical closeness and sexuality. But it is really much more than that.
Intimacy is the closeness and feelings of warmth we have with certain people. It is
an ongoing process of life with other people, and it has many components. Without intimacy with other human beings, life would be boring, cold, and lonely. Many
people in our culture place a high value on intimacy. Although intimacy is not restricted to marriage relationships, most of us get married in our search to find and
maintain intimacy. It is considered a reward and benefit of marriage.

Intimacy Versus Isolation

Intimacy is a prominent element in Erik Erikson's (1968) eight-stage theory of human development. Erikson was a follower of Sigmund Freud but transcended the
fatalism of Freud's psychoanalytic theory. He posited his own more optimistic beliefs, which emphasized success and the flowering of human potential. Whereas
Freud saw personality as being primarily established in early childhood, Erikson
argued that growth occurs across the life span, from birth to death. Even older
people are capable of making changes in their lives, if they choose to be flexible.

Erikson's theory focuses on psychosocial development, rather than on psychosexual development, Freud's primary focus. For Erikson, the individual moves
through eight predetermined steps (or stages) to become fully developed. Mastery
of the developmental tasks at one stage means the individual is ready to progress
to the next developmental stage. Failure or difficulty in meeting the challenges of
a particular stage does not mean an individual cannot move on. Rather, progress in
the next stage of psychosocial development will simply be more difficult or slower.
Each stage of life brings another "psychosocial crisis," as Erikson called it. Other
theorists prefer to say that each stage brings another "turning point" or "challenge."

The psychosocial crisis of young adulthood is intimacy versus isolation. The
challenge is to develop a close, warm relationship with another human being to
overcome isolation. If intimacy cannot be established with another, the risk of

According to Erikson's theory of psychosocial development, discovering how to create and build an intimate relationship is a particular challenge of young adulthood. As this young couple demonstrates, affection and trust are integral components of such a relationship.

experiencing loneliness and isolation is greater, Erikson contended. Falling out of love is a relatively common occurrence, and many individuals find that loss of intimacy can generate considerable pain. For some individuals, the failed quest for intimacy causes such pain that they conclude the search is not worth the effort. Most people, however, continue the quest.

"I wanted to crawl in a hole and die when Jim left me," said Sheila, a 27-year-old woman living in Buffalo, New York. "And I really did withdraw for a long time. It was winter—dark and incredibly cold outside—and I spent most of my free time sleeping or just lying in bed. Then I got superinvolved in my work at the office and in volunteer activities with the YWCA. I was coordinating a support group for teen moms at the Y. Anything that kept me away from men. Finally, a friend looked me in the eye and said, 'Why are you so gun-shy?'

"I looked straight back at her and acted as if I didn't know what she was talking about. But she knew me too well, and after a long talk I decided it was time to start looking again. I knew I was being irrational. I kept thinking, 'All men are creeps!' But what I really meant was, 'I'm so afraid of falling in love with a wonderful guy like Jim again and having him leave me.'"

Intimacy and Communication

Honest communication is essential to true intimacy. We cannot feel close to another person if we are hiding or withholding important thoughts or feelings about that person, or even about ourselves. This doesn't mean, however, that we should lay bare our every thought or emotion. High self-disclosure can be detrimental to the development of intimacy at the beginning of a relationship, and it can damage a more established relationship if the "brutal truth" is too brutal. In the former case, when a relationship is just beginning, we may be opening ourselves up to someone who doesn't have the same commitment to the relationship and who therefore would not share in return. In the latter case, when a relationship is established, "honesty" may be a thin disguise for hostility or anger against the partner or spouse.

Nevertheless, open communication in appropriate doses, at appropriate times, and with good intentions can enhance a relationship and lead to greater intimacy. A couple who tries to maintain peace and stability in their relationship by glossing over disputes or ignoring problems is headed for trouble. Finding a productive way of resolving differences, by meeting them head on and negotiating a workable compromise, is key.

Communication in intimate relationships is the subject of Chapter 8.

Intimate Experiences Versus an Intimate Relationship

One can feel close to another person in a variety of ways and in different areas of one's life. Some of these ways of being close include emotional intimacy, intellectual intimacy, social intimacy, recreational intimacy, and sexual intimacy.

An **intimate experience** is one in which we feel close or share ourselves in one area. For example, a deep philosophic discussion can be a very intellectually intimate experience for two people. Working together successfully on a project can lead to an emotionally intimate feeling. The most commonly thought of type of intimacy is sexual intimacy. People perceive experiences differently, of course. Whereas one person might feel strongly drawn to another after a discussion about life, or after a sexual experience, the other individual might not be nearly as moved. We can be intimate with a variety of people in a variety of ways.

An **intimate relationship** is one in which we share intimate experiences in several areas over time, with expectations that this sharing will continue. It is difficult to have and to maintain intimate relationships with more than a few people at once, because intimacy is time-consuming. For example, how many really good friends, intimate friends, do you have? Probably very few.

Also, it is quite clear from research with couples that no relationship can provide intimate experiences in all areas all the time. With apologies to Abraham Lincoln, "You can please some of the people some of the time, but you can't please all of the people all of the time." This is certainly the case with love relationships. A couple may be able to satisfy each other in a number of ways—emotionally, intellectually, sexually—but both partners will most likely satisfy other intimacy needs outside the relationship. We do not suggest sexual intimacy as one of these areas, because an extramarital affair can destroy intimacy in all other areas of the relationship. But both partners can have friends of either sex at work or in other areas of their lives, friends who are very special and who provide something that the mate does not or cannot. These friendships can add to each partner's happiness and thus be a positive force in the couple or marriage relationship, if the partners can minimize feelings of insecurity and jealousy.

The Paradox of Marriage and Intimacy

Most people in our culture seek marriage in their quest for intimacy. Marriage is an important source of intimacy, but paradoxically, intimacy too often declines, and sometimes is completely destroyed, after marriage. For many, marriage increases intimacy; for others, however, it becomes an "intimacy trap" and smothers the very thing the two people desperately seek to enjoy. On one hand, marriage is extolled as the path to happiness; on the other hand, it is seen as a source of conflict.

The basic question remains: Does marriage provide intimacy on a permanent basis? The answer is a qualified yes. Marriage can provide intimacy, but the partners must work to make it happen. Marriage in our society has become the classic great escape. People escape into marriage to avoid loneliness and to find intimacy. Later, when the marriage feels stifling or empty, some people escape from it to maintain their sanity and independence. The next section looks more closely at how couples can develop and maintain intimacy.

Developing Intimacy

Ten areas of marital and family dynamics have been identified that contribute to a couple's satisfaction or dissatisfaction with their relationship (Fowers & Olson, 1989.) Success in achieving intimacy in these areas increases the chances for success of the relationship as a whole. Most couples, of course, do not achieve complete satisfaction in all of these areas. But working toward a satisfactory level of intimacy in each area increases the chance of maintaining a healthy relationship.

Traits of Intimate and Nonintimate Relationships

In a large-scale study of 5,039 married couples, Blaine Fowers and David Olson (1989) looked at the relationship between level of intimacy and satisfaction with marriage. All the couples took a comprehensive marital inventory called **ENRICH,** which contained 10 categories of questions about the issues that are important in a married couple's relationship. The inventory is scored by comparing the responses of the two partners on all questions in each category, calculating the percentage of agreement for each of the 10 categories, and then averaging the results. The couples with high scores (high percentage of agreement) on the ENRICH marital satisfaction scale were identified as high-intimacy couples, and those with low scores on the marital satisfaction scale were called low-intimacy couples.

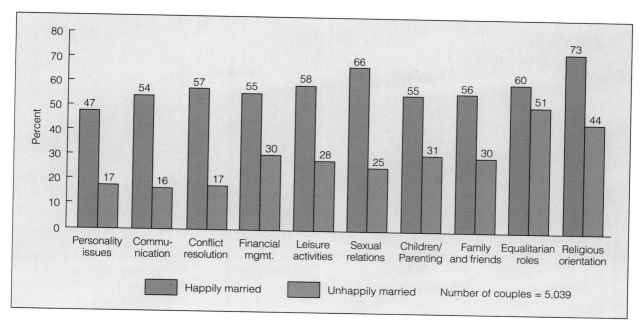

Figure 4.4 Happily Versus Unhappily Married Couples. *Source:* "ENRICH Marital Inventory: A Discriminant Validity and Cross-validation Assessment" by B. J. Fowers and D. H. Olson, 1989, *Journal of Marital and Family Therapy, 15* (1), 65–79. Copyright 1989 by American Association of Marital and Family Therapy. Reprinted by permission.

As hypothesized, the agreement scores of couples in the high-intimacy group were significantly higher than those of the couples in the low-intimacy group in 8 of the 10 ENRICH relationship-issue categories (Figure 4.4). The categories showing the most significant differences were sexual relations, communication, and conflict resolution. These three areas have been identified repeatedly in various analyses as significant to maintaining intimacy in a relationship. It is also noteworthy that almost all (86%) of the couples in the low-intimacy group had considered divorce.

Ten Essential Couple Relationship Strengths

Ten essential areas for developing and maintaining an intimate relationship, identified by Fowers and Olson (1989), are described below.

Personality Compatibility   Comfort with the partner's personality is important to a healthy relationship. The more we like and accept the personality traits and habits of our partner, the more satisfying the relationship. Conversely, personality traits such as tardiness, temper, moodiness, stubbornness, jealousy, and possessiveness are a few of the many that contribute to negative feelings and problems in a relationship. Couples need to realize that most of these traits will not change or disappear after marriage.

Communication Skills   Although definitions of communication differ, there is considerable agreement that good communication is essential for maintaining an intimate relationship (Olson, 1992). Some people are more comfortable talking

Open communication is an essential component of a successful relationship, but talking about feelings—especially feelings about the relationship—can be an excruciating experience for some individuals and couples. Fortunately, communication skills can be learned.

about feelings than others, especially feelings about the relationship. However, sharing even the most mundane thoughts or feelings can be a difficult experience for some people. Developing a satisfactory pattern of communication is critical to the development of an intimate relationship.

Conflict Resolution Skills   People have different attitudes about conflict—both its existence and its resolution— in a relationship. Some partners are more open than others to recognizing and resolving issues. Others believe it is better simply not to talk about problems and to hope they will somehow disappear. Couples who do well resolve conflict rather than avoid issues.

Financial Management Skills   Money is a key issue in any relationship, and intimacy is enhanced when a couple is in close accord on how to earn and spend it. Some people tend to be spenders; others are savers. Most are somewhere in between. Differences of philosophy about spending money can cause considerable conflict. Issues regarding whether to have separate and/or joint bank accounts are important to resolve.

Shared Leisure Activities   We all have different ways of spending our leisure time. If one partner wants to backpack but the other prefers ballet, there is a potential for conflict in the relationship. The couple must work out a satisfactory compromise, a solution preferred by neither but workable for both. Do one or both partners believe that leisure activities should always be shared exclusively between them, or is there room for friends to become involved? Sharing leisure activities can enhance relationship intimacy, but the potential for conflict in this area is always present.

Sharing leisure activities is one way couples can maintain and build the intimacy of their relationship. This couple has chosen an activity that allows for companionship, exercise, and adventure.

Sexual Relations   Sex is an emotional thermometer of the quality of the relationship. It is also an important aspect of human relations that couples generally have a difficult time discussing. When it comes to affection and sexual expression, differences are inevitable. Couples who have a good sexual relationship are able to express their affection freely and openly with each other, while respecting each others' needs and desires.

Attitudes About Children and Parenting   Couples must decide whether to have children and if so, how many. They also need to determine how they want to raise their children. Individuals have different views on the impact of children on the marriage relationship. They also differ greatly on how they prioritize children, marriage, and career. Discipline techniques vary widely, and the values and goals to be imparted to children can be a source of disagreement between spouses. Consensus on these issues can be beneficial to intimacy.

A Good Family and Friends   Relationships with relatives, in-laws, and friends can either strengthen or cause problems in a marriage. If the challenges of these family relationships and friendships are not handled carefully, they can be a sore spot for a couple's intimacy. Good friends, especially other couples, can be a valuable resource.

"We're friends with three other couples, and about every 6 weeks or so we get together at somebody's house for a potluck or whatever, just to talk," related Brenda, a mother of two teenage boys in Raton, New Mexico. "It's really good to hear what's happening to everybody. They're always short on

131

money, short on time, and long on stress, just like our family. Charlie's veterinary business is extremely demanding for him, and I put in long hours, too, keeping the books.

"It's comforting to share our lives. We laugh a lot. It puts my life into better perspective. Sometimes I get whiney and think, 'Woe is me.' But everybody's got problems, and our friends have a way of cheering me up."

Consensus on Roles   Does the couple agree on leadership in their relationship? Do they agree on roles and the division of tasks? Will one partner stop work if/when children arrive and stay home to care for them? Who will do the dishes, the laundry, the housecleaning? Who will maintain the car and do the yard work? A key to intimacy in this area is for a couple to find the type of role relationship that works best for them, whether it be equalitarian sharing or a division of tasks and responsibilities that follows the more traditional gender-role definitions. The rigors of daily life require couples to agree on many issues.

Shared Spiritual Values   Although it is intended to bring comfort to individuals and build bonds among family members, religion can drive a wedge between a couple. Some couples are in accord on spiritual values, and this agreement forms a strong bond between them. In studies of strong families, religious and spiritual values are mentioned repeatedly as an important family strength (Stinnett, Stinnett, DeFrain, & DeFrain, 1997, in press). But for some couples, the issue of religion is at the center of long and explosive arguments.

In sum, intimacy is a process that takes a great deal of time, effort, and hard work. Once achieved, it also takes a great deal of effort to maintain. Couples must constantly search for ways to vitalize and revitalize their intimate relationship. Although it may be easy to fall in love, it is very difficult to stay in love. Achieving and maintaining intimacy is a challenge worth pursuing.

Intimacy Games

One important aspect of an intimate relationship is that the partners be honest and straightforward about the things they want and don't want. When one partner asks for or tells the other what he or she wants, the partner is free to comply or not comply. But many people play **intimacy games** with their partner, concealing what they really want and attempting instead to manipulate the partner into doing or giving them what they want. Because intimacy games tend to be effective in the short run—people often get what they want using these techniques—they can be rewarding. But in the long run, they undermine relationships. Closeness and sharing suffer, resentment grows, and the relationship may ultimately be destroyed.

A popular notion is that of the competitive **zero-sum game.** In this type of game, there is a winner and a loser. What one person wins, the other loses; hence the sum is zero. A zero-sum game is in sharp contrast to more cooperative games

Table 4.1 Dimensions of Intimacy Games

CHARACTERISTIC	RELEVANT QUESTIONS
Name of game	What name describes the game?
Players	Who were the players/opponents? Who were the spectators? Who were the referees?
Playing field	Where was the game played? When was the game played?
Objectives	What were the short-term objectives? What were the long-term objectives?
Rules	What were the rules? Were they implicit or explicit?
Strategies	How was the game played? What strategies did the offense use? What counterstrategies did the defense use?
Communication style	Did the participants express themselves verbally, nonverbally, or both?
Rewards and penalties	What were the rewards? What were the penalties?
Outcomes	How effective was the game in the short term? In the long term? How enjoyable was the game? Was there a winner and a loser?

in which both people win by working together. In human relationships, zero-sum games usually lead to problems, especially if the rules are constructed so that the same person wins most of the time. One partner might say, for example, that he or she will make the final decisions about how the couple's money is spent because he or she works outside the home and the spouse doesn't.

Why do people play intimacy games? Sometimes people don't really know what they want from a relationship. Sometimes they're embarrassed to ask for what they want, or they assume they'll be turned down. Sometimes they perceive a situation to be so difficult that the only way they can see to handle it is by playing a game. Then, because playing games often works in the short run, people tend to play them again and again.

When we look closely at an intimacy game, we see that it has all the elements of games like chess, cards, or football: goals, players, rules, and strategies. But in a game like football, everyone knows what the goal is, who the players are, what the rules are, what the rewards and penalties are, when the game is over, and what the outcome is. In an intimacy game, many of these elements are hidden or unclear. Intimacy games can be identified and defined by asking the kinds of questions shown in Table 4.1.

Constructive Intimacy Games

Although most intimacy games are destructive, constructive intimacy games can enhance a relationship. Too often intimates focus on what they do *not* get from each other, rather than on how often the other person does good things for them. This sets up a negative cycle: As one person becomes more negative and less willing to give, the other person reciprocates. Soon neither person in the relationship is giving to the other in a positive way.

One way to reverse this type of negative interaction is to begin focusing on the positive, on what you can do for the other person and what the other person can do for you. Giving in a positive way encourages the other person to do the same. Also, telling the other person what you want increases your chances of receiving it.

Research by psychologists has indicated that when one partner does something positive for the other, the other will respond positively in return in the short term. They found that over a period of 2 weeks, if one spouse did 10 positive things for the other, that partner would receive about the same number of positives in return. In contrast, when individuals were negative, they received negative responses, and the negative pattern repeated itself. The researchers also did an interesting experiment in which they asked partners to double the number of compliments they gave to their spouses each day for a week. Although both spouses felt it would be strange to give and receive so many compliments, they found that the recipient not only accepted the compliments but returned about the same number over the next few days. This approach developed a positive complimentary cycle. The Beatles put it more poetically when they sang, "In the end, the love you take/Is equal to the love you make."

Unlike destructive intimacy games, constructive games help develop positive cycles. In addition, constructive games have objectives that are specific, rules that are explicit, strategies that are cooperative rather than competitive, and outcomes that are mutually rewarding. A constructive intimacy game called "Giving Compliments" is described in Box 4.2. Couples who would like instruction in constructive intimacy games can enroll in a couples communication workshop. Research indicates that such training can lessen manipulative and competitive interchanges between partners (Olson, 1992). Constructive games can be especially enjoyable with an intimate partner because you have a greater variety of ways in which you can reward each other, and it can be a way to develop more positive feelings toward each other.

Destructive Intimacy Games

Many intimacy games are destructive. Identifying and analyzing a few can illuminate their pitfalls and provide the basis for developing more contructive and positive ways of relating. Two destructive intimacy games are "I Don't Care; You Decide" and "The Ties That Bind."

"I Don't Care; You Decide"   Many times, we truly don't care what the decision is, and we genuinely want the other person to make it. However, when we know what we want but are afraid to tell the other person, or when we want to make

A Constructive Intimacy Game

Name of game	"Giving Compliments"
Players	*Co-players:* Two or more intimates (Marty and Pam). *Spectators:* Other family members. *Referees:* None needed.
Playing field	Any place or time players are together.
Objectives	Short term— *Marty:* To give as many compliments to Pam as possible for at least a day; to focus on the positives rather than the negatives and on giving rather than receiving. *Pam:* To receive compliments graciously; to not question why they are given. Long term— *Marty:* To improve the relationship in a positive way; to receive compliments from Pam in turn. *Pam:* To give compliments to Marty in turn; to improve the relationship in a positive way.
Rules	Explicit— *Marty:* To identify and compliment positive behavior by Pam; to not complain about not immediately receiving as much as is being given. *Pam:* To not question why so many compliments are being given. Implicit— None.
Strategies	*Strategy 1:* Marty gives appropriate compliments whenever possible. *Counterstrategy 1:* Pam accepts and enjoys the compliments. *Strategy 2:* Pam focuses on giving to Marty. *Counterstrategy 2:* Marty accepts the compliments and, in turn, continues giving to Pam. This is a cycle that feeds on positive giving and receiving.
Communication style	Verbal is generally best. Doing something nice is also acceptable.
Rewards	*Marty:* Feels good about being able to give to another. *Pam:* Appreciates compliments from another.
Penalties	None, if the game is played correctly. However, if either Marty or Pam stops giving, he or she will also stop receiving. Also, if Pam questions or does not accept Marty's compliments, the game will stop.
Outcome	If played effectively, this is a mutually enjoyable game in which both participants win. It can improve a relationship in both the short run and the long run and can be played anytime or anywhere.

the decision but want it to appear as if the other person has made it, these situations can become a game.

The initiator often begins playing this game when he or she is relatively sure the other person will make the decision the initiator prefers. The initiator often opens the game with a rhetorical or loaded question, such as, "Do you want to stop here for dinner?" This really means, "I want to stop here, and I hope you will know

Human relationships are too precious to risk by playing destructive games. Constructive interactions, positive feedback, and honest communication are the keys to successful, long-lasting relationships.

that and make that decision." When the other player says yes, however, she or he can then be held responsible if the food is bad, the service poor, or the bill too high.

Another common way this game begins is illustrated by this brief discussion between Jennifer and Tom. They received an invitation in the mail from a couple they haven't seen in some time. The party-givers are primarily Tom's friends, whom he has known for years. Jennifer doesn't enjoy them because they argue so much.

TOM: What do you want to do about this party? Should we go?

JENNIFER: I don't care . . . [even though she does].

TOM: Wouldn't you like to see them again?

JENNIFER: Well . . . don't you have other things you'd rather do this Saturday?

TOM: No, I'd rather go. Okay?

JENNIFER: Okay, but . . .

TOM: Are you sure you want to go?

JENNIFER: Yes, I guess so.

When Jennifer and Tom go to the party, Jennifer will go reluctantly and will probably be frustrated by the experience. Jennifer had hoped Tom would realize she didn't want to go to the party and would decide they shouldn't go. But by not expressing her true feelings and not actively involving herself in the decision-making process, Jennifer failed to achieve what she intended. This is one of the negative consequences of playing games.

Another negative consequence might be that when she gets home from the party, Jennifer will feel so miserable or annoyed that when Tom wants to make love, she will say quite honestly, "I don't feel like it tonight." Tom, not knowing whether Jennifer's playing a game, will speculate, "She didn't want to go to their house all along, and now she's punishing me by withholding sex!" The merry-go-round continues, and both people feel frustrated by the evening together.

"The Ties That Bind"   The parent-child relationship is fertile ground for destructive intimacy games, especially when the children become adults. Although supposedly played in the best interest of all concerned, these games are often disguised, and the players often do not enjoy playing them. Nevertheless, there is generally some game playing between parents and their adult children. Giving up the role of parent is difficult. Although many parents would agree intellectually with Kahlil Gibran's observations on children, they often have difficulty living this philosophy:

> *Your children are not your children.*
> *They are the sons and daughters of Life's longing for itself.*
> *They come through you but not from you,*
> *And though they are with you yet they belong not to you. . . .*
> *You are the bows from which your children as living arrows are sent forth.*
> *The archer sees the mark upon the path of the infinite, and He bends you with His might that His arrows may go swift and far.* (1923/1976, p. 24)

The degree and type of involvement parents have with their married children cause difficulty in many families. The prevalence of in-law jokes attests to the significance of this issue in marital and family relationships. Some mutually agreed-upon degree of balance is important. But it can be difficult to successfully balance the dimension of separateness as individuals with that of connectedness to our families of origin. Some parents have difficulty accepting the fact that their children are grown up and desire a more independent lifestyle, one that is free from past traditions. Parents who are frustrated in regard to their contact with their adult children often play games, such as the one described in Box 4.3 (p. 138) in which the ties that bind are maintained through implicit rules and subtle strategies.

Limiting Destructive Games

Over the years, researchers and family therapists have devised a number of useful techniques for limiting gamesmanship in families and maximizing true intimacy. First of all, it's important that everyone in the group knows the name of the game and identifies its rules, strategies, and objectives. Making implicit rules explicit helps. Identifying strategies and counterstrategies can quickly reveal the nature of the game. Also, discussing the disguised objectives and making them clear and specific can also limit many intimacy games. Each of these components is described in more detail below.

BOX 4.3

A Destructive Intimacy Game

Name of game	"The Ties That Bind"	*Adam's counterstrategy:* Not to accept gift, especially if it is money.	
Players	Parents (Lily and Pete) and their adult child (Adam).	**Communication style**	Usually nonverbal but sometimes in letters and by phone.
Playing field	Two separate households.	**Rewards**	*Lily and Pete's:* To maintain Adam's dependency.
Objectives	Short term— *Lily and Pete's:* To influence Adam's decisions. *Adam's:* To become independent.		*Adam's:* To get help paying bills and meeting other financial needs.
	Long term— *Lily and Pete's:* To maintain dependent relationship. *Adam's:* To become independent.	**Penalties**	*Lily and Pete's:* Attempt fails; Adam refuses help and achieves independence.
Rules	Implicit— No open discussion of issues, among others.		*Adam's:* Accepts help and remains dependent on parents or must forego help to maintain independence.
	Explicit— Avoided.	**Outcomes**	Mutual frustration. Game works in short run but fails in long run. Feels like a win-lose game.
Strategies	*Lily and Pete's:* To give economic support disguised as gifts.		

Naming the Game Catching yourself and others playing intimacy games can be fun, and it can also increase intimacy in your relationships—as long as it is done in a playful and good-natured manner. An intimacy game is a ploy someone uses to get something without directly asking for it. When you catch yourself or a loved one doing this, try very hard to describe what you see honestly. Encourage the loved one to be honest, too. Avoid blame or sarcasm. A matter-of-fact, caring approach is much more effective than a heavy-handed one.

Once the game playing is identified, try to give the game a catchy title. For example, everybody who has been in love is guilty at one time or another of playing the "If You Really Love Me, You'll Know What I Want" game. In this game we assume that the other person can read our mind at all times; if the loved one can't, then he or she must not care about us. Identifying and naming a game reduce the likelihood of its replay in the future. Simply focusing on the problem in a rational and calm manner is a major step in preventing it from occurring.

Making Implicit Rules Explicit Implicit (secret) rules are difficult for players to discover, and they add confusion to the intimacy game. Exposing implicit rules often destroys the game. The most common intimacy game rule is "Don't directly ask for what you want." This rule assumes that if you do ask directly, you will be refused. But playing by this rule puts you in a difficult situation. You don't ask directly because you think you'll be refused, but because you don't ask directly, people have to guess what you want. If they don't guess correctly, you won't get what you want.

By being direct, you give the other person a chance to choose how and when he or she might give you what you want. This places the responsibility for action on the other person and allows that person to feel more free in giving to you. And giving others what they want—making them feel good—makes the giver feel good also.

Unveiling Game Strategies Withdrawing quietly and sullenly from an argument is a common intimacy-game strategy. Its intent is to keep the other player in the argument from continuing on the offensive. The "opponent" may then respond with a counterstrategy, by saying, for example, "What's wrong, Dear?" And the obvious counterstrategy to this ploy is for the quiet and sullen "Dear" to respond, "[Sigh] Oh, nothing."

Unveiling game strategies like these can be an important step toward intimacy. This isn't easy because, as in cards or tennis, players often try to confuse their opponent. Your intimate opponent may set you up by unveiling one game strategy, only to substitute another. Unveiling strategies can help build intimacy in a relationship.

Identifying Disguised Objectives Rather than directly asking for what they want, some people disguise their objectives. The rhetorical question is a common technique for disguising what one really wants and for making the partner think that he or she is making the decision. For example, suppose your partner asks, "Wouldn't you like to go to this movie?" To identify the hidden objective, you can ask your partner what movie she or he wants to see.

Summary

- Love and friendship are alike in many ways, but there are crucial differences that make love both more rewarding and more volatile. Love relationships differ from very good friendships in that they have higher levels of fascination, exclusiveness, sexual desire, a greater depth of caring about the other person, a greater potential for enjoyment, and other positive emotions.

- The love triangle, developed by Robert Sternberg, has three dimensions: commitment, intimacy, and passion. Combinations of these dimensions are seen in eight different types of love relationships.

- Perspectives on love include Erich Fromm's, which maintains that love is difficult and requires work and practice; Stanton Peele's, which suggests that many people "in love" are addicted to it, just as people are addicted to alcohol, tobacco, or other drugs; and James Dobson's, which argues that demonstrating some independence from the relationship (tough love) can strengthen it.

- Intimacy involves feeling close to and sharing oneself with another. Although marriage is an important source of intimacy, intimacy often declines after marriage and sometimes disappears completely. Intimacy takes a great deal of time, effort, and hard work to develop and maintain.

- Ten essential areas of couple relationship strengths are personality compatibility, communication, conflict resolution, financial management, shared leisure activities, sexual relations, attitudes about children and parenting, family and friends, consensus on roles, and shared spiritual values.

- Intimacy games can be either constructive or destructive. To minimize destructive games, it's important to identify them, make their rules explicit, determine the hidden strategies, and make the disguised objectives clear and specific.

Key Terms

Passion Cluster	liking	consummate love
Caring Cluster	infatuation	intimate experience
commitment	empty love	intimate relationship
intimacy	romantic love	ENRICH
passion	fatuous love	intimacy game
non-love	companionate love	zero-sum game

Activities

1. In a small group, discuss your friendships and how they are similar to and different from love relationships.

2. What is romantic to you? In a small group, share a description of an especially romantic time in your life. What are the similarities and differences among the descriptions group members provide?

3. Take a class survey using anonymous written responses. How many times has each student been in love? What is the average number? What is the range (lowest to highest)?

4. Try this simple exercise. (Don't tell anyone what you're doing until you've completed it.) Count the negative comments you make to a loved one and, for every negative comment, try to give at least five positive statements. By this simple act of monitoring yourself, you will make your loved one feel better about himself or herself, make that person feel better about you, and generally improve the tone of your relationship. As you focus on positive behaviors, you will find that the need for criticism will lessen because each of you will become more and more sensitive to each other's needs, and your relationship satisfaction will improve.

5. Interview a divorced and/or remarried person, asking how the individual's definition of love changed as she or he went through the following phases: dating,

engagement, marriage, the period of marital dissolution and divorce, the single period, and remarriage. To do this exercise well, spend 45 to 60 minutes with the person, getting a good understanding of what happened to the marriage and why.

Suggested Readings

Bradshaw, J. (1992). *Creating love: The next great stage of growth.* New York: Bantam. *By one of America's most popular lecturers on intimate relationships.*

Buscaglia, L. F. (1992). *Born for love: Reflections on loving.* Thorofare, NJ: Slack/Random House. *Thoughts by excellent writer and public speaker Leo Buscaglia, a professor of education at the University of Southern California, who created one of the first university courses on love in the United States.*

Hendrick, S. S., & Hendrick, C. (1992). *Romantic love.* Newbury Park, CA: Sage. *An engagingly written social-psychological approach to romantic love, interweaving important facts and concepts from sociobiology, philosophy, history, family science, and sociology.*

Jampolsky, G. G. (1990). *Love is the answer: Creating positive relationships.* New York: Bantam. *Reports psychiatrist Jampolsky's attempt, after suffering through a particularly difficult period in his life, to learn what he could about how human beings find fulfillment.*

Johnson, S., & Marano, H. E. (1994, March/April). Love: The immutable longing for contact. *Psychology Today,* pp. 32–35, 64, 66. *Addresses our desperate need to connect, and our desperate fear of connection.*

Lerner, H. G. (1989). *The dance of intimacy.* New York: Harper & Row/Perennial. *The elaborate steps people go through to bond emotionally with each other, as identified by a clinical psychologist with the Menninger Foundation in Topeka, Kansas.*

McKinney, K., & Sprecher, S. (Eds.). (1991). *Sexuality in close relationships.* Hillsdale, NJ: Lawrence Erlbaum. *Useful readings on the joys and challenges of building a fulfilling sexual relationship with a partner.*

Osherson, S. (1992). *Wrestling with love: How men struggle with intimacy with women, children, parents, and each other.* New York: Fawcett Columbine. *A good book focusing on men's issues; useful reading for both men and women.*

CHAPTER 5

Singlehood, Dating, and Mate Selection

egardless of the intensity of a love relationship, there are both good and bad reasons for getting married. Similarly, there are both good and bad reasons for remaining single. Today, marriage is a personal choice, not a social dictate. In fact, more people are remaining single, and this choice is increasingly regarded as an acceptable alternative to marriage.

After a discussion of singlehood, this chapter examines theories that attempt to explain mate selection and the functions and stages of dating. The focus is on mate selection from a cross-cultural point of view, looking at arranged marriages around the world and comparing them with the customary "love matches" of modern developed societies. In American culture, physical attractiveness is the major factor in choosing a mate.

We also tend to find mates among those who are like us in some way, people from our group—ethnic, religious, or socioeconomic. But many of these rules are changing because of increased diversity in the U.S. population. So-called mixed marriages are a growing phenomenon, causing many families to examine their attitudes and behaviors toward people outside their particular cultural group.

The chapter concludes with a section on a serious problem in our society today: conflict and violence in dating, and the relationship between premarital violence and violence after marriage.

Being Single

Marriage is still very popular; 90% of young Americans expect to marry at some time in their lives. This proportion has remained relatively stable for the past quarter of a century. In spite of high levels of divorce, most young people expect their marriages to last. But there has been a change in recent decades. Young people are staying single longer and getting married at a slightly older age. In 1993 there were more men and, particularly, more women who had never been married than there were in 1960 (Table 5.1).

Government figures indicate that 40.8% of women and 36.6% of men over age 18 are single (U.S. Bureau of the Census, 1994, p. 57). In 1950, only 9% of all U.S. households were occupied by a single individual. By 1993, that figure had jumped to 25% (U.S. Bureau of the Census, 1994, p. 59). In the same period, single-parent homes jumped from 7% to 30% of all households (U.S. Bureau of the Census, 1994, p. 62).

Increasing Singlehood

Many factors contribute to the increase in **singlehood** today. For one, education and career are delaying the age at which young people are marrying. Linked to this trend is an increasing recognition in our society that singlehood can be a legitimate, healthy, and happy alternative to marriage. A. Shostak (1987) found that most young people interviewed said they would be "a little" bothered if they failed to marry. Relatively few said they would be "greatly bothered" by failing to marry

Table 5.1 Percentage of Women and Men Remaining Single				
	1960	**1970**	**1980**	**1993**
Women remaining single				
Ages 20–24	28.4%	35.8%	50.2%	66.8%
Ages 25–29	10.5	10.5	20.8	33.1
Men remaining single				
Ages 20–24	53.1	54.7	68.6	81.0
Ages 25–29	20.8	19.1	32.4	48.4

Source: U.S. Bureau of the Census (1994, p. 56).

at some time during their lives. The mothers of these same young adults also generally acknowledged that marriage was not a "must" for their children.

Shostak also concluded that marriage continues to be more important to young women than to young men. Although more and more young women are seeking jobs and careers, they still tend to value marriage and parenthood somewhat more than young men do. This is the case even though education and work opportunities have opened up for females in recent decades; if they choose to, women can make it on their own more easily than in the past. There is evidence that if an individual has experienced divorce in his or her family, that person is more likely to have both negative attitudes about marriage and positive attitudes about singlehood.

Some singles have been married before but are now in transition. About two thirds of divorced people remarry, usually 2–3 years after they divorce. But researchers are finding that even though most people remarry after a divorce, the rate of remarriage has dropped by more than 25% (Coleman & Ganong, 1991). The fact that individuals are not rushing back into marriage is another indication that the single lifestyle is becoming more and more acceptable in our society.

"I don't know, perhaps I'll never get married again," a middle-aged Alabama woman said. "At first after the divorce I was very panicky, like, 'Oh, I've got to be married, I've got to be married!' And then after several months of looking for the ideal mate, I discovered that I liked myself quite a bit and actually was quite content having my own private space in the world. I'm a dean now, and the college is developing pretty well. In a few years I might start applying for vice-chancellor jobs around the country. I think I'm capable of moving up a bit in higher education.

"Sure, it gets lonely sometimes. But I've got lots of friends, male and female. I get on the phone and call someone, and we get together and talk and laugh, and I think, 'Hmmm, it could be a lot worse. I could still be dealing with Jerome's drinking.'

[What about sex?] "Sex? Who needs it? . . . Just kidding! You can find sex without tying yourself down to a person forever. Gee, that sounds funny coming from someone who 20 years ago was so very, very conservative. But actually, I think I've got a realistic view of life now. If all I had in common with a fellow was sex, I'd be crazy to marry him."

Once considered a sad fate to be avoided at almost any cost, singlehood is today recognized as a legitimate, happy, and healthy alternative to marriage. This single man in his 30s demonstrates some of the benefits of being single, including self-sufficiency and the time and space to cater to one's own tastes.

Singlehood As an Alternative to Marriage

Singlehood is being seen as a legitimate alternative to marriage by more and more people in our society. This represents a major shift. Throughout most of American history, the failure to marry (note how even the terminology is loaded) was considered undesirable. Of course, not everyone married in 18th- and 19th-century America, and many married in their late 20s or their 30s. But social circumstances or pure economics probably contributed to not marrying more than personal desires did, for marriage was highly valued. "Old maid" and "spinster" were certainly not flattering descriptions for unmarried women (Degler, 1980).

In Colonial times (the 17th and 18th centuries), virtually all unmarried individuals lived in a family environment of some type—either in their parents' home or as servants in another's home. Unmarried people of all ages usually stayed dependent on the families with whom they lived until they married. Only then did they become fully independent members of society.

In the 19th century, the position of unmarried people began to change. They increasingly became involved in wage labor outside the family and often lived in boardinghouses. With the rise of the industrial system, many young people were needed to work in factories, often at some distance from the farms. The board-

Table 5.2 Living Arrangements of People Age 15 and Older, 1993

	MALES			**FEMALES**		
	Age: 15–19	20–24	25–34	Age: 15–19	20–24	25–34
Live alone	1%	6%	11%	1%	5%	7%
Live with spouse	1	17	52	4	28	60
Live with family of origin	95	60	23	91	52	25
Live with non-relatives	3	17	14	4	15	8
Total	100	100	100	100	100	100

Source: U.S. Bureau of the Census (1994, p. 57).

inghouses exercised family-type controls, but were still quite different from a traditional family environment. Although attitudes toward singlehood may have improved in the 19th and early 20th centuries, social custom held that marriage was by far the preferable state, and those who remained single continued to be stigmatized (Veroff, Douvan, & Kulka, 1981).

Today, an increasing number of single people live with their parents. In 1993, 60% of 20- to 24-year-old males and 52% of females of that age group lived with their families of origin (Table 5.2). In 1960, only 41% of 18- to 24-year-olds lived with their parents. For 25- to 34-year-olds in 1993, 23% of the males and 25% of the females still lived with their parents. In 1960, only 10% of that age group lived with their parents. Therefore, young adults are living with their parents more now than they did in the 1960s.

There are a number of reasons for this trend. Some young people postpone marriage until they are older and live at home until the wedding. College costs force many to stay at home to save money. Unemployment or divorce causes financial troubles for some. Single mothers often must stay at home with their parents for financial aid and help with the baby (Glick & Lin, 1986).

In sum, the lifestyles of single individuals have changed in recent decades. Singlehood is increasingly viewed as a viable option to marriage. More people are remaining single longer. Single young men and women are living together without being married—enjoying some of the benefits of marriage without the legal or religious commitments and with less stigmatization. There is at least one positive result of this trend toward longer singlehood and later marriage: The older one marries, the more likely one is to make a mature and permanent decision. Those who delay marriage until they have completed their education and found satisfying work increase their chances for marital stability.

The Pros and Cons of Singlehood

Some forces or factors attract people to marriage; other forces or factors may make singlehood more likely. Among the negative reasons for getting married are pressure from parents; the desire to leave home; fear of independence; loneliness; and not having a sense of the alternatives. Among the good reasons for getting married are desire for a family; emotional attachment and love for another; and security, social status, and prestige. Some of the negative forces that attract people to singlehood are poor communication with one's mate; boredom, unhappiness, and anger; and the feeling of being trapped in a relationship. Some of the positive reasons for choosing singlehood are career opportunities; the desire for self-sufficiency; the desire for mobility; and the freedom to change. Individuals should carefully examine their reasons for either staying single or getting married. Marriage today is a personal choice, not a social dictate.

Characteristics of Successful Singles

The adult single population today includes people who are single for a variety of reasons. One large and rapidly increasing group of singles are professional and career-oriented individuals. Highly educated and achievement oriented, many prefer to remain unmarried. Although employers used to believe that single professionals were less desirable employees (thinking perhaps that they could not adjust to marriage or were unstable or undependable), they are now beginning to appreciate the flexibility of "unattached" employees. Single individuals can transfer to new locations more efficiently than whole families, and they usually have fewer outside commitments, which can complicate a married employee's adjustment to a new locale. Single employees tend to devote more extra hours to their careers; they are as highly trained and capable as married employees.

Although single women have been subject to discrimination in salary and promotions (often because of employer expectations that they might marry and resign), firms are increasingly adopting affirmative action policies to provide more equitable treatment of female employees. As a result, singlehood is losing much of its negative stigma within professional groups.

Women who remain single are likely to be of above-average intelligence and high achievers. This can make it difficult for them to find an unattached man of equal status, because men often prefer to marry "down" (Macklin, 1980, p. 906). Because females outnumber males in the general population, men have a larger pool of potential marriage partners from which to choose. First-born girls (who are often achievement oriented) and "only" children are somewhat more likely to remain single than other children.

Although a few singles may lead the swinging lifestyle portrayed in Hollywood movies, the vast majority live very conventional lives. Career-oriented single people are likely to use the freedom their lifestyle provides to participate in a wide variety of experiences that individuals with families rarely have time for. They also like the flexibility to devote as much time as they like to career interests, to be able to travel wherever and whenever the job demands, and to alter their lifestyle as they desire or when new opportunities arise.

One of the biggest problems singles face is developing a network of friends and associates with whom to share social activities. To meet this need, a variety of churches, synagogues, and social organizations (as well as resort lodges and nightclubs) have created "singles' nights." Most employed singles report that their social life is as active as they want it to be, and few middle-aged career-oriented singles report being lonely or isolated. Although single people may at times feel they have missed something in life by not creating a family and may perhaps fear the prospect of loneliness in old age, they often can satisfy these needs by "networking" with other singles.

Singles and Sexual Intimacy

Single people have many of the same problems coping with their sex life as married people. Although they have the same basic desire to be sexually intimate and to be loved by someone, they have to use different approaches to fulfill their needs. Sexual satisfaction does not automatically flow into a marriage; both married and single individuals are engaged in a continual quest for tenderness, affection, intimacy, and satisfaction in life.

Perhaps the greatest change in the sexual behavior of singles in recent years has been the increased sexual activity of females (Miller & Moore, 1991). Single males have always been sexually active, but traditionally, females were expected to be reserved or limited in sexual expression. The revolution in sexual attitudes of the past three decades has allowed single women to become more sexual. Now approximately 90% of adult single females have experienced premarital intercourse.

For some, singlehood affords room to develop talent without the distraction of responsibilities to a mate and children. Would novelist George Sand (1804–1876) have achieved the same degree of literary artistry had she married Chopin? Would George Bernard Shaw (1856–1950) have given us, among other works, the play *Pygmalion* (on which the musical *My Fair Lady* is based) if he had been happily married?

Single people have the same basic desire for sexual intimacy that married people have, but they must take different approaches to fulfilling that need. For some, clubs like this offer the right mix of sociability, opportunity, and anonymity.

Although the "swinging singles" stereotype provides good movie material, few singles have the inclination or motivation to "swing" for any length of time. Most seem to prefer that sexual intimacy be tied to some degree of affection or companionship; one-night stands are of limited appeal. This has become even more true with the increasing risk of **sexually transmissible diseases (STDs),** particularly infection with the **human immunodeficiency virus (HIV)** that causes **acquired immune deficiency syndrome (AIDS).**

Singles and Loneliness

Singles are an enormously diverse group; no stereotype can describe them. Individuals are single for many different reasons. In addition to younger, never-married individuals, there are divorced single people, separated single people, and widowed single people. Thus, it is very difficult to generalize about singles. What does a 19-year-old college student who has never been married have in common with a 33-year-old career woman who has just separated from her husband? And what does a 27-year-old divorced father with custody of three young children have in common with a 78-year-old widow whose husband has just died of cancer?

One societal stereotype about single individuals is that they are lonely and lost. Though their circumstances differ greatly, single people do share the circumstance of being alone. Rollins insists that being alone is not synonymous with loneliness, noting, "Ninety percent of the singles in my study are not what I call lonely, they are alone" (cited in Peterson & Lee, 1985). In fact, Rollins found that of 99 singles between the ages of 21 and 66 who were surveyed, 65% were moderately happy or even happier. Rollins argued that the problem is not with singlehood but with society. "The sad part is that 33% of Americans 20–55 are single at any given time. The message we're giving them is you're lonely and atypical, and they begin to believe it." It's conceivable that the social stereotype of the distressed and lonely single could push an individual into a marriage he or she really doesn't want or need. The herd instinct is very strong.

John C. Woodward (1988) offers seven good ways to cope with loneliness. He maintains they will work for almost anyone:

- *Appraise yourself.* Ask yourself what kind of investment you have in loneliness. What is the payoff for being lonely? What are the good things about yourself? If you have difficulty making up your list, ask some people who know you.

- *Take a chance.* To relieve feelings of loneliness, you have to reach out and take risks. You must tell people how you really feel and what you need. Say, "I'm really lonely today. I wish I just had somebody to talk to." Until you do this, people can't help you.

- *Don't expect too much.* When you go out socially, go out just to have fun. Many lonely people go out with a different motive. They are trying to find the perfect person, a lifelong friend. When they don't succeed, they soon prefer to stay home and watch television, isolating themselves even more. Convince yourself, instead, that you can enjoy relationships that are less than perfect.

- *Depend on yourself.* Looking for someone else to make you feel all right is seldom effective. You have to depend on yourself and participate in activities you enjoy.

- *Rejoin your family.* Your family can be a great support. Regardless of how you treat your family or how they treat you, you still belong to that family. Families are often helpful to people coping with loneliness.

- *Find an outside interest.* Try to find something that really interests or excites you, and then work at it. If you join an organization, for example, don't just sit in the corner. Take some responsibility. Volunteer for things; really get involved.

- *Find a community.* A community can be any group in which you become a member.

Sociologist Duane Alwin surveyed 3,600 adults, a representative national sample, and found that individuals who live alone aren't socially isolated but actually have a more active social life than those who are married (cited in Elias, 1985). Alwin found that married couples did report a somewhat greater sense of well-being than unmarried people, but having children tended to lower couples' happiness scores. Alwin also found that if singles are unhappy, they don't see the reason as being because they are living alone: "Individuals who live alone tend to compensate. They have many more social contacts outside the home, much more social interchange, than married individuals do" (Elias, 1985, p. D6).

Alwin reported that, as a group, only single parents (90% of whom are women) experienced painful isolation and significantly poorer mental health as a result of living alone. He explained, "It's having the children that limits their friendship network; they have a limited ability to get away from the kids" (Elias, 1985, p. 6). As many parents and teachers will tell you, "Kids are great, but you've got to get some adult conversation in your life pretty soon or you go stir-crazy." Alwin concluded, "Our changing lifestyles don't necessarily bring negative consequences" (Elias, 1985, p. 6).

In a similar vein, sociologist Michael Hughes found in a study of 2,248 individuals that singles who live with another person give up privacy and have to adjust to the demands of roommates. "When you live with others, you must interact with them. If you live alone, you can choose to interact with others or not. Roommates drive some individuals crazy. . . . Living alone is no worse and in many circumstances better for non-marrieds than living with others" (cited in Peterson & Lee, 1985, pp. 8B, 9B).

Making Singlehood Work

Margaret Adams (1976) has argued that there are three essential criteria for a successful single life:

1. The capacity and opportunity to be economically self-sufficient.

2. The capacity and opportunity to be socially and psychologically autonomous.

3. A clearly thought-out intent to remain single by choice rather than by default.

Adams recognizes that finding a way to earn enough money to live is no easy task for some singles, especially single mothers with young children. The first step to success, then, is to be able to earn a decent salary. Second, single people must develop a sense of social and psychological independence. Although singles need a good network of friends to count on, they must also have the skill and determination to stand on their own two feet. Third, those who *choose* singlehood are more successful at it than those who feel they have no other choice. Singles by choice enjoy the opportunities for solitude and for developing a wide network of friendships. Singles by choice enjoy the freedom to invest as much time in their careers as they want and the freedom to spend money as they wish.

James Barkas noted that the most common route by which singles achieve fulfillment is a career. They also enjoy their friends, hobbies, cultural activities, charitable work, physical exercise, and romantic involvements—if and when these occur. It must be remembered that the idea of the "swinging single" is mostly myth. "The happy single enjoys life and seeks someone to enjoy it with, while the unhappy single wants someone to make him/her happy" (Barkas, 1980, p. 72).

Finding a Mate: Courtship Patterns

One of the chief reasons so many marriages fail is that the functions of a date and a mate differ radically—that of a date is to be charming; that of a mate to be responsible; and, unfortunately, the most charming individuals are not necessarily the most responsible, while the most responsible are just as often deficient in charm.

—SYDNEY HARRIS, *Journalist*

All societies have created some system for matching individuals for marriage and parenthood. These systems range from the practice of bride purchase or a village shaman selecting a mate according to astrological signs, to contractual systems in which a mate may serve as an indentured servant to the bride's parents, to individual choice based on personal attraction and love. In some cultures, couples are matched while they are still infants; others require that the bride or groom prove their fertility by producing children before they are eligible for marriage. Although the customs of mate selection vary widely, all perform the necessary function of matching a couple for marriage and eventual parenthood.

Parent-Arranged Marriages

Throughout most of world history, courtship was generally brief. In most cultures, the parents of the bride and groom selected the future spouse and made most of the arrangements for the marriage ceremony. If the prospective couple were granted any freedom of choice, they were expected to complete their arrangements in a few days. The pattern common in modern industrialized nations, in which a couple spends months or even years in dating and choosing a mate, developed largely within the past century.

Parent-arranged marriages are still practiced in much of the nonindustrialized world; up to three quarters of marriages in some cultures may be "arranged" (Fox, 1980). Although young adults in the United States today might view the practice as archaic and uncivilized, many people prefer parent-arranged marriages. For example, G. R. Gupta (1976) reports that most participants in such systems tend to view the process favorably. He says that in India, young people become distressed if they have to choose their own mate, fearing they might make the wrong choice.

Parent-arranged marriages are based on the principle that the elders in a community have the wisdom to select the appropriate spouse. Parents or elders are more likely to base their decision on economic, political, and social status considerations— to enhance the family's status and position through their choice. Considerations of lineage and family status are generally more important than love or affection in such decisions, although the parents may give the couple's preferences some consideration. Arranged marriages thus serve to extend existing family units rather than to create new units. They reinforce ties with other families in the community, strengthening the order and organization of the community (Lee & Stone, 1980).

Advantages of Arranged Marriages   Parent-arranged marriages are usually very stable, because it is the duty of the whole family to help the new couple get established in life. Divorce is almost unheard of—except for the reason of infertility—because the parents and members of the community who were responsible for the selection would disapprove of divorce. Although love between the potential mates before marriage is relatively unimportant, affection and respect usually grow through the years; arranged marriages are often quite harmonious. Because there is not really a courtship period, premarital intimacy is minimal or nonexistent.

In parent-arranged marriage systems, couples avoid many of the problems of dating "American style." There is virtually no risk of being rejected or of losing one's true love, and one does not have to determine whether one's partner is committed to the relationship. Although many people might not view these factors as advantages, they effectively ensure a stable marriage. Remnants of arranged courtship and marriage systems are still found in our culture today, in the limited number of professional marriage brokers still operating among urban ethnic groups. Further, as most single people know, relatives and friends are often only too eager to help find that "perfect" partner.

Patterns of Change   The world, in general, appears to be moving toward freedom of choice in marriage. This approach is sometimes referred to as the "love match," though love is not always the goal of marriage in Western industrial societies. Murstein reviewed a number of cross-cultural studies that looked at love marriages versus parent-arranged marriages (1980, pp. 52–54). He concluded that, cross-culturally, the absence of economic means for women leads to early marriage and little individual freedom. The ability of women to work leads to the decline of arranged marriages, enhances the possibility of love matches, and may slightly diminish the marriage rate. In general, the world is also moving toward monogamous marriage, although the rate of advance varies from country to country.

The movement away from arranged marriage appears to be related to industrialization. As countries change from more rural to urban/industrial societies, love marriages become more common. One study of Turkey, a relatively rural society, found that three quarters of the marriages were still arranged (Fox, 1980). Data from Africa, India, Israel, and Malaya indicate that love marriages are more likely among people who marry at a later age, have a higher level of education, have a higher socioeconomic status (or the promise of a higher status), and live in an urban setting. A woman who can support herself financially is more likely to want to decide for herself whom she will marry.

Cultural Variations   The ways people find marriage partners vary from culture to culture. In countries that are industrializing and moving away from arranged marriages, the influence of cultural tradition may be combined with modern sensibilities. In India, for example, it is commonly believed that there is one predestined mate who will share life with the spouse through reincarnation. Therefore, parents believe they should supervise their children's marriage choices to avoid mistakes. But many young people are unhappy with this approach, and a compromise is often reached. "Semi-arranged" marriages, in which parental approval is obtained before the marriage, are becoming more common (Bumiller, 1985).

In China, a marriage law passed in 1980 dramatically changed marriage pat-

Changing courtship patterns in Japan were reflected in the 1993 marriage of Crown Prince Naruhito to Masako Owada, a well-educated and independent-minded woman without a royal lineage. Nevertheless, their wedding ceremony was steeped in mysticism and in traditions dating back hundreds of years. In many cultures, there is an uneasy tension between the old and the new.

terns: from parent-arranged marriages in which a "bride price" was paid to the bride's parents to marriages based on free choice of a partner (Yi, 1984). Because opportunities for meeting eligible partners and for dating are limited, young people still depend on arranged introductions by friends and relatives. Dating is often difficult. Young men and women do not know how to act in this new role, and finding a place to be alone together can be a challenge.

Japan, the industrial giant of the Pacific, has generally moved from arranged marriages to love-based marriages. The traditional *nakode*, or matchmaker, is still used in some rural areas of Japan, but the matchmaker's role has become increasingly ceremonial. As more women have entered the labor force and gained financial independence, they have moved away from marriages arranged by their parents. Japanese young people find dating very awkward and uncomfortable, however, because they often do not have much social contact with members of the other sex.

The Scandinavian countries are perhaps the most liberal in the world in regard to marriage customs. Parent-arranged marriages disappeared decades ago in Scandinavia, and cohabitation has become the most common type of relationship until after the birth of a child. Research in Sweden indicates a steep drop in the marriage rate. Associated with this decline are cohabitation and state and/or parental support for children born outside of matrimony.

The American Dating System

Because the United States was one of the first nations to industrialize, it provides a good example of the changes in dating behavior that occur when a society evolves from an agrarian culture.

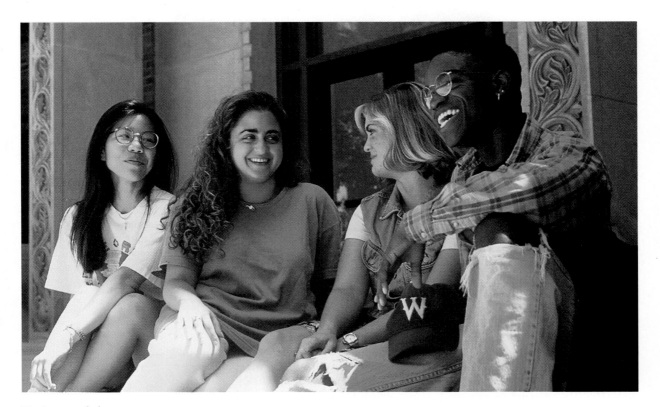

Dating trends have changed dramatically over the years. High school and college students today are likely to spend more time socializing in cross-sex groups of friends than as paired-off, exclusive couples.

The Emergence of Individual-Choice Courtship   Early in U.S. history, parents typically exercised considerable influence over dating and the choice of a mate. Young people were usually tied to the home and, except for the occasional community social event, had little opportunity to escape the watchful eyes of their parents. Opportunities for dating were infrequent. Courtship was a rather formal event, often conducted under parental supervision. Males were expected to get the permission of the female's parents and to initiate the acquaintance. Although the couple were generally allowed the privilege of making up their own minds, family members usually announced their approval (or disapproval) before the relationship got too serious. But young people were granted much more freedom of individual choice than exists in a parent-arranged courtship system.

As America became more industrialized and parents began to work away from the home, young people gained considerable freedom from parental supervision, as well as responsibility for organizing their free time. **Dating,** or individual-choice courtship, emerged as an activity in its own right, creating a new institution within the culture. This pattern, with some variation, appears to be common as societies change from agrarian to industrial.

Along with the emergence of individual-choice courtship and a defined period for dating, permissiveness in behavior also increased. The term **permissiveness** refers to the extent to which couples are physically intimate before marriage. Historically, males were permitted greater freedom and privilege than females and were likely to be more experienced in intimate relations than females. However, the same basic forces that produced the revolution in dating customs in industrial societies also fostered a decline in the **double standard**—different standards of sexual and social behavior for men than for women. As customs changed, women engaged in more sexual experimentation. The amount of sexual intimacy women experience before marriage still does not match that of men; but because female sexual involvement has increased rapidly, the difference between male and female sexual behavior is much smaller today than it was in the past. Although many females still expect males to call them, to plan dates, and to propose marriage, females are more assertive and participate to a greater extent in the dating process than they did in earlier generations.

By the 1980s, people were dating sooner—and also in a more casual fashion—than earlier generations had. Dating now commonly begins in preadolescence as a group experience where couples attend get-togethers as pairs. Peer-group values often advocate an individualistic approach to dating, stressing that people should "do their own thing." Steady dating is still popular, but adolescents have relaxed many of the requirements of exclusivity and commitment that were the norm in the past.

There is also evidence that young people are forming more cross-sex friendships than in earlier generations and placing more emphasis on relating to one another. Adolescents today are forming a more complete social system during the courtship period than earlier generations did, and this social system has much more influence on teenagers than parents or moral-religious systems do. On the other hand, courtship customs are less oriented toward marriage than in earlier periods; young people are less eager to become formally engaged and are delaying marriage. The divorce statistics appear to be influencing their thinking, causing them to approach marriage with more reservations. Cohabitation has become popular as a means of "testing" a relationship and exploring the nature of the marital experience.

Dating and Matchmaking Services   Although in an individual-choice courtship system young people make their own selections, many still want help in finding a mate. To fill this need, entrepreneurs all over the country have created a potpourri of dating services. The least expensive—and most risky—are the "Personals" or "Eligibles" sections in many newspapers and magazines (Box 5.1, p. 158). For a modest fee, individuals can buy a small space to describe their qualities, the qualities they seek in a partner, and the type of relationship they desire. The advertisements make interesting reading but can be a less-than-safe source for finding a dating partner.

Computerized dating services provide a more discreet but also more expensive approach. Some services call themselves "relationship agencies," and their approach is not too much different from that used by employment services. Dating services are rather popular in many major cities. For a fee, which might be $200, $400, or more, applicants fill out forms about themselves and describe their traits and the traits they want in a partner. Some services videotape applicants answering questions about themselves and their interests and include it in the package. All of this information is filed, and the files (coded by number, not name, to ensure some privacy) are open to those who have paid for the privilege. If questionnaire data on "Mr. X" looks good to a woman, she might ask to see his videotape. If she is interested in learning more about him, the agency might contact him by

BOX   5.1

A Singles Column from a Metropolitan Newspaper

F5907

FUN LOVING

Affectionate Black Female enjoys music, sports, dancing. Slender, nice looking wants to meet attractive male with the same interests.

F5910

WANTED
THE PERFECT RECIPE

1 Athletic, cute male (aged 29–39 years); 3 cups personality; 2 cups generosity; 3&3/4lb. gregariousness; 2 large pieces intelligence. Add to confidence, imagination and a GREAT SMILE. Sprinkle with adventure and serve immediately to one gorgeous petite (5'3"-105 lbs) nurse.

F5911

31 year old single White female who enjoys spending time going to Pops concerts, movies, dining out and jogging. I'm a college educated professional somewhat conservative, who values intelligence, honesty and time spent really getting to know somebody.

F5912

LOOKING FOR STYLE

In other words, Attractive, intelligent, self-assured, sensitive, caring, stable, and between the ages of 45 and 52. Does this describe you? If so, then you are that special someone that I have been looking to meet and explore life with. I am 44, 5'4", trim, attractive and looking for a quality relationship. Variety of interests but would like to seek out as much as possible that life has to offer. Note, phone number and photo, if possible. All replies answered.

F5913

Worth getting to know, fun to dance with, interesting to talk to, politically concerned, spiritually growing. 38, 5'7" female would like to meet male with similar characteristics.

F5914

ALCOHOL AND SMOKE FREE
NOT A FANATIC

Tall, attractive woman in early 30's is looking for someone (male) to enhance social life. Tennis and eating are a few of my enthusiasms. Photo optional.

ELIGIBLES

F5921

GIVE ME A CHANCE

to make you smile! Forty-five, fun loving, free of hang ups, no children. Professional. Enjoy theatre, jazz, aerobics, travel, dancing. I am slender, very attractive, enjoy good conversation. Photo please.

F5922

WANTED ONE WOMAN MAN

Somewhat shy, warm-hearted, French/Spanish woman, 30, 5'3", 100 lbs. wishes to meet single, sincere, honest, attractive, respectable male (approximately 33–43) to enjoy life with. Note, phone (photo optional). Prefer tall and slender, no druggies, please.

F5923

Attractive, fun loving woman wishes to meet single white male, 40–55, at least 6' tall, interested in outdoor activities, concerts, plays, picnics on the North Shore. Letter, picture.

F5924

FIRST AD EVER

Hard to find, attractive 49, slender, 5'6", blonde resembling Meryl Streep, wishes to meet slender professional gentleman who is thoughtful, trim, attractive, honest, financially secure and young at heart, prefer 45–55 years, non-smoker, social drinker with hope for special relationship. Multi interests include music, hiking, dining dancing. Share interesting moments. Note, phone, photo if possible.

F5925

Anoka Country girl seeking enhancement (not completion) from a whole individual, tallish, over 40, active and not "into preferably thin."

F5926

We are sick and tired of being set-up by well-meaning friends; you know, the ones who fix you up with social misfits and "nice guys." We are two tall, dark haired, professional career women who are intelligent, attractive out-going, risk takers. You just won't believe how wonderful we are!

F5932

MY BEST FRIEND

who happens to be a man, describes me as "Gracious, elegant and feminine." I'm petite, fifty-ish, a classical violinist, teach literature at the Univ. Somewhat intense, unconventional, ethical. Looking for a man with similar interests and values, my age, older or younger, non-obese, who has the courage to risk vulnerability and commitment for true intimacy and companionship.

F5933

Hi. I'm 34, cute, fit and a good person. I'm looking for a handsome man who likes renovating, restoring, creating, enjoying life and working together towards common goals. Let's talk.

F5934

WANTED: FISHING PARTNER. I promise to bait my own hook, clean and cook the catch and provide good relaxed company. You provide the boat and knowledge where the fish bite, a sense of humor and pleasant disposition would be greatly appreciated. I am 55 but could pass for 45? Maybe. Self employed professional woman who likes the outdoors, most creatures great and small, but also all the finer things in life and comforts of home. Interested? Drop me a line or two!

F5935

Spirited Petite Blond, media professional, comfortable in denim or silk, enjoys quiet interludes to new adventures. Interested in sharing positive energy with attractive, centered and secure 35–45 professional male. Photo appreciated.

F5936

Two tall, classy, single women in their 30's are looking for male counterparts. We have put a lot of energy into our careers, and now are ready to put energy into friendship/relationship. We are warm, fun-loving and have a lot to give the right person. Please send letter and phone number. Photos appreciated.

BOX 5.2

Dating Services Advertised in a Metropolitan Newspaper

Singles
NETWORK
Dating Service
Call us about our July Special SAVE $50 on a new membership
555-1824

- **Straight or Gay Columns**
- **Correspond Anonymously**
- **Fun, Private Inexpensive**

OFFICE (9 to 5, M–F)
555-1424
COMPUTER
555-5524

pc **2 Personal Columns On Personal Computers**
You Don't Need A Computer!

"I met a great lawyer at Introductions"
Introductions
a relationship agency
555-8488
fully complies with state law

Together
Established 1974
The Personal Introduction Service
555-3322
555-1100
555-2300

"Select-A-Date"
Let us introduce you to fun, frolic and adventure.

Be daring:
Tele: 555-0007

For Exciting Introductions

Jewish Dating Service
555-9790

phone or postcard, indicating the manner in which he can contact the interested woman. From that point on, what happens in the relationship is up to the individuals involved. A selection of advertisements from several dating services is included in Box 5.2.

The newest dating innovation is meeting people online, through subscription services or directly on the Internet. Some services offer chat rooms, such as America Online's "Romance Connection" and "Meeting Place" chat rooms, where strangers can get connected. As with personal ads, there are few safeguards to ensure the accuracy of the information people provide about themselves. Individuals often reveal only positive characteristics that they think will attract others to them. Although the subscription services and/or the Internet might be a simple and inexpensive way to meet someone initially, this approach to dating can be risky, and it can lack intimacy.

Dating Among Older People   The term *dating* has a decidedly youthful ring, but single people over 65 also date and are sexually active. The proportion of older individuals in the American population has increased dramatically since the turn of the century. In 1900, only about 4% of all Americans were 65 years of age or older; by 1990, 11% of males and 20% of females were over 65. As life spans lengthen, the percentage of older individuals is expected to increase to about 20% by the year 2050 (U.S. Bureau of the Census, 1992). People are not only living longer but are staying healthier and more active than in earlier generations. The older they are, the less likely they are to have children at home. There are now many generally healthy and active older adults looking for meaningful relationships.

Kris Bulcroft and Margaret O'Conner-Roden (1986) explored whether older people date, fall in love, and behave romantically in ways similar to the young. While observing singles' dances for older individuals at a senior center, the researchers noticed "a sense of anticipation, festive dress, and flirtatious behavior that were strikingly familiar to us as women recently involved in the dating scene." They interviewed 45 individuals aged 60 to 92 in Minneapolis, Minnesota. One difference the investigators noted between older and younger daters was their definition of dating. The older people defined dating as a committed, long-term, monogamous relationship, similar to going steady at a younger age. Unlike many younger individuals, who "play the field," the vast majority of the older people were not casual about dating.

But one facet of dating was similar for both older and younger daters: the "sweaty palm" syndrome. The elders turned "physiological and psychological somersaults" on their dates and experienced a heightened sense of reality, perspiring hands, heart palpitations, feelings of awkwardness, the inability to concentrate, and anxiety and longing when away from the loved one. The older individuals saw romance much like younger people do—candlelight dinners, long walks in the park, giving flowers and candy. For older men, romance and sex were closely linked: "You can talk about candlelight dinners and sitting in front of the fireplace," a 71-year-old widower explained, "but I still think the most romantic thing I've ever done was to go to bed with her."

What older people do on dates is similar to what younger individuals do but is often "far more varied and creative," the researchers concluded. In addition to the traditional youthful dates of pizza, movies, and dances, older couples went camping, enjoyed the opera together, and flew off to Hawaii for the weekend. Also, the pace of dating was greatly accelerated. Older people noted that they simply did not have much time to play the field. They favored a direct, non-game-playing approach in building relationships with someone of the other sex. Sexual involvements tended to develop, and sexual intimacy enhanced self-esteem. A 77-year-old woman explained, "Sex isn't as important when you're older, but in a

Although we usually think of dating couples as being young, more older couples are also dating.

way you need it more." For this woman, sex reaffirmed the fact that she was alive and important to at least one other person in the world.

Another major difference between older and younger daters, the investigators noted, was their definition of passionate love. Younger people tend to equate passionate love with real love; once the intensity fades, they think love is gone. Older daters looked at passionate love differently. They had learned from experience that the early intensity of passionate love simply cannot be sustained for very long. Most of the older individuals had learned through their marriages the value of companionate love—the "steady, burning fire" that endures and deepens over time. As one older man explained, "Yeah, passion is nice—it's the frosting on the cake. But it's her personality that's really important. The first time I was in love, it was only the excitement that mattered, but now it's the friendship, the ways we spend our time together that count."

Like younger individuals, older people face a number of dilemmas and difficulties in dating. Fear of disapproval leads many to be secretive about their dating activities. As a 63-year-old man said, "My girlfriend (age 64) lives just down the hall from me [in a retirement home]. When she spends the night, she usually brings her cordless phone just in case her daughter calls." And a 61-year-old woman reported that even though her 68-year-old boyfriend had spent three or four nights a week at her house in the past year, she had not yet told her family. "I have a tendency to hide his shoes when my grandchildren are coming over," the woman said.

Marriage is another dilemma for older people. They initially seek a marital partner, but many decide as time goes on that they are not willing to give up their independence. Women, especially, often like the new freedom divorce or widowhood has given them. Older individuals are not planning to raise a family together; many fear the burden of caring for someone in deteriorating health or being a burden themselves to someone else.

In general, family members and friends tend to support the older dater and to affirm the elder's right to seek personal happiness. One 64-year-old woman summed up dating rather well: "I suppose that hope does spring eternal in the human breast as far as love is concerned. Individuals are always looking for the ultimate, perfect relationship. No matter how old they are, they are looking for this thing called love."

Functions and Stages of Dating   Although dating customs have varied widely and have changed over the years, the basic functions of dating and courtship have remained consistent. Six basic functions that dating performs in our culture were identified by Robert Winch (1971). He noted that dating:

- Provides adolescents with training for adulthood. Because the adolescent period is becoming more distinctive as a stage of life, this function is likely to continue in the future.

- Is the focus for social activities other than courtship. Dating is a major recreational activity in its own right.

- Permits youths to establish their prestige and social position among their peers and to develop skills in human relations that they take into adulthood.

- Helps young people transfer their emotional orientation from their parents to their peer group and thus learn to function as autonomous adults.

- Lets youths learn gender roles and develop their sexual identity. Although parents serve as the initial gender-role models, young people expand their gender-role conceptions through exposure to their peer culture.

- Fulfills the instrumental role of mate selection for marriage.

Over the past decades, these functions have continued to be important in American culture. It is reasonable to expect that the process of dating will remain a viable part of our culture.

In a major study of the dating stages leading to marriage, Springer, Fournier, and Olson (1985) surveyed 960 students at the University of Minnesota. Students were first asked to describe the stage of their current premarital relationship and then to rate their commitment to that relationship on a 9-point scale (1 being the lowest level of commitment to the relationship; 9 being the highest level). The eight identified stages were friendship, casual dating, serious dating, steady dating, cohabiting, pre-engaged, engaged, and married. Figure 5.1 illustrates the average commitment scores for the students at each stage of dating and mating.

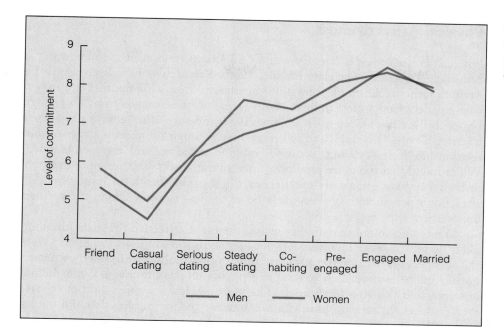

Figure 5.1 Levels of Commitment at Various Stages of Dating and Mating

Commitment increased as the relationship moved from the casual dating stage to marriage. Friends were given a higher level of commitment than casual dating, which averaged about 5 on the 9-point scale, but a lower commitment rating than serious dating. Engaged couples and married couples had the highest commitment ratings. The students did not rate being married as high on the commitment scale as being engaged, perhaps because engaged students idealized their level of commitment or perhaps because engaged students and married students defined commitment differently. The commitment level of cohabiting (living together) couples was similar to that of couples who were steady dating, but was lower than that of pre-engaged couples. Female students generally reported a higher commitment to their relationships than did males, although the difference was not statistically significant.

Criteria for Choosing a Mate

Americans tend to choose partners who are similar to them in a variety of ways—in ethnic and cultural background, age, educational and religious background, and socioeconomic status. Physical attractiveness also plays a large role in mate selection. This section discusses the criteria that influence mate selection in the United States.

Physical Attractiveness

Physical attractiveness is one of the most important traits related to frequency of being asked out on a first date (White, 1980). Researchers have been creative in devising rating scales to measure physical attractiveness. One method is simply to have a panel of judges rate individuals on a scale of attractiveness from low to high. Using this method, Gregory L. White (1980) measured the relative physical attractiveness of 123 couples and followed them through the various stages of their relationship (casual dating, serious dating, cohabiting, and engaged/married). White found that the more physically attractive a person was, the more likely she or he was to have friends of the other sex. On the other hand, the more physically attractive a person was, the less likely he or she was to worry about the partner's involvement with other people.

White also found that among males, the more attractive the male, the more likely he was to desire involvements outside the relationship. According to White, this was perhaps because the attractive male's opportunities with other women are greater and he is more likely to want to capitalize on this advantage. White did not, however, find this true for women: The more attractive women did not report a greater desire for relationships with men outside the partnership than did the less attractive women. In a follow-up study 9 months later, White found that couples of similar attractiveness levels were more likely to progress deeper into the relationship than were couples in which one individual was relatively more attractive than the other. People tend to "shop around." Most of us are aware of how good-looking we are compared with other people, and we tend to use this "attractiveness capital" as a bargaining chip in our negotiations with prospective partners.

One research group studied interpersonal attraction at a commercial video-dating service (Green, Buchanan, & Heuer, 1984). The researchers developed quantitative profiles of each dating-service member, based on a point system including age, judgments of physical attractiveness, social status, humor, and warmth. They found that people who were physically attractive got more calls for dates. Physically attractive males enjoyed more popularity, and popular females tended to be younger and more attractive than their less-popular counterparts. Females tended to select males with higher social status, whereas males tended to focus on female physical attractiveness. The researchers followed up on these dating couples to see how the dating progressed. They found that although men tended to prefer younger women, they did not continue to date them. A younger date might be attractive to the man on first glance, but the age difference was a crucial factor in ending the relationship. Women tended to choose older men but also tended to be more likely to reject them after dating them for a while. Differences in maturity level can be more important than attractiveness in a long-term relationship, this study suggests.

Male-Female Differences   It is commonly believed that men are more interested in physical attractiveness in a date but that women are more interested in personal qualities. Jeffrey S. Nevid (cited in Bozzi, 1985) surveyed 545 undergraduate men and women and concluded that there are some differences between the sexes in regard to the qualities they look for in a dating partner. Nevid's findings were relatively consistent with the stereotype that men are more interested in looks than women are.

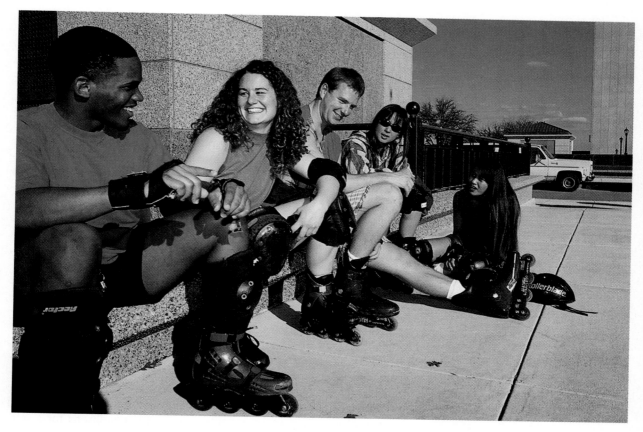

Nevid asked the students to rate the importance of 53 factors if they were looking for a purely sexual relationship and rate the importance of the same factors if they were looking for a more meaningful, long-term relationship. The 53 characteristics included physical qualities (such as facial features, buttocks, waistline, and overall attractiveness), personal qualities (such as sensitivity, honesty, warmth, and character), and demographic characteristics (including age and ethnic background).

When men and women rated characteristics for a long-term relationship, their lists were virtually identical, although in a slightly different order. For both men and women, the highest rated personal qualities were honesty, personality, fidelity, sensitivity, warmth, kindness, character, tenderness, patience, and gentleness. When asked to describe the qualities of an ideal sexual partner, however, the men and women diverged. Men described 10 purely physical qualities: figure, sexuality, general attractiveness, facial features, buttocks, weight, legs, breath, skin, and breasts, in that order. The women, on the other hand, blended physical and personal qualities in their top 10: general attractiveness, sexuality, warmth, personality, tenderness, gentleness, sensitivity, kindness, build, and character, in descending order of importance. The men obviously made a big distinction between a sex partner and a long-term friend.

When people are physically attractive, others assume they also have positive personal qualities, such as sincerity, honesty, and warmth.

Physical Attractiveness, Personality, and Life Success Another researcher studied the effects of physical appearance on personality and behavior (Agnew, 1984). Previous research had indicated that physically attractive people were more likely to be rated by others as also possessing good personal and behavioral qualities. Agnew found that overall appearance does make a difference in one's life in a number of ways: Attractive individuals do better in school, believe they have a more promising future, and feel better about themselves than do less attractive individuals. Young people who are attractive also have lower rates of juvenile delinquency, perhaps reflecting the fact that delinquency is lower among individuals who have a positive self-concept, good grades, and high expectations for the future. But physical appearance is not everything. Less attractive males date and interact socially just as often as attractive males. Furthermore, less attractive males are not any more angry or frustrated about life than are attractive males (Agnew, 1984).

One psychologist argued that attractive individuals are simply living up to the positive assumptions society makes about them (Berscheid, 1982). Attractive people are believed to be more sensitive, responsive, sincere, kind, interesting, strong, poised, modest, sociable, outgoing, and exciting. They are also assumed to have more potential for social, marital, and occupational success. Because they are seen to have all these qualities, attractive people get special treatment: "Beauty affects job opportunities, for example. Even when appearance has no conceivable relationship to a person's functioning in a job, the hiring decisions of experienced personnel consultants are significantly influenced by the applicant's physical appearance" (Berscheid, 1982).

Favorable treatment begins virtually at birth. From infancy on, attractive babies are hugged, cuddled, and kissed more often than less attractive babies. Mothers, fathers, nurses, and teachers all treat them better. Misbehavior in an attractive child is seen as a momentary slipup, whereas misbehavior in an unattractive child is seen as evidence of an antisocial personality. The classic conditions for a self-fulfilling prophecy are thus set up. We expect better things from attractive people, and they usually don't disappoint us.

The importance of physical attractiveness persists after years of marriage. Leslie Margolin and Lynn White (1987) surveyed more than 1,500 spouses who had been married for 10 or more years. They hypothesized—and found—that men, but not women, would report more sexual problems in their marriage if they believed that their spouse's attractiveness had decreased (e.g., the spouse had gained weight) while theirs had not. This study demonstrates that the male focus on physical attraction continues over time and is specifically linked to sexual satisfaction, as it is in younger men.

Age and Success Criteria

It has been estimated that in six out of every seven marriages in the United States, the man is as old as or older than the woman. Why is this the case? Physiologically, males mature more slowly than females and do not live as long. Furthermore, in the United States there are more males than females in their early 20s. Finally, there is the phenomenon social scientists have labeled the **mating gradient,** the tendency of women to marry men who are better educated or more successful than they are. Because men tend to "marry down" in terms of age and status, it can be difficult for successful older women to find a mate.

Table 5.3 Single Males and Females in the United States and Sex Ratio, 1993

AGE	MALES (IN THOUSANDS)	FEMALES (IN THOUSANDS)	SEX RATIO*
18–19	3,162	2,918	108
20–24	7,113	6,019	118
25–29	4,727	3,258	145
30–34	3,333	2,153	155
35–39	2,085	1,362	153
40–44	1,008	867	116
45–54	951	798	120
55–64	670	469	143
65–74	389	376	103
75+	180	419	43
Total	23,618	18,639	127

*Sex ratio indicates number of men to women: 100 means the number is the same; a ratio above 100 indicates more men than women.

Source: U.S. Bureau of the Census (1994, p. 56).

Although men tend to be as old as or older than women, the age difference between those marrying today isn't very pronounced, especially among younger people. In the United States in the 1980s, the average male marrying for the first time was between 23 and 25 years old, and the average female was between 21 and 22 years old. The average age difference between the two was 2–3 years. By the mid-1990s, however, the age of the male was 26.4 and of the female was 24.2, reducing the difference to slightly more than 2 years (U.S. Bureau of the Census, 1995). Age differences at the time of marriage are smallest between people marrying at younger ages, increasing between those who marry at older ages. But in all age groups, men tend to marry younger women.

The term **sex ratio** indicates the relationship between the number of men and the number of women of a given age. Due to differences in birth and infant mortality rates, the U.S. population has historically contained more men than women, and this situation continues today. In 1910, there were 106 single men for every 100 single women; now there are 127 single men for every 100 single women. If every single man in this country wanted to marry, there wouldn't be enough women to go around. This problem is true for men across all age groups, except those 75 and older (Table 5.3).

Endogamy and Exogamy

The pool of mates is often first narrowed by **endogamy,** the culturally prescribed practice or tradition of choosing a mate from within one's own group. These groups might include ethnic, religious, socioeconomic, or general age groups. The principle of endogamy makes it likely that middle-class Whites will marry middle-class Whites, Catholics will marry Catholics, and young people will marry young people.

Exogamy—the practice or tradition of choosing a mate from outside one's own group—is typically discouraged in our society. Although there are no laws against marrying someone of different socioeconomic status, religion, or ethnic group, these groups tend to be off-limits or less desirable as a source of marital partners. State laws do, however, forbid marriage between parents and children, brothers and sisters, grandparents and grandchildren, and children and their aunts and uncles. Many states also forbid marriage between stepparents and stepchildren and between a man and his father's former wife or his son's former wife. Legal marriage between people of the same sex is forbidden by state laws, though many gay men and lesbians decry these laws.

In 1967, the U.S. Supreme Court declared miscegenation laws, which forbade interracial marriages, to be unconstitutional. Miscegenation laws sought to prevent unions between Whites and African Americans, Whites and Native Americans, and Whites and Asians. In 1945, at the end of World War II, 30 of the 48 states had miscegenation laws.

Though legal prohibitions against marriage between people of different groups have disappeared, informal social codes remain. A particular community may not have a law against marrying a person of a different religion or ethnic group, but relatives and friends in the community are likely to disapprove of couples who deviate too far from the unwritten rules. There is some evidence, however, that our attitudes as a society are gradually becoming more open to viewing differences as a source of strength. In many parts of the country, people do not look twice if they see a Black-White couple walking down the street arm in arm or two women holding hands in public. But in other parts of the country, it still upsets some people to see love blossoming between a Catholic woman and a Jewish man.

Intercultural Marriages in the United States

The growing ethnic diversity in the United States and the increasing rate of marriage across ethnic groups are changing the "unwritten rules" regarding exogamy. This change reflects a common belief that in the United States all ethnic and cultural groups can live and work together. This belief is true to a certain degree—we have developed a relatively stable society and share certain democratic values—but the United States is by no means a blended and homogeneous society, as discussed in Chapter 2. Although the ethnic and cultural mix often works rather well, the elements that make it up remain distinct. Ethnic values and identifications endure for generations. When people marry out of their ethnic group, problems can arise; the difficulties inherent in intercultural marriage often intensify if the couple do not anticipate them. We confuse the idea that we are all created equal with the belief that we are all the same (McGoldrick & Preto, 1984, p. 347).

The marriage rate between members of different ethnic groups is difficult to assess accurately because the concept of race is elusive, and many people cannot be easily classified (see Chapter 2). The U.S. Bureau of the Census does, however, ask people to state their ethnic identity and calculates rates of Black-White marriage. The number of Black-White marriages increased from 65,000 in 1970 to 242,000 in 1993 (U.S. Bureau of the Census, 1994). Of those 242,000 couples, 75% were Black male/White female couples, and 25% were White male/Black female couples.

Marriages between individuals of different ethnic backgrounds involve special challenges. Partners must be aware of and appreciate differences, making them a strength of the relationship rather than a source of conflict.

Parents are often hesitant to bless an intercultural marriage. They may be aware of the problems their children will face, both within the relationship and in our society. They may also think the young couple are naive, idealistic, or blinded by love and need the guidance of their more experienced elders.

Some of these concerns are legitimate. When people marry, they are often idealistic in their beliefs. One common—and unrealistic—belief is that love conquers all. Another is that true love means the couple either has few differences or one partner can change the other after marriage. In the words of one family therapist, "Spouses tend to perceive their cultural differences as failings—either badness or madness. With insight, people are able to get some distance from their hurt feelings and stop taking inevitable differences personally" (Pearce, 1980). Although differences can be a source of strength in a marriage, they can also cause problems.

Ethnically mixed couples are more likely to divorce and to have a variety of marital and family problems, researchers suggest (McGoldrick & Preto, 1984). Children of intercultural marriages have more personal and relationship problems than children from ethnically homogeneous families.

The greater the ethnic differences between individuals, the less likely they are to marry, McGoldrick and Preto maintain. After marriage, the greater the differences, the greater the difficulty the couple will have adjusting to each other. These two family therapists identify eight factors that they believe most influence the degree of adjustment:

- *Values.* The greater the discrepancy in values between the cultural groups, the more difficulty the couple will have. For example, a Puerto Rican–Italian couple will probably have less difficulty due to disparity of values than will an Irish-Italian couple.

- *Acculturation.* The greater the difference in the levels of acculturation of each partner, the greater the probability of conflict. For example, couples are likely to have more difficulty if one is a recent immigrant and the other a fourth-generation American.

- *Religion.* Adding religious differences to cultural differences can compound adjustment difficulties. An Irish-Italian marriage will probably be easier than an Irish-Jewish marriage because Irish and Italian partners are likely to share a common Catholic heritage. This is one less area for misunderstandings.

- *Race (McGoldrick and Preto's terms).* Interracial couples are the most vulnerable of all couples, sometimes feeling isolated from both groups. The children of an interracial union are also sometimes subject to discrimination from both groups. As interracial children become more commonplace, however, this discrimination may decline.

- *Sex and sex roles.* Because women are generally reared to talk more about their feelings, an Irish wife, for example, will probably have an easier time adjusting to a Jewish husband than a Jewish wife would have adjusting to an Irish husband. Why? Because Jews are traditionally more verbal, and the family therapists presume that matching a verbal Irish wife and a verbal Jewish husband works out better than matching a verbal Jewish wife and a relatively less verbal Irish husband.

- *Socioeconomic differences.* Partners from different socioeconomic circumstances have added difficulties adjusting to each other. The financial issues with which couples must contend can become even more problematic if the partners have different life experiences and expectations regarding them.

- *Cultural familiarity.* Individuals who have some experience with the other's culture before marriage are more likely to understand and adjust to each other. Couples who live in a multiethnic neighborhood after marriage are also less likely to experience pressure and negative reactions from others.

- *Extended-family agreement.* If kin of both partners are supportive, the couple has a greater chance of success. If the couple feels forced to elope or if one partner's family refuses to attend the wedding, this can indicate future difficulties.

Box 5.3 relates one of McGoldrick and Preto's case studies of marriage between individuals from two different ethnic/cultural groups.

McGoldrick and Preto point out that every ethnic group has its own unique heritage, values, and behaviors that make it special. It is important for those who marry someone from a different group to be aware of these differences and to work toward making them an asset rather than a liability.

Family Therapy for a Troubled Ethnic Intermarriage

Mike, a 28-year-old Irish-Catholic lawyer, who had been married for three years to a Jewish social worker, suddenly left his wife, which precipitated her seeking therapy. Susan said she was not alone in being totally mystified by his suddenly leaving her and refusing to discuss it. Susan said she knew little of her husband's background, as he did not like to talk about it and she had always thought her family was a welcome replacement for him. She said his own father had deserted the family when he was eight and he had become the "man in the family." He had been a very responsible son, burying his bitterness about his father's desertion. Although his mother was very religious, he turned against religion from that time on.

Mike worked his way through law school, and from the time he met Susan had only occasional visits with his mother, who disapproved of his marrying a Jew. He had no contact with other relatives because of a cut-off that occurred at the time of his father's desertion. Six months prior to the separation he had received word through his mother that his father was still alive and had written that he was ill with cancer and wanted to see his son. Mike went to visit his father. Three weeks after the father's death, Mike announced he was leaving, and the next day he packed his bags and left. Susan became infuriated, but the more she raged, the more he withdrew. By the time she sought therapy, their communication had almost ceased, except for brief conversations about money.

The therapist, sensing that Mike had touched on long-buried cultural issues, requested permission to contact Mike. After some probing by the therapist, Mike indicated that he realized his marriage had been a sham. In spite of the warmth and expressiveness of his wife's family, he felt there was an unbridgeable chasm between them. He had tried to cover it up over the years with his jokes and friendliness, but reconnecting with his father had made him appreciate something about his own identity. He began to realize how he had hurt his mother by excluding her from his life because he could not find a way to integrate her into his wife's Jewish family. A resolution that would bring Mike back into Susan's family seemed impossible, but he was able to begin talking to her about feelings. The difference between the Irish difficulty with emotional expression and the Jewish need to articulate feelings about every experience was a major factor here. Susan gradually came to realize that, unlike her, Mike had been a great talker but had kept his real feelings hidden, even from himself.

It is interesting that within three years, both Mike and Susan had remarried, this time within their own ethnic groups. On follow-up four years later, both Mike and Susan said that it was only with the comfort of the cultural similarity in their second marriages that they had become aware of the depth of the differences between them that had made their divorce inevitable. One can speculate that if Mike and Susan had worked out their relationship with their families before their first marriages, the divorce might have been avoided.

Source: Excerpted from "Ethnic Intermarriage: Implications for Therapy" by M. McGoldrick and N. G. Preto, 1984, *Family Process, 23,* pp. 347–364. Copyright 1984 by *Family Process.* Reprinted by permission.

Joseph and Quinzola have been married for 15 years and have three children. Joseph is European American and Quinzola is African American. "I think Joseph and I have a pretty special relationship," Quinzola said. "He is a wonderful man, and I've always loved him. Sure, there was trouble with our families at first. Both families. And that took some working out between us.

"Joseph's parents grew up and lived in a small, White town all their lives. The biggest cultural difference they had in the whole town was fighting between Catholics and Lutherans. Joseph and I met at college in Cincinnati. When we went home to meet his parents for the first time after going out for a year, I felt you could cut the tension in the living room with a knife.

"But I have to admit my parents weren't much better. My dad was worse than my mom. He never has liked White people, in general. I'm sure he was convinced Joseph was after me just for sex. But after a while—Joseph would say it was a long while—my dad and Joseph became pretty good friends. I think they actually respect each other. Now his Aunt Wilson, I'm not so sure about her [chuckles]. I think she'll always hope for the return of slavery!"

Theories of Mate Selection

A number of theories have been developed over the years to explain how and why individuals choose a particular partner. No single theory appears to answer these questions completely, but several shed light on the subject.

Homogamy Versus Complementarity

Family theorists have maintained that people tend to marry others like themselves (Burgess & Wallin, 1943). This tendency to marry someone of the same ethnic group, educational level, socioeconomic status, religion, and values is called **homogamy.** But the fact that exceptions occur—African Americans marry Whites and Catholics marry Jews—indicates that there is much more to the mate selection process than simple homogamy.

Robert Winch (1958) caused a good deal of debate among social theorists when he proposed that people are attracted to those whose personalities are very different from their own. Winch called his idea the **complementary needs theory** because it asserted that "opposites attract"—that people are attracted to someone whose personality complements their own. He proposed, for example, that a dominant person and a submissive person would be attracted to each other.

Many family researchers tried to resolve the two theories—homogamy and complementary needs—and found very little support for Winch's ideas. Although there is evidence that people are attracted to those with similar background characteristics, there is little evidence one way or the other about personality similarities (Murstein, 1980). Perhaps one of the first to describe the importance of focusing on both similarities and dissimilarities was O. S. Fowler in his 1859 book *Matrimony* (Murstein, 1980). Fowler advised, "Wherein, and as far as you are what you ought to be, marry one *like* yourself; but wherein and as far as you have any marked *excesses* or defects, marry those *unlike* yourself in these objectionable particulars" (cited in Murstein, 1980, p. 259).

Bernard Murstein (1980) argued that all the studies cited earlier are consis-

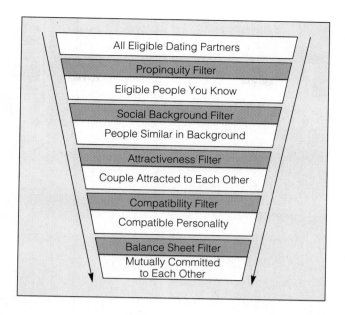

Figure 5.2 The Filter Theory of Mate Selection

tent with a theory that synthesizes the "opposites attract" and the "birds of a feather flock together" theories. After reviewing the studies, he reported finding that individuals with high self-esteem or high self-acceptance perceived themselves to be similar to their partner and that people with low self-acceptance were significantly lower in both perceived and actual similarity to their spouse. Murstein also argued that although complementarity of personality does describe some marriages, it is not typical of most marriages. "The only support of Winch's theory," he concluded, "was the work of Winch (1958) himself." Murstein and others tend to believe that, in general, similar qualities and characteristics tend to attract people to each other. Very dissimilar people do not usually marry, and if they do, they are often among the couples who are likely to divorce.

Filter Theory

Although under the law a person of legal age can marry any unrelated person he or she chooses, an analysis of mate selection suggests that people tend to go through a filtering process to narrow the pool of possible mates to a few prospective candidates. This idea was originally proposed by A. C. Kerckhoff and K. E. Davis (1962).

A graphic representation of the filter theory of mate selection is provided in Figure 5.2, which shows how the pool of prospective partners contracts as individuals are filtered out because of differences of one sort or another. The influence of **propinquity,** or nearness in time and space, is the first filter. In other words, the pool of available partners consists of those living within the same geographical area or with whom one is likely to come in contact. Years ago, the choice of a marriage partner was limited by the difficulty of traveling long distances; more

In the past, the pool of eligible partners was often limited by the difficulty of traveling long distances. Today, the Internet allows people from across the country to meet online, so the pool of potential partners is less restricted by physical proximity.

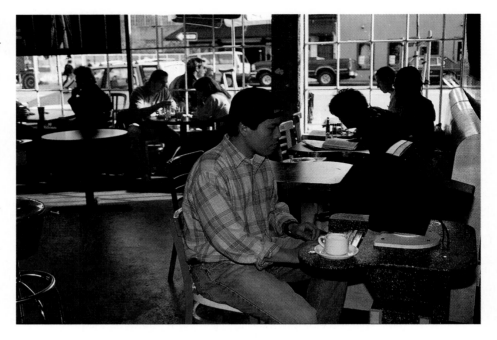

than half of the people married someone who lived only a few miles from their home. Although people now travel more extensively and have a broader range of social contacts, the pool of eligible partners is still influenced by the social circles we move in, the school or church or synagogue we attend, the job we hold, and the type of activities we choose to engage in.

The Internet is, however, changing the pool of possible dating partners. The potential pool is now less restricted to those physically nearby. A growing number of people are chatting online through subscription services or directly on the Internet and connecting with others of similar interests from across the country. This trend will increase as online commercial dating services and other Internet services help people meet a broader cross-section of potential partners.

The social background filter determines the ethnic group, socioeconomic status, and age of potential partners. Individuals who believe marriage outside their own socioeconomic group is unacceptable eliminate people who are not of their group from the pool of eligibles. As discussed earlier, an individual's physical attractiveness is important in selecting a date but less critical in choosing a mate. People tend to date individuals whom they consider equal to or more attractive than they are. Next, compatibility in personality, interests, and values acts as another filter in the mate selection process. At this more advanced stage, individuals are selecting from a smaller pool of eligible partners, which increases the possibility of finding an acceptable partner. Finally, people use the balance sheet filter: They evaluate what they are giving and what they are getting in the relationship. If their assessment is that this give-and-take is balanced, they often move on to a mutually committed relationship.

Stimulus-Value-Role Theory

A third theory of mate selection is known as stimulus-value-role theory. Murstein (1987) theorized that people are attracted to each other by an initial *stimulus* and then test their suitability for establishing a permanent relationship by comparing their *value* orientations and agreement on *roles*. In response to critiques by others in the field, Murstein has updated his stimulus-value-role (SVR) theory so that its three components are not distinct stages but rather work together to move a couple toward a committed relationship (Surra, 1991). Let's take a look at the way in which Murstein describes these three components:

- *Stimulus.* People are attracted to each other initially by a particular stimulus, such as an attractive physique or popularity. Each person evaluates how attractive the prospective partner is and how attractive he or she perceives himself or herself to be. The stimulus may act as a form of magnetism that draws the couple together, and that magnetism may be variously interpreted as "love at first sight," "magic," destiny, or infatuation. Whatever it is, the stimulus tends to energize the relationship beyond the bounds of simple friendship.

- *Value complementarity.* After a successful exchange during the stimulus stage of attraction, the couple begin to advance to the "value" stage of the relationship, in which they assess the compatibility of their basic beliefs and values. The couple often compare (in a very indirect, conversational mode) basic religious and political philosophies; attitudes toward money, work, and people; preferences for lifestyle and leisure activities; and feelings about character and personality. Although physical attraction is very important in drawing a couple together, it cannot overcome the strain of disagreement on many issues. Hardly a person has not thought at some time that "she (he) is beautiful (handsome), but I couldn't stand to live with her (him)." Thus, value complementarity becomes more important than physical attraction in selecting someone for an enduring relationship.

- *Role complementarity.* While comparing value complementarity, the couple also begin assessing role complementarity, or the extent to which they can establish a cooperative role relationship. Through interaction with each other, they discover each other's feelings and behaviors about power and authority (who is going to be the boss), the division of labor (who will perform what tasks), and the expectations each has for the other in the relationship. Each partner's values and roles emerge initially in the relationship, but eventually negotiation may be necessary to achieve a workable balance.

  Role complementarity can be tested only to a limited extent during courtship; the real test begins with marriage. Cohabitation can provide some indications of a person's style, but jointly dealing with important issues makes each partner's style more apparent. Everyone has different needs. Further, needs tend to change throughout life. A mate who might meet one's essential needs at age 20 could be incapable of meeting them at age 40. For example, one woman may desire a man who is assertive and dominant to "take charge" of her and their children; another might prefer an equalitarian mate who would support her professional career. Some men want their wives to be submissive; others admire an independent spirit of individualism. There is no end to the possible personality types that people seek in a partner. Each couple must determine if their combination is a workable one.

The three components of SVR theory act like filtering mechanisms for evaluating a dating relationship and determining whether to continue or end it. When a potential relationship ends, one or both parties may observe, "It just didn't work out." Often, there was attraction, but value or role complementarity could not be achieved.

Reiss's Wheel Theory of Love

Another theory of how a love relationship begins, is nurtured, and grows is Ira L. Reiss's wheel theory of love (Reiss & Lee, 1988). This theory describes four important components: rapport, self-revelation, mutual dependency, and intimacy need fulfillment. **Rapport** refers to the process of communication in which understanding and a sense of closeness between two people are developed. Two people have rapport when they are "on the same wavelength." Some people are quite good at building rapport with others. These skilled individuals are comfortable talking with different types of people. They tend not to be excessively judgmental about others, and they listen so they can understand others. Good rapport between two people often leads to **self-revelation,** which is the disclosing of personal information about oneself. Self-revelation, of course, is a two-way street. When they first meet, people are usually very cautious and do not reveal much. Gradually, they let a few "secrets" slip out, and the other person often reveals something very personal in return. Reiss notes that rapport encourages revelation of self, and this builds up what he calls **mutual dependency,** a relationship in which each person wants and needs the other person. This process takes time and can change over time. The fourth and final process in the development of love is what Reiss calls **intimacy need fulfillment,** the satisfaction one receives from having personal needs fulfilled, which leads to greater intimacy.

Reiss's wheel of love is graphically represented in Figure 5.3. Reiss describes his theory as a "wheel theory" of love because its four components are interdependent; that is, a reduction in any one of the components retards the development of a loving relationship. If, for example, a couple has an argument, self-revelation will diminish for a time. And if self-revelation diminishes in the relationship, the dependency and intimacy-need-fulfillment components will also diminish. The four components can also flow back and forth—even in the strongest of love relationships. In his model, Reiss indicates a flow in a positive direction with a plus (+) and in a negative direction with a minus (−). Every relationship has its rocky times; love ebbs and flows. But in healthy relationships that survive and develop, the flow generally moves toward increasing intimacy.

Reiss has surrounded the four components with an outer ring, which he labels "Social-Cultural Background," and an inner ring, which he labels "Role Conceptions." The four interpersonal components do not develop in a vacuum. Social-cultural background influences role conceptions, which in turn influence

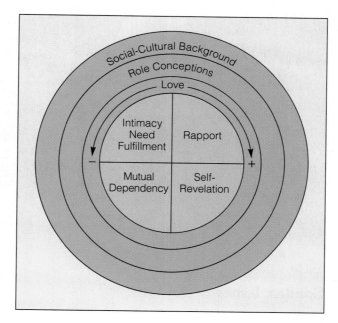

Figure 5.3 Reiss's Wheel of Love. *Source:* Adapted from *Family Systems in America* (4th ed.) (p. 103) by I. L. Reiss and G. R. Lee. New York: Holt, Rinehart & Winston. Copyright 1988 by Holt, Rinehart & Winston. Adapted by permission of the publisher.

the four components, because role conceptions are how we define what we expect in a love relationship and determine what we do to meet these expectations. Our religious values, our educational background, the family values we grew up with—all these influence how we think about love relationships, and our thinking influences our actions. It is important to keep in mind the tremendous diversity that exists in role conceptions within love relationships. Views differ greatly from one part of the world to another, and also among different cultural groups in the United States. In other words, we all are influenced by the society and cultural values around us.

Reiss notes that the wheel model applies not only to love relationships but also to other primary (close, intimate, face-to-face, and durable) relationships. It is useful in examining friendships, relationships with parents or children, and even casual relationships with colleagues, classmates, or roommates.

Conflict and Violence in Dating

Researchers have also looked at the issues of conflict and violence in dating relationships. Jealousy and differences in level of commitment are only some of the issues that can lead to conflicts between dating partners. These conflicts sometimes result in violent behavior, which can be a precursor to spouse abuse.

Conflict is an inevitable part of every relationship, but areas of conflict change as partners become more committed to each other. In the early stages of a relationship, jealousy and other personality issues are the greatest source of conflict; later, conflict arises from such issues as differences in background, the balance of power in the relationship, and parents.

Conflict Issues

Ten common sources of relationship problems were identified in one study of 960 students (Springer et al., 1985). These students reported 2,320 problems (an average of 2.5 problems per student) in their current relationships. Table 5.4 lists the 10 most frequently cited issues, in order from highest to lowest, at various stages of relationship development.

The most common sources of conflict for the students were personality issues, of which jealousy was the prime conflict issue. This finding is not surprising because commitment differences were the third most frequent source of conflict and these differences were particularly problematic in the early stages of dating. As couples approached marriage, jealousy was cited slightly less often as a source of relationship conflict, whereas parents were cited more frequently. Although they are a relatively minor source of conflict for couples at other stages of the relationship, parents are the second most frequent source of conflict for engaged couples. This is probably because the couple's parents become more actively involved in the relationship as it moves toward marriage—offering advice, visiting, giving parties and showers, and paying for the wedding. As might be expected for students, the second most frequent source of conflict was "not enough time together."

Conflict issues are different at each stage of the relationship, as Table 5.4 shows. Commitment differences were the most frequent source of conflict at the friend and casual dating stages and the second most frequent source of conflict at the serious dating stage. But commitment differences decreased in importance across the remaining relationship stages, most likely because commitment increases with each successive stage.

Values (such as how to handle money and gender-role issues) became more problematic as couples moved toward marriage. Communication, background, and power issues were rated across the stages as the 5th through 7th issues. Friends were the 10th most frequently cited issue across all stages.

Table 5.4 Top 10 Areas of Conflict Across Stages of Relationships

CONFLICT AREAS	OVERALL RANKING n = 960	FRIEND n = 154	CASUAL DATING n = 167	SERIOUS DATING n = 171	STEADY DATING n = 214	COHABITING n = 44	PRE-ENGAGED n = 89	ENGAGED n = 45	MARRIED n = 95
Personality (jealousy, esteem, moodiness)	1	2	4	1	1	2	1	1	2
Not enough time together	2	3	2	3	2	5	2	3	3
Commitment differences	3	1	1	2	3	7	6	7	9
Values (money, goals, lifestyle, gender roles)	4	8	6	4	7	1	7	5	1
Communication (disclosure, listening, honesty)	5	5	3	5	4	4	8	6	7
Background (different interests, religion, cultural, education)	6	7	5	6	5	3	3	4	6
Power (control, dependency, competition)	7	4	8	7	8	9	9	8	5
Parents	8	10	10	9	6	6	4	2	4
Sex (moral question, relative importance)	9	9	9	8	9	10	5	9	8
Friends	10	6	7	10	10	8	10	10	10

Source: Commitment and Conflict Across Premarital Relationship Stages by J. D. Springer, D. Fournier, and D. H. Olson, 1985, unpublished manuscript, Department of Family Social Science, University of Minnesota, St. Paul. Copyright © 1985 by David H. Olson.

Table 5.5 Types of Conflict in Dating (Sample = 272)

	CONFLICT USED (%)		CONFLICT RECEIVED (%)	
	Men	Women	Men	Women
Reasoning	100	100	100	99
Verbal aggression	87	93	87	89
Minor violence	22	38	32	29
Severe violence	3	19	16	8

Source: "Contextual Factors Surrounding Conflict Resolution While Dating: Results from a National Study" by J. E. Stets and D. A. Henderson, 1991, *Family Relations, 40(1)*, p. 32. Copyright 1991 by National Council on Family Relations, 3989 Central Ave. N.E., Ste. 550, Minneapolis, MN 55421. Reprinted by permission.

Courtship Violence

Violence between dating high school and college students is an area that was previously neglected by researchers (Cate & Lloyd, 1991). Professional findings about dating and courtship relationships are now indicating that they are more violent than initially expected. Few individuals completely accept the traditional romantic accounts of courtship relationships in America today. But popular songs, films, books, and television continue to depict premarital heterosexual relationships in an overly positive light. Young couples are shown as overcoming obstacles and achieving successful relationships. The stresses and strains inherent in these relationships are minimized, and aggression and violence are rarely mentioned.

In a study of aggression in 272 dating people, Stets and Henderson (1991) found the rate of physical aggression was highest in dating couples who were younger, were of low socioeconomic status, and had been drinking. The sample ranged in age from 17 to 26 years old and contained Whites (74%), African Americans (13%), Latinos (7%), Asian Americans (3%), and Native Americans (3%). The study asked about four approaches for dealing with violence: reasoning (discussing issues), verbal aggression (insulting, sulking, threatening), minor violence (pushing, slapping), and severe violence (kicking, hitting, choking) (Table 5.5). In terms of handling conflict, all males and females (100%) used reasoning, and most (87–93%) used verbal aggression. In terms of physical violence, more men (32%) than women (29%) were on the receiving end of severe violence. This concurs with the fact that fewer men (3%) than women (19%) reported using severe physical violence. Men are less often hurt than women in violent encounters, however, because women are generally not as physically able to cause serious injury as men.

One of the earliest studies of courtship violence among high school students was done by June Henton and colleagues (Henton, Cate, Koval, Lloyd, & Christopher, 1981). In surveying 644 students, they confirmed the existence of violence among teenage partners and observed that "adolescents do, indeed, experience violence in their dating relationships with considerable frequency and intensity" (p. 477). Some of their findings are particularly disturbing. For example, 27% of the victims of date violence interpreted the violence as an act of love; 31% of the perpetrators of the violence agreed, saying they had become angry only because they cared so much about their victim. In contrast, only about 5% of the victims and 3% of the perpetrators saw hate as the motive for the violent acts. According to the researchers, "Many adolescents are, thereby, constructing a topsy-turvy world for themselves where hate becomes love and violence indicates romantic passion" (p. 479). Adolescent victims and perpetrators often define abuse as love and assume the romantic notion that if problems arise, they will go away and that violence can be tolerated without undue stress. In short, the victim and the perpetrator conspire to pull the wool over each other's eyes by believing that violence is a consequence—if not proof—of intense love.

Young men often place the blame for violence on their partners. Most of the young women described their partner's acts of violence as being impulsive, spontaneous, or out of control or said that the male acted out of fear or sadness. These interpretations indicate that the young woman felt sympathy or pity for her assailant. The females often also conspired with the males by failing to let the secret out (Henton et al., 1981). Almost 25% of the violent incidents were not reported to anyone. In the cases where victims did report the violence, they commonly told friends (67%). But friends are not in a very good position to do anything about the violence, and most friends did nothing with the information.

> "I thought it would get better after the wedding. We had planned so long and carefully for it, and I knew the wedding would be wonderful," said Ronni from Chicago. "But even on the day of the wedding, Marty slapped me in the face. I don't know. He was frustrated about something my brother said or something. I don't know.
>
> "After we got married, it really got bad. He would stay out with his friends till all hours and when he came home, if I said even one word about it, he would hit me. Hard. I stayed with him 2 years, but when he pushed me down when I was 7 months pregnant, I couldn't stand it any more and I left for the domestic violence program shelter. He would have hurt the baby, and I would never have forgiven myself. I ended up leaving town, moving to my sister's in Indianapolis. I didn't have hardly anything . . . Alexis's baby clothes and her toys, my clothes, a small stereo system.
>
> "I didn't have anything, really, but I was free and that was what counted."

Courtship Violence and Later Spouse Abuse

Another research team was curious about the relationship between courtship violence and later spouse abuse (Roscoe & Benaske, 1985). Were abused wives likely to have been abused during courtship? In fact, 51% responded that they had been physically abused in a dating relationship at some time; however, 49% had not been abused during courtship. This means that for many women, physical abuse will come as an unpleasant surprise after the wedding. Violence in dating relationships was associated with the degree of involvement between partners; the higher the level of intimacy, the greater the likelihood of violence. The causes of violence were similar in courtship and in marriage. They were, in descending order of frequency, jealousy, alcohol, money, children, drugs, and sexual denial.

It is clear that if an individual is violent during dating, it is most likely that this behavior will continue after marriage. In general, a violent date is a poor marriage risk. Violence breeds violence and quickly destroys an intimate relationship.

Summary

- Young people are staying single longer and marrying at a slightly older age than in the past, partly because of their pursuit of education and career.

- Singlehood is seen as a legitimate alternative to marriage by more and more individuals in our society. This represents a major shift in thinking.

- Parent-arranged marriages remain common—and are effective—in many non-industrialized cultures today, but in the United States, individual-choice courtship is the norm.

- Research on dating among older individuals shows that they experience the same emotional effects as young people do but that their dates are often more creative than those of younger people. Sexual involvements do develop in older couples but are looked at in a more realistic manner.

- Eight distinct stages of commitment in dating and mating have been identified: friendship, casual dating, serious dating, steady dating, cohabiting, pre-engaged, engaged, and married. The level of commitment increases through the stages, as do the type and intensity of relationship problems and challenges.

- Factors that influence mate selection are physical attractiveness, personality, age, life success, and the principles of exogamy and endogamy. However, the rise in ethnic diversity in the United States is changing the unwritten rules regarding mixed marriages.

- Theories about mate selection include (1) homogamy theory, which proposes that people are attracted to others who are like themselves, and complementary needs theory, which suggests that opposites attract; (2) filter theory, which describes different characteristics people use to narrow the field of eligible partners; (3) stimulus-value-role theory, which holds that after the initial attraction (stimulus), value and role compatibility are the determinants; and (4) the wheel theory of love, which defines the process of love using the concepts of rapport, self-revelation, mutual dependency, and intimacy need fulfillment.

- Courtship violence, a formerly neglected area of research, has come under careful scrutiny in the past few years, and rates are rather high. Research shows that violent dates are likely to become violent mates.

Key Terms

singlehood

sexually transmissible disease (STD)

human immunodeficiency virus (HIV)

acquired immune deficiency syndrome (AIDS)

parent-arranged marriage

dating

permissiveness

double standard

mating gradient

sex ratio

endogamy

exogamy

homogamy

complementary needs theory

propinquity

rapport

self-revelation

mutual dependency

intimacy need fulfillment

Activities

1. Share your thoughts on these questions in a small group: What forces are pushing you toward marriage? What forces are pulling you toward marriage? What is pushing you toward singlehood? What attracts you to singlehood?

2. Share your values regarding sexual intimacy for single people in a small group. How do your values differ from those of others in the group?

3. Discuss your notions about singlehood with a group. Can a single person live a satisfying life? In general, do you think singles can be as happy as married individuals?

4. What initially attracts you to another person? Rank these five possibilities from 1 to 5 (1 being the highest and 5 the lowest): physical attractiveness, popularity, social status, personality, and character. Discuss your rankings in a small group.

5. Do opposites attract? Or do birds of a feather flock together? In a small group, discuss the theory of homogamy and the theory of complementary needs as they relate to friendships and love relationships.

6. Using Reiss's wheel theory of love, think about one intimate relationship in your life. Describe that relationship as it developed over time using the components contained in the wheel of love.

7. Discuss violence in dating as a small group. Be sure to address these questions, among others: How frequently have you experienced abuse? What was your reaction to it? What can be done to reduce courtship violence?

8. Find an older person (60 years or older) who is dating or has recently married. Ask this individual about his or her recent courtship experience and how it differs from the experience the person had in her or his 20s.

Suggested Readings

Cate, R. M., & Lloyd, S. A. (1991). *Courtship*. Newbury Park, CA: Sage. *Good, recent research on "going out," which is hard to find; a useful guide for understanding the courtship process.*

The mating game. (1993, July 19). *U.S. News & World Report*, pp. 57–63. *Traces the sophisticated courtship strategies of modern men and women back to the Stone Age. Concludes that women are more concerned about whether mates will invest time and resources in a relationship; men care more about a woman's physical attractiveness, which in ancient times reflected her fertility and health.*

Surra, C. A. (1991). Research and theory on mate selection and premarital relationships. In A. Booth (Ed.), *Contemporary families: Looking forward, looking back* (pp. 54–75). Minneapolis: National Council on Family Relations. *An excellent review of recent research.*

Whyte, M. K. (1992, March/April). Choosing mates—The American way. *Society, 29*, pp. 71–77. *Examines how we go about selecting the person we marry and asks whether there is something wrong with the process in the United States.*

Woodward, J. C. (1988). *The solitude of loneliness*. Lexington, MA: Lexington Books/Heath. *Outlines the results of more than 20 years of study by this family psychologist, who has done perhaps as much research on loneliness as anyone in the United States; offers suggestions for coping with one of the 20th century's most common problems.*

CHAPTER 6

Sexual Intimacy

Sex is everywhere in our society. Television dramas, music videos, and advertising abound with sexual images and innuendo. The average American child watches about 20 hours of television a week; sexuality therefore enters young people's consciousnesses regularly. As a result, young people are subjected to an implicit sex education. And those who use sex to sell products and increase TV program ratings are by and large in charge of sex education in this country, while the people who should be leading the way—parents, teachers, professors, religious educators—are often too embarrassed or otherwise ill-equipped to deal with the topic directly. The issue clearly is not whether to have sex education in the United States, but what kind of sex education we as a society want for our young people and what the source should be.

The purpose of this chapter is to present a reasoned and factual approach to sexuality, especially those issues central to the development of sexual intimacy in human relationships. It begins with an overview of sex and society, including historical and cross-cultural perspectives, current trends in sexual behavior in the United States, and sex education. Following this overview are sections on premarital sex, sexual satisfaction within marriage, extramarital sexual relations, sexual problems, achieving sexual health, and various approaches to sex therapy.

Sex and Society: An Overview

A person's sexual identity is an important part of who she or he is. A number of factors, including biology and culture, influence sexual identity. This section discusses these factors, looks at historical and cultural perspectives on sexuality, and explores the ways in which Americans receive information on sexuality.

Sexuality, Sex, and Gender

The formation of a person's sexuality is a complex process involving continuous interaction among a wide variety of biological influences, family and cultural influences, and each individual's relatively unique set of personality characteristics. **Sexuality** is a broad term that includes the set of beliefs, values, and behaviors that defines each of us as a sexual being. One aspect of an individual's sexuality is whether a person identifies him- or herself as **heterosexual, homosexual,** or **bisexual,** known as **sexual orientation.** Another aspect is whether the person is interested in having sexual experiences with a variety of partners or with only one partner. Yet another aspect is the type of sexual acts the person enjoys. There are countless beliefs, values, and behaviors associated with sexuality. Therefore, individuals vary widely in how they define themselves as sexual beings.

In our society, the term **sex** can refer either to being biologically female or male or to sexual activity. The term **gender** refers to the learned characteristics and behaviors associated with being male or female in a particular culture.

Historical Perspectives on Sex and Society

Throughout much of history, people's sexual behavior and thinking about sex were guided by religious teachings and cultural beliefs. Many religions, Christianity among them, attempt to regulate sex outside marriage by condemning it as sinful. Some religions, such as Islam, while also condemning sex outside of marriage, allow men to take more than one wife. Other ideas about sex evolve out of, and are part of, general cultural beliefs. For example, Western male-dominated culture has held the idea that women have little interest in sex. Other cultures—for example, that of the Inuit—consider female sexual activity to be on a par with male sexuality.

The rise of science led to a more scientific approach to sex. Little was known about the biological aspects of sexuality until Dutch microscopist Anton van Leeuwenhoek (1632–1723) and his student John Ham discovered sperm swimming in human semen. Oscar Hertwig was the first to observe fertilization of the egg by the sperm in sea urchins in 1875. The human ovum was not directly observed until the 20th century.

In the late 19th century, the psychological aspects of sex also came under the scrutiny of the scientist. Freud proposed that sexuality is central to the human experience, that even infants are sexual beings, and that human psychological and personality development proceeds through several stages in which the crucial experiences are essentially sexual.

Briefly, Freud proposed that individuals pass through five psychosexual stages:

1. *Oral stage.* Birth to 18 months, the period when an infant's pleasure-seeking activities involve the mouth.

2. *Anal stage.* From about 1.5–3 years of age, when the infant's pleasure seeking is centered around the anus and the function of elimination.

3. *Phallic stage.* Age 3–6 years, when the child's pleasure seeking involves the genitals. This is also the time, according to Freud, when the child competes with the parent of the same sex. This phenomenon is called the Oedipal complex (named for the character in Greek mythology who unknowingly killed his father and married his mother).

4. *Latency stage.* Age 6 to puberty, a period when the child represses sexual thoughts and engages in activities that develop social and intellectual skills.

5. *Genital stage.* Puberty through adulthood, a time of renewed interest in sexuality, which the individual fulfills through relationships with others.

Freud proposed his theories about psychosexual stages in a strict, repressive era in which sexuality was denied, especially for women. His ideas were at first considered scandalous, then gradually accepted. According to historian Peter Gay, it was "a devious and insincere world in which middle-class husbands slaked their lust by keeping mistresses, frequenting prostitutes, or molesting children, while their wives, timid, dutiful, obedient, were sexually anesthetic and poured all their capacity for love into their housekeeping and their child-rearing" (1984, p. 6). Freud's ideas continue to spark controversy today as his defenders present their

In our society, most information about sexual behavior and intimate relationships comes from the media. Not surprisingly, many people have misconceptions and distorted ideas about both the physical and the emotional dimensions of sexuality.

merits with perhaps as much energy as they did a century ago, while his detractors argue that he is little more than a historical artifact.

Today, we have a great deal of scientific knowledge about sex—about conception, contraception, and sexual functioning, as well as about how to treat infertility and sexual dysfunction. We talk openly about sex and are complacent about the ubiquity of sexual images in our society. Yet religion still plays a role in many people's sexual attitudes and behavior, and there is still conflict between those who espouse an open, objective, scientific, informational approach to sex and those who wish to regulate people's sexual behavior and their access to information on moral grounds. Some observers have concluded, however, that the influence of organized religion is declining. In 1989, the Christian Broadcasting Network commissioned the Gallup organization to interview 539 college students. The survey was conducted at 100 two-year and four-year campuses, and the sample of students was statistically representative of students nationwide. Nearly 80% of the students said that religion was important in their lives but that their faith had relatively little impact on their sexual attitudes and behavior. About two thirds (69%) of the students said they did not believe nonmarital sex was wrong, and more than half (56%) approved of living together in trial marriages ("Students' Sex Attitudes," 1989). When science, religious values, and sexuality collide, individuals need to find ways to resolve these often-conflicting ideas.

Sexuality Across Cultures

Attitudes toward sexuality and sexual behaviors vary markedly from one culture to another, and ethnocentrism encourages people to believe that their culture's thinking and practices are the only "right" or "natural" way to live. An important generalization cross-cultural researchers make about sexuality is that all societies regulate sexual behavior in some way, although the regulations vary greatly from culture to culture (Hyde, 1990). Sex is a powerful force, and societies around the world have found it necessary to develop some rules regarding sexual behavior. For example, **incest taboos,** which prohibit intercourse between parents and children and between siblings, are nearly universal; most societies also condemn forced sexual relations, such as rape (Hyde, 1990).

Standards of Attractiveness   Cultural standards of sexual attractiveness vary widely. In many non-Western cultures, a plump woman is considered more attractive than a thin woman. But in the United States, the ideal woman has a slim body, well-developed breasts, and long, shapely legs. The ideal man is tall and moderately muscular, with broad shoulders and narrow hips. Physical attributes are often more important for women in Western societies because women tend to be judged by their appearance, whereas men are judged by their accomplishments.

In some cultures, the shape and color of the eyes are most important; other cultures value good-looking ears. The Nawa of Africa value elongated labia majora (the pads of fatty tissue on either side of the vagina), and Nawa women are reported to tug on their labia majora to lengthen them. Although the specifics vary, most cultures identify certain physical traits as attractive and valuable (Hyde, 1990).

Standards we take for granted—such as those for physical attractiveness—are actually culturally determined. Although these two women are very different from each other in appearance, each is considered beautiful in her culture.

Sexual Behavior   Gender roles in sexual behavior differ considerably across cultures. In a few societies, including the Maori and the Kwoma of the South Pacific, females generally initiate love affairs. Although rape in American society is primarily committed by men, the anthropologist Bronislaw Malinowski (1929) reported groups of Trobriand Island women in the South Pacific regularly raping and sexually humiliating male strangers who were unfortunate enough to wander through the area near their village.

Sexual techniques also vary considerably from culture to culture (Hyde, 1990). Kissing is common in most societies; however, when the Thonga of Africa first saw Europeans kissing, they were amused and could not believe the Europeans were sharing saliva. In some societies, pain is inflicted on the partner during lovemaking. Apinayean women of South America have been known to bite off bits of their partner's eyebrows, Trukese women in the South Pacific poke fingers in the man's ear when sexually excited, and partners in some societies draw blood and leave scars as a result of sexual passion.

The frequency of sexual intercourse varies from society to society (Masters, Johnson, & Kolodny, 1992). American society today is apparently about average when compared with other cultures. The range of frequency of intercourse for married couples runs from a low of about once a month among the Keraki of the South Pacific to a high of a few times a night for young couples among the Aranda of Australia and the Mangaians of the South Pacific.

Sexual Attitudes   Attitudes toward **masturbation,** the self-stimulation of the genitals, vary widely from culture to culture. It is tolerated among children and adolescents in some societies but condemned at any age by other societies. Most societies tend to disapprove of adult masturbation; if it is discovered, the consequences range from mild ridicule to punishment (Gregersen, 1983).

Similarly, attitudes toward homosexuality vary widely from culture to culture. Although some cultures tolerate same-sex sexual activity among children, they disapprove when adults engage in it. Other societies force homosexual behavior on all their male members, most often during puberty rites. Despite variations in attitudes from culture to culture, investigators believe at least four generalizations can be made: (1) homosexuality is universal, occurring in all societies; (2) homosexuality is more common among males than among females; (3) homosexuality is never the predominant form of sexual behavior for adults; and (4) only about 5% or less of the population of any culture tends to practice homosexuality (Whitam, 1983).

Cultural Change   Cultural beliefs and attitudes regarding sexuality change, often dramatically, over time. In China, for example, a decade of economic and social reform spawned a new sexual permissiveness. The Shanghai Sex Research Center conducted a national survey of 23,000 people and found that the Chinese are having more sex outside marriage and are becoming increasingly adventurous in the ways they make love. The researchers also found an erosion of the strong tie between sex and marriage in the world's most populous nation. A vast majority of the people (86%) and about two thirds (69%) of married people approved of extramarital affairs. In the past, large families were revered in China, but today, China has a one-child policy (Burton, 1990).

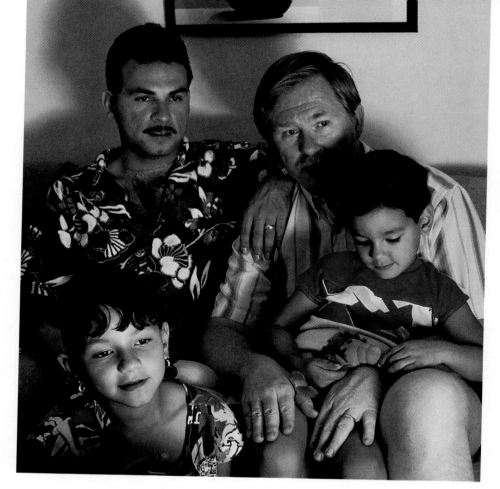

Homosexuality occurs in all human societies, but attitudes toward it vary. Although same-sex couples are becoming somewhat more visible in our society, homosexuality still has limited acceptance among the general population.

American Sexual Behavior Surveyed

There have been several significant sex surveys in the United States since Alfred Kinsey's landmark study in the early 1950s. These surveys reveal, among other things, information regarding the frequency with which Americans engage in sexual activity and the kinds of sexual activities they engage in.

The University of Chicago Study

In 1994 findings from perhaps the most extensive study of sexual behavior in the United States were reported. The research was based on face-to-face interviews with 3,432 American women and men between the ages of 18 and 59. Researchers looked at how age, gender, and marital status are related to sexual behavior; how women's and men's sexual lives and attitudes are similar and different; and how social factors including education, ethnicity, and religion affect sexual behavior (Laumann, Gagnon, Michael, Michaels, & Kolata, 1995).

Figure 6.1 Number of Sex Partners Among American Men and Women, 1994. *Source:* Data from Laumann, Gagnon, Michael, Michaels, & Kolata (1995).

Although our country is awash in sexual images that suggest we live in a very promiscuous society, this study indicates that sexual behavior does not measure up to those images (Cole, Dickerson, & Smilgis, 1994). The researchers found that although 17% of American men and 3% of American women had had sex with at least 21 partners since the age of 15, the sex life of the average American is more mundane (Figure 6.1). As the mass media put it, "The sex lives of most Americans are about as exciting as a peanut-butter-and-jelly sandwich" (Cole et al., 1994, p. 64).

Here are some of the results reported in the Chicago study:

- People fall into three groups: One third have sex twice a week or more, one third a few times a month, and one third a few times a year or not at all.

- People are largely monogamous. The majority (83%) have one or zero sexual partners a year. Over a lifetime, the average man has six partners, and the average woman two partners.

- Married couples, compared with single people, have more sex and are more likely to have orgasms when they do have sex. Nearly 40% of those married reported that they had sex twice a week, whereas 25% of singles said they had sex twice a week.

- Vaginal sex was ranked the most popular sex act (96% found it "very appealing" or "somewhat appealing"), watching a partner undress was ranked second in popularity, and oral sex was a distant third.

- Adultery is the exception, not the rule. Nearly 75% of the married men and 85% of the married women told interviewers they had never been unfaithful. Among the married people in the study, 94% said they had been faithful in the past year.

- Only 2.7% of the men and 1.3% of the women reported to the interviewers that they had had a same-sex sexual experience in the past 12 months.

Figure 6.2 (p. 194) indicates the frequency of sexual activity as reported in the study.

The study sparked a wave of controversy. The most common counterargument suggested that the results were relatively conservative because people are likely to lie to face-to-face interviewers about their sex lives. This U.S. study, though, mirrored recent studies in France and England that reported low rates of both homosexual behavior and extramarital sex.

Although most observers felt the research was well done, the University of Chicago research team admitted that the findings will remain debatable. First of all, 4,369 people were scientifically sampled for the study, but many were reluctant to participate. The 220 interviewers were trained to keep trying; some participants were visited 15 times before being persuaded to cooperate. In the end, 79% of those randomly selected for the research actually participated.

Even if people agree to participate in a study, will they tell the truth? "There is no way to get around the fact some people might conceal information," team member Stuart Michaels noted. For example, some gay men and lesbians are not likely to come out to an interviewer: "This is a stigmatized group. There is probably a lot more homosexual activity going on than we could get people to talk about" (Cole et al., 1994, p. 66).

Some of the other findings of the Chicago study included the following:

- The 1960s and the 1970s were a time of free love, compared with other decades; 40-something baby boomers were more likely to have had 21 or more sex partners, compared with respondents in other age groups.

- AIDS has changed sexual behavior to some degree. Among those who were especially active (five or more partners in the past year), 76% had decided to slow down, use condoms faithfully, or get tested for HIV.

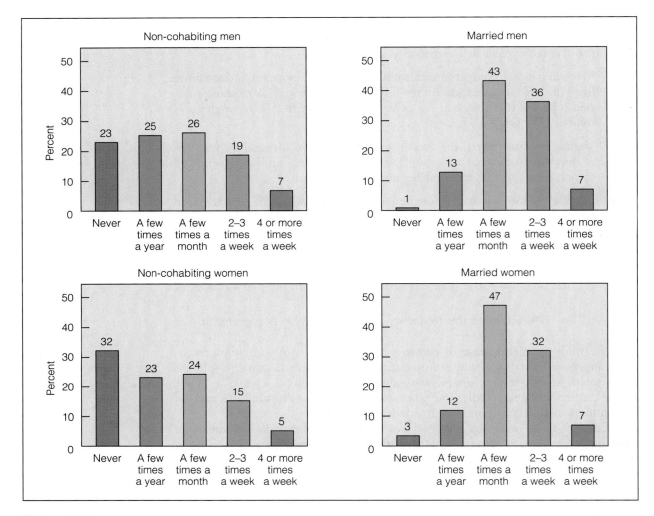

Figure 6.2 Frequency of Sexual Activity in the United States, 1994.
Source: Data from Laumann, Gagnon, Michael, Michaels, & Kolata (1995).

- The people who masturbate the most tend to be the people who also have sex the most. In team member John Gagnon's words, "If you're having sex a lot, you're thinking about sex a lot."

- Both men and women prefer receiving oral sex to giving it. White, college-educated men are more likely to have performed oral sex (80%) than Blacks (51%).

- Among women, 29% reported that they always have an orgasm during sex.

- Of women who had had an abortion, 72% had had only one.

- Fifty-four percent of men say they think about sex every day or several

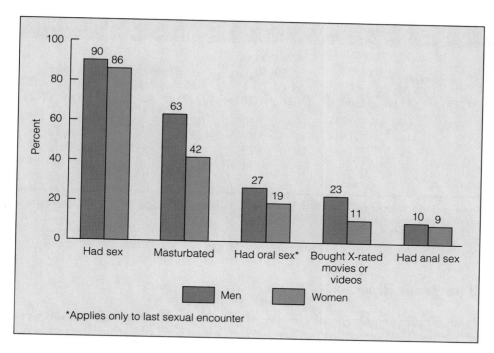

Figure 6.3 Sexual Practices Among American Men and Women, 1994. *Source:* Data from Laumann, Gagnon, Michael, Michaels, & Kolata (1995).

times a day; 67% of women say they think about it only a few times a week or a few times a month.

- Twenty-two percent of women say they have been forced by men to do sexual things they didn't want to do, but only 3% of men admit to ever having forced themselves on a woman.

Figure 6.3 summarizes the various sexual practices reported in the study.

Perhaps humorist Garrison Keillor has the last word on the University of Chicago study:

> Despite all you may have read lately, there is an incredible amount of normality going on in America these days, and it is good to know. Our country is not obsessed with sex. To the contrary. We wear ourselves out working, we are surrounded with noise and distraction and all manner of entertainment, we indulge our children as they run roughshod over our lives, the ghosts of old aunts and beady-eyed preachers lurk in the shadows watching us. Considering what the American couple is up against, it's astounding to think that once a week or once a month or maybe just on Memorial Day and Christmas or whenever the coast is clear, they are enjoying this gorgeous moment that is, despite its secrecy and long, shuddering climax, essentially the same experience as everyone else has had. It's almost worth all the misery of dealing with real estate people, bankers, lawyers and contractors—to have a home that has a bedroom where the two of you can go sometimes and do this. It is worth growing up and becoming middle-aged to be able to enjoy it utterly. (Keillor, 1994)

Table 6.1 Sexual Activity Across the Life Cycle Among American Men and Women, 1993									
FREQUENCY				**AGE (YEARS)**					
	16–26		27–38		39–50		51–64		65+	
Sample:	**M**	**F**	**M**	**F**	**M**	**F**	**M**	**F**	**M**	**F**
Numbers:	**(254)**	**(268)**	**(353)**	**(380)**	**(282)**	**(293)**	**(227)**	**(230)**	**(212)**	**(221)**
Daily	15%	13%	16%	8%	15%	10%	12%	4%	14%	1%
Few times a week	38	33	44	41	39	29	51	28	39	40
Weekly	19	22	23	27	29	29	18	33	16	33
Monthly	15	15	8	12	9	11	11	8	20	4
Rarely	13	17	9	12	8	21	8	27	11	22

Source: Adapted from *The Janus Report on Sexual Behavior* (p. 25) by S. S. Janus and C. L. Janus, 1993, New York: Wiley. Copyright 1993 by S. S Janus and C. L. Janus. Adapted by permission of John Wiley & Sons, Inc.

The *Janus Report*

In an excellent comprehensive survey of sexual behavior, Samuel Janus and Cynthia Janus (1993) compiled the *Janus Report*, which surveyed 2,765 Americans age 18 to over 65. This in-depth survey found that sexual activity was somewhat greater for men than for women across the life cycle, but that it decreased for both as they got older. However, sex continued to be rather common even for people in their 60s (Table 6.1). The researchers also found that sexual activity had begun earlier in life for members of each age group than it had for the next-oldest group among both males and females.

The *American Couples* Study

In a major study of sexual behavior among couples, Philip Blumstein and Pepper Schwartz (1983) surveyed 5,945 couples (11,890 individuals), of whom 3,574 (60%) were married couples, 642 (11%) cohabiting couples, 957 (16%) gay-male couples, and 772 (13%) lesbian couples. The results of their study were published in their book, *American Couples*. The couples interviewed were primarily White; about 40% had professional or technical careers, about 20% were managers and administrators, and the remaining 40% had a range of occupations. The value of this study lies both in its carefully conceived methodology and in the useful perspective it offers on various types of couples.

In terms of initiation of sex, about 50% of the husbands but only 12% of the wives felt they initiated sex more often than their partner. Thirty-three percent of the husbands and 40% of the wives felt they were about equal in initiating sex. The pattern was about the same for male and female cohabitors. Gay men and lesbians had very similar patterns, with 37% feeling that both partners initiated sex about equally, 31% feeling that they initiated more often, and the remaining 32% feeling that their partner was more often the initiator.

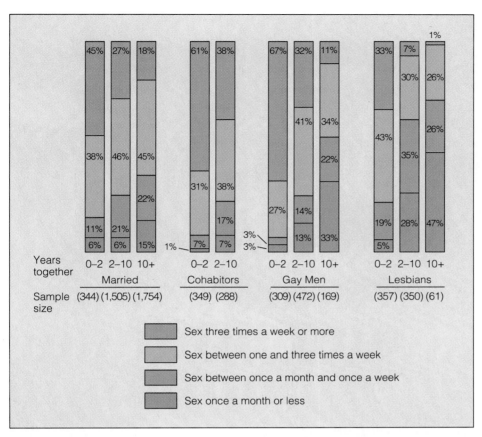

Figure 6.4 Frequency of Sexual Activity Among American Couples, 1983. *Source: American Couples* (p. 196) by P. Blumstein and P. W. Schwartz, 1983, New York: William Morrow. Copyright © 1983 by Philip Blumstein and Pepper Schwartz. Reprinted by permission of William Morrow & Co., Inc., pubs.

Sexual frequency was generally higher during the first 2 years of a relationship, with 45% of married couples having sex three times a week or more. In years 2–10, frequency dropped, with only 27% having sex three or more times a week. After 10 years of marriage, only 18% maintained that degree of frequency. Thirty-eight percent of couples married less than 2 years had sex one to three times a week. After 2–10 years of marriage, almost half (46%) of the couples dropped to this level. Cohabiting couples and gay-male couples who had been together less than 2 years were the most sexually active, with 61% and 67%, respectively, having sex three or more times a week. Again, as with married couples, frequency dropped after 2 years together. Lesbians were the least sexually active, and their frequency also dropped after 2 years in the relationship. Figure 6.4 shows frequency of sexual activity for all four groups during the time frames examined by the study.

In all of the couples, there was a direct relationship between sexual satisfaction and frequency of sex. Also, couples who were more satisfied with their relationship had sex more frequently. Couples who fought about things like parenting, household responsibilities, or how to spend money tended to have a less satisfying sexual relationship.

Research indicates that young people are becoming sexually active at an earlier age than in previous generations; they also tend to have more sexual partners. Currently, however, there seems to be a trend toward more conservative sexual behavior, perhaps because of the threat of sexually transmissible diseases.

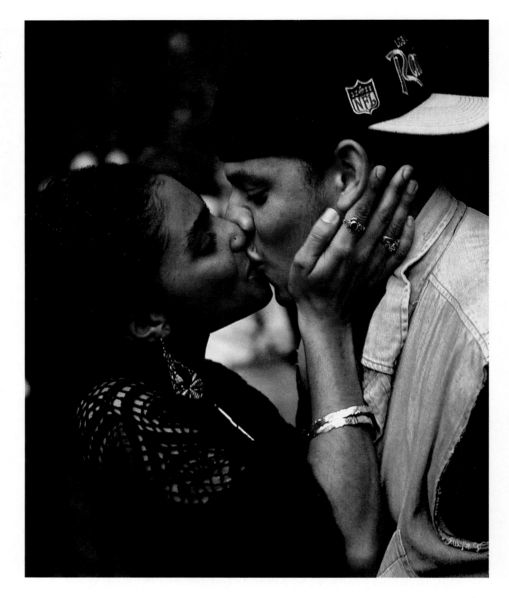

Gay-Male and Lesbian Sexual Behavior Surveyed

The Chicago study, the *Janus Report*, and the *American Couples* study all report different and sometimes contradictory data about lesbians and gay men. There are probably several reasons for these inconsistencies. One is the issue of definition and identity: Are you gay if you have one same-sex interaction? Or are you gay only if you identify yourself as gay?

Another issue is the stigmatization of homosexuality in our culture. Gay people are frequently the target of prejudice and sometimes of violence. Gay men and lesbians often experience discrimination in the employment and housing markets, and in most communities they hold little political power. Physical force is often used against them: Gangs of teenagers and young adults may terrorize homosexuals, and stories of police and the military using their power against gays are not uncommon.

Because of the stigma and the danger attached to "coming out," many gay men and lesbians choose not to reveal their sexual orientation to their families, friends, or co-workers—and certainly not to a stranger taking a survey! It is probably impossible to determine precisely what percentage of people in our society have engaged in homosexual behavior or consider themselves to be gay or lesbian. Kinsey and his associates found that by middle age, 50% of all males and 20% of all females reported some type of overt sexual experience with one or more members of the same sex (Kinsey et al., 1948). Furthermore, between adolescence and the later years of life, 37% of the men and 13% of the women had engaged in at least one sexual experience that culminated in orgasm with someone of the same sex. Four percent of the men and 2% of the women in Kinsey's studies reported that they were exclusively oriented affectionately only to members of their sex.

A study that appeared in 1989 reanalyzed data from a 1970 study of men and concluded that a minimum of 20% of the males had had sexual contact to orgasm with another male at least once in their life. About 7% had had such contact in adulthood; approximately 2% had had such contact in the past year. The researchers emphasized that these should be viewed as minimum estimates because people are likely to conceal such behavior (Fay, Turner, Klassen, & Gagnon, 1989). As we saw earlier, the Chicago study reported that only 2.7% of the men interviewed and 1.3% of the women said they had had a homosexual experience in the past 12 months.

Despite the prevalence of same-sex contact and despite the absence of evidence to support common stereotypes, society continues to discriminate against gay men and lesbians. For some people, aversion to homosexuals and homosexuality has developed into a phobia: **homophobia.** Many therapists and gays believe that people who are homophobic may be unconsciously or consciously hiding fears about their own sexual orientation. For example, many gay men who are out of the closet today (i.e., open about their sexual orientation) admit to having participated in "gay-bashing" incidents in the past, to convince others and themselves that they were straight.

In nearly all ways, gay-male and lesbian relationships are like heterosexual relationships. In general, gay men and lesbians have increasingly moved toward developing and maintaining ongoing relationships with one person. Because they have had to struggle with coming out and have often experienced considerable rejection by their families, gay men and lesbians, like other groups, frequently develop skills and strengths that are valuable in relationships. These include an ability to connect emotionally with other people of both sexes, flexible role relationships and an ability to adapt to a partner, an ability to negotiate and share decision-making power, caring and effective parenting among those who choose to become parents, psychological perceptiveness, and effective communication skills.

Many gay-male and lesbian couples build satisfying relationships. One study compared relationship satisfaction among comparable samples of gay-male, lesbian, and heterosexual couples and found no significant differences. All three groups rated their relationships highly satisfying (Peplau, Padesky, & Hamilton, 1981). Emotional expressiveness—"being able to talk about my most intimate feelings"—was cited by both heterosexual and homosexual women as very important. Lesbians placed a high value on equality in relationships; the most satisfying relationships were those in which both partners were equally committed, equally "in love," and equal in power (Peplau & Amaro, 1982).

Same-sex couples share other characteristics with heterosexual couples. For example, the frequency of sexual activity declines over time among gay-male, lesbian, and heterosexual couples. Like heterosexual couples, gays and lesbians sometimes have problems over who initiates sex. Although among heterosexuals the man is typically the initiator, in same-sex couples, the more emotionally expressive partner usually initiates sex (Blumstein & Schwartz, 1983).

Sex Education

Where do Americans get their sex education? Unfortunately, the *Janus Report* found that most people learn about sex "on the street" from their peers. Home ranked second as a source of sex education, followed by school and, rarely, church (Janus & Janus, 1993).

Consequences of Inadequate Sex Education

Because so little of our sex education is adequate, we have become a country with major sexual and parenting challenges, such as AIDS and adolescent motherhood. The United States leads the world in rates of teenage pregnancy and abortion (U.S. Bureau of the Census, 1994). Adolescent pregnancy in the United States could be described as epidemic: The rate is twice that of France, England, and Canada; three times that of Sweden; and seven times that of the Netherlands. Each year in the United States over 1 million unmarried women become pregnant, and 10,000 of those pregnancies are in girls 15 years of age or younger. In 1991, 30% of all births were to unmarried women; the rate for Whites was 22% and for African Americans, 68% (U.S. Bureau of the Census, 1994). Clearly, compared with other Western nations that have similar standards of living, levels of industrial development, and forms of government, the United States has a much higher rate of teenage pregnancy. This higher rate can be attributed to the increasing rate of sex among teenagers and to the irregular and ineffective use of contraception by American adolescents (Miller & Moore, 1991).

The rise in adolescent pregnancy in this country has a multitude of negative consequences. The problems associated with "children having children" are enormous. The father usually disappears from the picture, and the young mother ends up rearing the child alone. This often places an extra burden on the grandparents, who may not be overjoyed to be "parents" again. And although the young mother needs a decent education, she may find it difficult to continue in school. Young mothers often experience serious financial problems, inadequate housing, lack of transportation, loneliness, poor nutrition, physical health problems, and a cluster of other stressors that foster a situation where child neglect and abuse are common (Furstenburg, Brooks-Gunn, & Morgan, 1988).

"My parents were intelligent, sensitive individuals, and yet they treated the subject of sex like it was the plague," said Joyce, a 45-year-old single mother of three. "All I knew for sure was this must really be something if it was such a big secret! What happened with my brothers and sister (and me) was there were a lot of misconceptions and a lot of guilt.

"As a parent, what kind of message did I give my children? In my head I knew what I wanted to give them, but in my gut I was still at war with my own sexuality. So I, too, gave mixed messages to my children about sex. It wasn't until I went back to college full-time after my divorce and got into a human sexuality class that the shift really came for me internally. I began to stop feeling self-conscious and began to relax—to enjoy being human. I still have one child living at home, and I'm able to talk openly and honestly with him about any subject regarding sex.

"I feel strongly about good sex education for our children. Two years ago I would have been floored by the idea of showing films on sexual intercourse, masturbation, and gay and lesbian lovemaking to 12-year-olds and their parents in a church setting. Today, I would support it 100%. I wish sex education could be available to all children and their parents at least by the time kids are 12 years old."

Sex-Education Programs

The high rate of adolescent pregnancy and the long list of problems it causes in families have led to the development of a wide variety of sex-education programs across the country (Miller & Moore, 1991). (To find out how good your sex education has been, take the quiz in Box 6.1, p. 202.) A recent survey of 802 American adults indicated that a little more than half of the respondents had taken a sex-education class at some time in their life. Sixty-eight percent of the younger adults, those between the ages of 18 and 24, had taken such a class. Classes are commonly held in public and private schools and in churches and synagogues (Allen-Meares, 1989).

Currently, more than 80% of American adults favor sex education (Janus & Janus, 1993). The Janus survey found that sex education is favored by 86% of the population and that 89% want courses for children age 12 and older to deal with birth control information. About 75% of the adults want the courses to talk about homosexuality and abortion. Planned Parenthood, a national private nonprofit organization, has developed a wide variety of presentations and materials to benefit young people. The example of the organization's materials that is displayed in Box 6.2 (p. 203) lists some common misconceptions young people have about sex— "ridiculous ideas" that can lead to trouble.

BOX 6.1

Testing Your Knowledge About Sex

For more than 40 years, the Kinsey Institute at Indiana University has been pioneering in the scientific study of human sexuality. In a Roper poll conducted for the Kinsey Institute, 2,000 adults in the United States were asked a series of true-or-false and multiple-choice questions about sex. Only 45% of those tested answered more than half the questions correctly. See how you do on this sample of the questions.

CIRCLE
TRUE OR
FALSE

T F   1. Most women prefer a sex partner who has a large penis.

T F   2. Menopause does not cause a woman to lose interest in having sex.

——   3. When does the average American first have sexual intercourse?

——   4. Of every 10 women in the United States, how many would you estimate have ever masturbated?

T F   5. More than 25% of American males have had a same-sex sexual experience.

T F   6. Anal intercourse between uninfected people can cause AIDS.

T F   7. Most husbands have extramarital affairs.

——   8. What percentage of women engage in anal sex?

T F   9. Problems with erections are most often started by a physical problem.

T F   10. Almost all erection problems can be successfully treated.

——   11. What do you think is the average length of a man's penis?

T F   12. Lubricants like Vaseline Intensive Care or baby oil can cause microscopic holes in a condom or diaphragm.

T F   13. Homosexuality is usually difficult to tell just by people's appearance or gestures.

T F   14. A woman can get pregnant if she has sex during her menstrual period.

T F   15. A woman can get pregnant even if the man withdraws his penis before ejaculating.

Source: Adapted from *The Kinsey Institute New Report on Sex* (p. 45) by J. Reinisch and R. Beasley, 1994, New York: St. Martin's. Copyright © 1994 by The Kinsey Institute for Research in Sex, Gender, and Reproduction. Reprinted by permission.

Answers: 1. F; 2, T; 3. age 16 or 17; 4. 6–8; 5. T; 6. F; 7. F; 8. 30–40%; 9. T; 10. T; 11. 5–7 inches; 12. T; 13. T; 14. T; 15. T

Sex Education and Parents

Although people disagree about sexuality, there is agreement on one issue—that education about sexuality should begin in the home (Gordon & Snyder, 1989; Koop, 1988). The reason that the schools, religious institutions, and agencies like Planned Parenthood have become involved in sex education is that most parents feel incapable of or uncomfortable about talking seriously with their offspring about sexual matters. A subtle conspiracy of silence exists between parent and child. Parents tell themselves that they are willing to answer any questions their children might have about sex, but children sense that their parents really do not want to talk about these sensitive issues. Because both feel uncomfortable talking about sexuality, the subject is avoided.

B O X   6 . 2

Ten Ridiculous Ideas That Will Make You a Parent

1. You can count on your partner to use birth control.

2. Men have stronger sex drives than women do.

3. Men need to have sex with different women to learn to be better lovers.

4. If a woman uses birth control, then she has probably been sleeping around.

5. A woman would do anything to keep from getting pregnant.

6. It is easy for a woman to get on the pill.

7. If a man hasn't gone all the way by the time he's 16, then something is wrong with him.

8. Condoms are *not* cool.

9. When a woman says "no," she really just wants to be talked into it.

10. I could never talk to my partner about birth control.

Source: Adapted with permission from the brochure "Ten Ridiculous Ideas That Will Make a Father Out of You," © 1984, Planned Parenthood of Central Oklahoma, 619 N.W. 23rd Street, Oklahoma City, OK 73103.

Few children receive direct instruction from their parents in the areas of sexuality, sexual intercourse, or birth control (Miller & Moore, 1991). This is a sad state of affairs because good parental communication about sex may forestall or postpone a child's sexual activity. Among those daughters who are sexually active, parental verbal communication appears to help promote more effective contraceptive practices on the part of the adolescent. An interesting study of family interaction patterns in homes with teenagers found that adolescents who reported open communication and satisfaction with family interaction also reported more sex education in the home (Baldwin & Baranoski, 1990).

Sol Gordon and Judith Gordon (1990) concur that parents who accept their children's sexuality and help them learn to cope with it have a better chance of raising healthy and sexually responsible children than parents who avoid the issues. The Gordons urge parents to become "askable," positing that young people who can talk freely with their parents about sex will be stronger and more able to make wise choices as they grow to adulthood. Surveying more than 8,000 students, the Gordons found fewer than 15% reporting that they received a meaningful sex education from their parents. Girls were usually told about menstruation; the balance of their teaching could be summed up in one word: *don't*. Except for the occasional single prepuberty talk with Dad, who used vague birds-and-bees analogies and ended by mentioning the use of a condom, the boys were on their own.

Brent Miller and his colleagues studied how strictness of parenting was related to adolescents' sexual attitudes and behaviors (Miller, McCoy, Olson, & Wallace, 1986). These researchers hypothesized and found a curvilinear relationship between flexibility in parenting and sexual behavior. Sexual promiscuity and the experience

Because parents tend to be poor at providing their children with clear, useful information about sex, the responsibility for sex education in our society has fallen largely to schools and communities. Sex education is more effective when combined with access to a health clinic where contraceptives are available.

of intercourse were highest among teenagers who saw their parents as not being strict or as not having any rules (chaotic on the Circumplex Model), lowest among those teens who reported that their parents were moderately strict (flexible on the Circumplex Model), and intermediate among teenagers who saw their parents as being very strict and having many rules (rigid on the Circumplex Model). The results of this study suggest that if parents are concerned about adolescent sexual behavior, they can err in two directions: by being either too lenient (chaotic) or too strict (rigid). The more balanced levels (being structured or flexible on the Circumplex Model) are related to more responsible sexual behavior on the part of adolescents.

"It's very difficult finding the right balance with our kids," James, a middle-aged father in Cleveland, Ohio, noted. "I think we're doing okay, but you never know for sure until they're grown up and have made it safely through the difficult years of adolescence and young adulthood. We try to give them guidance, some things to think about when it comes to sexuality.

"But we try not to be too strict or moralistic because we know that can backfire. And really, they're going to do what they want to anyway, no matter what we say. We can only cross our fingers and hope their judgment is reasonably good.

"My own judgment as a young person was pretty good. I did make some mistakes, but I learned from them. I know my kids will make some mistakes, too, and I suspect they'll learn from them. I just hope the mistakes aren't irreversible."

A New Approach to Sex Ed

A recent approach for discouraging adolescent girls from getting pregnant is an 8-pound doll called Baby Think It Over. The doll looks innocent enough, but if you put it down for any length of time, it emits a high-pitched cry that sounds like a real baby. The shrieks occur at random intervals day and night. The only way to stop them is by inserting a key in the doll's back and holding it for 20–30 minutes, the average time it takes to feed a real newborn.

Teenage girls who have taken Baby Think It Over home for 3 days come back to school looking like they have been the subjects of a sleep-deprivation experiment. In other words, they look like real moms.

"I'm going to wait at least 10 years," said one exhausted San Diego high school student after her stint with the doll.

Source: From "Teens Need Dolls' Drastic Lessons" by David Grimes, 1994, Sarasota *Herald-Tribune*. Copyright © 1994 by David Grimes. Reprinted by permission of the Sarasota *Herald-Tribune*, Sarasota, FL.

Is Sex Education Effective?

Do sex-education programs work? After a 7-year study of nine programs around the country, a six-volume analysis by Mathtech Inc. concluded that certain conditions must be met if sex-education programs are to be effective (Leo, 1986). Two of the nine programs were very successful: They had strong backing from parents and the local community. The use of birth control increased only when the sex-education program was coupled with ready access to a health clinic. Graduates of sex-education programs were less permissive about nonmarital sex than young people in control groups.

A Minnesota-based program recorded 40% lower birth rates in schools with health clinics (Stark, 1986). Of the adolescent mothers who used the clinics, 80% stayed in school, and repeat pregnancies were almost nonexistent. Follow-up contact was necessary in such programs, however, because teenagers are poor at remembering to use birth control (Leo, 1986). This supports other studies reporting that only 14% of teenage girls used contraceptives the first time they had intercourse.

Most Western nations try to reduce adolescent pregnancy through programs emphasizing abstinence but offer the alternative of effective contraceptives to those who choose to remain or become sexually active. In the United States, "Just Say No" programs are promoted heavily, but there is little research evidence to conclude that they are very effective (Christopher & Roosa, 1990; St. Pierre, Mark, Kaltreider, & Aikin, 1995). As in Europe, the most effective American programs encourage abstinence but also offer an alternative for those who are already or who choose to become sexually active. Box 6.3 provides an example of a recent approach to discouraging teenage pregnancy.

Premarital Sexual Behavior

In the 1960s, about two thirds of American adults felt premarital or nonmarital sex was wrong, according to a Gallup poll. By the late 1980s, adults in this country were about evenly split, with half saying it was wrong "for a man and a woman to have sex relations before marriage" and about half saying it was not wrong. The pollsters believed this to be a dramatic turnaround in attitudes (Gallup Inc., 1989).

Sexual Behavior Among Adolescents

Young people have their own ideas about nonmarital sex, of course, and their behavior often does not square with adults' attitudes. A recent government survey found that 54% of the nation's high school students in grades 9–12 had had sex (Kolbe, 1992). Of that number, 39% said they had had sex in the 3 months before the survey. Among 9th graders, 40% of those surveyed said they had had sex. Among 10th graders, the figure rose to 48%. By 11th grade, it was 57%, and by 12th grade, 72%. This survey of 11,631 students, conducted in 1990, was the first the government had made. Although the researchers did not have data for earlier generations of young people, they believe that today's high school students are perhaps the most sexually active in history.

Students were asked to identify the birth control method they or their partner had used to prevent pregnancy the last time they had had sex. Forty-five percent reported using condoms, 33% reported using another method of contraception (e.g., birth control pills, withdrawal), and 22% reported not using any birth control (Kolbe, 1992).

Pregnancy is not the only concern for sexually active teenagers. They also risk contracting a sexually transmissible disease (STD), such as herpes or HIV infection. One in 25 students reported having had an STD (Kolbe, 1992).

Sexual Behavior Among College Students

Research on the sexual behavior of college students also indicates that premarital intercourse has continued to increase consistently (Robinson, Ziss, Ganza, Katz, & Robinson, 1991). Ira Robinson and his colleagues surveyed students about nonmarital sexual behavior every 5 years for more than 20 years (1965, 1970, 1975, 1980, 1985). They found that nonmarital sexual activity among college males increased 14.2% and that female nonmarital sexual activity jumped 34.3% between 1965 and 1985. As indicated in Table 6.2, the percentages of both males and females who had experienced intercourse increased from one time period to the next in almost every instance.

In addition to concluding that nonmarital sex has become more common over the years, Robinson and his colleagues (1991) also concluded that differences between male and female attitudes regarding sex decreased over the years. A certain contradiction in values was seen, however. Although more college students were engaging in sexual intercourse, the percentage of those who thought nonmarital

Table 6.2 Premarital Sex Among American College Students, 1965–1985

Year	Males		Females	
	Percentage	Number	Percentage	Number
1965	65.1	129	28.7	115
1970	65.0	136	37.3	158
1975	73.9	115	57.1	275
1980	77.4	168	63.5	230
1985	79.3	208	63.0	257

Source: From "Twenty Years of the Sexual Revolution, 1965–1985: An Update" by I. E. Robinson, K. Ziss, B. Ganza, S. Katz, E. Robinson, 1991, *Journal of Marriage and the Family*, 53, p. 217. Copyright © 1991 by the National Council on Family Relations. Reprinted by permission.

sex was immoral and sinful also increased. The old double standard gave males greater license for sexual behavior than females. The "new" double standard (reflected by the contradiction in attitudes) imposes greater sexual restrictions on others than on oneself.

The *Janus Report* found that the age of first sexual intercourse has become progressively younger over the years (Janus & Janus, 1993). The most dramatic difference was between people currently 18–26 and those over 65. Of males in the younger age group, 91% had had sex by age 18; only about 60% of the males 65 and older had had sex by that age. More differences were reported for women. By age 18, 83% of the 18–26 year olds had had sex; of the women 65 and older, only 41% had had sex by the age of 18. It is clear that younger people are having sex earlier than the group just ahead of them in age.

Marital and Extramarital Sexual Behavior

Surveys indicate that most young people have intercourse before marriage; in fact, premarital relationships are often highly sexual. After marriage, the sexual relationship gradually changes. Some people have jokingly asked, "Is there sex after marriage?" Research indicates there is.

Sex Within Marriage

When newspaper columnist Ann Landers asked her readers, "Has your sex life gone downhill since you got married?" 82% of the 141,210 people who responded said yes, sex after marriage was less exciting (Landers, 1989). However, intimacy—feelings of warmth and closeness between two people who love each other—does not appear to diminish with time. Within the intimate environment of a happy marriage, sexual experiences can become more satisfying and meaningful—and retain their excitement—over time.

Table 6.3 Sexual Activity Among American Married, Divorced, and Single People, 1993

FREQUENCY	MARRIED Sample Size: (1,552)	DIVORCED (246)	SINGLE (815)
Daily	14%	9%	11%
Few times weekly	44	33	32
Weekly	27	26	21
Monthly	8	10	17
Rarely	7	22	19
TOTAL	100	100	100

Source: Adapted from *The Janus Report on Sexual Behavior* (p. 159) by S. S. Janus and C. L. Janus, 1993, New York: Wiley. Copyright 1993 by S. S. Janus and C. L. Janus. Adapted by permission of John Wiley & Sons, Inc.

The *Janus Report* indicated that married couples have higher levels of sexual activity than divorced people and single people, as shown in Table 6.3 (Janus & Janus, 1993). More specifically, 58% of the married couples reported having sexual activity at least a few times a week, compared with 43% of singles and 42% of divorced people. Conversely, only 7% of married people rarely had sex, whereas the figure was 19% for singles and 22% for divorced people. In other words, married couples across the life cycle are even more active sexually than singles.

A hectic life often gets in the way of an active sex life. Long hours on the job and caring for children, continual interruptions, and countless other stresses tend to tire people out and decrease their sexual activity. For those couples with two jobs, the phenomenon has been called the **DINS** (double income, no sex) **dilemma.** Therapists have labeled it inhibited or hypoactive sexual desire. In addition to sheer fatigue, boredom is also cited as a factor by some individuals. Most of the time couples can resuscitate the sexual relationship with some tender care and concern, such as having dinner out together, seeing a movie, or going to bed early. Consulting a marriage and family therapist or a sex therapist may be useful for persistent sexual problems. The preeminent sex researchers and therapists William Masters and Virginia Johnson with Robert Kolodny (1988) argued in *Masters & Johnson on Sex and Human Loving* that half of all American couples are troubled by some type of sexual distress, ranging from disinterest to genuine sexual dysfunction. Some couples need therapy, but many others can benefit simply by heeding the 16 ideas outlined in Box 6.4.

For many people, sex is not the most important thing in life. A nationwide survey of 815 men found that the most important thing in a man's life is not sex, career, fame, or fortune, but marriage, according to 75% of the married men in the sample (Hellmich, 1990). About 90% of these husbands called their wife their best friend. Friendship, based on trust and sharing of responsibilities, becomes more important as life's challenges mount and sexual energy decreases (Hellmich, 1990).

Couples commonly reported that the number of times they had sex decreased somewhat as their years together passed. A study of 100 happily married couples reported that one third said they have intercourse about three times a month

BOX 6.4

Advice from Masters and Johnson on Sexual Health

1. Always remember that good sex begins while your clothes are still on.

2. Take time to think about yourself as a sexual being.

3. Take responsibility for your own sexual pleasure.

4. Talk with your partner about sex.

5. Make time to be together regularly.

6. Don't let sex become routine.

7. Use fantasy—you'll find it's one of the best aphrodisiacs.

8. Understand that working at sex doesn't work.

9. Don't carry anger into your bedroom.

10. Realize that good sex isn't just a matter of pushing the right buttons.

11. Nurture the romance in your life.

12. Don't make sex too serious.

13. Don't always wait to be "in the mood" before agreeing to have sex.

14. Realize that you and your partner don't have to see eye to eye sexually.

15. Don't be afraid to ask for help.

16. Try to keep your sexual expectations realistic.

Source: Adapted from *Masters and Johnson on Sex and Human Loving* (pp. 452–461), copyright © 1982, 1985, 1986, 1988 by William H. Masters, M.D., Virginia E. Johnson, and Robert Kolodny, M.D. By permission of Little, Brown and Co.

(Woodman, 1986). In some surveys, sex ranks low among the most rewarding aspects of life. In fact, sex ranked fifth—after love, health and fitness, friendship, and children—in the study of 100 happy couples (Woodman, 1986). Many family and sex therapists agree that some couples have happy, stable marital relationships with little sex. However, without sex, the relationship may develop a kind of coolness, and one or both partners may feel unfulfilled.

Although sex is clearly not everything, it is important to an intimate relationship. David Knox, director of the marriage therapy program at East Carolina University, explained it succinctly, "When sex goes well, it is 15 percent of a relationship, but if it goes badly, it's 85 percent." Sex is more than a simple physical need; "it represents identity, desirability, an affirmation of one's self. We attach many important psychological needs to our sexuality. That's why it's such a revealing area." In a similar vein, Gene Abel noted, "Anyone can say I care about you, and you may believe it or not. But during sex we naturally evaluate how our partner seems to feel about us. If loving feelings are there, they come through. If they are lacking, that comes through, too" (cited in Woodman, 1986, pp. 130–131).

Different people have different needs for sexual intimacy, and those needs affect how they perceive their sexual behavior. For this reason, couples must communicate clearly about sex if they are to maintain a satisfying relationship. The movie *Annie Hall* depicts two lovers with different perceptions of their sexual relationship. When a therapist asks them (separately) how often they have sex, the character played by Woody Allen answers, "Hardly ever, maybe three times a week." The character played by Diane Keaton replies, "Constantly, three times a week."

Overall, it appears that in many marriages sex is very important for long-term happiness. It has powerful symbolic value in a successful marriage, reaffirming the bond between the individuals. It is an indication that everything is still okay despite wrinkles, sags, and "love handles." To keep the spark in their lovemaking, married couples need to keep the relationship alive through communication and sharing. It is very difficult to have a successful sexual relationship if each partner does not feel good about himself or herself and the couple does not feel good about other aspects of their relationship.

> "Our sexual relationship is great today," noted Serena, a middle-aged woman living in St. Louis. "It's a lot better than it was early in our marriage. I don't know why exactly, but I think we're more used to each other, more comfortable with each other. Perhaps we really love each other more. As the years pass, you look back and see a long-term tradition of commitment and kindness, and recognize that you have really created a wonderful marriage together.
>
> "That's very special, and it makes you feel so very close to each other. It's hard to explain, but we do have a very sexy relationship with each other. Perhaps not as often as before, but it sure can be full of fire and tenderness."

Extramarital Sex

Where there is marriage without love, there will be love without marriage.
—Benjamin Franklin, 1733/1980, p. 347

Extramarital friendships are common in American society. As one husband put it, "It doesn't make a whole lot of sense to deny friendships across-the-board to half the human race. If I enjoy talking with a person at work, it doesn't make sense to lose this friendship just because she's a female." Ideally, couples should allow each other the freedom to develop relationships outside the marriage. But if they are not properly handled, friendships with members of the other sex can harm a marriage. These friendships can sometimes develop into extramarital sexual relationships, which are commonly cited as one reason for divorce. Opinion is divided on whether men and women can be friends—loving, affectionate, accepting, and so on—without becoming sexually involved.

"Have you had sex with someone other than your spouse?" Many researchers have asked American adults that probing question since the 1950s. In a 1990 Gallup telephone survey, fewer than 10% of the respondents said they had been unfaithful (Cox News Service, 1990). Recall that the 1994 University of Chicago study cited earlier found that about 25% of the husbands and 15% of the wives had been unfaithful at least once. The results of any study of the incidence of extramarital sex are highly debatable. There is the likelihood of underreporting because, as family therapist Frank Pittman notes, "if people would lie to their own husbands or wives, they would lie to a poll taker" (Cox News Service, 1990; Pittman, 1993a, 1993b).

Pittman, who has spent 30 years counseling people who have committed adultery, notes that affairs can be *very* different in terms of duration and intensity. The thousands of affairs he reports to have seen seem to fall into four broad categories: the most common, accidental infidelity (unintended and uncharacteristic acts of carelessness that really did "just happen"); romantic infidelity (falling in love, "the craziest and most destructive form of infidelity"); marital arrangements (calling in marital "aides" to keep one company while failing to deal positively with a deficient marriage); and philandering (although there are female philanderers, this is a predominantly male activity, in which infidelity is a hobby) (Pittman, 1993a, 1993b).

Pittman (1993a) identifies seven major myths about infidelity:

- *Everybody is unfaithful—it's a normal, expectable behavior.* Actually, we don't know how many people are unfaithful, but Pittman believes that most people are faithful most of the time.

- *Affairs are good for you; an affair can revive a dull marriage.* An affair can shake up a petrified marriage, and sometimes things work out, but in reality, an affair can "blow hell out of a marriage."

- *People have affairs because they don't love their marriage partners.* Pittman observes that "it routinely turns out that the marriage was fine before the affair happened and the decision that they were not in love with their marriage partner was an effort to explain and justify the affair."

- *People have affairs because they are oversexed.* Pittman argues, to the contrary, that "most affairs consist of a little bad sex and hours on the telephone." Most affairs are really about secrets: secret telephone calls and furtive lunches. "Affairs generally involve sex, at least enough to create a secret that seals the conspiratorial alliance of the affair, and makes the relationship tense, dangerous, and thus exciting."

- *Affairs are ultimately the wife's fault.* In a patriarchal society, it is assumed that when a man is unfaithful, it is because of the wife's aesthetic, sexual, or emotional deficiencies. But Pittman argues that "there is no point in holding the cuckold responsible for the infidel's sexual behavior unless the cuckold has total control over the sexual equipment that has run off the road. . . . Only the driver is responsible."

- *It's best to pretend not to know.* Silence fuels an affair, which can survive only on secrecy. "Adulterous marriages begin their repair only when the secret is out in the open, and the infidel does not need to hide any longer."

- *After an affair, divorce is inevitable.* With therapy, "most adulterous marriages can be saved, and may even be stronger and more intimate than they were before the crisis."

Family therapists counsel couples dealing with the crisis of infidelity and try to help them work through the situation in a cautious and rational manner. A professional therapist can be very helpful by encouraging spouses to be calm and honest in disclosing their motives. Infidelity can be a signal of the end of the relationship, or it can be a catalyst for dramatic and positive growth in the marriage.

Toward Sexual Health

Sex is an important part of human life, health, and happiness. It's a crucial ingredient in individual well-being and in intimate relationships, especially marriage. Problems in sexual functioning therefore need to be addressed if people are to have successful relationships.

Sexual Problems and Dysfunctions

When is sex a problem in one's life? In the words of sexologists Mary Calderone and Eric Johnson:

> Sex and human sexuality are not—or should not be—problems unless we human beings make them so. When and how do they become problems? In general terms, when they are used or expressed in ways that are harmful to any person or persons; when people are unable to express them in ways that they find satisfying and creative; and when they become associated with such negative feelings as anger, jealousy, fear, and guilt. (Calderone & Johnson, 1989, pp. 154–155)

Among the most common sexual problems are, for men, the inability to achieve and/or maintain an erection and, for women, the inability to reach orgasm. Many sexual problems arise from beliefs and attitudes about sex that are narrow or incorrect. Calderone and Johnson (1989) summarized a variety of general problems including the beliefs that sexuality is limited to the genitals, that sex equals intercourse, and that one's performance must be flawless. Unrealistic expectations about sex also played a role.

It is estimated that, at some time in their marriage, 50% of all married couples have sexual dysfunctions (Masters et al., 1992). Masters and his colleagues define **sexual dysfunction** as a state in which sexual behavior or the lack of it becomes a "source of anxiety, anguish, and frustration that often leads to general unhappiness and distress in personal relationships" (p. 367).

What Causes Sexual Dysfunction?   There are two causative categories for sexual dysfunction, according to Masters and his colleagues (1992). **Organic sexual dysfunctions** are related to physiological factors; **psychosocial sexual dysfunctions** are related to psychological, developmental, interpersonal, environmental, or cultural factors. The researchers note that it may not be possible to identify the precise cause of a particular form of dysfunction, and that some dysfunctions may have multiple causes. Organic factors cause 10–20% of all cases of sexual dysfunction and contribute to the dysfunction in another 15% of all cases, the researchers estimate. For example, a man may have difficulty achieving or maintaining an erection as a result of numerous medical conditions, including diabetes and alcoholism. Prescription medicines (e.g., drugs for high blood pressure) and street drugs (e.g., amphetamines, barbiturates, and narcotics) can cause erection difficulties (Masters et al., 1992).

Psychological factors that can result in sexual dysfunction are numerous. Developmental factors include troubled parent-child relationships, negative family attitudes toward sex and sexuality, traumatic childhood or adolescent sexual experiences, and conflict over one's gender identity (one's sense of being male or female). Personal factors include a variety of fears: of poor sexual performance, of pregnancy, of venereal disease, of rejection, of pain, of becoming close to someone, of losing control, or even of success. Interpersonal factors that can be related to sexual problems include poor communication and frequent power struggles between partners; hostility, distrust or deceit; lack of mutual physical attraction; and gender-role conflicts (Masters et al., 1992).

Types of Sexual Dysfunction Male sexual dysfunction is expressed in a variety of ways. These include **erectile dysfunction** (formerly called impotence), the inability to achieve or maintain an erection that is firm enough for intercourse. (Isolated episodes of the inability to achieve or maintain an erection are nearly universal among men.) **Premature ejaculation,** or rapid ejaculation, is difficult to define precisely, although it is a common sexual dysfunction. It causes problems in a sexual relationship when the woman is dissatisfied because the man reaches orgasm much more quickly than she does. **Retarded ejaculation,** the opposite of premature ejaculation, describes a dysfunction in which a long and strenuous effort is needed to reach orgasm. **Ejaculatory incompetence** is a man's inability to ejaculate in his partner's vagina despite a firm erection and a high level of sexual arousal. **Painful intercourse,** often believed to be a problem only for women, can also affect men. Pain can be felt in the penis and/or testicles or internally; the pain is often related to a problem with the seminal vesicles or the prostate gland (J.C. Coleman, 1988; Insel & Roth, 1996; Masters et al., 1992).

Female sexual dysfunctions include **vaginismus,** a condition in which the muscles of the outer third of the vagina respond with involuntary spasms to attempts at penetration, preventing intercourse. **Anorgasmia** is the inability to have an orgasm. **Rapid orgasm,** reaching orgasm too quickly, is the much-ignored female counterpart to male premature ejaculation. Painful intercourse, including burning, sharp or searing pain, or cramping, is also a common problem in women (J.C. Coleman, 1988; Insel & Roth, 1996; Masters et al., 1992).

Sexual dysfunctions are generally something people are uncomfortable admitting to themselves and discussing with others. We can laugh and leer about sex, but our culture has a difficult time talking honestly and openly about it.

Sex Therapy

Many people with sexual difficulties go without help for a long time. This is unfortunate, because most **sex therapy** is simply a process of education. Sex therapists instruct clients (people who seek sex therapy are not called patients) in the gentle art of lovemaking.

Reputable professional sex therapists are trained in the subjects of sex and sexuality and have experience working with many different people regarding sexual needs and dysfunctions. A national organization called the American Association of Sex Educators, Counselors, and Therapists (AASECT) has established criteria for certifying as sex therapists individuals who have met its training standards. AASECT has also developed ethical principles for the practice of sex therapy. The group will provide by mail a list of certified counselors and sex therapists for a small charge.*

Sex educators typically work with large groups of people and teach general information and principles that are useful to a variety of individuals. **Sex therapists** typically work with individuals, couples, or small groups of individuals and couples and focus more on individual concerns and problems. Based on content alone, it can be difficult to know whether one is witnessing a sex therapy session or a sex-education session. There is a good deal of overlap between the two approaches, so much so that some professionals do not distinguish between sex education and sex therapy.

Solving Sexual Problems   Sex therapy can involve a number of different components, including the following:

- Learning more about basic anatomy.
- Learning what one's true feelings are about the body.
- Learning what one's basic attitudes toward sex and sexuality are.
- Learning to relax with a partner and to get in a sexually responsive mood.
- Learning to sense one's own body and how the setting affects the body's responses.
- Learning sexual techniques.
- Exploring one's own and one's partner's body.
- Developing new sexual attitudes and techniques and maintaining them over time.

Sex therapists are quick to point out that couples with sexual problems should not rush into intercourse but should take the time to enjoy each other's company and to touch each other in a variety of loving ways. Masters and Johnson, for example, allowed no intercourse at all in the first weeks of sex therapy. Instead, couples were taught the art of touching as pleasurable in itself. Intercourse may happen, but it is not the goal (Cohen, 1987).

Therapists assert that a sure way to decrease lovemaking pleasure is to set intercourse and orgasm as its goals. Sex therapists Susan Dean and Adele P. Kennedy advise:

> When you are goal-oriented you are no longer in the present. You interrupt your responses when you try to anticipate the next step. Stay focused on the moment so that you receive all that is being offered. Touch is, in and of itself, the pleasure. Any by-product is coincidental to the experience, although it is to be enjoyed and appreciated. The motivation is to sensitize your body to its intrinsic capacity. (cited in Cohen, 1987, p. 87)

---

*AASECT, P.O. Box 238, Mt. Vernon, IA 52314; 319-895-8407.

The PLISSIT Model   One approach to sex therapy, developed by Jack Annon, is the **PLISSIT Model** (Annon, 1994). PLISSIT applies four levels of treatment, from the relatively simple to the more in-depth, in an ordered progression: permission (P), limited information (LI), specific suggestion (SS), and intensive therapy (IT). In the first and simplest level, clients received *permission* from an authority or another respected individual to engage in certain sexual behaviors. For example, many people in our society view sex negatively. They may need reassurance that a particular behavior is relatively harmless—for example, "Yes, masturbation is normal."

The second level is *limited information*, which can be picked up from a friend, a sexuality course, or reading. For example, a young man might be depressed and feel inadequate because he believes his penis is too small; this, in turn, may affect his sexual behavior. Through discussion with a friend, attendance at a course on human sexuality, or reading, the young man might learn that comparisons of penis size should not be made when the organ is in the flaccid state (that seen in the locker room) because erect penises differ less in size than do flaccid ones. He might also learn that there is no correlation between penis size and a woman's sexual satisfaction. With this information, the young man will feel better about himself and may be more sexually responsive. Without this information, his fears and feelings of inadequacy may develop into more serious sexual problems.

The third level, *specific suggestions*, includes behavioral exercises or suggestions for reducing stress. If the first two levels of treatment do not resolve a sexual problem,

Sexual interactions can be a source of frustration, disappointment, and anger in a relationship, but they can also be a source of happiness and great joy. A satisfying sexual relationship is a crucial ingredient in a healthy intimate relationship.

this third level, focusing on brief therapy with the help of a counselor, can be used. A way to begin on this level is to develop the history of the client's sexual problem.

The fourth level in the PLISSIT Model is *intensive therapy* with a trained and certified sex therapist or counselor. Only about 10% of clients with a sexual dysfunction need this level of help. The sexual problem a person is dealing with today may have roots in the person's past, and the distress resulting from the past needs to be resolved before progress can be made in the present. Specific suggestions regarding sexual technique may not get at the heart of the problem, but may simply be treating the symptom.

Other Approaches and Techniques   Two of the most common self-help techniques for overcoming sexual problems are body exploration and masturbation. Clinicians have found that masturbation exercises are helpful in treating orgasmic dysfunction in women, and lack of ejaculatory control in men. Once a woman learns how to reach orgasm through self-stimulation, she can teach her partner the best ways to bring her to orgasm through intercourse. Self-help techniques that help men slow down during masturbation often help them slow down while making love with a partner (Kelly, 1994).

Behavioral exercises may also be prescribed to help couples enrich and expand their sexual awareness and enjoyment. These exercises include sensate focus, the stop-and-go technique, and the squeeze technique.

- *Sensate focus.* Designed for couples, this technique teaches couples what gives each partner pleasure without expecting anything in return. The goal is not sexual arousal or intercourse, but education. Each partner directs the other, showing her or him what kinds of touches are the most enjoyable, where the sensitive places are, and how one likes to be touched. The exercise helps people learn to communicate better sexually.

- *The stop-and-go technique.* This technique teaches men how to control ejaculation and orgasm. The man's partner manually or orally stimulates his penis until he is just about to ejaculate. Then, the partner stops the stimulation, resuming it only when the man is in control. Stimulation and rest may be alternated several times in a session before orgasm and ejaculation are triggered. Repeated sessions over weeks or months help men control rapid or premature ejaculation.

- *The squeeze technique.* In this variation on the stop-and-go technique, when the partner stops stimulating the man's penis, the partner immediately applies pressure to the penis, squeezing it with the thumb and two fingers until there is a tolerable degree of pain. This pattern is repeated seven or eight times until the man learns to tolerate intense stimulation while delaying ejaculation. The squeeze technique further shortens the time it takes to resolve the problem of premature ejaculation (Hyde, 1990; Masters et al., 1992).

Does Sex Therapy Work?   Masters and Johnson treated more than 2,300 clients at their St. Louis clinic between 1959 and 1985. The researchers have written that 84.4% of men and 77.8% of women reported long-term cures to problems ranging from impotence and premature ejaculation to anorgasmia (Alpern, 1988).

At the Masters and Johnson Institute, whether the problem lies with the man or the woman, both partners are treated together for two weeks. Couples are tested for underlying physical conditions and are seen repeatedly by a male-female therapist team to discuss emotional problems. They are then sent back to their hotel room with suggestions on how to develop comfort and intimacy with each other. Fees run up to $10,000, based on the ability to pay. (Cost of treatment is often covered by medical insurance.) The therapists at the Institute treat not only sexual dysfunction but also cases of sexual compulsion, abuse, and incest (Alpern, 1988). The approach developed by Masters and Johnson has been expanded, modified, and used by sex therapists throughout the country.

In a review of a wide variety of sex therapy approaches, Joseph LoPiccolo and Wendy E. Stock (1986) pointed out that many people are helped by sex therapy even if they do not become fully functional sexually. At minimum, the therapy improves people's ability to understand their problems and to communicate with their partners about their needs and feelings.

Summary

- A scientific approach to the subject of sexuality began in earnest during the Victorian era in the late 19th and early 20th centuries. This work included that of Sigmund Freud, who proposed five psychosexual stages of development.

- Attitudes toward sexuality and sexual behaviors vary markedly from one culture to another.

- Sex surveys—such as the University of Chicago study, the *Janus Report*, and the *American Couples* study—reveal useful information about the sexual behaviors of Americans.

- Sex-education programs encouraging abstinence but also offering an alternative for those who are already or choose to become sexually active are among the most effective.

- Few children in the United States receive direct instruction from their parents in the areas of sexuality, sexual intercourse, or birth control. However, studies have shown that parental communication may forestall or postpone a child's sexual activity.

- Although sexual activity often decreases after marriage, this decline is not inevitable. Key elements in keeping the sexual relationship vital include communication, commitment, and investing the time to enjoy each other.

- According to the 1994 University of Chicago study, about 25% of husbands and 15% of wives have had an extramarital sexual affair; sometimes, but not always, the consequences are divorce.

- Types of male sexual dysfunction include erectile dysfunction, premature ejaculation, retarded ejaculation, ejaculatory incompetence, and painful intercourse. Female sexual dysfunctions include vaginismus, anorgasmia, rapid orgasm, and painful intercourse.

- Sex therapy involves a number of different components, including learning more about basic anatomy, learning what one's true feelings are about the body, and discovering one's basic attitudes toward sex and sexuality.

Key Terms

sexuality

heterosexual

homosexual

bisexual

sexual orientation

sex

gender

incest taboo

masturbation

homophobia

DINS dilemma

sexual dysfunction

organic sexual
   dysfunction

psychosocial sexual
   dysfunction

erectile dysfunction

premature ejaculation

retarded ejaculation

ejaculatory
   incompetence

painful intercourse

vaginismus

anorgasmia

rapid orgasm

sex therapy

sex educator

sex therapist

PLISSIT Model

Activities

1. Is sex truly everywhere in our society? For a day, keep a log noting what, when, and where you see or hear something with a sexual theme. Several people in the class can work together and report their findings to the larger group.

2. In a small group, generate as many synonyms or slang terms for various body parts as possible. On separate pieces of paper, write down these alternative words for *penis*, *vulva*, *vagina*, *buttocks*, and *breasts*. The goal of this exercise is to highlight the many indirect ways people talk about sex and sexual parts of the body. Discuss your findings.

3. In small groups, discuss the following situation: You are the parent of a 15-year-old son. He is interested in your views on nonmarital sex. What would you tell him?

4. What are your personal beliefs about nonmarital sexual behavior? Write a brief essay articulating and supporting your views.

5. Compare and contrast the results of Activities 3 and 4. How did what you would tell an adolescent differ from your personal views? In what ways were the two messages the same?

Suggested Readings

Berzon, B. (1990). *Permanent partners: Building gay and lesbian relationships that last.* New York: Plume/Penguin. *Suggestions by a psychotherapist specializing in same-sex relationships for resolving conflicts over power and control, jealousy, differences in sexual desire, money, and family demands.*

Boston Women's Health Book Collective. (1992). *The new our bodies, ourselves.* New York: Touchstone/Simon & Schuster. *The latest edition of a classic that has helped countless women understand their physical and emotional health for a quarter-century.*

Gullotta, T. P., Adams, G. R., & Montemayor, R. (Eds.). (1993). *Adolescent sexuality.* Newbury Park, CA: Sage. *Examines historical and theoretical perspectives; anatomy, physiology, and gender issues; heterosexual behavior; lesbian, gay-male, and bisexual youths; teenage pregnancy and parenting; aberrant (incestuous or involuntary) sexual experiences; sexually transmissible diseases; and sexual responsibility.*

Laumann, E. O., Gagnon, J. H., Michael, R. T., & Michaels, S. (1995). *The social organization of sexuality: Sexual practices in the United States.* Chicago: University of Chicago Press. Perhaps the most extensive study of sexual behavior ever conducted in this country. *A thinner companion volume for lay readers,* Sex in America: A definitive survey *(Boston: Little, Brown, 1995), was written with journalist Gina Kolata.*

Masters, W. H., Johnson, V. E., & Kolodny, R. C. (1992). *Human sexuality* (4th ed.). New York: Harper Collins. *An outstanding encyclopedic text covering an enormous number of topics in the area of human sexuality. An invaluable reference.*

Mathes, P. G., & Irby, B. J. (1993). *Teen pregnancy and parenting handbook.* Champaign, IL: Research Press. *A practical handbook with a matter-of-fact tone, appropriate for its target audience, teenage girls.*

Miller, B. C., & Moore, K. A. (1990). Adolescent sexual behavior, pregnancy, and parenting: Research through the 1980s. *Journal of Marriage and the Family,* 52 (November), 1025–1044. *A very useful review that distills the extensive research in this area.*

Ortiz, E. T. (1989). *Your complete guide to sexual health.* Englewood Cliffs, NJ: Prentice Hall. *A readable, practical guide.*

Pittman, F. (1993). *Private lies: Infidelity and the betrayal of intimacy.* New York: Norton. *A therapist reflects on 30 years of experience helping people "clean up the mess" created by their affairs.*

Rosenheim, M. K., & Testa, M. F. (Eds.). (1992). *Early parenthood and coming of age in the 1990s.* New Brunswick, NJ: Rutgers University Press. *A volume of interdisciplinary essays for families, educators, public health practitioners, and policy makers.*

Wincze, J. P., & Carey, M. P. (1991). *Sexual dysfunction: A guide for assessment and treatment.* Treatment Manuals for Practitioners Series. New York: Guilford Press. *An excellent overview of sex therapy today.*

Dynamics of Intimate Relationships

CHAPTER 7

Gender Roles and Power in the Family

Contemporary models of intimacy stress gender equality in marriage and other types of partnerships. Egalitarianism is the trend among many couples making a serious commitment to each other. But if women continue to make less money for the work they do outside the home and if men continue to avoid child care and household labor, the fabric of intimate relationships is threatened. The fragile bonds of intimacy can easily be damaged when one spouse is subordinate to the other, has more power than the other, or receives less respect and dignity in society.

Despite three decades of the feminist movement in this country, gender-based segregation of labor is alive and well in many families. This is especially true in the home, where men continue for the most part to do "men's work" and women to do "women's work." The problem with this arrangement is that the traditional roles also involve a disparity in power. Men's work receives more respect and better pay in our society than women's work; thus men tend to hold the upper hand in both the workplace and the home. Why this persists is the subject of ongoing debate. It is clear, however, that rigidly categorizing people and dictating their behavior in traditional masculine and feminine terms stifles individual creativity and diminishes the potential for achievement in both the world of work and the world of intimacy.

This chapter discusses gender roles and their origin, arguing that many of the behavioral differences between men and women stem not from biology but from culture. It also presents androgyny, an alternative to traditional masculinity and femininity, as a model of individual mental health. Four major theories about gender-role development are then considered. Finally, power in families is explored, with an emphasis on how couples establish and maintain a balance of power in their relationships.

Gender Roles

The different ways in which men and women behave are linked to, but not necessarily determined by, their physical sex. Individuals are identified as male or female on the basis of physical structures, which are determined by chromosomes, gonads, and hormones. This labeling occurs at birth and is the first step in the process of developing **gender identity**—a sense of being male or female and what that means in one's society (Cook, 1985).

Although nature determines an individual's sex, culture determines the attitudes and behaviors appropriate for an individual on the basis of her or his sex. In each culture, individuals learn to adapt to these expectations as they shape their personal and professional lives. **Gender roles** are expectations about people's attitudes and behaviors in life based on whether they are male or female. When a child is born, **gender-role stereotypes** come into play. People comment, for example, that he is "a strong, healthy boy" or she is "a darling, adorable girl."

Labeling affects a child's psychological development in a variety of ways. The child begins to adopt personality traits, attitudes, preferences, and behaviors considered appropriate to his or her sex, and these affect how he or she walks, talks, eats, exercises, thinks, and later makes love. The gender-role patterns assigned to males and females influence all our roles in life.

Gender-Biased Language

He	She	He	She
discussed	chattered	has character lines	has wrinkles
reminded	nagged	is assertive	is pushy
networked	gossiped	was tired	was depressed
complained	bitched	was upset	was emotional
is forgetful	is an airhead	dressed nicely	dressed "to kill"
is confident	is conceited	was friendly	was flirting
is careful	is picky	was upset	was moody
is articulate	is talkative		

Source: Based in part on *Sex Differences in Human Communication* (p. 131) by Barbara Westbrook Eakins and R. Gene Eakins. Copyright © 1978 by Harper & Row, Publishers, Inc. Reprinted by permission of HarperCollins Publishers, Inc.

Masculinity is the gender-linked constellation of traits that have been traditionally associated with men; **femininity,** the traits associated with women. In our society, the qualities stereotypically associated with masculinity include aggressiveness, independence, dominance, competence, and a predisposition for math and science. Qualities stereotypically associated with femininity include passivity, dependency, sensitivity, emotionality, and a predisposition for art and literature. These stereotypes are destructive because they imply that all males, and only males, have the so-called masculine qualities and that all females, and only females, possess the so-called feminine qualities. Obviously, any human being can have any of these qualities. Socially imposed gender-role stereotypes create inequality by prescribing—based on whether a person is male or female—certain qualities, behaviors, and opportunities and prohibiting or discouraging others.

Language is one of the most powerful tools people use both deliberately and inadvertently to establish and maintain rigid gender roles. The subtle ways we talk about people of the other sex reinforce stereotypes and segregate people by sex. We talk about men and women as being members of the "opposite" sex, reinforcing the notion that men and women are opposites and accentuating the differences rather than affirming the similarities. We thereby continue a hierarchical tradition in our culture that often places men on top and women on the bottom. It is more appropriate to talk in terms of the "other" sex, rather than the "opposite" sex. Box 7.1 illustrates how gender-biased language reinforces the misguided notion that men are more competent and rational than women.

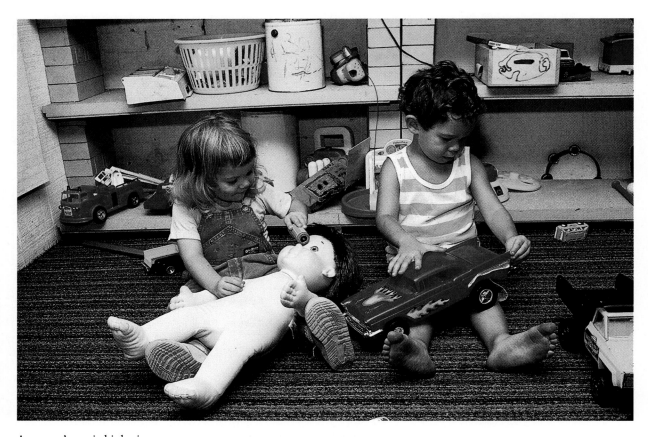

A person's sex is biologically determined, but the abilities, behaviors, activities, social roles, and other characteristics that are considered appropriate for males and females are determined by one's culture.

An International Survey of Male/Female Traits

In an international survey of 22 countries, the Gallup Poll (1996), found conventional stereotypes of women and men. Women were perceived as more affectionate, emotional, talkative, and patient than men. In the United States, 76% of those surveyed considered women to be the more affectionate sex; only 6% named men the more affectionate. When asked which sex is the more emotional, 88% said women, and only 4% said men. Men were perceived across cultures as being more aggressive, ambitious, and courageous than women. In most cultures, women and men were perceived to be equally intelligent.

Although none of the 10 traits surveyed were seen solely as male or female, the trait considered predominantly male was aggressiveness. The country with the highest margin was China, where 81% identified aggression as most characteristic of men and only 3% as most characteristic of women, a difference of 78 points. The differences favoring men were 58 points for the United States and 60 points for Canada and Britain. Both men and women across most of the 22 countries surveyed tended to agree with the opinions reported here.

Traditional Versus Contemporary Views of Gender Roles

In the traditional view of gender roles in our society, males are assumed to be superior to females and to have characteristics that are more desirable. The contemporary view holds that neither males nor females are superior; both have desirable—and undesirable—traits not based specifically on sex.

A Traditional View   The traditional view of gender roles in our society grew out of our male-oriented culture, but specific theories have been put forth in its support. One of the best known is that of sociologist Talcott Parsons (1955, 1965). Parsons's theory of the family assumed that highly contrasting gender roles were essential for families and society. For nearly two decades, Parsons's theory dominated sociology. This theory was in part developed to answer earlier observers who had argued that in urban industrial societies the family had lost its functions and was on the decline. Parsons countered that "the modern family" was an organized and functional unit that, instead of losing its value, was more important than ever.

Parsons believed that, in this modern family, society required that men be "instrumental" and women be "expressive." The man's instrumental role was to be the breadwinner, the manager, and the leader of the family. The wife-mother's expressive role was to take care of the emotional well-being of the family, providing nurture and comfort (Parsons, 1955, 1965). Parsons saw these two roles as separate, one to be performed by the husband and the other by the wife.

Parsons's theory has been attacked by numerous critics, and it is no longer a predominant family theory. His critics charged that it was a mistake to assume that the traditional family structure was both a universal and necessary social institution—that only this traditional family structure could fulfill the needs of the individuals within the family and of the greater society. Parsons, it was charged, focused on the positive aspects of this traditional family structure but deemphasized potential problems. He emphasized stability rather than change, focused on harmony rather than conflict, and saw function but ignored dysfunction. Parsons's theory also tended to stereotype masculine and feminine traits, reinforcing differences and denigrating women.

A More Contemporary View   Today, it is more commonly assumed that both sexes are capable and can be successful in a variety of roles at home and at work. Woman can be independent, strong, logical, and task oriented; men can be nurturing, sensitive, cooperative, and detail oriented. However, men and women can benefit by learning from each other. Men can learn the value of being more sensitive and caring from women. Women can learn the value of independence from men. And both can learn to work together and become interdependent.

Women may be at an advantage in this more cooperative approach to living. They have traditionally been encouraged to be good listeners, to be empathic, understanding, helpful, and supportive. These caring values fit well with the more cooperative approaches to group decision making that are gaining strength at home and at work.

Androgyny Life confronts us daily with situations in which both resiliency in the face of difficulty and sensitivity to other human beings are valuable traits. **Androgyny** refers to a blending of traditional masculinity and traditional femininity in the same individual. "Androgyny is a newly discovered old concept," according to Ellen Piel Cook (1985, p. 18). One definition of androgyny explains it this way:

> A condition under which the characteristics of the sexes—and the human impulses expressed by men and women—are not rigidly assigned. . . . [An androgyne is] a creature for whom . . . anatomy is not destiny; for whom the capacities to respond and make and be are irrelevant of gender. (Rosenstein, 1973, p. 38)

The concept of androgyny bridges the gap between masculinity and femininity, suggesting that individuals are free to create a personality based on their own personal needs and beliefs. Psychologist Carl Jung argued that both masculinity and femininity are inherent in everyone and emphasized the need for people to recognize and integrate both capacities. Jung believed the integration of masculinity and femininity was essential to the development of personal wholeness (Olds, 1981). Sandra Bem (1974, 1981a, 1981b) pioneered the development of a method for measuring psychological androgyny. Studies have found that people who have a good balance of both masculine and feminine characteristics are more loving than those who are stereotypically "macho" or feminine (Stark, 1985).

Dina Safilios-Rothschild (1976) speculated that gender-typed men and women tend to see members of the other sex as people to be manipulated rather than as partners in a give-and-take relationship. To maintain control, macho men learn not to express their feelings or to let themselves become dependent on others. Highly feminine women, on the other hand, often believe that the only way to relate successfully with men is to flirt, tease, and use other so-called feminine wiles to gain power. A successful love relationship requires a combination of traditional masculine and traditional feminine characteristics in each partner.

The androgynous model of the mentally healthy person is not mostly masculine in nature, as earlier models have been. Rather, this model is based on a workable mix of masculinity and femininity. Women's ways of knowing and living are treated with the same respect and dignity as men's ways of operating.

Soon after the term *androgyny* resurfaced in the early 1970s, discussions began on how to create a society without gender-role differentiation. An androgynous parent, for example, would be one who could be both expressive-affectional when the situation demanded it and instrumental-adaptive at other times (DeFrain, 1975, 1979).

The idea of androgyny came as a breath of fresh air to many people in the early 1970s, because many women felt overworked and underappreciated in the home and longed for contact with other adults and recognition in the working world. Countless women pointed out how demanding motherhood can be, involving round-the-clock, 7-day-a-week, year-in year-out responsibility. Many feminists called for men to become more active in childrearing. Influenced by these voices, a number of men responded with criticisms of conventional American fatherhood. They argued that fathers suffer from the inattention and emotional sterility of a life consumed by "careerism" at the expense of family and described the dreariness of the working world for fathers. "The guy who wins the rat race is still a rat," William Sloan Coffin pointed out (DeFrain, 1974).

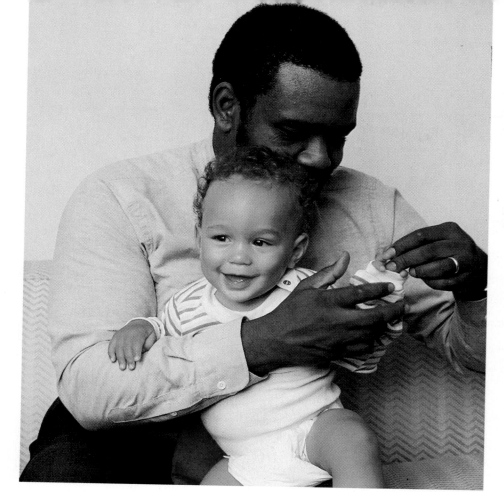

Gender-role stereotypes limit people's choices by dictating what they are believed to be able to do. Despite the stereotypes prevalent in our society, this man demonstrates that males can be sensitive, nurturing, patient, and capable of caring for children.

Beyond Androgyny   In 1993 Bem published another book on gender roles and relationships, *The Lenses of Gender: Transforming the Debate on Sexual Inequality.* Although she was instrumental in advancing the discussion of psychological androgyny in the 1970s and early 1980s, Bem argues in this book that the concepts of masculinity and femininity ought to be dropped altogether. The focus on androgyny, she claims, has merely heightened the focus on so-called masculine and feminine traits. This focus reinforces **gender polarization,** "the organizing of social life around male-female distinctions" (p. 192) and the linking of all aspects of human experience to sex and gender. The premise underlying gender polarization is not simply that men and women are different, she points out, but that men are superior to women.

Bem envisions a society in which gender polarization has been completely dismantled except for the purpose of reproduction. This vision is unrealistic, she acknowledges, because it challenges both the traditional belief that men are inherently dominant and the contemporary feminist focus on a woman-centered view of experience.

The Move Toward More Egalitarian Roles   American society in many ways is moving away from male dominance toward **egalitarian roles**—social equality between the sexes. The process of change has been long, and fraught with contro-

BOX 7 . 2

Contemporary Versus Traditional Dating and Marriage Patterns

Contemporary	Traditional
Both women and men initiate dates.	The man initiates dates.
The woman keeps her maiden name after marriage.	The woman takes the man's last name.
The couple cohabits before marriage.	The couple lives apart before marriage.
Premarital sex is expected.	No premarital sex.
Both continue their educations.	The wife supports the husband through school.
The birth of a child might precede marriage.	Children are conceived after marriage.
Both people work, and both may have careers.	The husband's work is the priority.
Roles are flexible.	Roles are rigid.
Spouses share child care.	The mother is responsible for child care.
Both initiate sex.	The husband initiates sex.
Both select the couple's friends.	The husband's friends become the couple's friends.

versy. The struggle occurs not only in society but is also played out each day in close relationships. Box 7.2 highlights some differences between traditional dating and marriage patterns and more contemporary practices. Looking back through the generations of one's own family gives a good picture of how dramatically times have changed.

One of the most telling indexes of change is the decline of the double standard, the social convention allowing men more sexual and social freedom than women. Women are claiming more freedom for themselves, although some don't realize or acknowledge they are doing so. A number of social scientists have commented that today many women shy away from calling themselves nontraditional or feminist but are clearly living very different lives than their mothers or grandmothers. What is apparently happening is that as women's roles change, the definition of "traditional" also changes.

Research indicates that younger couples are more egalitarian than older couples in their beliefs, feelings, and attitudes about marital and family roles. Olson, McCubbin, and colleagues (1989) studied 1,000 couples at seven stages in the fam-

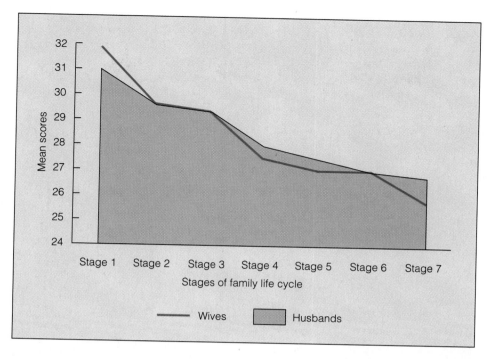

Figure 7.1 Egalitarian Roles Across the Family Life Cycle. *Source: Families: What Makes Them Work* (2nd ed.) (p. 108) by D. H. Olson, H. I. McCubbin, H. Barnes, A. Larsen, M. Muxen, M. Wilson, 1989, Sage Publications. Copyright © 1989 by Sage Publications. Used by permission of the publisher.

ily life cycle. The researchers developed a scale to measure egalitarian versus traditional values and roles. On the scale, the higher the score, the more the individual valued equality in the relationship; the lower the score, the more the person preferred traditional roles.

The seven stages of the family life cycle were (1) young couples without children, (2) childbearing couples, (3) couples with school-age children, (4) couples with adolescents, (5) couples in the launching stage, (6) couples in the empty nest stage, and (7) retired couples. Young couples without children were the most egalitarian in their views. Egalitarian views decreased steadily thereafter, reaching the lowest point among retired couples (Figure 7.1).

Does this mean that couples become more conservative as time passes? Or that younger couples are more contemporary in their views than older couples because times have changed? The study was not a longitudinal one, following the same people over time. Rather, it was a cross-sectional study in which seven groups of couples, representing the seven stages of the family life cycle, were surveyed at one point in time. The study therefore does not identify whether couples become more conservative over time. The study does tell us, however, that younger couples are more egalitarian than older couples. Attitudes and behaviors are clearly changing, and these differences among older and younger couples lead to interesting dialogues in many families. Younger couples are growing up and living in a different world than that of their parents—one that is more supportive of egalitarian relationships.

Relationships tend to be more egalitarian today than in the past. This young woman has many more options and opportunities than her mother or grandmother did, both in her relationships and in her other life choices.

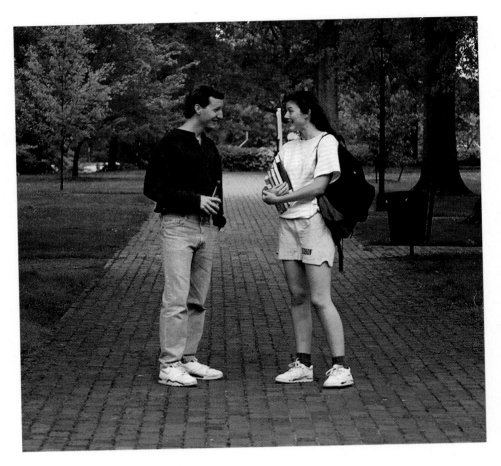

Persistent Gender-Role Patterns in Marriage Despite many changes in gender roles, old patterns persist. American couples still tend to exhibit gender-role family work patterns. In the home, men tend to do "men's work," and women tend to do "women's work." One research team found that, for families to achieve gender equality in the division of labor, "American males would have to reallocate 60 percent of their family work time to other tasks" (Blair & Lichter, 1991, p. 91). In a similar vein, other researchers have found that women carry a larger share of the responsibility for the children than do men (Leslie, Anderson, & Branson, 1991).

In many families, however, both fathers and mothers take a major responsibility for rearing children. In a *USA Today* poll (Ehrlich, 1984), 56% of the males and 46% of the females said both parents take primary responsibility for the children. *USA Today* found that financial management was divided relatively equally, according to husbands but not according to wives. Thirty-nine percent of the husbands said they took primary responsibility for money matters in the family, 41% said their wives took primary responsibility, and 19% said both spouses shared the responsibility. When the wives were questioned, 25% said their husbands took pri-

Copyright 1991 by Greg Howard. Reprinted with special permission of King Features Syndicate.

mary responsibility for money matters, 53% said they themselves took responsibility, and 22% said the responsibility was shared.

Household chores—cooking, washing, and cleaning—were the most clearly gender-segregated tasks for families in the *USA Today* study. Fourteen percent of the men said they did the most household chores, 86% of the men said their wives did, and no men said the division of labor was equal. Similarly, 7% of the women said their husbands did most of the household chores, 93% said they themselves did most of the chores, and no women said the division of labor was equal. Twenty-two percent of the women in the study felt their husbands should do more housework, and 9% of the husbands felt their wives should do more housework (Ehrlich, 1984).

Philip Blumstein and Pepper Schwartz (1983) surveyed nearly 3,000 couples and found that even among those working outside the home, women still bear almost all the responsibility for the housework. Although husbands of women who are employed did help out more around the house than husbands of homemakers, the contribution was minimal. And even if a husband was unemployed, he still did much less housework than a wife who was working a 40-hour week (Blumstein & Schwartz, 1983).

Though attitudes are changing, housework may be the last bastion of tradition in American families. Blumstein and Schwartz found that even among couples who professed egalitarian ideals, the reality was that the women did most of the housework. Even if a husband said he believed he should share responsibility for cooking, laundry, and grocery shopping, shared responsibility was more an ideal than a reality.

Working-class husbands were particularly vocal on the issue of housework. They did not believe they should be equal partners in the house, and thus did little housework. Among middle-class and upper-middle-class couples, Blumstein and Schwartz found two common patterns: in two-career couples in which the husband encourages the wife to work outside the home to contribute to the family income, husbands share some of the housework. When only the husband works outside the home, however, the wife does most of the housework herself.

Arlie Hochschild (1989) interviewed 50 two-job couples and found that most men don't really do much childrearing, cooking, cleaning, food shopping, or enough other chores to count. Hochschild's book, *The Second Shift*, described wives who plan domestic schedules and activities for their children while driving home from the office. At home, the women begin a second shift of work while their husbands tend to get off easy. These women did not resemble the beautiful, in-control businesswomen featured in magazine articles. Instead, they looked so exhausted that "at least for two-career couples who are trying to raise children . . . the information should be withheld from the young, or the race may not reproduce" (Hochschild, 1989, p. 62). In only 20% of the two-job families in the study did men share housework equally with their wives. Women who "do it all" tend to suffer chronic exhaustion, low sex drive, and more frequent illness. The result is that both partners forfeit their health, happiness, and often the vitality of their marriage.

Ongoing polls by the Roper Organization over the past 20-plus years have indicated that women's anger at men has risen steadily. (Box 7.3 reflects some of the reasons.) Relationships between the sexes have become more combative as more women have begun working outside the home. In 1970, 70% of women surveyed believed that "most men are basically kind, gentle, and thoughtful." In 1989, only 50% of the women believed that statement to be true (Gallup, 1989).

Social attitudes about men's and women's roles are changing, but the details have to be worked out in each relationship. This is no small task. For example, males are still expected to be "successful" in work. This means the man must demonstrate dominance, self-assurance, and coolness under fire. At home, he may be expected to shift gears and adopt the role of gentle father and loving husband, who is also willing to help with household chores. If he is used to "winning" in the world of work, he may have to get used to compromising—or "breaking even"—in the home. He may work in an autocratic office where he's the boss and go home to a democratic household where decisions are made in a more cooperative manner. If, on the other hand, he is not one of the few "winners" in the working world but just an "average Joe" who feels pushed around by his boss and "the system," he may be reluctant to give up his throne at home. Controlling his wife and children may give him some comfort, and he probably will not help much around the house.

In gay-male and lesbian couples, equality may be somewhat easier. Because both partners are the same sex, they do not have to contend with traditional gender-role stereotypes and may be more free to create a fair and equal division of labor in the home (Blumstein & Schwartz, 1983).

"You know, it's funny. We read all about the problems straight couples have with gender roles in their relationships. That just hasn't been an issue with Chris and me," said Janine, a young lesbian living in Des Moines. "Perhaps because we're both women, we don't get into the power struggles men and women get into. We both believe in a win-win approach.

"Maybe it's easier because both of us are good cooks and both of us like a tidy house. Perhaps the only hang-up is that neither of us is good at home repairs or maintaining the car. That's pretty stereotypical, isn't it? Two incompetent females when it comes to men's work. What we need is a good husband around here to take care of all the stuff we don't like to do."

B O X   7 . 3

A Woman's Struggle for Gender Equality

I am not a female suffering from "delusions." I am not "unstable," "psychotic," or "schizophrenic."

I was Minnesota's Business Woman of the Year in 1988. I was a delegate to the White House Conference on Small Business in Washington, D.C., in 1986. I was named one of *Corporate Report Minnesota's* Outstanding Women in Business in 1989.

But 10 years ago, in 1981, I was a divorced mother of two struggling with a small business. I made an appointment to meet with a traveling Small Business Administration representative about available loan programs. When I asked for an application, he rifled through his briefcase, then said, "I must have left that particular application in my motel room. Why don't you meet me there at 5 o'clock to fill it out?" It was clear what he meant. . . .

Let me try to make it easier for men to understand the social conditioning on females to keep their mouths shut.

Reverse the roles—and imagine growing up as a male in a world where everyone who has power is female: the president, Supreme Court, Congress, governors, judges, police, legislators, doctors, dentists, lawyers, school administrators, clergy. . . .

As you go through school, your female counselors steer you into the secondary positions; you can be the dental hygienist, but not the dentist. If you protest, you are told you are "unmanly" to want women's jobs. In this world, men earn 59 cents for every dollar women earn and rarely make it to the top, as the "glass ceiling" is firmly in place. Men—no matter how old or what their job—are still called "boys."

As a teacher, you are paid less than female colleagues with the same experience. You then start your own business—and are humiliated when you have to get your wife's permission for a bank loan even though she doesn't need your permission. You buy insurance through your business, and are appalled when the policy is issued in your wife's name and you are listed with the children under "dependents."

Not a pretty picture, is it? *Yet all of the above happened to me* and many women of Anita Hill's generation. These are not things that happen to men, which is why they cannot imagine the intimidating, fearful effect of society's long-term conditioning on women when they are treated like children and second-class citizens with little legal rights. No, baby, we have not come a long way.

Source: "No, Baby, American Women Have Not Come a Long Way" by L. Kraft, November 5, 1991, Minneapolis *Star/Tribune*, p. 6. Copyright 1991 by the Minneapolis *Star/Tribune*. Reprinted by permission of the publisher.

An International Perspective on Gender Roles

In its comprehensive survey of gender roles and the family, the Gallup Poll (1996) surveyed men and women in 22 countries with a combined population of 3.05 billion, or 53% of the world's population. The survey included countries in North America, South America, Europe, and Asia. The sampling error in the results is within plus or minus 3 percentage points.

Residents of nearly two thirds of the countries polled felt that their society was biased toward men. In 15 countries, either a majority or a plurality of those surveyed said that society favors men over women. Countries in greatest agreement that society favors men are Japan (78%), Germany (76%), Iceland (76%), France (76%), the United States (73%), and Britain (72%). In 7 countries, including El Salvador (63%), China (53%), and Thailand (52%), the consensus leaned more toward the belief that men and women are treated equally.

The survey showed some potential for change, however, because in 5 countries, about half those surveyed resented the gender-role expectations their society placed on them (Gallup Poll, 1996). Those countries are Germany (52%), Japan (52%), Thailand (52%), Chile (46%), and Panama (46%). In those 5 countries, at least half the women and more than 40% of the men expressed resentment.

The Gallup survey (1996) also demonstrated lessening support for the traditional family structure, in which the father is the breadwinner and the mother is the homemaker. In only 6 of the 22 countries did a majority of the population or close to it support the traditional roles: Hungary (66%), Chile (49%), the United States (48%), France (46%), and Japan (46%). Least supportive of the traditional family roles were Thailand (25%), Taiwan (26%), Spain (27%), India (28%), Germany (28%), and Lithuania (28%). These six countries were more supportive of the idea that both parents should work outside the home.

Multicultural Perspectives on Gender Roles

It is commonly believed that gender roles do not spring from innate characteristics individuals possess; rather, they are learned behaviors, rooted in the social context of the particular culture in which people live. The gender roles women and men play vary widely from culture to culture. This section examines some examples of cultural gender-role differences around the world and in the United States.

An Anthropological Perspective

Perhaps the classic description of how gender roles are rooted in culture comes from anthropologist Margaret Mead. In *Sex and Temperament in Three Primitive Societies*, Mead (1935) looked at "maleness" and "femaleness" in three New Guinea tribes: the Arapesh, the Mundugumor, and the Tchambuli. In American society, a traditional attribute of females is that they are gentle and unaggressive. Among the Arapesh, Mead found both the women *and* the men to be unaggressive. Not far away, among the Mundugumor tribe, Mead found that both males and females displayed an aggressiveness that Americans would call traditionally masculine behavior. In both the Arapesh and the Mundugumor tribes, Mead found little contrast in temperament between the sexes.

The third New Guinea tribe Mead studied provided further evidence of cross-cultural differences. Among the Tchambuli, both men and women behaved in ways that are opposite to traditional behavior in Western societies. Tchambuli women were independent and aggressive, acting like traditional Western men; Tchambuli men were gentle and sensitive, like traditional Western women. Mead's conclusion was that the varieties in temperament she observed among these three "primitive" societies were not dictated by biology but were largely the creation of the societies.

Mead's conclusion has been vigorously debated since it was published. Psychologist David Buss believes, for example, that innate biological differences between males and females have more to do with the differences in their social behavior than does the culture in which they live. He devised a questionnaire asking people to describe their ideal mate in five categories: earning capacity, industriousness, youth, physical attractiveness, and chastity. Buss then administered the questionnaire to 37 groups of men and women in 33 different societies around the world. Even though they came from different geographic and cultural areas, the people Buss surveyed consistently expressed the same patterns of preference. Females placed greater value on wealth and ambition, and males were more interested in signs of youth and fertility. Finding a mate who was a "good financial prospect" was more important to females in 36 of 37 groups. "Good looks" were more important to males than females in all 37 groups (cited in Cowley, 1989, p. 56).

Evolutionary theory, focusing on the notion that gender traits are to some degree transmitted through the genes, predicts that different cultures will have certain gender-role similarities due to the similar biological makeup shared by males and that shared by females. According to anthropologist John Tooby and psychologist Leda Cosmides, "The assertion that culture explains human variation will be taken seriously when there are reports of women war parties raiding villages to capture men as husbands" (cited in Cowley, 1989, p. 57).

Cross-cultural studies have found that women have been the primary caretakers of children in almost all known societies, whereas men have been much more likely to assume leadership roles in the economic and political arenas (Cowley, 1989). This division of labor by sex has almost always meant that women have found themselves in positions subordinate to men. Why do women do most of the child care from culture to culture? Biology is frequently cited: Women give birth to children, breast-feed them, and then continue in the role of a nurturing parent.

American society shows a clear trend toward establishing more egalitarian roles. However, the debate over nature, nurture, and gender differences has not been resolved. If men take more responsibility for child care and housework, women will have more opportunity for access to the economic and political world, likely resulting in a more even distribution of power in our society.

Mexican American Culture

Mexican American males are often stereotyped as being *macho*. Male exhibitions of aggressiveness—*machismo*—include bossing women around, being abusive to them, and having numerous extramarital affairs. But this macho attitude is not supported in the research literature (Vega, 1991). Even though some Mexican American males act macho, this is not the predominant pattern for those living in the United States. Researchers have found that warm, nurturing, and egalitarian male behavior is more likely in marriages in which the wife is employed, although it is also demonstrated in many more-traditional marriages.

There are different interpretations of why some Mexican American males display machismo. One viewpoint holds that machismo is an unconscious attempt to overcompensate for feelings of inferiority, powerlessness, and inadequacy. This inferiority springs from the fact that the man's indigenous Mexican ancestors were conquered by Spaniards (Whites), producing a "hybrid Mexican people having an inferiority complex based on the mentality of a conquered people" (Baca Zinn, 1980). Intermingling of the various cultures over the centuries produced a nation of mostly *mestizo* (mixed-"race") people.

An alternative explanation for the macho behavior asserts that it is a conscious reaction to the socially inferior position Mexican American males have been put in: "Men in certain social categories have had more roles and sources of identity open to them. However, this has not been the case for Chicanos or other men of color. Perhaps manhood takes on greater importance for those who do not have access to socially valued roles. Being male is one sure way to acquire status when other roles are systematically denied by the workings of society" (Baca Zinn, 1980, p. 39).

Men in a variety of ethnic groups are capable of exhibiting a macho, or aggressive, attitude as a way of asserting their need for respect and dignity. Macho behavior becomes less acceptable when it attempts to deny the inherent rights of other family members, particularly women.

African American Culture

African American men may have an advantage over White men in developing and integrating the "feminine" qualities that foster egalitarian relationships with women. According to one African American scholar, displaying dominant, aggressive behavior in the greater society carries considerable risk for African American males. As a consequence, "black male socialization includes a range of very positive results that young white men do not typically experience. From peers, for instance, young black men learn the concepts of 'brother' and 'blood'—a deep sense of identification with other black men that cuts across age, class, and geography. . . . From the women who raise us, black men learn firsthand to respect the strength of so-called feminine qualities—intuition, warmth, cooperation, and empathy" (Franklin, 1989, p. 278).

Is a strong women's movement that pushes for changes that benefit all women still needed in the United States? A recent poll found that African American women were more likely (85%) than White women (64%) or Latino women (76%) to respond in the affirmative (Cowan, 1989, p. 11). But many African American women see feminism from a different perspective than do White women. African American women have rarely served only in the housewife role because economic circumstances dictated that they work outside the home. African American women are also acutely aware of the disadvantages African American men have faced over the years, making it difficult for them to adopt a wholeheartedly feminist agenda. The dilemma: Am I more oppressed as a woman or as an African American? Because these two factors converge for African American women, life can be especially difficult for them.

Many African American women are hesitant about committing themselves to feminist goals that lead to conflict with African American men because, as Black psychiatrist Alvin Poussaint has said, "being a black man in American society is a high-risk adventure" (1982, p. 37). The U.S. Bureau of the Census bears out this statement. The following statistics are from the 1989 and 1994 editions of the *Statistical Abstract of the United States:* The life expectancy of African American males

Wilma Mankiller, former chief of the Cherokee Nation, was the first woman ever elected. Her election reflected the growing power of women in some Native American tribes.

is about 8 years less than that of White males, 9 years less than that of African American females, and 15 years less than that of White females (1994). African American males have a higher infant mortality rate than females (1989). They have a high adult death rate from illness and from homicide, a high unemployment rate, and a high rate of imprisonment (1994). African American males also have a higher rate of hospitalization for mental illness than do the other three groups, and higher rates of alcoholism and drug abuse than African American women (1989).

Native American Culture

Native American women confront many of the same problems that African American women face in American society, including a lack of political power that dates from the reorganization of Native American life in the 1920s. Native American cultures in the United States vary widely, but some include a matrilineal tradition in which women owned or still own houses, tools, and agricultural land. In recent years, there have been signs that Native American women are beginning to regain some of the power and prestige they had historically. In 1985 a woman was elected chief of the Cherokee nation, signifying "a revitalization of the role of women" in that tribe. In the 1986 Navajo elections, women won 72 of 327 local offices, and 62% of Navajo tribal scholarships were awarded to women (Robbins, 1987).

Many Native American families also face racism, unemployment, poverty, and the abuse of alcohol and other drugs (Robbins, 1987). Native American women play an important role in keeping the family and the tribe together. Some tribal traditions make it difficult for Native American women to attain leadership roles, and some tribes have religious beliefs against both contraception and abortion. But it has also been argued that tribal traditions are a source of strength for Native American women. In many cases, by upholding tradition Native American women have preserved tribal life despite the devastations of modern life. "If it wasn't for the women, their intestinal fortitude in keeping our traditions going, we would have disbanded as a tribe a long time ago," claims Alfred Benalli, Navajo director of an alcoholism program (cited in Robbins, 1987). The traditions give tribal members something around which to unite, and from this sense of oneness comes strength.

Cultural values and family life among Native Americans and the many other minority groups in American society offer fascinating comparisons and contrasts with the dominant culture. Although valid generalizations are difficult, the basic similarities between groups seem to outweigh the differences.

Japanese Culture

To understand the complex topic of power and gender roles in families in Japan, it is necessary to understand both the social system and the family system. The following overview, which applies to middle- and upper-class urban Japanese families, is provided by Shuji Asai (1996), a Japanese family therapist.

At the societal system level, Japanese culture is patriarchal. The male dominates; he plays the instrumental role in society and tends to be married to his work. Although women make up about 40% of the labor force in Japan, they face discrimination in terms of wages, assignments, and promotions.

Although Japanese society is patriarchal, within the Japanese family there is more of a matriarchal system, with the mother dominating. This is particularly true of childrearing and finances. Although the husband brings home the money, the wife controls it, including deciding how much spending money the husband receives each month. Part of the woman's financial power includes making decisions about when and where to invest and how much to pay for a house or remodeling.

In most Japanese families, family cohesion and family communication are also controlled by the mother. Japanese mothers often develop a very strong emotional connection with their children, serving as the communication link between the children and the father; the father may remain disengaged from the family. As a result, the mother dominates the family system while the father emphasizes his role at work.

Today, more Japanese women are seeking professional careers, and more are delaying marriage and even remaining single. These changes are moving Japan toward a more egalitarian society and are demanding that men and women renegotiate their traditional gender roles at work and at home.

Theories About Gender-Role Development and Change

Theorists interested in gender roles have focused on how children acquire gender-role identity during the early years of life. There is also interest in how changes in gender-role identity occur. Some observers believe that changes in gender-role identity are possible after early childhood, but it is generally assumed that once gender-role identity is formed, it remains stable and continues throughout adulthood. Four theories about gender-role development and change are described here: social learning theory, cognitive development theory, family systems theory, and feminist theory.

Social Learning Theory

Social learning theory is concerned with how individuals learn the behavior patterns considered appropriate for their sex. Social learning researchers have particularly focused on direct observation of behavior and how people reinforce each other's behavior. Early in life, reinforcement of sex-related behavior by others is of primary importance. As individuals grow and develop, they assess personal situations and develop standards and rules by which to live (Cook, 1985). In the case of gender roles, even very young children have already begun to internalize the standards and rules for being a boy or a girl in our society.

Social learning theorist Jerome Kagan (1964) argued that children at a young age dichotomize the world as female versus male and have a strong desire to match their own personal characteristics with the gender-role standards they learn from parents and society in general. Kagan believed that all children want to develop a gender-typed identity and that they see variations from the gender-traditional ideal as failures. He noted that certain aspects of gender-role standards cause unnecessary anxiety and restrictions for individuals, and he proposed that perhaps these standards should be changed.

Cognitive Development Theory

The **cognitive development theory** links gender-role development (the progressive acquisition of gender typing) to the more general maturation of the child's thinking processes. Lawrence Kohlberg (1966), the developer of this theory, argued that children themselves actively create gender identity, gender-role stereotypes, and values in their minds in their efforts to understand the world around them (e.g., "I can't do that! Only boys do that!"). He argued that the stereotypes do not necessarily become more rigid over time but follow a curvilinear pattern. In early childhood the stereotypes develop quickly and are quite rigid. When the child realizes that not all gender-typed characteristics (hair, clothes, sports, etc.) are crucial to maintaining gender identity, the child's thinking then becomes less

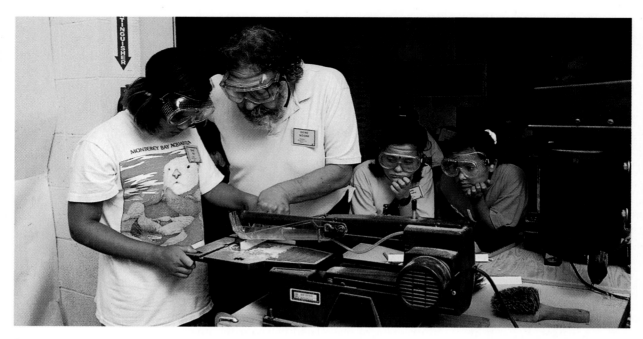

In previous generations, few girls had the opportunity to learn to use tools. Children today are no longer as limited by gender-role stereotypes as they were in the past.

rigid. With increasing maturity, the child learns that variations are possible and becomes more flexible in his or her thinking.

Paul Mussen (1969) synthesized social learning and cognitive processes in looking at gender-role development. Mussen noted that labeling occurs early in the child's life and that the child must see the label as positive, rewarding, lovingly applied, and accepted by the labeler. This linkage between the label and love and acceptance helps motivate the child to perform gender-typed behaviors.

Both the social learning and cognitive development theories have been attacked in recent years. First, it has been argued that these early theories erred by assuming that children of the same sex develop very similar gender-role identities (masculine for boys and feminine for girls). In fact, many boys engage in traditionally feminine behaviors, and many girls engage in traditionally masculine behaviors. Second, the early theories were criticized for considering the traditional gender-role identities desirable and divergence from the norm deviant. Today many children enjoy the freedom to engage in a broad range of activities, despite the dictates of tradition.

Third, the theories were criticized for assuming that early childhood is a critical period in gender-role development and that an adult's gender-role characteristics spring directly from early childhood experiences. Dramatic changes in gender-role behavior can take place later in life. Stories abound of female homemakers going back to school to become lawyers and of male engineers retiring early to take care of the home and garden while their spouses begin a new career outside the home. Subsequent theorists have explored human development after childhood and suggest that individuals retain the capacity for growth and change in regard to gender-role identity.

Family Systems Theory

Family systems theory, as you recall from Chapter 1, suggests that the family functions as a complete system; a change in one family member necessitates compensating changes in other family members, if the family is to achieve a new balance.

Family systems theory also acknowledges that change is a difficult process for both individuals and families. An individual wishing to go in a new direction in life must first struggle with herself, asking "Do I *really* want my role to be different from my mother's?" If the individual is successful in growing in new directions, family systems theory makes it clear that, unless the family changes with the individual, other family members will attempt to bring the individual back "into the fold."

Consider, for example, a young woman who desires more independence in a family that wants to maintain traditional family roles. The daughter feels stifled by the family's long list of rules and beliefs and finds support in feminist writings and rhetoric, but when she expresses her views, her parents react emotionally. "Are you telling me my life has been worthless?" her more traditional mother asks. "Those damned feminists!" her father sputters. Her mother becomes defensive because she has made a career of her children and her marriage. Her father becomes defensive because he felt he had done the right thing by supporting his wife and children.

Family systems that are balanced (on the Circumplex Model) tend to be more open to change and are more supportive of independence in family members (Tiesel, 1992). In contrast, some types of unbalanced family systems, particularly rigidly enmeshed types, are resistant to change and restrict independence in family members.

Feminist Theory

Traditional gender-role patterns—stressing the differences between men and women, masculinity and feminity—have been criticized by many observers of American society since the 1960s. Feminists have been among those critics. The gender-role constraints under which men and women traditionally lived have been revised considerably. Many women are doing things that their mothers would not have deemed possible. Many men are also gaining the freedom to function outside the traditional boundaries of masculinity. Making these profound changes in life is a struggle, but it would be difficult—if not impossible—for many people to go back to the traditional patterns.

Feminist scholars have focused on a variety of concerns (Walker & Thompson, 1984). First, they have worked to document the contributions women have made in the world. Feminists point out that although women have made countless contributions to culture and to human life, omission of these achievements from the historical record reflects the low status in which women have been held in society. Feminists point out that women have been exploited, devalued, and oppressed. In addition, as a result of their own experiences, feminists tend to be sensitive to other oppressed people.

A second focus of feminists is a commitment to change the conditions of women. Feminists strive to empower women by documenting oppression so that people recognize it when they see and experience it. Feminists take an affirming stance toward women, challenging the status quo of devaluation. This affirmation of women does not imply a rejection of men or all things masculine. Instead, both men and women are accorded equal respect and value.

Feminists found traditional gender-role theories to be highly suspect. They argued that Talcott Parsons's concept of instrumental and expressive activities falsely assumes that the two are mutually exclusive—that an individual cannot blend both. They pointed out that Parsons acknowledged the primacy of the father over the mother, which he felt was linked to the Western emphasis on achievement and instrumentality, and they criticized Parsons for not questioning male dominance (Thorne, 1982). The boxes males and females were put in, in sum, were seen as being too simple and too idealistic. In practice, many individuals—both men and women—felt stifled by the roles they were assigned and sought a way to transform the traditional family.

Power in Families

The fundamental concept in social science is Power, in the same sense in which Energy is the fundamental concept in physics.
—BERTRAND RUSSELL (1938)

The words *family* and *power* are inextricably linked. Power, control, and authority are continuously exercised in families, and struggles for personal power in families are exceedingly common. Tradition has dictated that considerable power go to the males in the family, but women often have more power than they or anyone else admits.

Power is defined as the ability (potential or actual) of an individual to change the behavior of other members in a social system (Olson & Cromwell, 1975, p. 5). Extending the above definition to families, **family power** is the ability of one member to change the behavior of the other members.

Many of the characteristics of power in close relationships were summarized by Kathleen M. Galvin and Bernard J. Brommel (1986, p. 123). Power is a system property—a feature of a family system—rather than a personal characteristic of any one family member. Power is an interactive process involving one family member who desires something from one or more other family members; these members may affect all other members in the system. Power is also a dynamic process, not a static one. It creates reciprocal causation (i.e., family members react to power attempts) in which one move leads to another, which leads to another, and so forth. Power also changes over time, particularly when the family is under stress. Power has both perceptual and behavioral aspects: The same power issue may be perceived differently by each family member.

A Family Power Model

Many disciplines have attempted to understand power, but it has proven to be a complex and elusive concept. "In the entire lexicon of sociological concepts, none is more troublesome than the concept of power. We may say about it in general

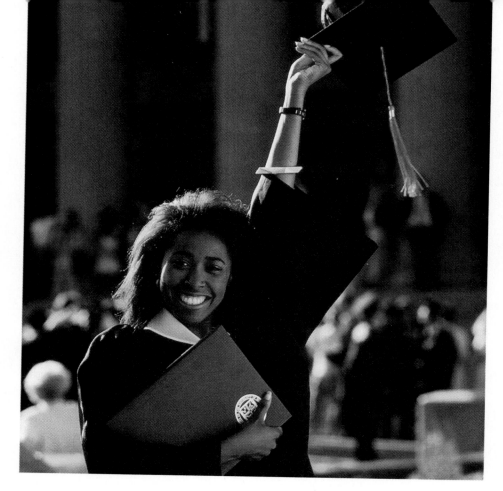

Educational level, occupational prestige, and income are all sources of power in our society—and in relationships as well. This college graduate is very likely to have more power in a marriage relationship than a high school graduate who chooses the role of full-time homemaker and mother.

only what St. Augustine said about time, that we all know perfectly well what it is—until someone asks us" (Bierstedt, 1950).

David Olson and Ronald Cromwell posed a series of relevant questions about power:

- Is power the actual ability to influence another person's behavior, or is it just the potential ability to do so?

- Is power an intentional or an unintentional process?

- Is power both overt and covert?

- Is power who decides or who does an activity?

- Is power who decides, or is it who decides who decides?

- Is power a process or an outcome?

- Does a power struggle mean there is a winner or loser, or is it possible for both individuals to win or lose? (Olson & Cromwell, 1975, p. 5).

Olson and Cromwell have divided family power into three areas: bases of family power, family power processes, and family power outcomes.

Bases of Family Power   Interest in the study of family power by family-focused social and behavioral scientists was sparked by Robert Blood and Don Wolfe's classic study, *Husbands and Wives* (1960), which developed a **resource theory of family power.** The researchers argued that the balance of power in a marriage is related to the relative resources each spouse has in that relationship. Blood and Wolfe focused on the resources of money, educational level, and occupational prestige and found that these were statistically related to the extent of the husband's perceived power in the marriage. In short, whoever has the most resources in the relationship has the most power.

Blumstein and Schwartz (1983) also found that money is an important resource that can affect the balance of power in a relationship. The sociologists studied heterosexual couples, gay-male couples, and lesbian couples. They found that money helped establish the balance of power among heterosexual couples and gay-male couples, but not among lesbian couples. Husbands had greater power over wives when the male-provider role was accepted. In more than 30% of the marriages in which the husband earned over $8,000 more than the wife, the husband was perceived to have more power. When the spouses' incomes were equal, however, the husband was more powerful in the relationship in only 18% of the cases.

Similarly, in gay-male couples, the individual who had the larger income was more likely to dominate. But among lesbian couples this was not true because the women tended to avoid dependence of one on the other. Among cohabiting heterosexual couples, a woman's income helped her establish equality in the relationship. Blumstein and Schwartz also found that money often means different things to men than to women. For men, money tends to represent identity and power. For women, money tends to represent security and autonomy (Blumstein & Schwartz, 1983).

Employment is also a source of power, studies of families in which the husband is the sole provider found. Blumstein and Schwartz divided the nearly 3,000 heterosexual couples in their study into three separate groups: couples in which the wife was a full-time homemaker, couples in which the wife was employed part-time, and couples in which the wife was employed full-time. The researchers found that the husband was more often perceived to be more powerful when the wife was a full-time homemaker than when the wife was employed full-time (Figure 7.2).

Some social scientists have argued that power in families is a function of more than income, education, and occupation. People find value in many different things, including intelligence, pleasing personality traits, personal appearance, skill in various areas of endeavor, social prestige, a sense of humor, and interpersonal skills (Berger, 1980). One husband has an intelligent, well-educated wife who has done very well in the professional world. But only half-jokingly, he admits that a big part of the power she has over him stems from her personality. She says that one of her husband's most powerful resources is his sense of humor: "He's crazy, I admit. But he sure is entertaining!" The ability to make a partner laugh often translates into power in a relationship.

An important nonmaterial resource that needs to be considered in any discussion of power is the individual's interest in maintaining the relationship. This "principle of least interest" was described by Waller (1951), who believed that the

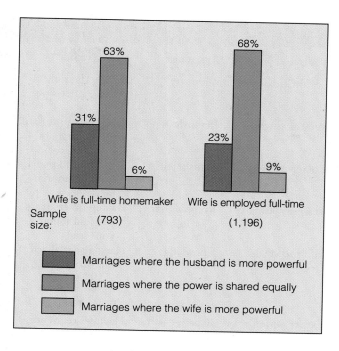

Figure 7.2 Wives' Employment and the Marital Balance of Power. *Source: American Couples* (p. 139) by P. Blumstein and P. Schwartz, 1983, New York: Morrow. Copyright 1983 by P. Blumstein and P. Schwartz. Reprinted by permission of William Morrow and Company, Inc.

individual who is least interested in maintaining the relationship has the most power. If one person is more dependent than the other or more concerned about keeping the relationship alive, the most-interested partner is likely to defer to the least-interested partner. In short, the least-interested partner will have more power. Even if the least-interested partner does not exploit the situation, he or she will be more powerful, and this is likely to be demonstrated in a variety of subtle and not-so-subtle ways.

Other researchers have approached the bases of family power in a somewhat more abstract way (Cromwell & Olson, 1975). Raven, Centers, and Rodrigues (1975) identified six bases of power. *Legitimate power,* also called authority, is based on an individual's legitimate or normatively prescribed right to change another's behavior. Legitimate power stems from one person's acceptance of a role relationship, believing that the other person has the right to request compliance. *Reward power* is the ability to provide rewards for desired behavior changes. *Coercive power* is based in the perception that punishment will occur if the desired behavior does not happen.

Referent power is based on identification with or attraction to another; these people have power that comes from being a role model or being physically attractive to others. *Informational power* is an individual's ability to use explanations and other persuasive communication to change someone else's behavior. The individual with informational power has carefully and successfully explained the necessity for change. *Expert power* is based on the perception that one person has superior knowledge or ability within a given area, the understanding and skill to lead

Table 7.1 Six Bases of Family Power

TYPE	RESOURCE	DEFINITION	EXAMPLE
Legitimate power	Authority	Having the right to make a decision	A single woman's right to decide if she has an abortion
Reward power	Rewards	Being able to reward for appropriate behavior	Praising a child for helping with household chores
Coercive power	Punishment	Being able to punish for inappropriate behavior	Punishing a child for staying out 2 hours late
Referent power	Respect and/ or love	Having others trust you and follow your lead	Following your parents' advice about how to handle their funerals
Informational power	Knowledge	Having specialized knowledge	Following the husband's advice on buying a car because he has carefully researched the topic
Expert power	Experience in an area	Having experience and respect in a field	Following the wife's advice about finances because she is a financial counselor

Source: Adapted from "The Bases of Conjugal Power" (pp. 217–232) by B. H. Raven, R. Centers, and A. Rodrigues. In *Power in Families*, edited by R. E. Cromwell and D. H. Olson, 1975, Sage Publications. Copyright © 1975 by Sage Publications. Adapted by permission of the publisher.

another to the best outcome. Examples of these six bases of family power are given in Table 7.1.

Family Power Processes Family power processes are those interaction techniques that occur during general family discussions, decision making, problem solving, conflict resolution, and crisis management. *Assertiveness* and *aggressiveness* refer to ways in which people attempt to change the behavior of others. People are being assertive when they express what they want or desire: "I would like you to pick up your clothes." People are being aggressive when they demand that others comply with their requests: "Pick up those clothes, or I won't fix dinner tonight." *Control* refers to how effective these attempts to change the behavior of others are. The more often others are willing to comply with a person's request, the more control that person has.

Family Power Outcomes The third area of family power—outcomes—centers on who makes decisions and who wins. There are several ways of measuring power outcomes. When doing observational research on power in families, researchers typically count the number of assertive statements individuals make and record how others respond to those statements. For example, in a family with two parents and an adolescent, if the husband makes 10 assertive statements and 8 of them

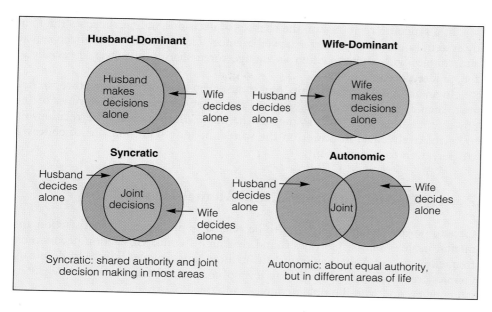

Figure 7.3 Power Patterns in Marriages. *Source:* Adapted from "The Measurement of Family Relationships" by P. G. Herbst, 1952, *Human Relations, 5,* pp. 3–35. Used by permission of the publisher.

are accepted by the rest of the family, the researchers calculate the husband's effective power in the family as 80%. If the wife makes 8 assertive statements but only 2 of them are accepted by the other family members, her effective power is 25%. If the adolescent makes 14 assertive statements and only 2 of them are accepted, the adolescent's effective power is 14%. On the basis of these observations, one could conclude that the husband in this family has more effective power than the wife or the adolescent.

Types of Power Patterns

According to one classic model (Herbst, 1952), power in a relationship can be divided in four basic ways: a **husband-dominated power pattern,** in which the man is basically the boss; a **wife-dominant power pattern,** where the woman is basically the boss; a **syncratic power pattern** (in essence, "to decide together"), in which authority is shared and decisions are made on a joint basis in most areas of endeavor; and an **autonomic power pattern,** in which each spouse has about equal authority but in different areas of life, and they essentially make decisions in their particular domains independent of each other. These patterns are illustrated in Figure 7.3.

In the early stages of a relationship, there can be a great deal of instability as the individuals struggle to work out the balance of power. As time passes, the partners assert themselves to establish some power in the relationship. A male- or female-dominated relationship, with one person leading and the other following, is difficult to maintain. Eventually the dominant one may tire of leading and the submissive one may tire of following. This can facilitate change to another type of power sharing.

In a syncratic relationship, the sharing of decisions and tasks causes the family system to come into a better power balance. The partners are relatively equal, and couples with children often encourage some sharing of power, especially as the children become older.

In an autonomic relationship, one spouse may have most of the power in one area, such as inside the home, whereas the other spouse may have most of the power in another area, such as outside the home. Both perceive the relationship to be relatively equal in power on the whole, because both domains of endeavor are perceived to be important.

Power, Marital Satisfaction, and Mental Health

Certain power arrangements tend to be related to higher marital satisfaction and mental health. Ramon Corrales found that high marital satisfaction occurs most frequently among egalitarian (syncratic or autonomic) couples. Husband-dominant couples are less likely to have a high level of marital satisfaction than are egalitarian couples, and wife-dominant couples rank third (Corrales, 1975).

Corrales found that many women do not seem satisfied in wife-dominated marriages. In a study of wives who perceived that they dominated the marriage, the women had relatively low scores on marital satisfaction. Corrales believed that these wives often exercised power by default, to compensate for a weak or ignoring husband. Husbands in these wife-dominant marriages reported that they were not as dissatisfied with the relationship as their wives were. Kolb and Straus (1974) suggested a "role incapacity" theory to help explain the wives' dissatisfaction. When a man relinquishes his traditional leadership role or fails to carry out his part of an egalitarian relationship, the wife is likely to become dissatisfied because she feels she married a less-than-competent man (p. 761).

A similar study of the relationship of power to marital satisfaction also revealed wife-dominant relationships to be problematic. Raven, Centers, and Rodrigues (1975) found that only 20% of the partners in wife-dominated marriages were "very satisfied" with the relationship, whereas more than two thirds of the partners in other types of power relationships were "very satisfied."

M. E. Madden (1987) measured power in 37 couples, looking at who made final decisions and the extent to which each spouse had control over the tasks he or she was responsible for. She found that for both husbands and wives, marital satisfaction was statistically related to perceived control over one's tasks. Who performed what task around the house was not so important as having a choice about who performed the tasks. The most satisfying relationship for both partners was one in which both had equal and moderately high control over tasks.

Premarital couples who are egalitarian in terms of roles also tend to have a more satisfying relationship. Alan Craddock (1984) studied 100 premarital couples who took the premarital inventory called PREPARE, which asks questions about roles, communication, conflict resolution, and other relevant topics. He compared four groups of couples: those in which both partners were egalitarian, those in which both partners were traditional, couples in which the male was egalitarian and the female traditional, and male-traditional/female-egalitarian couples. As predicted, premarital couples in which both were egalitarian were happier than the

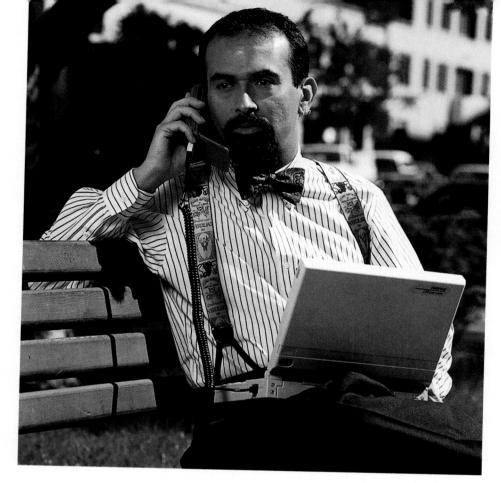

Men have as much to gain from egalitarian relationships as women do. The quest for power, money, and material success in which so many men are immersed is accompanied by higher levels of stress, higher rates of heart disease, and shorter life spans.

other three groups in terms of their communication, conflict resolution, personality compatibility, leisure activities, and family friends. The least satisfied were those couples where the male had a traditional role orientation and the female had an egalitarian orientation. Marriages with an unequal division of decision-making power are also associated with high levels of depression in both spouses, compared with more equitable relationships (Ross, Mirowsky, & Goldsteen, 1991).

In summary, power is a vital issue in intimate relationships. Sensitive use of power and the creation of a balance of power are two important keys to relationship satisfaction and mental health.

"In my parents' marriage, my mother always acted like my father had the power, but you could tell that she was constantly figuring out ways to manipulate him into thinking something was his idea," said Emily, a young woman living in Northampton, Massachusetts. "I realize she felt that, in the culture of her time, that was the best way she could ensure a reasonable measure of power in the family. It was the 1950s. Dad was a minister and everyone expected him to act like God, and he did.

"Today, I like how my own marriage works better. The assumption in society leans more toward equality, even though I think men still hold most of the cards. But in our family, the assumption is pretty much that power will be balanced out. We don't say this in so many words, but it's quite clear that when a decision is made, it's a shared decision. I wouldn't have it any other way, and I think David is pretty much in agreement on this, also.

"If we didn't do it this way, somebody would be pretty cranky pretty quick, until things got worked out fairly."

Communication and Power Dynamics

Researchers who study communication have identified several ways in which spouses exert power in their interactions with each other or make an effort to avoid the use of power in communication (Fitzpatrick, 1988, pp. 116–117). Conversations can be either symmetrical or complementary. A **symmetrical interaction** is one in which partners send similar messages that are designed to control how the relationship is defined. Researchers further divide symmetrical interactions into three types: competitive, submissive, and neutralized. The three are similar in that both spouses adopt the same tactic: both compete, both submit, or both are relatively neutral in the search for a solution to the issue. They differ in the tactic used and in the results.

In **competitive symmetry,** the conflict between partners escalates. He says, "I don't want to go to your relatives' birthday party. I'm real tired from work." She says, "You may be tired, but the real reason you don't want to go is you simply don't like my relatives. You never have." He says, "Well, I don't. They're boring and bigoted, and I've heard everything they ever had to say years ago." The discussion becomes a competition in which both aim to defeat the other. This win-lose approach sets the stage for escalating hostilities.

In **submissive symmetry,** both spouses try to give control of the situation to the other. He says, "Look at the checkbook. How will we ever get out of debt?" She says, "I don't know. We never seem to have enough money." He says, "I'm afraid they'll repossess the new car if we don't send in the payments on schedule." She says, "It would be a shame. I love that car. . . . " Both partners avoid taking control of the situation, attempting to win by passing responsibility to the other.

In **neutralized symmetry,** spouses respect each other and try to avoid exerting control over each other. She says, "I noticed the toilet has a little leak again. I have a meeting this evening, but tomorrow after work I can fix it." He says, "You're better at figuring out mechanical things than I am, but I could pick up the parts." She says, "That would free us both up by 6:30 to go out to dinner together." These spouses have avoided a power struggle over the toilet by offering ideas in a gentle spirit, approaching the matter as equals on the same team instead of boss and servant. Each gives a little, and both come out ahead. This win-win approach ensures that partners will have time to enjoy each other instead of fighting.

A **complementary interaction** differs from a symmetrical interaction in that the participants adopt two different tactics: One is dominant and one is submissive. He says, "Would you iron my shirt? I've got an important meeting tonight." She says, "Sure." If a relationship is to remain vital, it is important that partners try not to exert power over each other but, instead, work together for mutual benefit. Equality nurtures intimacy.

Suggestions from Family Therapists

Richard B. Stuart (1980) offers several useful principles for couples interested in keeping a balance of power in their relationship. Remember that power is a characteristic of relationships, not of people. Power is always relative, changing, and useful only to the extent that it is legitimate. Many of the conflicts that cause relationship stress are struggles over power process (the way decisions are made) rather than disagreements about a specific issue. The person holding the authority to make each decision must have the responsibility for carrying out the action. Decision making should be balanced by the value of the areas each partner controls, not by the number of areas each has. It is more efficient and more realistic to assign each partner primary responsibility for making decisions in certain areas, whether or not the other has veto authority, than to make all decisions a matter of mutual agreement.

Men may think they have a lot to lose by giving up some of their power over women and children, but in fact, they have a great deal to gain. Men tend to die younger than women, often from a variety of illnesses related to stress and poor lifestyle choices. A macho, "win-at-all-costs" attitude is commonly thought to contribute to men's health problems. "Having to continually prove oneself by outperforming others, and being fearful about losing, can become an obsession that leads only to anxiousness and uncertainty," according to family therapist Larry Frahm (1987). Rigid gender roles may mean that men have more power in our culture, but it is lonely at the top. The path toward intimacy is best walked side by side.

Summary

- Gender roles—the expectations every society has about people's attitudes and behaviors based on whether they are male or female—are rooted in biology but heavily influenced by culture.

- A traditional view of gender roles was articulated by sociologist Talcott Parsons, who proposed a theory of family roles that assumed men should be "instrumental" and women "expressive." Parsons's theory has been vigorously challenged and is no longer accepted.

- In many ways, American society is moving away from male dominance toward egalitarian gender roles. The concept of androgyny refers to a blend of traditionally masculine and feminine personality traits in one person. Recent writings on gender appear to be moving the discussion beyond androgyny. Rather than defining mental health as a blend of masculinity and femininity, observers argue that these concepts are cultural constructs rather than biological realities. It makes little sense, they declare, even to talk about "maleness" and "femaleness" because individuals are all so different.

- Persistent gender-role patterns in marriage mean that women do much more of the housework in the family than men do; this can lead to exhaustion, lack of sex drive, and anger.

- In Mexican American, African American, and Native American cultures, as in White society, men have often been dominant in their families, but signs of change are also apparent in these cultures. Japan, too, is moving toward a more egalitarian societal and family system.

- Historically prominent theories of gender-role development include social learning theory, which is concerned with how individuals learn the behavior patterns considered appropriate for their sex; cognitive development theory, which links the progressive acquisition of gender typing to the general maturation of the child's thinking processes; family systems theory, which holds that the entire family must change when an individual member changes; and feminist theory, which argues that women are exploited, devalued, and oppressed and affirms their equality with men.

- Family power is the ability of one family member to change the behavior of other family members. Researchers have looked at three areas of family power: bases of power, power processes, and power outcomes. Power in a family is related to how much money an individual earns, to educational level, and to occupational prestige.

- Heterosexual couples divide power in their relationship in four basic ways: a husband-dominant pattern; a wife-dominant pattern; a syncratic pattern, in which authority is shared; and an autonomic pattern, in which each spouse has about equal authority but in different areas of life.

- One way power is exerted or avoided in families is through patterns of communication. The most successful relationships appear to have a relatively even balance of power between the partners.

Key Terms

gender identity

gender role

gender-role stereotype

masculinity

femininity

androgyny

gender polarization

egalitarian roles

social learning theory

cognitive development theory

power

family power

resource theory of family power

husband-dominant power pattern

wife-dominant power pattern

syncratic power pattern

autonomic power pattern

symmetrical interaction

competitive symmetry

submissive symmetry

neutralized symmetry

complementary interaction

Activities

1. In small groups, discuss whether American society will ever evolve into one in which one's sex is relatively unimportant, except in relation to reproduction. How

far can we go in removing the old gender-role stereotypes? How far do you, as an individual, want society to go? Report what you decide to the larger group. Did you reach any consensus on these issues?

2. Study Box 7.2, "Contemporary Versus Traditional Dating and Marriage Patterns." If you are in an intimate relationship, decide which aspects from the "contemporary" list and which from the "traditional" list apply to your relationship. Also have your partner do the same exercise, then compare answers.

3. In small groups, discuss family power: How was power distributed in your family of origin? How do you know? (Give examples.) How do you want power to be distributed in the family you hope to create in the future? Do you think this will be possible? How? Report your findings to the larger group.

Suggested Readings

Bem, S. L. (1993). *The lenses of gender: Transforming the debate on sexual inequality.* New Haven, CT: Yale University Press. *An important theorist discusses how we can move beyond masculine and feminine to human.*

Cook, E. P. (1985). *Psychological androgyny.* New York: Pergamon. *An excellent overview of research and theory on the notion that human beings can be both masculine and feminine, tough and tender.*

Gilmore, D. D. (1990). *Manhood in the making: Cultural concepts of masculinity.* New Haven, CT: Yale University Press. *Explores what it means to be a man in many cultures around the world.*

Goodrich, T. J. (Ed.). (1991). *Women and power: Perspectives on family therapy.* New York: Norton. *Excellent discussions from a feminist perspective on the empowerment of women in family therapy.*

Lips, H. (1997). *Sex and gender.* (3d ed.). Mountain View, CA: Mayfield. *An encyclopedic text explaining the biological and psychosocial processes of becoming male and female, masculine and feminine.*

Taylor, R. J., Chatters, L. M., Tucker, M. B., & Lewis, E. (1991). Developments in research on Black families. In A. Booth (Ed.), *Contemporary families: Looking forward, looking back* (pp. 275–296). Minneapolis: National Council on Family Relations. *A very good review of research on African American families, packed with useful ideas and directions for study and understanding.*

Thompson, L., & Walker, A. J. (1991). Gender in families: Women and men in marriage, work, and parenthood. In A. Booth (Ed.), *Contemporary families: Looking forward, looking back* (pp. 76–102). Minneapolis: National Council on Family Relations. *An excellent review of research on gender roles in families.*

Vega, W. A. (1991). Hispanic families in the 1980s. In A. Booth (Ed.), *Contemporary families: Looking forward, looking back* (pp. 297–306). Minneapolis: National Council on Family Relations. *Reviews research on Hispanic families and gives direction for future studies.*

CHAPTER 8

Communication and Intimacy

Communication is at the heart of intimate human relationships—it is literally the foundation on which all else is built. Communication is the way humans create and share meaning, both verbally and nonverbally. The ability to communicate is one of a handful of essential skills individuals must master if they are to enjoy close relationships. In fact, the ability and the willingness to communicate have been found to be among the most important factors in maintaining a satisfying relationship.

This chapter focuses on the art of interpersonal communication. It discusses several important principles of communication, as well as gender and cultural differences in communication styles. It offers ways for people to become more aware of their communication patterns and styles. Finally, it suggests various approaches and techniques people can use to improve communication in their relationships, thereby increasing the level of intimacy they enjoy with friends, partners, and family members.

Perspectives on Communication

Communication difficulties often arise when participants have divergent communication styles. This section sheds light on the two most significant sources of communication-style differences: gender and culture.

Gender Differences in Communication Style

Common gender-related differences in communication often cause conflict between men and women. It sometimes seems as if there are two separate styles of communication: a masculine style and a feminine style. A better understanding of the differences between these styles by both men and women can reduce some of the friction between them.

Jane Tear (cited in Meier, 1991) summarizes what many authorities believe to be common differences between male and female communication styles (Box 8.1). Men often use conversation in a competitive way, perhaps in an attempt to establish dominance in the relationship, whereas women tend to use conversation in a more affiliative way, hoping to establish friendship. Females tend to use good listening behaviors (such as eye contact, frequent nodding, focused attending, and relevant questions), whereas men seem less focused on listening and more focused on responding. Males also tend to talk more but to disclose less personal information about themselves. Females tend to speak as a way to connect with people and ideas.

Deborah Tannen's work complements Tear's synthesis of communication styles. In her book, *You Just Don't Understand: Women and Men in Conversation*, Tannen (1990) reported a conversation between a couple in their car. The woman had asked, "Would you like to stop for a drink?" Her husband had answered truthfully, "No," and they hadn't stopped. He was later frustrated to learn that his wife was annoyed because she had wanted to stop for a drink. He wondered, "Why didn't she just say what she wanted? Why did she play games with me?" The wife was

BOX 8.1

Conversational Style and Gender

Listening Style

Male

Irregular eye contact

Infrequent nodding

Infrequent use of "uh-huh"

May continue another activity while speaking

Interrupts in order to speak

Questions are designed to analyze speaker's information

Female

Uninterrupted eye contact

Frequent nodding

Frequent use of "uh-huh"

Usually stops other activities while speaking

Waits for pauses in order to speak

Questions are designed to elicit more information

Speaking Style

Male

Few pauses

May abruptly change topic

Speaks until interrupted

Speaks louder than previous speaker

Frequent use of "I" and "me"

Personal self-disclosure rarely included

Humor delivered as separate jokes or anecdotes

Humor often based on kidding or making fun of others

Female

Frequent pauses

Connects information to previous speaker's information

Stops speaking when information is delivered

Uses same volume as previous speaker

Frequent use of "us" and "we"

Personal self-disclosure often included

Humor interwoven into discussion content

Humor rarely based on kidding or making fun of others

Note: This chart was developed by Jane Tear, a New York City–based consultant who specializes in gender dynamics in the workplace. She stresses that although most people have a speaking style fairly typical of their sex, each person's individual style reflects gender-typical tendencies to a greater or lesser extent.

Source: "War of the Words: Women Talk About How Men and Women Talk" by Peg Meier, January 6, 1991, Minneapolis *Star/Tribune (First Sunday,* p. 8). Copyright 1991 by Minneapolis *Star/Tribune.* Reprinted by permission.

annoyed not so much because she had not gotten her way but because her husband had not considered her preference. From her point of view, she had shown concern for her husband's wishes, but he had shown no concern for hers.

Tannen believed that in this instance the spouses had used different but equally valid styles of communication and that both need to learn how to decipher each other's approaches to communication:

> In understanding what went wrong, the man must realize that when [his wife] asks what he would like, she is not asking an information question but rather starting a negotiation about what both would like. For her part, however, the woman must realize that when he answers 'yes' or 'no' he is not making a non-negotiable demand. (p. 22)

Competition Versus Connection   Men are generally socialized to be competitive; they live in a hierarchical world in which each encounter with another person is seen as a challenge to their position. When the match is over, the man often evaluates himself as one-up or one-down. Male conversations are almost symbolic struggles in which the competitor tries to gain the upper hand, protect himself from threatening moves, and not allow himself to be pushed around. Men are therefore more uncomfortable talking about feelings than women are, because feelings can be interpreted as signs of weakness.

Women tend to approach the world not as competing, independent individualists but as individuals intimately interconnected with one another. Women tend to "network"; men tend to "compete." Tannen argues that for women, conversations are "negotiations for closeness in which people try to seek and give confirmation and support, and to reach consensus" (1990, p. 25). Women tend to seek out a community and to work to preserve intimacy and avoid isolation. Although they are also concerned with achieving status and avoiding failure, these are not their major focuses in life.

Though we all apparently need to have both a sense of independence from others and a sense of intimacy with others, men lean toward independence and women lean toward intimacy. The greater the difference in communication style between a man and a woman, the greater the potential for misunderstanding. A woman, needing closeness, will naturally want to tell her spouse where she's going, whom she'll be with, and when she'll return. A man, needing independence and control, may find it more difficult to see why it is important to share this information.

Similarly, a woman, being more concerned with building a close relationship, will want to tell her spouse about every purchase she would like to make—even those that are rather minor in terms of dollars. Her husband may resist seeking permission from her for every little purchase, seeing any lessening of control over the family purse strings as a loss of control in life (Tannen, 1990, p. 26).

Communication in an intimate relationship involves a continuous balancing of competing needs for intimacy and independence. Tannen points out that intimacy implies that "we're close and the same," whereas independence implies that "we're separate and different." Independence can also be the foundation of a hierarchy in a relationship—that is, "If I'm independent of you, and you're dependent on me, I'm higher on the totem pole. I'm in power." Perhaps that is why men, socialized to pursue power and control, tend to place more emphasis on independence than women do. Independence fits better into the world in which men have been trained to live (Tannen, 1990, p. 28).

Tannen explains women's "nagging" by arguing that it comes from a different approach to living. Women are inclined to do what people ask them to do, whereas

Gender differences in conversational style can lead to misunderstandings if people are not aware of them. Women tend to view conversation as an opportunity to connect with another person; men tend to view conversation as an arena for establishing dominance. These young women are probably able to communicate with each other more easily than with a member of the other sex.

men tend to resist even the slightest hint that someone else—especially a woman—has the authority to tell them what to do. Women tend to repeat their requests of men—to "nag"—because they assume men think like they think. "He would, of course, want to do what I'm asking if he only understood what I want."

So who's at fault? Neither. Both are simply reflecting masculine and feminine gender roles in their conversational styles. Tannen is careful to point out that women also value freedom and independence but tend to emphasize the interdependence and connection more. Similarly, men find comfort in closeness, but are socialized to see independence as more important.

Affiliation Versus Action   Women are often seen as the "talkers" in the family, whereas men may play the "strong and silent" role. This phenomenon also springs from differences between masculine and feminine gender roles. Women, seeking to affiliate, do so by talking. Men, being competitive, tend to be careful about talking. So when men go out with their friends, they are likely to do things together rather than to just talk. Women, on the contrary, tend to seek social situations centered around conversation, such as having lunch together. A good heart-to-heart talk builds intimacy and warm feelings. (Gay men also tend to favor a conversational style that focuses on building intimacy.)

In groups of people, men tend to be the talkers, but much of this talk is performance oriented, an attempt to establish dominance. When the topic is politics, sports, or other controversies that can be vigorously disputed, men lead the discussion. This performance-oriented talking is not really about establishing intimacy but about clarifying who has the power.

Men also tend to focus on solutions to problems, whereas women focus on sharing what they are feeling about problems. Because of this difference in focus, men often feel that women "only talk" about problems, and women often feel frustrated and misunderstood.

Male and female gender roles begin to influence boys and girls at a young age. Boys generally play outside more and do so in larger, hierarchically structured groups. Girls tend to play more in small groups or pairs, and the center of their life often is developing a best-friend relationship. For girls, intimacy is an essential ingredient of a relationship (Tannen, 1990, p. 43). During adolescence, males and females struggle to integrate with each other. Although they are attracted to each other, they have difficulty understanding each other. These difficulties continue throughout dating and into marriage. It is logical to argue that gender-role differences contribute to the unhappiness many people experience in marriage.

Tannen (1990) concludes that both sexes could learn from each other. Women could learn to accept some conflict and difference without considering it a threat to intimacy; men could learn from women that interdependence is not a threat to personal freedom. Tannen believes that the "best" style of communication is a flexible one: finding that delicate balance between separateness and connectedness. To determine your gender communication quotient, take the quiz in Box 8.2.

Cultural Differences in Communication Style

The uses and interpretations of both verbal and nonverbal communication vary widely from culture to culture. In England, for example, gestures are considered to be bold and undesirable additions to the communication process. But in Italy, France, and the Polynesian islands of the southwest Pacific, among other places, gesturing is common.

Cultural differences can affect not only how well a message is understood but also the way in which the messenger is perceived as an individual. A graduate student from India related the following incident, which occurred when he first arrived in the United States. The student was fairly fluent in English, but he was totally unfamiliar with American customs. One day he was walking down the street with a fellow student with whom he had become good friends. Without giving it much thought, he reached toward his friend and began holding hands with him as they walked down the street. Having assumed his friend was heterosexual, the American student was somewhat startled and asked his friend why he wanted to hold hands. The Indian graduate student became confused and said it was customary in India for two close friends to hold hands to show their friendship.

Clearly, actions may be interpreted quite differently in different cultures. The nature and scope of our nonverbal repertoire are largely determined by our cultural

Your Gender Communication Quotient

How much do you know about how men and women communicate with one another? The 20 items in this questionnaire are based on research conducted in classrooms, private homes, businesses, offices, hospitals—places where people commonly work and socialize. The answers are at the end.

TRUE FALSE

1. Men talk more than women.

2. Men are more likely to interrupt women than they are to interrupt other men.

3. There are approximately ten times as many sexual terms for males as females in the English language.

4. During conversations, women spend more time gazing at their partner than men do.

5. Nonverbal messages carry more weight than verbal messages.

6. Female managers communicate with more emotional openness and drama than male managers.

7. Men not only control the content of conversations, they also work harder at keeping conversations going.

8. When people hear generic words such as "mankind" and "he" they respond inclusively, indicating that the terms apply to both sexes.

9. Women are more likely to touch others than men are.

10. In classroom communications, male students receive more reprimands and criticism than female students.

11. Women are more likely than men to disclose information on intimate personal concerns.

12. Female speakers are more animated in their conversational style than are male speakers.

13. Women use less personal space than men.

14. When a male speaks, he is listened to more carefully than a female speaker, even when she makes the identical presentation.

15. In general, women speak in a more tentative style than do men.

16. Women are more likely to answer questions that are not addressed to them.

17. There is widespread sex segregation in schools, and it hinders effective classroom communication.

18. Female managers are seen by both male and female subordinates as better communicators than male managers.

19. In classroom communications, teachers are more likely to give verbal praise to female than to male students.

20. In general, men smile more often than women.

Answers: 1. T; 2. T; 3. F; 4. T; 5. T; 6–9. F; 10–15. T; 16. F; 17. T; 18. T; 19., 20. F

Source: "How Wide Is Your Communication Gender Gap?" by Hazel R. Rozema, Ph.D., Milliken University, and John W. Gray, Ph.D., University of Arkansas at Little Rock. Reprinted by permission.

Many aspects of communication are matters of culture, including such nonverbal elements as eye contact, facial expression, physical proximity, and touching. These Latino men find it natural to greet each other on the street with a hug. Most Northern Europeans would be more comfortable with a handshake.

heritage, as well. For example, the different ways in which men react to beautiful women around the world have been documented: The American male lifts his eyebrows, the Italian presses his forefinger into his cheek and rotates it, the Greek strokes his cheek, the Brazilian puts an imaginary telescope to his eye, the Frenchman kisses his fingertips, and the Egyptian grasps his beard (Parker Pen, 1985).

Westerners consider direct eye contact important, but many cultures see it as a personal affront, conveying a lack of respect. In Japan, for example, when shaking hands, bowing, and especially when talking, it is important to glance only occasionally into the other person's face. The gaze should instead focus on fingertips, desk tops, and carpets. In the words of one American electronics representative, "Always keep your shoes shined in Tokyo. You can bet a lot of Japanese you meet will have their eyes on them" (Parker Pen, 1985, p. 40).

In most Latin countries, from Venezuela to Italy, the *abrazo* (hug) is as common as a handshake. Men hug men, women hug women, men hug women. In Slavic countries, this greeting is better described as a bear hug. In France, the double cheek-to-cheek greeting is common among both men and women. But the Japanese are averse to casual touching, preferring a traditional bow from the waist. Americans may feel uncomfortable with bowing, but to the Japanese, it means "I respect your experience and wisdom."

Using Communication to Develop Intimacy

When close relationships succeed, couples are likely to cite good, positive communication as an important element leading to this success. A man might say, "We're best friends. We talk about everything. I don't know what I'd do if she weren't around to listen to my problems. She lets me know, very clearly, when she's upset about something. But I don't feel attacked. It's like, we both just sit down and work out a solution." On the other hand, when a close relationship fails, poor communication is commonly seen as a major factor. People may say, "We don't communicate." "He never talks." "She always nags." "He doesn't understand me."

Communication is important at every stage of a close relationship. The seeds of marital failure are often sown early in a relationship—sometimes even before marriage. Poor communication before marriage is likely to continue after marriage. One study of couples used the PREPARE premarital inventory (introduced in Chapter 1) to assess premarital individuals' feelings and attitudes toward communication in their relationships. The assessment focused on the level of comfort each partner felt in sharing feelings and in understanding each other. Couples who scored low on communication were more likely to be dissatisfied in their marriage or divorced 3 years later (Larsen & Olson, 1989).

In a national sample of 5,039 married couples, Fowers and Olson (1989) used the ENRICH marital inventory (introduced in Chapter 4) to discriminate between happily and unhappily married couples. The researchers found that background factors (socioeconomic status, age, education, years married) were less predictive of marital satisfaction than were the dynamics of the relationship itself. The top two predictors of a happy couple were good communication and skill in conflict resolution.

Communication is also important for families across the family life cycle. When children arrive, the complexities of family life increase, and positive communication becomes even more important. One of the challenges for families is parent-adolescent communication. Often adolescents have more-negative perceptions than their parents of how well things are going in the family. A study of 540 families with adolescents found that families with open communication patterns and problem-free communication tended to be stronger. Open communication focuses on the ability to share feelings and ideas with one another; problem-free communication is the extent to which communication lacks conflict and difficulties. Figure 8.1 (p. 266) shows that both mothers and fathers tended to rate the quality of communication between themselves and their teenagers higher than the teens rated the communication (Olson, McCubbin, et al., 1989).

Figure 8.1 Parent-Adolescent Communication. *Source: Families: What Makes Them Work* (2nd ed.) (p. 233) by D. H. Olson, H. I. McCubbin, H. Barnes, A. Larsen, M. Muxen, M. Wilson, 1989, Sage Publications. Copyright © 1989 by Sage Publications. Used by permission of the publisher.

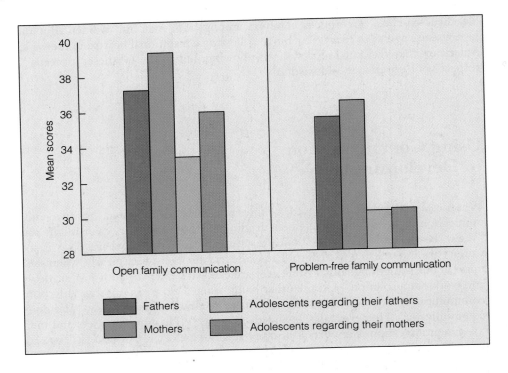

Communication is a complex process, but understanding certain principles can help individuals improve their interactions with others. For example, it is useful to know that people send subtle verbal and nonverbal messages to each other no matter what they say or do, even when they aren't consciously trying to say or do anything. Therefore, one important principle of communication is that "you cannot *not* communicate." Noncommunication is also a form of communication.

Communication as a Cooperative Endeavor

Communication depends on both the skillful sending and the skillful receiving of messages. Believing that you sent a clear message is no guarantee that it was decoded (understood) in the way you intended. The only way to know whether the message you sent is what was received is to ask the other person what he or she heard. Having the receiver restate what was said enables the sender to see if the message was understood.

When disagreement and conflicts arise, there is a natural tendency to blame the other person and deny or minimize personal responsibility for creating and maintaining the conflict. For example, a couple has an argument over the husband's refusal to discuss issues in the relationship that the wife considers important. The more she pushes him, the more the husband withdraws. He says to her, in effect, "I wouldn't withdraw so much if you stopped nagging me." To which the wife retorts, "I wouldn't nag you if you would discuss these important things with me." The discussion finally ends with the husband withdrawing even more, which only reinforces the wife's negative feelings. This potential dialogue ends in a monologue, with each blaming the other for what has happened and neither accepting responsibility for the outcome.

One model of interpersonal communication assumes a linear cause and effect. In the battle just described, the husband blames the wife because she nags and the wife blames the husband because he withdraws. This is an example of the principle represented by the **linear causality model,** which says that there is a direct, or linear, relationship between cause and effect. Although individuals often use this linear model, it totally misrepresents what has happened and is usually destructive, not productive. Both people end up saying, in effect, "If it weren't for you, I wouldn't act this way."

A family systems model better explains both what has happened and how to escape this type of situation. A **circular causality model** shows how both people are responsible for what has happened and that both are therefore responsible for changing it and preventing it from happening again. In a circular causality model, one person sends out a message, which causes a change in and a response from the other person. That response causes a new response in the first person, and so on. The communication cycle escalates into conflict. The husband's and wife's responses to each other's comments trap them in a vicious circle of causality: He says, "I withdraw because you nag," and she says, "I nag because you withdraw." Each spouse sees his or her behavior only as a reaction to the other's behavior, not as a determining factor in the other's response. In essence, they are both escalating the conflict.

It is best to avoid the "blame game" and to focus on working together to find solutions that are acceptable to everyone involved. Whereas blaming is a competitive endeavor in which one side tries to beat the other, genuine communication is a cooperative endeavor in which the participants focus on agreement.

Content and Relationship Messages

When people communicate with each other, they send out two kinds of information. The most obvious component of communication is content facts—that is, opinions and experiences. This can be called the "report" or "content" component of communication. The report component is usually relatively straightforward and for the most part is given verbally. The other component of communication is the message individuals send out about the relationship they have with the person with whom they are communicating—for example, whether it is a friendly relationship. This has been called the "relationship" or "command" component of communication. More subtle than the report component, the relationship component is often conveyed nonverbally. Although the content of the message being communicated may be straightforward, it is always interpreted in light of the accompanying message about the relationship between the people involved in the communication.

Nonverbal Communication

In communicating with other people, it is important to pay close attention to nonverbal messages. In fact, some researchers estimate that nearly 65% of all face-to-face communication is nonverbal. It is ironic, then, how carefully we select our

People send some of their most powerful messages nonverbally. With her head pushed forward aggressively, the corners of her mouth turned down, and her eyes set in a fixed stare, the woman on the right conveys an intense and intimidating presence. Her conversational partner responds by pulling her head back, smiling tentatively, and clasping her hands together. We don't know the content of their conversation, but we can guess something about their relationship.

words, when they comprise only 35% of the communicated message, and how little attention we sometimes pay to the nonverbal message we are also conveying.

Verbal communication includes both spoken and written words. Spoken communication has various nonverbal aspects to it: tone of voice, volume, pitch, speed of speech, and rhythm of speech. Written communication also has nonverbal aspects: style of writing (handwritten, printed, typed, sloppy, neat) and the medium (personal stationery, a card, a napkin) (Argyle, 1988).

Nonverbal communication takes a wide variety of forms (Argyle, 1988; Brockman & Peterson, 1990). It includes facial expressions, eye contact, gestures and other body movements, spatial behavior (e.g., how close to one another people stand or sit), body contact, nonverbal vocalizations (e.g., sighs, grunts), and posture. Nonverbal communication is just as difficult to interpret as verbal communication. Is that yawn boredom, or is it a reflexive action?

One component of communication that has a central influence on the accurate transmission and interpretation of nonverbal messages is the relationship context. For example, if you saw two people hugging at the airport, you would assume they have a close relationship. In other words, people make guesses about a relationship based on nonverbal behavior and the context in which they observe the behavior.

Daniel Sternberg and Ernest Beier (1977) demonstrated nonverbal communication in couples by combining observational measures with written measures designed to assess each couple's level of couple harmony. They were able to correlate characteristic nonverbal behaviors with certain types of marital relationships. They found that couples who had little disagreement during topical discussions tended to sit more closely together, touch each other more frequently, and establish a greater amount of eye contact than couples who experienced a great deal of disagreement during these discussions. Moreover, they found that when both the husband and the wife were described as high complainers, the couple sat farther apart, established minimal eye contact, and talked more than any other type of couple tested. Conversely, couples described as low complainers seemed to evidence the greatest amount of nonverbal affection and caring, including touching each other, assuming open-arm and leg postures, and maintaining eye contact.

Mixed Messages and Double Binds

People often send **mixed messages**—messages in which there is a discrepancy between the verbal and the nonverbal components. The receiver hears one thing but simultaneously feels something else. When the verbal and the nonverbal messages conflict, people tend to rely more on the nonverbal information. An example of a mixed message is when a person collapses into his or her favorite chair to watch a long-awaited television show and says, "Is there anything you want me to help you with now?" Although the verbal message conveys a willingness to help, the nonverbal actions express just the opposite. The person sending the message is hoping that the listener notices the discrepancy and responds to the nonverbal cues, enabling the speaker to watch the program while at the same time giving the impression of being willing to help out.

We all send mixed messages for a variety of reasons every day, but they often stem from an unwillingness to be direct and honest in our communication. Mixed messages can become a barrier to real understanding. Directness in communication minimizes misunderstanding and confusion.

Whereas a mixed message is a conflict between the verbal and the nonverbal components of a communication, a **double bind** occurs when the verbal and nonverbal messages (interaction component) relay information that causes some question or conflict about the relationship between the speaker and the receiver (the relationship context). The receiver is in a double bind when the speaker creates a situation—legitimate or not—that calls into question the type of relationship the receiver has with the speaker.

An example of a double bind is when one person tells a friend a secret and later learns from other people that the friend told them the secret. Because the supposed friend told a secret that was not to be shared, the speaker questions not only the trustworthiness of the friend but also the existence of the friendship. When one questions the relationship, one is caught in a double-bind situation.

Although a double bind can occur in any relationship, the probability of its occurring is greater if the relationship component is unclear. When the relationship between the two parties is established and clearly defined, the relationship component plays a less significant part in the interpretation of the message, and consequently, the content can be more accurately understood. For example, if you say to someone, "You really are feeble minded," that message could be interpreted in a variety of ways, depending on the relationship you have with that person. If the person is a close friend, she or he would probably realize that you were just joking and might respond in a similar fashion. If the other person is someone you have just recently met, however, he or she might not only *not* know how to interpret what you said but might also question whether she or he would want a relationship with you.

The more clearly defined the relationship is, the less chance there is that a double-bind message will occur. If a husband brings his wife flowers, for example, the way she interprets this behavior will depend on the mood of their current relationship. If she is feeling good about the relationship, she would likely interpret the flowers as a sign of affection. Depending on recent events, she might see them as a bribe, an apology, or preparation for something to come. She could worry about what this act means, an indication that she is unsure or distrustful of her husband's behavior. Again, the interpretation depends on the quality and current mood of their relationship and on past experiences related to this event.

In summary, when the relationship between the two parties is established and clearly defined, the relationship component plays a less significant part in the interpretation of the message, and consequently, the content is more accurately understood.

Metacommunication: Clarifying Your Communication

In the original description of double-bind communications by Gregory Bateson (Bateson, Jackson, Haley, & Weakland, 1956), a situation was described in which a hospitalized male schizophrenic was visited by his mother. When the man tried to embrace his mother, she stiffened, pulled away from him, and asked, "Don't you love me anymore?" On the verbal level she was implying love, but nonverbally she was rejecting him. Because of his dependent relationship with her, he was unable to respond verbally to the double-bind situation she had created.

The primary way of preventing or unbinding a double bind is known as **metacommunication**—simply, communicating about communicating. It is sometimes easier for children to pick up and respond to conflicting messages than it is for adults, as illustrated in this incident. A man was talking with a 5-year-old boy he liked very much. The boy was describing how much he disliked girls; the man commented that he really liked girls but disliked boys. After a moment of perplexity, the boy responded, "You're teasing!"—and they both laughed. In spite of the conflicting message about their relationship, the child was able to understand and to point out the incongruence. Because the man acknowledged the discrepancy, they were both able to see the humor in the situation. It did not turn into a double bind.

It is more difficult to respond to a double-bind message when it is from someone with whom one has a close and dependent relationship. Because of the significance of the relationship, the possibility exists that metacommunicating might create more problems. Paradoxically, the more dependent the relationship in which the double-bind messages occur, the greater the resistance to clarifying these messages.

Although double binds are usually seen as detrimental to a relationship, they can also prove beneficial. They can, first of all, create a situation in which one person feels the need for a clearer definition of the relationship. This can be accomplished by discussing the nature of the relationship directly, to clarify and possibly to renegotiate its nature.

A second paradox is that to feel free enough to improve a relationship, one must be willing to risk losing the relationship. Consequently, the more one has in-

B O X   8 . 3

Improving Your Communication Skills

1. *The foundation of all communication is effective listening.* There are a number of ways to enhance one's listening skills:

   a. Face your partner and maintain eye contact if at all possible.

   b. Provide appropriate nonverbal feedback—nod, smile, frown, and so forth.

   c. Don't interrupt; wait for the person to complete her or his message; avoid unsolicited advice, comments, and criticism.

   d. Use the "two-question" approach: Ask a question; listen to the answer; ask a second question in response to the answer. Following up on what the person is saying shows that you are interested.

   e. Use "how," "what," "where," and "when" questions instead of concentrating on "whys."

   f. The goal of questions is to better understand the other person's point of view, not to interrogate the person so blame can be affixed.

   g. Make sure your biases don't interfere with your listening skills.

2. *Take responsibility for your messages by using "I" statements and avoiding statements beginning with "you."*

3. *Make constructive requests which seek to change the way you interact with the other person.* Requests should: (a) begin with "I would like . . . " statements; (b) call for positive actions; (c) be respectful by using words like "please"; (d) be couched in the language of wants rather than needs.

4. *Consistently praise your partner for fulfilling your requests, and be sure to respond to your partner's requests.*

5. *Offer each other ongoing, positive feedback.* Negative feedback is likely to make things worse, but positive information will probably help keep the relationship open to positive change.

6. *Clarify your understanding of what your partner is saying by restating what you have heard or seen in your own words; ask your partner to confirm if you are understanding correctly.*

Source: Helping Couples Change (p. 97) by R. B. Stuart, 1980, New York, Guilford Press. Copyright 1980 by R. B. Stuart. Reprinted by permission.

vested in a relationship, the less willing one is to discuss or change it, even though change is often necessary if the relationship is to remain vital or to grow. Because many individuals are not willing to take this "existential risk," their relationships become increasingly predictable and routine. It can be very difficult, but relationship issues need to be discussed and clarified if the relationship is to be enhanced.

Using Communication to Maintain Intimacy

Developing and maintaining communication skills is a lifelong process. Being good at communicating takes time, practice, and attention to detail. This section focuses on specific speaking and listening skills. A good overview is provided by psychologist Richard B. Stuart, who offers suggestions for improving your communication skills in Box 8.3.

Speaking: The Art of Self-Disclosure

It is very important that as a speaker you speak for yourself, not for others. Communication problems often occur when a person tries to speak for another person, especially in a close relationship. Another way to avoid unnecessary friction is to stay away from "you shoulds" and "we's." Again, the issue is one of power and control.

Self-disclosure occurs when an individual reveals to one or more people some personal information or feelings that they could not otherwise learn. We acquire information about an individual in many ways—from mutual acquaintances, from the person's behavior, and even from the clothes she or he wears. Self-disclosure differs from these other ways of acquiring information in that the individual willingly and with some forethought discloses the information. (Self-disclosure does sometimes also occur inadvertently.)

Self-disclosure requires both an awareness of information (reactions, goals, feelings, etc.) about oneself and a predisposition to disclose that information. For example, an adolescent may want to discuss her vocational goals with her parents, goals that do not include college. Her parents, however, are set on her going to a particular college. The daughter complies with her parents' wishes to avoid conflict and never discloses her true feelings about going to college. Thus, although this individual was aware of her feelings, her predisposition to disclose did not overcome her desire to avoid conflict.

Self-Disclosure and Intimacy Patterns of self-disclosure vary with the type of relationship individuals have, but relationship type is not the sole determinant of self-disclosure. High and low levels of disclosure occur between strangers, friends, and intimates. But factors such as motivation for and frequency of disclosure are likely to be related to relationship type. Let's look at three different relationships—between strangers, between friends, and between intimates—and compare the patterns of self-disclosure among them.

If you were to ask why a person did not reveal personal information to a bus driver, the probable reply would be that it did not seem "right." What this means is that disclosure did not seem appropriate in light of the fact that the individual and the bus driver do not know each other. Personal disclosure to strangers seems inappropriate because there is no relationship history to serve as a foundation for the disclosure. There are, of course, exceptions to the general rule. When one stranger discloses to another, it may be because the discloser knows that he or she will never see the other person again and therefore feels there is little risk.

"I was on a plane trip from Texas to Chicago," related Lydia, a young art student. "I found myself seated next to a young man who, like myself, was a student. We talked casually for a few minutes, mentioning where we had spent our vacations. However, by the time the plane had reached cruising altitude, he began asking me questions about my relationship with my boyfriend, future plans for marriage, motivations for marrying, and a host of other pointed and personal questions.

"I was rather surprised to be asked to reveal such personal information, but I was even more surprised to find myself answering his questions. At first I was wriggling with discomfort at disclosing to a complete stranger.

SALLY FORTH   BY GREG HOWARD

Copyright 1987 by Greg Howard. Reprinted with special permission of King Features Syndicate.

But although the questions were startling, his manner was not at all offensive. In fact, he seemed rather likable. As he also revealed some information about himself, I revealed more personal information and feelings to him. I guess I felt I had nothing to lose because I would never see him again."

A second type of situation in which strangers may disclose is in a structured support group like Weight Watchers, Alcoholics Anonymous, or group psychotherapy. Here, disclosure is encouraged so that the group may help the person work through feelings related to a specific goal or task. Because the groups's purpose is to help the group member deal with problems that he or she might feel uncomfortable expressing in another situation, there is less concern about the appropriateness of disclosure.

Self-Disclosure in Friendships and Intimate Relationships   Although self-disclosure is not expected between strangers, it is expected and desired between good friends. The discloser is usually aware of how the receiver will react to a disclosure, based on what has gone on previously in the relationship. Although self-disclosure between friends may be quite selective, it may also become quite intimate and personal as the friends increase their mutual trust and exclusivity. In a relationship between friends, self-disclosure increases the listener's obligations because the listener also feels compelled to self-disclose. Mutual disclosure helps the friendship develop more equally on both sides. Friends' close relationship and previous knowledge about each other let them move quickly from impersonal to personal communication: One moment they may be talking about a mutual friend's wedding and the next, about their personal feelings about their own marriages.

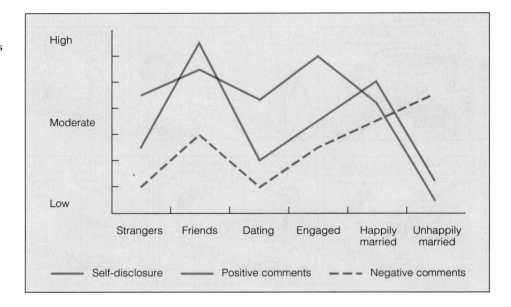

In some intimate relationships, including marriages and parent-child relationships, there is unfortunately less self-disclosure than in close friendships.
Among married couples, partners often assume they know each other. Some even
finish each other's sentences. But this assumption can be problematic, inhibiting
communication. Also, couples often allow themselves only "leftover" time to share.
At the end of the day, they may exchange pleasantries, review the day's activities,
and talk about friends and the children, but they rarely take the time to talk with
each other about their relationship, their hopes, and their dreams. Most married
couples take their intimacy for granted. Consequently, they stop exploring new aspects of each other's personality and feelings. Some husbands and wives think that
love alone will make the spouse understand all their needs and desires: "*If* she (he)
loved me, she (he) would know what I want." However, spouses cannot guess their
partner's inner feelings. Two people must *tell* each other what they need and want.
Revealing new information to the partner enables the partner to share in one's
changes and increases the intimacy of the relationship. Failure to reveal changes
can result in partners "growing apart" from each other.

Figure 8.2 summarizes some research on self-disclosure, positive comments,
and negative comments in various types of relationships. (The positive and negative comments were about the partner and sometimes about the relationship.) Interactions with strangers tend to be low to moderate on self-disclosure, involving
many more positive than negative comments. The greatest degree of disclosure
and a high level of positive comments are seen in close friendships, which also involve a moderate amount of negative comments. Dating relationships tend to have
a higher level of expression of positive feelings and lower levels of both self-
disclosure and negative comments. As couples move toward engagement, positive

comments are at their highest, and both self-disclosure and negative comments increase. Happily married couples tend to be moderate to high on both positive and negative comments, as well as on self-disclosure. In contrast, unhappily married couples show very few positive comments and very low self-disclosure; however, negative comments are high.

Listening: A Difficult Skill

We hear only half of what is said to us, understand only half of that, believe only half of that, and remember only half of that.
—MIGNON McLAUGHLIN, *Journalist* (1963)

Comedian Lily Tomlin urges us to "listen with the same intensity reserved only for talking." If one communication skill could be considered a foundation for intimacy, it would be listening. A very perceptive person once said, "Listening is really a lot more fun. When I'm talking, I'm not learning a thing."

People have a tendency to judge one another, listening to what others say and then deciding whether they are "right" or "wrong." Being right usually means that the other person agrees with us, and being wrong, that the person disagrees with us. Good listening skills require suspending judgment and spending more energy trying to understand other people. An important listening skill is to restate the speaker's ideas and feelings for verification. Although this approach slows down communication, it minimizes misunderstanding and conflict. When the goal of communication is to control other people, listening skills are of little importance. If the goal is to connect with other people and to develop genuine emotional intimacy, however, listening is essential.

Sherod Miller and his colleagues considered listening to be the process of developing a full understanding of another person's "story" (situation, concern, point of view). Effective listeners are aware of and make choices about how much they will attempt to direct or influence the speaker's telling of the story. Miller and his colleagues noted that the listener's motives are paramount and identified three basic motives, or goals, among listeners: (1) to lead by persuading, (2) to clarify by directing, and (3) to discover by attending (Miller, Wackman, Nunnally, & Miller, 1988).

The distinguishing factor of each of these three listening approaches is the degree of control, or power, the listener desires over the situation. Does the listener follow the leader, allowing the speaker to relate the story in her or his own way? Or does the listener become the leader—getting the speaker to tell the story in the way the listener wants to hear it? The answer affects the quality and integrity of the information that is exchanged. The attentive, or discovery, mode is clearly the most effective for building rapport and trust.

Persuasive listening is hardly listening at all; the "listener" is really looking for an opening to jump in and control the direction of the conversation. Sometimes the persuader resembles a television reporter trying hard to get that 10-to 15-second "sound bite" for the evening news. **Directive listening** involves less control than persuasive listening, but does attempt to channel, or direct, the conversation. Studies indicate that excellent salespeople (those most likely to make the

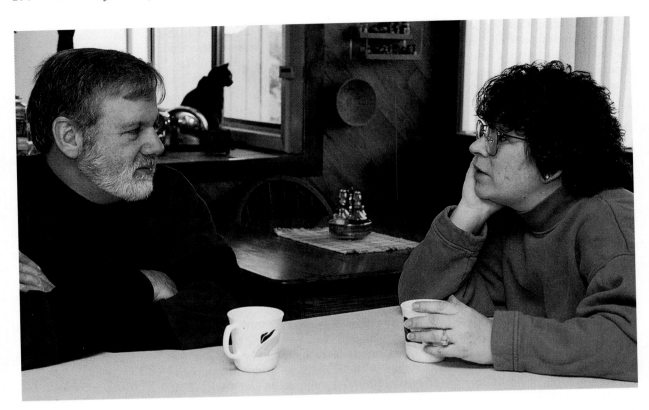

Attentive listening is a rare skill worth cultivating. It not only builds trust and intimacy in a relationship but also most efficiently allows a speaker to get her point across—without interruption or distraction.

sale) ask four times as many questions as the average salesperson asks (Miller et al., 1988). The questions control the direction of the conversation, steering it where the directive listener wants it to go.

Directive listening has certain advantages. It quickly focuses a conversation, and if the speaker cooperates, it allows the directive questioner to take charge of the dialogue. The major disadvantage of directive listening, however, is that in the interest of efficiency, crucial elements of the story may be lost. Directive listeners who use the approach in a very curt manner often fail to really understand what they are being told. By controlling the direction of the conversation, the directive listener may also lead the speaker down a blind alley into a trap.

Attentive listening is a mode in which the listener simply lets the speaker tell the story spontaneously and without interruption, encouraging rather than directing the teller. Busy people sometimes feel that attentive listening is too time-consuming. In fact, it is more efficient than the other approaches because it lets the speaker get to the *real* point, avoiding misunderstanding and confusion.

"I hope I don't sound immodest," said Francis, a retired newspaper editor in Charlotte, North Carolina, "but I think the main reason people have always liked me over the years is because I'm a good listener. I really enjoy hearing

Table 8.1 Effects of Passive, Aggressive, and Assertive Behaviors on Senders and Receivers

PASSIVE BEHAVIOR	AGGRESSIVE BEHAVIOR	ASSERTIVE BEHAVIOR
As sender	**As sender**	**As sender**
Self-denial	Self-enhancement at another's expense	Self-enhancement
Inhibition, hurt, anxiety	Self-expression	Self-expression, good feelings about self
Allows others to choose	Chooses for others	Chooses for self
Does not achieve desired goal	Achieves desired goal by hurting others	May achieve desired goal
As receiver	**As receiver**	**As receiver**
Guilt or anger	Self-denial	Self-enhancement
Lack of respect for sender	Hurt, defensiveness, humiliation	Self-expression
Achieves desired goal at sender's expense	Does not achieve desired goal	May achieve desired goal

Source: Adapted from *Your Perfect Right: A Guide to Assertive Living* (6th ed.) (p. 16) © 1990 by Robert E. Alberti and Michael L. Emmons, San Luis Obispo, CA: Impact. Adapted by permission of Impact Publishers, Inc., P. O. Box 1094, San Luis Obispo, CA 93406.

what other people have to say. I don't have any desire to sit in judgment of them, or to feel superior, or to give out a lot of advice. I simply like to listen and try to understand how their world works. It's always very interesting.

"People take this as a supreme compliment. They smile when they see me coming, and they're always coming up to me to tell me the latest story about their lives because they know I'll appreciate it if it's funny or sympathize with them if it's sad. It's really kind of fun. I always know what's happening, more than anyone else I know. My ability to listen served me well all those years in the newspaper business, too.

Passive, Aggressive, and Assertive Communication

Researchers have identified three styles of responses in interpersonal situations: passive, aggressive, and assertive (Alberti & Emmons, 1983). Each response style has effects on both the respondent and the partner. Assertive statements were consistently found to be the most accurate, expressive, self-enhancing, and productive in terms of achieving a goal. Table 8.1 summarizes the basic characteristics and effects of assertive, aggressive, and passive behaviors.

Passive communication is characterized by an unwillingness to say what one thinks, feels, or wants. Passive behavior is frequently associated with feelings of anxiety about other's opinions, overconcern about the feelings of others ("I just didn't want to hurt her"), and fears about saying or doing anything that can be criticized ("I was afraid of saying the 'wrong' thing"). Passive responses reinforce feelings of low self-esteem, limit expressiveness, leave a well of hurt and anxious feelings, and make achievement of personal goals unlikely. Receivers of passive responses often feel anger at and lack of respect for the sender, realizing that their goals have been achieved at the sender's expense. Passive behavior does little to enhance either person's feelings about self or the other and creates distance rather than intimacy.

Aggressive communication aims to hurt or put down another person and to protect the self-esteem of the aggressor. Aggressive statements are characterized by blame and accusations: "You always . . . ," "You never . . . ." Aggressive behavior is associated with intense, angry feelings and thoughts of getting even. When people act in an aggressive manner with their partners, it reinforces the notion that the partner is to blame for the aggressor's frustration, that it is the partner's responsibility to make things "right." Aggressiveness is expressive behavior, but it is all too often self-enhancing at the other's expense. Goals may be achieved, but only by hurting and humiliating the other. The partner may also retaliate in kind. Because aggressive behavior focuses on the negative aspects of people rather than the negative aspects of the "situation," it generally escalates in negative spirals, leaving both partners feeling hurt and frustrated and creating distance in the relationship.

Assertive communication involves the expression of thoughts, feelings, and

Table 8.2 Communication Patterns and Intimacy

COMMUNICATION PATTERN		RELATIONSHIP	WHO WINS	LEVEL OF INTIMACY
Person A	**Person B**			
Passive	Passive	Devitalized/Boring	Both lose	Low
Passive	Aggressive	Dominated	I win, You lose	Low
Aggressive	Aggressive	Conflicted	Both lose	Low
Assertive	Assertive	Vital/Growing	Both win	High

desires as one's right as an individual. It is self-expressive, with frequent use of the personal pronouns "I" and "me." Assertiveness is associated with feelings of self-esteem, self-confidence, and determination to express opinions or feelings. Assertiveness, in a word, is giving yourself the right to be who you are without infringing on the rights of your partner to be who he or she is. Assertiveness enables people to feel good about themselves and increases the likelihood of achieving personal goals. Because assertiveness encourages expressiveness rather than defensiveness, it facilitates intimacy between partners.

Assertiveness, passiveness, and aggressiveness are not personality traits; they are types of responses or behaviors. In most cases, it is inappropriate to label oneself or another a passive, aggressive, or assertive person. Some people use certain types of behaviors in specific situations or with certain people. For example, some women report that they have difficulty expressing their feelings or desires assertively in sexual relationships.

Because passive and aggressive responses affect intimacy negatively, becoming aware of the kinds of situations that elicit these nonintimate behaviors can enable you to practice more assertive responses. Table 8.2 illustrates how various communication patterns affect intimacy. For example, if both Person A and Person B have a passive style of communication, the relationship is likely to be devitalized and boring. In a conflict, both tend to lose because neither makes an effort to say what he or she thinks or wants. And in the end, the level of intimacy in the relationship is low, and the relationship is unsatisfying to both. Intimacy has the best chance of growing when both persons are assertive because this creates a win-win situation.

Types of Talk

Another useful way to describe communication is to divide the world of talk into four major types: small talk and shop talk, control talk, search talk, and straight talk (Miller et al., 1988).

Small Talk and Shop Talk

Small talk is the friendly, conventional, sometimes playful communication that makes the world go around smoothly. When not overdone, it is a useful approach for building rapport with other people. Common topics include weather, news, sports, daily routines, and other generally superficial events. Small talk is pleasant talk that aims at establishing a connection with another person with a minimum of hassle. A history of healthy small talk between individuals is important because it builds a reservoir of pleasant times both people remember.

Shop talk focuses on work-related matters, whether one's work is in the home, the school, the office, or elsewhere. Shop talk is a bit more formal than small talk, but its purpose also is to connect with another person. It can focus on organizational politics and events, and at its best, it helps to maintain the organization. Shop talk is also comfortable talk in social situations (e.g., "Well, what do you do?"). Shop talk can be overdone, however, especially if people spend so much time talking about their work that they fail to deal with other aspects of life.

Control Talk

The main purpose of **control talk** is to gain agreement or compliance from another person. This type of talk is very common in society and can be heard when individuals compliment, praise, persuade, or direct other people. Miller and his colleagues (1989) note that most selling, directing, bargaining, supervising, teaching, advocating, and preaching activities can be classified as control talk.

Too much control talk—directing of each other—usually signals that partners are experiencing mounting pressures in their daily lives. They find themselves mired in an "efficiency dance," doing what they *have* to do simply to get through the current situation. Too much control talk can lead to **fight talk,** an especially negative type of control talk. Miller and his colleagues found that when one partner acted negatively toward the other, the second partner reacted negatively 80% of the time. If the first person reacted to that negative response with another negative response, a conflict often began. In short, you get what you give. Fight talk usually comes from anger and frustration and clearly puts down the other person. The words are direct, aggressive, and punitive. When people use fight talk, they are letting out their feelings and desires rather than trying to figure out positive ways of coping with them. The focus of fight talk is on winning, on getting one's way, rather than on developing consensus and compromise. Miller and his colleagues argue that fight talk is a reactive rather than a proactive style of communication. Rather than giving in to the impulse to attack, it is better to shift to a more useful communication style.

Fight talk is conventional warfare: **spite talk** is guerilla warfare. Spite talk communicates a "poor me" attitude. It may reflect long-term low self-esteem, or it may simply be a temporary response to a particular situation. Spite talk drains the listener's energy. It often makes the listener want to change the subject or flee from the spiteful person.

People engaged in fight talk and spite talk have been likened to dancers. In fact, one popular book on anger is entitled *The Dance of Anger* (Lerner, 1985). As with dancing, the actions of people engaged in fight talk and spite talk influence each other. If one of the "dancers" is clearly winning on the pure aggression scale, the other dancer can counter by becoming more withdrawn, quiet, or passive. This passivity may make the aggressor even "crazier." Physical violence may be the aggressor's next move against the passive partner.

Fight talk and spite talk are hazardous to the self-esteem of both parties because they focus on people rather than on their behavior or the issue at hand. It is difficult to love another when one disagrees with the partner's attitudes or behavior. Fight talk and spite talk are signals that important work needs to be done in the relationship. They should not be seen as signs of disaster (interchanges of this type are common between people who love each other) but as catalysts for exploration and growth. In the long run, however, couples need to minimize fight talk and spite talk. There are more efficient and less painful ways of communicating.

Search Talk

The goal of **search talk** is to stop the communication dance, step aside for a while, and see what is happening. Search talk is similar to metacommunication, in that its aim is a better understanding of complex, difficult-to-define issues. Search talk is an objective, intellectual, and rational exploration of facts and possibilities—a trying-out of ideas without preconceived notions of what is "right" and what "should" be done. It can also be defined as brainstorming. Search talk reduces pressure by increasing people's information. Its nonthreatening, nonjudgmental nature helps to build rapport and trust between people. Because search talk is rational and objective, it may overintellectualize the situation, omitting some points that are essential to understanding it emotionally.

"He's so very good at intellectualizing everything," declared Ellen about her lawyer husband. "He's so cool and rational, and he can always beat me in a serious argument. I always feel like I'm being interrogated. He picks me apart logically. But he always seems to miss the *real* point. We're arguing from two different planes of existence, really. He's all head and forgets the heart. He doesn't know how to connect with me emotionally. Or maybe he's afraid to try."

Ellen later divorced her husband because he was unable to develop feelings of closeness and affection.

Search talk works well when it is used to genuinely try to understand and connect with another person. When used to win over or hide from another person, however, it can have disastrous consequences for the long-term health of the relationship.

Straight Talk

The kind of talk that comes from both the head and the heart is called **straight talk**—the effort to deal completely and congruently with the issue. The goal of straight talk is a genuine connection. The parties do not try to manipulate each

When a couple wants to really connect with each other, they have to use all their communication skills—speaking honestly, listening attentively, requesting clarification, giving constructive feedback. Such efforts pay off in high-quality moments like the one this couple is enjoying.

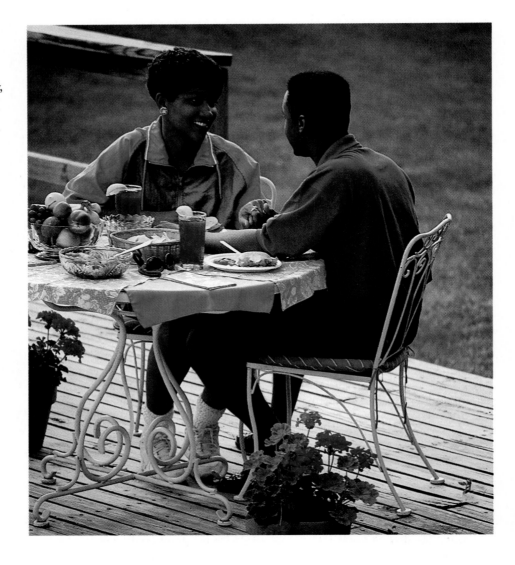

other, but try to manage their own behaviors so that a solution can evolve naturally. The core of the issue is examined honestly, and tension and disagreement are dealt with without blame, demands, defensiveness, or deceit.

After a straightforward, honest, and respectful exchange of thoughts, feelings, and desires, the couple commits themselves to positive future action. The goal is to ensure that future interchanges go more smoothly so that intimacy in the relationship can increase. (For some guidelines on how to increase intimacy through effective communication, see Box 8.4.) Straight talk continues until both partners feel that all the issues have been discussed adequately and a plan of action has been agreed upon. If one or both still have a "gnawing feeling," there is likely something deeper that needs to be discussed.

BOX 8.4

Using Communication to Increase Intimacy

1. Look for the good in your partner, and give him or her compliments.

2. Praise your partner as much as possible.

3. Take time to listen, listen, listen.

4. Listen to understand, not to judge.

5. After listening carefully, summarize your partner's comments before you share your reactions or feelings.

6. Share your feelings by using "I" statements (i.e., "I feel" or "I think").

7. When issues arise, avoid blaming each other, and talk directly about how to deal with the issue differently.

8. If issues persist, focus on creating as many new solutions as you can, and then try them one at a time.

9. If problems still persist, seek counseling early, when it's easier to find solutions.

10. Give your relationship the priority and attention you did when you were dating.

Summary

- Communication, the process of sharing messages, is an integral part of intimacy.

- Men and women tend to have different communication styles because of gender roles established in the cultures in which they grow up. Although the differences can easily be exaggerated, men tend to be more competitive in their communication and women tend to be more focused on connecting emotionally with others.

- Basic principles of communication include the following: one cannot *not* communicate; the message sent is often not the message received; when communication fails, both people are to blame; all messages convey both content information and relationship information; nonverbal communication carries about 65% of the meaning in an exchange; incongruent verbal and nonverbal communication can cause misunderstanding; and metacommunication (talking about talking) is useful for unbinding double binds.

- Self-disclosure—individual revelations of personal information or feelings—is a key to the development of intimacy.

- Listening is the process of developing a full understanding of another person's "story" (situation, concern, point of view). Persuasive listeners and directive listeners try to control the conversation. Attentive listeners aim at fully understanding the other person's point of view, an approach that encourages the development of genuine intimacy.

- Passive communication is characterized by an unwillingness to say what one thinks, feels, or wants. Aggressive communication aims at hurting or putting down the other person. Assertive communication assumes that expressing thoughts, feelings, and desires is the right of the individual.

- Types of talk include small talk, which is friendly, conventional, and sometimes playful; shop talk, which focuses on work-related matters; control talk, which is used to gain agreement or compliance from another person; search talk, which, like metacommunication, aims at analyzing the exchange; and straight talk, which is an effort to deal completely and congruently with the issue at hand.

Key Terms

linear causality model	persuasive listening	shop talk
circular causality model	directive listening	control talk
nonverbal communication	attentive listening	fight talk
	passive communication	spite talk
mixed message	aggressive communication	search talk
double bind		straight talk
metacommunication	assertive communication	
self-disclosure	small talk	

Activities

1. Study Jane Tear's chart, "Conversational Style and Gender," in Box 8.1. In small groups, discuss the hypothesis that men tend to use conversation in a competitive way in an effort to "win," whereas women tend to use conversation to build a relationship. Is this true, or is it a stereotype? What are the values and limitations of each style?

2. Because males and females are socialized differently, adult male culture differs somewhat from adult female culture. What can parents do for their children in the early years to minimize confusion and misunderstanding between the sexes later on?

3. Use the Family Circumplex Scale in Resource Section A to rate the communication in your family of origin now or at some time in the past. Identify the most positive and most negative aspects of that communication.

4. Use the Family Circumplex Scale in Resource Section A to rate the communication at various stages of a current relationship (friendship, dating, cohabiting, marriage). How has the communication changed over time on each aspect of the scale?

5. Focus on assertive, passive, and aggressive behavior in this exercise. Form groups of four. Two people will role-play the styles listed below for 2 or 3 minutes while the other two people observe. After each segment, discuss what it felt like to play the assigned role and have the observers give their reactions. When your group

has role-played all three styles, compare and contrast the various styles.

a. Assertive and Assertive (both people are assertive)

b. Passive and Aggressive (one person acts passive; one acts aggressive)

c. Assertive and Passive (one acts assertive; one acts passive)

Suggested Readings

Alberti, R. E., & Emmons, M. L. (1983). *Your perfect right: A guide to assertive living.* San Luis Obispo, CA: Impact. *Tips for learning to express oneself in direct, assertive ways, without being aggressive.*

Cupach, W. R., & Spitzberg, B. H. (Eds.). (1994). *The dark side of interpersonal communication.* Hillsdale, NJ: Lawrence Erlbaum. *An exploration of family violence, distressed marital relationships, paradoxes, equivocation, conversational dilemmas, double binds, and so forth.*

Lerner, H. G. (1993). *The dance of deception: Pretending and truth-telling in women's lives.* New York: HarperCollins. *From sexual faking to family secrets, reveals how the struggle to tell the truth is at the center of women's deepest longings for intimacy, authenticity, and self-regard. The third volume in the author's trilogy, which includes* The Dance of Anger *and* The Dance of Intimacy.

Miller, S., Wackman, D., Nunnally, E., & Miller, P. (1988). *Connecting with self and others.* Littleton, CO: Interpersonal Communication Programs.

Miller, S., Wackman, D., Nunnally, E., & Miller, P. (1988). *Connecting: Skills workbook.* Littleton, CO: Interpersonal Communication Programs. *Excellent, practical, and readable guides by a team of researchers and writers who have labored for many years to help people learn how to communicate better and to build intimate relationships.*

Parker Pen Co. (1985). *Do's and taboos around the world.* Elmsford, NY: Benjamin. *A fun collection of examples and anecdotes illustrating how communication and cultural practices around the world differ greatly. Fosters understanding of and sensitivity to these differences.*

Tannen, D. (1990). *You just don't understand: Women and men in conversation.* New York: Morrow. *Analysis by a communication specialist of the ways in which women and men talk differently and how these differences can lead to difficulty. Useful couples reading.*

CHAPTER 9

Conflict and Conflict Resolution

Because people view the world from a wide variety of perspectives and have different goals, conflict is an inevitable part of intimate human relationships. In fact, the more intimate our relationships, the more chances there are for interpersonal conflict. Although conflict may be "normal" in a statistical sense, it does not have to escalate into verbal and physical violence. There are many constructive approaches to settling disagreements.

This chapter describes some simple and practical approaches to resolving the conflicts we experience every day. The focus is on the prevention of serious problems in intimate relationships and on rational ways to build healthy intimate relationships. Chapter 15 discusses domestic violence and how it can be effectively resolved.

Conflict and Anger: An Overview

If conflict is not resolved, it continues to grow. This section focuses on the hierarchical process of conflict and illustrates the value of early decision making in preventing problems and crises. Anger can be a major problem in intimate relationships. Myths about anger and taboos associated with it limit our ability to express it in a constructive manner.

The Hierarchy of Conflict

The hierarchy of conflict, illustrated in Figure 9.1, can be thought of as a continuum ranging from exchanges on daily events to crises. The lowest three levels in the conflict hierarchy represent common reasons that individuals get together to relate: namely, to chat about daily events, to discuss ideas, and to express feelings. These discussions generally operate at a low level of tension, and there is usually little or no pressure for any decision to be made. The next four levels in the hi-

Figure 9.1 The Hierarchy of Conflict

If this couple is in a situation that requires a decision, they should deal with it as early as possible. When decisions are avoided, problems arise; when problems are ignored, crises occur.

erarchy involve increasing tension and need for discussion. An awareness of the need for a decision precedes decision making. If a decision that should be made is not made, this could lead to the development of a problem, which would then need to be solved. If a problem is not solved, it could lead to a crisis, which is more difficult to resolve.

As an example of the hierarchical process of conflict, let's consider a couple, Joanne and Gary, who need to make a decision about birth control. The process involves three phases: the decision-making phase, the problem-solving phase, and the crisis-resolution phase.

Decision-Making Phase   If Joanne and Gary are aware that they need birth control, then they need to make a decision about the type of method(s) to use. If they are not aware, then they won't make a decision. This could lead to pregnancy (a potential problem), and pregnancy could become a crisis if they did not want a child at that time. Even if they are aware of the need for a decision, however, they may not be willing or able to make a decision. That also could lead to crisis. In other words, deciding not to decide *is* in fact a decision, but it is one that often produces undesirable consequences. Even if they do make a decision, it may be either effective or not effective. An effective decision might be to use the birth control pill, which would maximize the chance that an unwanted pregnancy would not occur.

Problem-Solving Phase   Problems can arise for Joanne and Gary either because they made no decision or because the decision they made was not effective. If Joanne becomes pregnant, they have reached the problem level. In the problem-solving phase, Joanne could consider whether to have an abortion. If she does not want an abortion or fails to decide within 3 months, the problem becomes more serious.

Crisis-Resolution Phase   If Joanne and Gary did not want to have a child, not dealing with the unwanted pregnancy could lead them into a crisis. A crisis has the highest level of tension and creates the most pressure for a decision. Both tension and pressure increase the difficulty of making an adequate decision. Failure to make a decision earlier (to decide, for example, on a type of birth control) forces Joanne and Gary to make a more difficult decision (whether to have the child or an abortion, whether to get married, whether to relinquish the child for adoption).

Logic would indicate that individuals would be aware of potential problems and would therefore make early decisions to prevent those problems and avert crises. However, many times the opposite is true. Many individuals, couples, and families put off making easier, less complex preventive decisions. As a result, they are later faced with problems or crisis situations. This hierarchy of conflict model illustrates the sequential flow toward crisis and points up the importance of awareness and early decision making in preventing problems and crises.

Anger and Conflict Taboos

Most couples are afraid of negative emotions—anger, resentment, jealousy, bitterness, hurt, disgust, and hatred—and have a difficult time learning how to deal with them. A common tactic is to suppress negative emotions, hoping they will disappear with time.

There are two predominant reasons for suppressing negative emotions (Crosby, 1991). One is sociological in nature; the other is psychological. Our culture and many others have a taboo against the expression of anger. This message, transmitted verbally and nonverbally from generation to generation, says that nice and competent people do not show anger, that anger is wrong, and that anger indicates that something is terribly wrong in a relationship. This message requires individuals to deny their genuine feelings and keeps them from being in touch with what they are experiencing in life.

> "I don't know what to do or think anymore," said Doris, married for 5 years to Edward. "I know he loves me . . . I guess. He's just got so many rules he lives by, and so many rules I'm supposed to live by and the kids are supposed to live by. Maybe it's easier for him to live by these rules. Maybe he doesn't really think about them. I don't know. I just can't live by them anymore. The tension in me is volcanic. I find myself crying uncontrollably sometimes. I never have been able to express my feelings. My body expresses them. And now my feelings have built up so I can't seem to keep from exploding."

The psychological reason for suppressing negative emotions has to do with human insecurity. Individuals think, "If I let other people know what I am really thinking and who I really am, they won't love me and I will be abandoned." In intimate relationships, individuals struggle to find a delicate balance between dependence on

FEIFFER®

each other and independence from each other. Some observers call that balance *interdependence*. In families, too, children and adolescents struggle to differentiate themselves from their parents and their siblings, to stake out territory and beliefs that are their own. People search for individuality while at the same time trying to maintain close relationships.

Some couples have been socialized to believe that all disagreements in a relationship are wrong. Some falsely assume that the essence of marriage is harmony at any price. Such beliefs can be devastating to the relationship in the long run.

"When I was growing up, my parents gave me the impression that fighting was wrong in a happy family and that kids should be shielded from it." The speaker was Drew, a 30-year-old man from a Catholic background. "When they wanted to have a good argument, they would wait until we kids were out of the house or asleep. I grew up believing that my mom and dad never fought. Estelle, my wife, is from an alcoholic family. Her father would get drunk and pull the telephone cord out of the wall, push her mom around, and hit the kids. The meeting of these two approaches to conflict in one marriage was quite perilous for a number of years. My wife sometimes pushed and pushed until I blew up. I would try to hold in my anger, but eventually I couldn't stand it any longer. One evening I got so mad I picked up a hamper full of clothes and was going to throw it at her."

Fortunately, Drew and Estelle were both intelligent, creative, and committed to the marriage. They stuck with each other long enough to find out how to face and deal with conflict in a positive and productive way.

People tend to have negative attitudes toward conflict due to the popular assumption that love is the opposite of hate. Love and hate are both intense feelings. Rather than being opposites, however, they are more like two sides of the same coin. The line between the two is a fine one, with feelings of love often preceding those of hate. However, when negative feelings are stifled, positive feelings also die. People often say, "I don't feel anything toward my spouse any more. Not love or hate. I'm just indifferent." Indifference—lack of feeling—is the opposite of anger and love and hate. In the words of one loving father about his children, "If I didn't give a damn, I wouldn't get mad." Anger and love are connected; we often are angriest with the ones we love.

Rollo May described the dynamic connection between love and hate when he said:

> A curious thing which never fails to surprise persons in therapy is that after admitting their anger, animosity, and even hatred for a spouse and berating him or her during the hour, they end up with feelings of love toward this partner. A patient may have come in smoldering with negative feelings but resolved, partly unconsciously, to keep these as a good gentleman does, to himself; but he finds that he represses the love for the partner at the same time as he suppresses his aggression. . . . The positive cannot come out until the negative does also. . . . Hate and love are not polar opposites; they go together. (May, 1969)

Myths, Theories, and Facts About Anger

In all matters of opinion, our adversaries are insane.
—Mark Twain

Bill Borcherdt (1989) offered an insightful perspective in his discussion of anger. "Of all the human emotions, anger has created the most harm and caused the greatest destruction within individuals, couples, families, and between social groups and nations" (p. 53). Anger is a double-edged sword; when a person is angry at others, the anger also negatively affects the angry person. As Borcherdt put it: "It is impossible to hate, despise, or resent somebody without suffering oneself." Although anger can sometimes make people feel good, it often can also make them feel guilty and less positive about themselves.

Anger can also produce a feeling of strength and power. It deludes people into thinking that they are doing something constructive about the problems they face, when actually they are only making things worse. Anger lets people substitute feelings of superiority for those of hurt and rejection. It also allows them to think anything they want about another person without fear of retaliation.

Four common but false beliefs about anger are that it is externally caused; that it is best to express anger openly and directly; that anger can be a helpful and beneficial emotion; and that if you don't get angry, other people will take advantage of you (Borcherdt, 1989). Let's take a closer look at these beliefs.

- *Anger is caused by others.* Many people believe that "somebody or something outside of you magically gets into your gut and makes you angry or gets you upset" (Borcherdt, 1989, p. 54). However, one's happiness or unhappiness is not externally caused, Borcherdt points out. Anger, like any other

B O X   9 . 1

Anger: Myths and Facts

<table>
<tr><td>

Facts

- Anger is a feeling, with psychological components.

- Anger is universal among human beings.

- The nonexpression of anger leads to an increased risk of coronary heart disease.

- The venting of anger—"catharsis"—is of value only when it sets the stage for resolution.

- Aggression leads to further aggression, not resolution.

- Most anger is directed toward those close to us, not toward strangers.

- Depression, shyness, and suicide are expressions of anger at oneself.

</td><td>

Myths

- Venting (by yelling or pounding pillows) "releases" anger and therefore "deals with" it.

- Women get less angry than men.

- Some people never get angry.

- Anger always results from frustration.

- Aggressive behavior is a sure sign of an "angry person."

- TV violence, active sports, and/or competitive work "releases" anger.

</td></tr>
</table>

Source: Adapted from *Your Perfect Right: A Guide to Assertive Living* (6th ed.) (p. 107), © by Robert E. Alberti and Michael L. Emmons, 1990, San Luis Obispo, CA: Impact. Adapted by permission of Impact Publishers, Inc., P.O. Box 1094, San Luis Obispo, CA 94306.

human emotion, is self-created, usually when someone else does something we don't like.

- *The best way to deal with anger is to "let it all hang out."* The trouble with this idea is that it may make people feel better for the moment, but it won't help them get any better. Letting it all hang out does not resolve the underlying issues. Also, venting of feelings tends to bring out those same feelings in others, increasing both people's anger.

- *Anger is a beneficial emotion.* Individuals may find that, in the short run, they get their way more often by getting angry. But in the long run, they will push their partner away from them. The partner may also try to get even.

- *You're a "wimp" if you don't get angry.* This myth about anger holds that if people don't counterattack every time they are attacked, they are weak, inferior "patsies."

Borcherdt urges people to decide how they want to feel, rather than how someone else is going to make them feel. Firm and assertive statements, such as "I disagree" or "I don't like that," let us take more control of situations. We do not have to get angry; we choose to get angry—and we can therefore choose a different approach. Other common myths and facts about anger appear in Box 9.1.

Intimacy and Conflict

Someone once joked, "The major cause of divorce is marriage." Living together as a couple can be one of the most difficult challenges people face in life. This section focuses on how intimacy and conflict are bound together, the difficult balance between love and anger, the dance of anger that couples and families perform, and the sources of conflict in intimate relationships. This section also emphasizes the significance of anger in all intimate relationships.

Intimacy Breeds Conflict

The more one knows about another person, the more possibilities there are for disagreement and dislike. If a relationship is to survive and thrive, each of these differences has to be worked through in some way. Folk wisdom tells us that "you always hurt the ones you love." Sociologists who have studied violence in America tell us that statistically "it is safer to be with strangers than with your spouse or lover." Police officers report that domestic calls are among the most dangerous types of calls to which they respond.

Verbal conflict is not only acceptable but highly desirable if it is constructive, George Bach and Peter Wyden (1969) argued in their book *The Intimate Enemy: How to Fight Fair in Love and Marriage.* Couples who fight together stay together, Bach and Wyden argued, provided they know how to fight properly. Couples who don't fight and therefore don't resolve issues can end up in an emotional divorce. Bach and Wyden's approach to conflict generated controversy when it first appeared; many felt the idea was too radical. However, by encouraging couples to discuss issues openly rather than denying them and assuming they would fade over time, the approach helped many people.

Love and Anger in Balance

One challenge, or "growing edge," couples commonly bring up in marriage counseling is the issue of balancing "separateness and togetherness" (the cohesion dimension on the Family Circumplex Model) (Mace, 1982b). The challenge is for couples to preserve "a comfortable balance between the freedom of the individual partners to act independently and to develop their own individual patterns and abilities, while at the same time enjoying the rewards of a deeply shared life" (p. 113). With too much togetherness, marriage becomes a form of bondage. With too much separateness, the relationship dies from lack of attention.

Love and anger must also be kept in balance. "In every marriage the two dynamic forces are love, which seeks to draw the couple together, and anger, which tends to drive them apart" (Mace, 1982b, p. 115). Anger can be a healthy emotion if it helps couples create an interdependent relationship.

Anger becomes an ally of the partners when they use it to help them attend to those areas in the relationship that need work. If the couple does not find a constructive way to use anger in the relationship, however, it can create distance between them until they gradually drift apart. The common divorce scenario is not one of fireworks but one of a gradual loss of closeness (Mace, 1982b, p. 116). In short, fear of anger can lead to disengagement, and disengagement can lead to emotional divorce, which often leads to legal divorce.

In a mature marriage, anger is seen not as an enemy but as a friend. Experts suggest that couples make a contract never to attack each other when angry (Mace, 1982b, p. 116). Instead, they should consider the feelings of anger a sign that something is not right with the relationship. When they have calmed down and cooled off, they should calmly and rationally try to work things out. In other words, if they use anger as a barometer to signal an impending storm, the couple can work together to prevent major damage to the relationship.

The Dance of Anger

It is our job to state our thoughts and feelings clearly and to make responsible decisions that are congruent with our values and beliefs. It is not our job to make another person think and feel the way we do or the way we want them to.
—HARRIET GOLDHOR LERNER (1985)

In her book *The Dance of Anger*, Harriet Goldhor Lerner urges people to closely observe how they manage anger, and graphically describes her own style of managing anger when she is under stress:

> When stress mounts, I tend to underfunction with my family of origin (I forget birthdays, become incompetent, and end up with a headache, diarrhea, a cold, or all of the above); I overfunction at work (I have advice for everyone and I am convinced that my way is best); I distance from my husband (both emotionally and physically); and I assume an angry, blaming position with my kids. (Lerner, 1985, p. 190)

Lerner developed a guide to various styles of anger management and labeled these styles pursuer, distancer, overfunctioner, underfunctioner, and blamer. Lerner's styles can be categorized in terms of the Family Circumplex Model based on the types of intimate relationships they tend to lead to.

Using Circumplex Model terminology, **pursuers** tend to want to create connected or enmeshed types of intimate relationships that are very high in cohesion. Lerner describes pursuers as people who react to their anxiety by seeking greater togetherness in a relationship. Pursuers place a high value on talking and expressing feelings, believe other people should do the same, and tend to criticize a partner who can't tolerate feelings of closeness. Pursuers feel rejected when the partner wants more emotional space and pursue the partner more vigorously in this situation before coldly withdrawing.

Distancers tend to want to create disengaged or separated types of intimate relationships that are low in cohesion. Distancers want emotional space when stress is high. They value self-reliance and are private people rather than help-seekers. They have difficulty showing neediness, vulnerability, and dependency. Partners tend to describe them as being emotionally unavailable, withholding, and unable

Different relationship styles often emerge when people are under stress. "Pursuers" tend to seek greater closeness as their anxiety increases; "distancers" tend to retreat to get more space. All couples need to find a comfortable balance between togetherness and separateness.

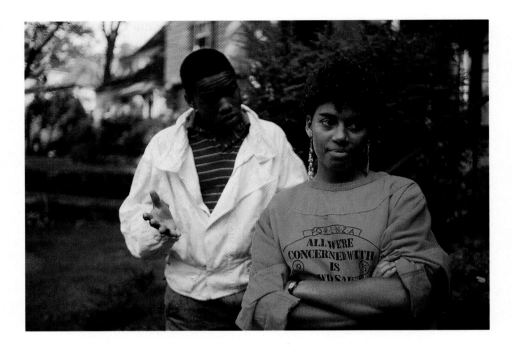

to deal with feelings. Distancers often manage anxiety by retreating into their work and may terminate a relationship entirely when things become too intense. Distancers tend to open up the most when they are not pushed or pursued.

The **dance of anger** refers to Lerner's use of the metaphor of a dance to describe how human beings relate to each other. Think about the dance of a pursuer and a distancer. As the pursuer moves closer, the distancer retreats. Then, as the pursuer unhappily backs off, the distancer's comfort level increases and the distancer moves toward the pursuer. The pursuer warms up again and moves in on the distancer, who again begins to retreat. Back and forth, ebb and flow. Just as people have different tastes in food, clothing, and cars, they have different feelings and needs about closeness. Using the vocabulary of the Circumplex Model, pursuers and distancers have difficulty finding a comfortable balance between separateness and togetherness. Left to their own devices, family relationships would move back and forth between the extremes of being enmeshed or being disengaged.

Lerner describes **underfunctioners** as people who in many areas of life just can't seem to get organized. These people are too high in flexibility (chaotic). Underfunctioners tend to become less competent under stress, letting others take over or fill in. These people are described at work and in the family as "the fragile one," "the sick one," "the problem," "the irresponsible one." Underfunctioners have difficulty showing their strong and competent side to intimates.

Overfunctioners, on the other hand, know what is best not only for themselves but for everybody else as well. These people are low in flexibility (rigid or structured). In difficult times, overfunctioners move in quickly to advise, rescue, and take charge. They can't seem to stay out of the way and let other people solve their own problems. In this way they avoid thinking about their own problems.

Overfunctioners are commonly labeled as "always reliable" and "always together" and have difficulty showing their vulnerable, underfunctioning side, especially to people who are having troubles.

Using Lerner's dance metaphor, how would a couple composed of an over-functioner and an underfunctioner dance? The overfunctioner would hide feelings of inferiority and incompetence by swooping in to "save" the underfunctioner. This act of saving would make the underfunctioner's task more difficult in the long run because it deprives the underfunctioner of the opportunity to develop personal strengths.

Couples sometimes think that a team made up of an overfunctioner and an underfunctioner is a complementary one. However, this type of relationship is vulnerable. The overfunctioner will eventually tire of saving the underfunctioner, or the underfunctioner will tire of looking and feeling so incompetent. If the relationship is to endure and become strong, the partners must find that delicate balance between one person creating chaos and the other rigidly fixing situations.

Lerner's fifth style, the **blamer,** is a person who has a short fuse and responds in times of stress with emotionally intense feelings. Blamers often fall in the rigidly enmeshed style, an unbalanced type of family system. Blamers spend a lot of energy trying to change other people. They involve themselves in repetitive cycles of fighting, which may relieve tension but which also perpetuate old patterns. Blamers hold others responsible for their feelings and see others, rather than themselves, as the problem.

Lerner notes that women in our society are encouraged to overfunction in the areas of housework, child care, and "feelings" work. In all other areas of endeavor, however, women are socialized to be pursuers and underfunctioners. Men, on the other hand, are socialized to be distancers and overfunctioners. Both sexes are good at blaming other people, but Lerner believes that today women do it more conspicuously than men because most women still feel they have less power in our society and resent their subordinate status.

All five ways of managing anger can be useful at times, but problems occur when one style dominates. It is important to find a balance between pursuing and distancing, underfunctioning and overfunctioning, blaming and taking the blame. In Lerner's (1985) words, "You will have a problem . . . if you are in an extreme position in any one of these categories or if you are unable to observe and change your pattern when it is keeping you angry and stuck" (p. 193).

"I think dance of anger is a good metaphor for how we operated in the early years of our marriage," said Curt, a writer, as he talked over coffee in the Pike Place Market in Seattle. "It almost seemed choreographed, it was so predictable. Eileen would do her part of the dance, and then I would respond with my part of the dance, back and forth, back and forth, and then all hell would break loose. It could get really ugly. I was so mad at her once, I thought I could kill her.

"I think a big part of the problem was we were simply replaying old videotapes of the families we grew up in. Her family in Puyallup was a soap opera par excellence. They loved to fight and did it well all their lives. My dad was an attorney in Bellingham, and he could really pour on the B.S. as well. He'd filibuster over the dinner table in his melodramatic way for ages, and my

Most people have an impulse to blame others when things go wrong, but some people habitually avoid responsibility for their part in problems. "Blamers" like these people tend to expend a great deal of energy trying to get others to change.

mother would finally crack and become a bitch on wheels. It was pretty predictable. It made me sick to my stomach. I left home when I was 17.

"Fortunately, Eileen and I could see the pattern in our own marriage. We read some books and articles about more positive approaches to settling our differences. We experimented and finally found better ways to get along. Luck probably played a part in it all—as did the fact that we mellowed a bit with age and just simply didn't enjoy a good brawl anymore. For whatever reason, we don't dance and brawl as much. Nobody's thrown anything for a long time. We don't fall into the old habits. We simply sit down and work things out. Thank God."

Sources of Conflict in Couples

Although many assume that newlyweds rarely fight, it has been found that they do fight; the top five issues generating conflict are money, family issues, communication style, household tasks, and personal tastes (Arond & Pauker, 1987). See Table 9.1 for the specific issues and the percentage of times they were mentioned by couples.

A survey found that nearly 40% of the 530 participating newlyweds had had at least one "fight" a week, and that nearly 70% had had at least one fight a month (Arond & Pauker, 1987). "Fights" lasted from minutes to days; almost two thirds (63%) of the newlyweds checked minutes, another third (33%) checked hours, and only 4% indicated that their fights lasted days. When a "big conflict" occurred, the styles of resolution varied considerably. The top three approaches were "discussing things calmly" (59%), "suffer silently" (41%), and "screaming" (47%).

Table 9.1 The Most Common Topics of Arguments Between Newlyweds

TOPIC	PERCENT	TOPIC	PERCENT
Money	23	Time for each other	5
Family issues	14	Value differences	4
Communication style	12	Job obligations	3
Household tasks	12	Religion	2
Personal tastes	11	Friendships	2
Decision making	5	Shared interests	1
Sex	5	Marital goals	1

Source: The First Year of Marriage (p. 124) by M. Arond and S. L. Pauker, 1987, New York: Warner Books. Copyright 1987 by Miriam Arond and Samuel Pauker, M.D. Reprinted by permission of Warner Books, New York.

The sources of conflict often change as time passes in a relationship. Edward Bader and his colleagues gathered data about the content of couple conflict over a period of 5 years (Bader, Riddle, & Sinclair, 1981). The researchers first interviewed couples just before marriage and then reinterviewed them 6 months, 1 year, and 5 years after marriage. Before marriage, the man's job and issues of time and attention were tied for first place in terms of arousing the most conflict. Six months after marriage, household tasks rose to number one, and handling money was number two; time and attention issues had fallen to third place in the conflict sweepstakes. At the end of the first year of marriage, household tasks were still number one, time and attention was second, and handling money was third. At the end of 5 years, household tasks were tied with time and attention for first place, but sex had moved from a lowly thirteenth position to third. The researchers concluded that the basic tasks of living together (how to divide housework, how much time and attention to give to each other, how to handle money, and related issues) created the most conflict for couples.

Box 9.2 (p. 300) summarizes findings on communication in stable and unstable relationships.

Approaches to Conflict Resolution

Grant me the serenity to accept what can't be changed, The courage to change things that can be changed, And the wisdom to know the difference.
—REINHOLD NIEBUHR (1951, in Carruth & Ehrlich, 1988, p. 600)

If anger is a normal part of intimate relationships, then fights and disagreements are likely to occur. The issue is how to "fight" fairly and constructively. This section offers some suggestions for resolving conflicts in ways that preserve and enhance relationships.

B O X   9 . 2

Communication Patterns in Successful and Unsuccessful Relationships

Psychology professor John Gottman and his colleagues have been conducting scientific experiments for 20 years on more than 2,000 couples, using video cameras, EKG monitors, and specially designed instruments for observing what happens when couples interact (Gottman & Silver, 1994). Researchers observe how couples talk to each other, examining facial expressions, gestures, fidgeting behaviors, and so on, as well as physiological changes like heart and respiration rates during conflict. They also note listening skills and expressions of sarcasm and contempt. The results are like a "CAT scan of a living relationship."

Gottmann now believes he can identify responses and physiological reactions that are essential to a sound marriage and those that damage a relationship. In one study, he was able to predict divorce within 3 years with 94% accuracy. Gottmann believes there are three types of stable marriages:

- *Validating couples*, who listen to and understand each other's point of view and compromise often.

- *Volatile couples*, who fight passionately and often, but are more affectionate and romantic than most couples.

- *Conflict-avoiding couples*, who resolve their problems by minimizing or avoiding them, accentuating the positive aspects of their marriage and accepting the rest.

The common denominator of all three types of stable marriage is, according to Gottman, that the couples are "nicer to each other." The ratio of positive to negative moments in their relationship is 5 to 1. "Positive moments nurture the affection and joy that are crucial to weather the rough spots," Gottmann states.

And what about divorce-prone couples? If there is a negative interaction for every positive one, the couple is divorce bound. Danger signs include *criticism* (attacking a spouse's personality or character), *contempt* (insulting and psychologically abusing a spouse), *defensiveness* (denying responsibility, making excuses, whining), and *stonewalling* (retreating from the conversation into stony silence). When these behaviors become routine, the marriage has serious problems.

To argue in a healthy manner, Gottmann offers these strategies:

- Call a time-out and cool off.

- Edit the argument, responding only to constructive criticisms and ignoring the nastiness.

- Stay focused, rather than wandering around verbally.

- Put the fight into perspective, and be willing to see that most issues are not all that important.

- Be affectionate, understanding, empathetic, and validating.

- Use humor, and be able to laugh at yourself.

Source: Adapted from *Why Marriages Succeed or Fail*, copyright © 1994 by J. Gottmann Ph.D., New York: Simon & Schuster; with permission of the publisher.

Fighting Fair

The terms *fight* and *fighting* are commonly used in our society to describe verbal disagreements between people. They are also used to describe boxing matches and other physically violent encounters. When family therapists talk about rules for fair fighting, they are talking about rules to govern verbal exchanges. Calling verbal conflict a fight is useful. It draws attention to the fact that verbal disagreements

BOX   9 . 3

Sixteen Rules for Fair Fighting

1. Negotiate from the Adult position.

2. Avoid ultimatums.

3. If one loses, both lose.

4. Say what you really mean.

5. Avoid accusations and attack.

6. Own your own feelings first.

7. Always check out your perceptions.

8. State your wishes and requests clearly and directly.

9. Never use sex to smooth over a disagreement.

10. Repeat the message you think you received.

11. Refuse to fight dirty.

12. Resist giving the silent treatment.

13. Focus on the issue and focus on the present.

14. Call "time-out" and "foul."

15. Use humor and comic relief.

16. Always go for closure.

Source: Illusion and Disillusion (pp. 170–180) by J. Crosby, 1991, Belmont, CA: Wadsworth. Copyright 1991 by J. Crosby. Reprinted by permission of the publisher.

are serious business and should be treated with caution and good sense (Crosby, 1991). Tension and anger build up during these exchanges, and verbal conflict can turn into physical conflict.

People should observe certain conventions when arguing with each other, because they will feel safer voicing disagreement if they know that it will not get out of hand. Crosby argues that "if we can trust—really believe—that our partner will not abandon us or take advantage of our vulnerability, we can then learn to interact in an aboveboard, straightforward manner" (p. 170). Without this basic trust, people will become defensive when they are accused or will hide their defensiveness with a strong counterattack when they are attacked. The 16 ground rules for fair fighting (Crosby, 1991) are listed in Box 9.3 and explained below.

1. Negotiate from the Adult Position   Using terminology from transactional analysis, Crosby argues that each partner should make a firm commitment to negotiate from the Adult position, rather than from the Child or the Parent position. Transactional analysis theorizes that people often replay old "tapes" in their minds and, under stress, are likely to act as they did when they were a child or as a parent acted toward them. Negotiating from the Child position, a person will act vulnerable and will often feel hurt or threatened. Negotiating from the Parent position, a person will rigidly repeat arguments and views held by her or his parents rather than interacting in new ways in this new situation. Negotiating from the Adult position, the person can listen carefully to the other, respond assertively and rationally, and work with the other person to find a solution acceptable to both.

2. Avoid Ultimatums   An ultimatum is a nonnegotiable demand—"You do this or else!"—and is a hallmark of dirty fighting. Fair fighting emphasizes negotiation, allowing each person room to bargain. Ultimatums generally lead to counter-ultimatums, leaving little room for genuine negotiation. An ultimatum puts the receiver in the Child position, with the sender in the Parent position. Neither person gets a chance to negotiate from the Adult position.

3. If One Loses, Both Lose   American society emphasizes competition in the marketplace, but in families competition can be problematic. Sometimes one partner is especially good at debating and may "win" most of the arguments. The other person may accuse the partner of using big words or sophisticated logic and is not likely to be happy about the situation.

The better debater may have won the argument but has lost just as surely as the partner has. The relationship has lost openness and a spirit of cooperation. The goal of fighting fair in a family is not to win or lose the argument but to work together to find solutions that are acceptable to everyone. Clearly, if one person loses, both lose.

4. Say What You Really Mean   As conflict increases, people often fail to say what they really mean. They may become agreeable on issues when they don't really want to accommodate. They do this to protect the other person's feelings, but they are also protecting themselves from pain or embarrassment. The more people get in touch with and share how they really feel about an issue, the earlier it will be to find a solution.

Take, for example, the issue of cohabitation. Should the couple move in together or wait until marriage to live together? One person may feel positive about cohabiting; the other person might feel ambivalent, seeing both the positive and the negative consequences. Because cohabitation is a complex issue, it can be useful to write down the pros and cons: "I love him"; "Mom and Dad will be mad"; "I'm afraid he will take advantage of me and I'll end up doing all the housework"; "I'm afraid I'll have to support him financially, and I can't even support myself now." After listing the pros and cons, the ambivalent individual can more clearly see why she or he is feeling undecided. The next important step is to share this clearly with the other person.

5. Avoid Accusations and Attack   When people are accused, they tend to react either by accusing the other person of something or by withdrawing. "You" statements are implicit or explicit signals of attack: "You make me mad," "You always do that," or "It's all your fault." Most people become defensive and angry in response to statements of this sort.

6. Own Your Own Feelings First   Instead of attacking with "you" statements, use "I" statements: "I feel hurt," "I feel rejected," or "I feel disappointed." Although the difference between saying "I" and saying "you" may seem small, it is significant. With "I," the speaker is clearly pointing out that something is wrong in the relationship and is simply putting the issue on the table for discussion. The "I" statement indicates the other person is innocent until proven guilty, rather than vice versa.

A key to positive communication is taking responsibility for one's own feelings. "I" statements set the tone for a constructive interaction.

7. Always Check Out Your Perceptions   Miscommunication is often the catalyst for disagreements. Don't assume that you know what is really going on until you have talked with the other person. Also, don't try to guess what the other person is thinking or feeling. It is your responsibility to ask.

8. State Your Wishes and Requests Clearly and Directly   Dogs and cats often do a better job of communicating their needs than humans do. Because they are afraid of being turned down or rejected, people often do not directly say what they want. One common approach is to ask a leading question, one that hints at the desired result without directly asking for it. For example, someone who wanted to go to a movie might ask, "Wouldn't you like to see that movie tonight?" The indirect approach may work sometimes, but people should not rely on it to get them what they want.

9. Never Use Sex to Smooth Over a Disagreement   People sometimes use sex as a tool or a weapon in an argument. When people use sexual persuasion to get their mate to agree with them, the underlying issue or conflict often remains unresolved, or if the disagreement is about some immediate decision, it is likely that no decision will be made. Also, the partner who feels pressured into a decision might later resent the partner doing the pressuring.

10. Repeat the Message You Think You Received   Active listeners let their partners know that they correctly heard what the partner was saying. Crosby calls this process "football": "You can't throw the ball (the message) back to your partner until you prove to your partner that you caught the ball (the message) he or she threw to you" (1991, p. 176). Active listeners don't repeat the message verbatim but simply restate it in their own words to show their partner that they understand it. Active listening does three valuable things: it forces people to listen; it slows down reaction time, which keeps the discussion calmer and more rational; and it aids understanding of the message.

11. Refuse to Fight Dirty   Dirty fighters lose the battle before they begin the attack. They prove their inability to deal positively and fairly with the situation. Crosby (1991) lists a variety of dirty fighting techniques:

- *Gunnysacking.* **Gunnysacking** is an alienating tactic in which participants stuff their true feelings into a deep sack and do not let the other person know what they are really feeling. The problem is that the gunnysack can hold only so much. When the sack overflows it all "hangs out," and gunnysackers may verbally or physically attack the other person.

- *Passive-aggressive behavior.* Like gunnysackers, people using **passive-aggressive behavior** feign agreement or act like everything is okay when in fact they really disagree with what is happening. People who act this way for some time eventually tend to become hostile and aggressive.

- *Rapid-fire questioning.* Rapid-fire questioning is an adversarial technique often used by police and lawyers to confuse a suspect or a witness. People who use adversarial techniques in their profession may try the same approach with their partners, but such techniques do not build intimate relationships or resolve conflicts.

- *Verbal abuse.* Name-calling, yelling, pouting, and sulking all belong in the category of dirty-fighting techniques. None of them are helpful in resolving conflict.

12. Resist Giving the Silent Treatment   Refusing to talk—the silent treatment—is an attempt to get even with or manipulate the partner. Shutting out the other emotionally in the hope that the partner will give in is a form of psychological torture. This approach rarely resolves the conflict. Disagreements don't go away by themselves; they may lie dormant for a while, but they will eventually resurface, often in a less manageable form than before. The shut-out partner's anger and frustration will also tend to increase, even though that may not be the intent of the partner who refuses to argue.

13. Focus on the Issue and Focus on the Present   Constructive arguments focus on the here-and-now and stay on the topic. Arguments that leap from one issue to another accomplish very little. Bringing up the past usually is a ploy for placing blame. In a fair fight, the relevant question is not "Where have we been?" but "Where are we going from here?"

14. Call "Time-Out" and "Foul"   When verbal interchanges get too intense, a time-out can be useful. The length depends on how emotionally overwrought the participants are. Sometimes an hour is sufficient; sometimes a day is needed. Time-outs shouldn't last too long, however, because one or both partners may refuse to deal with the issue again.

Another helpful tool in a conflict is calling a "foul" when fair-fighting rules are broken. If one person brings up the past or uses a dirty fighting technique, call a "foul." This gives both partners a chance to calm down and think things through before trying again to resolve the disagreement.

15. Use Humor and Comic Relief It's often just as useful to laugh as to cry. In a similar vein, it's better to laugh than to yell. People in an argument usually look and sound pretty foolish to an objective third party. In a conflict, people need to step back, look at the situation from a new perspective, and laugh at themselves if possible. Sarcasm or laughing at the partner rarely helps resolve the dispute, however.

A useful form of humor for families is **incongruity humor,** which focuses on seeing the incongruous things in life—the things that don't fit together logically—rather than on blaming others or putting them down. For example, a divorce court judge laughs when he tells of listening for 3 hours to the attorneys and the divorcing couple argue over who was to have possession of a 9-foot-long metal pipe. The judge tried to help the couple see the humor in the situation.

16. Always Go for Closure **Closure** is the resolution of an issue. Strive for closure as soon as possible or practical. Letting the argument drag on increases the likelihood of gunnysacking, passive-aggressive behavior, or the silent treatment. The sooner people reach genuine agreement, the better. Resolution lets the feelings of bonding and respect return in the relationship.

Constructive and Destructive Approaches

Peace cannot be kept by force. It can only be achieved by understanding.
—ALBERT EINSTEIN (1931, in Eigen & Siegel, 1993, p. 690)

In destructive approaches to conflict resolution, old issues are brought up and only negative feelings are expressed. The information shared is selective, and the focus is on people rather than issues. Differences are emphasized, and the goal is to minimize change. There is often a winner and a loser, which decreases intimacy.

Conversely, constructive conflict resolution focuses on current rather than past issues, involves sharing of both positive and negative feelings, and provides information in an open manner. Mutual blame is accepted, and the search for similarities allows both parties to win. As a result, intimacy increases and trust grows in the relationship. A comparison of constructive and destructive ways of resolving conflict is given in Table 9.2 (p. 306).

Styles of Conflict Resolution

Learning how to deal effectively with conflict is one of the most important things people can do in their efforts to create a strong family. Because conflict resolution

Table 9.2 Constructive and Destructive Approaches to Conflict Resolution

AREA OF CONCERN	CONSTRUCTIVE APPROACH	DESTRUCTIVE APPROACH
Issues	Raises and clarifies issues	Brings up old issues
Feelings	Expresses both positive and negative feelings	Expresses only negative feelings
Information	Complete and honest information	Selective information
Focus	Conflict focuses on issue rather than person	Conflict focuses on person rather than issue
Blame	Accepts mutual blame	Blames other person(s) for the problem
Perception	Focuses on similarities	Focuses on differences
Change	Facilitates change to prevent stagnation	Minimizes change, increasing conflict
Outcome	Both win	One wins and one loses, or both lose
Intimacy	Resolving conflict increases intimacy	Escalating conflict decreases intimacy
Attitude	Trust	Suspicion

is so critical, many therapists focus their efforts on understanding and describing useful approaches and identifying counterproductive ones.

A useful way of looking at conflict resolution styles and comparing one's own style with that of others is presented in Figure 9.2. The model is based on the belief that each style of conflict is composed of two partially competing goals: concern for self and concern for the other person. Concern for self is measured by how aggressive one is, and concern for others focuses on the level of cooperation. This model of conflict resolution identifies five styles: the competitive style, the collaborative style, the compromise style, the avoidance style, and the accommodating style (Kilmann & Thomas, 1975). There are advantages and disadvantages to all five styles.

1. *Competitive style.* People who use a **competitive style** of conflict resolution tend to be aggressive and uncooperative, pursuing personal concerns at the expense of the other. Those with a competitive style gain power by direct confrontation and try to "win" without adjusting their goals and desires in light of the other person's goals and desires. Life is a battleground for people with this type of style. They tend to agree with the following statements: "Once I get wound up in a heated discussion, I find it diffi-

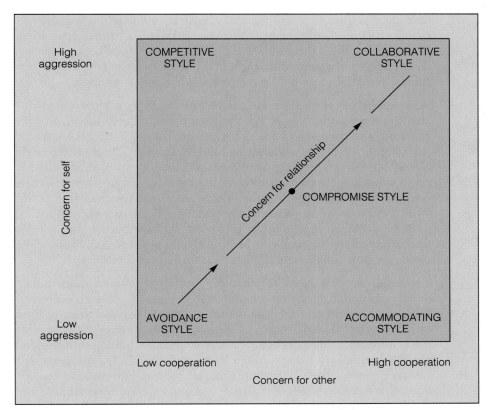

Figure 9.2 Styles of Conflict Resolution. *Source:* "Interpersonal Conflict: Handling Behavior as Reflections of Jungian Personality Dimensions" by R. Kilmann and K. Thomas, 1975, *Psychological Reports, 37*, pp. 971–980. Copyright *Psychological Reports* 1975.

cult to stop," and "I like the excitement of engaging in verbal fights" (Hocker & Wilmot, 1985, p. 41). A competitive style is usually not conducive to developing intimacy.

2. *Collaborative style.* People who have a **collaborative style** of conflict resolution are highly assertive in regard to reaching their goals but at the same time have a great deal of concern for the other person. People who use this style would agree with statements like these: "When I get into a conflict with someone, I try to work creatively with them to find new options," or "I like to assert myself, and I also like to cooperate with others" (Hocker & Wilmot, 1985, p. 114). Because collaboration takes a good deal of energy, it may not be worth the investment if one sees little value in continuing the relationship. Another problem with collaboration is that good collaborators are powerful and may use their strength to manipulate others.

3. *Compromise style.* People who use the **compromise style** (which is intermediate on both the aggression and cooperation axes, as shown in Figure 9.2) would agree with these statements: "You have to be satisfied with part of the pie," or "When disagreements occur, you each have to give a little" (Hocker & Wilmot, 1985, p. 117). The compromise style is more direct

than the avoidance style, but it does not push the issues as much as the collaborative style. Compromise is less time-consuming than collaboration, but it also reinforces the notion that the relationship is one between equals. Disadvantages of compromise include the fact that an easy "formula" for conflict resolution may not be the best solution for all involved.

4. *Avoidance style.* Nonassertive and passive behaviors characterize the **avoidance style** of conflict resolution. Avoiders pursue neither their own concerns nor the concerns of the other person. They sidestep the issue by changing the subject or withdrawing from the conflict. The avoidance style has certain advantages: It gives the avoider time to think about whether any good will come from continuing the fight and about whether others could manage the situation better. There are several disadvantages of this style: It conveys the message that the avoider does not care enough to deal with the problem, it puts the problem on the back burner, and it reinforces the notion that conflict is bad and should be avoided at all cost. The avoidance style usually sets the stage for further conflict.

5. *Accommodating style.* Nonassertive but cooperative behavior characterizes the **accommodating style.** Accommodaters put aside personal concerns to satisfy the wants and needs of the other. Advantages of accommodation include the fact that giving in and showing reasonableness are good ideas if you discover you are wrong. Also, accommodation minimizes losses and possible harmful consequences in a losing situation. There are also disadvantages to this style: Accommodation tends to reduce creative options because it sacrifices genuine dialogue; it may also produce resentment and the desire to get even.

No one style of conflict resolution is automatically superior to another (Hocker & Wilmot, 1985). Each has advantages and disadvantages in certain circumstances and between different individuals. Clearly, there are no simple or easy ways to resolve human conflicts. Each situation must be approached with caution and thoughtfulness. People in conflict have to consider many factors, including the personalities of those involved, the merits of the argument, and the level of investment each has in continuing the relationship.

Resolving Conflict: Six Basic Steps

Let us begin anew, remembering on both sides that civility is not a sign of weakness, that sincerity is always subject to proof. Let us never negotiate out of fear, but let us never fear to negotiate.
—John F. Kennedy (1961, in Baker, 1990, p. 101)

Family therapists assume that most tension and fights between couples signal that something needs to be resolved. This section summarizes the basic strategies authorities generally agree are useful for successful negotiation within intimate relationships. The steps are: clarifying the issue, finding out what each person wants, identifying various alternatives, deciding how to negotiate, solidifying the agreements, and reviewing and renegotiating. Each of these strategies is discussed with special attention to the various communication skills presented in this text. It is during periods of conflict that good communication skills take on additional importance.

1. Clarifying the Issue   Conflicts and fights are probably caused as frequently by misunderstanding as they are by genuine differences. People find themselves arguing over something they don't really disagree on, but only thought they did. Clarifying the issue helps; sometimes true differences get pushed aside or covered over by side issues. These types of misunderstandings can be minimized by using the following techniques:

- Each partner can take the responsibility for spending some time alone to think through what is bothering her or him. During this time, the individuals should ask themselves questions that focus on the issue and on their thoughts, feelings, and desires about the issue. Guiding questions include: "I'm feeling upset now; what situation(s) triggered that?" "What was going on that made me feel uncomfortable?" "How would I like things to be different?" "What are some things I want for myself?"

- Individuals should try to understand fully what the partner is saying. Using good listening skills, the listener should repeat back to the speaker what is being "heard"—both its content and its feeling—until the speaker is satisfied that the listener has understood the message. In addition, the listener can ask questions to clarify or to elicit more information from the speaker. By focusing questions directly on what the speaker is sharing, the listener facilitates identification of the conflict.

- Each person is responsible for keeping the discussion focused. This can be done by agreeing to talk about other issues that emerge at another time or by using reminders such as "Let's refocus" or "Now, where were we?" to keep the discussion from drifting.

- Each person should sum up what the other has said after each person has had an opportunity to talk. Checking out with each other what each one sees as the problem ensures that both agree on what the issue is.

2. Finding Out What Each Person Wants   After both people are clear about what the issue is, the discussion should shift to identifying what each person wants. Omission of this part of the process often leads to unsatisfactory negotiations and repetitive fights. Its inclusion helps to minimize hurtful exchanges between frustrated couples because each partner has to identify what he or she wants, rather than recounting "how bad things have been." This identification of needs can be a difficult process for some couples, but it can be facilitated by genuinely asking each other to express desires. If one partner says, "I don't know what I want, but I just know I don't want things to be the way they have been," this is a straightforward signal that this part of the process has not been completed.

3. Identifying Various Alternatives   The concept of alternatives assumes that there are several ways the partners can be satisfied. Looking at the various options

Brainstorming—thinking of as many solutions to a problem as possible—is a creative way to address conflicts in a relationship. Generating alternatives highlights the fact that many possibilities exist even when the partners think they're at an impasse.

often leads to new insights. **Brainstorming** ideas can be a fun and creative process because both partners are working together to find ways to deal with the issue. Research indicates that brainstorming increases people's skill at identifying useful alternatives (Warmbrod, 1982).

4. Deciding How to Negotiate   After the various alternatives have been identified, it's time to try to work out some agreements, or plans, for change. There are several strategies couples can use to negotiate differences. Each has advantages and disadvantages.

- *Quid pro quo.* Latin for "this for that," **quid pro quo** is a negotiating strategy by which parties agree that "I'll do this if you'll do that." For example, the Smiths have been hassling over the weekly household chores. Each feels that he or she is doing more than the other. After discussing the alternatives for dividing the tasks more equally, they readily move into a quid pro quo bargain. Jack agrees to do a certain number of the tasks, and Marlene agrees to do certain tasks. This strategy is most effective when it is used as a way to "divide and conquer" because it clarifies what each is going to do. The major disadvantage of this strategy is that it can easily break down if one person fails to keep her or his agreement. Another disadvantage is the difficulty of finding relatively equivalent divisions.

- *Quid pro quid.* Meaning "this for this," **quid pro quid** is an agreement to do something the other person asks you to do in exchange for being able to do something you want to do. For example, Brent's wife, Nancy, wants him to accept more responsibility for taking care of the children. He agrees to be fully responsible for the children for two nights, in exchange for a night out with his friends. This bargaining strategy has advantages over the quid pro quo method in that the consequences for not living up to the bargain are clear and are not based on what the other partner does. This strategy works especially well when one partner is asking the other to change because it enables the partner who agrees to the change to give himself or herself something he or she wants as well. This helps avoid power struggles in which one partner feels she or he has to change simply because the other demands that things be different.

- *Agreeing to disagree.* After exploring all the alternatives, a mutually agreeable solution is not always possible; the negotiating strategy in this case is **agreeing to disagree.** For example, Len wanted to invest the couple's savings in some lakefront property, and Lesley wanted to take a trip to Europe. After long hours of discussion, both felt even more strongly about what they wanted. Because they couldn't agree on either course of action, they agreed to disagree—and left the money in the account. When the issue is not critical to the maintenance of the relationship, agreeing to disagree leaves open the possibility of finding a solution later. Where the differences are more basic, however, such as one partner wanting children and the other not or one partner wanting to get married and the other wanting just to continue living together, agreeing to disagree will only work in the short run.

5. Solidifying the Agreements   Partners may need to try several negotiation strategies before reaching agreement. But when an agreement is reached, it's important to make sure that both people are clear about what has been agreed to and that both do indeed agree. This can be facilitated by not bulldozing the other into agreement. Too often, in their haste to "get things wrapped up," people make agreements they know they can't stick to. Couples should take the time to fully explore what the agreement means for each person before giving it the final stamp of approval. They should be sensitive to each other's reservations. It's a good idea to avoid making agreements while either partner is upset. Pressure tactics, such as implied threats, often win the battle but lose the war. When both partners are in agreement, they should make a contract by writing down everything they've agreed to in simple, clear language. Couples should post the agreement as a reminder of what each is to do. They should also agree to review the situation within a short period of time.

6. Reviewing and Renegotiating   Once an agreement has been negotiated, it is easy to assume that "that's settled once and for all." Unfortunately, this is rarely the case. Carrying out an agreement often brings other issues to light. It is not unusual to discover that the agreement does not really resolve the problem. A timely review ensures that bad feelings about the agreement do not go on too long.

When agreements break down, partners distrust or are disillusioned about each other's genuine interest in working together. Broken agreements should be reviewed as soon as possible. Couples often discover that one or the other simply "forgot" to do what was agreed upon. It is important for people to remind themselves that change is rarely smooth and that it is also rare for any person to live up to any agreement completely. But if both partners are invested in each other's personal well-being and want their relationship to grow, couples can positively resolve just about any conflict.

Summary

- Conflict is inevitable in any intimate relationship. It can be thought of as a process that builds along a hierarchy from decision making to problem solving to crisis resolution; making decisions when they are called for helps prevent crisis.

- Most couples are afraid of negative emotions and have a difficult time learning how to deal with them. A common tendency is to suppress anger for fear of damaging the relationship. Because love and hate are so closely tied, however, the suppression of anger can lead to loss of affection for the partner.

- Popular myths about anger include the belief that anger is caused by others, that the best way to deal with anger is to "let it all hang out," that anger is a beneficial emotion, and that you're a "wimp" if you don't get angry.

- Intimacy and conflict are inextricably tied together. Anger keeps people from developing unhealthy dependencies on each other. Interdependence, a balance between dependency and independence, seems to work best.

- People manage stress and anger in a number of ways. Pursuers seek greater to-getherness in a relationship, distancers want emotional space when stress is high, underfunctioners become less competent under stress, overfunctioners tend to take charge in tough times, and blamers believe everyone else is responsible for their problems.

- The top five issues that generate conflict between newlyweds are money, family issues, communication style, household tasks, and personal tastes.

- People should observe certain conventions, or "rules for fair fighting," when they are voicing disagreement; such conventions make the argument safer and more likely to lead to a satisfactory conclusion.

- Some styles of conflict resolution are the competitive style, pursuing personal concerns at the expense of others; the collaborative style, being highly assertive in regard to reaching one's goals while also showing great concern for the other person; the compromise style, an intermediate style between aggressiveness and cooperativeness; the avoidance style, avoiding conflict by changing the subject or withdrawing; and the accommodating style, which involves nonassertive and cooperative behaviors.

- Family therapists and other authorities generally agree on six steps for resolving conflict: clarify the issue, find out what each person wants, identify various alternatives, decide how to negotiate, solidify the agreements, and review and renegotiate.

Key Terms

pursuer

distancer

dance of anger

underfunctioner

overfunctioner

blamer

gunnysacking

passive-aggressive
   behavior

incongruity humor

closure

competitive style

collaborative style

compromise style

avoidance style

accommodating style

brainstorming

quid pro quo

quid pro quid

agreeing to disagree

Activities

1. Using Harriet Lerner's ideas about characteristic styles of managing anger, focus on someone with whom you have an important relationship. Does one of you tend to be a pursuer or a distancer? An overfunctioner or an underfunctioner? A blamer or a blame-taker? Rate each of you on a continuum from 1 (low) to 10 (high) on each of the dimensions. Are you performing any dances based on these style differences? If so, how might you create a healthier dance?

2. Use John Crosby's 16 rules for fair fighting as the basis for a small-group discussion. Group members should first rate themselves on each of the rules. Then members should discuss some practical things they can do to become fairer fighters.

3. Select a disagreement you have with someone in an important relationship, one that has been difficult for you both to resolve. Agree to discuss the issue. See if you can work out the disagreement using the six basic conflict resolution steps discussed at the end of this chapter.

Suggested Readings

Borcherdt, B. (1989). *Think straight! Feel great! 21 guides to emotional self-control.* Sarasota, FL: Professional Resource Exchange. *Sound advice for dealing with frustration in one's life and anger in one's soul.*

Crosby, J. F. (1991). *Illusion and disillusion.* Belmont, CA: Wadsworth. A guide to positive communication and the development of intimacy. *Helps readers see through the illusions they create about their loved ones and explains how to overcome the disillusion that inevitably follows to create a sound relationship.*

Gottmann, J., & Silver, N. (1994). *Why marriages succeed or fail.* New York: Simon & Schuster. *An excellent in-depth analysis of couple interaction patterns that are predictive of successful versus divorcing couples.*

Lerner, H. G. (1985). *The dance of anger.* New York: Harper & Row. *An excellent exploration of the very predictable, almost choreographed ways in which people deal with anger in intimate relationships, along with suggestions from a clinical psychologist for dealing positively with that anger.*

Markman, S. S., & Blumberg, S. L. (1994). *Fighting for your marriage.* San Francisco: Jossey-Bass. *Provides an overview of the authors' PREP communication program for couples; contains very useful suggestions for resolving couple conflict.*

CHAPTER 10

Managing Economic Resources

Financial issues are the most common stressor for families across the family life cycle, regardless of how much money they make (Voydanoff, 1991). In addition, one of the most problematic areas for couples planning to marry is talking about financial issues; many couples are unwilling or unable to do so. On a more positive note, however, research has consistently demonstrated that couples who handle their money and finances well also tend to be more happily married (Olson, McCubbin, et al., 1989).

Money, of course, cannot buy family happiness. As one observer noted, "The best things in life are not things." There are countless examples of financially secure people who have not figured out how to have a fulfilling relationship with their partner, their parents, or their children. The media remind us of this almost daily with stories of rich but unhappy politicians, business people, royalty, movie stars, and so forth. On the other hand, there seems to be little truth to the "poor but happy" scenario, either. Economic hardship and problems in family relationships are often related. Researchers have found that divorce, marital separation, domestic violence, and the abuse of alcohol and other drugs are more likely among the poor than in any other socioeconomic group (Voydanoff, 1991). Earning an adequate income and managing money efficiently and effectively are important for family well-being. If a family has enough money to meet its basic needs, the members can turn their attention to enhancing the quality of their lives personally and as a family.

This chapter focuses on financial issues, particularly as they relate to intimate relationships and to family life across the life span. Money problems in a family are often related to an inability to develop an open and well-organized couple or family system. These financial problems then lead to more stress and conflict in the family. Ideas for successfully managing family finances are presented with the goal of demonstrating how to achieve economic goals and harmony in intimate relationships.

The Stresses of Family Finances

To some people, money means power; to others, love. For some the topic is boorish, in bad taste. For others, it's more private than sex. Add family dynamics to the mix, and for many you have the subject from hell.
—KAREN S. PETERSON (1992a)

Although Americans make more money per person than most people in other countries, financial issues tend to dominate our lives, and dissatisfaction with money matters remains high. A recent national poll found that only 62% of the people in a random sample of U.S. households were satisfied with their current standard of living (M. Levinson, 1991).

An enduring paradox about money is that no matter how much families have, they always seem to need more.

"When our first daughter was a toddler 20 years ago, my take-home pay was about $3,100 a year," related Paul, a contractor and writer of children's books. "Adjusted for inflation today, that might be about $10,000. Things were tight, but we lived pretty well in many respects. We traveled a lot—cheaply, of course—and we enjoyed life. We were, for the most part, happy. Today, we have three teenagers and our family income is approaching $60,000 a year. Frankly, money causes me just as much anxiety today as it did way back then. And I really can't say we're any happier."

Most people, no matter what their income, are likely to say that if they only had $1,000, $5,000, or $10,000 more a year, things would look pretty good for their family. Family economist Karen Craig (personal communication, 1991) put it this way, "Wants are insatiable. The more you make, the more creative you are in spending." There never seems to be enough money, whether the family income is $10,000 or $100,000, and many families find themselves with some debt each month. Many people assume that material things will bring them happiness but find instead that their possessions have a certain power over them. The house and car must be repaired; the clothes cleaned; the swimming pool maintained; any extra money invested wisely. As one observer said, "Everything you own owns you."

Clearly, *money* is a powerful word. It evokes a variety of emotions: envy, fear, anger, hope, scorn, lust, disgust. Pollsters consistently find that the most common source of disagreement in U.S. families is money matters. For example, a survey of 2,555 randomly sampled American adults found that money was the biggest fighting word in their families (Goodman, 1986). Thirty-seven percent of the respondents said money was the major problem, followed by children and child-rearing issues (29%), household chores (26%), and diets and health (21%). Family therapists point out, however, that many of these arguments are not really about money. They are actually battles over power and control in the family, over competing hopes and dreams, over different visions of the good life and how to live it.

Finances: A Family Problem

For most Americans, money is a source of anxiety and discomfort that continues across the life span. Olson, McCubbin, and colleagues (1989) found in their study of 1,000 families that money is the most commonly reported source of stress and strain that families face. Many families at each stage of the family life cycle felt finances were problematic. The most difficult periods of the family life cycle financially were the childbearing stage, the adolescent stage, the launching stage, and the retirement stage. About half of the families in the childbearing stage reported stress and strain related to finances. During the adolescent stage, money-related problems apparently peaked, with 60% of the families reporting they felt stress in this area. This dropped to 40% at both the launching and the retirement stages.

Finances and Couple Conflict

It's not surprising that conflict over money is common among couples because becoming a couple means exchanging financial independence for financial interdependence. Partners have to decide together on the level of rent or mortgage responsibility they can afford. It is likely that the two will have different ideas about how to spend

Money—the lack of it or different ideas about how to spend it—is the most common source of family conflict. Although having expenses that exceed income will always cause stress, money causes fewer conflicts for couples who have learned to compromise and to share financial decision making.

money. Working out a successful compromise can take a good deal of negotiation. "Partners who feel they have equal control over how money is spent have a more tranquil relationship," according to Blumstein and Schwartz (1983, p. 89).

Why do couples fight over money? In a survey of 400 physicians, mostly psychiatrists, nearly half (49%) believed that the primary reason that quarrels over money occur in marriage is that one spouse uses money as a way of dominating and controlling the other (Mace, 1982a). Thirty-four percent of the physicians believed that the primary reason for money quarrels was the differences in spouses' spending priorities, and 14% of the physicians saw differences in spouses' thriftiness as the primary source of conflict.

In another study focused on how newly married couples handled finances and made family decisions over the first 10 years of their marriage (Schaninger & Buss, 1986), the investigators were especially interested in differences between those who divorced and those who remained happily married. They found that happily married couples practiced role specialization. There was greater influence by the wife and less dominance by the husband in the handling of family finances. There was also greater joint decision making about family issues and more influence by the wife in family decision making. Equality at an early stage was important for the vitality of the marriage.

What specific financial stressors cause problems for families across the life cycle? That is one of the questions Olson, McCubbin, and colleagues (1989) wanted to answer in their study of 1,000 families. Their findings are useful in pinpointing common difficulties across the family life cycle.

The most stressful financial issue was increased strain on the family's money for food, clothing, energy, and home care as the family grew. Forty-five percent of the families reported increased strain on financial resources due to these issues. A close second in the list of the top ten financial stressors across the family life cycle was the purchase of a car or another major item. Third, and closely related to number two, was stress due to taking out or refinancing a loan to cover increased expenses. Number four on the list of financial stressors was increased strain due to the cost of child(ren)'s education, and number five was a change in conditions (economic, political, weather) that hurt family investments and/or income (Olson, McCubbin, et al., 1989). See Table 10.1 (p. 320) for a summary of these and other stressors across the life cycle.

Money problems are likely to have a negative effect on individual well-being and family relationships (Voydanoff, 1991). Family members simply don't get along as well with each other when they are suffering from economic distress. Employment instability—job loss or uncertainty over the future of a job—can be a major stressor. Those who are unemployed have an increased likelihood of suffering from depression, anxiety, and psychophysiological distress (stress-related physical problems). If a man is unemployed, his wife is also likely to experience psychological distress from trying to deal with the situation. Low income is also related to several types of psychological distress (Voydanoff, 1991).

Coping with Financial Stressors

Why do some families survive economic hard times whereas others are torn apart? Researchers have focused on coping resources and coping behaviors in trying to answer this question (Voydanoff, 1991). Coping resources can come from oneself and from the family. Foremost among **personal coping resources** are self-esteem and mastery. To survive economic hard times, individuals need to feel good about themselves, to feel as if they are capable of standing up to the onslaught. They need a sense of mastery, confidence in their ability to learn new skills and techniques to meet changing situations.

Family coping resources include cohesion, adaptability, and a willingness to adopt nontraditional family roles in the face of changing economic circumstances—all characteristics of a healthy family system. For example, perhaps a mother has never worked outside the home. Her husband has lost his job at a manufacturing plant. He has been out of work for 6 months, and the family has used up its savings. To keep the family afloat, the wife finds a job as a clerk at a convenience store. In this crisis situation, the family coping resources include cohesion (the ability to stick together in tough times and to empathize with each other's plight) and adaptability (the ability to change to deal with the crisis).

Social support, or help from other people, can be critically important in times of economic distress. Major types of social support include instrumental aid (such as money, goods, and services), emotional support, and information (such as advice and feedback). Social support can come from a variety of people, including a spouse or an immediate family member, extended family, co-workers, neighbors, self-help groups, and human-service professionals. When social support is available and is used by an individual in financial crisis, it generally provides increased psychological well-being and improved quality of family life (Kessler, Turner, & House, 1988; Voydanoff, Donnelly, & Fine, 1988).

Table 10.1 The Top 10 Financial Stressors for Families Across the Life Cycle

	Average Across Stages	Stage 1 Couples n: (207)	Stage 2 Childbearing (269)	Stage 3 School-Age (232)	Stage 4 Adolescents (494)	Stage 5 Launching (352)	Stage 6 Empty Nest (230)	Stage 7 Retirement (234)
1. Money for food, clothing, and energy	45%	50%	57%	46%	62%	54%	30%	15%
2. Purchase of a car or other major item	43	50	49	49	43	51	32	23
3. Taking out a loan	31	38	33	29	33	35	17	*
4. Child(ren)'s education	29	29	13	21	30	51	*	*
5. Problems with family income	26	24	32	26	34	24	27	13
6. Medical/dental expenses	23	20	31	29	31	23	13	17
7. Purchase or construction of a home	16	24	21	10	*	*	11	*
8. Bad investments	16	12	18	12	18	18	18	14
9. Overuse of credit cards	15	17	11	15	16	14	*	*
10. Starting a business	10	10	*	11	*	*	10	*

*Less than 10%.

Source: Adapted from Families: What Makes Them Work (2nd ed.) (pp. 285–288) by D. H. Olson, H. I. McCubbin, H. Barnes, A. Larsen, M. Muxen, M. Wilson, 1989, Sage Publications. Copyright © 1989 by Sage Publications. Used by permission of the publisher.

When the major wage earner loses a job, there are several things the family can do to cope:

- Other family members can go to work outside the home.

- The family can increase its participation in the so-called informal economy, exchanging goods and services for cash or by barter.

- The family can decide together how to cut back expenditures dramatically.

Cutting the budget is not easy, and families have reported depression, low marital satisfaction, and high tension when forced to do so. On the other hand, certain approaches have been found to make things worse in times of economic distress. Denying that there is a problem; keeping feelings to oneself; or eating, drinking, or smoking to relieve tension tends to increase marital stress (Wilhelm & Ridley, 1988).

> "I was out of work for 26 months over a period of 40 months, but who was counting? It was probably the most devastating experience in my life," Stan, a middle-aged man living in Boston, said. "I applied for 205 jobs before I finally found one that worked out. People say, 'All you have to do is get off your butt and you can find work.' I used to believe that myself. But it's not that easy. With a master's degree in education, I was happy at one point to find work delivering newspapers on Sunday morning at 3 A.M.
>
> "My self-esteem was so low I felt I wanted to die. One morning I was so depressed that I was lying on the living room floor, just feeling broken. My daughter stepped over me as she went out the front door to high school. My son stepped over me on his way out the door to college. My wife stepped over me on her way out the door to her job. At the time, it felt like I had died and they didn't even notice. They simply stepped over the body and went about their business.
>
> "Now I know that they really were upset about my unemployment. My wife, Sally, was probably as upset about it as I was. But there was nothing any of them could do at the time but go on with their own lives. They tried to comfort me, but many times I was beyond comforting. Fortunately, I found a good job that I enjoy. It doesn't pay all that well, but I love having it. Being without work was terrifying. Even talking about it still upsets me today, 10 years later."

Why Do Finances Cause Problems?

There are several reasons finances cause problems for families:

- Money is a taboo topic in many families.

- Couples tend to have unrealistic expectations about finances.

- Many couples do not create and stick to a budget.

cathy®   **by Cathy Guisewite**

- Some families overspend and rely too heavily on credit.
- Partners have different styles of spending and saving.
- One partner uses money as a tool to gain power and control over the other partner.
- Partners have different ideas about the meaning of money.

Money: A Taboo Topic

In the dating phase, many couples are more likely to talk about their past relationships than their financial situations. It is not very romantic to talk about potential income, the use of credit cards, and views on savings. Yet among married couples, money matters are the most commonly discussed topic (Blumstein & Schwartz, 1983).

> "I thought we talked about everything before marriage," said Marcia, a 42-year-old computer technician. "But we never seemed to get around to money—what it means to each of us and how it should be spent. Because I saw money as a symbol of security, I wanted to scrimp and save. I wanted to build a house, a nest, and feel safe inside. Because he saw money as a tool to achieve freedom and independence, he wanted to use it for adventure. We were doomed from the beginning to fight over money."

Even after children are born, many couples still find it difficult to talk about money, especially with their children. But many financial advisors and counselors argue that it is essential to break a family pattern of financial silence. If parents refuse to help their children learn how to manage money, it "creates people who depend on us," according to psychologist Jane Nelsen. "When we don't teach kids responsibility, their self-esteem suffers. They feel inadequate. That teaches them

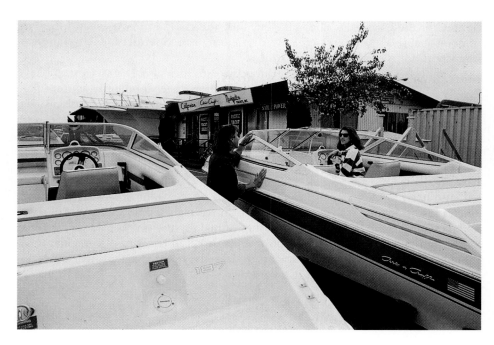

Money is not just the paper, coin, or plastic used to buy things. It can be a source of status, security, enjoyment, or control. If partners have incompatible attitudes about money, extravagant purchases are likely to cause conflicts between them.

to manipulate us to get what they want. They don't develop their own capabilities" (cited in Peterson, 1992b). Emotional struggles with teenagers can be prevented by setting a budget for adolescent spending.

Common Financial Pitfalls

Before marriage, many young couples have unrealistic expectations about how much money they can expect to earn and how much things will cost (Arond & Pauker, 1987). Most couples also do not invest time or effort in the careful construction of a budget. Although budgeting requires some attention to detail and record keeping, a budget can keep couples out of financial trouble and alleviate emotional struggles between partners.

Overspending is another common financial problem, one closely associated with buying on credit. Credit paves the way for many family financial crises, and credit cards make it easy to overspend and get into debt. And the high interest rates on credit-card balances (often double the rate on bank loans) can make it difficult for many to pay back more than the interest on their debt. It can be very difficult for many families to get out of debt without a realistic budget.

When it comes to spending and saving, individuals have a wide variety of personal styles, which can create considerable conflict between partners and in families. Ideally, it is a good idea for couples to talk about their spending patterns before marriage; however, most couples do not find out until after marriage how different their spending/saving styles are. The greater the difference in styles, the greater the possibility of conflicts over money. Two very common—and conflicting—styles are spenders and savers. **Savers** compulsively save money, often keeping very little free for the essentials. They may buy only the cheapest items, even if they are of poor quality and not cost-effective in the long run. **Spenders** love to purchase items both for themselves and for others.

Although most people do not exhibit the extremes of either style, many have a tendency toward one of the two styles. It is often easier to identify another person's style than to describe our own. It's wise for potential partners to discuss the spender and saver styles.

Money can also be a means of gaining and maintaining power over a partner or other family members. Power struggles complicate financial issues. Couples can minimize conflict by setting up clear rules about handling money. If both partners have an income, they may each retain power over what they personally earn. They will also need to pool part of those earnings to pay for joint expenses (rent, food, and so forth) or to make large purchases or investments. This takes mutual trust, openness, and solidarity on financial issues. If one partner makes most or all of the money in the family, this can be a powerful weapon in times of disagreement. Although the "earning" partner may not admit it, the other partner often senses the attitude "I earned it, I'll spend it my way."

The Meaning of Money

Arond and Pauker (1987) have identified four common orientations toward money:

- *Money as status.* A person with a status orientation toward money is interested in money as power—as a means of keeping ahead of one's peers.

- *Money as security.* A person with a security orientation is conservative in spending and focuses on saving.

- *Money as enjoyment.* A person with an enjoyment orientation gets satisfaction from spending, both on others and on him- or herself.

- *Money as control.* A person with a control orientation sees money as a way of maintaining control over her or his life and independence from a partner or other family members.

It is possible for a person to have more than one orientation, but not two conflicting approaches—for example, enjoyment *and* security. A questionnaire for assessing your money orientation is provided in Box 10.1.

Family Income and Expenses

This section focuses on the average income of U.S. families and on income variations among different ethnic and cultural groups. It also explores typical family expenses and differences in family net worth. Finally, it examines whether it is worth it financially for both spouses to work outside the home, especially if they have children.

Money: What Does It Mean to You?

1 = Strongly disagree; 2 = Disagree; 3 = Uncertain; 4 = Agree; 5 = Strongly agree

Use the scale above to respond to each of these items:

_____ 1. It is important to me to maintain a lifestyle similar to or better than that of my peers.

_____ 2. In making a major purchase, an important consideration is what others will think of my choice.

_____ 3. Since money equals power, I am willing to work hard for money in order to have more power.

_____ 4. I really enjoy shopping and having nice things.

_____ 5. Saving money for a rainy day is an important principle to live by.

_____ 6. If I had a moderate amount of money to invest, I would be more likely to put it into multiple resources that are relatively safe than into one fairly risky source that has the potential to make a lot of money.

_____ 7. Being "flat broke" is one of the worst things that could happen to me.

_____ 8. Saving for retirement is an important financial goal for me.

_____ 9. If I suddenly came into a windfall of $1,000, I would use the money for something I have always wanted to do or have.

_____ 10. Since "You can't take it with you," you might as well spend it.

_____ 11. Money can't buy happiness, but it sure helps.

_____ 12. Few things in life give me greater pleasure than making a great buy.

_____ 13. I like/would like having my own business because I can/could control my financial destiny.

_____ 14. I like being able to make decisions about how to spend the money I earn.

_____ 15. It bothers me to de dependent on someone else for money.

_____ 16. I feel uncomfortable if someone offers to "pick up the tab" at a meal we have shared because I feel indebted to them.

Scoring and Interpretation After taking the quiz, add up your answers to the four questions for each category and record your scores below. Scores for each category can range from 4 to 20, with a high score indicating more agreement with that approach. It is possible to have high or low scores in more than one category. General guidelines for interpreting your scores appear in the box below. Record the interpretation for your score in each category on the scoring chart.

Category	Items	Your Score	Interpretation of Score
Money As Status	1-4	_____	_____
Money As Security	5-8	_____	_____
Money As Enjoyment	9-12	_____	_____
Money As Control Over Life	13-16	_____	_____

Score	Interpretation
17-20	Very High
13-16	High
9-12	Moderate
4-8	Low

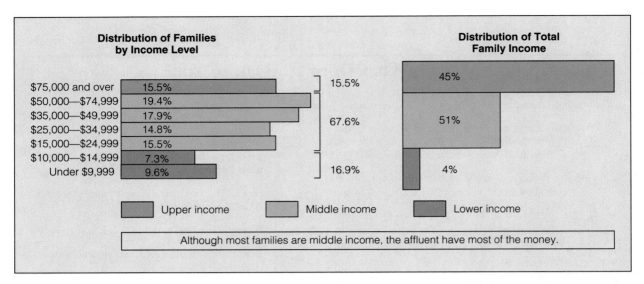

Figure 10.1 Income Levels of U.S. Families, 1995. *Source:* U.S. Bureau of the Census, 1995.

Family Income

More than half the families in the United States are considered middle-income families. The U.S. Bureau of the Census currently defines the middle-income range as between $15,000 and $75,000 per year. Lower-income families make less than $15,000 per year, and upper-income families make more than $75,000. Figure 10.1 breaks the lower- and middle-income categories down into various subcategories. It also illustrates that although most U.S. families (67.6%) are middle income, a majority of the money in this country goes to affluent families: Roughly 45% of family income goes to only 15.5% of America's families. By contrast, lower-income families comprise 16.9% of U.S. families, but make only 4% of the money. The rich have gotten richer since the mid-1980s, and both middle-income and lower-income families have lost ground.

Ethnic Income Differences   There are considerable income differences across ethnic groups in the United States (Table 10.2). For example, among all types of family households, the median income for White families is $39,320; Black families, $21,761; and Hispanic families, $24,926. Table 10.2 also indicates that for these three ethnic groups, married couples earn substantially more income than the average in their group, and single parents make significantly less.

Families in poverty are a large group, especially in all ethnic groups except Whites. Though the United States is one of the most affluent nations in the world, many American children live in poverty. There are approximately 66 million children in the United States under 18 years of age; 13.9 million (21.1%) of these children live in poverty. Looking specifically at the 16.5 million single-parent families in this country, 8.1 million (49%) live in poverty. Among the 23.6 million children under the age of 6, 24% (5.7 million children) live in poverty. Of children younger than 6, broken down by ethnic group, 14.4% of White children, 50.7% of African American children, and 44% of Hispanic children live in poverty (U.S. Bureau of the Census, 1994).

Table 10.2 Income Levels by Ethnic Group and Family Structure

ETHNIC GROUP/TYPE OF FAMILY	MEDIAN INCOME
All groups	
All families	$37,222
Married couples	42,140
Female householder, no husband present	18,587
White	
All families	39,320
Married couples	42,820
Female householder, no husband present	32,412
Black	
All families	21,761
Married couples	34,290
Female householder, no husband present	12,606
Hispanic	
All families	24,926
Married couples	29,007
Female householder, no husband present	13,994

Source: U.S. Bureau of the Census (1994, p. 466).

What does living in poverty mean in human terms? It means that people might not have adequate food or a decent place to sleep. (In the case of the homeless, it could mean living in a refrigerator box in an alley or under a bridge.) It means people cannot afford to see a physician when they are ill or to purchase medicine when they need it. Being poor may mean having no telephone, no radio, no television, no means of transportation. It often means that children attend substandard schools or that their parents move so often looking for work that the children do not attend school at all. To all who live a financially impoverished life, poverty is a very stressful state of affairs.

Lower-middle-income families, although not officially "poor" by government definition, also find it quite difficult to make ends meet (Schuchardt & Guadagno, 1991). In both two-parent and single-parent families at the lower-middle-income level of earnings, about three quarters of all family expenditures can go for housing, food, and transportation. This leaves little money for anything else.

Many people have argued that excessive wealth, like poverty, can be burdensome. "Growing up rich is not an unmixed blessing," according to Frank S. Pittman, a psychiatrist who has worked with both poor and rich families. He states, "Great wealth has undoubted benefits, but it is not good for children. It distorts their functional relationship with the world, it belittles their own accomplishments, and it grotesquely amplifies their sense of what is good enough. It is addictive" (Pittman, 1985, p. 464). However, the problems of the rich are qualitatively different from those of the poor. Writer James A. Michener, who has been both rich and poor in his long life, concludes, "For anyone to claim, as some do, that the damage from having too much is comparable to that from having too little is nonsense, pure and simple nonsense" (1991, p. 249).

A medical degree costs at least 8 years of college tuition, but the expense is small in comparison to a lifetime of high earnings, which the degree virtually guarantees. Women graduates will probably earn less, however, than their male counterparts because they are more likely to defer career opportunities while their children are young.

Gender Income Differences   There is a large difference in the average income of males and females at all educational levels, with men making more than women at each level (U.S. Bureau of the Census, 1994). The average American man working full time earns $37,180 per year, whereas the average American woman working full time earns $24,798. The discrepancy between the incomes of males and females in Black and Hispanic families is smaller than that in White families (U.S. Bureau of the Census, 1991).

Education pays off financially; income rises dramatically as education increases. Individuals with 8 or fewer years of formal education in this country earn on average $13,388. Those with a high school diploma average $29,006. People with a college degree earn an average of $49,539 (U.S. Bureau of the Census, 1994). The financial benefit of education for White males is greater than it is for females and other minority groups. Women with 4 years of college earn less than men with only a high school diploma.

Economists and other social observers cite a number of reasons for the higher incomes of males. Women often drop out of the labor force to have children and then stay at home caring for them for a few years. Meanwhile, men gain seniority in the labor force and get more job-related experience. Although it is illegal to pay women less for doing the same job, women have little legal recourse when they are paid lower wages for jobs that may require essentially similar skills. Also, salaries in fields traditionally dominated by women tend to be lower than those in fields traditionally dominated by men. This situation is seen by many people as discriminatory and sexist.

The "equal pay for comparable work" approach takes a fresh look at "men's" and "women's" work. Proponents argue that pay should be based not on traditional gender-role assumptions but on the comparative difficulty of the job. How much

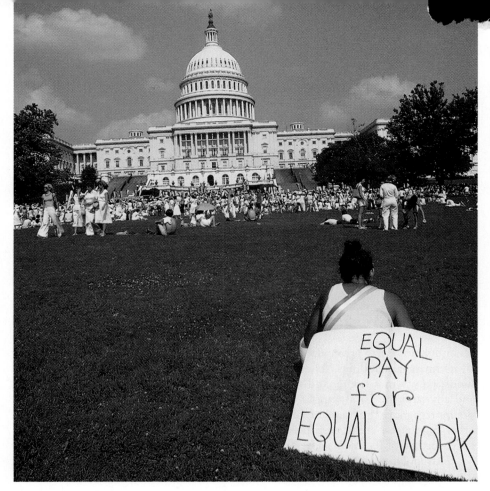

As more women have joined the workforce and more families need two incomes to meet their expenses, debates have increased about the differences in salaries paid to men and women for similar kinds of work. If a female secretary and a male computer technician, for example, have the same amount of education, experience, and job responsibility, why is the secretary apt to be paid less?

should a secretary be paid in comparison with a plumber? A child-care worker in comparison with a computer service technician? Some states have developed elaborate formulas. A job's worth, in terms of salary, is calculated on the basis of the number of years of education, training, and experience it demands and the difficulty or risk it involves.

Why do Whites tend to make more than African Americans and Hispanics, even when their educational levels are similar? Many observers argue that racism is still active in the United States, and that the difference in income can be traced to discrimination. It has been argued, however, that a number of other factors also play a part. The first is urban residence. Many jobs sought by minorities have moved from the cities, where most people of color live, to the suburbs, where there are fewer African Americans and Hispanics. The second factor is type of company. Minorities are more likely than Whites to work in service industries, where salaries are lower. Third is time with a company. Many college-educated minorities are relative newcomers to the labor market and have had less time than Whites to be promoted and earn higher pay.

The controversy over the income gap between White males, females, and minorities in our society is not likely to end soon. The disparity in income between the haves and the have-nots is a problematic issue in a society where millions of people are living at or near the poverty level.

Annual Household Expenses

The proportion of income allocated for various categories in a family budget depends on income level. For example, poor people spend a higher percentage of their income on food and housing than rich people do. After meeting their basic needs, the rich can afford many luxuries that are out of reach of most people's budgets. Table 10.3 presents U.S. Census Bureau figures for all urban households in this country. (Urban households are those in cities and surrounding suburbs that have a population of more than 100,000.) The largest expenditure is for housing, followed by transportation and then food. The amount dedicated to various categories varies widely among families, however, according to personal taste, philosophy of life, and decisions to skimp in one area and spend freely in another. Expenses that vary widely include food, housing, vehicles, and clothing.

Family Net Worth

A family's net worth is calculated by adding up all its financial assets and subtracting all its financial liabilities. Assets include cash on hand or in savings or retirement funds; equity in a home; and the value of the family car, household possessions, and any land the family might own. Liabilities include the balance remaining on the mortgage on the home or land; money owed on installment loans for a car and other purchases; credit card debts; and other debts. A family's net worth gives a good picture of its financial health.

Extrapolating for 1991 from Census Bureau data, researchers reported that the median net worth of White households was $50,876; Hispanic households, $6,387; and African American households, $4,416 (Garman & Forgue, 1991). As measured by their median net worth, most White families have some cushion against financial hard times. Hispanic and African American families on the average live much closer to the financial edge. This can be a source of stress.

As expected, net worth and education are closely related. Households headed by college graduates had a median net worth of $78,542, those headed by high school graduates had a net worth of $4,246, and those headed by individuals with less than a high school diploma had a net worth of $3,048.

Households headed by a married couple had a median net worth of $65,151; the figure dropped to $18,051 for households headed by an unmarried male and to $12,848 for those headed by an unmarried female. The researchers concluded that two people can earn, save, invest, and create significantly more net worth than a single person (Garman & Forgue, 1991).

Does It Pay to Work Outside the Home?

Financially and emotionally, there are both advantages and disadvantages to women working outside the home when there are children. By the year 2000, an estimated 61.6% of all women in the United States will be working outside the home, up from 57.5% in 1990 and 43.3% in 1970 (U.S. Bureau of the Census, 1994). This means that there will be more two-income families at all age levels.

One of the sobering facts of life for two-income families is that the second in-

Table 10.3 Average Annual Expenditures, by Category, for All Urban U.S. Households

ITEMS		AMOUNT
Housing, total		**$ 9,477**
Shelter	$5,411	
Fuels, utilities, and public services	1,984	
Household operations and furnishings	1,749	
Housekeeping supplies	433	
Transportation, total		**5,228**
Vehicles	2,189	
Gasoline and motor oil	973	
Other vehicles and public transportation	2,066	
Food, total		**4,273**
a. Food at home, total	2,643	
b. Food away from home	1,631	
Tobacco products and smoking supplies		**275**
Health care		**1,634**
Pensions and Social Security		**2,397**
Life and personal insurance		**353**
Apparel and services		**1,710**
Alcoholic beverages		**301**
Other expenditures		**4,198**
Total		**$29,846**

Source: U.S. Bureau of the Census (1994, p. 460).

come often seems to disappear when the expenses associated with earning it are paid. A hypothetical example: Assume the second income in the family is a reasonably good one—$28,000 a year, or $2,333 a month. Each month, federal, state, and Social Security taxes could conceivably take about $942. Child care for two children under school age could easily take another $550 a month. Working outside the home increases the cost of clothing—say, $110 extra a month; personal-care and dry-cleaning bills go up an extra $45 a month. Lunch costs go up about $110 monthly, and transportation to work could add at least $55 a month. After all is said and done, the $2,333 is reduced to $521 a month—about $3.25 an hour—in real income.

One woman who quit her $7-an-hour job in a family decision to rely solely on the husband's income said, "I had the feeling that all my money was going for clothes, lunch, and day care for my daughter." It is important to emphasize, however, that there are many reasons beyond financial ones for working outside the home, including personal and professional development, networking with others, and getting a break from child care at home.

Financial Resource Management

Family resource management is a field that studies the processes of planning and using human resources toward the optimal development of both the individual and the family. It focuses on relationships and activities within the home as well as outside it (Rettig & Hogan, 1992). Resource management is an important aspect of family living because it involves the mobilization of resources toward important values and central life purposes, helping family members meet changing goals and concerns across the life span. Family resource management looks at the family as a problem-solving group and views management as a means of achieving some of the most prized qualities of life (Rettig & Hogan, 1993).

The decision-making process in family resource management can be broken down into the following specific actions (Rettig, 1986):

- Perceiving desired or necessary changes
- Facing the problem
- Agreeing to solve the problem
- Discussing the meaning and definition of the problem
- Identifying personal needs
- Negotiating and mediating the issues
- Imagining and creating desirable alternative outcomes
- Agreeing on value priorities, goals, and policies
- Planning the mobilization of resources for high-priority goals
- Implementing policies and plans
- Controlling and adjusting plans
- Evaluating and assessing results
- Planning for the future

The Process: Stages and Steps

Building on a management model developed by Bea Paolucci and her colleagues, Bauer and Wollen (1990) have illustrated the value of a systematic approach to managing resources. The two basic stages are organizing and planning, and implementing decisions.

Organizing and Planning   The organizing and planning stage of family resource management includes three steps: value clarification, goal setting, and resource allocation.

VALUE CLARIFICATION   **Values** are ideas individuals have about what they consider desirable in life—what they believe is right, what they hold dear, and what they feel committed to. Values are personal and deeply ingrained, and individuals use them to organize the world around them and to direct their plans and activities. Even when individuals are unaware of it, their values influence all their choices (Bauer & Wollen, 1990).

One reason arguments over money can become so heated is that decisions about money stem from values. When someone else questions or attacks our financial decisions, we often feel personally attacked. In family money management, it is important that individuals clarify their personal values and then find a way to work together so that each individual's values can be expressed. Compromise may be necessary to maintain the well-being of the family unit.

GOAL SETTING   When they have clarified their values and found a way to preserve individuality, family members can begin to set goals together. **Goals** are objectives, or purposes, an individual or a family wants to achieve; and economic, human, and environmental resources are the tools for attaining them. Because the basic purpose of any kind of management is achieving goals, goals must be discussed, clarified, and prioritized as part of the financial management process (Bauer & Wollen, 1990).

Goals must be attainable and realistic, and they also must be stated in specific and measurable terms. A well-conceived goal indicates exactly what needs to be done and when it needs to be done. Goals can be set for both the short term and the long term. We organize our daily lives around short-term goals: "Today I'm going to fill out the forms at the credit union to make sure money is deducted each month from my paycheck." But these short-term goals generally relate to long-term objectives: "Eventually, I will have saved enough money for a down payment on a house."

RESOURCE ALLOCATION   Successful family resource management at all stages of the family life cycle depends on a realistic assessment of individual and family resources. **Resources** are the tools, talents, and possessions a person uses to create a lifestyle, solve everyday problems, and reach goals. A complete assessment of family resources includes an examination of economic, environmental, and human resources.

Economic resources can be divided into four types: income, fringe benefits, credit, and wealth. *Environmental resources* include the physical environment (land, plants, and water), political and community resources (schools, police, and social service agencies), and social resources (religious bodies, community groups, and service organizations) available to the family. *Human resources* include the mental, emotional, and physical qualities individuals possess: physical skills (such as woodworking, typing, gardening), social skills, and mental skills (such as problem solving, planning, decision making); interests (a desire or willingness to be involved in a particular activity); attitudes (a willingness to adapt, self-confidence, friendliness); human energy (an individual's capacity for mental, physical, and emotional activity); and time (Bauer & Wollen, 1990). This list makes it clear that human beings have a wealth of resources on which to draw. The process of resource allocation means using the best resource to do the job effectively and efficiently.

Implementing Decisions   The implementation of decisions is the second stage of family resource management; it includes three steps: facilitating, checking, and adjusting.

FACILITATING   This stage begins with facilitating the decisions agreed upon in the organizing and planning stage. Family members facilitate their efforts to implement their decisions by drawing upon all the resources they command. Human resources are probably a family's greatest resource. Enthusiasm for the task at hand makes the work go more smoothly. Good judgment, initiative, and skill in communication all make the implementation process easier.

CHECKING   During the implementation stage, it is essential to monitor the situation regularly and to carefully evaluate whether the plan is working. For example, did we really make as much money at work this month as we had hoped? Were expenses as low as we predicted? Can we handle the 17% health insurance increase this year?

ADJUSTING   Most likely, families find that their initial assessment of the financial picture was less than perfect. Minor (and sometimes major) adjustments to plans are usually necessary. Say, for example, that you didn't know much about roofing when you bought your old house, and now winter rains are turning your king-sized bed in the upstairs bedroom into a water bed. A new roof will cost $8,000. Finding the money for the roof may require numerous adjustments to your financial plans. No matter what the stage of the family life cycle, unexpected expenses are bound to arise.

Budgeting Guidelines

Budgeting is the regular, systematic balancing of income and expenses. It is a personal system for making sure there is enough money to cover the essentials and, one hopes, a few extras.

To construct a workable budget, individuals need to examine their personal values about saving and spending; they must also have a good idea of what things really cost. To begin with, a couple needs to establish how much income they can count on. They should then outline their expenses by category: shelter, transportation, food, clothing, and so forth. After developing categories that reflect their particular circumstances, they must estimate how much money they will need to pay for each category.

Most people don't take the time to create a budget. An accurate budget requires that a couple or family record their expenses on a regular basis so they know how much they are spending in each category. At the end of the month, the couple can look at the recorded expenditures and develop a budget for the next month. Individuals usually find budgeting easier than families do. Individuals don't need to negotiate decisions and work out priorities that are appropriate for the entire family.

Budgeting is a continuous process of assessment and adjustment. A good budget is simple; it is also realistic and clear. A good budget builds in some personal control for each family member. It also distinguishes between wants and needs, with needs given priority but a few wants satisfied if possible. A good budget treats credit as debt, not income. Charging something or deciding to pay for it "on time"

Table 10.4 A Monthly Budget for a Two-Income Couple	
Income (after taxes, Social Security, retirement, and health insurance)	
Husband's take-home pay	$ 1,430
Wife's take-home pay	1,010
Interest earned on savings	30
Total Income	**$2,470**
Fixed Expenses	
Rent	$ 485
Bank loan (automobile)	150
Utilities	110
Telephone	45
Insurance	95
Furniture payments	170
Savings	260
Day-to-Day and Discretionary Expenses	
Food	$ 280
Clothing	175
Entertainment	130
Personal care	80
Gas, oil, insurance, and car maintenance	140
Miscellaneous	290
Total Expenses	**$2,460**
Surplus	**$ 60**

Source: Adapted from *Financial Management Extension Consultant Program: Young Singles and Young Couples* (MI-3891) (p. 28) by J. W. Bauer and B. J. Wollen, 1990. Copyright © Minnesota Extension Service, University of Minnesota. Reproduced with permission of the publisher. Copies available from Distribution Center, 20 Coffey Hall, 1420 Eckles Ave., St. Paul, MN 55108-6064.

creates a fixed expense that adds to a family's debt.

A sample budget for a married couple who both work outside the home is shown in Table 10.4. In looking at the budget, remember that a good budget is a unique budget. No one is "average" or "typical." This two-income couple had only a $60 surplus at the end of the month. Unfortunately, too many couples go deeper into debt each month, rather than developing savings. Careful planning and use of resources is the difference between comfort and crisis. A look at the hard realities of budgeting is provided in Box 10.2 (p. 336).

Pooling Money: Pros and Cons

Should two-income couples pool their money? This is a difficult question that partners have to answer together. It is also one that couples should discuss before marriage. Couples who favored pooling money were neither more nor less satisfied with money management issues in their relationship than those couples who insisted on keeping money separate. Each group of couples believed their system was the right way to handle money (Blumstein & Schwartz, 1983, p. 108).

BOX 10.2

A Lesson in Budgeting

"It is always an instructive experience to watch a class of unmarried undergraduate students draw up a budget for the first year of marriage," according to sociologist Carlfred Broderick, who teaches marriage and family courses at the University of Southern California.

Inevitably the students assume two substantial incomes. One or possibly both are expected to bring a car with them into the marriage. They are scandalized to learn how much of their paychecks they will never see due to deductions for various federal and state taxes. They are not aware that some companies also deduct substantial amounts for pension or retirement funds, insurance, or parking privileges. Even so, the diminished total is still substantial, and they plunge into the list of monthly expenditures with some zest. They allot so much for a decent apartment and utilities, so much for food, so much for eating out, for entertainment or hobbies, for clothes, for insurance, for transportation, for medical and dental expenses, for personal allowances, for laundry, for subscriptions to newspapers and magazines, for church or charity, for gifts.

The married students in the class sit shaking their heads as the numbers are put on the board. Inevitably there is an overrun on the first approximation, so the class painfully and reluctantly cuts back a few dollars here and there. Finally they come up with a balanced budget and a feeling of relief that it is really not so bad after all. Then someone says, "But what if the woman gets pregnant and they lose her income?" A grim silence settles over the class. Someone else says, "She just can't. They can't afford a baby, even on both incomes." "What? Not ever?" "Well, I don't see how—not on that budget." Yet it is clear that couples do it all the time.

Eventually a married student will confess that he or she and spouse live on a fraction of the money listed. How? Well, they almost never eat out, they drive only one car, and they don't have much furniture because they can't afford it. Not infrequently students accuse me of having set up this situation to discourage them from ever getting married. That is not true. But it is true that some of the toughest issues to face in the transition from romantic courtship to the realities of marriage are in the area of money.

Source: Marriage and the Family (4th ed.) (pp. 231–232) by C. Broderick, 1992, Englewood Cliffs, NJ: Prentice-Hall. Copyright 1992 by C. Broderick. Reprinted by permission of the publisher.

Many newly married couples find it difficult to avoid pooling, believing that a refusal to do so might be interpreted as lack of commitment by the spouse. Married couples tend to favor pooling more than cohabiting couples. But those who remarry after divorce are more likely to maintain separate funds, perhaps because they worry about the permanence of the new relationship or because they bring financial assets or liabilities to the new relationship (Blumstein & Schwartz, 1983).

Pooling is simpler because there are fewer accounts to balance. But each spouse must keep the other informed about financial actions, and there is a loss of independence. For example, if one partner forgets to record a check written on the joint account and causes an overdraft, a conflict is inevitable.

"We had a very organized system all worked out when we got married," explained Janice, a middle-aged Kansas City woman who was talking about her second marriage. "We were older. Frank was 49 at the time. I was 35. We were very logical. We kept separate accounts, not wanting to pool our income. He had his business expenses to cover, and I had my business expenses. I had the three kids, from my first marriage. It seemed logical for him to pay for his things and for me to pay for my things. Keep it separate, keep it orderly.

"Our logical system worked for about 3 months, and then he got cancer and was out of work for 11 months. No income. I had to pay for everything out of my income. It was tight, but we made it financially. And Frank recovered from the cancer and has a good prognosis.

"Then not long after the cancer episode, almost as if to even things up a bit, my first husband came roaring back and took us into court in an extended custody battle over the children. He charged that I was a rotten mother and that he should be awarded the kids. His charges were complete nonsense, but the fight lasted 2 1/2 years and cost $35,000 before we finally won. There was no way I could pay for all that, so Frank dipped into his savings and helped me out.

"He said he did it because it was only fair: I had saved him in his time of crisis, the cancer, and he loves the children and feels like a father to them and wanted me to be happy. All our logical ideas about separating funds and keeping accounts very, very straight flew out the window.

"Actually, I'm glad they did. We have created a really good marriage by not keeping the books so precisely. We don't worry so much about money anymore."

Savings

Thrift used to be a basic American virtue. Now the American virtue is to spend money.

—DAVID BRINKLEY

Most poverty-level and lower-income families are incapable of saving much money. They spend a high percentage of their income to meet basic needs such as food, clothing, shelter, and utilities. However, middle- and upper-income families are in a good position to save something each month, and there are very good reasons for them to do so.

Perhaps the best reason for saving is that most people will face a financial crisis at some time. Accidents, illness, pregnancy, job loss, divorce, and many other crises are all too common—and they all have financial consequences. At least 6 months' salary should be saved for emergencies. By following a few simple guidelines, couples and families can save 10–20% of their income per year. Thomas Garman and Raymond Forgue (1991), experts in financial management, offer six guidelines for those who want to save money:

- *Don't buy on impulse.* Know what you're shopping for, and don't buy anything you don't really need.

- *Avoid buying on credit.* The high interest rates credit cards charge can double the cost of an item.

		INTEREST RATE		
YEARS	AMOUNT INVESTED	6%	12%	DIFFERENCE
10	$12,000	$16,766	$23,586	$6,820
20	24,000	46,791	96,838	50,047
30	36,000	100,562	324,351	223,789
40	48,000	196,857	1,030,970	834,113

Table 10.5 The Results of Saving $100 a Month at Different Interest Rates

- *Buy at the right time.* Avoid peak-demand, and therefore peak-price, periods. Watch for sales, but don't buy something just because it's cheap. Look for quality.

- *Don't pay extra for a brand name.* Generic items are often as good as and are usually cheaper than brand-name goods. Again, look for quality.

- *Recognize that convenience costs money.* The local store may be handy, but a once-a-week trip to the discount center may yield savings.

- *Question the need to go first class.* Do you really need the "best"? Can you really afford the most expensive version of a given product or service?

One of the facts of the financial world is that interest on savings compounds. Money invested in a safe place at a good rate of return grows at a steady rate. By saving a few hundred dollars a month over 30 or 40 years, a person can become a millionaire. It takes some planning and careful budgeting, but the result is relative financial gain and security. Table 10.5 shows the result of saving $100 a month and investing it at 6% and 12% interest for various periods.

Credit: Uses and Abuses

There are both advantages and disadvantages to using credit. Credit can be an easy choice, but it is important not to overuse it. Excessive debt can result in bankruptcy. Financial counseling can help those who have gotten into problems with credit.

Advantages and Disadvantages of Credit

Buying on credit is very popular, for a number of reasons (Bauer & Wollen, 1990). They include enjoying something while paying for it, taking advantage of sales, shopping convenience, and having something in case of an emergency. The disadvantages of credit are the generally high interest charges and the potential for overuse. Credit should be used with caution. Unfortunately, it is a very seductive luxury.

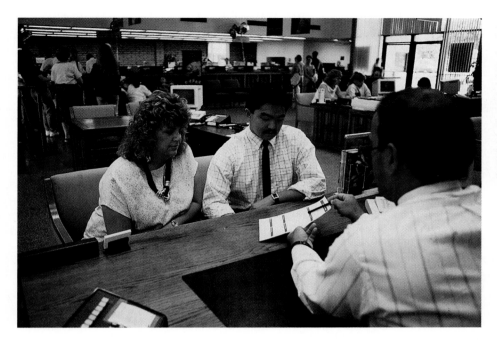

Buying a home is by far the biggest and most complicated financial decision a family makes. It requires not only planning several years ahead to save enough money for the down payment, but also shopping carefully for the best loan and for the best affordable house.

Purchasing a Home

The family dwelling has psychological significance in virtually all cultures. It provides the family's space and binds them together as a unit. It can be a haven, a place of rest and enjoyment, somewhere to kick off one's shoes and escape the pretenses of polite society.

A home is usually the most expensive item Americans buy. Careful deliberation should go into its purchase. One rule of thumb is that whether renting or buying, a family should spend no more than one week's take-home pay per month for housing expenses. Housing expenses are either rent or the total of all house-payment expenses (mortgage payment, insurance, and real estate taxes). Families who can find adequate shelter for 20–25% of their take-home pay are likely to be in relatively good financial health. Unfortunately, many lower-income families find themselves paying 50% of their income or more for housing.

Renting Versus Buying   Generally speaking, it is wiser to buy a home than to rent. Rent money is gone forever, whereas each mortgage payment gradually increases one's equity in the home while inflation increases the net worth of the dwelling. There are, however, many exceptions to this rule of thumb, and families must carefully analyze their financial situation.

There are numerous advantages to both renting and buying (Garman & Forgue, 1991). The advantages of renting include mobility, the possible amenities of an apartment complex (pool, tennis courts, party rooms, laundry facilities), and a lifestyle that involves fewer responsibilities. No large down payment is needed (only a security deposit), and the fixed housing expenditure (rent) makes budgeting easier.

The advantages of buying include pride of ownership, a better credit rating,

	CALCULATING THE COST TO:	
	RENT	BUY
Cash-Flow Considerations		
Annual rent ($580/month) or mortgage payments ($619/month)	$6,960	$ 7,428
Property and liability insurance	270	425
Real estate taxes	0	2,000
Maintenance	0	800
Less interest on funds not used for down payment (at 8%)	(1,245)	0
Cash-flow cost for the year	**$5,985**	**$10,653**
Tax and Appreciation Considerations		
Less principal repaid on the mortgage loan	$ 0	$ (293)
Plus tax on interest from funds not used for down payment (28% tax bracket)	348	0
Less tax savings due to deductibility of mortgage interest (28% tax bracket)	0	(1,998)
Less tax savings due to deductibility of real estate property tax (28% tax bracket)	0	(560)
Less appreciation on the dwelling (4% rate)	0	(3,200)
Net cost for the year	**$6,333**	**$ 4,602**

Table 10.6 Should You Buy or Rent?

Source: Personal Finance (3rd ed.) (p. 347) by E. T. Garman and R. E. Forgue, 1991, Boston: Houghton Mifflin. Copyright © 1991 Houghton Mifflin Co. Reprinted by permission of the publisher.

and a monthly payment that can remain constant for many years. The federal income tax deductions for mortgage interest and real estate property taxes are a major advantage, as is the potential for the home to increase in value over time. Owning a house forces one to save as one makes payments on an asset that is growing in value. A homeowner can also borrow against equity as the value of the home increases. Owners can make home improvements and alterations, which can increase the value of the home and/or add to the enjoyment of the dwelling.

The disadvantages of renting are that it offers no tax deductions and no potential gain from the rising value of the property. Rents rise with inflation, and many rental units have restrictions on noise level, pet ownership, and/or children. The disadvantages of buying are that a substantial down payment is needed; this can reduce available funds for other things. Also, the cost of maintenance and repairs can be high. A home is a big commitment in time, emotion, and money.

The financial benefits of buying versus renting are illustrated in Table 10.6. The example is based on renting a home for $580 a month, or buying a similar home for a slightly larger mortgage payment of $619 a month. Careful study of the table shows that renting in this particular situation costs more than buying by about $1,700 a year.

The Cost of Home Loans Family resource management specialists advise people to shop carefully for a loan when purchasing a home. The difference in the monthly payment between a 9% and a 10% home loan might not be much, but over the life of the loan, which is usually 15–30 years, the savings on interest payments can be substantial. A modest 25-year mortgage loan of $60,000 will cost the borrower more than $151,000 at 9% interest but more than $157,000 at 10% interest. One percentage point makes a $6,000 difference over the 25-year life of the loan. These figures also show that a $65,000 or $75,000 home (assuming a $5,000 or $15,000 down payment plus a $60,000 loan) really costs more than double its price when the interest on the mortgage is considered.

Credit Overextension

Credit overextension, a situation in which excessive debts make repayment difficult, is a serious problem that can cause considerable stress on families. The following danger signs suggest credit overextension (Bauer & Wollen, 1990; Garman & Forgue, 1991):

- *Debt exceeds normal limits.* People who spend more than 15–20% of their disposable income to repay debts (excluding mortgage loans) are likely to be in trouble. If the percentage is increasing each month, the situation is even more serious.

- *Monthly expenses exceed income.* When too much income goes to debt repayment, people may use credit cards to purchase things they would normally buy with cash. They may also use high-interest-rate cash advances from their credit cards. Both actions increase the overall debt load.

- *Using savings to pay for everyday expenses.*

- *Paying the minimum payment only.* Rather than paying each month's bills in full, people begin to pay only what they must, increasing their debt from month to month.

- *Reaching or exceeding credit limits.* People who are at or near the limits of their various lines of credit or those who are requesting increases in their credit limits may be in trouble.

- *Picking which creditors to pay.* As monthly bills mount and sources of additional credit are exhausted, people begin to pick and choose among creditors, paying a few one month and others the next.

- *Borrowing from one source to pay another.* People who use a cash advance from one credit card to pay the monthly bill on another credit card are likely to be in trouble.

- *Total debt is unknown.* People who cannot quickly estimate how much they owe often have multiple creditors to whom they owe large amounts.

- *Loss of a job would mean immediate financial disaster.* When a wage earner loses a job, it is a serious financial crisis for most families. But the full effects may not be felt immediately by families who have a savings cushion. Those who are already overextended in terms of credit have no resources with which to weather any loss of income.

Debt and Bankruptcy

Bankruptcy is a legal term indicating that a person is financially insolvent and unable to pay her or his debts. More than 900,000 people declare personal bankruptcy in the United States each year (Bauer & Wollen, 1990). Although bankruptcy offers some protection from creditors, it is not a solution to financial problems because the bankruptcy is a blemish on one's financial record for many years, making many financial matters more difficult. In our society bankruptcy signifies an individual's inability to handle money wisely, and society exacts various punishments on those who declare bankruptcy.

To stay out of debt and avoid bankruptcy, it is helpful to know why some people assume too much debt. It is interesting that level of income is not clearly related to debt. Debt-free families can be lower, middle, or upper income. Debt-ridden families also come from all socioeconomic levels.

Excessive debt may be due to any or all of these: credit spending, crisis spending, careless or impulsive spending, and compulsive spending. Unwise *credit spending* can lead to overextension. *Crisis spending*—resulting from unexpected events in life like unemployment, uninsured illness, and business income decline or failure—can throw personal finances into turmoil. *Careless or impulsive spending* is paying more than is necessary, purchasing inferior merchandise that does not last, and buying things one does not really need. *Compulsive spending* occurs because some people simply can't say no to salespeople, or because they have an uncontrollable impulse to acquire material things.

The healthiest of families can become financially overextended. It is not necessarily a sign of stupidity, a personality defect, or an indicator of immorality. A miscalculation can lead to financial problems. Ignorance in a highly technical area, or a financial downturn beyond one's control in a global industry, can precipitate trouble. Fortunately, there are a number of time-tested strategies for families who have become overextended. Although these solutions are not easy, they are far better than the bankruptcy alternative:

1. *Develop and stick to a balanced budget.*

2. *Avoid making any new financial commitments.* Do not incur any new debt.

3. *Destroy all credit cards.* Alternatively, lock them up so that they can't be used.

4. *Develop a plan for repaying all debts.* If the budget cannot handle the repayment schedule, try to negotiate lower payments and lower payback periods.

5. *Pay off debts with the highest interest rates first.*

6. *Work to reduce the total number of debts.*

7. *Make a plan to pay at least a small amount on each debt each month.*

8. *Avoid debt-consolidation loans.* These can set the stage for new borrowing, especially on credit cards.

Financial Counseling

If no progress has been made in 3–6 months, people who are overextended should seek financial counseling. Many large employers have budget counselors available through the human resources department or an employee assistance program. When financial difficulties are a symptom of a deeper marital or personal problem (alcohol or other drug abuse, depression, violence), a therapist may be the best way to approach the crisis.

For example, a single parent continues to support her 25-year-old son, even though his cocaine addiction is dragging her down financially. The son deals cocaine to come up with some of the $3,000 or $4,000 a month he needs to support his drug habit. He also constantly borrows money from his mother and even steals and pawns her possessions. Consumed by guilt, she covers up for him, pays the bills, and loans him money, denying his drug habit. This mother needs a competent financial advisor to help her deal with the mountain of debts she has accumulated and a personal therapist to help her come to grips with her son's drug problem, for which he must take responsibility.

People seeking financial counseling should avoid "credit clinics," which charge fees of $250–$1,000 or more for their services. Some of these businesses advertise that they will negotiate new repayment schedules with creditors, but people in financial trouble can work directly with their creditors or can find help from non-profit personal counseling organizations (Bauer & Wollen, 1990; Garman & Forgue, 1991). The human-services section of most local telephone books lists resources. Another possible resource is the network of 450 Consumer Credit Counseling Service (CCCS) agencies across the United States. Each year about a million people seek credit and budget counseling advice from CCCS.

> "We were near bankruptcy when we finally decided to go to a family therapist who specialized in financial issues," said Vera, a 35-year-old woman from Birmingham, Alabama. "It was the best thing we could have done. She helped us see that we both looked at money differently, and she helped us reconcile our differences. We had to cut up a lot of credit cards and go on a strict financial diet.
>
> "But it worked, and today we are in good shape financially. More important, we understand each other much better and know how to avoid ugly arguments while still maintaining genuine communication."

Summary

- Financial issues are the most common stressor for U.S. families across the family life cycle, regardless of how much money they make. The most difficult periods are the childbearing, adolescent, launching, and retirement stages.

- Family money problems are often related to an inability to develop specific spending and saving plans. Some arguments are not really about money, however, but about power and control in the relationship.

- Personal and family coping behaviors that help people through difficult economic times include self-esteem, cohesion, and adaptability. Social support from family members and others, and the use of family service agencies, are also important. Coping strategies that make things worse include denying the problem and failing to disclose feelings.

- Finances cause problems for couples and families because people consider the topic of money taboo, have unrealistic expectations about finances, do not create and stick to a budget, overspend and rely too heavily on credit, differ in their spending and saving styles, use money as a tool to gain power and control over their partner, and have different ideas about the meaning of money.

- More than half the families in the United States are considered middle-income families, defined by the U.S. Bureau of the Census as earning between $15,000 and $75,000 per year. However, a disproportionate share of the money in this country goes to affluent families, with only 15.5% of families receiving roughly 45% of the personal income. About 16.9% of U.S. families are lower-income families, but they make only 4% of all personal income.

- White families in the United States make more money, on average, than Hispanic and African American families. Males make more money than females, and there is a clear relationship between educational level and income. The median net worth of White households is $50,876; of Hispanic households, $6,387; and of African American households, $4,416.

- The two major stages in the process of managing family financial resources are organizing and planning, which involves value clarification, goal setting, and resource allocation; and implementing decisions, which involves facilitating, checking, and adjusting.

- Budgeting is the regular, systematic balancing of income and expenses. To budget successfully, individuals need to examine their personal values about saving and spending and to monitor their plan monthly.

- Couples who pool their money are neither more nor less satisfied with money management issues in the relationship than couples who have separate accounts.

- Most poverty-level and lower-income families are incapable of saving much money because they must spend most of their income to meet basic needs. Middle- and upper-income families should put aside at least 6 months' income in savings for financial emergencies.

- Monthly housing expenses should consume no more than one week's take-home pay. Generally, buying a home is a better investment than renting.

- Credit spending, crisis spending, careless or impulsive spending, and compulsive spending are four reasons people go into debt. Families who cannot reduce their debt over a period of 3–6 months should seek financial counseling.

Key Terms

personal coping resources	spender	resources
family coping resources	values	budgeting
saver	goals	bankruptcy

Activities

1. Write a few paragraphs describing how money was handled in the family in which you grew up, and how you handle money today. Then form groups of five or six for discussion. After members have read their essays to the group, identify similarities and differences that emerge. Have someone record these, and report them to the class. Identify the common themes among the group reports.

2. Are you a spender or a saver? How about your partner? Consider the similarities and differences between your style and your partner's style.

3. Pair off into "couples" and discuss the following questions (Dyer & Dyer, 1990) as if you were planning to marry. Then report your discussions to the class.

    a. Do you believe that all your assets belong to both of you and that all your debts are your joint responsibility?

    b. Do you expect to share equally in financial decisions? If not, how do you plan to make financial decisions?

    c. Do you plan to use a budget? Why or why not?

    d. How do you feel about each partner's having a personal allowance for which he or she is not accountable to the other?

    e. How do you feel about buying on credit? Small items? Large items?

    f. What will you do about the debts each of you brings into the marriage?

    g. Who will be the treasurer? The checkwriter? The bookkeeper? The investor?

4. Figure out your own personal budget, using the Personal Budgeting Form on page 346. Fill in each blank, estimating how much you spend in each area. How much can you put into savings? How much surplus will you have at the end of each month?

Suggested Readings

Anderson, E. A., & Koblinsky, S. A. (1995). Homeless policy: The need to speak to families. *Family Relations, 44*, 13–18. *A summary of current research on the characteristics of homeless families, with an overview of government policy.*

Bauer, J. W., & Wollen, B. J. (1990). *Financial Management Extension Consultant Program: Young singles and young couples.* St. Paul, MN: Minnesota Extension Service. *A useful tool that helps young people manage money successfully.*

Blumstein, P., & Schwartz, P. (1983). *American couples.* New York: Morrow. *Based on research with thousands of heterosexual, gay-male, and lesbian couples, an excellent discussion by two sociologists of the challenges people face in their quest to create an intimate relationship. Focuses on money, sex, and power.*

Burkett, L. (1989). *The complete financial guide for young couples.* Wheaton, IL: Victor Books. *A practical, nuts-and-bolts approach to money management.*

Dyer, P., & Dyer, G. (1990). *Growing together.* Minneapolis: PREPARE/ENRICH. *How people can continue to change without becoming estranged from one another, with good advice about money management.*

Personal Budgeting Form

Monthly Income $_____

Expenses

Food, total $_____
   Meals and snacks at home
   Food away from home
   Alcoholic beverages
   Other_____

Housing, total $_____
   Rent or mortgage
   Fuels, utilities, and public services
   Household operations and furnishings
   Housekeeping supplies
   Other_____

Apparel and services $_____

Transportation, total $_____
   Vehicles
   Gasoline, oil, insurance
   Public transportation

Health care $_____

Life and other personal insurance $_____

Pensions and Social Security $_____

Other expenditures $_____

Savings $_____

Monthly Expenses $_____

Surplus (if any) $_____

Olson, D. H., McCubbin, H. I., Barnes, H. L., Muxen, M. J., Larsen, A. S., & Wilson, M. A. (1989). *Families: What makes them work* (2nd ed.). Newbury Park, CA: Sage. *Contains especially useful sections on money.*

Rubin, L. B. (1992). *Worlds of pain: Life in the working-class family* (2nd ed.). New York: Basic Books. *The current edition of the 1976 classic qualitative study of working-class couples, providing "flesh and blood" insights.*

Rubin, L. B. (1994). *Families on the fault line: America's working class speaks about the family, the economy, race, and ethnicity.* New York: HarperCollins. *A study based on 162 interviews with working-class and lower middle-class families in various U.S. cities.*

VanderStaay, S. (1992). *Street lives: An oral history of homeless Americans.* Philadelphia: New Society. *Sensitizes the reader to the human dimensions of extreme poverty in the United States.*

PART IV

Stages of Marriage and Family Life

CHAPTER 11

Cohabitation, Marriage, and Early Married Life

It [marriage] happens as with cages: The birds without despair to get in, and those within despair of getting out.
—MONTAIGNE (1595, in Beck, 1980, p. 165)

Marriage is full of paradoxes. It is much easier to get into than to get out of. It is also a risky venture, with roughly a 50% chance of divorce. Yet most people want to get married; without thinking about it much, they assume their marriage will last a lifetime. But very few couples prepare themselves in any meaningful way for marriage. Should it be a surprise, then, that millions of unhappy people end up puzzling over why their marriages fail?

This chapter examines cohabitation, getting married, and the early years of marriage. We discuss the personal and social factors that increase the likelihood of a successful marriage and explore the positive and negative reasons for getting married. The relationship between parental marital status and couple relationship satisfaction is also discussed.

We then turn to premarriage preparation and the importance of premarital programs. A discussion about how behavioral and social scientists have learned to predict marriage success or failure with 80–85% accuracy follows. The remainder of the chapter addresses the difficult challenges couples face in their first years of married life and offers some recommendations for strengthening the marriage during its early years.

Cohabitation

For many people, marriage is no longer considered a prerequisite for living with a romantic partner. In fact, by the time they reach their early 30s, almost half the U.S. population has cohabited at some time (Nock, 1995). **Cohabitation** is defined by the federal government as two unrelated adults of the opposite sex sharing the same living quarters. A broader definition would include same-sex couples who have an emotional and sexual relationship. Between 1980 and 1993, the number of couples cohabiting doubled, to 3,510,000 (U.S. Bureau of the Census, 1994). Among cohabiting couples, about half (54%) the partners had never been married, about one third (37%) had been divorced, and the rest were widowed.

It is clearly safe to say that cohabitation is becoming more common in America. It is also true that cohabitation has sparked a good deal of controversy. Numerous studies have been conducted to evaluate this phenomenon, but the results are somewhat difficult to interpret. Marriage is a risky proposition. Conflict is inevitable, and the likelihood of divorce is high. For these and numerous other reasons, more people are deciding to live together rather than marry.

People cohabit for many reasons and have various types of cohabitation arrangements. In a highly instructive review of research and the observations of counselors, Carl Ridley, Dan Peterman, and Arthur Avery (1978) identified four common patterns of cohabitation: Linus blanket, emancipation, convenience, and testing.

The number of unmarried couples living together in the United States doubled between 1980 and 1993, a trend that some observers believe is the most dramatic family-related change ever to occur in American society. Couples live together for many different reasons, including the opportunity to see how their relationship withstands the pressures of daily living.

- **Linus blanket.** Named after the character in the comic strip "Snoopy" who carries a security blanket with him, the Linus blanket type of cohabiting relationship occurs when one partner is so dependent or insecure that he or she prefers a relationship with anyone to being alone. The insecure partner often finds the open communication on which a successful relationship thrives to be difficult, and the stronger partner does not feel that he or she can criticize the more "fragile" partner. After shouldering the planning and decision-making burdens for too long, the stronger partner often becomes frustrated and leaves the relationship. When the relationship ends, the insecure partner's fragile self-esteem falls even lower, and the departing partner feels guilty.

- **Emancipation.** Some people use cohabitation as a way to break free from their parents' values and influence. Women who grew up in very conservative religious traditions sometimes seek sexual emancipation not permitted by their parents or their faith through cohabitation. Guilt often overwhelms these women, however, and they break off the relationship. But because the business of emancipation is not finished, they often enter into another cohabiting relationship. The partner suffers in this type of situation because the individual seeking emancipation brings too much unfinished business to the relationship and is trying to gain independence at another's expense.

- **Convenience.** Relationships in which one person is the giver and the other is the taker are often relationships of convenience. Cohabiting relationships of this type may involve a man who is in the relationship mainly for sex and to have a housewife (although women may cohabit for economic, sexual, and social reasons also). The woman supplies loving care and domestic labor—and hopes, but dares not ask, for marriage. It is obvious what the man gets out of the relationship. The woman gains a few hard-earned lessons: that unconditional giving can go unreturned and that reciprocity is essential for the long-term survival and ultimate success of a relationship. The partners usually part company, older and wiser.

- **Testing.** Cohabitation can be a true testing ground for marriage if the partners are relatively mature and clearly committed to trying out their already mutually satisfying relationship in a situation more closely resembling marriage. If the test goes well, they marry; if not, they separate. Either way, they have learned important lessons.

Cohabiting as Preparation for Marriage

Many couples state that cohabitation is a test of future marital compatibility. Eleanor Macklin (1980) found, for example, that the majority of the participants in her study would not consider marriage without first having lived with the potential mate. Similarly, the majority of cohabitants in a separate study stated that the arrangement was primarily preparation for marriage (Lewis, Spanier, Atkinson, & Lehecka, 1977).

The growing prevalence of cohabitation among middle-class youth adds a new step in the mate selection process. Traditional courtship has been severely criticized by counselors because it emphasizes recreation and avoids conflictual issues. Also, the strong erotic needs of the not-yet-married couple sometimes make it possible for them to solve problems more easily. As one husband said in counseling, "When you're in love, you're willing to compromise on anything!"

Traditional courtship provides partners with idealized views of each other, making early marriage a period of more severe and difficult adjustments for most couples. In contrast, some argue that those who cohabit before marriage will experience the realities of life together before they decide to tie the knot. Another obvious area of disagreement is on moral, religious, or philosophical grounds. Some see cohabitation as inherently immoral. They argue that it violates religious dogma. Another area of disagreement is whether cohabitation is a true testing ground for marriage. Because it is not truly a marriage, some argue, it cannot serve as a test of marriage. Cohabitation is only "playing house," in the opinion of many observers.

Finally, some argue that living together as a test of marriage really doesn't make much sense. To test marriage, they say, you need to actually get married. However, living together won't keep you from experiencing pain and misery if the relationship breaks up. For some couples who have cohabited, dealing with the pain of a broken relationship can be as difficult as it would have been if they had been legally married.

Angela and George had been living together for a little over 3 years. He was a 26-year-old computer salesman; she was a 26-year-old quality control

Figure 11.1 Living Arrangement and Premarital Satisfaction. *Source:* From *Predicting Premarital Satisfaction on PREPARE Using Background Factors* by K. L. Stewart and D. H. Olson, (1990) (p. 17), unpublished manuscript, Prepare/Enrich, Inc., Minneapolis, MN. Copyright © 1990 Prepare/Enrich. Used by permission of the publisher.

manager at a competing firm. They had met through mutual friends nearly 5 years earlier. Now they shared a condominium in Los Angeles and two Irish setters.

One evening as they were lying in bed, Angela rolled over and gave George a big kiss on the cheek. "Honey," she said, "what do you think about getting married?"

George looked at the ceiling for a few long seconds and said, "Angie, what would you say if I said 'Maybe' ?"

Angela rolled over and looked at the wall. George rolled over and looked at the other wall. After a long time, George rolled over and hugged Angela as she looked at her wall. "Angie, will you marry me?" he asked, pleading ever so slightly.

"Yes!" she responded, rolling toward him and giving him a big kiss. "Of course!"

Cohabiting and Relationship Satisfaction

There is no clear-cut answer to the question of whether cohabitation really does help prepare people for marriage. It might be useful for some; for others, it is not a positive experience.

In a study of 4,271 engaged couples, Kenneth Stewart and David Olson (1990) found that cohabiting couples had a less satisfying premarital relationship than engaged couples who lived apart (Figure 11.1). To determine engaged couples' levels of satisfaction, a total sample of 17,025 couples completed a comprehensive premarital inventory called **PREPARE,** which evaluated their satisfaction in 14 aspects of their relationship. From the total sample, the most satisfied (numbering 2,124) and the least satisfied (numbering 2,147) were selected (total = 4,271) for comparison. Of the couples selected, about one third (31%) were cohabiting; in another third (34%), one person lived with her or his parents and the other lived with others. In one fifth (22%) of the couples, both partners lived with their parents; in only 13% of the couples did both partners live alone.

In this study, cohabiting couples had the lowest level of premarital satisfaction, whereas premarital couples in which both people lived alone had the highest level of premarital satisfaction. Although about two thirds of the cohabiting couples fell into the low-satisfaction group, about two thirds of the couples with both living alone fell into the high-satisfaction group.

It also appears that engaged couples with both partners living alone are more satisfied than couples in which one or both partners still live with their parents. One possible explanation for these findings is the way in which the couple became independent from their family of origin. Cohabiting couples may be rebelling against their families to some degree; couples in which both partners live with their parents might be too dependent on their parents. Those engaged couples who are both living alone might have achieved a more satisfactory degree of independence from their families of origin.

Cohabiting as a Courtship Stage

One of the earliest studies of cohabitation was done by Robert Watson (1983), who studied 87 Canadian couples in his efforts to find out if cohabitation is, indeed, "a new stage of courtship which, in replacing dating, may provide a more realistic basis for the selection of a mate" (p. 139). He found that about two thirds (64%) of the couples studied had engaged in some form of cohabitation before marriage. Watson was interested in seeing if couples who had cohabited before marriage would display a higher level of adjustment during the first year of marriage than couples who had entered marriage in a more traditional manner. Watson was surprised to find that noncohabitors were better adjusted during the first year of marriage than those who had previously cohabited. What might account for this difference? Watson offered two possible explanations. First, researchers know that the first decade of marriage is characterized by consistently declining marital satisfaction. As the years go by, happiness with the relationship tends to diminish. The cohabitants had been living together longer than the noncohabitants. Therefore, the cohabitants' satisfaction scores would probably tend to be lower because the excitement and romance of early marriage had already worn off. The cohabitants were simply further down the path than the noncohabitants.

An alternative theory argues that people who cohabit and those who do not cohabit have very different perceptions of what marriage is all about and that those perceptions influence how they adjust to marriage. To cohabitants, marriage may be a relatively insignificant rite of passage. Young people living together have said, "Our love is in our heart. We don't have to go before a preacher or a judge to prove it." Cohabitants have already established a household, they have already defined their roles to each other and their friends, and they have probably had to defend their relationship to parents who may disapprove of it. Noncohabitants, on the other hand, tend to look at marriage as "a liberating ritual through which new possibilities, notably, the public establishment of a common household, are opened to a couple and are celebrated" (Watson, 1983, p. 146).

To cohabitants, then, marriage does not bring freedom; it is not a liberating ritual. Cohabitants have already been liberated. For them, marriage only brings more tightly defined responsibilities. This reality may be reflected in the cohabitants' lower adjustment scores after marriage. Did the people who cohabited before marriage have any regrets about their behavior, looking back? Not many did; fully 94% reported they had no regrets. And did the people who had not cohabited before marriage have any regrets? Ninety percent said they did the right thing.

Cohabiting and Relationship Longevity

Researchers have found that cohabitation is associated with a greater risk of marital dissolution than noncohabitation (DeMaris & Rao, 1992; Hall & Zhao, 1995). A comparison of couples who did and did not cohabit before marriage found that those who had cohabited reported lower-quality marriages, a lower commitment to the institution of marriage, more individualistic views of marriage (wives only), and a greater likelihood of divorce than those who had not (Thomson & Colella, 1992).

Robert Schoen (1992) sheds more light on the issue of cohabitation. He found that cohabitation is generally associated with a higher risk of marital dissolution but that the differential is smaller in comparisons of recent cohabitants and noncohabitants than it is between those whose experiences took place some years ago. Cohabitation was a highly controversial proposition 25 years ago and perhaps was an attractive option for a small group of people who were also rather different from the norm in other ways. Those characteristics may have made them more likely to divorce after marriage. Today, cohabitation is relatively commonplace. Schoen hypothesizes that as cohabitation has become more common over the years, the relatively "select nature of those who cohabited" may have largely disappeared. Perhaps the difference between cohabitants and noncohabitants will shrink even more in the future as cohabitation becomes more and more statistically normal.

Other researchers have concluded that cohabitation can prepare a couple for marriage, but how successful the arrangement is depends on a number of factors, including the needs, goals, motivations, and competence of the individuals cohabiting. "It would seem unfortunate to conclude that cohabitation is inherently good or bad preparation for marriage, but rather it should be viewed as having the potential for both" (Ridley et al., 1978, p. 134). The characteristics of the people cohabiting determine the long-range effects on the relationship.

Concerns in the popular press that cohabitation poses a threat to the institution of marriage and indicates a lack of commitment to long-term relationships are probably not justified. Cohabitation has become a part of the courtship process for many college students. It is not an alternative to marriage, but rather a step in the direction of marriage. A study of 231 college-aged Boston couples found that most college students who cohabit expect to marry at some time in the future. It also found no significant differences between couples who were "going together" and those who were cohabiting as to whether they broke up or got married (Risman, Hill, Rubin, & Peplau, 1981).

Legal Issues in Cohabitation

In the minds and spirits of the cohabiting couple, they may be married, but in the eyes of the law, the matter is more complicated. To some people, the most important aspect of marriage is the spiritual and religious dimension—the melding of two kindred souls. To other people, the psychological and emotional aspects—the development of intimacy—are the most important.

But marriage is also a legal contract. Couples should consider the legal issues carefully before entering into a cohabitation arrangement. As long as the living arrangement goes well, there is not a whole lot to worry about. But what about separation? Cohabitants are no more stable in their relationships than married people; in fact, they are probably less stable. So when a cohabiting couple breaks up, they have issues to resolve. Problems can arise in the areas of personal property, wills and estates, and income earned while cohabiting. Attorney Barton Bernstein concludes that "individuals choosing to cohabit should consider the ramifications of cohabitation prior to or early in the development of their relationship in order to avoid devastating legal complications" (Bernstein, 1977, p. 361).

Bernstein's rhetoric may sound a bit melodramatic to young people who don't have a lot of money or property to fight over after a relationship has broken up. But the stakes are higher for some cohabitants. Until recently, unmarried couples who were living together could end their relationships without legal hassles. But the much-publicized 1976 court ruling in *Marvin* v. *Marvin* changed this.

Actor Lee Marvin and Michelle Triola had lived together from 1964 to 1970. She had adopted his last name, calling herself Michelle Marvin. When the couple separated, the actor supported her for a period of 2 years. When the support ceased, Michelle Marvin sued Lee Marvin on the grounds that he had broken his verbal promise to her: If she would live with him and abandon her career as an actress, he would support her for life, sharing his earnings. She argued that she had kept her part of the bargain, but he had not kept his. The California Supreme Court made a landmark decision in the case, for the court had no existing legal guidelines from which to make a judgment. The court set a value on Michelle Marvin's services in the relationship so that it could make a property settlement. When the first round of legal maneuvering ended in 1979, Ms. Marvin was awarded $104,000. This money was to compensate her for the lost years of her career, and part of the money was to help her reestablish herself in the working world.

Michelle Marvin thus became the first unmarried woman to obtain "equitable relief"—in a sense, alimony. This suit also resulted in the coining of a new term: **palimony.** As a result of *Marvin* v. *Marvin* and related issues, lawyers now advise couples who wish to cohabit to draw up a legal agreement to protect themselves. If the relationship ends, the agreement serves as a guide for the rational and orderly division of property. The document should cover such issues as future earnings, who will receive custody of any offspring, and who will pay child support.

In one legal arrangement called *contract cohabitation*, one cohabitant in essence hires the other as a live-in companion. The agreement specifies each partner's rights

Although love and intimacy are apparent between the partners in this lesbian relationship, commitment may be harder for them to develop and maintain. Because of societal pressures, many individuals in long-term, same-sex relationships are deprived of the opportunity to have their commitment to each other acknowledged and celebrated publicly.

and obligations and is especially useful for middle-aged couples with considerable financial assets. The contract cohabitation agreement may be canceled at any time. The "employer" is thus protected from having to pay palimony or having to divide up his or her property, as might be required without such a contract.

Same-Sex Cohabitation

Same-sex cohabitants (both gay men and lesbians) often feel stigmatized by society. As cohabitants, they have no legal status, and as homosexuals, they are stigmatized for their sexual orientation. Their relationship may cause great discomfort to their parents, other family members, and friends. As a result, they may choose not to divulge their sexual preference to people who would disapprove.

Commitment, essential to a sound and long-lasting relationship, is especially difficult to build in an "invisible" relationship, which many same-sex relationships tend to be. Philip, himself a partner in a same-sex relationship, had this to say about these issues:

> Right, they [gays] don't have the externals imposed by the institution of marriage. They don't have the in-laws; they don't have the children; they don't have the PTA; they don't have the office parties. . . . All of these things, you know, are great supports for couples, those straight couples, to try to keep their marriage together. You know, gay people don't have that, none of those institutional supports to back them up. So it's got to come out of some real need, some real commitment to each other to try to keep it together and to try to remain allies against what is ultimately a hostile world to them. (Denneny, 1979, p. 72)

A research team received completed questionnaires from 32 lesbians and 50 gay men in Philadelphia who had lived together for at least 6 months (Lewis, Kozac, Milardo, & Grosnick, 1981). The investigators were especially interested in the

<head>B O X   1 1 . 1</head>

Is Cohabitation the Right Choice for You?

1. *How did each of you come to the decision to live together?*
   Good signs: Each individual has given considerable thought to the decision, including both pros and cons.
   Bad signs: One or both partners hasn't thought much about it.

2. *What do you think you will gain from living together?*
   Good signs: Each person wants to learn more about self and the partner.
   Bad signs: One or both wish to live together for convenience only, or they seek independence from peers or parents.

3. *What responsibilities do you have to each other? What are your expectations of each other?*
   Good signs: Expectations are compatible between partners.
   Bad signs: One or both have given little thought to this, or they disagree.

4. *Identify your partner's primary physical and emotional needs, and estimate how well you are fulfilling those needs.*
   Good signs: Each has a clear understanding of the other's needs and is willing and capable of meeting them to a good degree.
   Bad signs: One or both are not fully aware of the other's needs or are unwilling to or incapable of satisfying them.

5. *What makes the relationship important to you? How do you feel about your partner?*
   Good signs: Partners care deeply for each other, and there are many significant elements bonding them together.
   Bad signs: There is an emotional imbalance, with one partner more committed than the other. Or neither partner is deeply committed.

6. *What will your family and friends think?*
   Good signs: Both people are aware of how the other intimates in their lives will react. The family and friends are either supportive of the cohabiting relationship, or the couple has carefully considered how they will deal with opposition.
   Bad signs: One or both individuals are not aware of their families' or their friends' reactions, or families and/or friends are not supportive of the couple's decision to cohabit.

7. *How open are you with each other in terms of honestly sharing feelings?*
   Good signs: Each individual usually can open up to the partner.
   Bad signs: One or both partners have a difficult time being honest.

8. *Can each of you discuss the other's strengths and weaknesses together? How much are you trying to change your partner?*
   Good signs: The partners know each other's feelings about strengths and weaknesses, and there is little effort on either's part to mold the loved one into something different.
   Bad signs: The partners have trouble accepting each other for who each one is.

9. *How do you manage conflict?*
   Good signs: The partners express their differences and mutually work out solutions. There is evidence of give and take on both sides.
   Bad signs: One or both can't express himself or herself. The couple avoids problems rather than making a genuine effort to solve them.

level of commitment homosexual couples had developed, despite the constraints society puts on them. A quarter of the gay men reported that they had known each other for less than a year; half the lesbians had known each other for 1–2 years. The respondents were asked to describe how "formal" their commitment was. Among the gay men, 48% reported that they had developed a "long-term commitment" to each other; among the lesbians, 38% reported a long-term commitment. Furthermore, 62% of the gay men and 31% of the lesbians reported that their relationship "will probably result in a formal, recognized commitment," such as a "holy union."

The study found that lesbian couples were slightly more apt to do things together and spent less time away from each other with other people than gay-male couples. Lesbians were also more likely to confide in each other, talking things over together. And they were more certain of the value of their living arrangement and rarely fantasized about breaking up. But the researchers noted that the similarities the study uncovered between gay-male cohabiting relationships and lesbian cohabiting relationships were much more noteworthy than the few differences.

Questions to Consider Before Cohabiting

Professionals are just beginning to answer some of the basic questions about cohabitation. Cohabitation works for many people, but others remain opposed to it. Happy marriages have been developed by those who lived together before marriage and by those who did not. Before cohabiting, it is important for partners to discuss questions like those in Box 11.1. Ridley, Peterman, and Avery, the authors of the discussion points, also offer some guidelines—"good" signs and "bad" signs—for determining, on the basis of the answers, whether living together is a positive step.

Clearly, there are a number of things for a couple to consider before deciding to cohabit. In many ways, cohabitation is just as complicated a relationship as marriage. And it is probably no buffer against the painful decisions people must make in their lives regarding loved ones. Eventually, individuals must make choices about how committed they are to their partner. Whether one is married or not, the decision can be very difficult.

A Formula for a Successful Marriage

A loving relationship with another human being offers enormous benefits and can be therapeutic, helping to heal many wounds. But people with major psychological deficits bring barriers to intimacy into a relationship. Most counselors would agree that it is a mistake to marry someone who is playing a therapist or a patient role. Chances of marital success are greater if one marries a friend.

A careful review of research and clinical experience reported by many professionals indicates that a marriage has a better chance for success if potential partners meet the following conditions:

Independence and maturity make for a successful marriage because the partners are likely to have acquired the self-knowledge and self-confidence necessary for an intimate relationship. Because they can express their needs honestly and assertively and respond unselfishly to each other's needs, such couples are more likely to be friends as well as lovers.

- *Both individuals are independent and mature.* The more mature and independent two people are, the easier it is for them to develop an interdependent relationship that can facilitate intimacy. Independence and maturity often increase with age, a good reason for waiting to marry. In fact, the single best predictor of a successful marriage is the age of the couple. This is partly because older people are typically more stable and know what they want in marriage.

- *Both individuals love not only each other but themselves.* Self-esteem is very important in an intimate relationship. It is difficult to truly love another person without also loving oneself. People need to feel secure and self-confident before they can be truly giving and loving to another.

- *Both individuals enjoy being alone as well as together.* To balance the separateness and togetherness that an intimate relationship requires, people need to enjoy separate activities and time apart. Time apart reminds partners of the value of the relationship and increases the importance and value of time together. Too much togetherness can lead to such negative behaviors as attempting to control the partner and failure to appreciate the partner.

- *Both individuals are established in their work or occupation.* A stable and satisfying occupation or job fosters both financial and emotional security. When people's jobs are going well, they are able to devote more time and energy to their relationships. Conversely, the greater the stress at work, the less positive energy there is for a relationship.

BOX   1 1 . 2

Facts About Marriage

- Approximately 2.4 million couples marry each year.

- Approximately 1.2 million couples divorce each year.

- In about half of all marriages, one or both people have been married at least once before.

- In 1995, the bridegroom's average age was 26.7; the bride's age was 24.5. In 1960, the average age was 22.8 for the bridegroom and 20.3 for the bride.

- Engagements last an average of 9 months.

- The average U.S. wedding costs about $15,000.

- Approximately half of all marriages end in divorce. The average length of a marriage is 6 years.

Source: U.S. Bureau of the Census (1992, pp. 90–94); U.S. Bureau of the Census (1995).

- *Both individuals know themselves.* An intimate relationship requires openness and honesty between the partners. They must be able to evaluate their personal strengths and failings objectively and not blame their problems on other people. They must also know what they want from another person and also what they can give to a partner.

- *Both individuals can express themselves assertively.* One key to developing intimacy is assertiveness—expressing oneself in a direct and generally positive manner. People who are not assertive in their communication often adopt a passive-aggressive approach. The more clearly partners can ask for what they want from each other, the better the chances that the partner will comply.

- *Both individuals are friends as well as lovers.* When people focus on their lover's needs, they find that the loved one tends to focus on their needs. This has been called the law of enlightened self-interest. Developed by social exchange theorists to describe successful relationships, the principle holds that being less selfish is in a person's best interest because it helps to build cooperative and intimate relationships that benefit everyone. Nonpossessive caring encourages the partner to grow and to reach his or her potential. Both partners generally benefit.

Some facts about marriage in the United States today are presented in Box 11.2.

Reasons for Marrying

Couples can give many positive reasons for getting married, but they often have difficulty identifying reasons not to marry. This section explores a variety of positive characteristics that facilitate intimacy in marriage and also looks at some negative issues that can create problems in marriage.

Positive Reasons

There are many good reasons to get married, and marriages based on positive motives have a higher chance of success.

Companionship   Sharing one's life with someone is one common reason for marriage. Companionship provides a partner for sharing the journey of life. However, although some people falsely assume that marriage will end loneliness, it seldom does unless both partners feel good about themselves.

Love and Intimacy   The need for love and intimacy is related to the need for companionship. A good marriage can be a precious gift. Actor Bill Cosby was interviewed about his feelings for his wife, Camille, after 22 years of marriage. The couple met on a blind date. They have four daughters, and friends view their relationship as a kind of "marital miracle." Cosby has been described as a very strong and purposeful individual, but he is said to melt in Camille's presence. "I've seen Bill walk into a crowded room, suddenly spot her, and start crawling toward her across the floor," one colleague reported. "Every time he looks at her, it's as if he's seeing her for the first time. It's like they're still on a high-school date." One reporter noted that when the subject of Camille came up, Cosby's eyes misted over and his voice quavered as he said, "It's hard to describe a relationship with so much growth in it. It goes past just missing her when she's not here. I'm just very, very fortunate that the person I trust the most trusts me and the person I love the most loves me. I love her so much" (Waters, 1985). It is difficult to maintain such intensity in a long-term relationship; most couples report that passion decreases over the years.

Supportive Partnership   Another good reason for marriage is the opportunity it provides for growth as a human being and for nurturing the growth of one's partner. A marriage cannot survive if the partners think only of their own development, career needs, or needs for recognition and accomplishment. But sharing each other's successes and genuinely supporting each other in the quest for betterment and achievement enhance and stabilize a relationship. To achieve this, both people must be willing and able to give of themselves. A mutual-admiration marriage has an excellent chance of success.

Sexual Partnership   Marriage has long been seen as a stable source of sexual satisfaction for both partners, although this view declined in the 1970s and 1980s following the "sexual revolution." Many people concluded that sex and marriage did not necessarily have to go together. The AIDS epidemic, however, has again changed sexual attitudes to some degree. Marriage is often seen as a way to legitimize one's sexual feelings and behavior. But if sex is the major reason for marrying, the marriage will not have a very good chance of surviving.

Sharing Parenthood   Another traditional reason for marriage is to have children, but parenthood can be a mixed blessing. Most parents find rearing children to be a challenging and often frustrating task, but also a very satisfying one. When the

The marriage of two successful people can have unique challenges, but Bruce Willis and Demi Moore seem to have created a supportive partnership. They not only share each other's successes but also provide a strong family life for their children.

children are grown up and independent, most parents say that they have had enough parenting for one lifetime, but they also say that if they had it to do all over again, they would again decide to have children. Parenthood clearly is not for everyone, and it can unite or divide a couple. Parents who successfully raise children forge important bonds between them. Approached realistically, parenthood remains a very sound reason for marriage.

Negative Reasons

There are also a number of poor reasons for getting married. Unless these issues are dealt with before marriage, they can create considerable challenges for a couple.

Premarital Pregnancy   "Having to get married" because of premarital pregnancy is not a good way to go into marriage. Although the partners have shared sex, they may have not yet developed other aspects of true intimacy and may lack a real understanding of who they are marrying. Sex partners are not necessarily friends.

Almost one out of three children (30%) are born out of wedlock (U.S. Bureau of the Census, 1995). The rate of children born out of wedlock varies considerably by ethnic background: for African Americans the rate is 68%; for Native Americans, 55%; for Hispanics, 45%; for Caucasians, 23%; and for Asian Americans, 10%. These rates have increased dramatically in the past decade, and there are indications that they will not decrease unless interventions are developed to address this growing problem.

Rebellion Against Parents   Although many people are uncomfortable admitting that conflict with parents is a reason for marrying, it too often is the case. Marriage as rebellion against repressive parents or a dysfunctional family of origin may be a rational option for a young person. People who have suffered in the cross fire of long-term conflicts between their parents are ripe for rebellion. People who have been the victims of parental alcohol or drug abuse or of physical, emotional, or sexual abuse all have legitimate reasons to flee from their families. But a legitimate reason for leaving one's family of origin is not necessarily a legitimate reason for getting married. It is better to develop one's independence and to come to terms with one's family of origin before thinking about marriage.

Independence   Closely related to the need to escape or rebel is the need to be independent. Young adults have a drive to succeed on their own. But becoming independent from one's family of origin is something that only an individual can do. People cannot rely on their partner to do it for them.

Rebounding from Another Relationship   The rebound syndrome—another negative reason for getting married—seems to be easier to detect in other people than in ourselves. The common reply to a warning is "Oh, no! I understand what you're saying, but this relationship is *different*." People tend to frame new relationships in positive terms, focusing on the joys and ignoring the fact that they may be reacting against their previous relationship. People on the rebound may "need" the new partner for emotional support. A marriage works better, however, when two people "want" rather than "need" each other. A rebound relationship is in danger from the start because the object of affection is seen not only as a friend or lover, but also as a therapist or healer of the wounds of the old relationship.

Family or Social Pressure   Many families put subtle and not-so-subtle pressure on young people who do not marry relatively early. Both males and females may be pressured, but women often feel more pressure as they reach their late 20s. Many students who go to college find that the classmates whom they left behind in their hometown are soon married and pregnant. People who choose for many good reasons not to marry young or who choose not to marry at all should not succumb to this pressure. Marrying against one's own desires is unlikely to produce a happy relationship.

Economic Security   Although economic security has been a traditional reason for marrying, it has dubious merits today. With half of today's marriages likely to end in divorce, young women simply cannot afford to be dependent financially on their husbands. Add widowhood to this equation, and it becomes quite clear that all women need to know how to support themselves financially.

There is the genuine possibility of unemployment for one or both spouses over the course of a marriage. Many people experience the trauma of being out of work for an extended period. Marriage does not automatically produce economic security, but couples continue to search for the elusive goal. Financial problems are the most common marital problem Americans cite in national polls.

In summary, there are many positive and negative reasons for marrying, and

BOX 11.3

Warning Signs of a Problem Marriage

Monica McGoldrick, an eminent family therapist, has compiled the following list of warning signs of a problem marriage. She observes that the more characteristics that are true, the higher the potential for marital problems.

1. The couple meets or marries shortly after a significant loss.

2. The wish to distance from one's family of origin is a factor in the marriage.

3. The family backgrounds of each spouse are significantly different (religion, education, social class, ethnicity, age of the partners).

4. The spouses come from incompatible sibling constellations.

5. The couple resides either extremely close to or at a great distance from either family of origin.

6. The couple is dependent on either extended family financially, physically, or emotionally.

7. The couple marries before age 20.

8. The couple marries after an acquaintanceship of less than six months or after more than three years of engagement.

9. The wedding occurs without family or friends present.

10. The wife becomes pregnant before marriage or within the first year of marriage.

11. Either spouse considers her or his childhood or adolescence an unhappy time.

12. Either spouse has a poor relationship with siblings or parents.

13. Marital patterns in either extended family were unstable.

Source: Adapted from "The Joining of Families Through Marriage: The New Couple" (p. 231) by M. McGoldrick. In *The Changing Family Life Cycle: A Framework for Family Therapy* (2nd ed.) by B. Carter and M. McGoldrick, 1989, New York: Gardner Press. Copyright © 1989 by Allyn & Bacon. Reprinted by permission.

people in love are often not objective when it comes to analyzing their motives and actions. Being rational and realistic about reasons for marrying is not easy. But people who marry mainly for positive reasons are likely to have sounder marital relationships. For warning signs of potential marriage problems, see Box 11.3.

Parental Perspective and Influence on Marriage

A marriage is influenced by the parents of both partners. Folk wisdom tells us that when you get married, you marry a whole family, not just one person. This becomes increasingly clear as a couple moves toward marriage.

To examine the influence of parents on the premarital relationship, Stewart and Olson (1990) studied 5,128 premarital couples. Although all these couples were planning on marriage, not all were satisfied with their premarital relationship. People get married for many reasons, as discussed earlier. For a marriage to be strong and to last, the relationship must be healthy. Unfortunately, some premarital couples planning to marry are not getting along well even before marriage. Of all the premarital couples, two groups were studied: those who were very satisfied with their premarital relationship (the upper third of the total group) and those who were the least satisfied with their premarital relationship (the lower third of the total group). The middle third of the total group was not included in this analysis.

Stewart and Olson asked each of the engaged couples if their parents were positive or negative about the upcoming marriage. They found that if both sets of parents were negative about the upcoming marriage, 88% of the engaged couples had low premarital satisfaction. If only one set of parents was negative about the upcoming marriage, 73% of the engaged couples said they had low premarital satisfaction. Looking at the data from the positive side, if both sets of parents were positive about the upcoming marriage, 58% of the engaged couples reported that they had a positive premarital relationship. This study demonstrates that parents are very accurate in their perception of a premarital couple's relationship, particularly if the couple is having problems. This is because "outsiders" like parents are often more realistic and less idealistic than a couple in love. It is, therefore, important for a premarital couple to pay attention to parental feedback, particularly if their parents have serious concerns.

Another important issue is the relationship between the parents' marital status and the premarital satisfaction of the engaged couple. As presented in Figure 11.2, when both sets of parents were married, 57% of the premarital couples reported that they were highly satisfied with their relationship. On the other hand, when both sets of parents were divorced, 67% of the engaged couples reported low premarital satisfaction.

Will a couple with divorced parents also divorce? And will a couple with happily married parents have a good marriage relationship like that of their parents? Although there clearly is a strong tendency in the direction of the parental pattern, the premarital couple with divorced parents might simply need to work harder and smarter to overcome the issues and problems they have experienced in their families of origin.

> "Divorce was no fun in our family," said Shelley as she sat on her living-room couch in her home in Omaha. "I was 12 at the time and I thought my family was the only awful family in the world. Dad was running around with his girlfriend, and Mom cried all the time. I can't think of many good things to say about divorce.
>
> "But there is one: It made me very, very careful about getting married. I just didn't jump into it like some friends I know. Maybe I was even a bit too picky. I turned down two guys—one, I was even engaged to.
>
> "Finally, though, after I had been going with Dave for 2 years, he broke down my barriers. I was 27 at the time and never married. He had been married for 3 years in his early 20s. I was really hesitant about getting involved with a guy who had been divorced. But he passed all my tests and put up with my gun-shy attitude toward marriage.

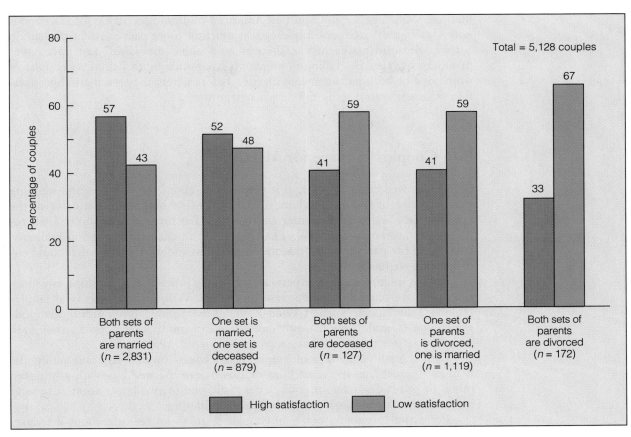

Figure 11.2 Parents' Marital Status and Couples' Premarital Satisfaction. *Source:* From *Predicting Premarital Satisfaction on PREPARE Using Background Factors* by K. L. Stewart and D. H. Olson, (1990), unpublished manuscript, Prepare/Enrich, Inc. Minneapolis, MN. Copyright © 1990 Prepare/Enrich. Used by permission of the publisher.

"We've been married 8 years now and I think it's going to work. But I still don't count on anything, because of what happened to Mom and Dad. We're careful to take good care of our marriage. Every day."

Preparing for Marriage

The dignity of a vocation is always to be measured by the seriousness of the preparation made for it. How then do we appraise marriage?
—R. Herbert Newton

Couples who marry for the first time often spend months of preparation and thousands of dollars on their wedding, which will last only a few hours, but most invest little time or money preparing for their marriage, which is intended to last a lifetime. Weddings are an important American tradition; preparing for marriage is not. Although divorce probably causes as much or more pain in America than do automobile accidents each year, there is no "behind-the-wheel" test for couples planning to marry. But failing to prepare is like preparing to fail. Many couples in which one or both partners were married before agree; they see marital preparation as essential to making the new marriage work.

Can Couples Prepare for Marriage?

Before the wedding couples find it easy to talk about the flavor of the wedding cake, the size of the diamond and the design of its mounting, the color of the groomsmen's ties, and other entertaining issues. But finances, in-laws, and role relationships are rarely discussed. The fear is that to challenge or seriously discuss issues with the partner might threaten her or him and start a battle that could endanger the wedding.

People are not naturally experts at developing intimate relationships, any more than they are naturally experts at a profession. Writing about his own family-building experiences, Norbert Wiener, one of the original developers of the modern computer, said, "One has only one life to live and there is not time enough in which to master the art of being a parent" (Wiener, 1956, p. 224).

Only a small percentage of couples take a course on marriage and family life. A higher percentage spend an hour or two before the wedding with a minister, rabbi, or priest discussing marital issues. Still, one or two hours seems a meager investment in a relationship expected to last a lifetime.

Premarital programs can help couples learn to be realistic about marriage. Couples need to know that marriage takes a tremendous investment of time, effort, and energy, and that they must work at their relationship throughout their life together. Premarital preparation can get the marriage off to a good start.

Good educational programs for premarital couples should be more available (Olson, 1992). After the wedding, couples would be well-advised to continue their education about marriage. They might read and discuss books on marriage, or they might attend marriage enrichment seminars or workshops as preventive maintenance.

If concerned clergy did not insist that couples meet with them at least once before marriage, many couples would have no premarital preparation. In fact, about 35% of all couples (usually those who are not married in a church or synagogue) receive no premarital services or programs. About 25% of couples meet once or twice with their clergy to discuss marriage issues. About 20% of couples attend church-sponsored small-group couples workshops or retreats where they discuss marriage. Because many clergy feel inadequately trained to work with couples, an increasing number are using a premarital inventory to help them assess the relationship. About 15% of couples both consult with clergy and complete a premarital inventory. However, only about 5% of premarital couples obtain the most intensive and effective type of premarriage counseling, which includes structured programs to build both communication and problem-solving skills (Olson, 1992).

BOX   11.4

The PREPARE Premarital Program

Goals

- To help a couple explore their relationship strengths and growth areas.
- To help a couple increase their communication skills (i.e., their ability to share feelings and to listen attentively).
- To help a couple learn how to resolve conflict using the ten-step conflict model.
- To help a couple discuss their families of origin and current relationship style.
- To motivate a couple to invest time and energy to keep their marriage strong.

The 14 Relationship Areas Assessed

Communication styles	Financial management	Family and friends
Conflict resolution	Personality issues	Religious values
Egalitarian roles	Sexual relationship	Cohesion in family of origin
Idealistic distortion	Children and parenting issues	Flexibility in family of origin
Realistic expectations	Leisure activities and interests	

Source: Adapted from Olson, Fournier, & Druckman (1989).

How Effective Are Premarital Programs?

Some approaches to premarital counseling are clearly more effective than others. Lectures are intended to produce attitude change about family topics, but large lecture courses for groups of couples are not an effective way of helping premarital couples prepare for marriage. Five different premarital education programs were evaluated by Rosalie Norem and her colleagues (Norem, Schaefer, Springer, & Olson, 1980). The programs ran for 6–8 weeks, were judged by professionals to be well conceived, and were creatively presented. But no attitude change was produced as a result, and the researchers concluded it was much like pouring water over a duck's back. Another negative outcome of the large-group lecture format was that it discouraged most couples from considering future marriage enrichment programs. It also decreased couples' willingness to go to a marriage counselor if marriage problems occurred in their relationship. In general, the lectures disappointed rather than excited the couples.

Another study evaluating premarital counseling found that using a premarital inventory with couples was clearly superior to traditional discussion sessions with clergy and to the group-lecture format (Druckman, Fournier, Olson, & Robinson, 1981). The researchers used a premarital inventory called PREPARE, which assesses 14 content areas of the engaged couple's relationship (Box 11.4). The inventory was administered to the couples by counselors and clergy; the couples' answer sheets were scored; and an 11-page computer report was sent to the counselor or clergy, who then interpreted the results for the couple and worked with them for one or two sessions. The advantage of this approach over the large-group lecture format is that premarital inventory encourages the couple to look at each other and at the relationship more realistically.

Bernard Guerney and his colleagues also found that their Relationship Enhancement Program for both married and premarital couples is effective (Guerney & Maxson, 1991). This program increases the premarital couple's empathy and self-disclosure skills so that the partners can put themselves in the other person's shoes and communicate more honestly and openly. Guerney's program also increases the premarital couple's positive feelings about their relationship. The researchers studied couples 6 months after the program ended and found that the skills they learned persisted, although they had dropped considerably from the level achieved immediately after the program ended.

Bader, Microys, Sinclair, Willett, and Conway (1980) developed a pioneering program for premarital couples designed to improve their conflict-resolution skills. The researchers concluded that these kinds of skills can be taught to couples and that the skills were still present when the researchers retested the couples a year later. More important, the researchers found that the skills of couples who took the course improved as time passed, whereas a control group (which did not take the course) showed no change in conflict-resolution skills a year later. A study by Norman Wright (1980) also indicated that marriage preparation can be useful. He surveyed 1,000 couples after marriage and found that those who had had at least six premarital sessions felt they had benefited from the experience and had a lower rate of divorce than those who had not participated.

"I think the lectures were very helpful and the readings were good," said Jean. "We would discuss some of the articles they assigned us on our dates. It helped." Jean and her husband, Jeff, are a middle-class couple living in Minneapolis. She is an accountant, and he runs a small advertising firm.

"But really, what I liked the best were the discussions with other couples," Jeff added. "The leader got us going, and we really took off. It was great to hear other couples talk about what was happening in their relationships. I thought Jean was pretty cranky when she would complain about my buddies from the basketball team and how we would always go out drinking together.

"When I saw similar situations from other women's perspectives, though, it made more sense. I kind of scaled back on my go-go attitude," he concluded.

"It's lucky you did," Jean smiled. "I was pretty mad at you at the time."

What Constitutes an Effective Premarital Program?

It is evident from the research that there are at least three essential components to an effective premarital program:

1. *The couple should take some type of premarital inventory and should receive feedback on the results.* A premarital inventory increases the couple's awareness of the strengths and potential problem areas in their relationship. It also helps them discuss their relationship. In addition, the process establishes a relationship with a member of the clergy, a counselor, or a married couple with whom the couple can consult should they need intensive counseling for serious problems. Finally, it prepares them for later marriage enrichment.

2. *The couple should participate in a small discussion group in which couples share their feelings.* This increases a couple's ability and willingness to share with other couples, lets the couple see how other couples relate and deal with issues, and may foster friendships with other couples.

3. *The couple should receive training in communication and problem-solving skills.* These skills help the couple deal with various relationship issues by teaching them empathy as well as techniques for self-disclosure, resolving conflict, and problem solving.

The premarital program should last 6–8 weeks. Unfortunately, most premarital couples do not begin marriage preparation until 2 or 3 months before their wedding. Ideally, marriage preparation should begin at least 1 year before marriage. When a couple cannot complete a comprehensive program before marriage, they should continue some sort of program after marriage.

Predicting a Successful Marriage with PREPARE

Love is not enough to make a successful marriage. The truth of this can be seen in divorce statistics: Most people who marry are in love, but roughly half of those who marry eventually divorce. If love at the time of marriage is a poor predictor of marital happiness, what characteristics *do* predict a happy marriage? Studies demonstrate that the type of relationship a couple has before marriage is very predictive of whether they will have a successful and happy marriage.

To identify factors that predict marital satisfaction, two long-term studies of couples were completed. Engaged couples were questioned 3–4 months before their marriage and then followed to a point 3–4 years after their marriage. The first study was done by Blaine Fowers and David Olson (1986); the replication study was done by Andrea Larsen and David Olson (1989). Both studies found that 80–85% of the time it was possible to predict, on the basis of their PREPARE Inventory scores *before* marriage, whether a couple would be happily married or divorced.

PREPARE is a premarital inventory of questions that couples answer to identify the strengths in their relationship and also the areas where growth is needed. Using PREPARE helps couples learn how to communicate and resolve conflicts; it also helps motivate couples to invest the time and energy needed to improve their marriage. PREPARE, developed in 1980 by David Olson, David Fournier, and Joan Druckman (1989), contains 125 questions grouped into 14 different categories (see Box 11.4).

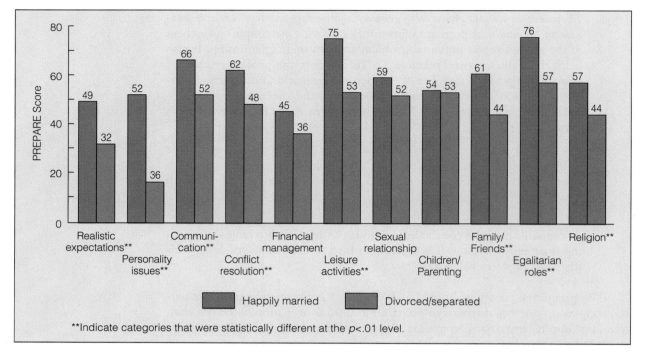

Figure 11.3 PREPARE Scores of Happily Married Versus Divorced/Separated Couples. *Source:* "Predicting Marital Satisfaction Using PREPARE: A Replication Study" by A. S. Larsen and D. H. Olson, 1989, *Journal of Marital & Family Therapy, 15,* p. 318. Copyright 1989 by *Journal of Marital and Family Therapy.* Reprinted by permission.

Fowers and Olson (1986) wanted to see if problems up to 3 or 4 years *after* marriage could be predicted 3 or 4 months *before* marriage. The couples who were happily married after 3 years had had significantly higher scores *before* marriage in 11 of the 14 categories in the PREPARE inventory than couples who had divorced. The characteristics that best predicted a happy marriage were relationship characteristics. Before marriage, couples who were still happily married after 3 years had been more realistic about their relationship, had felt good about the personality of their partner, had enjoyed communicating with their partner, had felt good about their methods of resolving conflicts together, and had agreed on their religious/ethical values.

The replication study (Larsen & Olson, 1989) found very similar results. This study found that the happily married and divorced/separated groups differed significantly on 13 of the 14 PREPARE categories before marriage. Only on questions in the area of children and parenting were the two groups similar before marriage.

As Figure 11.3 shows, the couples who were happily married after 3 years scored on the average higher in every category except children and parenting. One new finding in the replication study was that having more egalitarian role relationships and a good balance of individual versus joint leisure activities also were important predictors of a happy marriage. In other ways, the results of the replication study were very similar to those of the initial study.

Another interesting finding from both studies has to do with couples who took the PREPARE inventory and then decided not to marry. Generally, 10–15% of the couples who take PREPARE and receive feedback make that choice. In comparing the couples who canceled their upcoming marriage with those who were happily married or divorced/separated after 3 years, the researchers found that the couples who canceled were almost identical to the group who later divorced or separated. The researchers concluded that the couples made a good decision in not marrying because they had few relationship strengths and therefore a high probability of getting divorced.

PREPARE is not, however, a test to be passed or failed. It is a questionnaire that can help couples discuss more fully their strengths and areas in which they need to grow. It is important for couples with many unresolved relationship issues to try to resolve these differences before marriage. Researchers have consistently demonstrated that problems in premarital relationships do not magically disappear after marriage. Rather, these problems often intensify.

About 500,000 premarital couples have taken PREPARE, and more than 20,000 counselors and members of the clergy have been trained nationally to administer the questionnaire and to use the results in premarital counseling. Couples interested in taking PREPARE should ask their clergy or a counselor about it or should contact the Life Innovations office for referral to a trained person in their area. (See address in Activities section.)

Marriage problems and divorce cause tremendous pain for millions of people in the United States. Although further research will help refine PREPARE, it is already well established that couples whose marriages are happy tend to have a successful premarital relationship. In summary, happy premarital couples—who generally become happily married couples—are those who:

- Are realistic about the challenges of marriage.
- Communicate well.
- Resolve conflicts well.
- Feel good about the personality of their partner.
- Agree on religious and ethical values.
- Have egalitarian role relationships.
- Have a good balance of individual and joint leisure activities.

Awareness of these research findings and accurate assessment of the strengths and problem areas of a relationship *before* marriage can avert a great deal of heartbreak and pain later in marriage.

Using the Family Circumplex Model in Premarital Counseling

The Circumplex Model can be used to help partners discuss and compare their **families of origin**—the families in which they were raised during childhood—before they marry. This is important because when a couple gets married, each part-

Figure 11.4 Family of Origin and Ideal Type of Marriage

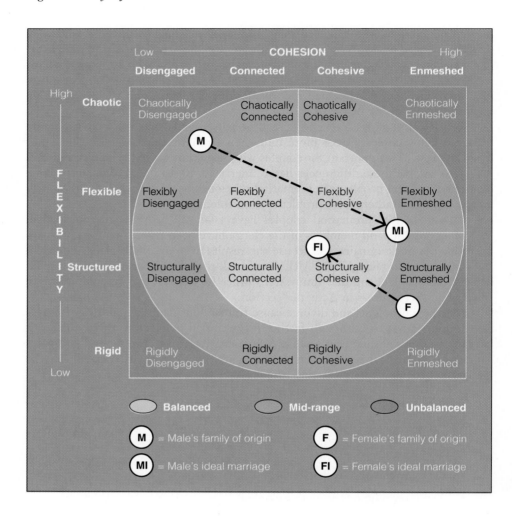

ner is also joining the other's family. The case study that follows involves Kathy and Jim, a couple whose family backgrounds are quite different. They explored these differences in premarital counseling.

A Structurally Enmeshed Family of Origin

Kathy grew up in a *structurally enmeshed* family (Figure 11.4). She is the third oldest of six children, who at the time of counseling range in age from 18 to 27. Kathy's parents have been married for 28 years. All of the children except Kathy live and work in the town in which they grew up. Kathy's family is structured on the flexibility dimension of the Circumplex Model for the following reasons: While growing up, the children knew what was expected of them. The parents were firm yet fair with discipline and enforcement of family rules. The mother was strong and a thorough organizer, and the father was equally strong and even stubborn at times. The father acted as the head of the household but respected his wife's education, contributions, and ability. The mother was comfortable playing a somewhat traditional role and worked hard at keeping the family organized.

Kathy's family is enmeshed on the cohesion dimension. They are a close-knit Catholic family from a small town. Except for 18-year-old John, all of the children have left home, and all except Kathy have settled in the local community. The children drop by the family home several times a week. On weeknights, they play cards or just sit around and talk. The whole family gets together at least every other Sunday for dinner. The mother is heavily involved in each of her children's lives. She feels excited when they are excited and guilty when they are down, and she is always trying to help them. The father is less involved in the lives of his children but expects them to visit often, especially on weekends.

A Flexibly Disengaged Family of Origin

Jim grew up in a *flexibly disengaged* family (see Figure 11.4). He is the older of two children; his brother is four years younger. His parents have been married for 27 years but are now separated. After several years of frustration, the mother decided that she had had enough and asked her husband for a separation; he moved out several months ago. He has been asking for a reconciliation, claiming he's changed, but she is suspicious of these "instant" changes and has decided to "wait and see" if they are permanent.

Jim's family is currently flexible in terms of how it functions, but over the past several years, it has undergone certain changes. For many years, it was closer to a structured family: The mother and father had traditional male and female roles, with the father handing down the rules and the mother backing him up. After 15 years as a homemaker, however, Jim's mother went back to school and got a 2-year certificate in bookkeeping. Her self-esteem improved, and she became more confident and assertive in her relationship with her husband. The family system became more flexible. Jim's father began helping out around the house. He became more lenient with the boys when he saw that they were fairly responsible and willing to pitch in around the house.

In terms of cohesion, the family is currently disengaged. When they were young, the boys were very involved in school activities, and the parents each had separate interests. The father had his hunting and fishing, and the mother had her church activities. The father took the boys hunting and fishing when they got old enough, and they went on several canoe trips together. But these outings were the only times they were together. Most of the time, family members went their own ways and did their own thing. Each person in the family had his or her own friends, and these friends were sometimes more important to each person than family members were.

Goals for the Relationship

Kathy and Jim disagree somewhat on how cohesive (close) they want to be in their marriage, in part due to their families of origin. These two diverse family systems present some problems for this couple. Kathy would like a *cohesive* type of marriage, but one in which she would have more emotional space and greater autonomy than in her enmeshed family of origin. Jim would like an *enmeshed* marriage, in reaction to his disengaged family of origin (see Figure 11.4). He has experienced a lot of pain and disappointment due to the breakup of his parents' marriage and has vowed not to make the mistakes they did. He doesn't want to be in another disengaged system where people go their own way and do not connect emotionally.

One of the struggles this couple is having is negotiating just how much closeness they want from the relationship. Because it's hard for Jim to say what he is really feeling and to share his need for closeness in a direct way with Kathy, she sometimes interprets his desire for closeness as an attempt to control her. But Kathy wants to avoid the overcontrolling atmosphere of enmeshment that existed in her family. So she sometimes backs away from Jim when he is needy and wants closeness. Jim isn't always aware of how he tries to control Kathy or even why he wants to. He is more aware of the outcome of his efforts—her withdrawal.

What both Jim and Kathy have in common is the desire for a *structured* type of marriage. Although Jim sympathizes with his mother, he emotionally leans toward his father's value of a more structured type of system, with more stable male-female roles and predictable family rules and patterns. This is the level of flexibility with which he is most comfortable. Kathy would also like a structured marriage with fairly stable roles but with a distribution of responsibilities. She likes the predictability of a structured system but does not want it to become rigid like her family of origin. The desire for a structured system is a goal they both share and one they can work together to achieve.

From the Wedding Through the Early Married Years

This section provides some guidelines for planning a wedding and then looks at the difficult process of adjustment newlyweds face during the first few years of marriage.

The Wedding

Despite the massive investment it often entails, a wedding is not a marriage. Today, the average cost of a wedding is about $15,000. This figure includes the wedding ceremony, sit-down meals, reception, entertainment, gifts, honeymoon, and so forth. The average engaged couple spends about $4,000 of their own money on their wedding and honeymoon.

Although the wedding ceremony is an important celebration and can help friends and families bond, it can also create some problems. Decisions about the guest list and the kind of reception can create intense struggles between family members and the bride and groom.

Arond and Pauker (1987) have developed some useful guidelines for couples planning their wedding:

Whether a wedding is simple or extravagant, it is a milestone in the lives of two families, not just two people. Decisions about the date, the place, the kind of ceremony, the size of the wedding party, the guest list, and the reception often require negotiation among the couple and their relatives so that everyone will feel that their preferences have been considered.

1. Begin planning at least 1 year in advance.

2. Try to consider the feelings of others, particularly family members.

3. Consider what is important to you and what your budget is.

4. Be assertive—it's *your* wedding.

5. Use the preparations as a time to share and make decisions as a couple.

6. Try to keep it simple so that you can enjoy it.

As the wedding approaches, many couples become concerned about the ramifications of this critical decision to marry. In a survey of 1,000 couples who were soon to be married, the researchers found that 67% of the individuals questioned whether they were making the right decision; 51% were concerned whether they had enough money to get married; 48% were concerned about getting along with in-laws; and 42% wondered whether they would "goof up" the ceremony.

Newlyweds: The Difficult Adjustment

There is hardly any activity, any enterprise, which is started with such tremendous hopes and expectations and which fails so regularly as love.
—Erich Fromm

The first year or two of marriage are for many couples the most difficult, even if they lived together before the marriage and feel they have a good relationship.

He likes to make a quick circuit of the store, picking up whatever appeals to him. She likes to make a list of what they'll need for the week and shop for bargains. Newlyweds discover differences in their habits and preferences every day and must find ways to accommodate them if their marriage is to succeed.

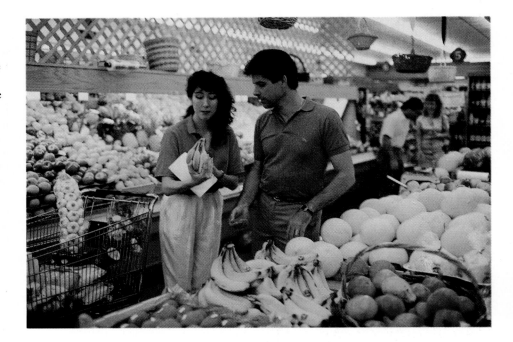

Marriage is a more difficult transition than most couples anticipate, often because couples expect marriage to be easy and to be similar to what they have experienced with each other previously.

In a comprehensive study of newlyweds, Arond and Pauker (1987) surveyed 455 newlyweds and also asked 75 couples who had been married for a few years to look back on their first year of marriage. The newlywed stage is a difficult transition because the partners must leave their families of origin, give up their previous independence, and begin to function as a couple. This study found that about half the couples doubted their marriage would last and felt they had significant marital problems during this first year. About 40% found marriage harder than they had expected and also felt that their partner had became more critical after marriage. Sixty-three percent had marital problems related to money; 25% had sexual problems, even though 85% had engaged in sex before marriage; and 35% said relationships with single friends worsened after marriage.

Many of the couples studied had gone into marriage with a wealth of experience together (Arond & Pauker, 1987). Sixty-three percent had vacationed together before marriage, 48% had shared household expenses before marriage, 22% had bought a house or a car together before marriage, and 85% had had a sexual relationship before marriage. But the study found no statistical relationship between living together before marriage and happiness with the sexual relationship or the total relationship after marriage. In fact, the researchers found that couples who had lived together before marriage had significantly lower marital satisfaction scores than those who had not cohabited before the wedding.

One of the major reasons newlywed couples find the adjustment to marriage

Premarital Fantasies and Marital Realities

She married him because he was such an assertive male;
She divorced him because he was such a domineering husband.

He married her because she was so gentle and petite;
He divorced her because she was so weak and helpless.

She married him because he could provide a good income;
She divorced him because all he did was work.

He married her because she was so attractive all the time;
He divorced her because she spent too much time in front of the mirror.

She married him because he was so romantic and sociable;
She divorced him because he was a fun-loving playboy.

He married her because she was so quiet and dependent;
He divorced her because she was so boring and clinging.

She married him because he was the life of the party;
She divorced him because he was such a dud at home.

He married her because she was so sociable and talkative;
He divorced her because she could only discuss trivia.

She married him because he was such a good athlete;
She divorced him because he was either playing or watching sports.

He married her because she was so neat and organized;
He divorced her because she was too compulsive and controlling.

so difficult is that they typically are idealistic. Premarital relationships are often filled with fantasies and myths, especially the notion that the partner will change undesirable traits after the couple is married. Unfortunately, marriage neither changes people nor makes it easier for others to change them. In fact, marriage often magnifies undesirable traits. A person who arrives late before marriage will typically arrive late after marriage. A person who is sloppy before marriage will be sloppy after marriage—but the sloppiness will become more apparent in the closeness of marriage.

One young woman reported that her fiancé was kind and gentle with her until the night before the wedding. Then, he became angry and shoved her in an argument over the cost of the ceremony. She thought he did this because he was tense about the upcoming ceremony, so she went through with the wedding. In the first 6 months of marriage, she was physically abused on eight separate occasions, with the severity of the abuse increasing as the months passed. She divorced her groom after 1 year of marriage. Box 11.5 shows how some premarital fantasies look as marital realities.

For an easier adjustment in the early years of marriage, Arond and Pauker (1987) offer five recommendations to newlywed couples:

Happy couples learn to weather the stresses of life. They are, above all, best friends and enjoy spending time together. In fact, they are likely to find each other more interesting as the years go by.

- *Acknowledge and handle hostility.* Anger and aggressiveness are natural in an intimate relationship. They must be acknowledged and the feelings expressed in constructive ways.

- *Tolerate imperfections and differences.* Differences between two people are natural and should be seen as a strength, an important aspect of individuality. Couples need to learn how to agree and how to agree to disagree.

- *Separate from your families of origin.* Although families of origin are important, couples must invest in their marriage and not let parents interfere with it. Partners should also avoid using parents as leverage against each other.

- *Be committed.* A marriage cannot be taken for granted. Partners need to remind each other of their ongoing commitment.

- *Realize that marriage has its ups and downs.* Marriage can produce many good times. It also has its share of struggles, challenges, and differences. These provide opportunities for growth both personally and in the relationship.

The Early Years of Marriage: Issues and Strengths

As already noted, couples face many challenges in establishing a life together during the early years of marriage. Their resources as individuals and as a couple are tested, sometimes severely. Some couples find that these challenges strengthen their relationship; for other couples, the challenges signal the beginning of the end of

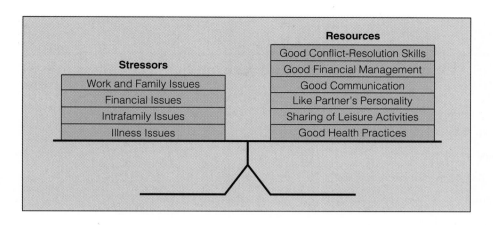

Figure 11.5 Resources of Young Couples Who Effectively Coped with Stress. *Source: Families: What Makes Them Work* (2nd ed.) (p. 209) by D. H. Olson, H. I. McCubbin, H. Barnes, A. Larsen, M. Muxen, M. Wilson, 1989, Sage Publications. Copyright © 1989 by Sage Publications. Used by permission of the publisher.

the marriage. A national survey of marriage across the life cycle focused on the stressors at each major stage (Olson, McCubbin, et al., 1989). For married young couples who did not have children, the major stressors were work and family issues, financial issues, intrafamily issues, and issues related to illness.

Among *work and family issues*, 40–54% of the couples had had to deal with problems related to a promotion or change of job, a decrease in job satisfaction, or difficulty with people at work. About one in four had lost or quit a job. Whether positive or negative, all of these changes are stressful. *Financial issues* were also a major concern among the young couples, with half feeling they needed more money. Over half had purchased a car or another major item, and more than a third had taken out a major loan. One in four had purchased or built a home, and one in five was faced with increased medical/dental costs. Among *intrafamily issues*, more than one third reported that chores were not getting done. Nearly a third complained that the husband was away from home too much, and about 20% noted that the wife was away from home too much. One in five couples felt that disagreements and problematic issues were not getting resolved. Finally, *illness issues*, including the death of parents and close relatives, caused stress in as many as 30% of the relationships.

This survey also studied why some couples were able to cope with these stressors more effectively than others (Figure 11.5). The couples who coped most successfully had good conflict-resolution and communication skills, were able to manage their money effectively, liked each other's personalities, shared leisure activities together, and had good health maintenance practices. In other words, couples who coped well drew on personal and relationship strengths to overcome the stressors.

Numerous studies have focused on the qualities of a happy marriage. Jeanette Lauer and Robert Lauer (1985) studied 351 couples, most of them happily married. They asked the couples to identify the major characteristics that kept their marriages strong and vital. The Lauers found that in marriages that survive, the spouses saw each other as best friends and as someone they liked to spend time with. The couples also felt that marriage required a long-term commitment and that it was sacred. They felt that they agreed on life goals and noted that they found their spouses more interesting over time. In addition, they enjoyed fun times

What Keeps a Marriage Going?

	Priority	
	Husbands	Wives
My spouse is my best friend.	1	1
I like my spouse as a person.	2	2
Marriage is a long-term commitment.	3	3
Marriage is sacred.	4	4
We agree on aims and goals.	5	5
My spouse has grown more interesting.	6	6
I want the relationship to succeed.	7	7
An endearing marriage is important to social stability.	8	10
We laugh together.	9	8
I am proud of my spouse's achievements.	10	15
We agree on a philosophy of life.	11	9
We agree about our sex life.	12	14
We agree on how and how often to show affection.	13	10

together and they liked their sexual relationship. In sum, these happy couples valued their relationship and gave it the priority it required to be mutually satisfying. Note the high level of similarity in ranking between husbands and wives (Box 11.6).

Some Recommendations for a Happy Marriage

A review of the research and clinical observations produces a number of recommendations for a meaningful and vital marriage relationship:

- Individuals should not be pressured to marry early; they should mature emotionally and establish themselves in their chosen profession before making a marriage commitment.

- Marriage is not for everyone. Family members and friends should recognize this and not pressure anyone who has chosen the single life into getting married.

- Individuals and couples should experiment with a variety of lifestyles so they can make an informed decision about the lifestyle most appropriate for them.

- Couples should be encouraged to relate openly and honestly rather than to play traditional dating/mating games.

- Couples should spend 1 year in premarital counseling before they marry, and they should not marry until they have established a meaningful relationship and resolved major difficulties.

- The decision of parenthood should be made jointly, and it is best if it follows the decision to marry. Couples should establish a strong and viable marriage relationship before they have children.

- Couples should be creative and flexible in their roles and mutual responsibilities, not only during the initial phase of marriage but throughout the marriage relationship.

Summary

- Cohabitation raises legal issues in such areas as personal property, wills and estates, and income earned while cohabiting.

- Positive reasons for marriage include companionship, love and intimacy, growth of the individuals and the partnership, sexual satisfaction, and parenthood. Negative reasons for getting married include a premarital pregnancy, rebellion against or escape from parents, independence, replacing a lost love (rebound relationships), family or social pressure, and economic security.

- Couples spend too little time preparing for marriage. They often fear that exposing their differences will end the relationship. Resolving differences before marriage provides a better chance for marital happiness, however.

- A very low percentage of couples in the United States go through a comprehensive marriage preparation program. The most useful programs include (1) a premarital inventory to assess strengths and areas of potential growth and discussion of the assessment results with a trained counselor; (2) participation in a small discussion group in which couples share feelings and concerns with each other, and (3) training in communication and problem-solving skills.

- Researchers have developed an inventory that couples can take before marriage to assess the strengths in their relationship. The inventory can predict a couple's chances of marital success or failure with 80–85% accuracy.

- Love is not enough to make a successful marriage. Researchers have identified the following relationship characteristics to be predictive of marital happiness:

realism about the relationship, acceptance of the partner's personality, good communication, good conflict-resolution skills, agreement on religious/ethical values, egalitarian role relationships, and a balance of individual and joint leisure activities.

- The first year or two of marriage are, for many couples, the most difficult. Some tips for a less stressful adjustment in the early years of marriage include acknowledging and handling anger and aggressiveness openly, tolerating imperfections and differences, separating from families of origin, being committed to the marriage, and realizing that there are ups and downs in marriage.

- Major stressors for newlywed couples include work and family issues, financial issues, intrafamily issues, and illness. Couples who cope well tend to have a strong and vital marriage with good communication and conflict-resolution skills.

Key Terms

cohabitation	convenience	palimony
Linus blanket	testing	family of origin
emancipation	PREPARE	

Activities

1. List what you feel are positive and negative reasons for getting married. Share the list with a partner or with others in a small discussion group.

2. How do you know if you are ready for marriage? Discuss this issue with a small group, and formulate some guidelines to help people decide whether they are ready to marry.

3. *For dating or engaged couples:* Both partners should write down five things they like about their partner and five things that sometimes bother them. Then both partners should communicate the items on the list very carefully, discuss them, and listen to each other so that the discussion is positive and constructive.

4. For those dating or engaged couples interested in taking the PREPARE Inventory, first contact a counselor or a member of the clergy in your area. If you cannot locate someone trained in PREPARE, send a stamped self-addressed envelope to Life Innovations (P. O. Box 190, Minneapolis, MN 55440-0190) for a list of trained counselors in your community.

Suggested Readings

Arond, M., & Pauker, S. L. (1987). *The first year of marriage.* New York: Warner. *A practical book that can help couples make it through this most difficult period, the year in which divorce is most likely to occur.*

Arp, D., & Arp, C. (1989). *60 one-minute marriage builders.* Brentwood, TN: Wolgemush & Hyatt. *Concise, useful ideas for enhancing a marriage.*

Dinkmeyer, D., & Carlson, J. (1989). *Taking time for love.* New York: Simon & Schuster. *Tips from two family psychologists for slowing down and focusing on one of the most satisfying aspects of life, emotional intimacy with another human being.*

Duff, J., & Truitt, G. (1991). *The spousal equivalent handbook: A legal and financial guide to living together.* Houston: Sunny Beach. *Practical advice on legal and money matters for cohabitants.*

Ihara, T., & Warner, R. (1990). *The living together kit: A detailed guide to help unmarried couples deal with legal realities.* Berkeley, CA: Nolo Press. *Advice for preventing or avoiding many of the legal problems that can occur when a relationship goes sour.*

Miller, S., Nunnally, E., & Wackman, D. (1990). *Talking together.* Littleton, CO: Interpersonal Communication Programs, Inc., 7201 S. Broadway, Suite 6, 80122. *An excellent guide for couples in their first year of marriage who need to learn how to talk with each other.*

CHAPTER 12

Parenthood

Parenthood is the process of raising children who will provide continuity within the family. There is no greater responsibility or challenge, and for many people who do the job well, there is no greater satisfaction than seeing one's children grow, learn, and enjoy life. Parenthood has been called the world's most difficult job—offering no pay, no fringe benefits, no vacation, and precious little thanks. Counselor Jennifer James wryly remarked that "the first half of our lives is spoiled by our parents, and the last half by our children" (James, 1984). But as one observer noted, and many would agree, "Children fill a space in your life you never knew was empty."

A parent's job is to give a child both "roots and wings" (Orr & Van Zandt, 1987, p. 87). This is no easy task. Rearing children may indeed be life's greatest mixed blessing. It is full of good times and bad times, frustrating challenges and elating successes. A baby's first stumbling steps and first words, a teenager's first love, a grown child's first baby—all are important transitions that parents remember. At the same time, children bring heavy responsibilities and drain energy, finances, and time. There is no book on rearing children that answers all the questions and no clear path to family happiness. The road is difficult, and there are no guarantees. Governor Christine Todd Whitman of New Jersey, in addressing a Wheaton College graduation-ceremony audience, noted, "I don't mind saying that I have the most important and fulfilling job in the world. It demands responsibility, knowledge of finance, being on call 24 hours a day, combining firm leadership with careful negotiations, and keeping one's promise. That job is being a parent" (Whitman, 1995).

This chapter begins by examining the challenge of parenthood, first taking a look at some of the conventional wisdom that surrounds it. Among the challenges are the effects of parenthood on marriage, the decision whether to have children, and the financial burdens of raising children. Various parenting styles, and their correlations with the family styles of the Circumplex Model, are examined next. Ways in which parenting styles change over the family life cycle are also discussed.

A look at issues in parenting follows. Some practical approaches to raising children, including coparenting, are explored, and the benefits of parent education and family therapy are detailed. The chapter concludes with some of the many satisfactions parents cite about childrearing.

The Challenge of Parenthood

Many authorities have noted that parenthood is the last bastion of amateurism in our society. Plumbers, bookkeepers, computer analysts—all need some kind of formal training, certificate, or license. About the only job that doesn't require some special kind of education is nurturing the young to adulthood.

Our society tends to shy away from "intruding" into family matters, and rearing children is certainly a family matter. But some have gone so far as to argue that education and even something like an internship should be mandatory before people can become parents—that is, that a license should be required for parenthood. Although such a proposal has little chance of passing today, its proponents

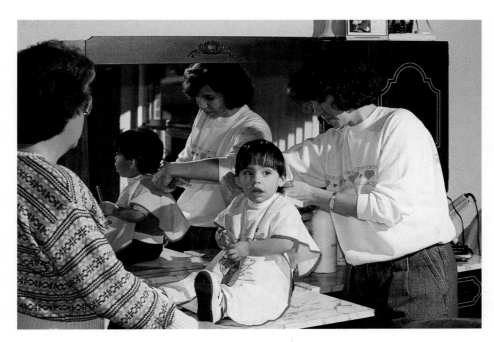

A first haircut is one of the many milestones that mark a child's growing up. Although this toddler may not remember the experience, his mother and grandmother will remember this event in his transition from baby to little boy.

point out both the importance and the difficulty of parenting. Society benefits from parents' successes but also suffers from their mistakes.

Adults with problems often had problems as children, and many times they pass their problems on to the next generation. For example, one therapist described a counseling session with an abused woman who had fled from her husband after repeated beatings; the woman's 18-month-old son was with her. During the session, the toddler became angered over some minor issue and ran at his mother. In his frustration, he put his hands around her neck and tried to strangle her. He was imitating almost precisely what he had seen his father do a few days earlier. With counseling, this pattern could be changed so that the boy would not repeat his father's behavior.

Conventional Wisdom About Parenting

All societies have a series of folk beliefs, which are widely accepted and rarely examined. They may be commonplace, but they are not necessarily common sense. For the purposes of our discussion, we will call these common beliefs *conventional wisdom*. Although conventional wisdom often contains a grain of truth, it does not usually tell the whole story. As one observer has noted, we do not need common sense at all; what we need is uncommon sense, because conventional wisdom can often get us into trouble. Conventional wisdom on parenthood often sugarcoats the subject, romanticizing a task that is too important for people to undertake with rose-colored glasses. What follows is a list of commonly held folk beliefs in our society, along with our comments, which we hope offer a more balanced and realistic view:

How Active Are Young Children?

When young parents first hear the term *hyperactive*, it seems to describe their own child almost perfectly. And, indeed, every young child is hyperactive at times, although only a small percentage are hyperactive in a clinical or dysfunctional sense. John DeFrain and Patricia Welker wanted a better understanding of just how active a young child is, so Welker followed 18-month-old Alyssa DeFrain around for a "typical" day in the child's life. During this 24-hour period, Alyssa was asleep for 12 hours.

Welker recorded everything the toddler was doing at 15-second intervals on long sheets of paper in tiny handwriting. In sum, Alyssa did 4,652 separate and recognizable activities. She never appeared frantic in her work or play, but she rarely did nothing. In fact, much of the time she was doing two or three things at once: looking at her big sister, drawing a picture, and curling circles in the rug with her toes.

Alyssa's 4,652 actions were divided into 221 different behavioral categories. The activities included: watches/looks at something 643, manipulates/experiments with an object 96, gives something to someone 46, takes something from someone when offered it 48, lies down 26, listens 172, talks 529, grunts incoherently 78, cries 62, fusses 25, screams 17, sings 22, dances 16, falls down 9, resists 11, points 85, hits something 16, picks up a book 24, walks 299, picks up something other than a book 210, changes body position during 58-minute nap 41, laughs/giggles 34. It's not surprising that a parent who has to supervise all these activities, run interference for the busy child, and keep the youngster out of trouble sinks into bed exhausted at the end of the day.

- *Rearing children is nothing but fun.* Although childrearing can be fun, it is also a thankless and very demanding job. Parents have to *make* childrearing fun if they are to enjoy it.

- *Children are always sweet and cute.* Although children can be adorable, they can also be selfish and destructive, as well as extremely active physically. In fact, they possess the full range of human qualities—positive and negative—that adults must deal with in each other. Parents who have no break from watching over children can easily become exhausted. Box 12.1 reports the results of a research project that explored one young child's high level of activity.

- *Children will turn out well if they have "good" parents.* Parents are an important factor in a child's development, but they are only one influence among many, including school, the mass media, and the child's peer group. The goal of parenting must be to instill values and model positive behaviors with the hope that children will internalize and use them in their lives. But there are no guarantees. Some good parents work hard at parenting, only to see their children get into great difficulty in life.

- *Children improve a marriage.* Rearing children is a team effort. The bond between partners can intensify as a couple raises children together. But children also tend to put tremendous pressure on an intimate relationship.

Television families of the 1950s, 1960s, and 1970s, like the Brady Bunch, were often idealized portraits. They resembled few real families of their era, but they helped create the conventional wisdom that parents then were better than parents today.

- *Good parents can manage any child, no matter what the child's nature.* This myth is based on the notion that a human being is born a *tabula rasa*, a blank slate upon which the environment writes its script. But research on infants indicates that to some degree temperament is present at birth: Some babies are calm and content; others are cranky. Although the family environment parents construct for their young is tremendously important, it is not, as mentioned earlier, the only influence or the sole determinant of outcome. Children also strongly shape their parents' behavior.

- *Today's parents are not as good as yesterday's.* Standards for raising children have gotten higher, making the challenge for today's parents greater. Society now expects more democratic approaches, ones that take the child's feelings into account when decisions are made and that involve older children in the decision-making process.

- *Couples without children are frustrated and unhappy.* Many singles and couples without children are very happy and content. Many of them do, however, have close relationships with children of extended-family members or of friends.

- *One child is too few.* Although many believe that only children are spoiled and selfish, that is not necessarily the case. Studies have found that there are both advantages and disadvantages to having only one child. One child is less expensive to raise, is less demanding on the parents, places fewer limits on the parents' freedom, and receives more parental attention. The disadvantages of having only one child are that the parents may focus too much attention on or overprotect the child and the child may feel lonely and need more peer companions.

- *There are no bad children, only bad parents.* Most parents want the best for their children and do what they can to see that their wish comes true. Parents fail in parenting because of ignorance, lack of support, or their own unhealthy family background.

- *All parents are adults.* As reflected in our nation's teenage pregnancy rates, many adolescents are unfortunately becoming parents. The most recent statistics indicate that 12.8% of all birth mothers are teenagers (U.S. Bureau of the Census, 1995). Childrearing is difficult for adults; it is particularly challenging for teenage parents.

- *Children appreciate the sacrifices their parents make and the advantages they provide.* Most parents want appreciation for the sacrifices they make for their children. Unfortunately, children often do not realize their parents' importance until they themselves become parents. Parents need to learn to enjoy the everyday pleasures and satisfactions of raising their children and to appreciate any small thanks they may receive along the way.

- *Sex education creates more sexual behavior.* Most people support sex education in the home, but some question its value in the schools. They inaccurately assume that sex education in the schools stimulates interest in sex and creates more sexual problems (King, Camp, & Downey, 1991).

- *Parenthood receives top priority in our society.* Making money—not parenthood—receives top priority in our society. Parents are pressured to put their jobs first if they want promotions, and sometimes if they simply want to hold onto them.

- *Love is enough to guarantee good parental performance.* Love helps parents put up with the many difficulties they encounter in childrearing. But success at parenting also requires hard work and good parenting skills.

- *Single-parent families are problematic.* Although rearing children is hard enough for two-parent families and can be more difficult for a single parent, a stable one-parent family is superior to an unstable two-parent family (DeFrain, Fricke, & Elmen, 1987).

- *Parenting ends when the children leave home.* For most parents, parenting does not end when a child leaves home. Adult children may come back home to live after their divorce, loss of a job, or some other life crisis. Adult children may have children and need help with child care. Grandparenting brings joy, but it can also be exhausting.

- *The "empty nest syndrome" leaves many parents lonely and depressed.* One observer has noted, "After the kids leave home, some parents suffer from the empty nest syndrome; others change the locks." Many parents enjoy the freedom that comes with not having adolescents at home. The middle-aged parent may get a job or change jobs, travel, or take up a new avocation. After they leave home, adult children are often surprised to watch their parents blossom and enjoy life in a variety of new ways.

- *Parents alone should rear the young.* Parents are ultimately responsible for raising their children. But society has a stake in the outcome and needs to support parents in this challenging process.

The Transition to Parenthood

Parenthood isn't something that happens gradually. The 9 months of a normal pregnancy should give prospective parents time to think about parenthood and to plan for the arrival of the baby, but many are unprepared for the challenges that will confront them when the infant arrives. They most likely took classes to prepare for childbirth, but none to prepare for parenting.

Parenthood As Crisis: Effects on Marriage   When the baby is born, parenting begins. For some it is a crisis. E. E. LeMasters gained prominence in the 1950s with the report in *The New York Times* of a study entitled "Parenthood as Crisis." LeMasters argued that due to romantic notions about parenthood, people go through a process of disenchantment when they have children. LeMasters was flooded with letters from parents, most of whom agreed with his findings. In his research, LeMasters had interviewed 46 couples and had found that 83% defined the coming of a child as a "crisis" for their marriage (LeMasters, 1957). Other researchers have been debating these findings every since; the definition of the term *crisis* remains controversial (Belsky, 1991).

Parenthood means that a married couple will have less time for each other. Before the baby, the couple could focus attention on their relationship and had time to enjoy each other's company. "Free" time markedly diminishes with the birth of a child, and a couple's focus shifts to nurturing the baby. Parents often find themselves exhausted, awakened often in the night for feedings or due to crying or illness. Few parents know much about caring for an infant until they have one of their own.

As a child grows older, the parents' job does not get any easier. Change only creates new challenges. The colic may end, but the child is soon toddling around sticking fingers in wall sockets, emptying houseplant soil on the living-room rug, or spreading Vaseline from the medicine cabinet all over the bathroom. Fortunately, most parents have a sense of humor and patience—and also realize the importance of covering sockets, locking cupboards, and putting other things out of the reach of a toddler.

The playfulness and pleasure of pre-parenting days disappear for some couples, and life takes on more seriousness. The couple's sexual relationship is often affected by the demands of raising a child. Most couples find that their sexual ac-

BOX 12.2

Mother Murphy's Laws for Raising Children

1. Parenthood is much easier to get into than out of.

2. If your spouse hasn't already driven you nuts, your kids will.

3. Nobody really wants your job, but everyone thinks they can do it better.

4. Those who think they can do it better messed up when they had the chance.

5. Bad traits are inherited from your spouse's side of the family.

6. Good traits are inherited from your side of the family.

7. By the time you've finally learned something about raising children, you're a grandparent.

8. Your mother knows best. About everything. And she'll never let you forget it.

9. You don't have to be a Supermom to succeed in both your career and childrearing. All you need is a $100,000 job and live-in help.

10. The day after you get a raise at work, your day-care center will inform you that tuition is being increased.

11. The increase in tuition will exceed your raise.

12. Taking care of your baby is easy, as long as you don't have anything else to do.

13. The more experts you consult, the more solutions you'll find for any parenting problem.

14. Psychologists know best. About writing books.

15. When you're pregnant, everyone gives you advice.

16. After you've had your baby, everyone gives you advice.

17. When your baby becomes a teenager, everyone gives you advice—especially your teenager.

18. When your teenager "leaves the nest," everyone gives you advice.

19. When you become a grandparent, you get to pass on all that good advice to your children.

20. By the time you can afford to start a family, you're too old to do it. (And you know enough not to.)

Source: Adapted from *Mother Murphy's Law* by B. Lansky, 1986, New York: Meadowbrook/Simon & Schuster. Copyright 1986 by Bruce Lansky. Adapted by permission of the publisher, Meadowbrook Press.

---

tivity decreases because they are exhausted. Spontaneity in social patterns can diminish. For example, parents of infants don't just "drop in" on friends when dropping in means packing baby bottles, diapers, plastic pants, and a change of clothes.

"Mother Murphy's Laws" in Box 12.2 poke some fun at the common challenges of parenting and grandparenting.

The Child-Free Alternative   The terms applied to the choice not to have children—among them, nonparenthood, voluntary childlessness, and the **child-free alternative**—all seem to ask whether a person can be happy and fulfilled in life without having children. Government figures indicate that 9.3% of American

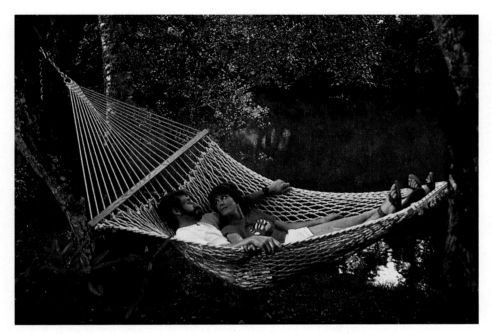

Parenthood is not for everyone, and couples who have decided not to have children can find happiness and fulfillment with each other, with their careers and avocational interests, and with friends and family.

women between the ages of 18 and 34 do not expect to have children (U.S. Bureau of the Census, 1994). More couples are considering not having children because they know how difficult parenting is, and they want more freedom and more time for their marriage. A review by Jean Veevers (1980) of 22 studies of child-free marriages revealed some interesting answers to common questions about childlessness:

- *What long-term effects does voluntary childlessness have?* Two studies on this aspect of childlessness found that although adult children are often very important to their parents in old age, older people without children also do quite well. Aging parents may find themselves rejected or neglected by their adult children. Those without children often prepare for their later years by developing a network of friends and relatives to help meet their needs. Also, they learn how to cope with isolation if necessary (Rempel, 1985).

- *Is there something wrong with people who don't wish to have children?* Veevers found that the majority of studies on this topic concluded that nonparents exhibit no more psychopathology or deviance than a control group of randomly sampled parents. It has been found that African Americans, Native Americans, and Mexican Americans tend to be more family oriented than Whites and consider children an important part of marital life (Mindel, Habenstein, & Wright, 1988).

- *Do people without children do better in their careers?* Apparently, many people without children do very well. Voluntary childlessness leaves people with time and energy that can be focused on career goals. Among women of eminence, a disproportionate number are childless.

- *Is the quality of a child-free marriage as good as that of a marriage with children?* Recent studies have found more vital and happy relationships among child-free couples than among those with children (Olson, McCubbin, et al., 1989; Somers, 1993). This is, in part, because child-free couples can devote more time to their marriages and because those who do not have a good relationship are more likely to divorce if they do not have children.

Financial Issues and Children

One of the surprises for most parents is how much children cost, not just in terms of time and energy but also financially. Raising children is a very expensive venture, no matter what a family's income. An analysis of the expense of raising a child, based on data from the Family Economics Research Group at the U.S. Department of Agriculture, was summarized by Mark Lino (1991a, 1991b). The data were broken down into six major categories: housing, food, transportation, clothing, health care, and education. As expected, the amount of money spent on a child varied with the income level of the family. For families earning less than $29,900, the cost of raising each child from birth to 17 was $86,100. For middle-income families earning $29,900–$48,300, the cost of raising each child was $120,150, and for families earning more than $48,300 the cost increased to $168,480 (Lino, 1991b). Specifics for the two-parent middle-income family ($29,900–$48,300) for the six expense areas and by the age of the child are presented in Table 12.1.

> "When the last of our three children finally left home this summer," said Dick, the CEO of a software company in Phoenix, "I calculated that my wife and I would have more than $1,000 a month extra to spend. But it doesn't really matter. We'll have more money, and the house will be a lot quieter, but I can't say we'll be any happier. We'll probably pay off a few bills with the extra money and buy some new furniture and a living-room rug as soon as we don't have adolescents clomping about, spilling food everywhere." He paused, then added wistfully, "But I'm not sure the money will bring us happiness. That big old, empty house will be kind of hard to rattle around in at night."

An important aspect of socializing children is helping them learn to understand and manage finances. Sharon Danes (1992) did a systematic study of 182 parents to learn when they thought it appropriate to introduce their children to a variety of financial activities. About 70% of parents felt that children 8 years or younger were mature enough to receive an allowance, and 64% felt that they could open their own savings account. Almost half the parents surveyed felt that 12- to 14-year-olds could be responsible for their own clothing budget, and 29% believed that they were mature enough to be told the family's income. About half the parents felt that 15- to 17-year-olds should know about car insurance and have their own checking account. More than half the parents believed that by age 18–20,

Table 12.1 Expenditures on a Child by U.S. Middle-Income Two-Parent Families

AGE OF CHILD	TOTAL	HOUSING	FOOD	TRANSPORTATION	CLOTHING	HEALTH CARE	EDUCATION, CHILD CARE, AND OTHER
0–2	**$ 6,140**	$ 2,330	$ 830	$ 990	$ 400	$ 290	$ 1,300
3–5	**6,540**	2,270	960	1,050	440	280	1,540
6–8	**6,500**	2,280	1,220	1,130	470	290	1,110
9–11	**6,330**	2,150	1,370	1,060	480	300	970
12–14	**7,050**	2,090	1,450	1,370	790	310	1,040
15–17	**7,490**	2,060	1,620	1,630	750	320	1,110
Total	**$120,150**	$39,540	$22,350	$21,690	$9,990	$5,370	$21,210

Source: "Expenditures on a Child by Two-Parent Families" by M. Lino, 1991b, *Family Economics Review, 4*(1), p. 32. U. S. Department of Agriculture.

adult children should have and be responsible for their own credit card and be able to apply for and make the payments on a loan.

Adoption: Moving Toward Openness

Since the mid-1970s, adoption practices in the United States have changed dramatically, with the confidentiality maintained in the past no longer the norm (McRoy, Grotevant, & Ayers-Lopez, 1994). The trend is toward "openness" in adoption, which means that there is contact between the adoptive family and the birth parent(s). The contact may be either direct or mediated (e.g., through an adoption agency). Some adoption professionals argue that fully open adoption should be standard practice and that the secrecy of confidential adoptions has been harmful to all those involved. Others argue that openness is experimental and may prove to be harmful: Confidential adoption has worked well, so why change it?

To understand the issue of openness in adoption, Harold Grotevant and Ruth McRoy recruited a nationwide sample of adoptive families and birth mothers with a "target" adopted child between the ages of 4 and 12 when the first interview occurred between 1987 and 1992. The sample included 720 individuals: both adoptive parents in 190 adoptive families, at least one adopted child in 171 of the families, and 169 birth mothers. Families were sampled across the full range of openness in adoption: *confidential* (no information shared between birth parents and adoptive parents); *mediated* (information shared, with the adoption agency as the go-between); and *fully disclosed* (ongoing direct contact between birth and adoptive family members). Adoptive families were interviewed in their homes.

As predicted, when compared with parents in confidential adoptions, parents in fully disclosed open adoptions reported higher levels of acknowledgment of the adoption, more empathy toward the birth parents and child, a stronger sense of permanence in the relationship with their child projected into the future, and less fear that the birth mother might try to reclaim the child (Grotevant, McRoy, Elde, & Fravel, 1994).

Many adoptive parents failed to involve the child in the open adoption process, however (Wrobel, Ayers-Lopez, Grotevant, McRoy, & Friedrick, 1996). Almost half the children in mediated adoptions did not participate in the contact their adoptive parents were having with their birth mother, but most of these children were not aware they were being excluded. However, most of the children in fully disclosed adoptions were included in meetings with birth parents.

It appears that couples who have greater openness in the adoption process also have better family communication (Mendenhall, Grotevant & McRoy, 1995). Adoptive couples' interviews were coded for communication skills using Olson's Family Circumplex Rating Scale. Couples who had greater openness in adoption showed significantly higher levels of self-disclosure, listening skill, empathy, tracking, and respect.

Relationships between the adoptive family and the birth mother are also being examined through the lens of boundary ambiguity, which is said to exacerbate family stress because of family members' inability to determine who is inside and who is outside the family system (Boss, 1988). Boundary ambiguity occurs when a family member is physically absent but psychologically present, or vice versa. Fravel (1995) examined the psychological presence of the birth mother in the adoptive family system. It appears that boundary ambiguity is almost inevitable in adoptive families. Adoptive families who have a higher level of tolerance for ambiguity seem to handle open adoption more effectively.

Parenting and the Family Circumplex Model

The Circumplex Model can be useful in integrating the variety of parenting models and variables that have been developed and identified by professionals studying relationships between parents and children. Much of this research has been done by child-development professionals, who are increasingly adopting a more systemic approach to parent-child relationships. Although much of the earlier work of child-development professionals focused on the influence of the parent on the child, these professionals began to recognize how much the child also influences the parent. A now-classic book by Richard Bell (1977) demonstrated the importance of focusing on the child's influence on the parent. Even at that time, the idea was not new to proponents of family systems theory, but it was a breakthrough for traditional child-development researchers. In the 1980s, a strong consensus developed about the need to study **bidirectional effects**—both the effects of the child on the parent and those of the parent on the child—in order to understand parent-child dynamics. A systemic perspective takes this one step farther, viewing the parent-child relationship as an interactive cycle, a circular process of mutual influence.

Styles of Parenting

Diana Baumrind (1991) has identified four parenting styles and has done considerable work using those styles. Baumrind's four styles are the authoritative (democratic), the authoritarian, the permissive, and the rejecting styles of parenting. We added the uninvolved style, which was identified from the Circumplex Model. Baumrind also identified three styles of behavior in preschool children—energetic-friendly, conflicted-irritable, and impulsive-aggressive—and correlated those behaviors with her parenting styles.

Authoritative (Democratic) Style In **authoritative parenting,** parents establish clear rules and expectations and discuss them with the child. Although they acknowledge the child's perspective, they use both reason and power to enforce their standards. Children of authoritative-style parents exhibit what Baumrind describes as energetic-friendly behavior. These children are very self-reliant and cheerful. They cope well with stress and are achievement oriented. Many other observers concur with Baumrind (Rueter & Conger, 1995; Steinberg, Lamborn, Darling, Mounts, & Dornbusch, 1994).

Authoritarian Style In **authoritarian parenting,** parents establish rigid rules and expectations and strictly enforce them. These parents expect and demand obedience from their children. In Baumrind's observations, children of authoritarian-style parents are often conflicted-irritable in behavior: moody, unhappy, vulnerable to stress, and unfriendly.

Permissive Style In **permissive parenting,** parents let the child's preferences take priority over their ideals and rarely force the child to conform to their standards. Baumrind observed that children of permissive-style parents generally exhibit impulsive-aggressive behavior. These children are often rebellious, domineering, and low achievers.

Rejecting Style In **rejecting parenting,** parents do not pay much attention to their child's needs and seldom have expectations regarding how the child should behave. As a result, children from these homes are often immature and have psychological problems.

Uninvolved Study In **uninvolved parenting,** parents often ignore the child, letting the child's preferences prevail as long as those preferences do not interfere with the parents' activities. The uninvolved style of parenting is not often discussed in published research, but it is in many instances combined with the rejecting style. Children of uninvolved parents are often loners, withdrawn, and low achievers.

Parenting Styles and the Circumplex Model

Many of the concepts proposed by researchers to describe parent-child relationships can be correlated with the dimensions of cohesion and flexibility in the Circumplex Model. Much parent-child research has focused on the concept of

Authoritative-style parents are actively involved with their children. They set standards and discuss them with the child. Children of these parents tend to be self-reliant and achievement oriented, and they cope well with stress.

parental warmth, which is closely related to the cohesion dimension of the Circumplex Model, and on the concept of parental power, which is related to the flexibility dimension of the Model. In addition, the five parenting styles defined above can be placed on the Circumplex Model, as shown in Figure 12.1.

The *democratic (authoritative) style* of parenting falls into the balanced area of the Circumplex Model because it is either structured or flexible on the flexibility dimension and connected or cohesive on the cohesion dimension. Many in our culture consider the democratic style of parenting ideal because it makes the child an active participant in the family and its decisions.

The *permissive style* of parenting is often very high in both cohesion (enmeshed) and flexibility (chaotic). It can be a problematic style of raising children because it lets them get away with almost anything. The *authoritarian style*, its opposite, is similar to the Circumplex Model's rigidly enmeshed family style: very high in cohesion (enmeshed) but very low in flexibility (rigid).

The *uninvolved style* of parenting is very low in cohesion (disengaged) and high in flexibility (chaotic). The *rejecting style* is low in both cohesion (disengaged) and flexibility (rigid). Because these styles fall at the extremes of the Circumplex Model, they are ineffective and problematic ways to rear children.

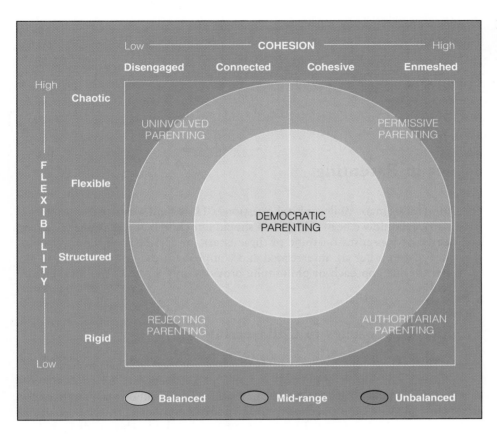

Figure 12.1 Parenting Styles and the Circumplex Model

The Effects of Children on the Family Across the Family Life Cycle

As noted in Chapter 3, Olson, McCubbin, and their colleagues (1989) found that in healthy families the levels of family cohesion and family flexibility varied across the family life cycle in very predictable ways and appeared to be related to the presence and age of children in the family.

Family Cohesion   Young couples without children had the highest level of cohesion, with 71% at the cohesive level. Among families with young children, the percentage at the cohesive level dropped to 63%. More than 60% of the families with adolescents were connected (lower in cohesion), with only 40% at the cohesive (higher) level. These findings indicate that healthy parents are closer when they have younger children and less close when they have adolescents (see Figure 3.7).

Family Flexibility   The level of family flexibility also differed among healthy families based on the presence and age of children. Sixty-two percent of the younger couples without children felt their relationship was flexible. Among families with young children, 63% were structured, which is appropriate for that stage of the life cycle. More families with adolescents were flexible (55%) than structured (45%). And among older couples whose children had left home, 62% had returned to a flexible style (see Figure 3.8).

Issues in Parenting

Parenting raises many philosophical questions: "How shall we raise the children?" "How strict should we be?" "How soon should our child be toilet trained?" There is a degree of consensus on some of these issues, in part because the myriad approaches to parenting are interrelated and complement each other. Focusing too narrowly on one approach or philosophy provides only a part of the total picture of parenting.

Practical Approaches to Childrearing

Several theories of child development have been proposed and have had an impact on approaches to raising children. Freud and his followers focused on the importance of childhood, when the foundation for later life is laid down. Freudians and other proponents of the **psychodynamic theory** emphasized the importance of providing a positive emotional environment for the child, who needs to believe that the world is a safe and good place and that parents can be trusted to be kind and consistent. Freudian theory also identified stages of development building on the libido, or psychic energy, which is expressed at the various stages through different regions: the mouth in infancy (oral stage), the sphincter in toddlers (anal stage), the genital area in early childhood (phallic stage), a period with a lack of focus (latency stage), and a reemergence of the genital area at puberty (genital stage). Though much of Freud's psychodynamic theory has fallen out of favor today, his place in history is secure for his efforts in establishing the importance of healthy development in infancy and early childhood. Though individuals who have suffered enormously in childhood can make dramatic, positive changes later in life, it is best if we can help children succeed from the very beginning.

Whereas Freud was interested in psychological and personality development, Piaget and later proponents of **organismic theory** were interested in cognitive development, the development of the mind. Piaget held that the mind develops through various stages over the course of childhood and adolescence. He observed that children think very differently than adults do. Child-thought is primitive and mystical; young children have only the beginnings of logical reasoning. Thought processes develop slowly toward higher forms into adulthood. This theory encourages parents to select toys and activities that are at an appropriate developmental level for their children and not to expect more than their children are capable of.

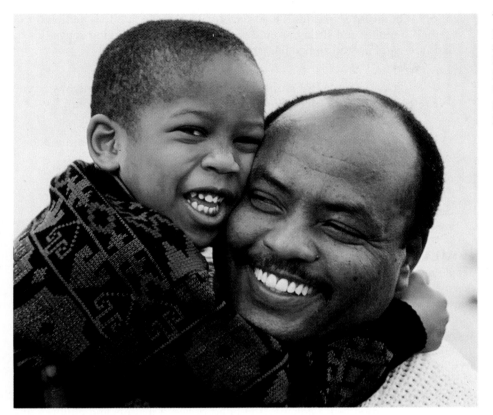

Teaching a child appropriate behavior does not necessarily mean punishment for bad behavior. A more effective technique is reinforcing good behavior with praise and a hug.

The **behaviorists,** operating from **learning theories,** have developed some practical, positive approaches for dealing with children's behavior. Rather than focusing on punishment, behaviorists encourage "accentuating the positive," known as **reinforcement.** When a child does something positive, reward the child. Picking the appropriate reinforcer is not easy; "different strokes for different folks" often applies. Most children respond quite well to money, but praise and a hug are usually equally or even more effective. (Adults, too, appreciate praise from a boss for giving that extra effort.) A parent's job is to be creative in developing new reinforcers.

Perhaps the greatest positive reinforcement is simply enjoying each other's company. For example, when invited to speak about our research on strong families at a conference, we often go on a "journey of happy memories" with our audience. We ask people to recall the "best time" they can remember as a child: "Close your eyes. Think back to when you were a kid. Picture the best time you can remember with your family. Go right back to the scene as if you were there once again. What are you doing with your family? What's happening? Who's there? Get into it. Feel it. . . . "

After the audience has done this, we ask them to open their eyes, and then we call for volunteers to describe what they just saw in their mind's eye:

> "I'm in the living room. It's Thanksgiving. The whole family is gathered together, standing and sitting around the piano. We're all singing songs. Us kids are giggling and squirreling around, too. It's wonderful."
>
> * * *
>
> "We're on vacation. We're at the lake 2 hours north of our hometown. We're camping out. We're telling ghost stories around the campfire."
>
> * * *
>
> "I remember how we'd play games every Friday night. Just lie on the floor in the living room and play simple board games and laugh together."
>
> * * *
>
> "When I was 12, my job was to scrub the kitchen floor with Mom every Saturday morning. We'd be on our hands and knees—just the two of us—scrubbing and laughing and flicking water at each other. It was great!"

We have gone on this journey of happy memories with literally thousands of people over the past 20 years, and the most remarkable thing we find is that when asked to recall the "best times" of their childhood, adults rarely recall something that cost a lot of money. On only a handful of occasions have we heard a happy memory that was very expensive: a costly vacation to a theme park, a big meal in a fancy hotel. The vast majority of our happiest memories from childhood come from experiences that cost almost nothing. The key element is this: People who love one another are together, enjoying each other's company, being kind to one another.

It's very clear: Simple things can be tremendously reinforcing to a good relationship. These good times enhance the bond between parents and children and make it likely that children will be cooperative.

Increasing Use of Day Care

As more mothers work outside the home, one consequence is the increasing demand for day care facilities (U.S. Bureau of the Census, 1995). In 1991, only 23% of parents used organized day care; in 1995, the number was 30%. Dependence on grandparents and other relatives for day care decreased somewhat between 1991 and 1995, dropping from 53% to 48%. Use of non-relatives to care for preschool children is expected to increase as more mothers return to the workplace.

Coparenting

A growing number of parents have adopted a cooperative approach to parenting, known as **coparenting.** Traditional family roles—in which dad was the provider and mom the nurturer; dad was "tough" and mom "tender"—are changing. More mothers are working outside the home, and more men are sharing in parenting tasks. An increasing number of mothers are providing income for their families and enjoying the connection to the world outside the home, and an increasing

Doonesbury

BY GARRY TRUDEAU

Doonesbury © 1986 G. B. Trudeau. Reprinted with permission of Universal Press Syndicate. All rights reserved.

number of fathers are experiencing the joy of watching their children grow and learn.

Some share the responsibilities equally: Mother and father each do half the child care, half the housework, and half the work outside the home. But most couples do not divide up the tasks exactly equally. One young father explained, "I'm a better cook, so I tend to do more of that. She likes to see a neat, clean house, so she concentrates on that. We both like taking care of the girls, but I do baths and bedtimes because she's so tired at the end of a day of nursing." Flexibility is the key.

Researchers have found a number of advantages to the coparenting model. Parents maintain that they are quite satisfied with their marriage and family life, arguing that they get along better with their spouse than they did before they adopted the approach and that their relationships with their children have improved. Some partners were considering divorce before they changed their attitudes about childrearing. Coparenting frees men to spend more time relating to, caring for, and relaxing with their children and at the same time frees women to pursue outside interests. Both parents have much to gain from active involvement in their children's growth. Parenthood is much too important and much too time-consuming to be left up to one person (DeFrain, 1979; Schwartz, 1994).

Another important benefit of coparenting is that it brings fathers into the family on an emotional level. Some observers have concluded that fathers often "draw on their life at home to take care of their emotional needs, but . . . distance themselves from the emotional needs of other family members" (Larson & Richards, 1994). Some fathers enjoy being nurtured at home but don't want to nurture others in the home or don't have the capacity to do so. The experience of coparenting can help men learn how to attend to the emotional needs of others. This is a skill that has often been neglected because in our culture we tend to socialize men for competition, not cooperation.

A problem with coparenting is that sometimes the marriage gets lost in the shuffle. The mother is working outside the home, caring for the children, doing housework; the father is doing the same. Two outside full-time jobs and the job of maintaining a family and household add up to at least three full-time jobs for only two people. Often the marriage is neglected while the spouses concentrate on their employment responsibilities and their family and household tasks. The couple might be doing great at the office and great with the kids, but still end up getting divorced because they forgot to focus on their relationship with each other. They need to remember that the foundation for the whole operation is a strong marriage.

Fatherhood Today

Coparenting may be gaining popularity as an ideal, but the reality in many cases is quite different (Kouneski, 1996). Although the images of father as breadwinner and mother as nurturer are slowly breaking down, new images—especially for fathers—have not yet taken hold. More than half of American mothers with children under 18 are now in the workforce, but many fathers have not become proportionately involved in nurturing tasks. The value of fatherhood has not increased.

Some scholars have gone so far as to ask, Is the father even a part of the family? D. Blankenhorn (1995) has found that nearly 40% of children live in homes where the biological father is not present. Wade Horn (1995) estimates that 6 out of 10 children born in the 1990s will be "fatherless" before reaching adulthood. What forces are responsible for these trends? And what can be done about them?

The Absent Father   Two major threats to a father's presence in a child's life are divorce and nonmarital childbearing, both of which are increasing. Marriages are continuing to fail at a high rate, and a growing number of families are starting out without a father (U.S. Bureau of the Census, 1995). One-third of births are to single women. Virtually all children born outside of marriage live with their mothers, and in two thirds of these cases, the father never establishes paternity.

In 90% of divorce cases, the children reside with their mothers. Many fathers, no longer living with their children, struggle to stay involved with them. But research has shown a pattern of gradual withdrawal by nonresidential fathers and growing alienation between fathers and children. One large national study found that about two thirds of children of divorce had a poor relationship with their fathers; among children whose parents were not divorced, less than a third (29%) had a poor relationship with their fathers (Zill, Morrison, & Coiro, 1993). Conflict between the former spouses also affects the quality of the father-child relationship. It can create strains on the child that offset any advantages of having the father actively involved.

When fathers remain in frequent contact and conflict between the parents is low, fathers are more likely to make regular child support payments (Seltzer, 1991). There is a strong association between a divorced father's economic support and the well-being of his children. So frequent contact, low parental conflict, and economic support have a positive effect on the child's well-being, but many fathers would like to have the opportunity to contribute to their children's lives in deeper and more meaningful ways.

The Father as Nurturer   Research in child development has shown that fathers are just as capable as mothers in performing nurturing tasks (assuming the fathers are living with their children). Children can establish attachment relationships with fathers as they do with mothers. Fathers respond to the needs of their infants, picking up on their cues, just as mothers do. When mothers are present, however, fathers tend to back off and defer to them.

Fathers are more likely to be involved in the care of children if the parents are dual earners, but only when the mother works different hours than the father. When parents work the same hours, mothers tend to come home to a "second shift" of family work (De Luccie, 1995).

Some studies report that women want men to be nurturing in their families, but other studies have shown that many mothers do not want increased father involvement (Hogan, 1993). The home is said to be a place of power and control for women, whereas the workplace is where men have traditionally dominated. Some women do not want to share their power or their role as the "more important parent." Men's involvement as fathers can be shaped, positively or negatively, by the mothers' expectations and support.

In sum, it seems that fathers are fully capable of nurturing and caring for their children, but other factors—social, cultural, and interpersonal—tend to discourage them from doing so whole-heartedly. This is particularly unfortunate in light of the belief, put forth by some feminist scholars, that as more men become involved in nurturing tasks, inequalities in the workplace and the family will be reduced (Silverstein, 1995).

Responsible Fatherhood   What is the appropriate role for a father? It must first be acknowledged that every society constructs and defines roles for men and women; the role of father is no exception. In our society today, there is no single definition or description of this role. If a father is living at home with his children, he may be married and coparenting or single and parenting alone. Living apart from his children, he may be young and unwed, with or without paternity established. If divorced, he may have joint physical or legal custody or just visitation rights.

Although single fathers and divorced fathers with custody have nurturing roles thrust upon them, it appears that fathers in our society are given quite a wide latitude in how involved they want to be in the family. Unlike mothering, fathering appears to be a choice that men make in the face of contextual pressures. They can be very involved—or they can walk away.

To develop new roles, fathers need the support of mothers. They also need the support of society in general—in the workplace, in the courts, and in the social service agencies that serve families. This support may be forthcoming. Recognizing the holistic nature of family health, family service programs now attempt to involve fathers when they work with families. Additionally, new community-based programs have emerged to support fathers in their efforts to be responsibly involved in their families. Jim Levine and Ed Pitt (1995), discussing their experience as practitioners who work with families, advance this definition of responsibility: A responsible father waits to have children until he is prepared to support the child, financially and emotionally; he establishes legal paternity; and he actively provides physical and emotional care for the child, as well as financial support, in cooperation with the mother.

Given the pressures of living in our society, it may be that mothers and fathers will never achieve equal coparenting. Perhaps it is more important that they nurture a loving, cooperative marriage relationship. In a 1996 report prepared for the federal Health and Human Services Department, William J. Doherty, Edward F. Kouneski, and Martha F. Erickson recommend that fathering programs involve mothers and focus on the well-being of the mother-father partnership. They believe that new programs should be developed to promote caring, committed, and collaborative marriages. The future of fathering, it seems, is intricately linked with healthy relationships between men and women who have formed equal partnerships meant to last.

Parent Education and Family Therapy

In meeting the challenges of raising children, parents often turn to professionals for guidance, either for education or for therapy. **Parent education** usually involves a presentation of information in a group setting followed by a group discussion of generic parenting problems, such as communication, discipline, imparting values to children, sibling rivalry, and choosing adequate day care. **Family therapy** usually involves a therapist working with a single family with one or more specific problems, including sexual abuse, spouse abuse, child abuse or neglect, a runaway child, a child's attempted suicide, a child's coming out as a gay man or a lesbian, or the abuse of alcohol or other drugs.

Both parent education and family therapy take place in a variety of settings, and fees range widely. Services through public agencies are often less expensive than those offered by private practitioners. Parent education programs are usually much cheaper than therapy, and many are free or cost very little. One of the main advantages of parent education programs is their ability to show parents that they are not the only ones having trouble figuring out how to raise their kids; this can be tremendously comforting to troubled parents. In an effective parent education session, a professional might present ideas for 15–30 minutes; then parents break into small groups and discuss their own family trials and tribulations. Parents soon learn that they are all "in the same boat." Breaking the tension and discussing common issues can be the foundation for positive change and growth in the family.

Many parent education programs have been developed over the years (Anglin, 1985; Arcus, Schvaneveldt, & Moss, 1993a, 1993b). Any community of reasonable size offers a surprisingly rich variety of programs, including programs for abusive and neglectful parents, foster parents, adoptive parents, single parents, bereaved parents, and chemically dependent parents; programs for stepfamilies; childbirth education programs; family stress management programs; marriage and family enrichment programs; and sex education and other programs for parents and teenagers.

The mass media also provide a steady supply of ideas and advice for parents. Parents avidly seeking answers to difficult questions are often dismayed by the diversity of advice available, wondering how to make sense of it all. A useful strategy is for parents to gather a number of opinions from a variety of sources on an important parenting topic and then to carefully consider what they think is best for their own family, taking into account the specifics of their personal situation. Parents are the ones who are responsible for the rearing of their children; they must make the important decisions that affect their children's lives.

Challenges and Pleasures of Parenthood

An enduring problem for parents is how to translate philosophy into action. One important goal is to provide children with a basic foundation upon which they can build, as illustrated by Kahlil Gibran's poem "On Children":

Your children are not your children.
They are the sons and daughters of Life's longing for itself.
They come through you but not from you,
And though they are with you yet they belong not to you.
You may give them your love but not your thoughts,
For they have their own thoughts.
You may house their bodies but not their souls,
For their souls dwell in the house of tomorrow,
which you cannot visit, not even in your dreams.
You may strive to be like them, but seek not to make them like you.
For life goes not backward nor tarries with yesterday.
You are the bows from which your children
*   as living arrows are sent forth.*
The archer sees the mark upon the path of the infinite,
and He bends you with His might that His
arrows may go swift and far.
Let your bending in the archer's hand be for gladness;
For even as He loves the arrow that flies,
so He loves also the bow that is stable.
(Gibran, 1923/1976, pp. 18–19)

Each day parents are confronted with difficult questions that have complex answers. To find these answers, parents must learn to relate their personal philosophy to what is actually occurring with their children:

- "I don't believe in spanking, but this kid is driving me crazy!"

- "I love to watch my children grow, but I also need a life of my own. How do I balance the two?"

- "He flunked his math test again. I told him I would help him study for it, but he didn't want to study. Should I let him suffer the consequences of failing?"

	PERCENT RECORDING
SPECIFIC SATISFACTION	THE RESPONSE
Watching children grow and develop	74
Love for children	65
Pride in children's achievement	62
Sharing	54
A growth experience	45
Passing on values	44
Fun to do things with	43
General enjoyment	41
Feeling of being part of a family	40
Self-fulfillment	39
Feel needed	39
Enjoying physical contact	37
Feeling closer to spouse	36
A purpose for living	32
Enjoying the simple aspects of life	31
Companionship	27
Hope for the future	26
New appreciation for my parents	25
Adds stability to life	25
Shared marital project	24
Keeps me young	19
Pleasure for grandparents	16
More things to talk about with spouse	15

Table 12.2 Common Satisfactions of Parenthood

Source: "Parent Satisfactions: Implications for Strengthening Families" (p. 147) by W. H. Meredith, N. Stinnett, and B. F. Cacioppo. In *Family Strengths 6: Enhancement of Interaction*, edited by R. Williams, H. Lingren, G. Rowe, S. Van Zandt, P. Lee, and N. Stinnett, 1985, Lincoln, NE: Department of Human Development and the Family, Center for Family Strengths, University of Nebraska. Copyright 1985 by Center for Family Strengths. Reprinted by permission.

There are also myriad pleasures associated with being a parent. Bill Meredith, Nick Stinnett, and Benjamin Cacioppo (1985) surveyed 702 Midwestern parents, focusing on the satisfactions they experienced in their parental role. The study found that 76% of the sample were satisfied with parenthood, 16% were neither satisfied nor dissatisfied, and 8% were dissatisfied with the parenting role in general. Table 12.2 identifies the specific satisfactions surveyed parents cited.

"I can't imagine a life without my children," said Karim, a 45-year-old businessman from Detroit. "Sure, I get mad at them. They bug me, and I yell at them once in a while. But I love them so much, and their journey through life is so much fun to watch. I keep wondering: "What's the next chapter of the story going to be? What are they going to do next? What will they all become?

"I suppose I could have concentrated on my career more if I hadn't had children, but love has always counted far more to me than money. You can't hold a $100 bill in your lap and read a story to it."

One of the best-known sources of childrearing advice today is Dr. T. Berry Brazelton. As a scientist, he developed a widely used assessment of the neurological condition of newborns, and as a popular author, he has focused on the development of attachment between parents and children and on children's emotional and behavioral development.

Summary

- Parenthood is both extremely challenging and, for most parents, very satisfying emotionally.

- Conventional wisdom on the subject of parenthood in our society is commonplace. Though many people might believe the conventional "truths," research on parenthood indicates that the picture is more complex.

- Parenthood changes a couple's world: They have less time for each other and for individual interests, they may have money problems, and parenting can be physically exhausting, especially for mothers.

- Researchers have found that voluntarily childless individuals and couples can have just as satisfying a life as those who have children. Child-free people have more time for intimate relationships and for their careers, and in old age they often rely on friends and relatives for support. Of American woman aged 18–34, 9.3% do not expect to have children.

- A middle-income ($29,900–$48,300) U.S. couple will spend about $120,000 to raise each child through the age of 17.

- Parenting styles differ, and some are more effective than others. The authoritative (democratic) style is favored today because it appears to produce self-reliant children who cope well with stress. Other parenting styles are authoritarian, permissive, rejecting, and uninvolved.

- Many parenting styles can be related to the cohesion and flexibility dimensions of the Family Circumplex Model. The authoritative (democratic) style falls into the balanced areas of the model because it exhibits dynamic balances on both the dimensions. Because other styles fall near the extremes of the model, they can be problematic approaches for rearing children.

- Across the family life cycle, a healthy family's level of cohesion and flexibility changes dynamically with the presence and age of children. Couples without children are generally both more flexible and more cohesive. Couples with young children become a bit less cohesive and far more structured in their attempts to cope with the challenges of parenthood. As children grow into adolescents, healthy families become considerably less cohesive (although still connected) and far more flexible, giving their teenagers room to develop as individuals. The majority of empty nesters are high on the flexibility dimension.

- Positive approaches to childrearing include reinforcing (rewarding) children's positive behavior rather than punishing negative actions, and coparenting, a sharing of traditional male and female roles between parents.

- A vast array of parent education programs exists in the United States in response to the challenges of raising children and the diversity of American families. Many trained professionals provide both information and one-on-one therapy. The media also offer advice. But in the final analysis, parents must decide how they wish to raise their children.

Key Terms

child-free alternative	rejecting parenting	learning theories
bidirectional effects	uninvolved parenting	reinforcement
authoritative parenting	psychodynamic theory	coparenting
authoritarian parenting	organismic theory	parent education
permissive parenting	behaviorist	family therapy

Activities

1. Read Kahlil Gibran's poem "On Children" carefully and write a brief essay analyzing his philosophy of parenthood. On what points do you agree, and on what points to you disagree?

2. Set a time and place to interview your father and/or mother about their beliefs on rearing children and the challenges and joys they have experienced over the years as parents. A good interview takes careful planning: Write down 15–20 questions you want to be sure to ask. Then describe your findings from the interview in a short paper and share it with the class or a small group. You might like to audiotape or videotape the interview; these tapes can become family treasures.

3. Parenthood can be a thankless task; children are often too busy and too overwhelmed by their own problems and concerns to think about their parents' feel-

ings. Write a letter to your parents, thanking them for all the things they have done for you and for their unique human qualities.

4. Spend an afternoon with some children you know—your brother and sister-in-law's children, a neighbor's children, or a friend's kids. Write down your reactions to this brief "parenting" experience.

Suggested Readings

Arcus, M. E., Schvaneveldt, J. D., and Moss, J. J. (Eds.). (1993). *Handbook of Family Life Education: Foundations of Family Life Education*, Volume I; and *The Practice of Family Life Education*, Volume II. Newbury Park, CA: Sage. *Excellent resources for parent educators.*

Biller, H. B. (1993). *Fathers and families: Paternal factors in child development.* Westport, CT: Auburn House. *Culmination of the efforts of a scholar who has probably written more about the father's role in child development than any other author in the past 30 years.*

Bozett, F. W., & Hanson, S. M. H. (Eds.). (1991). *Fatherhood and families in culture context.* New York: Springer. *Chapters on historical and cross-cultural perspectives, social class and fatherhood, religion and fatherhood, rural and urban influences, the future of fatherhood, and more.*

Dinkmeyer, D., & McKay, G. D. (1990). *Parenting teenagers* (2nd ed.). Circle Pines, MN: American Guidance Service. *One of many useful books on this subject by two psychologists.*

Fine, M. J. (Ed.). (1989). *The second handbook on parent education: Contemporary perspectives.* New York: Academic Press. *Valuable readings for parent educators, edited by a University of Kansas professor.*

Gilbert, L. A. (1993). *Two careers/one family.* Newbury Park, CA: Sage. *Up-to-date information on families in which both parents work full-time.*

Kagan, S. L., & Zigler, E. F. (1987). *Early schooling: The national debate.* New Haven, CT: Yale University Press. *An excellent discussion of the pros and cons of early childhood education.*

Klagsbrun, F. (1992). *Mixed feelings: Love, hate, rivalry, and reconciliation among brothers and sisters.* New York: Bantam Books. *A rather scholarly yet readable book that focuses on the complexity of our feelings about our siblings.*

LeMasters, E. E., & DeFrain, J. (1989). *Parents in contemporary America: A sympathetic view.* Belmont, CA: Wadsworth. *Places parenthood in its social context; includes sections on myths of parenthood, the American mother, the American father, single parents and stepparents, programs for parents, and much more.*

McCarney, S. B., & Bauer, A. M. (1989). *The parent's guide: Solutions to today's most common behavior problems in the home.* Columbia, MO: Hawthorne Educational Series. *A useful tool for parents.*

Spock, B., & Rothenberg, M. B. (1992). *Baby and child care.* New York: Pocket Books. *The latest edition of the top-selling parenting book in the world.*

Utne, E. (1994). My worthy foe: How familiarity breeds contempt (and love). *Utne Reader* (May/June), 2. *A fun look at brotherly love.*

Zigler, E. F. (1992). *Head Start: The inside story of America's most successful educational experiment.* New York: Basic Books. *A look, by a professor at Yale University who has been involved in the program from its early days, at this approach to early childhood education.*

CHAPTER 13

Midlife and Older Couples

As the life expectancy of the average American has increased dramatically over this century, interest in midlife and older couples has also grown. Understanding families in the middle and later years provides a perspective on life's journey. What happens to couples and their marriages in these years directly affects the lives of the younger generations. Middle age can be a time of personal and relationship growth, but it also offers many challenges. And aging has as much to do with psychological and social factors as it does with chronology and biology.

This chapter focuses on several key issues of middle age, beginning with a look at the effects of midlife on job satisfaction, sexuality, and the marriage relationship. Reasons for divorce in middle age are explored, and suggestions for strengthening a marriage are presented. A look at some contemporary phenomena—the "empty nest," the "cluttered nest," and the conflicting generational demands between which middle-aged individuals are often "sandwiched"—follows, as well as a discussion of grandparenthood.

The discussion of family life in the later years attempts to answer the question "How old is 'old'?" and also debunks the conventional wisdom about old age. A look at retirement and at family dynamics among aging couples follows. The chapter concludes with a section on the death of a spouse.

Family Life in the Middle Years

What images does the term *middle age* conjure up? The most vivid way for a youthful college student to picture this age is to think of mom and dad. Middle age can be a relaxing time, a time of thankfulness that the challenges and fears of youth have been overcome. But middle age can bring new pressures, new challenges.

"Life begins at 40," an old saying goes. The kids may leave the nest. Family income may reach a peak. But "middlescence" can set in. In the middle years, some people mourn lost opportunities, the road not taken, and wonder what their lives would have been like if only they had been bolder, smarter, or luckier. "Middlescents" also often yearn for a taut young body and freedom from the grind.

In Erik Erikson's schema, middle age can be a time for generativity or stagnation (1950). The question of middle age is "Can we remain productive despite boredom and malaise? (Can an old dog learn new tricks?)" Millions of people transform their lives in the middle years by starting new careers or falling in love. Those who are flexible, who can adapt to new circumstances and "roll with the punches," will be much more likely to succeed. The inflexible ones may survive but will probably not excel—and they will be less likely to enjoy the process of living as much as those who are flexible.

Defining Middle Age

A popular societal definition of **middle age** is the years between 35 and 65, but age alone does not tell one a lot, especially when applied to the middle years. The

One of the biggest changes of middle age is the children's leaving home for college or a job. Parents who are flexible usually enjoy the freedom from daily responsibility for their children and are likely to develop new interests or even start a new career.

eminent gerontologist Bernice Neugarten notes, philosophically, that the middle years are the time when people begin to think about how many years they have left, rather than how many they've already lived (1968).

One middle-aged man described life as a rainbow: At the bottom left are infancy, early childhood, adolescence, and young adulthood; around the very highest point of the rainbow are the middle years; and on the lower right side of the rainbow are the later years of life. When one reaches the crest of the rainbow, the middle years, one can clearly see the remainder of life for the first time. "When I reached middle age," the man explained, "I saw the rest of my life clearly. It looked like more of the same old stuff I had grown tired of over the past 10 years. Some people might call it a middle-aged crisis," he continued. "I thought of it as a middle-aged opportunity, and I've been changing steadily ever since."

Evelyn Duvall, a distinguished family sociologist, worked with Reuben Hill to develop the family life cycle stages and family development theory. From Duvall and Hill's perspective, middle age is that time between when the last child leaves home and retirement (Duvall & Miller, 1985). This, very roughly speaking, is the 15 years between 50 and 65. This chapter takes a somewhat broader view of middle age, including families with teenagers, families launching young adults, middle-aged parents with an empty nest, and retirement. All four stages put together roughly span the years 35–65, neatly coinciding with society's definition of the middle years.

The size of the 50–59 age group, often called the 50-something population, will increase about 50% by the year 2006 (U.S. Bureau of the Census, 1995). This group will gain 12.4 million people, growing from 25.3 million today to 37.7 million people in 2006. Because of their numbers, these aging baby boomers will be able to focus more attention on the retirement, health care, and empty nest issues that will be important to them. Their buying power will also mean that purveyors of health care and other consumer products will be designing with them in mind.

The Middle-Aged Person and the Working World

The biggest challenge in midlife, especially for men, is how to thrive (or even survive) in the working world while maintaining a successful family life. Three pioneers in research and thought on the middle years, Daniel Levinson, Roger Gould, and Gail Sheehy, also emphasize *crises* in midlife.

Levinson (1978) observed that the middle years can bring on a tumultuous struggle within individuals. "Every aspect of their lives comes into question, and they are horrified by much that is revealed. They are full of recriminations against themselves and others. They cannot go on as before, but need time to choose a new path or modify the old one" (p. 199).

Gould (1975), looking at middle age from a developmental perspective, suggested that between ages 43 and 50, people come to terms with life, develop a reasonable picture of themselves, and are comfortable with their strengths and limitations. After 50, a general mellowing seems to occur. A lot of things have been accomplished, and the sense of urgency diminishes. A lot of other things have not been accomplished, but that becomes more acceptable.

Sheehy (1976) packaged these ideas in her popular book *Passages: Predictable Crises of Adult Life*. Whether the middle years are a time of "transition" or a time of "crisis" or simply a time of "challenge" is essentially up to the individual.

For many people, **routinization** is a major problem on the job. In their 20s or early 30s, individuals tend to bounce from job to job. But, especially if they are members of the middle class, individuals are likely sooner or later to settle into a relatively comfortable position—one that provides a reasonably good income, requires expertise the individual possesses, and involves interacting with amiable co-workers. The job, in short, is as comfortable as an old shoe. But after 10 or 15 years, the leather may be starting to wear a bit thin. Maybe, for example, the person can't "go anywhere" in the job; leveling off means it will be years, or never, before some type of vertical or even horizontal change occurs.

Middle-aged people often feel their work position is risky. It is usually very difficult to make a career change in midlife, and the tradeoff for a new, more interesting job may be a pay cut. If a person cannot figure out how to make the old job fulfilling again, however, the danger is that boredom, anxiety, or anger will build up to the boiling point. Fights with bosses and co-workers (and one's family) often have their roots in these common "middlescent" feelings.

Women who return to college or to work outside the home when their children reach a more independent age develop two distinct careers in their life. Middle-aged women returning to the work marketplace after a long absence are at a certain disadvantage because they are older but lack "on-the-job" experience. Although they usually have tremendous insights and skills from work in the home and in the community that would translate well on the job, they often experience discrimination. Employers sometimes demean these talents. Worse yet, women

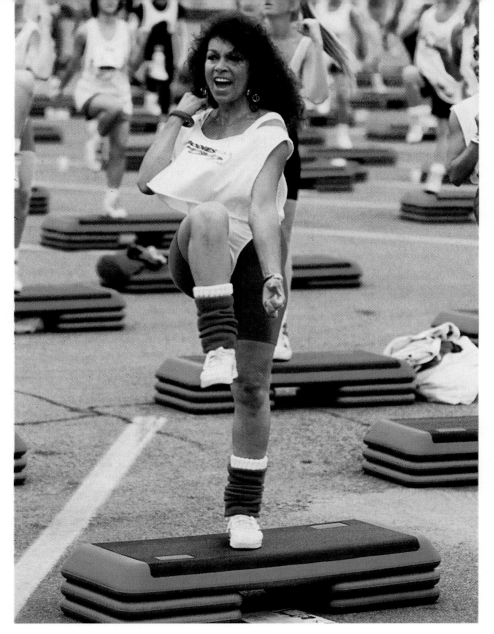

Between 43 and 50, people usually come to terms with life and are able to realistically assess their strengths and weaknesses.

themselves often do not realize how competent they are and suffer from feelings of inferiority.

The good news about this two-step career approach to life is that just when one career, parenthood, is running out of steam and may be becoming burdensome, a new career in the working world is waiting in the wings. Delighted with her new job teaching at a community college, one woman stated, "I've been recycled. I've been a mother of four children for 15 years. And now I'm a *person* again!" At age 42, to use a common term, she was "born again."

Box 13.1 (p. 420) presents a broad-ranging study of family stress in the middle years, detailing both the types of stressors families face and their strategies for coping with stress.

B O X   1 3 . 1

Family Stress in the Middle Years

A team of university-based family researchers in nine states conducted the largest study ever undertaken of family stress and coping in the middle years. More than 1,900 families in Indiana, Iowa, Kansas, Kentucky, Louisiana, Michigan, Minnesota, Missouri, and Nebraska responded to a 27-page questionnaire about the stressors they faced and how they coped. The research focused on intact families, middle-aged husbands and wives with at least one child still living at home. The study found that it is difficult for couples to find time and energy for their own wants and needs during this period of life.

Types of Stressors

Families in the study were asked to rank various stressors. The top 12 stressors identified by both husbands and wives were the following:

1. A family member's involvement with the judicial system.

2. A major financial loss.

3. Serious emotional problems.

4. The serious illness or accident of a child.

5. The serious illness or accident of the primary wage earner.

6. Marital separation.

7. The death of an adult brother or sister.

8. Loss of the primary wage earner's job.

9. The death of own or spouse's parent.

10. The illness of own or spouse's aged parent.

11. Expenses that exceed the total family income.

12. Intrusive relatives.

This list is an average of events reported by both husbands and wives. Wives perceived family-related matters to be more stressful, in general, whereas husbands considered job-related and financial concerns to be more stressful.

The researchers found that stressors have an additive effect. The greater the number of stressors, the more likely a family is to experience emotional, relational, and health difficulties. In short, the more troubles we have, the more likely we are to become physically and emotionally ill, and the more likely our family relationships are to suffer.

Stress-Related Symptoms

Reported symptoms of stress, from most common to least common, were:

1. Irritability.

2. Weight problems.

3. Muscle tension or anxiety.

Sexuality in Middle Age

As noted in Chapter 6, sexual activity often declines steadily over the years of a marriage, as stress and boredom take their toll. Fortunately, among couples who are creative and committed, sex can remain a source of intense pleasure throughout the middle years. Two issues of concern during this time are menopause and "male menopause."

Menopause   The most dramatic age-related change in female reproductive functioning, after puberty, is **menopause,** the end of monthly menstrual periods. Sheehy (1992) refers to menopause as the "silent passage" because it is so rarely

Family Stress in the Middle Years *(continued)*

4. Use of prescription drugs.

5. Difficulty relaxing.

6. Use of tobacco.

7. Depression.

8. Headaches.

9. Frequent colds or flu.

10. Difficulty sleeping.

11. Use of alcohol.

12. Accident-proneness.

Parents generally reported more symptoms of stress than children. Wives reported more symptoms than husbands.

Coping with Stress

The families were asked how they coped with life's stressors. They ranked their stress-management techniques in descending order:

1. Attending church services.

2. Sharing concerns with friends.

3. Facing problems head-on and trying to find solutions.

4. Participating in church activities.

5. Sharing difficulties and doing things with relatives.

6. Seeking information and advice from their family doctor.

7. Seeking information and advice from people in other families who had faced similar problems.

8. Asking for and accepting help from neighbors.

9. Seeking help from community agencies and programs.

10. Seeking professional counseling.

The researchers concluded that physical and emotional problems can be indicators of high stress levels. If the signs appear in a family, the family needs to find help. First and foremost, the results support talking. Talk to other family members, to relatives, to friends. The researchers also stressed the importance of proper nutrition, adequate rest and sleep, plenty of exercise, and fun activities to add some spice to life.

Source: Adapted from "Stress, coping and adaptation in the middle years of the family life cycle," by the Cooperative Extension Service, Iowa State University, Ames on research conducted by the North Central Regional Committee 164. Agriculture Research Service, U.S. Department of Agriculture, Washington, DC, 1989.

discussed openly. Menopause occurs, on average, around the age of 50 but can begin as early as a woman's mid-30s or as late as her early 60s. Because of reduced estrogen production and other hormonal changes, menopause signals the cessation of a woman's ability to have children. Reproductive organs shrink, and the amount of fatty tissue in the breasts and other parts of the body decreases. The vulva becomes thinner, losing its capacity to engorge with blood, and the vagina shrinks and loses some elasticity. Vaginal secretions that provide lubrication during intercourse diminish.

Some women experience distress—including irritability, insomnia, "hot flashes," headaches, and depression—during menopause. Some physicians recommend taking hormones orally, by injection, or by use of a patch for transdermal absorption under the skin to relieve these symptoms, which result from temporary hormonal imbalances. Hormone replacement therapy is a common approach to relieving some of the discomfort that menopause can bring. It can also minimize the loss of bone mass that can occur after menopause.

In general, most women perceive menopause as a transition period rather than a problem. Even though physical responses change, a woman's perception of pleasure and satisfaction in intercourse remain the same or may even increase. A number of factors may be involved, including freedom from fear of pregnancy and the fact that the couple may be rediscovering each other after losing contact during the challenging full-time parenting years (Boston Women's Health Book Collective, 1992; Hyde, 1990; Masters, Johnson, & Kolodny, 1993; Sheehy, 1992).

"Male Menopause"   Sexual changes related to age also occur in men. Production of the male hormone **androgen** declines slowly and steadily in most men until about age 60, when it levels off. For most men, this decline in hormone production does not cause the emotional and physical changes that some women experience during menopause. In other men, the symptoms are so similar to those experienced by menopausal women that physicians diagnose the condition as **male menopause,** a term that generates some controversy in the medical community.

As men get older, the amount of fluid ejaculated with orgasm tends to diminish, as does the strength of the ejaculation. The testicles become smaller and less firm; erections become less frequent and also less rigid. By age 50 the average male may require 8–24 hours after orgasm before he is capable of having another erection. Most men also require more time to reach orgasm, but this can be viewed as simply lengthening the period of pleasure for both the man and his partner (Hyde, 1990).

The Middle-Aged Marriage

Many marriages are happier before children arrive and after they leave home (Olson, McCubbin, et al., 1989). For many couples in the middle years, marital satisfaction may be at a low point, increasing as the adolescents leave home.

Divorce in the Middle Years   Maggie Hayes (1979) conducted one of the first studies of the phenomenon of divorce in the middle years, exploring why it occurs and what people can do to strengthen their ties to each other to prevent it. Marriages that ended in divorce in the middle years had generally survived that long for two major reasons: children and money. The couples had generally gotten off to a good start in their marriages. Two thirds felt that the early years of the relationship had been good but that it had deteriorated very gradually as time passed. Hayes was especially interested in the dynamics of this deterioration process and reported a number of important contributing factors:

- *Dominance of the husband.* Only 17% of the people in Hayes's study considered their marriages to be equal partnerships. The vast majority of both spouses viewed the husband as dominant, with many wives describing their position in the relationship as little more than that of an indentured servant. "He wouldn't let me" was a phrase Hayes heard repeatedly. The men appeared to fear their wives' personal growth or independence. They

FOR BETTER OR FOR WORSE   BY LYNN JOHNSTON

squelched the woman's efforts to get a job, go back to school, handle money, or even learn to drive a car—describing these desires as "overindependence." Both partners often referred to their marriage as "boring."

- *Failure to communicate and to share.* About 75% of the people interviewed considered their partner hard to talk with. Husbands were especially unable to share their feelings; wives often accused them of being too judgmental, too much of a know-it-all, or fearful of conflict. Most of the couples seldom talked with each other. One in five often quarreled, but almost half said they "seldom" quarreled, indicating little interest in the relationship. The vast majority of people said their partner contributed little or nothing to their self-esteem. Women tended to have lower self-esteem than men.

  Shared couple activities had decreased over time in most of these marriages. Work, children's activities, housework, and individual interests took precedence. When Hayes asked, "What did you do together that gave you the most pleasure?" many people could think of nothing to say. There was no reservoir of happy memories from which to draw. Couples failed to express love and concern verbally, and the desire for closeness, warmth, kissing, and touching had disappeared. Sex had become a bore, and innovative behavior was resisted by the spouse.

- *Excessive career involvement.* The husband's career successes had often had a negative effect on the marriage, drawing him away from a spouse whom he no longer considered interesting. A husband's lack of career success was also perceived as damaging to the relationship. Among couples who divorced in middle age, 75% of the wives were working. The effects cut both ways: The positive effects of more income and personal growth for the wife were often offset by the husband's resentment of the time and attention the wife gave to her work.

- *Extramarital involvements.* Some 75% of the men and 25% of the women whose marriages ended in divorce had been sexually unfaithful. More of the men had been unfaithful earlier in the marriage without the wife's knowledge. Affairs in the middle years tended to become serious emotional involvements. Women who had an affair often said that they viewed it as a way of affirming themselves as women after being ignored as wives. Both men and women viewed affairs as destructive to the marriage.

- *Midlife change.* The male **midlife crisis,** a term often used in the popular literature to describe certain changes during the middle years, was cited in many of these broken marriages. The most common story Hayes heard from wives was that the husband had developed an obsession with his appearance: buying a new wardrobe, exercising, losing weight, changing his hairstyle. This was followed by absences from home, irritability, absent-mindedness, and self-centeredness.

Strengthening Marriage in the Middle Years   Hayes observed that we can all learn a lot about marriage from divorced people. Based on the experiences of the people she interviewed, Hayes offered several recommendations for strengthening marriage during the middle years:

- Establish priorities early in marriage, with the spouse at the top of the list. Do not allow parenthood to overshadow the marriage.

- Be alert for warning signs of marital problems, which include nagging, sarcasm, possessiveness, criticism, and personal discontent.

- Strive toward equality in all aspects of the marriage. Each partner should feel important and powerful.

- Seek a balance between togetherness and personal growth; either extreme can be harmful to a marriage.

- Good sex in a relationship in the middle years does not come naturally; it is a result of a positive daily life together.

- Develop a network of friendships with other couples who are concerned about maintaining a quality marriage.

- Evaluate the marriage from time to time, and attend a marriage enrichment workshop.

- Avoid boring or frustrating work situations; a midlife career change may be beneficial.

- Consider a lifestyle change rather than a partner change in middle age to add pizzazz to the marriage.

A happy marriage is the key to a content spouse. The best way to deal with infidelity is to prevent it from occurring.

Empty Nest or Spacious Nest?

The term **empty nest syndrome** describes the feelings of malaise, emptiness, and lack of purpose that parents can have when their children leave home. Some par-

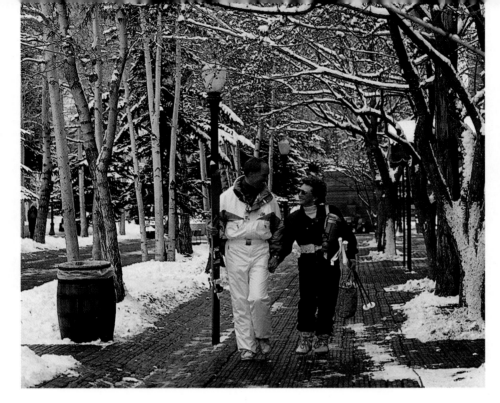

Successful middle-aged couples have managed to share feelings and activities throughout their marriage, in spite of competing demands of jobs and children. They continue to express love and concern both verbally and physically.

ents do suffer from these feelings, and most go through a period of adjustment when their children leave the nest. But the empty nest is a boon for many parents, giving them more time and energy to invest in their marriage. To emphasize the positive aspects of this time, we prefer the term **spacious nest**. There is more room in the home for the parents' things—and more money and time in the marriage for each other.

The opposite of the spacious nest is the parental nest refilled with **boomerang kids**—adult children who return home as a result of divorce, job loss, or an inability to make it in the "real world" (Okimoto & Stegall, 1987). Bernice Neugarten and Dail Neugarten have noted, "The so-called 'empty nest' . . . is not itself stressful for most middle-aged parents. Instead, it is when the children do not leave home at the appropriate time that stress occurs in both the parent and the child" (1987, p. 35).

Today, middle-aged parents of young adults are less likely to find themselves with empty nests than were their counterparts 20 or 30 years ago. More young adults are postponing marriage or are marrying and divorcing. This phenomenon has also been called the **cluttered nest**—adult children returning to the parental nest to live after college graduation while they get established professionally and financially and save enough money to move into their own apartments or homes (Schnaiberg & Goldenberg, 1989).

Recent data from the U.S. Bureau of the Census indicate that about one in four (27%) of those 18–34 years of age in this country are living with their parents, according to Andrew Cherlin (1993), a family demographer. Low wages and high unemployment contribute to the difficulty young people have in making it on their own. Dividing this age group into two subgroups, the researchers found that in 1992, 54% of all 18- to 24-year-olds and 12% of all 25- to 34-year-olds were living with their parents. "Very, very few people will live with their parents when they get married, but if you aren't married, being at home can look like a reasonable alternative. Thirty years ago, it wasn't that acceptable to still be living at home after you were 20 years old. Now it's very common" (Cherlin, 1993).

Those who have studied this phenomenon offer some practical suggestions to help parents launch their adult children (Okimoto & Stegall, 1987). They suggest that parents should:

- Remind their children that they are living in the parents' home.

- Consider charging their children for room and board.

- Set the house rules.

- Limit financial support.

- Support all signs of independence and encourage their children to seek employment, even in a less-than-desirable job.

However, the problems associated with boomerang kids and cluttered nests may be exaggerated. Parents generally understand the difficulties young people face in trying to make it on their own in the working world and are usually willing to help out. Most parents like their adult children and enjoy their company. Research on parents who have adult children living at home indicates that the majority are satisfied with the living arrangement and have mostly positive relationships with their adult children (Aquilino & Supple, 1991).

"What was I supposed to do?" one middle-aged mother in suburban Washington, D.C., asked rhetorically. "Slam the door in her face?" This woman was talking about her daughter, who returned home with two preschool-aged children after her divorce. "She had no money. Her husband's lawyer was threatening to take the kids away, and she was so depressed I thought she might overdose on pills. I had to help. I love my daughter and I love my grandchildren.

"I knew they wouldn't be with us forever. I knew she would be getting back on her feet soon enough. I knew I could help. What are families for?"

Caught in the Middle: The Sandwich Generation

Besides struggling with adolescents, young adults leaving home, and boomerang kids, those in their middle years are also apt to have growing responsibilities for aging parents. For this reason, middle-aged parents have been described as the **sandwich generation.**

Caring for an elderly family member can be a burden for the caregiver. But it can also increase intimacy between a parent and an adult child. One study of 133 pairs of adult caregiving daughters and their elderly mothers reported that about half the mothers and daughters saw their relationship as having been positively affected by the caregiving situation, while most of the rest reported no change in the quality of their relationships (Walker, Shin, & Bird, 1990). Caregiving also gives the younger generation the opportunity to return in some small way the many kindnesses the older generation bestowed upon them early in their life (Allen & Walker, 1992; Walker, Pratt, & Oppy, 1992).

Caregiving is not a one-way street. Even very troubled and frail older adults have many things to offer to the younger generation, including good advice, the wisdom and perspective that comes from a long life, financial aid, and friendship.

For some middle-aged parents, though, the stress of caring for both adolescent and young-adult children and for frail aging parents can be too great. Exhaustion and anger can boil over, generating intergenerational conflicts. These can also produce neglect or abuse of the elderly, unfortunately relatively common in the United States (Stull, Bowman, & Smerglia, 1994; Winston, 1994).

Grandparenthood

If I had known grandchildren would be this fun, I would have had them first.
—BUMPER STICKER

The most recent data available from a national survey of people aged 65 or older reveal that 75% have living grandchildren. Many people become grandparents long before age 65; the first grandchild is often born when individuals are in their early or mid-40s (Aldous, 1995; Troll, 1989).

For most people, the grandparent-grandchild interaction is very enjoyable. Three fourths of those with grandchildren have contact with them weekly (Troll, 1989). Although grandparents are not directly responsible for the well-being of this younger generation, they do have a vested interest in the development of their grandchildren. They want their grandchildren to pass on family traditions, and they may offer suggestions from a distance.

In one study, 90 grandmothers were asked about the value of the grandparent-grandchild relationship to them (Timberlake, 1980). Eighty percent said they valued the intergenerational relationship because it provided a continuation of themselves through another generation. Statements like "Oh, she certainly has Grandma's eyes!" or "He sure is stubborn—just like Grandpa was" reflect this attitude. Timberlake also found that three of five grandmothers said grandchildren filled a need for creativity, accomplishment, competence, and a reconfirmation of their own identity. Building a relationship with a grandchild is certainly a creative endeavor and gives the grandparent a sense of accomplishment. Further, nurturing such a relationship takes great skill and reinforces the grandparent's sense of self-worth and sense of importance to the family as a whole (Doress & Siegal, 1987).

Because grandparents usually do not have day-to-day responsibility for child-rearing and do not have to discipline the child, they can often build a more stress-free relationship with the grandchild than the parents can. From the parents' perspective, the grandparent is often accused of "spoiling" the youngster. From the grandparent's perspective, the good fortune of grandparenthood is accentuating the positive. One anonymous humorist explained that "the reason grandparents and grandchildren have such strong affection for each other is that they have a common enemy."

Because they do not have to bother with the daily chores of child-rearing, grandparents are free to develop a more creative relationship with their grandchildren, sharing activities and interests with them. For most grandparents, one of the greatest satisfactions of grandparenthood is seeing a continuation of themselves through another generation.

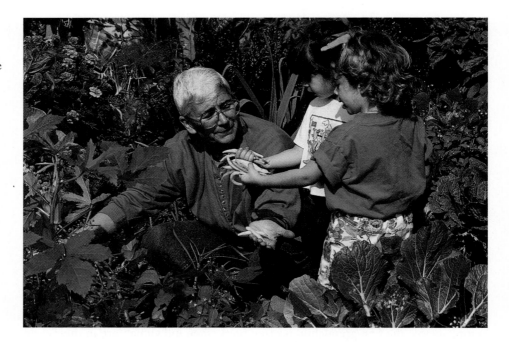

By and large, the grandparent role is mutually enjoyable for grandparents and grandchildren, and it gives the parents a welcome break. It is not without cares, however; the stress of grandparenting can sometimes overwhelm and tire out grandparents. But most often the role is one of joy. "I can enjoy these kids so much now . . . so much more than I really could my own kids. I don't have to worry about them. Their mom and dad can do the worrying."

Clarice Orr and Sally Van Zandt have written movingly about the importance of grandparents:

> Grandparents are significant family resources to enrich the lives of their grandchildren. Perhaps through more intergenerational contact, grandparents can "patch and mend" some of the "raveled ends" and "tattered seams" of the new extended family. They will realize that by their actions they can sprinkle stardust in the eyes of their grandchildren. Above all, elders need to learn there are but two lasting bequests they can give their children and grandchildren: one is roots and the other is wings. (Orr & Van Zandt, 1987, p. 87)

Family Life in the Later Years

The later years of life can be bittersweet. For those who were successful in raising a family and planning for retirement, the later years are easier than for those who have family or financial problems. Some older adults experience loneliness and isolation. Many must make do on limited funds, and elder abuse by younger family members occurs in some families. Suicide is slightly more common in the later years than in the earlier years (McIntosh, 1991).

U.S. society is going through a "demographic revolution" as the life span of the population increases. Since 1900, the average life expectancy in the United States has increased from 47 years to 75 years (Brubaker, 1991). Average life expectancy differs somewhat between men and women: For men it is 72.0 years; for women, 78.8 years. Also, the longer individuals live, the longer they can be expected to live. When individuals reach age 45, their life expectancy increases to 78 years. When they reach age 65, their life expectancy rises to 82. If they live to age 85, on average, they will live 6 years longer (Metropolitan Life Insurance Co., 1993).

Due to increased life expectancy, our society is growing older. At the turn of the century, fewer than 1 in 8 Americans was over age 55, and only 1 in 25 was 65 years old or older. By the mid-1980s, about 29% were 55 or older, and about 1 in 9 Americans was at least 65 years of age. More older people were women: Among those ages 65–69, there were only 81 men for every 100 women; and among 70- to 74-year-olds, there were only 72 men for every 100 women (Brubaker, 1991).

Defining Old Age

Old age is often said to begin at 65, which in our society is the typical age of retirement. But any exact chronological starting point for old age is bound to be arbitrary. In some parts of the world, where life expectancy is lower, a person might be old at 35 or 40. Even in our own society, we see enormous variation among older adults. We all know active 75-year-olds and feeble 50-year-olds.

Part of the reason for this variation is that "old age" is quite a long period of time, encompassing many phases and changes. Duvall and Brent Miller (1985) divides older adults into three distinct groups: (1) the young-old, those between 55 and 65, who are still working and at the peak of their social and vocational status in life; (2) the middle-old, those between 65 and 75, the majority of whom are retired and in good health and who have abundant time to follow their interests; and (3) the old-old, those over age 75, who as a group tend to be the frailest, loneliest, and poorest of the old.

Aging is in part a psychological phenomenon. How an older person feels depends largely on his or her mental attitude toward both the accomplishments of the past and the possibilities of the future. For most purposes, a person who feels "young at heart" *is* still young.

Of course, aging is also a biological reality, and some variations among older adults are a result of their different genetic heritages. Aging is also a social phenomenon. If society forces people into retirement at 65, it is in effect declaring them to be old. Such social definitions are powerful influences on how a person feels and acts. Finally, aging is part of the family process, one that occurs in the context of ongoing interpersonal relationships with spouses, parents, children, and other family members. The attitudes of these important others help us redefine ourselves as we grow older.

Older couples often have more time to enjoy leisure activities together. They may also return to hobbies or activities they previously did not have time to enjoy while working.

Despite the challenges of aging—the wrinkles, the lower energy levels, the failing eyesight or poor hearing—many people adapt to those changes and continue to live fruitful lives. How we as individuals, and as members of families and communities, define the later years powerfully influences our well-being during this time.

Conventional Wisdom About Old Age

Grow old along with me! The best is yet to be, The last of life, for which the first was made.

> —ROBERT BROWNING (1864, in Jack, 1970, p. 811)

Many people in our society accept the conventional wisdom about old age. It is important to set the record straight about these false beliefs, though, because older adults suffer from prejudice in much the same way that other groups in our society do. When one judges an older person negatively without even knowing the person, one is guilty of **ageism.**

At 65, You're "Over the Hill"   Attitude has a good deal to do with how "old" one is. People whose attitudes toward life remain positive generally lead happier and more fulfilling lives in their later years. Many symptoms popularly associated with old age—cognitive impairment, falling, dizziness, loss of bladder control, and loss of appetite—are symptoms of disease, not of normal aging.

Table 13.1 Sexual Activity Among Older Adults

FREQUENCY OF SEXUAL INTERCOURSE	39–50		51–64		65+	
	M	**F**	**M**	**F**	**M**	**F**
A few times a week	54%	39%	63%	32%	53%	41%
Weekly	29	29	18	33	16	33
Monthly	9	11	11	8	20	4
Rarely	8	21	8	27	11	22

Source: The Janus Report on Sexual Behavior (p. 25) by S. S. Janus and C. L. Janus, 1993, New York: Wiley. Copyright 1993 by S. S. Janus and C. L. Janus. Reprinted by permission.

Most Older Adults Are Poor   Median annual income decreases after people reach about age 55. For example, households with adult members age 45–54 have the highest median income before taxes: $44,540. In households with adult members age 55–64, median income before taxes is $34,062; for the 65-and-older age group, median income falls to $17,160 (U.S. Bureau of the Census, 1994, p. 465). However, almost 75% of those over age 65 own their own home free and clear, and their household expenses are generally lower because their children no longer live with them.

A Harris poll found that 68% of all the people in the United States under age 65 thought that money was a problem for older people but that only 17% of those 65 or older considered money a problem (Hunt, 1982). Older adults have relatively lower incomes than younger people, but most do not perceive this to be troublesome.

Older Adults Lose Their Sex Drive   Young people find it difficult to imagine that their parents make love, let alone their grandparents and great-grandparents. Yet most older people enjoy sex, but they have sexual intercourse less often than when they were younger (Cross, 1993; Hodson & Skeen, 1994; Mayo Foundation for Medical Education and Research, 1993). In one study of 202 healthy retirement-home residents ages 80–102, the researchers found that 88% of the men and 72% of the women fantasized about being intimate with a partner (Bretschneider & McCoy, 1988). Sexual feelings and sexual behaviors can continue across the life span. Notable exceptions can be people who have some kind of physical disability and those who believe they shouldn't enjoy sex at their age.

The *Janus Report*, a national survey of sexual behavior, found that sexual activity was higher in men than in women. There was some decrease in frequency as people become older, but the rate did not decrease as dramatically as many assumed (Table 13.1).

Older Adults Are Usually Sick   People over 65 have about half as many *acute* illnesses as those between 17 and 44. It is true, of course, that *chronic* conditions tend to accumulate over time, and older adults commonly suffer from sensory losses—hearing, vision, and taste. But as the American Association of Retired Persons (1986) points out, these problems do not keep most older adults from enjoying an active, healthy life. People who have adapted to change throughout life will likely find ways to cope with most of the changes that aging brings.

Older Adults Become Senile   The term *senility* is not often used by gerontologists today because it has little specific meaning. Although brain damage can be caused by a series of small strokes, most progressive organic brain impairment is caused by disease, such as Alzheimer's disease. Assuming that memory loss or change in behavior in older adults is a function of age can cause one to neglect looking for a disease that might be successfully treated. Why should an older person's depression or anger be attributed simply to the aging process? Might it not have roots in some life occurrence? (See Blieszner & Shifflett, 1990; Rybash, Roodin, & Santrock, 1991.)

Most Older Adults End Up in Nursing Homes   Eighty percent of older adults who are sick and need long-term care are cared for by their family. On any given day, less than 5% of the people in the United States over age 65 are in a nursing home, and most of those people are over age 85. African American families are less likely to institutionalize their elderly family members than are White families (J. Burr, 1990). Few families abandon their loved ones in their later years, and few families wantonly "warehouse" older members in a nursing home. It is also probably safe to say that the vast majority of nursing homes have dedicated staffs and try very hard to meet the needs of infirm older people.

Most Older Adults Are Lonely   The conventional wisdom about the lonely elderly brings to mind a picture of a frail old man sadly rocking in his chair on the front porch of a public home for the aged. No one comes to visit him, and he babbles to himself of times gone by. There are certainly cases like this, but older adults as a group are not necessarily lonely. John Woodward (1988) has studied loneliness across the life span for more than 25 years and has found that older adults have, on average, the lowest loneliness scores. His findings argue against the stereotype that the later years are a time of emptiness and endless reminiscence.

Woodward cautions, however, that his research does not indicate that older adults are *not* lonely, only that of all the groups he and his colleagues have studied, they are the *least* lonely. "Loneliness is a central and inevitable theme in human existence," Woodward contends. "Everyone gets lonely. Some elderly are abjectly lonely, and some adolescents are rarely lonely."

Older Adults Are Isolated from Younger Family Members   More than half of all people over age 65 who have children live either in the same household with an adult child or in the same neighborhood as their child (Troll, 1989, 1994). Contact with other family members, especially adult children, is rather frequent. Most older adults enjoy their privacy, preferring not to live in the same house as their adult children and their grandchildren. Of older people who have adult children but live alone, however, half live within a 10-minute distance of a child. Half of the older people with children had seen one of their adult children the day they were interviewed for this national study, and about three quarters had seen at least one of their adult children during the week preceding the interview. Even in those cases where the geographical distance between them is considerable, older and younger family members tend to stay in contact (Dewit, Wister, & Burch, 1988).

What about the quality of these contacts—a much more difficult characteristic to measure? One way to measure quality is to ask if people help each other. In a national study, 7 out of every 10 older adults with children said they helped their children and 7 out of every 10 older adults helped their grandchildren. Five out of every 10 even helped their great-grandchildren. Seven out of 10 older people also said they received help from their children. This help included home repairs and housework, care in an illness, and different kinds of gifts. In addition, older people helped their adult children by caring for grandchildren. In short, it appears that older people are not isolated from younger family members and that these contacts are generally happy ones (Mancini & Blieszner, 1991).

Retirement

The stereotyped view of retirement is as a dreary, downhill period of life in which people lose their self-esteem and immerse themselves in memories of better days. They stop being productive working citizens and slowly waste away. To the contrary, research shows that retired people are no more likely to be sick or depressed than people of the same age who are still on the job. In fact, most people adapt satisfactorily to retirement, with few long-term changes in their health, psychological well-being, or family relationships (Fletcher & Hansson, 1991).

There are, of course, examples of people who find retirement difficult and depressing. A woman said of her recently retired husband, "He used to be a powerful executive with 200 employees under him. He would work long, hard hours and then come home to relax and enjoy his hobbies. He retired 5 years ago, and ever since he's been terribly depressed."

Fortunately, positive retirement stories are the general rule. Most men and women report they adjust quite well to voluntary retirement, and studies consistently find that satisfaction with life remains fairly high for the majority of retired people. Those who have difficulty with retirement are often those who have had difficulty making major transitions in life, those who are shy or lonely, and those with few instrumental (task-oriented or proactive) and communal (social) abilities (Fletcher & Hansson, 1991).

Retirement from the working world has traditionally not been as difficult a task for women as for men because women usually have household responsibilities that make the transition smoother. But Carolyn Kitchings Johnson and Sharon Price-Bonham (1980) point out that employment is not a secondary role for *all* women. Some women find retirement quite difficult, and the proportion of women in this category will presumably increase as the percentage of women in the workforce grows.

As with any major life transition, retirement takes some adjustment. Retired people report a number of problems associated with this transition, including sleep difficulties, difficulty figuring out what to do with themselves, and sadness over not seeing work friends and colleagues regularly. But other retirees are quick to point out that they have gotten involved in so many new activities that they have less free time than they did when they were working and would like to slow down a bit.

Most older people adjust well to voluntary retirement, especially those who get involved in new activities.

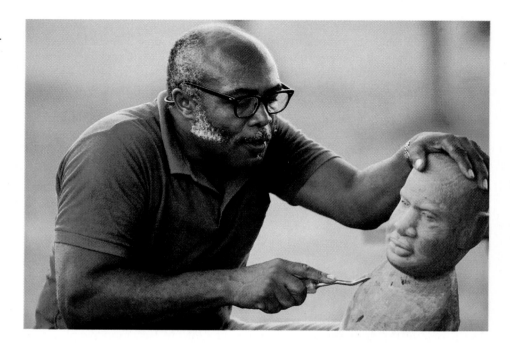

Retirement affects marriage in different ways. For couples who place a high value on intimacy and family relationships, retirement can bring more freedom to enjoy each other and the family. Some wives—especially those who always assumed traditional roles and traditional divisions of labor—are pessimistic about the husband's impending retirement, perhaps fearing the retiree will intrude on their domestic territory.

Family Dynamics and the Aging Couple

A number of family researchers have studied long-term marriages, and their findings give a picture of the quality of such relationships. When interviewed about **longevis marriages**—marriages that last 50 years or more—George Rowe and Marcia Lasswell divided them into three categories: (1) couples who are very happy and blissfully in love, (2) couples who are very unhappy but who continue the marriage out of habit or fear, and (3) couples in between, who are neither very happy nor very unhappy and accept the situation (cited in Sweeney, 1982). Lasswell estimated the "very happy" number at roughly 20% of the total, and the "very unhappy" number at 20%. Both researchers also found a negative relationship between the number of children couples had and marital happiness: Couples with larger families tended to have less happy marriages. "We can't explain that, except the study indicated a dip in marital happiness is almost always concurrent with the time the children are a heavy responsibility for parents," Rowe said (p. 23). He theorized that the more children a couple has, the longer this period of responsibility lasts.

Spouses who got along well in their early years are likely to get along well in their later years, too. For some couples, in fact, marriage gets better with age.

Timothy Brubaker (1985) reviewed 25 studies of older couples' relationships and identified three common patterns in the studies:

- Some couples experience a decline in marital quality during the middle years of the marriage, and then the marriage improves in the later years.

- For some couples, the marriage declines gradually in quality as the years go by, with the trend line from the newlywed days to later life moving steadily downward.

- For some couples, the trend line remains stable in the middle years and into the later years. Those who were happy when the children were at home will remain happy when the children leave home and when they retire. Those who were unhappy as a couple when the kids were at home will continue to be unhappy when the nest empties and they retire.

In general, the quality of the marital relationship shows continuity over the years. Couples who did not get along well in their early years together are likely not to get along well in the later years of their marriage. "In the later years, those who have vital, rewarding relationships will most generally experience continued positive interactions within the marriage, while those who have difficult, unsatisfying relationships will most likely experience continued negative marital interactions" (Brubaker, 1991, p. 229).

Losing a Spouse

The death of a spouse is a difficult life transition for most, and for some it is a devastating personal crisis (Van Zandt, Mou, & Abbott, 1989). Brubaker (1985) outlined three characteristic stages of the grieving process:

1. **Crisis-loss stage of grief.** In the first few days and weeks after the loss, the survivor is in a chaotic state of shock. Common reactions are "I can't believe this is happening to me." "I'll do anything to bring her back." "What am I going to do now?"

2. **Transition stage of grief.** In the transition period, the survivor begins trying to create a new life. Grief lessens in its intensity, and the bereaved person begins to see the possibility of a life ahead.

3. **New-life stage of grief.** The survivor changes her or his lifestyle and proves to the world and to herself or himself that it is possible to live satisfactorily as a single person. The widow or widower develops an identity without the partner.

Grief lasts longer than was long believed to be the case—up to 2 years, according to research on widows. A widow's grief can include a range of feelings, from sadness and anger to fear and anxiety. The prevalence of anxiety in the first 3 years after a husband's death led one researcher to see its role in mourning as crucial (Sable, 1989). Other researchers see depression as a significant risk among bereaved spouses (Gilewski, Faberow, Gallagher, and Thompson, 1991).

"We were married for 54 years," an older woman in Fort Myers, Florida, explained. "It wasn't all perfect, but we were pretty good friends. He's been gone now for 7 months and I'm still adjusting. I'm doing okay, but not great. I'm trying to get involved in some church groups, and in a senior aerobics class.

"I'll make it through this, but I don't like it. The hardest part is the evenings. It's just so quiet without him around. This is going to take a while. We were together for 54 years, and now all of a sudden he's gone. This is going to take some time.

"When you lose someone who's been so much a part of your life for so long, you're never going to be the same. Think about it: How could you be?"

In the United States, 11 out of every 12 people who have lost a spouse are women. This is because women live about 7 years longer on average than men and because they tend to marry men older than themselves. Three out of 4 wives can expect to become widows. Widowhood involves a number of challenges: the shaping of a new identity (from a partner in a couple to a single individual), financial problems (which may force many back into the job market), and health problems. Important factors in successfully coping with the loss of a spouse include maintaining a sense of autonomy and involving oneself in social relationships and community affairs (Day, 1991).

Summary

- Middle age roughly spans the years 35–65, a period during which many couples are still raising teenagers, launching young adults and then coping with their absence from or return to the home, and entering retirement.

- The challenges of middle age include thriving (or perhaps surviving) in the working world; for many women, developing a second career outside the home; the transition of menopause and for men, "male menopause": maintaining the emotional and sexual health of the marriage; coping with the "empty" or the "cluttered" nest; and dealing with the demands of aging parents.

- Marriages fail in the middle years for five main reasons: dominance of one partner (usually the husband) in the relationship; failure to communicate and to share; excessive career involvement; extramarital involvements; and midlife changes.

- Recommendations for strengthening a marriage in the middle years include making the spouse number one, being alert to warning signs of trouble, establishing an equal partnership, helping the spouse feel important and powerful, balancing togetherness and personal growth, working to keep the sexual relationship exciting, networking with other committed couples, evaluating the marriage and attending marriage enrichment workshops, changing frustrating job situations, and changing the relationship rather than the partner.

- One of four 18- to 34-year-olds in the United States is living with his or her middle-aged parents—a phenomenon that has been called the "cluttered nest." Suggestions for launching or relaunching adult children include charging for room and board, setting house rules, limiting financial support, and encouraging all signs of independence and employment-seeking.

- People in their middle years are often "sandwiched" between two or more competing responsibilities: caring for adolescents, dealing with "boomerang kids" (adult children returning to the parental nest), and caring for their own aging parents. The results can be both positive (a closer relationship between the caregiver and the aging parent) and negative (too much stress). Social support is available to those who may need help.

- Grandparenting reinforces continuity of the generations and brings satisfaction to most grandparents. Of those 65 or older, 75% have living grandchildren.

- U.S. society is undergoing a "demographic revolution" due to the increasing life span of its population. Today, average life expectancy is 75, and at least one in nine individuals is 65 or older.

- Aging involves biological, psychological, and social factors. How individuals feel about their lives and how others view them have a lot to do with how "old" they feel.

- Conventional wisdom about old age includes that at 65, you're "over the hill"; most older adults are poor; older adults lose their sex drive; older adults are usually sick; older adults become senile; most older adults end up in nursing homes; most older adults are lonely; and older adults are isolated from younger family members. All these beliefs are untrue.

- Contrary to stereotypes of retirement as a negative period of life, approximately 75% of those who retire voluntarily adapt satisfactorily to retirement, with few long-term effects on their health, psychological well-being, or family relationships.

- Not all marriages of long duration are happy. People stay married out of habit, out of fear, or in about 20% of these marriages, because they are happy. The fewer the number of children, the happier the marriage seems to be.

- The death of a spouse is a difficult life transition for most and a devastating personal crisis for some. More women than men will lose a spouse. Important factors in successfully coping with the loss include maintaining a sense of autonomy (a belief in one's ability to direct one's own life) and being involved in social relationships and community affairs.

Key Terms

middle age	empty nest syndrome	ageism
routinization	spacious nest	longevis marriage
menopause	boomerang kids	crisis-loss stage of grief
androgen	cluttered nest	transition stage of grief
male menopause	sandwich generation	new-life stage of grief
midlife crisis	old age	

Activities

1. Discuss career issues with a middle-aged man or woman, asking the individual to trace her or his career development. What conclusions can you come to?

2. Interview your parents (if they are middle-aged) or other middle-aged individuals about the stresses of midlife and their means of coping with them.

3. Interview a middle-aged person who is caught in the middle, trying to support adolescent or young-adult children and at the same time care for an elderly family member. Prepare 10 or 15 questions for the interview, and record 5 or 6 general conclusions about the middle years from the interview. Share your ideas with other class members who have done the same thing.

4. After reading the section on grandparenthood, write down some questions for a grandparent, then interview him or her. This can be an easy and rewarding interview for young adults because grandparents and young adults often have an automatic bond.

5. Interview an older couple. Ask them to tell you the story of their family, including information about their parents and grandparents. Focus part of the interview on intergenerational relationships.

6. Write down your feelings about death and share them in a small-group discussion. Record the similarities and differences in the feelings that emerge.

Suggested Readings

Blieszner, R., & Alley, J. M. (1990). Family caregiving for the elderly: An overview of resources. *Family Relations, 39* (January), 97–102. *A wide variety of potential sources of support for families caring for an aging member with special needs.*

Bolles, R. N. (1996). *What color is your parachute? A practical manual for job-hunters and career changers.* Berkeley, CA: Ten Speed Press. *A very popular nuts-and-bolts approach for people looking for a good job.*

Boston Women's Health Book Collective. (1987). *Ourselves, growing older.* New York: Simon & Schuster/Touchstone. *An excellent book on the biological changes and social and psychological needs of older women.*

Brubaker, T. H. (1991). Families in later life: A burgeoning research area. In A. Booth (Ed.), *Contemporary families: Looking forward, looking back* (pp. 226–248). Minneapolis: National Council on Family Relations. *An excellent review of research in this area by a noted student of aging.*

Conrad, R. T. (1993). *"What should we do about mom?" A new look at growing old.* Bradenton, FL: Human Services Institute. *A loving approach to the challenge families face when older members need a great deal of specialized care.*

Hanson, R. O., & Carpenter, B. N. (1994). *Relationships in old age: Coping with the challenge of transitions.* New York: Guilford. *Predictable transitions in old age when social supports are needed.*

Kübler-Ross, E. (1986). *Death: The final stage of growth.* New York: Simon & Schuster. *A thought-provoking exploration of the meaning of death by a psychiatrist who has worked with dying people for many years.*

"Making wise decisions for long-term care." (1989). Washington, DC: American Association of Retired Persons. (AARP), 1909 K St., NW, 20049. *One of many very useful resources of interest to older people and their families produced by this organization.*

Mancini, J. A., & Blieszner, R. (1991). Aging parents and adult children: Research themes in intergenerational relations. In A. Booth (Ed.), *Contemporary families: Looking forward, looking back* (pp. 249–264). Minneapolis: National Council of Family Relations. *An excellent overview.*

Moody, R. A. (1988). *The light beyond: New explorations by the author of* Life After Life. New York: Bantam. *Fascinating reading on the question of life after life, with many people's stories of "near-death experiences," by a writer who rekindled interest in serious research on the subject.*

Sheehy, G. (1992). *The silent passage: Menopause.* New York: Random House. *A useful reference for those approaching menopause by a writer whose* Passages, *on predictable crises in middle years of life, made national headlines in the late 1970s.*

Turner, B. F., & Troll, L. E. (1994). *Women growing older: Psychological perspectives.* Thousand Oaks, CA: Sage. *Adds to the limited literature exploring how one's sex affects the aging process.*

PART V

Challenges and Opportunities

CHAPTER 14

Family Stress and Coping

Problems within families, and the stress related to those problems, are growing. More than half of all couples currently planning to marry will end up divorcing. Violence between spouses and family members occurs in 30% of all families. Sixty percent of all siblings experience at least one violent episode in their dealings with each other. One in five murder victims is killed by a family member. Roughly 4 million children are abused and perhaps 5,000 are killed by adults each year in the United States. And caseworkers estimate that for every physically abused child, 5–10 others may be neglected (U.S. Bureau of the Census, 1995). Untold numbers are emotionally battered by their parents. Alcohol-related problems plague roughly one in three U.S. families, and the use and abuse of other drugs is widespread. Stress-related maladies—including heart attack, ulcers, migraine headaches, hypertension, back troubles, and possibly even cancer—are increasing.

Stress is a fact of life for individuals and families. The important question is how to manage it. Stressful events and issues can bring families closer together—or they can divide and shatter them.

This chapter looks at stress from various perspectives, exploring whether stress can be beneficial, how much stress is too much, the connection between stress and physical health, and why the ability to deal with a stressor varies from family to family. Researchers have found both that families experience certain common types of stressors and that some of these are more prevalent at certain stages of the family life cycle than at others. These subjects are explored, along with the characteristics of families who deal with stress successfully.

Cultural Perspective on Family Stress

Some of the commonalties about family stress across cultural groups are as follows:

- *Families from all cultural groups experience family stress.* Although the causes of family stress and the types of issues that are most stressful may vary by cultural group, all families seem to experience and understand the concept of family stress.

- *All stressors either begin or end up in the family.* No matter what the origin of a stressor, it most likely will end up affecting the family system and its members.

- *All families must find resources (internal and/or external) to help them cope with or manage the stress in their lives.* Families from various cultural groups probably differ in the specific resources they use to manage family stress. Although research on understanding successful coping strategies in various cultures is under way, little work focuses on identifying the range and variety of coping resources used by different cultural groups. This type of information could greatly enhance our cross-cultural understanding of stress and coping.

- *All families have some internal strengths for managing stress in their family system.* Many studies of various ethnic groups have assumed a deficit model of family functioning—that is, a model based on the premise that something is wrong or missing. More often than not, this model is Eurocentric as well, assuming that the features of Western families are essential in all families. Cross-cultural studies of families have seldom sought to identify family strengths within a cultural group; instead, they have focused on the problems in families from different cultures. By building on a family strengths model, it is possible we will more clearly identify useful coping strategies across cultures.

- *To manage their stress, families tend to first use internal resources (those inside the family system) before seeking external resources (those outside the family system).* Across cultural groups, most families rely on their internal resources first, seeking external help only after internal resources have proven to be inadequate.

"When the tractor rolled and Dad was killed, we were stunned," Joanne said. "We were in a state of shock for several days. It was like walking through a terrible dream world. I was 17 at the time. After the funeral and after all the food that people had brought over ran out, we kind of had to start picking up the pieces of our lives. We clearly had no choice. The cows needed milking. Life was going on without us.

"We relied on ourselves, first and foremost. I took on a lot of Mom's responsibilities, and Mom took on much of what Dad had been doing. Tommy, who was 15 at the time, became a big part of Dad, too.

"But we couldn't do it alone, without Dad, so Uncle Harley and Uncle Bud jumped right in. I love them for it. They each gave us a couple hours a day for several months till we could get adjusted, and countless hours at planting time and harvest. The neighbors all jumped in, too. Fortunately, in a small farming community people look out for each other. The work they put in was helpful, but I still think the most helpful thing was we didn't feel so all alone out there on the 640 acres. That could get to you, terribly quick."

In addition to seeking commonalties, it is also important to be open to differences, which increase our appreciation of diversity and our opportunities to learn. The definition of the family system used here is broad and includes both the nuclear and extended family systems. In many cultures, the extended family system often plays a more significant role as a resource for managing family stress than the nuclear family system.

The Curvilinear Nature of Stress

Hans Selye, the pioneer of stress research, defined stress as "the nonspecific response of the body to any demand made upon it" (1974, p. 14). It is immaterial

Figure 14.1 The Curvilinear Nature of Stress

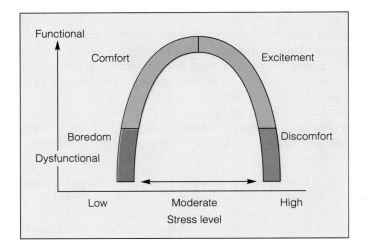

whether the demand is positive or negative; both create the same physiological response. **Stress** is the body's reaction to the demands of life. **Stressors** are external events that cause an emotional and/or a physical reaction. Although people often think of stress as negative, its impact depends on how it is viewed by each individual. Stress is a very personal issue.

A paradoxical aspect of stress is that both too much and too little stress are problematic for individual and family functioning, but moderate levels of stress are usually positive. In other words, there is a *curvilinear relationship* between stress and functioning (Figure 14.1). Thor Dahl (1980) described four reactions to different levels of stress: boredom, comfort, excitement, and discomfort. Too little stress is unhealthy and is associated with boredom and lack of motivation. Too much stress is also unhealthy and leads to feelings of discomfort, or **distress.** Low to moderate levels of stress are healthy and can feel comfortable. Moderate to high levels of stress can also be healthy, creating excitement and energy. This motivating, positive kind of stress is called **eustress.**

Another paradoxical aspect of stress is that individuals continually need to seek an appropriate balance between too much and too little stress. This dynamic balance can often be difficult to achieve; most people feel pushed toward higher levels of stress. A major aspect of life is the attempt to cope with stressors effectively. Happiness is not so much the absence of stress as it is the ability to manage stress effectively.

Stress and Life Events

Much of the current research on the relationship between life changes and signs of emotional and physiological stress in individuals has been heavily influenced by the work of T. H. Holmes and R. H. Rahe (1967). These researchers developed a scale of 43 "life events" that require some type of change of behavior, or readjustment. The scale is called the Holmes and Rahe Social Readjustment Rating

Table 14.1 Holmes and Rahe Stress Rating Scale	
EVENT	**IMPACT (POINTS)**
* 1. Death of spouse	100
* 2. Divorce	73
* 3. Marital separation	65
4. Jail term	63
* 5. Death of close family member	63
6. Personal injury or loss	53
* 7. Marriage	50
8. Fired at work/lost job	47
* 9. Marital reconciliation	45
*10. Retirement	45
*11. Change in health of family member	44
*12. Pregnancy	40
*13. Sex difficulties	39
*14. Gain of new family member	39

Note: Impact points indicate the severity of the impact of the stressor on individuals, couples, or families.
*Stressors related to couples and families.

Source: "The Social Readjustment Rating Scale" by T. H. Holmes and R. H. Rahe, *Journal of Psychosomatic Research, 11,* p. 213. Copyright 1967 by Elsevier Science Inc. Reprinted by permission of the publisher.

Scale, but it is often referred to as the Holmes and Rahe Stress Test. These life events include personal, family, financial, and occupational stressors. Table 14.1 lists the top 14 stressors identified by Holmes and Rahe. It is noteworthy that 11 of the top 14 stressors are marriage and family issues. In fact, the scale could legitimately be called a Marriage and Family Stress Test.

Holmes and Rahe found a relationship between life changes and health. Of those people who scored between 0 and 150 points on the scale, more than 30% experienced a serious negative health change in the 2 years that followed. (A serious negative health change might be the development of an ulcer, enduring depression, cancer, the onset of alcoholism, or a heart attack.) Of those who scored between 151 and 300 points, about 50% experienced a serious negative health change in the 2 years that followed. And of those who scored more than 300 points, almost 90% experienced a serious negative health change in the 2 years following the rating.

Holmes and Rahe theorized that physical and emotional problems are likely to occur when individuals experience a cluster of major and minor changes in life. It is noteworthy that the life events on the scale are not necessarily negative. Having a baby is usually seen as a positive occurrence, for example, but it is also stressful and requires readjustment.

One middle-aged woman scored above 700 on the Holmes and Rahe Stress Test. She received her divorce in January and remarried in August, her new hus-

Figure 14.2 Interrelationships Between Various Types of Stress

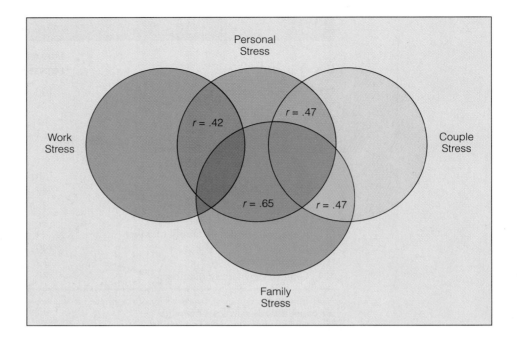

band moved out 3 months later, and by late November she had a new live-in companion. Her mother died during the year, and the woman started and lost two jobs. She had a sprinkling of other life changes during the year, including two car accidents and many bills. As might be predicted, she became very depressed and considered suicide.

Stress Pile-Up

An important concept is that of **stress pile-up:** the occurrence and after-effects of several stresses within a short period of time. For example, stress in a couple's relationship is often taken by each person to their job, and stress at work is often brought home. In a study of stress in 400 people, Kenneth Stewart (1988) asked questions about stress in each area of the person's life. He found that stresses in the various areas of life were interrelated. For example, family stress was highly related to personal stress, and couple stress and family stress were also very related, as were couple stress and personal stress (Figure 14.2). This study clearly demonstrated that focusing on stress in only one area of life gives at best a partial picture of the total stress in a person's life.

Stressors for Families

Researchers have provided answers to many questions about family stress, and we explore some of their work in this section.

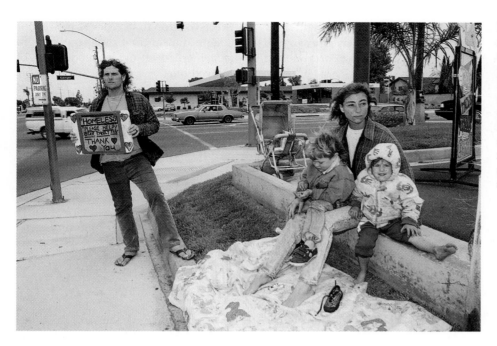

Homeless families experience a pile-up of stressors: no income, no place to live, difficulty in obtaining health care, disruption in the children's schooling, and isolation from relatives and friends. Only the most resilient families are able to survive against these odds.

Common Types of Family Stressors

Pauline Boss has done extensive research on family stress theory and has summarized many of her ideas in the book *Family Stress Management* (1988). Boss has identified 12 different types of family stressors, grouped into 6 pairs: internal and external, normative and non-normative, ambiguous and non-ambiguous, volitional and non-volitional, chronic and acute, and cumulative and isolated. She has defined these types of stressors as follows:

Internal: Events that are initiated by someone inside the family, such as getting drunk, suicide, or violence.

External: Events that are initiated by someone or something outside the family, such as earthquakes, terrorism, the inflation rate, or cultural attitudes toward women and minorities.

Normative: Events that are expected over the family life cycle, such as marriage, birth, launching an adolescent, aging, or death.

Non-normative: Events that are unexpected, such as winning a lottery, getting a divorce, dying young, war, or being taken hostage. Such events are often, but not always, disastrous.

Ambiguous: The facts surrounding the event are unclear. You may not even be sure that it's happening to you and your family. For example, your employer announces that it plans to lay off 20% of the workforce but doesn't say who.

Non-ambiguous: The facts surrounding the event are clear, including what is happening, when, how, how long, and to whom. For example, a severe thunderstorm is moving into the area for the next 2–3 hours.

Volitional: Desired, sought-after events, such as a freely chosen job change, college entrance, or a wanted pregnancy.

Chronic: A situation of long duration, such as diabetes, chemical addiction, or ethnic discrimination.

Cumulative: Events that pile up, one after the other, so that there is no time for resolution between them. In most cases, such a situation is dangerous.

Non-volitional: Events that are not sought out but that just happen, such as being laid off or the sudden loss of a loved one.

Acute: An event that lasts a short time but is severe, such as breaking a limb, losing a job, or flunking a test.

Isolated: An event that occurs alone and that can be pinpointed easily.

Boss's well-organized description of various types of stressors has helped clarify why people perceive and react differently to stress and how their reactions depend on the type and severity of the stressor.

Stressors Across the Family Life Cycle

A study of 1,000 intact families looked in a systematic way at the stressors families face at each stage of the family life cycle (Olson, McCubbin, et al., 1989). The researchers asked husbands and wives in each life cycle stage to identify the stressors and strains that their family had experienced in the past year. The percentages of couples reporting eight different types of stressors and strains at each of the seven life cycle stages are shown in Figure 14.3.

Stage 1: Young Couples Without Children Young couples indicated the most stress and strain in four areas of life: work-family strains, financial and business strains, intrafamily strains, and illness and family "care" strains. In this period, many young couples face changes in job/work situations and other problems at work, including increasing workload, dissatisfaction with the job, and conflict with the boss and other employees. Couples struggle with debts and increased expenses, as well as with the husband's absences for work-related concerns and uncompleted home tasks. Young couples also experience some personal illnesses, and illnesses of parents and relatives.

Stage 2: Childbearing Stage It is no surprise that when one or more children arrive, demands on the parents increase substantially. Families at the childbearing stage struggled primarily with financial and business strains but also with intrafamily strains, pregnancy and childbearing strains, work-family strains, and illness in the family. Financial strains increased in this period. Especially noteworthy were the strains caused by taking out or refinancing a loan; the purchase of a car; medical expenses; or a change in economic, political, or weather conditions that adversely affected the family's income. Stressors that occurred during the childbearing stage included greater involvement in outside activities, decrease in satisfaction with the job, and illness of a relative or friend.

Stage 3: Families with School-Age Children Families involved in the day-to-day routine of rearing school-age children have a new set of stresses and strains to

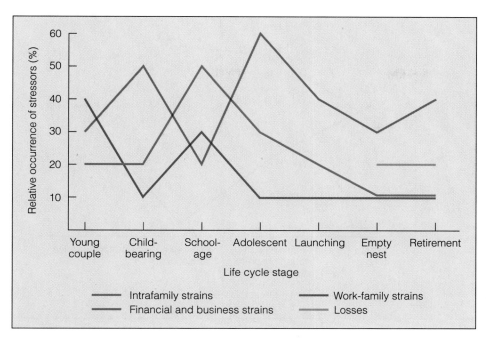

Figure 14.3 The Occurrence of Stressors Across the Family Life Cycle. *Source:* Adapted from *Families: What Makes Them Work* (2nd ed.) (p. 123) by D. H. Olson, H. I. McCubbin, H. Barnes, A. Larson, M. Muxen, M. Wilson, Sage Publications. Copyright © 1989 Sage Publications. Used with permission of the publisher.

struggle with. Although financial strains (the pressure of paying off a loan or two, and increased expenses) continue to stress some families, the majority of stressful life events associated with Stage 3 fall into the categories of intrafamily stressors and strains and work-family problems. Families with school-age children faced an increase in family-related demands, such as children's outside activities, chores that did not get done, sibling rivalry and conflicts, and child management problems. Also, father/husband absence was a concern for a good many families. Decreased job satisfaction was felt by some, work responsibilities were increasing for many, and others were changing jobs or careers.

Stage 4: Families with Adolescents   A new configuration of stressors and strains challenges families with adolescents. Financial strains concern most of these families, intrafamily strains concern some, and work-family strains concern a few. More than two thirds experienced an increase in outside activities related to adolescent children, almost half felt tasks and chores were not getting done, and about a third were having difficulty managing their teenagers. But money was the greatest concern at this stage. Teenage children are expensive. Providing food and clothing, paying the utilities, and maintaining the home were a strain on the majority of families. Some also faced payments on major loans, and changing economic conditions were hazardous for others. With adolescents nearing college age, the cost of children's education was seen as a stressor.

Stage 5: Launching Families   Financial and business strains will plague many families in the fifth stage of the family life cycle. Over half of the parents complained about increased expenses for food, clothing, energy, and home care; chil-

Figure 14.4 Family Stress and Family Satisfaction. *Source:* From *Families: What Makes Them Work* (2nd ed.) (pp. 122, 181) by D. H. Olson, H. I. McCubbin, H. Barnes, A. Larson, M. Muxen, M. Wilson, Sage Publications. Copyright © 1989 by Sage Publications. Reprinted by permission of the publisher.

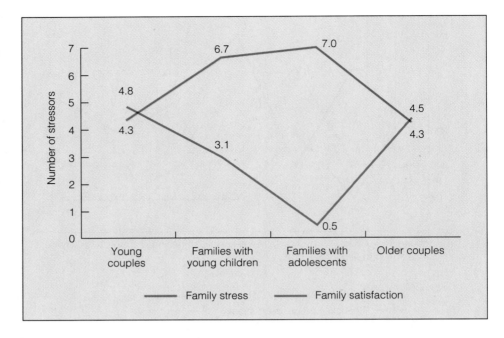

dren's education continues to be a major source of stress in the family; and loans or refinanced loans are burdensome for more than a third. Families in this stage struggle with transitions (young adult members leaving home), with nearly half of the adolescents beginning college. Families in the launching stage also experience intrafamily strains, including an increase in children's activities and an increase in tasks or chores that do not get done.

Stage 6: Empty Nest Families   As young adults leave the family to assume new roles and responsibilities, couples face additional demands. Financial strains still rank highest, followed by illness, losses, intrafamily strains, work-family strains, and marital strains. Some families struggled with chores not getting done, and about one in five couples reported increased difficulty with the husband and wife's sexual relationship. Financial hardships caused by a change in economic, political, or weather conditions were reported by more than a quarter of the couples. Other problems included the stresses of major purchases; food, clothing, energy, and home care costs; a decrease in job/career satisfaction; serious illness of a relative or friend; and death of a spouse's parent, close relative, or close friend.

Stage 7: Families in Retirement   For families in retirement, the major stressor continues to be financial, followed by serious illness or death of a parent, spouse, relative, or close friend. Work-family and intrafamily stresses are also present. Financial strains continued to be a major source of stress for 40%. A few couples were faced by threats to family investments or income. Major purchases were troublesome for some; increased expenses for medical and dental care were troublesome for others; and food, clothing, energy, and home care costs were also stressful.

Conclusions Some general conclusions can be made about stressors and strains across the family life cycle:

1. Stressors and strains are common at all stages of the family life cycle.

2. Financial strains are reported across all stages, ranking first in five of the seven stages, and intrafamily and work-family strains are also present across the stages.

3. A major pile-up of stressors and strains occurs at the adolescent and launching stages, at which couples also report the lowest level of family satisfaction (Figure 14.4).

4. A dramatic drop in stress and increase in family satisfaction occurs among older couples whose children have left home.

5. Husbands and wives generally agree in their assessments of the number of demands upon them. However, wives report slightly more demands at four stages (childbearing, school-age children, launching, and empty nest) than husbands.

Common Life Events at All Stages of the Life Cycle

Olson, McCubbin, and their colleagues (1989) also identified specific common life and family events that affected at least 10% of the families at all seven life cycle stages:

- *Incompleted tasks.* The myth is that the "normal" intact American family is well-functioning, efficient, and effective. However, incomplete tasks are a problem in every stage of the life cycle for almost half of all families.

- *Emotional difficulties in family life.* At every stage of the family life cycle, an average of 15–20% of families reported experiencing emotional problems, with the highest rates at the adolescent (19%) and launching (28%) stages.

- *Sexual difficulties between husband and wife.* An average of about 20% of couples at all stages reported sexual problems, with more problems occurring in the adolescent and launching stages.

- *Unstable economic conditions.* Because this study was conducted during a period of some economic uncertainty, it is not surprising that 25–30% of families in all stages of the life cycle reported problems associated with hard economic times. High unemployment, crop failures due to weather, political turmoil leading to cuts in government budgets, and other conditions kept many families on edge.

- *Major economic investments and purchases.* Homes, children's educations, and business investments were other major financial expenses that caused worry for families in all stages, especially those at the launching stage. Nearly half

Perhaps people who have a high tolerance for messiness and lateness come from families who have difficulty completing tasks. This difficulty is common not only among families with young children, when clutter and unfinished chores are to be expected, but during every stage of the family life cycle among almost half of all families.

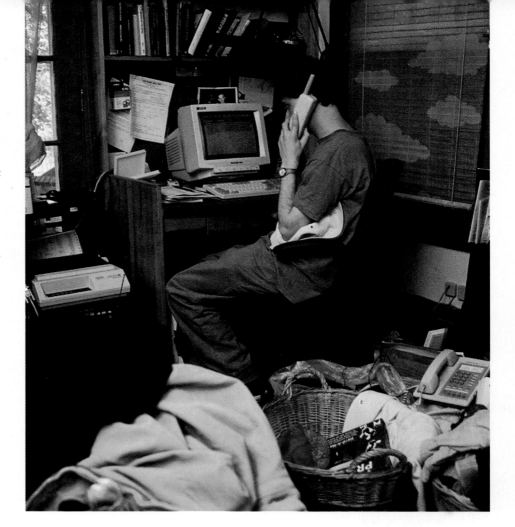

of all families had purchased a car or another major item for which they had taken out a loan.

- *Medical and/or dental expenses.* Rising interest rates, the higher cost of living, and increases in health care costs made it difficult for some families at every stage to adequately cover medical and/or dental bills, with 25–30% of families identifying these expenses as concerns. Health care expenses were especially troublesome during the childbearing and childrearing stages. Low-income families tended to sacrifice quality of care and preventive health care to reduce medical/dental expenses.

- *Money for the basics of family living.* Almost half of the families in every stage reported stress caused by the struggle to provide food and clothing, pay utilities, and cover housing costs. Families with adolescents were the most heavily burdened, with 62% reporting this concern.

- *Changing jobs and/or careers.* The challenges of the working world put a good deal of stress on families at all stages of the life cycle, but especially at the young couple stage, where nearly half (46%) experienced this issue as they

On *Día de los Muertos,* when, according to custom, the dead are permitted to visit living relatives and friends, Mexican families decorate family graves and picnic in the cemetery. This tradition, which juxtaposes the joys of life with an unsentimental acceptance of death, allows people to explicitly acknowledge the physical and psychological absence of family members who have died.

sought to establish themselves in a career. Another particularly stressful period was the launching stage, when one third of the families experienced this situation. Wives often were reentering the workforce after rearing children, and husbands were growing dissatisfied with the career they had been in for 10 or 20 years.

- *Losing, quitting, or retiring from a job.* When a family member leaves a job—by choice or by the employer's decision—there is usually a good deal of stress in the family. Although this situation can occur in any stage of the family life cycle, it was particularly common in the young couple and launching stages.

- *Illness and death in the family.* The serious illness of a close relative or family member is not confined to the later years. It affects roughly one third of families at all stages but is especially prominent in the launching and empty nest stages. Death affects about one fifth of families throughout the life cycle, but it is most prevalent in the launching, empty nest, and retirement stages.

Boundary Ambiguity and Family Stress

A valuable contribution to family stress research is Boss's (1988) definition of **family coping** as "the management of a stressful event or situation by the family as a unit with no detrimental effects on any individual in that family" (p. 60). The family system uses cognitive, affective, and behavioral processes to manage the stress.

Figure 14.5 Boundary Ambiguity and Family Stress. *Source: Family Stress Management* (p. 75) by P. Boss, 1988, Newbury Park, CA: Sage Publications. Copyright © 1988 by Sage Publications. Reprinted by permission of Sage Publications.

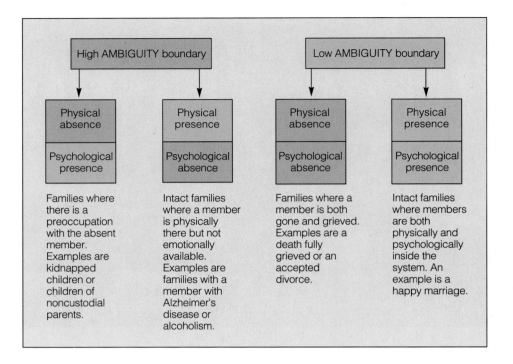

Boss also suggested that "managing stress" (rather than "coping with stress") be used to describe the outcome.

An understanding of stress is further enhanced by Boss's (1988) introduction of the term **boundary ambiguity,** a lack of clarity about whether a person is in or out of the family system. The two related variables in boundary ambiguity are physical and psychological presence or absence. Boss also linked this concept to the level of stress that a given situation creates (Figure 14.5). Low ambiguity (congruence between physical and psychological presence or absence) is related to low stress. When there is both physical and psychological absence, as in the death of a family member or an amicable divorce, it is possible for the family to grieve and then to move on with their lives. Likewise, situations in which there is both physical and psychological presence, as in a happy family or marriage, are also low in stress.

At high levels of boundary ambiguity, family stress is highest and most difficult to manage. Physical absence and psychological presence keeps the grieving process from occurring because the whereabouts and condition of the person are not known. This situation occurs when a child is kidnapped; it is also seen in noncustodial parents' concerns for their absent children. Physical presence and psychological absence, as occurs when a family member suffers from alcoholism or has Alzheimer's disease, is also very stressful. Because the member is not emotionally available, family members cannot adequately resolve issues.

Family Stress Theory

Family stress research started with the early work of Reuben Hill (1949), who began studying American families separated during World War II and reunited when the men came home. He was interested in the fact that families faced with the same event—separation—varied so widely in their ability to adjust or adapt to the event. Some families who were separated by the war adapted rather well to the situation and reunited with relative ease. Others did not weather the storms of separation and were quick to divorce upon the soldier's return.

The ABC-X Model of Family Stress

Hill's explanation of this phenomenon became known as the **ABC-X Family Crisis Model** (1958). The model states that:

A = the stressor

B = the family's crisis-meeting resources

C = the definition the family gives to the stressor

X = the crisis

Hill defined a **stressful life event** as "an event that creates a change in the family system" and a **crisis** as "any sharp or decisive change for which old patterns are inadequate." One dictionary definition of crisis is simply a turning point in life. A turning point can lead in either a negative or a positive direction. Therefore, contrary to popular view, a crisis does not have to be negative.

One could use the ABC-X Model to describe, for example, the outcome of an adolescent's running away from home. The event (A), the adolescent's running away, will turn into a crisis (X) if family members do not use their interpersonal skills as a resource (B), and if they do not (C) define the event in a way that minimizes the seriousness of the adolescent's behavior.

The Double ABC-X Family Stress Model

Hill's colleagues, H. I. McCubbin and J. Patterson (1982), developed what they called a **Double ABC-X Family Stress Model,** which they believed more accurately described family adjustment and adaptation to stressors or crises. The Double ABC-X Model builds on Hill's ABC-X Model of family stress, but whereas Hill's model focused on a single stressor event, McCubbin and Patterson's model looks at the cumulative effects of stress. The Double ABC-X Model relabels Hill's "A" factor (the stressor) "Aa," or "Family Pile-Up" of events. Aa includes family hardships and prior strains that continue to adversely affect the family, along with the stressor.

In the Double ABC-X Model, a stressor is seen as a life event (either expected or unexpected) that affects the family unit at a particular point in time. This event produces change in the family system. **Family hardships** are defined as demands on the family that accompany the stressor event. For example, the stressor event of losing one's job leads to the family hardship of reduced income. **Prior strains** are lingering residual effects of family tensions and prior stressor events that may still trouble the family.

In the Double ABC-X Model, McCubbin and Patterson take into account Holmes and Rahe's finding that stress pile-up is a factor in how people cope with crisis. Pile-up of stress can help explain why one event can be the "straw that breaks the family's back." For example, parents who abuse their children are often found to have high scores on the Holmes and Rahe Stress Test (Holmes & Rahe, 1967). They may be lonely and isolated; be stuck in a terrible marriage; have little money, education, and earning potential; and live in poor housing, with no car or telephone for contact with the outside world. A normal child growing up with a parent in this type of situation is at risk for abuse because any action on the child's part can be the "last straw" for the vulnerable parent.

When the family unit encounters a new stressor event, prior strains often worsen as the pressure builds. A married couple may be in intense conflict over money; the wife's career may set the stage for major conflict when the couple find out that their daughter has a serious and chronic illness. The daughter's illness raises questions about whether the wife, who is just beginning to advance in her career, should now stay home and care for her daughter, cut back on the hours she works, hire outside help to care for the child, or ask the father to help more with the daughter's care. This "last straw" may create so much stress for the couple that they end up getting a divorce. Hill's ABC-X Model has proved fruitful for researchers trying to understand families in crisis; McCubbin and Patterson's refinement, the Double ABC-X Model, has made the theory even more useful.

A Roller Coaster Course of Adjustment

Hill (1958) also studied families in crisis and described the course of family adjustment to a crisis as a "roller coaster course of adjustment." According to Hill, family adjustment involves: (1) a period of disorganization, (2) an angle of recovery, and (3) a new level of organization.

As an example, consider how the birth of a stillborn baby affects most families. Such an event is, of course, terribly painful for the parents, surviving siblings, and other family members; all of them initially experience loneliness and despair (DeFrain, Martens, Stork, & Stork, 1986). The course of adjustment for the average parent of a stillborn child is charted in Figure 14.6.

The process of recovering from a crisis like the birth of a stillborn baby takes a long time. Two to three years seems to be about the average for parents, but five years of grief is not uncommon. The recovery process lasts longer for families who believe it is not healthy to talk about death. This conspiracy of silence probably makes a couple's pain much greater than it might otherwise be. Couples who grieve openly, talking and crying with loved ones and friends, recover more quickly. It also appears that recovery takes about the same amount of time for men and women.

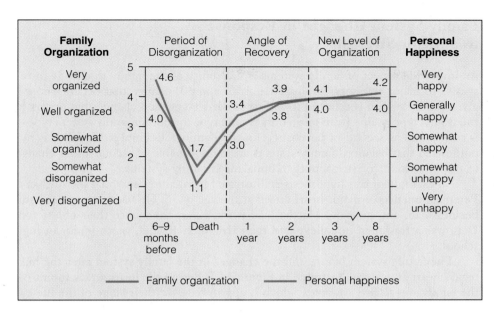

Figure 14.6 Family Organization and Personal Happiness After a Stillborn Baby (couple scores). *Source:* Reprinted and adapted with permission from *Stillborn: The Invisible Death* by John DeFrain, Leona Martens, Jan Stork, and Warren Stork. Copyright © 1986 Jossey-Bass. First published by Lexington Books.

A common myth is that men are somehow "stronger" than women, that they can stand up better against pain. Men who act tough and do not have the courage to reach out for the help they need take longer to heal than those who are not afraid to admit their hurt.

> "It was very difficult for me after the baby died," Joseph said. "Allison was in the hospital for a week after the stillbirth with complications from the delivery. She was very, very ill. Somehow I had to keep on going. I went to work every morning because my boss is about as understanding as a rock. I snuck out to the hospital during lunch break every day.
>
> "Right after work ended at 4:30, I'd run over to our child care provider's, get the kids, take them home, and feed them. Then I'd jump in the car with them again and go get my mom, and she'd come over and watch them while I went to the hospital for a couple of hours with Allison. Then home, crash, sleep a second, and start all over the next morning at 5:30. On and on and on. I thought I would lose my mind, but I just couldn't because Allison was so ill.
>
> "She recovered slowly from it all, and I had to be terribly, terribly strong. I had to go into a kind of trance to get through it. After a couple of months, though, she was getting a little better, and one Saturday I just cracked. I was looking out the back window at our neighbor holding her new baby, and I threw a cookie jar at the wall. Man! Peanut butter cookies flying everywhere.
>
> "Allison knew right away what was happening. She took me in her arms, and we sat down on the couch and I cried and cried. It was finally my turn to grieve for baby Jamie. I had never had time before that."

Family System Changes in Response to a Major Stressor

An important aspect of family systems is the ability of the family to change in response to major stressors. As discussed in Chapter 3, change that occurs *within* a given family system is referred to as first-order change, and change that occurs in the system type itself—from one family system type to another family system type—is referred to as second-order change. In the Family Circumplex Model, it is hypothesized that balanced family systems are more capable of second-order change in response to major stressors than unbalanced family systems.

An example of this hypothesis is illustrated by a family in which the husband, Peter, experienced a major heart attack at the age of 56. He had been a successful businessman, and his wife, Martha, had worked part-time since their oldest son, Dan, was a freshman in college and their daughter, Rachel, was a junior in high school.

The family system before and the changes in the family system after the husband's heart attack are illustrated in Figure 14.7. Before the heart attack (point A), the family was *flexibly separated*, which is appropriate for their stage of the life cycle. Immediately after the heart attack (point B), the family system became *chaotically enmeshed* because the family did not know if the father was going to live. The family, along with close relatives and friends, gathered at the hospital and huddled together in a mutually supportive way. This high level of closeness and bonding created enmeshment, and the fact that the family had to change all of its daily routines and roles created a chaotic system.

During the first and second week after the heart attack, the family became a little less enmeshed, but they developed a more rigid style of operating, creating a *rigidly enmeshed* system (point C). This rigidity was an attempt to bring some stability to the chaos by reorganizing some of the family routines. From about the third to the sixth week, the family changed again, becoming a *structurally connected* system (point D). Some of the rigidity was no longer needed and some of the enmeshed closeness decreased, but the family remained closer than they were before the crisis.

This example illustrates one family's ability to change system type to adapt to a crisis. The family changed several times over the 6-week period following the crisis, and these changes were beneficial in helping the family deal with this major stressor.

Families Who Manage Stress Successfully

To learn why some families cope well with stress whereas others fail, Olson, McCubbin, and their colleagues (1989) focused on specific family resources and also evaluated the type of family system around which families were organized. Two conclusions were very evident from the study: (1) balanced families coped better with stress than unbalanced families, and (2) balanced families had better communication and a larger behavioral repertoire. Balanced families cope more effectively with stress because they have more personal and relationship resources,

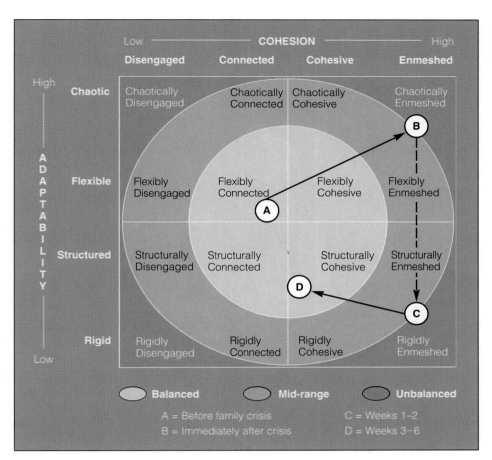

Figure 14.7 The Family System Before and Changes After the Husband's Heart Attack

including better communication and problem-solving skills. Families who cope well also have the ability to see problems as challenges to be confronted or dealt with head-on, rather than avoided or denied.

At the adolescent and launching stages of the life cycle, when family stress is the highest and family satisfaction the lowest, the researchers studied why some families with adolescents coped more effectively with stress than others did. The most significant finding was that families who coped well were headed by couples with a strong marriage relationship. Although the strength of the relationship was important across the family life cycle, the marriage became more important when adolescents were challenging authority and seeking their own independence.

The study identified the specific stressors (demands) at the adolescent and launching stages and the specific resources of the couples and families who coped well. The stressors included financial strains, intrafamily struggles, work-family issues, and family transitions. The resources of the parents in families who coped well included good financial management, liking the personality of the partner, and a good network of families and friends on which they relied for support. In

Families who cope successfully with stress communicate well, have good problem-solving skills, and are usually headed by a couple whose marriage is strong and who are happy with the quality of their lives.

addition, the couple had a good sexual relationship and were very happily married. Last, they felt good about their overall quality of life, regardless of how much money they made.

Family Coping Strategies

The Chinese symbol, or pictograph, for the word *crisis* is a composite of two other pictographs: the symbols for "danger" and "opportunity" (Figure 14.8). For thousands of years, the Chinese have known that a crisis can be a dangerous time but also a time to look for new opportunities. Strong families tend to agree with that idea. Researchers found that fully 77% of the strong families reported that in the midst of the hurt and despair of a serious crisis, there were also positive occurrences (Stinnett, Sanders, & DeFrain, 1981). Eighteen percent of the families were uncertain whether anything "good" had developed out of the crisis, and only 5% were convinced that the crisis was all "bad."

What good could possibly come out of a disaster? Many families say that after they have weathered a crisis together, their relationships with each other are stronger, more positive, and more loving. People who have gone through a crisis often relate how they became stronger as individuals as well as closer to their partners and families. They grow to appreciate their families more and become more willing to share with them.

Danger   **Opportunity**

Figure 14.8 The Chinese Symbol for *Crisis*

Theoretical Perspectives

Boss (1988) clarified the difference between coping as a family resource and coping as a process and provided reasons why the concept of **managing stress** is more useful than the concept of "coping with" stress. The family's coping resources are considered strengths of individual family members, but having these strengths available does not mean the family will use them. Describing the family as "managing stress" is more accurate than saying the family is "coping." Boss (1992) also maintains that resources are derived from all aspects of life: psychological, economic, sociological, and physical.

S. E. Hobfoll and C. D. Spielberger (1992) completed an excellent overview of family stress models and research, observing the commonalties and differences among family stress theories and identifying the important family resources across a variety of models. The major resources and strengths were cohesion rather than separateness, flexibility/adaptability rather than rigidity, communication rather than privacy, boundary clarity rather than boundary ambiguity, and order and mastery rather than chaos and helplessness.

W. R. Burr and S. R. Klein (1994) have provided a systemic model of family stress that is considered less linear and deterministic than the ABC-X Model. Focusing on nine dimensions of family life (cohesion, marital satisfaction, communication, daily routines, contention, family development, leadership, family rituals, and emotional climate), the researchers interviewed 46 families who had experienced one of the following six stressors: bankruptcy, troubled teens, displaced homemaker, child with a handicap, child with muscular dystrophy, or infertility. They assessed how the family's response to the stressor influenced the functioning of the family system (roller coaster, increased functioning, no change, mixed, or decreased functioning). Their descriptive analysis demonstrated the diversity of resources that families used to manage stress.

Burr and Klein (1994) also provided an excellent summary evaluation of the coping strategies found in past studies to be the most useful for families. They identified six general coping strategies that encompass numerous specific strategies. The six major family coping strategies fall into the categories cognitive, emo-

Table 14.2 Major Family Coping Strategies	
GENERAL	**SPECIFIC**
Cognitive	Gain knowledge
	Reframe situation
Emotional	Express feelings
	Resolve negative feelings
	Be sensitive to other's emotional needs
Relationships	Increase cohesion
	Increase adaptability
	Increase trust and cooperation
Community	Seek help and support
Spiritual	Be involved in religious activities
	Maintain faith
Individual development	Develop autonomy, independence

Source: Adapted from *Reexamining Family Stress* (p. 133) by W. R. Burr and S. R. Klein, 1994, Thousand Oaks, CA: Sage. Copyright © 1994 by Sage Publications. Reprinted by permission of Sage Publications.

tional, relationships, community, spiritual, and individual development (Table 14.2).

A Case Study

Let's look closely at a family experiencing the crisis of unemployment, using the general concepts from the Burr and Klein model (see Table 14.2). The Newman family has five members: Natalie, the mother, who has been at home caring for three daughters for the past 12 years; Albert, the father, an aeronautical engineer who specializes in electrical system design for a large airplane manufacturing company; and the girls, Sylvia, 12, Natasha, 9, and Alexis, 5. The Newmans have been accustomed to a good income for the past 10 years as Albert has moved up through the ranks of his company. He rose quickly to middle management, but the bottom has fallen out of the airplane industry for the forseeable future and Albert is one of hundreds who have been laid off.

The family listens in shock as Albert explains what has happened, and in the days and weeks and months that follow, the family creates and recreates a series of plans to reorganize itself in the face of this severe crisis. The crisis is not resolved in 30 minutes as it would be in a television sit-com but becomes a jigsaw puzzle for the family, working together, to solve. Each day, solutions take form as new pieces are connected.

Being a strong family, the members are good at using many coping strategies. First, at a family meeting at the dinner table a few days after the initial shock fades, they agree that it's a bad situation but it's nobody's fault and they all will help to find solutions (a cognitive strategy and a relationships strategy). Albert notes that over the years they have accumulated enough savings to be able to hold out for at least a year if they can all work together to figure out ways of reducing their spending (a cognitive strategy and a relationships strategy).

Natalie redefines the situation, noting that it is not only a crisis but an opportunity for growth: "I had been thinking about finding a part-time job now that the girls have gotten older, and this will give me the chance to get back and polish up my accounting skills" (a cognitive strategy). Five-year-old Alexis sees the distressed look on her father's face and crawls up on his lap. "You'll be okay, Daddy. I'll take care of you," she promises, bringing tears to her father's eyes (an emotional strategy). Albert takes a deep breath and allows that if Natalie could find a part-time job, that would be great. "What I'd really like," he notes, "is to get out of the business world altogether. You know, I haven't been very happy for a long time. I'd like to find a part-time job for a while also and see if I could go back to school. I'm not too old to go in a new direction, and if I could get my master's degree or even aim toward a doctorate, maybe I could get a job teaching in a high school or college. I like young people" (a cognitive strategy).

"You're great with kids!" chimes in 12-year-old Sylvia (an emotional strategy). Natasha and Alexis add that they'll be sure to help Mom more around the house now that she's going to be working outside the home (a relationships strategy). "You won't have to pick up so much around the house because of me," Natasha adds. "I can give myself a bath now, Mom," Alexis volunteers (individual development strategies). Natalie notes that "we should tell all our friends at church about the layoff. You don't have to feel ashamed, Albert. They know how bad the industry's business has been. Someone at church might be able to find some part-time work for both of us" (a community strategy).

"I think we can get through this!" Albert concludes. "We're good people. We have each other. We will do it, and we'll be better as a family because of this" (spiritual and cognitive strategies).

> "For a period in our marriage, we made the mistake of focusing totally on the kids and our jobs and we forgot about our own personal health and our marriage," Jack said. "Something jolted us back into reality. It was when our friends Sarah and Michael divorced. It was such a shock to us. They seemed to be in such good shape together.
>
> "But when it was all over, Sarah told Mary how life had gotten to going so fast and she and Michael had just drifted further and further apart. One day, it had seemed to her like 'poof . . . it's gone.' She had asked Michael quietly to leave, and he quietly left.
>
> "We talked and talked about them, and we grieved for them and for ourselves because we could see the same thing happening with us. And we changed things for the better: We focused on our marriage, deciding it was the foundation for the whole operation.
>
> "It's really good with us now."

A Cross-Cultural Analysis

In an important study, Mary Hanline and Steven Daley (1992) observed the coping strategies used by African American, Hispanic, and Caucasian families with a disabled child and similar families without a disabled child. Each family member

Especially in times of trouble, families need a social support network. Contrary to the notion that strength means facing a problem without any help, research indicates that the strength to cope with problems comes from close connections with friends, neighbors, and relatives.

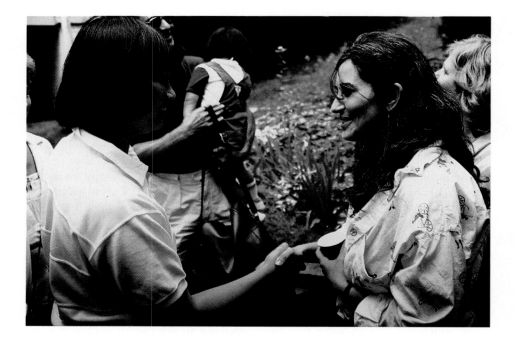

completed the F-COPES and the Family Strengths scales. The F-COPES scale measures family coping resources, including social support, spiritual beliefs, reframing, and passive appraisal. The Family Strengths scale measures family pride and family accord. To avoid reinforcing stereotypes, the researchers emphasized the strengths of each family, rather than directly comparing families from the different ethnic groups.

The strongest families used more social support from family and friends and had higher levels of spiritual beliefs. Another consistent finding was the importance of **reframing,** redefining the stressor as a challenge rather than denying the problem; this action enables family members to deal with the problem directly, building pride. Hispanic and Caucasian families, with and without a disabled child, tended more often to use passive appraisal, the denial of problems, which in turn leads to more family conflict.

Social Support

Support from one's social network is often very important in the face of problems. This **social support network** includes kin, friends, neighbors, social service institutions, and special self-help groups. Americans historically have placed tremendous emphasis on self-reliance. Most people are taught to take care of themselves, and they try to keep their problems close to home. This approach can be useful because it encourages us to "tough it out," but it is not of much help in many situations. When individualistic spirit is carried to extremes, people suffer in isolation. An important element of healthy or strong families is their ability to reach outside the family into the community for help. All families need to draw on outside resources for help, and they also need to support other families in exchange for the aid those families provide. Families should strive neither to be totally independent of nor to be overly dependent on one another. Rather, families should establish interdependence.

Carolyn Attneave (1982) has illustrated the importance of interdependence for families dealing with a crisis. A medical clinic wanted to know who would be the best risk for a new type of kidney dialysis machine. This machine could be taken home and run by patients with a little help from their family. The investigators found that families who had a large support network (15 people or more) were more likely to be successful in helping the dialysis patient than were those with a small support network (less than 15 people). Who makes up this life-saving support network? Simply put, it is an interdependent network of friends and acquaintances who share good times and bad times and who trust that they will get what they need from all the members.

The Biopsychosocial Approach and Family Problems

The family is increasingly being considered an important resource in dealing with people's psychological and physical problems. There is also growing evidence about the interrelationships among a person's physical symptoms, psychological issues, and social context (family and environment).

The **biopsychosocial approach** to stress management and health care integrates biomedical and psychosocial approaches. The idea and term originated with George Engel (Doherty & Campbell, 1988). The biopsychosocial approach contrasts with the biomedical approach, which assumes a separation between the mind and the body and does not make a connection between physical problems and a person's emotional and social context.

Within a biopsychosocial framework, an individual's physical and emotional problems are also the family's problems. Both the individual and the other family members are actors and reactors to each other. For example, a child who has a serious asthma attack and needs to go to the emergency room naturally creates a major stressor for the family. The asthma affects the family, and the family's reaction influences the care the asthmatic child will get. Asthma, then, becomes part of the family system—and thereby becomes a family problem.

The family is potentially a major resource for dealing with physical and psychological problems. A wealth of clinical research indicates that a family system can increase a patient's compliance with treatment plans and improve the success of a variety of health care programs, such as weight reduction, smoking cessation, and recovery from chemical dependence (Becker, 1989; T. L. Campbell, 1995).

Family stress is also a good predictor of serious physical symptoms and poor mental health in an individual. In a major study by G. R. Parkerson, E. Broadhead, and C. J. Tse (1995), researchers used the Duke Social Support and Stress

Scale, developed by Parkerson, to investigate the relationship between family stress and physical symptoms. They found that family stress scores were better predictors than social stressors or social support variables of severe illness, more hospitalizations, and higher medical expenses.

Medical Care and the Family

Theodor Litman (1974) states: "The family constitutes perhaps the most important social context within which illness occurs and is resolved. It consequently serves as a primary unit in health and medical care" (p. 497). Effectively implementing a biopsychosocial approach requires moving toward a more family-focused approach to medical care. As already discussed, the family provides a primary social context for dealing with stress and with physical symptoms. In their classic 1983 book, *Family Therapy and Family Medicine*, William Doherty and Mac Baird identified several reasons for the close linkage between the family and medical care:

- Family members transmit diseases to one another.

- Health behaviors (such as food preferences and exercise) are learned and maintained in the family system.

- Individual and family stress affects health and recovery from illness.

- The family helps define health and illness in its members.

- The family often decides when and where to go for health care.

- The family is the social group most immediately affected by an individual's illness and medical treatment.

- Family support facilitates recovery from illness.

As a result of the growing importance of the biopsychosocial approach to stress management and health care, more professionals are working with families as a way to help treat physical symptoms. Susan McDaniel, Jeri Hepworth, and William Doherty's 1992 book, *Medical Family Therapy: A Biopsychosocial Approach to Families with Health Problems*, discusses the values and techniques that are important for helping families help themselves. The most basic assumption is that "*all human problems are biopsychosocial systems problems:* there are no psychosocial problems without biological features and no biomedical problems without psychosocial factors" (p. 26).

Another outcome of the biopsychosocial approach is a new professional career called **medical family therapy.** McDaniel, Hepworth, and Doherty (1992) define the field as *medical* because the focus is on a variety of health problems, including chronic illness and health behaviors. It is called *family therapy* to identify the foundation for the work as family systems theory. This approach emphasizes collaboration; the patient, the family, and health care providers all work together for the best interest of the patient and family.

Copyright 1988 by Greg Howard. Reprinted with special permission of King Features Syndicate.

The Family's Influence on Health Behaviors

As suggested by the biopsychosocial approach, families can help their members cope with illness as well as help them stay healthy. A Gallup poll of 1,011 adults focused on why people take steps (such as quitting smoking, cutting down on alcohol, exercising more, losing weight, and eating a healthier diet) to improve their health habits. The poll found that a spouse or a "significant other" (for single people) had much more influence on a person's decision to adopt more positive health behaviors than did the person's doctor (Gurin, 1985).

Married people live longer than single people. Although death, heart disease, cancer, stroke, and accidents affect married people, statistically speaking, singles—especially those who are widowed or divorced—are more likely to be hit by these problems. The Gallup survey tried to discover why this is so and concluded that healthy families have the power to help their members deal constructively with stress. Healthy, supportive families also help members change their health behaviors. They are more likely than others to help their loved ones quit smoking, change their dietary habits, and establish and maintain an exercise program.

Of the adults sampled by the Gallup organization, 87% had made a behavior change to try to improve their health in the previous few years. Of those, 15% had quit smoking, 39% had reduced their alcohol consumption, 44% had learned ways of controlling job stress, 45% had started exercising more, 46% had lost weight, and 60% had become more careful about their nutritional intake.

Married men were twice as likely to have quit smoking as single men (22% versus 11%), and they were more likely to have lost weight (42% versus 31%).

Who helped these men make these difficult health-behavior changes? According to the researchers, the data were quite clear on this point: "Family and loved ones shape our health habits more than doctors do." Medical doctors were influential, especially in regard to smoking and diet and among those over 50 and those who were divorced, widowed, or separated. But in general, more people were helped by family and loved ones than by doctors.

Before family members can be helpful, however, individuals must be open to being helped. The Gallup study identified profound differences among women, single men, and married men in their ability to accept help or encouragement from other people. Single men were found to be the "real rugged individuals," the ones most likely to insist that they didn't need help from anyone in changing their behavior. Married men were much more open to help and also tended to rely on their wives for help. Many husbands credited their wives with helping them to change, but few wives felt their husbands had been of much help to them. Even though gender roles in this country are slowly evolving, women still appear to be the caretakers of the family's health.

Doherty and Thomas Campbell (1988) have written extensively about the relationship between the family and health behaviors. They have found, for example, that research clearly demonstrates that smokers tend to be married to other smokers and that married smokers often smoke about the same amount as their partner. Adolescents are more likely to smoke if the same-gender parent smokes. Smokers find it easier to quit if their partner quits at the same time. Positive reinforcement from the smoker's partner helps to prevent a relapse; nagging tends to increase the relapse rate. In other words, smoking is related to family dynamics.

Doherty and D. Whitehead (1986) studied family dynamics and cigarette smoking in more detail using the Family FIRO Model, a model with three dimensions: inclusion (being together or alone), control (who is in charge), and intimacy (personal closeness). They found that a person's ability to quit smoking was related to these family dynamics and that these dynamics could either encourage or hinder relapse.

> "I was so stubborn about my smoking addiction," said Bill, a 34-year-old electrician living in Indianapolis. "Jan would nag and nag at me, and I'd just hunker down more and more. Get more stubborn. Finally, I think she just gave up."
>
> "Yes," Jan explained, "I became totally convinced I was going to have a dead husband. His coughing in the morning was getting worse, and I figured he had irritated his lungs so totally that he would develop lung cancer. I wasn't angry with him anymore because I saw he was completely convinced he couldn't stop and was deep-down ashamed he was hooked. I finally just got depressed and stopped talking about it."
>
> "Several months later," Bill continued, "I was still puffing away, and one morning I walked into the bathroom and our 5-year-old son Joey had cut out a little red construction-paper heart and taped it on the bathroom mirror. It said in his little scrawl: 'Daddy, I don't want you to die.'
>
> "I never smoked another cigarette."

Summary

- Families in all cultures experience stress, even though the types of issues that cause the stress vary by cultural group. All stressors either begin or end up in the family, affecting family members. Families usually try to use resources within their family system to cope with problems before turning to resources outside the family.

- The relationship between stress and functioning is curvilinear. Too little stress creates boredom; too much creates discomfort and frustration. Eustress, a moderate to high level of stress, is positive, motivating, and exciting.

- Much of the early research on stress focused on life events (e.g., divorce, personal injury, pregnancy) and how those events caused stress. Holmes and Rahe developed one of the most popular stress scales, which identified how many events a person had experienced in the past year. This scale assumes that stress pile-up, the accumulation of stressful life events, is what is most problematic for people.

- Boss identified six pairs of family stressors: internal/external events, normative/non-normative events, ambiguous/non-ambiguous events, volitional/non-volitional events, chronic/acute events, and cumulative/isolated events.

- New stressors appear at each stage of the family life cycle; others are common across all stages. Financial issues concern families at all stages and all income levels. Intrafamily and work-family strains are also seen at all stages of the family life cycle.

- Stress is highest among families with adolescents, and family satisfaction is lowest at that stage. Young and older couples without children in the home tend to have less stress and higher couple satisfaction.

- Common family life events at all stages of the cycle are uncompleted tasks, a family member's emotional difficulties, sexual difficulties between spouses, unstable economic conditions, major economic investments/purchases, medical and/or dental expenses, money for the basics of family living, job-related concerns, and illness or death in the family.

- In Boss's concept of boundary ambiguity, the variables of physical and psychological presence or absence describe both the existence of ambiguity and the level of stress associated with it. Stress is high when ambiguity is high: when a person is psychologically absent but physically present or is physically absent but psychologically present. Concurrence of the variables reduces stress.

- Family stress theorist Hill's ABC-X Model and McCubbin and Patterson's expanded Double ABC-X Model seek to describe why families react as they do during times of stress or crisis. Hill's variables include the stressor, the family's crisis-meeting resources, and how the family defines the event; the Double ABC-X Model recognizes the additive effect of family hardships that accompany the stressor and prior strains, the sum of which may cause a stress pile-up.

- The roller coaster course of adjustment to stressors, described by Hill, involves a period of disorganization, an angle of recovery, and a new level of organization.

- An important aspect of a family is whether it is able to change its system type to deal with a major stressor affecting it. This type of change is called second-order change. Balanced families are more capable of second-order change and are typically better able to deal with stress effectively than unbalanced families.

- In families who cope successfully with stress, the parents possess these resources: good financial management skills, appreciation for the personality of the partner, a strong social support network of families and friends, a good sexual relationship, a happy marriage, and satisfaction with the quality of their life.

- Families draw on a variety of resources and related coping strategies to deal with stressful issues: cognitive resources (reframing the situation), emotional resources (expressing feelings), relationship resources (increasing cohesion), community resources (support from the health care system), spiritual resources (praying; seeking help from a pastor, priest, or rabbi), and individual resources (problem-solving skills).

- The biopsychosocial approach to stress management and health care assumes that people's biological, psychological, and social aspects are interconnected. This systemic model focuses on the way physical symptoms relate to a person's emotional health and takes a comprehensive approach to a person's overall well-being.

Key Terms

stress	ABC-X Family Crisis Model	prior strain
stressor	stressful life event	managing stress
distress	crisis	reframing
eustress	Double ABC-X Family Stress Model	social support network
stress pile-up	family hardship	biopsychosocial approach
family coping		medical family therapy
boundary ambiguity		

Activities

1. Identify a major stressor that you and your family experienced. Then plot how your family changed over time to deal with this major stressor, using the Family Circumplex Rating Form, Table A.2 in Resource Section A. Identify your family's position at four points in time: before the event, during the event, 1–2 months after the event, and 6 months after the event. Review Figure 14.7 if necessary.

2. List the family stressors and strains you recognize at the launching stage of the family life cycle. Then discuss family stressors and strains at the launching stage

with your parents. Have each parent describe what the stressors are (or were) for her or him. Look at those areas in which your mother's response differs from your father's. Also compare their descriptions with yours.

3. Select a major stressor in your family and describe how your family reacted as a group. It can be the same stressor as the one you identified in Activity 1, or it can be a different one. Indicate what your family did that was helpful and not helpful in dealing with the stressor. What resources did you and your family find most useful for managing your stress?

Suggested Readings

Boss, P. (1988). *Family stress management.* Newbury Park, CA: Sage. *A very comprehensive and useful book by a professor of family social science at the University of Minnesota, St. Paul, who has invested more than two decades in studying how families cope with stress and crisis.*

McCubbin, H. I., Thompson, E. A., Thompson, A. I., and Fromer, J. E. (Eds.). (1994). *Sense of coherence and resiliency: Stress, coping, and health.* Madison, WI: University of Wisconsin. *Ways to assess how well families are functioning, developed over many years by a team led by Hamilton McCubbin, dean of the School of Family Resources and Consumer Sciences at the University of Wisconsin.*

Ross, C. E., Mirowsky, J., & Goldsteen, K. (1991). The impact of the family on health: The decade in review. In A. Booth (Ed.) *Contemporary families: Looking forward, looking back* (pp. 341–360). Minneapolis: National Council on Family Relations. *An excellent review of research supporting the thesis that an individual's physical health is related to the emotional well-being of his or her family.*

CHAPTER 15

Family Problems, Domestic Violence, and Alcohol Abuse

For most people, the family is a shelter from the storms of the outside world, a secure base from which to cope with stressful times. But for a significant minority, family life is a source of stress. It is shattered by domestic violence, neglect, emotional cruelty, incest, or the abuse of alcohol and other drugs. Violence and abuse are too common in our society. And all too often these behaviors become a vicious cycle—with adults abused as children repeating these destructive patterns with their own children.

This chapter focuses on the dark side of family life, looking first at the physical and sexual abuse of children. It then turns the spotlight on spouse abuse and on sibling and child-to-parent abuse. Finally, it looks closely at the abuse of alcohol in families, because alcoholism or problem drinking is often related to domestic violence.

Family Problems and Family Systems Theory

Do families create problems for their individual members, or do individuals create problem families? For example, is schizophrenia in a family member "caused" by other family dynamics, or does a schizophrenic family member "cause" problems for and within the family? Is hyperactivity in children caused by inadequate parenting, or is the inadequate parenting a response to the difficulty of dealing with a hyperactive child?

According to family systems theory, these questions are difficult if not impossible to answer. Because family members are tied together in an intricate web of relationships, what one member does automatically affects the other members and the family system itself. Rather than trying to identify "causes," family therapists focus on helping families identify and resolve their unresolved issues. They ask families to ask themselves, where do we go from here?

Studies of family problems using the Family Circumplex Model bear out the premises of family systems theory. These studies have looked at chemical abuse, physical abuse, sexual abuse, and psychological abuse. Overall, they show that a family with one troubled individual is often a family that is not functioning well as a whole.

The Family and Mental Illness

What are the families of troubled individuals, those with mental or emotional disorders, like? Researchers have used the Circumplex Model to study the families of individuals with schizophrenia and with anxiety neurosis. According to the *Diagnostic and Statistical Manual of Mental Disorder*, 4th ed. (American Psychiatric Association, 1994), **schizophrenia** is a mental disorder characterized by bizarre or

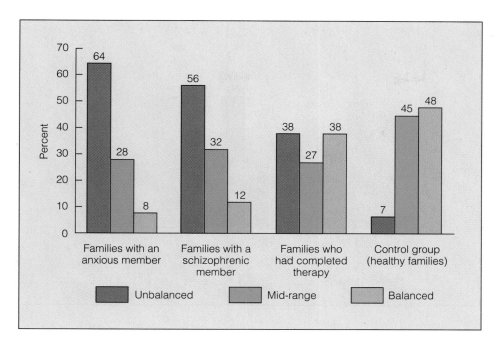

Figure 15.1 Problem Families and Their Family Types. *Source:* Adapted from *The Family Types of Schizophrenics, Neurotics, and "Normals"* by J. Clarke, 1984, unpublished doctoral dissertation, Family Social Science, University of Minnesota, St. Paul.

grandiose delusions (such as delusions of being controlled or persecuted or of being God); auditory hallucinations (hearing voices); incoherent, illogical thinking; and very grossly disorganized behavior. **Anxiety disorders** are mental disorders characterized by panic attacks not caused by life-threatening situations or extreme physical exertion. Symptoms of panic attacks include heart palpitations, chest pain or discomfort, choking or smothering sensations, dizziness, feelings of unreality, tingling hands or feet, hot and cold flashes, sweating, faintness, trembling or shaking, fear of dying, and fear of losing control.

To test the hypothesis that balanced family types are more functional than unbalanced family types, researchers have conducted a number of studies. One of the earliest was done by John Clarke (1984), who found strong support for this hypothesis (Figure 15.1). Clarke studied four groups of families: families with a schizophrenic member, families with a member with an anxiety disorder, families who had completed therapy in the past, and healthy families (the control group). Clarke found that a high percentage of families with anxious and schizophrenic members were unbalanced family types (64% and 56%, respectively) compared with the healthy families (7%). Conversely, a high percentage of the healthy families were balanced family types (48%) compared with the families with an anxious member (8%) and the families with a schizophrenic member (12%). Basically, what Clarke found is that individuals with problems are likely to live in families with problems. A person with an anxiety disorder or a person with schizophrenia is commonly found in a family having difficulty establishing a healthy sense of togetherness and having difficulty coping with stress and crisis in life.

Figure 15.2 Alcoholic Families (adults) and Their Family Types. *Source:* from *Alcoholic Families and the Circumplex Model*, p. 26, by D. H. Olson, 1989, unpublished manuscript, Family Social Science, University of Minnesota, St. Paul.

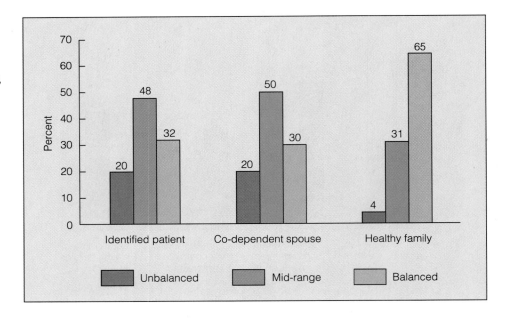

The Family and Alcohol Abuse

One study found that families who had a chemically dependent family member were significantly different from families who did not have a chemically dependent member (healthy families) (Killorin & Olson, 1984). This study focused on alcoholism and found that 20% of the families of alcoholics were unbalanced family types but that only 4% of the healthy families were unbalanced types. Furthermore, 65% of the healthy families were balanced, but only about one third of the families with an alcohol-dependent member were balanced. In other words, families of alcoholics tended to lack cohesiveness and the ability to adapt successfully to change.

> "The drinking drove a wedge between us as family members," said Julia, an exhausted-looking woman of 39. "We were so traumatized by the crisis, we withdrew from each other. I hid out from Bill because I didn't know what to do to help him with his disease, and the children hid out from both of us. They disappeared a lot, both emotionally and physically. Just left the discussion, left the house. It was heartbreaking."

Figure 15.2 illustrates the findings of the study. The "identified patient" is the alcoholic himself or herself. "Co-dependent spouse" refers to the partner of the alcoholic. Family systems theory uses the term **co-dependent** to describe a person, such as a spouse, whose actions enable the alcoholic to continue the drug dependence. **Enabler** is another term for someone with this behavior pattern. Both terms are intended to acknowledge that the co-dependent or enabler, often unknowingly, helps the alcoholic partner continue to drink.

"Rather than forcing the issue and demanding that Emily go into treatment, I kept making excuses for her: to her boss, to her parents, to her friends. I'd say she was ill and wouldn't be in to work today, or that I'd forgotten to tell her about her brother's birthday party, or whatever." The speaker was Conrad, age 45, a businessman living in Petersburg, Virginia.

"In the short run, this worked. In the long run, it was a disaster. Emily didn't get the professional help she needed because I was so ashamed of what was happening to her and to our family. I was afraid it would hurt my business and our status in the church and the community. It ended up destroying our family, which was the greatest loss of all."

Physical Abuse and Neglect of Children

In a statistical sense, the American family is the most violent social institution in our society.

        —M. A. STRAUS AND R. J. GELLES (1986, p. 466)

Child abuse is the physical or mental injury, sexual abuse, or negligent treatment of a child under the age of 18 by a person who is responsible for the child's welfare. Child abuse includes not only physical assault but also malnourishment, abandonment, neglect, emotional abuse, and sexual abuse (Finkelhor & Araji, 1986). The U.S. Advisory Board on Child Abuse and Neglect (1990) stated, "Beating children, chronically belittling them, using them for sexual gratification, and depriving them of the basic necessities of life are repellent acts and cannot be permitted in a civilized society."

Professionals who work in the area of child abuse point out that abuse and neglect occur in families from all social classes and at all income levels. Being a child of rich, well-educated parents does not necessarily guarantee safety, but research does indicate that abuse is seven times more likely among families with a yearly income of less than $15,000 (Straus, 1990)—perhaps a reflection of the stress such families experience.

Incidence

More than 1 million children are abused each year in the United States. Child neglect, the most commonly reported type of abuse, accounts for an estimated 49% of the cases reported in this country each year. Physical abuse (major and minor physical injuries) accounts for about 23% of reported cases, and sexual abuse accounts for 14% of all reported cases. Emotional abuse (psychological mistreatment or mental cruelty), although prevalent in our society, accounts for only 5% of the reported cases of child abuse each year (U.S. Bureau of the Census, 1995). Sibling abuse is probably the most common form of physical abuse of children. In a study of 733 families, 82% of the children ages 3–18 reported sibling violence in their family in the preceding year.

Emotional abuse of a child is a dramatic and destructive sign that a family is not functioning well. To treat this problem, family systems therapists seek to help the family work through unresolved issues rather than to eliminate the "cause" of the abuse.

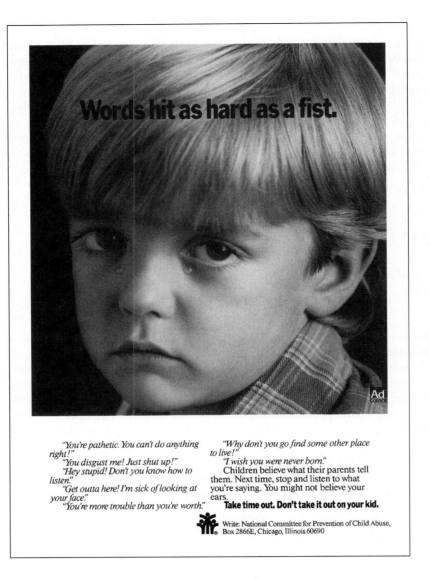

American society tends to condone violent rather than nonviolent approaches to the discipline of children. Research indicates that most American parents approve of spanking and slapping their children, and almost two out of three parents do so in a given year (Straus, Gelles & Steinmetz, 1980). Even though spanking and slapping are clearly violent behaviors, they are not generally viewed as child abuse in our society. But why does our society consider it relatively acceptable to hit a child, a brother, or a spouse but unacceptable to hit an employee, a co-worker, or a salesperson?

In a national survey of parents, Straus and Gelles (1986) found that 10.7% admitted to using severe forms of punishment, including kicking, biting, punching,

Running away from home is the way many children cope with abuse by a family member. For these youngsters, the bleak and often frightening experience of life on the streets is preferable to violence at the hands of someone who is supposed to care for them.

beating, hitting or trying to hit their children with an object, or wielding a gun or knife against them. Mothers are apparently slightly more likely than fathers to be violent or severely violent toward their children (Gelles & Straus, 1988), perhaps because they spend more time with them. Boys are more likely than girls to have violence inflicted upon them by their parents (Gelles & Cornell, 1985).

More than 1 million cases of child abuse are reported in the United States each year. In 1963, before laws were passed requiring physicians and other professionals to report actual or suspected cases of abuse, only 150,000 cases were reported (Children's Defense Fund, 1988). Even though the number of reported cases has increased dramatically since the early 1960s, most authorities agree that much abuse still goes unreported.

More than 1,200 children in the United States die each year due to abuse or neglect (Gelles & Straus, 1988). Homicide is the fifth leading cause of death among children in American society. The murder rate for infants under the age of one is 8 per 100,000, and two thirds are murdered by a parent. Among children ages 1–4, 3 per 100,000 are murdered each year, and a parent is responsible for one in four of these deaths. The murder rate for children ages 5–14 is 2 per 100,000 each year (U.S. Bureau of the Census, 1995).

The Impact on Children

Abused babies tend to be extremely difficult to nurture and to rear because of what they have experienced. This reflects the vicious cycle of abuse between a parent and a child, in which a negative act by the parent produces a negative response

B O X   1 5 . 1

The Impact of Violence on Children

Murray Straus and Richard Gelles have been studying family violence for more than two decades. In one study, the research team interviewed 3,206 parents of children under 17 years of age who were living at home. The interviewers asked parents about problems their children had experienced and about their use of violence toward their children in the previous year.

The list of difficulties the parents talked about included difficulty making friends, temper tantrums, failing grades in school, disciplinary problems, misbehavior and disobedience at home, physical fights with other children, physical fights with adults, deliberately damaging or destroying property, stealing money or other items, drinking, using drugs, and getting arrested.

The risk of these problems happening in the life of a child growing up in a violent home was nearly double the risk of these problems for a child whose home was free of violence. More than 40% of the children from violent homes had some problems in school, were aggressive, and/or had problems with drugs or alcohol. Only 23% of the children growing up in nonviolent homes experiences these same troubles. Children living in violent homes were also three to four times more likely to break the law and be arrested. A child growing up in a violent home often becomes part of a cycle of violence.

Source: Adapted from "The National Family Violence Surveys" by M. A. Straus. In *Physical Violence in American Families* (pp. 3–16) edited by M. A. Straus and R. J. Gelles, 1990, New Brunswick, NJ: Transaction Books.

from the child, which in turn produces another negative response from the parent, and so on.

Researchers have found that abuse can compromise children's intellectual and social development in a variety of ways. Abused children tend to have lower IQ scores, learning problems, lower grades, and poorer school performance than do children who are not abused. Many abused children are aggressive, oppositional, and extremely wary. Other possible problems related to abuse include bedwetting; tantrums; inability to trust other people; difficulty relating to both peers and adults; generalized unhappiness; poor self-image; and the tendency to engage in juvenile delinquency, join a gang, run away from home, be truant from school, and become involved in violent crime (Gelles & Straus, 1988). Box 15.1 presents the results of a study on the effects of violence in the home on children and adolescents.

Transcending Abuse

Many abusive parents were themselves abused as children, but being abused as a child does not necessarily doom a person to pass the misery along to the next generation. Some abused children grow up to be happy and healthy adults, although transcending the pain of a violent childhood is very difficult. Since the early 1980s, researchers and clinicians have begun to focus efforts on understanding these "resilient" or "invulnerable" individuals. What they have found is that a nurturing relative, adult friend, or teacher often helped the troubled individual find a more positive approach to living.

Edward Zigler and his colleagues have estimated that the rate of "cross-generational transmission" of child abuse is about 25–35%. This means that about one quarter to one third of those who are physically or sexually abused or neglected as children will subject their own children to similar abuse. However, the majority (65–75%) of people abused as children "will care for their offspring as well as the general population." According to the researchers, "many adults abused as children remember the agony they once suffered and have sworn to give their own children a better start." The research team did make it clear, however, that individuals with a history of abuse are still about six times more likely to abuse their own children than is the average person, who has about a 5% likelihood of doing so (Zigler, Rubin, & Kaufman, 1988).

In our own study of surviving and transcending childhood trauma, a man named Robert told us about years of physical and emotional abuse in his family. When he was a teenager, Robert had intervened one afternoon when his father was beating his mother. His father had stormed into the basement after him, warning that he was going to kill him. Robert had grabbed a hunting rifle and shot his father, who died soon after. When a police officer had come to pick up the youngster a few hours later, the officer had said he understood that the shooting was in self-defense.

"He told me that I was a good boy, and that it wasn't my fault," Robert said. "I felt like the first time anyone had ever said anything kind to me in my whole life."

Robert healed from his childhood trauma and went on to become a police officer himself, working with troubled young people. "I dedicated my life to the memory of that officer who made such a difference in my view of myself," he told us.

Abuse in childhood clearly does not preordain a person to go on in life to abuse others.

Families at Risk

A number of factors are related to the likelihood of child abuse occurring in a family.

- *Economic distress.* Unemployment, low income, illness in the family, and inability to pay for adequate medical care are stressors in the lives of many abusive parents (Krugmann, Lenherr, Betz, & Fryer, 1986).

- *Inadequate parenting skills.* Abusive parents often hold unrealistic expectations about children, have little knowledge of child development, and demonstrate an inability to bond with infants (Azar & Rohrbeck, 1986).

- *Parental personality problems.* Abusive parents often have low self-esteem, and they are more likely to be immature, lacking in empathy, and self-centered than nonabusive parents. They tend to be prone to anger, rigid, domineering, self-righteous, and moralistic (Dubowitz & Egan, 1988; Krugman, et al., 1986).

The likelihood of child abuse is greater when the parents are under stress because of unemployment, low income, or illness, especially if they are immature and know little about the development of children. During times of stress, parents need friends and other sources of support to help them cope with frustrations and relate to their children in a positive way.

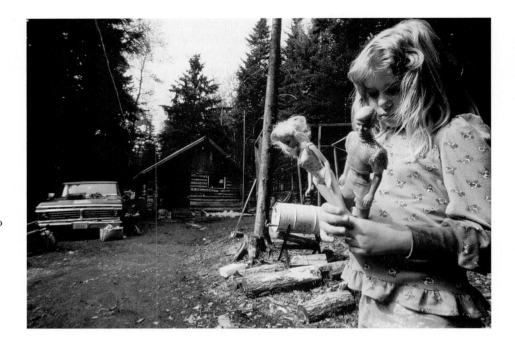

- *Chemical abuse as a means for coping with stress.* Abusive parents often have high stress in their lives but have a difficult time dealing with stress in a proactive, rational manner. Many use alcohol and other drugs to forget their troubles (Hamilton, Stiles, Melowsky, & Beal, 1987).

- *Social isolation.* Abusive families are likely to be isolated from their community, with few friends or sources of outside support (Gelles & Cornell, 1985).

- *A special child.* Children with a chronic illness, an emotional disturbance, hyperactivity, mental retardation, or a physical handicap are at higher risk for abuse (Hawkins & Duncan, 1985). Children who were unplanned and are unwanted are also more likely to be abused, as are children whose birth was difficult for the parent (Krugman et al., 1986).

- *Family size.* Researchers have found that the likelihood of child abuse tends to increase with family size. Parents of two children are 50% more likely to abuse their children than parents of a single child. The rate of child abuse has been found to peak at five children and to decline in larger families (Gelles & Cornell, 1985).

- *Domestic violence in the family of origin.* Abusive parents were likely to have witnessed domestic violence between their parents and were likely to have been physically punished themselves as children (Gelles & Cornell, 1985).

- *A violent subculture.* Some cultures and subcultures appear more tolerant of violent behavior toward children. For example, children who live in an unsafe neighborhood characterized by high levels of violence are at greater risk of being abused than are children growing up in a more peaceful neighborhood.

- *A violent marriage.* Parents who abuse their spouse are more likely to abuse their children than parents whose marriage is peaceful.

- *Single parent.* Children who live with a single parent are more likely to suffer abuse than those who live with two parents (Daly & Wilson, 1985), perhaps due to the stresses often associated with single parenthood.

- *Stepparent.* Children living with a stepparent are more likely to be abused than those living with both natural parents. One study of preschoolers found the likelihood for abuse to be 40 times greater for stepchildren; the stepparent's lack of a biological tie with the child may make her or him less tolerant (Daly & Wilson, 1985).

Treatment and Prevention

A growing body of professional literature demonstrates that Americans can do something about child abuse. Parents can learn how to deal more positively and effectively with their children. Education is the key to preventing abuse; education and therapy are needed to help abusive families.

Child abuse is now commonly seen by the professionals who work in this area as a family and societal problem. Treating the problem involves three interrelated strategies: (1) increasing the parent's self-esteem, (2) increasing the parent's knowledge of children and positive childrearing techniques, and (3) devising community support networks for families under stress (Goldstein, Keller, & Erne, 1985).

Parents who mistreat children are commonly viewed as people who need more positive ways of coping with their many problems. Counselors working with abusive parents are often quite successful in facilitating positive behavioral changes. By focusing on the strengths these troubled parents do have, a therapist can enhance the development of the parent's self-esteem and parenting skills. A counselor can also provide referrals to other community services: financial aid for families in economic distress; food stamps; aid in finding better housing; family planning and adoption services; and day care.

Many programs for troubled parents include a parent discussion and support group component. A group of parents, often facilitated by a professional, gets together to share stories about life's ups and downs and to offer advice and support. Child abuse hotlines are also useful. Parents can call in at any time for help in dealing with difficult childrearing situations.

There are a number of things we as a society can do to prevent abuse of children (Baumrind, 1994; Gelles & Straus, 1988; Lore & Schulz, 1993; Swift, 1986). They include working to reduce sources of social stress, such as poverty, racism, inequality, unemployment, and inadequate health care. Other tasks include eliminating sexism in the workplace and the home, providing adequate child care across the nation, promoting educational and employment opportunities for both men and women, supporting sex education and family planning programs in an effort to reduce unplanned and unwanted pregnancies, and working to end the social isolation of families in our culture.

Sexual Abuse of Children

Sexual abuse of children is a growing problem but one that is still underreported. There were 375,000 allegations of child sexual abuse in the United States during 1990, a 20-fold increase since 1980. By age 18, an estimated 27% of girls and 16% of boys have been sexually abused (Darnton, Springen, Wright, & Keene-Osborn, 1991). There are two basic forms of child sexual abuse: incestuous abuse (intrafamilial abuse), which occurs between family members, and nonincestuous abuse (extrafamilial abuse), which occurs between nonfamily members (Finkelhor, 1984).

Incest is sexual activity of any kind between members of the same family, including grandparents, adopted children, stepparents, and in-laws. Incest is forbidden today in virtually every human society. **Incestuous abuse** is the sexual exploitation of a child under age 18 by a relative. It is far more frequent between brothers and sisters, fathers and daughters, stepfathers and stepdaughters, and uncles and nieces than between mothers and sons (Peters, Wyatt, & Finkelhor, 1986; Russell, 1986). It is often an intensely damaging psychological experience, contributing to persistent, long-term sexual and social difficulties.

During the past decade the definition of incest has broadened. In addition to sexual intercourse, incest is now considered to include fondling, rubbing one's genitals against a child, and excessive or suggestive washing of a child's pubic area. It does not matter if the child is perceived by the adult as freely engaging in the sexual activity or even enjoying it. A child cannot give informed consent to the activity. Incest, thus, is an abuse of power and authority (Gorman, 1991).

Dynamics of Incestuous Families

Clinicians and researchers have invested a great deal of energy in understanding the causes of incest and the dynamics of incestuous families. C. A. Courtois (1988) cites four general dynamics that need to be examined to better comprehend an incestuous family: (1) the psychodynamic, which centers on the personalities and backgrounds of the family members; (2) the sociological or sociocultural dynamic, which focuses on social and cultural factors; (3) the family system dynamic, which examines the family as a unit; and (4) the feminist dynamic, which analyzes family gender roles and patterns.

Focusing on the family system dynamic, clinicians and researchers often find that incestuous families tend to be isolated and withdrawn from the outside world. Family members suffer from social, psychological, and physical isolation and try to meet most of their individual needs within the nuclear family. Appropriate boundaries do not exist between family members across generational lines. Individuation and independence are discouraged and even punished. Role reversal between parents and children is common. Emotional and physical deprivation predominate. Affection is most commonly expressed sexually (Courtois, 1988).

There are apparently two broad family system types in which incest occurs: the chaotic family and the normal-appearing family. The **chaotic family** is the stereotypical incestuous family. These families often have a multitude of problems

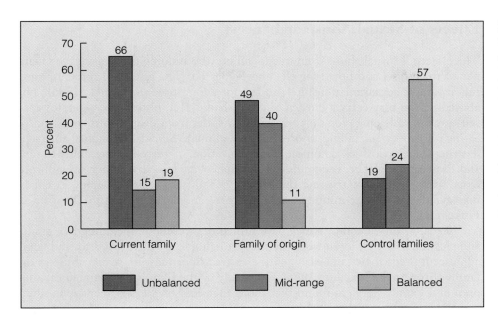

Figure 15.3 Sex Offenders and Their Family Types. *Source:* "Sexually Addicted Families: Clinical Use of the Circumplex Model" (p. 127) by P. J. Carnes. In *Circumplex Model* edited by D. H. Olson, C. S. Russell, and D. H. Sprenkle, 1989, New York: Haworth Press. Copyright 1989 by Haworth Press. Reprinted by permission.

reaching back through the generations. They tend to be of low socioeconomic status, and many individuals in the family are only marginally functional, with limited educational and vocational achievements. Substance abuse and trouble with the law are common. Abusers in a chaotic family are more likely to be punished for incest than are abusers in a normal-appearing family—and their punishment is likely to be more severe (Courtois, 1988).

The **normal-appearing family** appears healthy and functional to outsiders. The family is socially and financially stable and is usually well integrated into the community. The parents' marriage has lasted a long time. The family is often a traditional one, with the husband as head of the household. From the inside, however, the normal-appearing family is in trouble. Family members lack emotional energy and cannot nurture one another. The parents are emotionally needy; abuse of alcohol or other drugs is likely. The children must not only care for themselves but are often caretakers for the parents. When a child discloses incest, denial and disbelief are the responses. In the case of a trial, the family's financial resources are used to defend the perpetrator and attack the child's credibility. The perpetrator, often the father, is rarely found guilty (Courtois, 1988).

Sex offenders generally live in and come from family types that are unbalanced on the Circumplex Model, families that lack genuine emotional closeness, have poor communication skills, and have limited skill in dealing successfully with everyday stresses and major crises in life. Patrick Carnes (1989) found that 66% of sex offenders were living in unbalanced types of families and that 49% had grown up in unbalanced families. In contrast, most families in the control group (no sex offender in the family) were balanced or mid-range types of families (Figure 15.3).

Effects of Sexual Abuse and Incest

The effects of sexual abuse seem to depend on who is doing the abusing, the manner of the abuse, and how long the abuse goes on. The effects of forceful, hurtful, exploitive sexual relationships can last for a long time (Kilpatrick, 1986). The abused person may carry a burden of guilt, shame, fear, bitterness, anger, lowered self-esteem, and depression for years and may suffer from sleep disturbances and/or eating disorders (including anorexia and bulimia). Suicidal thoughts and self-destructive behaviors are common. Revictimization, increased vulnerability to rape and to marital violence, is common. Individuals may also have other sexual problems, such as difficulty trusting the partner, inability to relax and enjoy lovemaking, avoidance of sex, inhibited sexual desire, and lack of orgasm (Browne & Finkelhor, 1986).

Sexually abused children may have difficulties in school, including low grades and truancy. Many children who run away from home are incest victims, and many adolescent pregnancies and early marriages are associated with sexual abuse in the family (Browne & Finkelhor, 1986). One study by the Illinois Department of Children and Family Services found that more than half of the 445 teenage mothers questioned had been sexually abused as children or had been forced to have sex. The average age for the first incident was 11.5 years ("Teen Moms," 1987).

In general, the effects of incest have been likened to those of **post-traumatic stress disorder.** Individuals regularly reexperience the trauma through recurrent invasive thoughts and uncontrollable emotions. They often feel detached from the external world and may feel compelled to avoid situations that remind them of the original trauma (Edwards, 1989).

Treatment and Prevention

In the case of father-daughter incest, the traditional solution was to protect the victim by removing the father from the home and imprisoning him. This left the victim and her family to fend for themselves in the wake of a great emotional trauma. Today the judicial system and the community family support network often work in concert to evaluate the family situation and recommend an approach appropriate for the family's circumstances. The goal might not necessarily be to incarcerate the perpetrator. In some situations he might be moved out of the home into a treatment setting, while all members of the family are helped in a variety of ways to come to terms with the trauma. Therapists might work on developing family members' self-esteem and improving family relationships. Referral might be made to an alcohol or other drug treatment program. Self-help groups for victims, perpetrators, and other family members operate in a number of cities. One goal is for family members to learn how the incest has affected each of them (Nadelson & Sauzier, 1986).

The conspiracy of silence surrounding incest is beginning to crumble in American society. A number of prominent people—among them, Roseanne, Oprah Winfrey, former Miss America Marilyn Van Derbur, and LaToya Jackson—have come forward to describe the abuse they experienced as children (Gorman, 1991). These very public disclosures often encourage less well known people to tell their stories

Because very young children do not know the words to describe an act of sexual abuse, therapists ask them to use anatomically correct dolls to show what happened. A demonstration with dolls is more reliable than direct questions because small children often attempt to guess what answer the interviewer wants even though they do not understand the question.

and begin the long process of healing. Support groups for incest survivors provide safe places for sharing painful secrets with trustworthy individuals.

In an effort to prevent sexual abuse, many organizations and schools in this country have educational programs for children on "good touch and bad touch." Children are taught how to avoid potentially abusive situations, how to react when approached, how to say no so that people know they mean it, and the importance of telling adults they trust what has happened until someone believes them.

Education can also help adults protect children from sexual abuse. Parents, teachers, physicians, mental health professionals, and police officers are key figures in the child protection team. Parents must overcome their reluctance to talk about these issues with their children. Finally, as a society we need to abandon some of our stereotypic sexual games. Sexuality should not be a commodity for exploitation but a positive gift for bonding and the expression of affection.

Spouse Abuse

The home is actually a more dangerous place for American women than the city streets.
> —Dr. Antonia C. Novello, *former U.S. Surgeon General*
> ("Family Violence," 1991, p. 3)

Although the family is usually considered to be a loving and supportive social institution, it is, in fact, more violent than the military, except in times of war (Gelles & Harrop, 1989). More than a third of the women who are murdered in this coun-

Figure 15.4 Knowing the Attacker. *Source:* U.S. Bureau of the Census (1995, pp. 202–205).

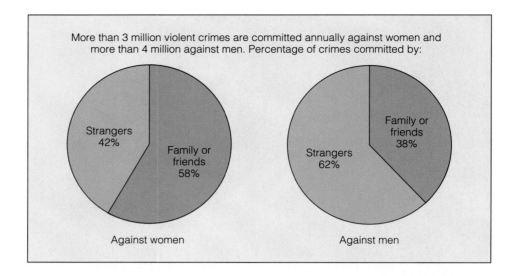

try die at the hands of their husbands or boyfriends. Domestic violence is the single greatest cause of injury to women, ranking higher than automobile accidents, muggings, and rapes combined ("Family Violence," 1991; Straus, 1989). A recent Johns Hopkins University study found that one in three U.S. women has been the victim of domestic abuse and half have been assaulted before the age of 18 ("Study," 1995). About 20% of all police officers killed each year in this country die while intervening in a family dispute (U.S. Department of Justice, 1989). Most violence (58%) against women is caused by husbands, family members, or male friends; about 47% is perpetrated by strangers. However, 62% of the violence against men is perpetrated by strangers; only 38% is at the hands of a wife, another family member, or a friend (Figure 15.4).

Incidence

Researchers estimate that approximately 3 million people, mostly women, are severely assaulted each year by their spouses (Gelles & Straus, 1988; Straus & Gelles, 1986). Most cases are not reported, for a variety of reasons. Victims often do not recognize the violence as abuse because in some ethnic and cultural groups violence toward women is the norm. Society's traditional respect for family privacy also inhibits reporting. Victims may feel guilt or shame for being abused or may fear their partner will retaliate if they report the incident.

Husband abuse does occur, but because men are generally bigger and stronger than women, husbands have higher rates of inflicting the most dangerous and injurious forms of violence on wives. Much violence by wives appears to be in self-defense (Straus & Gelles, 1986).

Although the number of cases reported to authorities has risen dramatically in recent years, the actual rate of spouse abuse declined slightly according to a national survey conducted in 1975 and repeated in 1985 (Straus & Gelles, 1986). In 1975, 12.1% of the husbands admitted that they were violent toward their wives, and 3.8% said they were severely violent (15.9% total). In 1985, 11.3% of the husbands were violent toward their wives, and 3.0% were severely violent (14.3% total).

In 1975, 11.6% of the women reported being violent toward their husbands, and 4.6% were severely violent (16.2% total). In 1985, 12.1% of the wives were violent toward their husbands, and 4.4% were severely violent (16.5% total). The actual rate of violence was probably higher than reported because people are not comfortable admitting to being violent. An unexpected finding was that the rate of wife-to-husband violence was somewhat higher than that of husband-to-wife violence (Straus & Gelles, 1986).

Straus and Gelles (1986) speculate that the small decline in reported domestic violence between 1975 and 1985 can be traced to an increase in the average age of marriage (younger couples tend to be more violent than older couples), a more prosperous economy in 1985 (violence has been linked to financial stress), and increasing public awareness that violence toward women is unacceptable.

A dating relationship is apparently more likely to be violent than a marital relationship. The National Family Violence Survey of 5,768 couples found that 20% of the dating couples had experienced a physical assault during the previous year, compared with 15% of the married couples (Stets & Straus, 1989). Courtship is a training ground for marriage and also, apparently, a training ground for spouse abuse.

"In the beginning I thought Jerry was abusive because he was drunk, but then it happened when he wasn't drunk, too." The speaker was Norina, a 20-year-old college woman. She went on, "I ignored it at first. I guess I thought it would quit. I also loved him so much I tried to cover it up.

"He became very demeaning toward me, and there was a lot of mental abuse. I wanted to quit seeing him, but he wouldn't accept it. I needed to get away, but he followed me wherever I went and watched every move I made. I didn't realize how bad the situation had become until one night at a party. He had followed me there but didn't speak to me most of the night. He left—or so I thought. Because I was upset, I started to talk with a male friend of mine. Out of the blue my boyfriend returned, picked me up, and carried me outside behind a building. I was scared and started crying. I was so upset I couldn't listen to him. He kept slapping me and telling me to shut up and listen. A few of my friends were watching. They confronted my boyfriend, and he started fighting with them.

"The best thing I did was to go to a counselor. She taught me how to deal with my feelings. She made me realize that there was nothing more I could do in the relationship except get out. She also made me aware that there was nothing I could do about my boyfriend until he recognized that what he was doing was wrong and would go for help himself."

Spouse or partner abuse can be physical, sexual, or emotional. Spouse abuse and child abuse are closely linked. Seventy percent of the men who batter their partners also batter their children (Bowker, Arbitell, & McFerron, 1988; Jouriles & Norwood, 1995).

Factors Contributing to Spouse Abuse

Researchers and clinicians have hypothesized that a number of factors contribute to the likelihood of spouse abuse in a family. These factors are quite similar to those related to child abuse.

Violence in the Family of Origin   Family systems theory attributes a tendency toward domestic violence as an adult to growing up in a violent home, where the child learns to be a victim as well as a potential **victimizer.** Abused male children typically learn to be victimizers. They often develop a sort of "pecking order" attitude toward violence: You get beat up when you're small; then when you're big, you repeat what you learned. Female children typically learn to be victims in their family of origin and are likely to become victims again in their marriage (Gelles & Cornell, 1985; Kruttschnitt, Heath, & Ward, 1986; Lincoln Family Service Association, 1991; Simons, Johnson, Beaman, & Conger, 1993; Steinmetz, 1987). As with child abuse, however, growing up in a home where spouse abuse occurs does not guarantee that one will become a victim of a victimizer as an adult (Gelles & Cornell, 1985; Stark & Flitcraft, 1985). People can and do make positive, life-affirming choices.

Those theorists with a psychodynamically oriented approach might see some abusers as having a personality disorder that is facilitated by a "willing" victim. The abuser's sadism is reinforced by the victim's masochism. In a similar vein, **learned helplessness theory** postulates that battered women often have learned from childhood that they cannot afford to appear competent around competitive men who like to win. These women give power away to men, and this ingrained passivity leads to a lack of options in life. When abused, they feel they have no way out: nowhere to go, no job skills or career opportunities, no choice except to continue to take their punishment.

Low Self-Esteem   Low self-esteem is a factor in domestic violence. The abusive spouse may feel inadequate and may use violence to gain control. The abused spouse may passively accept the violence, feeling that she or he deserves nothing better.

Youth   Age and spouse abuse are statistically related. Marital violence is twice as likely among couples who are under age 30 than among those over age 30 (Gelles & Cornell, 1985).

Economic Stress   Although spouse abuse occurs in families at all income levels, it has been found that economic stress increases the likelihood of wife battering. Spouse abuse is more likely in low-income families, and unemployed men are twice as likely to batter their wives as employed men are (Gelles & Cornell, 1985; Steinmetz, 1987).

Isolation   Social isolation is also a factor in abuse. Abusers often feel isolated and alone. They have fewer contacts with friends, neighbors, and relatives and engage in fewer social activities than nonabusers do. In stressful times they have no social support network upon which to call (Gelles & Cornell, 1985).

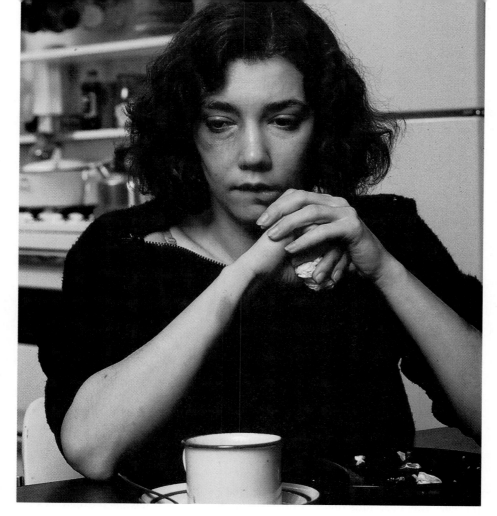

Most women who are physically abused by their husbands or partners are reluctant to report the abuse and even more reluctant to end the relationship. One theory for this masochistic behavior is that these women were abused as children and know only the role of victim. Another theory is that throughout their lives they have been conditioned to act passively and as a consequence have few skills and little self-esteem and see no alternative to a brutal relationship.

Alcohol   Alcohol is implicated in a high percentage of domestic violence incidents. Many men who assault their wives have been drinking (Gelles & Cornell, 1985). Does drinking cause violence? Some observers argue that alcohol facilitates violence by helping to break down the abuser's inhibitions. But alcohol cannot be seen as the sole cause of the violent episode. Drinking is no more an excuse for assaulting another human being than it is for killing someone in a car accident.

Male Dominance   Professionals and clinicians studying abuse from a feminist perspective have identified clues as to why men batter women. They note that many in our culture believe that males have the right to control or try to control their partners. Men have also been socialized to believe that aggression is an acceptable, normal response to stress and anger. A patriarchal family system influences males to assume the head-of-the-household role and women to accept subordinate status. Egalitarian decision making is associated with nonviolence in families. Levels of wife-beating and husband-beating were higher among husband-dominant couples than democratic couples (Straus, Gelles, & Steinmetz, 1980).

493

Other Cultural Factors   Some observers are especially critical of sports in this country, saying that hypercompetitiveness and a win-at-any-cost attitude can lead to brutality in the home. Social philosopher Myriam Miedzian believes that boys today are being raised in a culture that discourages nurturing behavior and leads many to grow up to be men who denigrate and beat women. Miedzian cites studies which have found that boys who are involved in competitive sports demonstrate a lower degree of sportsmanship and fair play than boys who have not been involved in competitive sports. Miedzian concludes that "if you combine the emphasis on winning at any cost with the negative attitude toward women, it is not at all surprising that approximately one-third of the sexual assaults on college campuses are by athletes" (cited in Levy, 1991, p. 17).

In our culture the depersonalization and objectification of women are reinforced by pornography and by advertising that uses sexy women to sell products. Victim blaming is common, as rape trials often reveal. We live in a society with a high tolerance for overt coercion and the use of physical force to gain control over others (Pence, Duprey, Paymar, & McDonnell, 1989). All of these social factors are viewed as contributing to the epidemic of domestic violence in this country.

Patterns of Spouse Abuse

Clinicians commonly see a three-phase, cyclical pattern to wife battering: (1) a tension-building phase; (2) an explosion phase, in which the actual beating occurs; and (3) a loving or honeymoon phase, in which the battered woman is rewarded for staying in the relationship (L. Walker, 1979). The third phase can be very pleasant. Many women stay with their spouses or boyfriends because of the promises and gifts that often follow a violent incident.

A common belief in our culture is that venting anger verbally can prevent physical violence. This theory of **catharsis conflict,** as it has been called, is simply not true. Verbal aggression is not a substitute for physical aggression but actually goes hand-in-hand with physical aggression. The more verbally aggressive a couple is, the more likely they are to be physically aggressive with each other (Straus & Sweet, 1992).

Treatment and Prevention

Many clinicians and prefessionals who work in women's shelters are skeptical that batterers will change their behavior without professional help and without the genuine desire to change. Some argue that battering men "have a good thing going" because a terrified wife and children jump every time the batterer says jump.

Counselors commonly advise battered women to leave their husbands and go to a relative or friend's home or to a shelter for battered women. But this is easier said than done. Some men panic when women leave because they feel they are losing control. Panic can lead to even more violent behavior. "It's extremely rare that you read about a man who has beaten a woman to death while she's living with him," according to Ellen Pence, who works with battered women. "It's when she leaves him that he kills" (Simpson, 1989).

Fortunately, there have been many advances in treatment services for spouse abuse in the past two decades. The first shelter for battered women opened in 1974; today there are several thousand shelters across the country. Shelters provide safety for the abused spouse and children; temporary housing, food, and clothing; counseling to build a stronger self-concept; and guidance in finding employment, legal assistance, and other practical kinds of help (Straus, 1989).

Responding to pressure from the women's movement, police departments are now more likely to make arrests in cases of domestic violence. Assault against a spouse is seen as a serious offense (Straus, 1989). After studying research findings indicating that men who had spent time behind bars were less likely to assault their partners again, the Duluth, Minnesota, police department was the first in the United States to make arrest mandatory for suspected batterers. The Duluth program requires batterers to attend at least 6 months of counseling and classes. If a man misses two meetings, he risks serving up to 10 days in jail. Studies done 2 years after the program was initiated found that 80% of the women whose partners had completed the program were no longer being battered (Simpson, 1989; Knudsen & Miller, 1992).

As a society, our ultimate goal should be the prevention of domestic violence. To do this we need not only to treat those families in which violence has occurred but also to address the causes of violence. We still live in a society that devalues women and children and glorifies power, the use of force, and the macho behavior associated with alcohol abuse.

To help prevent the next generation from falling into the sexism/violence trap, Miriam Miedzian suggests encouraging schools to teach positive approaches to conflict resolution in the classroom and on the playground, to show children there are alternatives to violent behavior. Television should be prosocial and nonviolent, rather than filled with sexism and violence. We need to restrict violent pornography, which both demeans women and glorifies killing. Also, boys should be encouraged from a young age to be empathetic rather than aggressive (Levy, 1991).

Sibling and Child-to-Parent Abuse

Domestic violence is not initiated only by adults, nor is it directed only at children and spouses/partners. Siblings may engage in violence, and children sometimes attack their parents.

Sibling Abuse

One of the most common forms of family violence is **sibling abuse.** Seventy-five percent of siblings experience at least one violent episode a year. Fifty percent of siblings are punched, kicked, or bitten each year, and 16% beat each other up. Guns or knives are used or their use is threatened in less than 1% of these incidents (Gelles & Cornell, 1985).

Siblings often learn physical violence in the home, usually from their parents. Of children who were repeatedly abused by their parents, 76% severely assaulted a sibling; only 15% of children whose parents used no physical punishment or other violence during the year assaulted a sibling (Gelles & Cornell, 1985).

To prevent sibling violence, parents can do the following things: (1) not be violent toward each other, (2) be supportive and nurturant toward their children, (3) give their children a strong, clear message that violence between them is not acceptable, (4) monitor their children's behavior and be watchful, and (5) avoid coercive discipline, which is associated with higher rates of fighting between siblings (Loeber & Dishion, 1984).

In sum, parents need to take the time to teach their children nonviolent ways of relating to each other. Older children, in particular, can be instructed to sit down together and come up with a nonviolent solution to their conflict. Their efforts at conflict resolution can be surprisingly creative.

Child-to-Parent Abuse

Although some authorities in our culture believe that it is acceptable for parents to hit children, few believe it is all right for children to hit parents. Because parents are usually physically and socially more powerful than their children, we assume that parents are immune to abuse by their children. But **child-to-parent abuse** occurs in many families.

In a nationwide survey of family violence, nearly 10% of the parents reported that they had been hit, bitten, or kicked at least once by their children. Three percent of the parents reported that they had been the victim at least once of severely violent behavior on the part of a child 11 or older. The researchers concluded that "children are capable of violent behavior that is as devastating as violence inflicted by adults" (Gelles & Straus, 1988). The research team heard stories of children pushing parents down stairs, setting the house on fire with the parents in it, and attacking parents with guns or knives in an effort to seriously injure or kill them. The majority of children who attack their parents are between the ages of 13 and 24.

Mothers are abused more often than fathers, probably because women usually are not as physically strong as men and because women are commonly viewed as acceptable targets for aggression. Mothers who have been abused by their husbands are more likely to be abused by their children (Gelles & Cornell, 1985). Teenagers who were once victims of parental violence often grow up to fight back.

Finally, family caseworkers report many situations in which an adult child physically or emotionally abuses her or his elderly parents. The stress of caring for an aging parent can be great, and abusive adult children sometimes argue that they are paying their parents back for abuse they suffered as children: "He did it to me. Now I have my chance to get even." Fortunately, many treatment programs are available to help people find positive and satisfying ways to relate to one another across the generations.

B O X   1 5 . 2

Warning Signs for Alcohol Abuse

The following are common warning signs that a person is abusing alcohol. The more warning signs that are relevant, the greater the severity of the problem with alcohol use.

1. Drinking alone or secretively.

2. Using alcohol deliberately and repeatedly to perform or to get through difficult situations.

3. Feeling uncomfortable on occasions when alcohol is not available.

4. Escalating alcohol consumption beyond an already established drinking pattern.

5. Consuming alcohol heavily in risky situations (for example, before driving).

6. Getting drunk regularly or more frequently than in the past.

7. Drinking in the morning or at other unusual times.

Source: Core Concepts in Health (7th ed.—1996 Update) (p. 260) by P. M. Insel and W. T. Roth, 1996, Mountain View, CA: Mayfield. Copyright 1996 by Mayfield Publishing Company. Reprinted by permission.

Alcohol Problems in Families

A family with a drinking problem is always a family in trouble.
—Marcia Lasswell and Thomas Lasswell (1991, p. 256)

Alcohol is a drug that acts as a depressant to the central nervous system. It is the mood-altering ingredient in wine, beer, and hard liquor. Alcohol is absorbed into the bloodstream and travels to virtually every part of the body. When ingested in large amounts and/or over a long period of time, alcohol can kill. It can damage the liver, heart, and pancreas; other consequences include malnutrition, stomach irritation, lowered resistance to disease, and irreversible brain or nervous system damage (National Council on Alcoholism, 1989). **Alcohol abuse** is a generic term that includes both **alcoholism,** addiction to alcohol characterized by compulsive drinking, and **problem drinking,** alcohol consumption that results in a functional disability.

An estimated 12 million men, women, and children suffer from alcoholism in the United States; 16–19 million adults are problem drinkers. About 100,000 people die prematurely each year as a result of alcohol misuse (National Council on Alcoholism 1989). Alcohol-related death is the leading cause of death for people between the ages of 16 and 24. Alcohol is a factor in almost half the murders, suicides, and accidental deaths in this country. Drunk drivers are involved in half of all fatal motor vehicle crashes, and 65 of every 100 people in the United States will be involved in an alcohol-related motor vehicle crash sometime in their life (R. H. Lauer, 1989; Lord, 1987; Taylor, 1988). To see if you have a problem with alcohol, review the warning signs in Box 15.2.

Alcohol As a "Cause" of Family Violence

A federal survey by the National Center for Health Statistics found that 4 in 10 adult Americans have been exposed to alcoholism in their families ("Alcohol Impacts," 1991). Alcohol is commonly associated with marital disruption, domestic violence, and many other family problems (Roosa, Tein, Groppenbacher, Michaels, & Dumka, 1993). Countless thousands of children are born each year with fetal alcohol syndrome, a constellation of birth defects, including mental deficiencies and low birthweight, that have been found to be associated with heavy drinking during pregnancy.

Alcohol abuse is far more common among men than among women, although alcohol abuse by women is growing. Most literature has focused on the husband as the alcohol abuser and the wife and children as victims, but it is increasingly being recognized that many wives also have alcohol dependence problems.

Alcohol abuse and family violence are statistically related. A national sample of more than 2,000 couples found in general that the more often a spouse was drunk, the greater was the likelihood of physical violence in the marital relationship. The exception to this finding was when the alcohol abuse was extreme. In this case, when the spouse was "almost always" drunk, the level of physical violence dropped to a lower level (Straus, 1990).

Abused women often see drinking as the "cause" of their husband's violent behavior. Richard Gelles concluded that "most of the wives subscribe to the 'conventional wisdom' that alcohol affects people in such a way as to release pent-up violence. The wives feel that if their husbands did not drink, they would not become violent" (Gelles, 1972, p. 113). Husbands involved in violent incidents in which alcohol played a part often concurred that drinking was the problem. "He would say, 'Look, this isn't me. It's the drink that is making me act this way'" (Dobash & Dobash, 1979, p. 118). A study of convicted child molesters found that those men who had been drinking at the time of the crime said that the drinking caused the offense: "I was intoxicated and I couldn't account for myself." "If I were sober, it never would have happened." "Drinking is the reason" (McCaghy, 1968, p. 48). The trouble with these interpretations on the part of both the victim and the abuser, however, is that drinking is used to excuse the violent behavior and to lessen the drinker's responsibility for it. The perpetrator has no reason to change the violent behavior.

Even if there is no violence in the family of an alcoholic, there is likely to be a high degree of marital dissatisfaction and a large number of disagreements. Tension and verbal conflict are likely to be frequent (O'Farrell & Birchler, 1987). Researchers have estimated that half the divorces and half the juvenile arrests for delinquency in the United States occur in families with at least one alcohol-abusing member.

Spouses and children of alcohol abusers are at risk for developing serious physical and emotional problems. Although the majority of children reared in alcoholic homes are not likely to suffer some kind of pathology, they are more likely to exhibit a variety of behavioral and emotional problems than are children from families that do not include an alcoholic member. These problems include conduct disorders or delinquency, alcohol abuse, hyperactivity, difficulties with school work, anxiety, depression, or other health problems (West & Prinz, 1987). Box 15.3 relates a story about the results of alcohol and domestic violence.

The Voice of a Survivor

I'm a survivor of domestic violence; my Mom was a victim. My real father left when I was three years old. Prior to my thirteenth birthday, my Mom remarried. They were only married six months before the abuse started. He was only violent when he was drinking, and he never physically abused us three kids. He was abusing our Mom, the only person in our lives who ever loved and protected us. The abuse lasted less than three years.

On March 26, 1958, my Mom was killed by her batterer. He was drinking that Easter Sunday and insisted Mom accompany him for a car ride (she knew better than to refuse). They left the house around 4 p.m. This was to be the last time any of Mom's children saw her

alive. My Mom was declared a fatality in a car accident, but that is not the real cause of Mom's death. My Mom died a victim of domestic violence.

Sixteen years after my Mom's death, through counseling, I was encouraged to go back and settle the destruction my Mom's death caused. To forgive my Mom was easy, probably the easiest thing I have ever done. But to forgive the abuser was altogether a different matter. My Mom never got out of the violence, but I did, and I've put the past in its proper place. I work with victims of violence, in the hope that victims become survivors. I sense my Mom agrees.

Source: Adapted from "Voices of Survivors," 1990, *Nebraska Domestic Violence Sexual Assault Coalition* (Spring), p. 6.

The Family's Reaction to Alcohol Abuse

In a classic article, Joan K. Jackson (1954) was the first to describe how families attempt to live with an alcohol-abusing father. Jackson studied a sample of families of Alcoholics Anonymous members and outlined a seven-stage process. It is widely recognized today that there are many families with alcohol-abusing mothers or other members, and Jackson's insights are useful for understanding these families. The stages can also be useful in thinking about other chemical dependence problems.

Stage 1: The family attempts to deny the problem. The problem drinker, when confronted by the sober adult about the drinking behavior, denies there is a problem. The family accepts this statement and tolerates or rationalizes the abuser's drinking episodes.

Stage 2: The family tries to eliminate the problem. When the drinking can no longer be ignored, the sober spouse tries to control the problem drinker with threats, bribes, and/or by hiding the alcohol. Marital conflict increases, and family members isolate themselves from friends and neighbors in a futile effort to conceal the drinker's problem.

Stage 3: The family becomes disorganized. The sober spouse realizes that the problem cannot be rationalized away or concealed from the children or the drinker's employer and co-workers. The sober spouse also recognizes that it is futile to try to curtail the drinker's alcohol consumption. Conflict increases, with the children often caught between arguing parents.

Stage 4: The family makes a first attempt at reorganization. The sober spouse recognizes that the drinker cannot function adequately in the family—a recognition often precipitated by the drinker's mismanagement of family funds or by the drinker's violence toward the sober spouse or the children—and takes action. The sober spouse may assume the alcohol abuser's role in the family or may decide to leave the alcohol abuser. The sober spouse may seek assistance from various public agencies, counselors, and self-help groups like Al-Anon. This network of support helps the sober partner gradually regain self-esteem and find the strength to go on. During this stage, the problem drinker is likely to bargain with the family, hoping to regain the lost family role and stature. If the family accepts the drinker's bargain but the drinker then does not quit drinking, the destructive cycle begins again.

Stage 5: The family attempts to escape the problem. The sober spouse seeks a legal separation or divorce. The alcoholic often gives up drinking for a while, but the sober spouse has already shifted from inaction to action.

Stage 6: The family makes a second attempt at reorganization. After legal separation or divorce, the sober spouse assumes the roles formerly held by the drinker, and family life without the drinker is generally much better for all family members than was life with the drinker. The sober spouse may feel guilty for having left the troubled partner. The drinker may attempt to reenter the family or may try to "get even" with the family.

Stage 7: The family reorganizes, with the substance abuser seeking help. If the alcohol-abusing member seeks help and learns to control the drinking, the family may be able to reunite successfully. The process can be difficult; family roles will have to be reassigned once again, and family members will need to reassess their feelings toward the alcohol abuser.

Later researchers built on Jackson's work and outlined a number of coping strategies women commonly use when dealing with alcohol-abusing husbands. These include emotional withdrawal from the marriage; infantilizing the husband; threatening separation or divorce or locking the spouse out of the house; trying to avoid family conflict; assuming control over family finances; and acting out themselves by drinking, threatening suicide, or becoming involved with other men.

Treatment and Prevention of Alcoholism

In a classic model for treating alcoholism, Johnson (1973) outlined a five-stage process. First, alcoholics need to be confronted about their condition by people they trust and in a form they can receive. Even in the most advanced phases, alcoholics can recognize and accept some reality. Second, when the alcoholic has indicated a willingness to receive treatment, a carefully phased detoxification is begun. Medical treatment is necessary to deal with the acute symptoms. Third, it is essential to educate the alcoholic about the facts of alcoholism. Fourth, in individual and group therapy the alcoholic learns to identify defense mechanisms and break them down. The person gains a realistic insight into who he or she has become and begins to rebuild feelings of self-worth. Fifth, professionals and volunteer lay therapists help the alcoholic become established in the community again

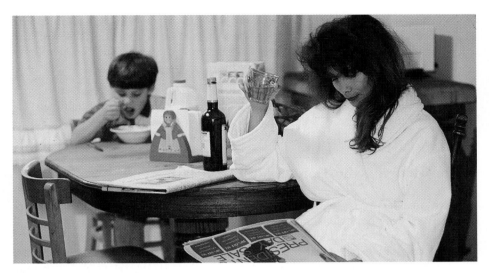

Alcoholics need to be confronted about their condition by people they trust and in a form they can receive. Even in the most advanced phases, alcoholics can recognize and accept some reality.

by helping the individual find a job, repair strained or broken family and personal relationships, and gain society's acceptance.

Self-help groups such as **Alcoholics Anonymous (AA)** (for alcoholics) and **Al-Anon** (for families of alcoholics) are active in most cities and towns in this country. In some metropolitan areas, many different AA meetings are held at a variety of locations each week. These groups offer advice and support for troubled individuals and families. **Alateen,** founded on the AA model, has proven to be helpful for young people with alcoholic parents. In weekly meetings members discuss their problems and learn from others in similar situations.

Some family therapists have been critical of programs that treat the alcoholic outside the context of the family, whereas some alcoholism treatment therapists have criticized family therapists for assuming that alcoholism can be cured simply by eliminating dysfunctional family patterns (Fenell & Weinhold, 1989). It is probably safe to say that problems in families can contribute to alcohol abuse in individual members and that the alcohol abuse then contributes to problems for that family. Those who work with alcohol abusers are becoming increasingly aware that family therapy is an important tool in the treatment of alcoholics and their family system (O'Farrell, 1992).

The National Council on Alcoholism and Drug Dependence (NCADD, 1995) in New York City argues that the disease can be stopped, citing the fact that 1.5 million Americans are in recovery. Some of NCADD's recommendations for people dealing with an alcoholic:

- *Recognize that alcoholism is a disease*. It is not a moral failure or a simple lack of willpower.

- *Learn as much as possible about alcoholism*. Most libraries have many books and articles on alcoholism and other addictions.

- *Do not become an enabler*. Do not support someone's drinking by pretending there is no problem (denial) or by protecting or lying for the alcoholic.

- *Avoid home treatments.* Do not try to solve the loved one's problem by preaching, complaining, acting like a martyr, or trying to reason with the drinker. Alcoholics need expert help from organizations such as Alcoholics Anonymous.

- *Get help for yourself.* The illness of alcoholism affects everyone close to the alcoholic. Many organizations help not only the alcoholic but family members and friends.

Acknowledging the Dangers of Legal Drugs

Our national fervor to stamp out addiction to illegal drugs has tended to overshadow concern about the serious harm legal drugs cause in our society. Alcohol and tobacco cause many times the number of deaths attributable to illegal drugs—and their costs, in terms of lost time from work and medical bills, are much greater. NCADD (1995) estimates that about 180,000–200,000 Americans die each year from alcohol abuse (including alcohol-related medical problems, motor vehicle crashes, homicides, suicides, and other unintentional injuries).

Elizabeth Whelan, president of the American Council on Science and Health, reports that 500,000 smoking and nonsmoking Americans die each year from diseases related to legal cigarette smoking, whereas an estimated 30,000 die from illegal drugs (Whelan, 1995). Environmental tobacco smoke is one of the most widespread and harmful indoor air pollutants, according the U.S. Environmental Protection Agency (Schepers, 1991). An estimated 30,000–53,000 nonsmoking Americans die each year from breathing other people's smoke (B. C. Coleman, 1995). And chewing tobacco and snuff, especially popular among adolescent males, have been linked with mouth cancer and throat cancer (Newman, 1990).

Medically, alcohol and cigarette addictions are the most difficult habits to break, according to Dr. William Brostoff. It is easier to withdraw or undergo detoxification from cocaine or even heroin than from alcohol or cigarettes ("Nation's Legal Drugs," 1986). It has been found that actively involving the spouse in the smoking cessation program increases the program's success (Doherty & Whitehead, 1986).

Almost all adult smokers begin to smoke before age 20, researchers have found. Recent studies indicate that poorer family functioning is related to adolescent cigarette smoking. For example, William J. Doherty and William Allen (1994) found that families who were low in family cohesion (togetherness) and had a parent who smoked were the most likely to have a young adolescent who smoked. Similarly, Janet N. Melby and her colleagues found that harsh and inconsistent parenting was related to adolescent tobacco use and that nurturant and involved parenting was not (Melby, Conger, Conger, & Lorenz, 1993).

The family clearly is a major influence in our lives, either as a foundation for health and happiness or as an unhappy battleground. Emotional, physical, and sexual abuse does occur in families, and many families are plagued by alcoholism and addiction to other legal and illegal drugs. But these problems can be treated effectively. Fortunately, most families find ways to create relatively supportive and satisfying relationships among their members, which helps prevent family problems of all sorts.

Summary

- Because family systems theory sees family members' behaviors as interrelated, with each member's actions affecting the other members and their actions, it focuses on helping families resolve issues rather than on identifying "causes" of family problems.

- The family systems of individuals with mental disorders and those who abuse alcohol are more likely to be unbalanced on the Circumplex Model than they are to be balanced (healthy).

- Child abuse includes not only physical assault resulting in injury but also abandonment, neglect, emotional abuse, and sexual abuse. More than 1 million American children are abused each year. Abuse and neglect occur in all social classes and at all levels of income, although they are far more prevalent among low-income families.

- Children exhibit two extreme behavioral adaptations to abuse: aggressive, acting-out behavior or passive acceptance. Many abusive parents were themselves abused as children, but only about one quarter to one third of all children who are abused grow up to abuse their own offspring.

- Parental and family risk factors for child abuse include economic distress, inadequate parenting skills, parental personality problems, chemical abuse, social isolation, a special child, family size, domestic violence in the abuser's family of origin, a violent subculture or marriage, and single parenthood or stepparenthood.

- Treatment of child abusers involves increasing the parent's self-esteem, educating the parent about children and childrearing techniques, and helping the parent develop a support network.

- Sexual abuse of children is categorized as intrafamilial (incestuous) or extrafamilial (nonincestuous). Incestuous abuse is the sexual exploitation of a child under age 18 by a relative. Child sexual abuse is seen in chaotic families (those with multiple problems over many generations) and in normal-appearing families (especially those in which roles are traditionally structured but parental nurturing skills are lacking). Most sex offenders live in and grew up in families that are unbalanced on the Circumplex Model.

- Reports of child sexual abuse have increased dramatically in recent years, most likely because the law now requires professionals who suspect it to report it.

- The effects of sexual abuse on the victim include difficulties in school, guilt or shame, anger, lowered self-esteem, depression, sleep and eating disorders, self-destructive thoughts and behaviors, increased vulnerability to rape or marital violence as an adult, and sexual difficulties. Support groups can help incest survivors resolve the effects of sexual abuse.

- Domestic violence is the single greatest cause of injury to women. An estimated 3 million people, most of them women, are severely assaulted each year in the United States by their spouses. Most incidents are not reported.

- Many of the risk factors for spouse abuse in a family are similar to those for child abuse: victimization as a child, low self-esteem, youth, economic stress, social isolation, alcohol abuse, and a male-dominated relationship. Cultural factors that implicitly support the objectification and denigration of women may also play a part.

- Counselors generally advise battered women to leave their husbands. Shelters for abused women and their children offer emotional support and counseling as well as practical help. Arrest of perpetrators of domestic violence is more likely today, and research indicates that men who spend time behind bars are less likely to assault their partners again.

- Sibling abuse and child-to-parent abuse are more common than might be expected. An estimated 75% of siblings are involved in a violent episode each year, and 10% of parents are victimized by violent behavior on the part of their children, generally those 13–24 years of age.

- An estimated 12 million men, women, and children in this country are alcoholics and 16–19 million adults are problem drinkers. Alcohol abuse and family violence or marital discord are related. An estimated half of the divorces and the juvenile arrests for delinquency in the United States occur in families with an alcohol-abusing member.

- In dealing with an alcohol-abusing member, families commonly go through seven stages: attempting to deny the problem; attempting to eliminate it; disorganization; a first attempt at reorganization, in which the sober spouse takes action; legal escape through separation or divorce; a second attempt at reorganization; and the seeking of help by the alcohol-abusing member.

- Successful treatment for chronic alcoholism involves five stages: confrontation by trusted people in a form the alcoholic can receive; detoxification under medical supervision; education about the facts of the disease; individual and group therapy to help the alcoholic identify and break down defense mechanisms; and reestablishment in the family and community.

- Legal drugs cause more deaths than illegal ones. An estimated 180,000–200,000 Americans die each year from alcohol abuse, and about 500,000 Americans die from diseases linked to smoking. The highest estimate of deaths attributable to illegal drugs is 30,000 per year.

Key Terms

schizophrenia	chaotic family	child-to-parent abuse
anxiety disorder	normal-appearing family	alcohol abuse
co-dependent	post-traumatic stress disorder	alcoholism
enabler	victimizer	problem drinking
child abuse	learned helplessness theory	Alcoholics Anonymous (AA)
incest	catharsis conflict	Al-Anon
incestuous abuse	sibling abuse	Alateen

Activities

1. Describe in one or two paragraphs the most violent incident you have witnessed in your family. Note who was involved, what the dispute was about, and what happened. Read and discuss your description with a small group. How do you plan to avoid such violence in your family in the future?

2. Describe a recent incident in which you saw physical punishment used to discipline a child. Then describe how the child could have been disciplined in a more positive (nonviolent) way. Keeping in mind the principle "Teach children, don't hit them," brainstorm nonviolent approaches to disciplining children.

3. Conduct a class survey focusing on class members' perceptions of alcohol and other drug problems in their families. If appropriate, discuss the relationship of these problems to any violence that has occurred in their families.

4. In small groups, discuss the extent of alcohol and other drug abuse on campus. Also discuss any violent incidents, such as date rape, related to chemical abuse.

Suggested Readings

Gelles, R. J., & Loseke, D. R. (1993). *Current controversies on family violence*. Newbury Park, CA: Sage. *Discusses the disagreements among family violence researchers about how to conceptualize the problem, how to study it, and how to interpret the findings in the effort to recommend appropriate interventions.*

Gelles, R. J., & Straus, M. (1988). *Intimate violence*. New York: Simon & Schuster. *An excellent resource from the pioneers in family violence research.*

Hampton, R. L. (Ed.). (1991). *Black family violence: Research and theory*. Lexington, MA: Lexington Books. *A worthwhile compilation of interdisciplinary research.*

Jacob, T. (1993). Family studies of alcoholism. *Journal of Family Psychology, 5* (March/June), 319–338. *A useful review of research on the family and alcohol addiction.*

Kaplan, L., & Girard, J. L. (1994). *Strengthening high-risk families: A handbook for practitioners*. New York: Lexington Books. *Offers guidance for those interested in becoming part of the revolution in social services, focusing on home-based family treatment.*

Kirschner, S., Kirschner, D. A., & Rappaport, R. L. (1993). *Working with adult incest survivors: The healing journey*. New York: Brunner/Mazel. *An integrated procedure for treating adults who have experienced abuse.*

Lockhart, L. L., et al. (1994). Letting out the secret: Violence in lesbian relationships. *Journal of Interpersonal Violence, 9* (4), 469–492. *Reports an exploratory study aimed at understanding violence among lesbian couples, which is not rare but which has until recently been largely ignored.*

O'Farrell, T. J. (Ed.). (1993). *Treating alcohol problems: Marital and family interventions*. New York: Guilford. *A systematic description and evaluation of family therapy techniques for each stage of alcoholism.*

Schroeder, B. (1990). *Helping kids say no to drugs and drinking: A practical prevention guide for parents*. Lincoln, NE: Alcohol and Drug Abuse Council of Nebraska. *A very useful reference for parents, teachers, and others who work with children.*

Wurtele, S. K., & Miller-Perrin, C. L. (Eds.). (1992). *Preventing child sexual abuse: Sharing the responsibility*. Lincoln, NE: University of Nebraska Press. *An excellent book for anyone interested in starting or improving a prevention program or simply wanting to learn more.*

CHAPTER 16

Divorce and Adjustment

People don't generally marry with the expectation that they will divorce, but the odds are good that it will happen to them. Despite the prevalence of divorce, our society sees it as a tragedy and a sign of the breakdown of the American family. But divorce can have a positive outcome, freeing individuals from painful or difficult marriages that cannot be changed. Many who have experienced divorce feel it was a sad necessity in their lives. They see it as the first step in a journey of healing and growth that has led to a satisfying single life or, perhaps, a successful marriage to a new partner.

This chapter examines the complicated process of marital dissolution, separation, and divorce. It begins with a look at various trends in the termination of marriage in our society: statistical trends, historical trends, and legal trends. Different ways of looking at divorce are then presented, in a search for a better understanding of the reasons people divorce. Finally, various processes of adjusting to divorce are outlined.

Trends in Divorce

Divorcees are people who have not achieved a good marriage—they are also people who would not settle for a bad one.
—PAUL BOHANNAN (1970, p. 54)

Marriage continues to be popular, but, unfortunately, the likelihood of a marriage being successful, as discussed throughout this book, is less than 50%. Some researchers argue that the 50% rate may be too conservative for future estimates, predicting that two thirds of all marriages in the United States today will end in divorce (Martin & Bumpass, 1989). The projection for second marriages is closer to 60%. But marriage is so popular that about 75% of younger people who divorce are likely to remarry—three out of four divorced women and five out of six divorced men (U.S. Bureau of the Census, 1995). Figure 16.1 illustrates the divorce-remarriage patterns that can be expected with a 50% divorce rate.

Statistical Trends

In 1993, there were approximately 2.36 million marriages and 1.21 million divorces in the United States (U.S. Bureau of the Census, 1994). Divorce is part of a lengthy series of relationship processes, including dating, perhaps cohabitation, marriage, marital dissolution, marital separation, divorce, singlehood, dating, usually cohabitation, and remarriage. After a comprehensive review of research on divorce, Lynn White (1991) found that divorce is higher among lower-income couples, higher among Blacks than Whites, higher among people who marry at a younger age, and higher among religiously mixed marriages. The highest rate of divorce, 50–80%, is among women who marry in their teens, are of lower socioeconomic status, drop out of high school, and are pregnant when they marry.

The average age at divorce is 35 for men and 33 for women. The average length of first marriages that end in divorce is about 7 years. So, of the half of all

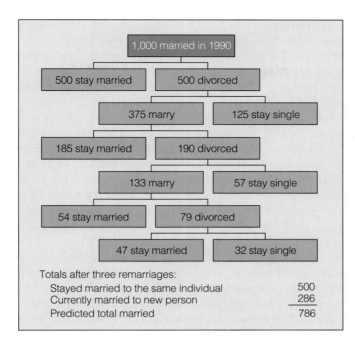

Figure 16.1 Estimated Divorce and Remarriage Rates for 1,000 Individuals Married in 1990. *Source: Family Science* (p. 445) by W. R. Burr, R. D. Day, and K. S. Bahr. Copyright © 1993 by Wadsworth, Inc. Reprinted by permission of Brooks/Cole Publishing Company, Pacific Grove, California 93950.

first marriages that end in divorce, half of those end within the first 7 years (U.S. Bureau of the Census, 1994).

Divorce most often occurs during the first year or two of marriage. By the end of 5 years, 19% of couples are divorced; by the end of 10 years of marriage, 14% more are divorced. Another 7% divorce before 15 years of marriage; 7% more divorce before their 25th anniversary; and 3% more, before their 50th anniversary (L. K. White, 1991).

Historical Trends

The U.S. divorce rate is much higher than it has been in previous decades. In the two decades before World War II (1920–1940), there were roughly 5–8 divorces per 1,000 people each year. By the end of World War II (1946), this rate had sky-rocketed to more than 17 per 1,000 per year. The rate dropped dramatically in the 1950s, to 9–10 per 1,000, but in the late 1960s it began a steep climb to a peak of more than 22 per 1,000 at the close of the 1970s and in the early 1980s. In the remainder of the 1980s and early 1990s, the divorce rate averaged about 21 per 1,000 people (U.S. Bureau of the Census, 1994).

Many explanations have been offered for the dramatic increase in divorces that began in the 1960s. Some say that changes in divorce laws in the 1970s influenced the divorce rate, but this has been seriously contested by others. Some of a conservative orientation argue that "women's liberation" is the cause. Others look at a whole complex of social factors, including economic conditions, level of education of women, and attitudes toward divorce (L. K. White, 1991).

Educated women still face discrimination in the working world today, but their chances for economic survival on their own are better than were those of past generations of women. With education comes the freeing knowledge that "I don't need a man to lean on. I can take care of myself." However, divorce rates among poor and low-income families are even higher than among the educated and the better off. For most families, having a skilled, educated wife is an advantage in terms of family stability. But if an educated and skilled woman is not happy in her marriage, economics do not require her to stay with a man she does not love.

It is true that as the percentage of women working outside the home has increased over the years, the divorce rate has also increased. But a woman's working outside the home does not necessarily cause divorce; many happy marriages involve two wage earners. Working outside the home helps alleviate financial stress for families, but the workplace adds other stressors. Some marriages can withstand these stressors; other marriages cannot. Stress alone, however, does not cause divorce.

Although the United States has the highest divorce rate of all the Western industrialized nations, divorce rates in other nations are increasing to match ours. Economic prosperity brings with it more autonomy in mate selection for young people. In rural agrarian societies, where parents choose marriage partners for the young, divorce rates are relatively low. Free choice and the relative economic independence of women in Western cultures are two important contributors to the higher divorce rate.

The marriage bond has lost some of its religious significance and has become more of a personal commitment between two people. Some churches and synagogues have not welcomed those who are divorced, but others have encouraged their participation. Discussion and support groups for divorced people now operate under the umbrella of more churches. Marriage is increasingly being regarded as a voluntary commitment between two people, one which they continue to keep as long as the relationship is mutually satisfying. This definition is far different from the traditional notion that marriage is for life.

Legal Trends

Since 1970, when the state of California instituted the first no-fault divorce law, major changes have occurred in divorce laws across the United States. These changes came about as an almost direct response to the rising number of divorces and to the changing roles of women in this country. Today all 50 states have laws similar to California's (Parkman, 1992).

No-fault divorce abolished fault ("guilt" of one party) as the basis for dissolving a marriage. Under no-fault law, one party's assertion that "irreconcilable differences have caused irremediable breakdown of the marriage" is sufficient for the granting of a divorce.

Traditional Divorce Law   Lenore Weitzman and Ruth Dixon have identified the four major elements of traditional divorce law that were transformed by the no-fault system of divorce (Weitzman & Dixon, 1980; Weitzman, 1985). These elements are:

Because divorce can be traumatic for both adults and children, lawyers should not act as adversaries doing battle for their clients but rather should try to facilitate responsible communication. The lawyer's most important task is to help the divorcing parents restructure the family and minimize the emotional damage to both themselves and their children.

1. *Gender-based divisions of role responsibilities.* Traditional family law assumed that the husband would provide financial support in a lifelong marriage. If the marriage ended and if the wife had been virtuous, she was granted **alimony**—continued financial support. This gender-based division of labor was also recognized in regard to children. The husband remained responsible for their economic support after the divorce, and the wife was the preferred custodial parent.

2. *Grounds for divorce.* Traditionally, **fault**—legal blame for the end of a marriage—had to be assigned, and only serious offenses were considered sufficient grounds for divorce. Evidence for misbehavior varied from state to state, but husbands charged with cruelty were often alleged to have caused bodily harm to their wives. Wives were more likely to be charged with neglecting their husbands or their homes.

   In practice, many couples wishing to divorce simply agreed privately to an **uncontested divorce**—one in which one party, often the wife, would charge the other party, generally the husband, with mental cruelty and the "accused" would agree not to challenge the "accuser" in court. Even though the parties had colluded in the matter and often perjured themselves in court, the courts considered the grounds "appropriate violations" of the marriage contract.

3. *Adversarial proceedings.* In the traditional system, lawyers "did battle" for their clients and divorces had to be "won." One partner was "guilty" and the other was "innocent."

4. *Linkage of the financial settlement to determination of fault.* A finding of "guilty" or "innocent" had important financial consequences. Alimony

could be awarded only to an innocent spouse: A wife found guilty of adultery, for example, could not receive alimony. Property awards were also linked to the determination of fault. This linkage produced heated accusations and counteraccusations.

No-Fault Divorce Law   Weitzman and Dixon (1980) have also explained how no-fault divorce law altered the four elements of traditional divorce law discussed above:

1. *Redefinition of the traditional duties of husbands and wives and establishment of equality between the genders as a norm.* Under no-fault laws, the husband is no longer considered by law to be the head of the family. Both spouses are presumed to be equal partners, with equal obligations for financial support and care of their children. Spouses are treated equally in respect to child custody, as well as finances and property.

   The so-called **tender years doctrine,** which presumed that young children would automatically do better with their mother than with their father, has been replaced by the notion of joint custody as being in the "best interests of the child." Fathers are at least theoretically equal to mothers in questions of custody. In a small minority of cases, fathers are winning not only custody but also child support.

2. *Elimination of fault-based grounds for divorce.* Under no-fault laws, one spouse does not have to prove the other's adultery, cruelty, or desertion. The concept of "irreconcilable differences" recognizes that discussion of the reasons for the marital dissolution is irrelevant.

3. *Elimination of the adversarial process.* Proponents of divorce reform had argued that the adversarial nature of traditional divorce proceedings was harmful to all parties involved, but especially to the children. Under no-fault, by facilitating accurate and responsible communication rather than doing battle, lawyers could help divorcing parents restructure the family and prepare to fulfill their post-divorce parenting responsibilities. Many spouses neither love nor hate each other at the end of a marriage; they are capable of an "amicable divorce" and are good candidates for joint custody of their children (discussed in Chapter 17).

4. *Basing of financial decisions on equity, equality, and economic need rather than on fault or gender-based role assignments.* In a no-fault system, each spouse's economic circumstances are assessed under the principle of equality between the sexes. No-fault laws adhere to the notion that divorced women should be self-supporting but that if that is not possible, they should receive fair compensation. Under the newer no-fault divorce laws, older homemakers are more likely to receive alimony than younger homemakers. In some cases, a woman might receive support while she goes back to school for retraining. Recently, attorneys have been forcefully arguing that women who put their husbands through professional school are entitled to a share of their earnings for a period of time after the divorce.

   Reformers had argued that with an increasing number of women entering the labor force, alimony was rapidly becoming an anachronism.

This, however, ignored the fact that female workers earn on average only about 60% of what male workers earn.

There has been a backlash to the financial aspects of no-fault divorce (Parkman, 1992). They are seen by many as anti-women and as punishing women financially for divorce. Divorced women and their children suffer an immediate drop of 27% in their standard of living, whereas their ex-husbands experience an increase of 10% in their standard of living (Parkman, 1992).

No-fault divorce laws are based on the theory that equality results in a more positive outcome for all involved. How the theory works in practice depends on the decisions of individual judges who must adjudicate the more than 1 million divorces in the United States each year.

Effects of the Change   In evaluating the results of the no-fault system, researchers report a mixture of expected and unexpected findings. Though Dixon and Weitzman (1980; Weitzman, 1985) observed that no-fault divorce had no discernible effect on the divorce rate, more recent research reports that it did increase the divorce rate across the 50 states (Nakonezny, Shull, & Rodgers, 1995). The mandatory counseling feature of the system apparently did not bring about many reconciliations; it proved to be too little, too late for most marriages.

No-fault has eliminated the hypocrisy of the old system, which forced spouses into pointing the finger whether they wished to or not, and it seems to have somewhat reduced the bitterness of the battles. The number of hearings before a final decree of divorce has declined markedly, and these hearings were where many of the most bitter battles were fought. Property settlements and spousal and child support appear to be fairer under the new guidelines. However, no-fault did eliminate one benefit of traditional divorce law for those who have a valid grievance. Because men could no longer be punished for obvious wrongdoing, women, in particular, lost a bargaining advantage in negotiating property settlements and alimony (Dixon & Weitzman, 1980; Weitzman, 1985).

Judges joke that divorce court service is like a sentence in Siberia. Despite changes in divorce laws, divorce court remains "the saddest room in America." But no-fault laws have alleviated some of the tremendous pain of divorce and have facilitated greater cooperation in coparenting after the divorce.

Understanding Divorce

Both partners in a divorce will most likely spend considerable time trying to unravel the reasons why their marriage ended. Although the task is difficult, it is essential to the postdivorce recovery process. The search for the "causes" of a divorce must take into consideration a number of factors and many points of view. This section looks at several important things to consider in trying to understand why people divorce.

Table 16.1 Major Reasons Marriages Fail (sample = 500)

	LISTED FIRST (NUMBER)	(RANK)	TOTAL NUMBER OF TIMES LISTED	(RANK)
Infidelity	168	(1)	255	(1)
No longer in love	103	(2)	188	(2)
Emotional problems	53	(3)	185	(3)
Financial problems	30	(4)	135	(4)
Physical abuse	29	(5)	72	(8)
Alcohol	25	(6)	47	(9)
Sexual problems	22	(7)	155	(5)
Problems with in-laws	16	(8)	81	(6)
Neglect of children	11	(9)	74	(7)
Communication problems	10	(10)	18	(11)
Married too young	9	(11)	14	(12)
Job conflicts	7	(12)	20	(10)
Other	7		19	

Source: "Correlates of Marital Happiness Among the Remarried" by S. L. Albrecht, 1979, *Journal of Marriage and the Family, 41* (4), p. 862. Copyright 1979 by National Council on Family Relations. Reprinted by permission.

Why Couples Divorce

"Marriage causes divorce!" is the facetious reply to the question "What causes divorce?" The stresses and strains of living together are simply too difficult for many couples. But the picture is more complicated. What are some of the factors that interweave to cause divorce? Why do some people divorce, whereas others in apparently more troubled relationships stay married? Family researchers and family therapists have spent considerable time exploring what causes divorce.

A classic study by Stan Albrecht (1979) of 500 divorced people who remarried found that the top four reasons given for the failure of these marriages were infidelity, no longer loving each other, emotional problems, and financial problems. The complete list is presented in Table 16.1, and some of the reasons are discussed below.

Infidelity   "The grass is always greener" in some people's minds. Marriage becomes boring, the relationship with the spouse becomes difficult or unsatisfying, or another person is seen as being a much better partner. Married people seek solace outside marriage for many reasons, but **infidelity**—having sex with someone other than the marriage partner—can mean the end of the relationship.

After studying separated and divorced people, G. S. Spanier and L. Thompson (1984) found that extramarital sex often occurred before the divorce but argued that it was a result of rather than the cause of marital problems. In about one third of these marriages, the extramarital sex first occurred before separation appeared likely. These affairs were less likely to be "one-night stands" for either sex and often involved some emotional commitment and long-term involvement. Although these affairs were generally satisfying, females felt more guilty than males.

Most real-life divorces bear little resemblance to soap-opera divorces. They are not the result of infidelity, criminality, or betrayal, but rather of gradual marriage burnout. If one of the partners continues to hide unhappiness rather than discussing it, all feelings for the spouse may gradually disappear, leaving only disinterest.

The Absence of Love   One of the most common scenarios for divorce is the **devitalized (burned-out) marriage,** one that has died not with a bang (as in the case of marital violence) but with a whimper, because the partners are no longer in love. Some researchers argue that this divorce scenario is the most common of all (Hayes, Stinnett, & DeFrain, 1980).

Marriage burnout comes on so slowly that couples often are not aware of it. Both spouses may feel that things are okay but not great, or one spouse may harbor ill feelings but not admit them to the other. There may be no dramatic signs that things are very wrong until the end. One young man told of a wonderful vacation with his wife. "We joked and laughed and cuddled and made wonderful love. When I went to work the day after we got home from vacation, there was a letter waiting at the office for me from her lawyer. It said she wanted a divorce." The young man was crushed by this experience. The divorce was a total shock to him and to his parents. His spouse had kept her unhappiness a secret.

People do not want to fail in marriage, and so they tend quite often to cover up their true feelings. If they do this long enough, all feeling for the spouse can disappear. They neither hate nor love the spouse, and in the absence of any feeling at all, they end the marriage. This same thing also occurs in many marriages that survive. Couples may fight frequently about a variety of issues, leading to growing dissatisfaction with the marriage. These couples often develop a disengaged relationship, with little emotional connection, but they often stay married because of their children, their religious values, or for economic reasons.

Physical Abuse   Many divorces are associated with violence. Spouses attack each other verbally and physically. In the heat of marital disputes (often when one or both have been drinking), people can do and say almost unbelievably abusive things. Many times neighbors, good friends, and relatives may be unaware that anything is wrong in the marriage. People hide their emotional and physical bruises rather than risk being considered failures by others. When divorce occurs, outsiders often say, "I just don't understand it. They were such a perfect couple."

Unhappy Versus Happy Couples

To learn more about the characteristics of happily married versus unhappily married couples, Fowers and Olson (1989) studied a national sample of 5,039 married couples. There were 2,375 unhappy couples in the study, most of whom were in marriage counseling. The other 2,664 were happily married couples who had attended a marriage enrichment program. To confirm how satisfied the couples were, spouses were asked whether they had "considered getting divorced." As expected, among the happy couples, 95% of the spouses said that neither partner had considered divorce, whereas among the unhappy couples, 95% of the spouses had considered divorce.

In terms of background characteristics, the mean age of the males was 33 and of the females, 32. The couples had been married an average of 9.7 years, they had an average of 2.9 children, and the majority of the spouses had some college education. The surprising thing about the background characteristics was that there was very little difference in age, years married, and number of children among the couples. These variables did not discriminate between the unhappy and the happy couples.

All the couples took the ENRICH marital inventory developed by Olson, Fournier, and Druckman (1989), which was explained in Chapter 4. Discriminate analysis (a statistical approach that permits determination of how well a set of scales can discriminate between two specific groups) was used to see how well the ENRICH scales of couple agreement could discriminate between the happily and the unhappily married couples. The analysis showed that the scales could discriminate with about 90% accuracy between happily and unhappily married couples. Five of the scales were the most predictive: sexual relationship, communication, conflict resolution, children and parenting, and leisure activities. However, scores of happy and unhappy couples differed significantly on almost all the scales, with happily married couples getting significantly higher positive couple scores on all of the scales except financial management and egalitarian roles. The three scales on which the two groups showed the most significant differences were the quality of their communication, skills at resolving couple conflict, and the quality of their sexual relationship. Figure 16.2 illustrates the average scores for the happily and the unhappily married couples.

Communication and Conflict Resolution Some authorities might say that communication problems are the central reason for divorce. Most divorcing people relate how communication, including the ability to resolve conflict and deal with problems, broke down in their marriage. Communication and conflict resolution are interrelated. Both are necessary skills in a happy marriage, as demonstrated by the Fowers and Olson (1989) study.

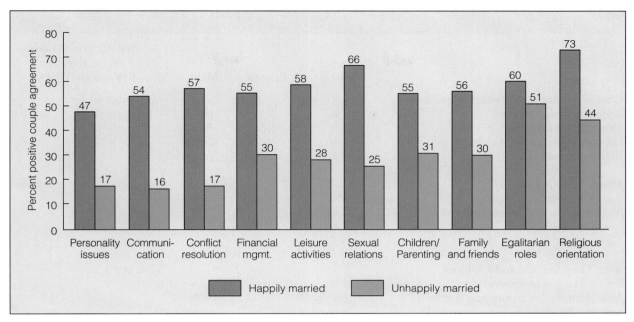

Figure 16.2 Agreement on Important Issues in Happily Married and Unhappily Married Couples. *Note:* Based on ENRICH couple agreement scores (*n* = 5,039 couples). *Source:* "ENRICH Marital Inventory: A Discriminant Validity and Cross-validation Assessment" (p. 71) by B. J. Fowers and D. H. Olson, 1989, *Journal of Marital and Family Therapy*, 15, 1, 65–79. Copyright © 1989 by American Association of Marital and Family Therapy. Reprinted by permission.

Sexual Problems   An unsatisfying sex life is often associated with divorce. Some divorcing people contend that sex is only the battleground, not the cause of the war. But an unsatisfactory sex life can be a significant source of stress in a marriage, and divorcing people often talk about the failed sexual relationship. Spanier and Thompson (1984) asked separated and divorced individuals to compare sexual satisfaction early in the marriage with sexual satisfaction just before they separated. The researchers found a dramatic decrease in sexual satisfaction.

Adjusting to Divorce

The divorce process can be stressful and even traumatic for some, but the most difficult time for most people is the period leading up to the decision to divorce. After the divorce, most generally feel good about the property settlement, and they generally feel that their life is better overall than it was during the marriage. After divorce, some people withdraw from activities for a while but gradually become involved with others again. For more details, see Table 16.2.

Paul Bohannan (1970) has described the divorce process as an intense journey including "six stations of divorce." These stations, or experiences, often overlap, occur in different sequences, and vary in intensity for each individual. The six experiences are:

Table 16.2 The "Best" and "Worst" Periods of Divorce

	COMBINED SAMPLE	FEMALE	MALE	SPOUSE FOR WHOM SITUATION IS BETTER OR WORSE
Characterization of Divorce Experience				More stressful for wife
Traumatic, a nightmare	23%	27%	16%	
Stressful, but bearable	40%	40%	40%	
Unsettling, but easier than expected	20%	19%	24%	
Relatively painless	17%	13%	20%	
Most Difficult Period				Both rate predivorce as worse
Before decision to divorce	55%	58%	50%	
After decision, but before final decree	22%	20%	25%	
Just after the divorce	21%	19%	23%	
Now	3%	3%	3%	
Best Time for Self and Children				Wife better now
Before decision to divorce	13%	8%	22%	
After decision, but before final decree	6%	6%	5%	
Just after the divorce	14%	15%	12%	
Now	67%	71%	62%	
Feeling About Property Settlement				Wife more satisfied
Good or very good	70%	73%	68%	
Frustrated, unhappy	26%	22%	32%	
Just glad to get out	4%	6%	1%	
Post-Divorce Income				Wife's income much lower
Much lower	31%	48%	7%	
Somewhat lower	16%	18%	12%	
About the same	39%	27%	57%	
Somewhat higher	11%	6%	17%	
Much higher	3%	1%	7%	
Change in Contact with Relatives				Wife has more contact now
More contact	32%	37%	25%	
No change	55%	52%	60%	
Less contact	12%	10%	15%	

Source: Adapted from "Reactions and Adjustments to Divorce" by S. L. Albrecht, 1980, *Family Relations, 29* (1), pp. 61, 63. Copyright 1980 by National Council on Family Relations. Adapted by permission.

1. **Emotional divorce.** Deterioration of the marriage, the breakdown of bonding and communication, and replacement by feelings of alienation.

2. **Legal divorce.** Dissolution of the marriage by the legal system and the courts.

3. **Economic divorce.** Financial and property settlements.

4. **Coparental divorce.** Decisions about child custody, single parenting, and visitation rights.

5. **Community divorce.** Changes in relationships with friends and community members.

6. **Psychological divorce.** Regaining individual autonomy.

Emotional Divorce

Deciding to marry feels so good because you have found someone you love. Divorce feels so awful because that love has been lost. Divorce involves a vast spectrum of emotions, and no two individuals react to it the same way. There are, however, some common patterns that appear in most divorces.

Anger and violence are very common with divorced couples. A spouse who is losing a mate can be very angry. Many people try to escape the pain of loss or their rage in chemicals. Even those who had not been prone to abusing drugs before sometimes can figure out no other way to cope. "I just needed to turn my brain off for a while," one husband said. "It hurt too much to think, and I couldn't stop thinking painful thoughts any other way."

Other people may fall into total emotional disrepair and depression, finding it impossible to function. They may sleep a lot and may think about suicide. One woman who lost her husband to her best friend put it this way, "I was so depressed I wanted to kill myself, but for three days I couldn't find the energy to get out of bed to get the pills in the bathroom to do it." Many physicians argue that the misery of a dissolving marriage can also weaken the body's resistance to disease. As noted in Chapter 14, colds, pneumonia, headaches, ulcers, and even cancer have been found to be related to marital stresses. One physician has even called marital conflict the "number one killer."

The crisis of divorce, like many other crises in life, often adds to the common human feeling of loneliness. Listen to this divorced mother of two young children: "This weekend is pretty lonely. All my weekday friends have weekend husbands. I've painted Billy's room, baked 10 dozen oatmeal cookies (Elizabeth's request), and got two weeks of shopping done and it is still only Saturday. Maybe I got married because weekends are so long."

Even though we know it isn't true, when we're in the midst of a crisis, we may think, "No one can understand how terrible I feel now. No one has ever gone through this before." John Woodward, who has done a great deal of research on loneliness, argues that to feel lonely is a universal human condition. The crisis of divorce exacerbates these feelings of loneliness (Woodward, 1988). In the words of Robert Weiss, "Of all the negative feelings of the newly separated, none is more common or more important than loneliness. Only a minority fail to suffer from it, and even those who most keenly desired the end of the marriage often find the initial loneliness excruciating" (1973, p. 83).

The decision to divorce is most often not reached easily or quickly, and it may be fraught with ambivalence. Even though a spouse has moved out of the home, there is still a chance that he or she will return. Emotions run deep. Hate may exist in tandem with love. One minute an individual is thinking, "There's no way that I can survive this marriage"; the next, "Oh, I miss her so much."

Legal Divorce

When Bohannan first conceived his six stations of divorce, he included the adversarial legal process as a significant challenge. No-fault laws have eliminated the element of blame, or fault, to some degree, but they have not removed all conflict from the proceedings. As Norman Krivosha (1983), former chief justice of the Nebraska Supreme Court, has noted, "If people don't want to live together, then let them divorce. By moving to no-fault divorce, we shifted the fight from divorce to property and custody." Competing attorneys do battle for their clients, and these "hired guns" try to get the most they can for whoever is paying the fee.

The adversarial system may work reasonably well for resolving disputes between businesses or strangers, but families with children thrive on trust and cooperation. Divorcing parents have to deal with each other because they remain connected by their children. Rather than helping to mend the wounds of a broken family, the legal system often makes things worse. One judge commented, "Criminal court is easier, and a lot more fun."

In recent years, a nationwide movement toward the mediation of divorces has gained ground in the United States. A network of professional and volunteer mediators is growing with the intent of keeping family disputes out of the legal system to minimize the emotional damage to ongoing family relationships. Rather than partners each hiring a lawyer to represent them in the divorce, families can go to a trained mediator, who tries to work out the dispute in the best interest of everyone involved. The mediator works to find a win-win solution, rather than the win-lose approach of the courtroom.

Economic Divorce

Some spouses simply don't want to argue about the money, the house, the cars, the furniture. The pain of divorce seems too much to bear, and the financial details exceed their coping abilities. But the economic realities must be faced and resolved. Lawyers are useful for sorting out all the complications—and to represent your better interests when you don't have the energy to do so yourself. Many people are so relieved to get out of an unhappy marriage that they don't want to think about the details. "Let him have anything he wants," many a lawyer has heard. "I just want to forget the whole thing."

Divorce can have a crippling financial legacy. Drastic downward mobility, a sort of reverse American dream, is one major consequence of divorce for many. A. Stroup and G. E. Pollock (1994) found, for example, that the incomes of divorced people are lower than the incomes of married people, by 30% for women and by 10% for men. Because children still usually remain with their mother after a divorce, it's especially important for women to get a fair income and property settlement.

After a divorce, many women are forced into the job market, some for the first time. They may have little job experience because they've been home caring for children. Their self-esteem is at a low ebb as a result of the breakup of the marriage, and they may have little confidence in their ability to find and hold a good job in a tight job market.

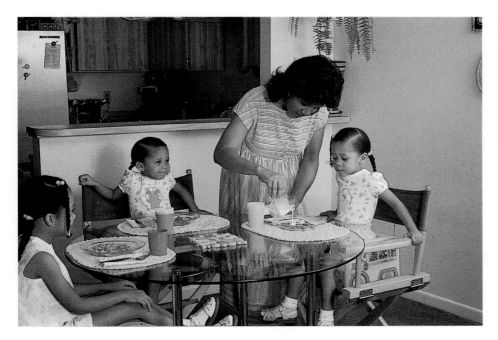

Many newly divorced mothers with young children face the double challenge of finding affordable child care and a job that pays a livable wage but does not require special skills or extensive experience.

The term **feminization of poverty** refers to the statistical fact that the percentage of female single parents in the total percentage of people who are poor in this country is increasing. Much of this increase of women in poverty is the result of the increasing divorce rate and the severe reduction in divorced women's income. The divorced woman, especially the mother with young children, is in a difficult fix. Her marriage proved unworkable and ending it was probably a good idea, but life after divorce often proves to be financially punishing.

Coparental Divorce

Children play a role in making a satisfactory marriage relationship more difficult to achieve in some respects, but they are also a bond between parents, even in divorce and after it. About 60% of divorces involve children (Kitson & Morgan, 1991; L. K. White, 1991). Spouses may divorce each other, but parents cannot divorce their children. The most difficult dilemma facing divorcing partners with children is the question of what will happen to the children. The coparental divorce experience reflects the reality that parents must work out how they will coparent even though they will no longer be married or live together.

It has been estimated that 80% of the children in divorced families live with their mothers, 6% live with their fathers, and 14% live with other relatives (Kitson & Morgan, 1991; L. K. White, 1991). Traditionally, women have taken the lion's share of the responsibility for the children in a divorce. Fathers have often found themselves with minimal visitation rights and little control over the situation. This does not foster coparenting.

Most children want to maintain contact with both parents after a divorce. For the good of the children, the parents need to control any hostility they may feel toward each other. If the custodial parent makes visits too unpleasant for the noncustodial parent, that parent may find it easier to simply fade out of the picture.

The majority of children wish to have continued contact with both parents after divorce (Kitson & Morgan, 1991; L. K. White, 1991). The youngsters, in essence, continue to love both parents even though the parents don't love each other. Ensuring that both parents have ongoing contact with their children is a difficult goal to achieve. If hostilities continue between the parents and the mother has been granted custody of the children, the father often finds himself in an uncomfortable situation. Although he may want to see his children, the visits can be punishing emotionally both for him and for the children. Many fathers simply fade out of the picture in this type of arrangement. They find that going to the zoo or on a picnic with their kids a few days a month is too bittersweet an experience. The father in this type of situation often charges that the mother has poisoned his relationship with his children.

The mother often maintains that the father showed no interest in the children before the divorce and that this pattern continued after the divorce. She may say that the children want to be with their friends on the weekend rather than with their father. Objectively judging who is to blame in these circumstances is difficult, but the end result is generally quite clear. The father often drifts away from his children emotionally and feels little inclination to pay child support because he doesn't feel connected to them any more. If he marries again, he is likely to marry a woman with children of her own and may feel pressure from his new wife to be involved with "their" children. "I've got two sets of kids to support now," one father said. "One set isn't even really mine, and my own set, I can only see every other weekend."

There have been numerous studies on the effects of divorce on children (Amato, 1993; Demo & Acock, 1991; Wallerstein & Blakeslee, 1989). These studies suggest three conclusions regarding the effects. First, divorce is a very difficult crisis in the lives of the vast majority of children who experience it. Most children grieve over the divorce and wish it were not happening. This is especially true in the case of marriage devitalization or burnout, in which the divorce may have come as a complete surprise to the children.

Second, many children are angry at their parents, and many are angry at themselves.

> "My best friend's parents got a divorce, and I felt so sorry for her," 11-year-old Jenna said. "I imagined once what it would be like if my parents got a divorce. I did this so I could understand what my friend was going through. Then when my parents got a divorce, I felt so guilty. I thought they got a divorce because I had imagined they got one."

When parents break up, children often feel responsible. It takes sensitive parents to help guide the children through their grief. Some parents, overburdened with their own anger and sadness, are of little help to their children.

Third, although divorce is difficult for almost all children, subjection to long-term marital hostilities is even worse. After reviewing many studies of the effects of divorce on children, Lynn White (1991) concluded that family discord has more of a negative impact on children than the type of marital structure in which they live. A stable one-parent family is better than an unstable two-parent family. A tension-filled home can have negative consequences for all living there. Children respond to this type of environment with depression, anger, troubles in school, and various physiological symptoms.

Community Divorce

Divorce comes as a shock not only for members of the nuclear family, but for relatives, friends, neighbors, and colleagues at work. When someone is divorcing, people are not quite sure how to respond to them. The best approach is to listen when they want to share and to be a caring and supportive friend. Friends, parents, sisters, and brothers are often the most supportive. Conversely, most in-laws become out-laws; they tend to support and defend their relative, regardless of the reasons for the divorce. Parents are particularly stressed when their adult children divorce. As one research team described it, "The effects of divorce spread outward like the vibration rings caused by dropping a stone in a quiet pond. Our attention is drawn to the point where the stone hits the water, and less interest is given the larger area which is also disturbed by the impact" (Bader, DeFrain, & Parkhurst, 1982, p. 93).

Divorce research has tended to focus on the impacts on the divorcing couple and their children but not on the effects on others, such as grandparents (Spitze, Logan, Deane, & Zerger, 1994). When Bader contacted the middle-aged parents of divorcing individuals, she found that although some were glad their child was getting a divorce, the overwhelming emotion most of them felt was sorrow. In the words of one mother, "At first it was like a death in the family to think that our son-in-law would not be a part of the family any longer."

Dating after a divorce can be both scary and enjoyable. However, newly divorced people should not rush the emotional process of divorce, which can take anywhere from several months to a few years. They should ease into dating slowly, and they definitely should not rush into another marriage on the rebound.

Couple friends also have difficulty figuring out how to respond to a divorcing couple. Which of the partners should the couple friends continue to have contact with? It would be difficult to keep both ex-partners as friends, and as a couple, it would seem awkward to invite just one person. The divorcing couple often feel bitter about losing their couple friends. However, couples who were primarily connected to only one of the partners often offer valuable support after a divorce.

Psychological Divorce

Many people getting divorced find it useful to talk with a marriage and family therapist or another professional skilled in working with personal and relationship problems. Counselors can provide insights and suggestions for adjusting to the single life.

Many people find it useful to join support groups. Parents Without Partners and similar groups across the country can be very helpful to divorcing people seeking to grow through their crisis. These support groups can help people see that they're "all in the same boat." Others with similar problems can be mutually supportive and caring. Groups of divorced people also set up educational programs and social activities (dances, potlucks, camping trips) at which members can meet others. The main thing is to become actively involved with other people again.

The worst thing a newly divorced person can do is to marry again quickly "on the rebound," but dating can be enjoyable. Friends can often be a valuable source of potential dating partners. It is important to get back into dating gradually and not to rush the process. Those whose friendship network does not contain sufficient potential dating partners may wish to consider a commercial dating service. These businesses were described in Chapter 5.

How Long Does It Take to Adjust?

How long does the divorce journey take? The answer is different for each person. The emotional process of divorce may last from several months to a few years after the divorce. The legal process may take only 6 months, but if children are involved and a custody fight occurs, the struggle could last several years. One father, who had been fighting for custody of his youngsters for 6 years, had incurred legal costs of close to $35,000.

The economic process of divorce may also last a long time. For example, if the ex-wife goes back to school after the divorce, she may be in school for 3 or 4 years. Both spouses suffer financially, but usually the wife is the primary financial loser.

The coparental divorce process can last from several months to years. If the couple is on friendly terms, they may work out a joint-custody arrangement that functions well in a few months. If not, battles over custody and child visitation may last a long time. The psychological divorce may also take a long time: Some people take several years to shift to a more independent lifestyle; others make the transition in a few months. These stations of divorce usually run concurrently and often overlap.

Divorce is often less problematic for people who can talk openly about it. When individuals accept the divorce as an important part of their life, they can then move on as independent and happy single people. Divorce is something that most people do not willingly choose, but it can often be a very valuable learning experience. As one man said, "Going through a divorce was an important part of my life that I wouldn't let anyone take away from me for a million dollars. And it was something I wouldn't want to go through again for a million dollars!"

Summary

- Statistics indicate that the average length of first marriages that end in divorce is 7 years. But marriage is so popular that about 75% of younger divorced individuals are likely to remarry: three of four divorced women and five of six divorced men.

- In the late 1960s, the U.S. divorce rate began to climb, leveling off in the late 1980s and early 1990s. Some explanations for the increase include the effect of no-fault divorce laws, the "women's liberation" movement, economic conditions, women's increasing education, and changes in attitudes toward divorce.

- No-fault divorce laws eliminated fault as grounds for divorce, gender-based division of responsibilities, the adversarial nature of divorce, and linkage of the financial settlement to the determination of fault. Some argue, however, that no-fault's principle of equity between the sexes penalizes women financially in divorce.

- The top four reasons for divorce are infidelity, no longer loving each other, emotional problems, and financial problems.

- Bohannan identified six different but overlapping separation experiences with which divorcing individuals must contend: emotional divorce, legal divorce, economic divorce, coparental divorce, community divorce, and psychological divorce.

- Research on the effects of marital discord and divorce on children suggests that divorce is a crisis in the lives of most children who experience it. In addition to sadness and regret, many children experience anger at their parents and at themselves. However, living in a two-parent home fraught with hostility and discord is worse for children than living in a stable one-parent home.

- When is the healing process complete? When a divorced person can talk openly about the divorce without considerable anger, guilt, remorse, or feelings of failure and can accept the divorce as a part of her or his life, divorce has been a valuable learning experience.

Key Terms

no-fault divorce	infidelity	economic divorce
alimony	devitalized (burned-out) marriage	coparental divorce
fault		community divorce
uncontested divorce	emotional divorce	psychological divorce
tender years doctrine	legal divorce	feminization of poverty

Activities

1. Interview someone who is divorced, focusing on the individual's account of the divorce. Use Bohannan's six stations of divorce as a guide for your questions. Compare and contrast the results of the interview with others in a small-group discussion.

2. Interview a young adult whose parents have gone through a divorce. What perspectives can you gain from your discussion with this individual? Discuss your conclusions with others in a small group.

3. Role-play a child-custody dispute. Have one class member be the father, arguing why he should have custody of the preschooler. Have another class member be the mother, arguing why she should have custody. Question these people carefully, as a good attorney would, and come to your own conclusions. Check your perceptions of the situation with other members of your class.

Suggested Readings

Briles, J. (1988). *The dollars and sense of divorce: The financial guide for women.* New York: Master Media. *A useful tool for women dealing with the financial challenges of divorce.*

Goldman, L. (1994). *Life and loss.* Bristol, PA: Accelerated Development. *A workbook designed for parents and teachers who are helping children deal with their feelings of loss.*

Kayser, K. (1993). *When love dies: The process of marital disaffection.* New York: Guilford. *An interesting book with broad appeal.*

Kitson, G. C., & Morgan, L. A. (1991). The multiple consequences of divorce: A decade review. In A. Booth (Ed.), *Contemporary families: Looking forward, looking back* (pp. 150–161). Minneapolis: National Council on Family Relations. *An excellent review of research on the wide-ranging effects of divorce.*

Parkman, A. M. (1992). *No-fault divorce: What went wrong?* Boulder, CO: Westview Press. *Examines the financial consequences of no-fault divorce from an economist's perspective, and proposes legal reforms to make divorces economically efficient and fair, as well as easier to obtain than before no-fault divorce laws were passed.*

Stevenson, M. R., & Black, K. N. (1995). *How divorce affects offspring: A research approach.* Madison, WI: Brown and Benchmark. *A review of the research literature.*

Teyber, E. (1992). *Helping children cope with divorce.* New York: Lexington Books/Macmillan. *Wisdom from a counselor with extensive experience.*

Vaughan, D. (1986). *Uncoupling: Turning points in intimate relationships.* New York: Oxford University Press. *Describes the social and psychological process of breaking up.*

Wallerstein, J. S., & Blakeslee, S. (1989). *Second chances: Men, women and children a decade after divorce.* New York: Ticknor & Fields. *Insights from researchers who have been studying divorce for two decades.*

White, L. K. (1991). Determinants of divorce: A review of research in the eighties. In A. Booth (Ed.), *Contemporary families: Looking forward, looking back* (pp. 141–149). Minneapolis: National Council on Family Relations. *A comprehensive review of the research in this area, by an investigator who has invested a great deal of time and energy learning why people divorce.*

CHAPTER 17

Single-Parent Families and Stepfamilies

Most divorces today involve children. Divorced single parents must deal with challenges that include loneliness and isolation, financial problems, and work overload. Despite these challenges, however, many divorced single parents develop healthy and functional families. Meanwhile, the parent who is not living with the children is also struggling to establish a new identity and to maintain a relationship with the children he or she has "lost" in the divorce.

Most divorced people sooner or later begin looking for a new mate, but they are generally much more skeptical about marriage than they were "the first time around." Even more difficult than finding a new partner is finding one who also cares about the children, and vice versa. Single parents who marry again then face the challenge of developing a stepfamily system that works.

This chapter looks at how people with children "pick up the pieces" after divorce and establish new family systems. It compares these systems with the nuclear family and also explores the stresses and strengths of both single-parent families and stepfamilies.

The Changing Picture of the Family

Single-parent families have also been called one-parent, lone-parent, or solo-parent families. Some observers have suggested that single-parent families are problem families, but this is an inaccurate picture. Many divorced single parents are doing an excellent job raising their children; the children are thriving at home and at school. Stepparent families, too, are succeeding. Single-parent families and stepparent families face many of the same challenges that other families do. But in addition, these families also must cope with unique challenges.

The Increase in Single-Parent Families

Nearly one third of all American families were headed by a single parent in 1994; the number has increased rapidly over the past two decades. The proportion of single-parent families was about 11% in 1970 and rose to 20% in 1980. By 1990, the number had increased to 28%, and it reached 31% in 1994 (U.S. Bureau of the Census, 1995).

By far the majority of single-parent households are headed by females. There were almost 10 million single mothers heading households in 1994, compared with 1.6 million single fathers. Single fathers were twice as common in White families (16%) as in Black families (8%).

During the past several years, the number of single-parent households has increased most dramatically for families of color (Figure 17.1). In 1994, 25% of the Caucasian households were headed by a single parent; the rate was 34% for Mexican American households and 65% for African American households.

The rapid increase in the divorce rate since the late 1960s is seen by some observers to be simply an accentuation of a long-term upward trend. The rate of re-

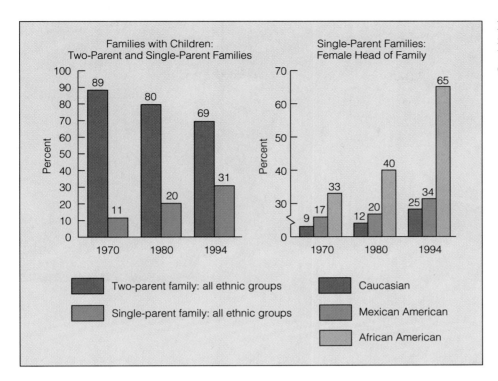

Figure 17.1 The Family in Transition. *Source:* U.S. Bureau of the Census (1995, p. 54).

marriage went up during the 1960s but then declined steeply until the late 1970s, when it moderated. As noted in Chapter 16, perhaps 75% of younger men and women who divorce will eventually marry again (Glick & Lin, 1986). About two thirds of recent second or subsequent marriages were preceded by cohabitation (Bumpass & Sweet, 1989).

On the average, first marriages that end in divorce last about 7 years. Those who marry a second time do so on the average in 2–3 years. Many second marriages also end in divorce, tending to do so in 4–5 years. There are only minor differences among Caucasians, Mexican Americans, and African Americans in these three sets of statistics (Norton & Mooran, 1987).

Authorities on marriage and divorce statistics on the national level believe that divorce rates and rates for subsequent marriages have probably peaked but are likely to remain high in the future (Glick & Lin, 1986; Norton & Mooran, 1987). These high rates are by-products of modern life. Some people will marry only once, but the majority will divorce and marry again (Glick & Lin, 1986).

Family Terminology

The changing nature of the family in our society has made new vocabulary necessary. This section defines the new terminology.

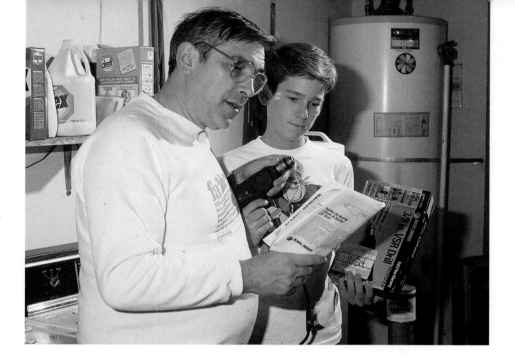

After divorce, many families are not really single-parent families but binuclear families. Children whose parents have joint custody have two homes and usually move freely between the two. Binuclear families resulting from an amicable divorce may even come together for holidays and other celebrations.

Binuclear Families Versus Single-Parent Families Constance Ahrons and Morton Perlmutter have suggested that divorced parents use the term *binuclear* rather than *single-parent* to describe their family. This term reflects the fact that the process of divorce is not necessarily all bad but that it interweaves positive and negative elements. Divorce is "a process that results in family reorganization rather than disintegration" (1982, p. 35). This reorganization of the nuclear family after divorce frequently results in the establishment of two households, the mother's and the father's. If one ex-spouse does not drop out of the family after the divorce and the two households continue to interrelate, then a **binuclear family** has been established.

In some binuclear families, children have a primary and a secondary home after divorce. In these families, one parent has **sole custody** of the children and they live with that parent in the primary home; the other parent in the secondary home has rights of visitation with the children. In a smaller proportion of families, the homes of both divorced parents have equal importance—"one child, two homes." This arrangement has been termed **joint custody.** In an even smaller proportion of families, one parent has sole custody of one or more of the children, and the other parent has sole custody of the other child or children. That arrangement is called **split custody** (DeFrain, Fricke, & Elmen, 1987).

In binuclear families, relationships between the two households can vary greatly. A few binuclear families share some holidays and birthdays, but many rarely get together as a group. Four types of relationship behaviors between ex-spouses in binuclear families have been identified by Ahrons and Roy Rodgers (1987). Some ex-spouses get along wonderfully, whereas others continue the predivorce wars into the postdivorce years. The researchers gave the four types of ex-spouse relationships the descriptive names "perfect pals," "cooperative colleagues," "angry asso-

Many people who remarry have children from a previous marriage, and the resulting combination can be a large stepfamily with complex dynamics. The children must establish relationships with their stepparent and their stepsiblings, and the adults must learn new roles as stepparents.

ciates," and "fiery foes." The researchers called a relationship that was completely over a "dissolved duo."

Marriage Versus Remarriage   A few words need to be said at this point about the term **remarriage.** The dictionary definition includes both marrying the same person again (a rare occurrence) and marrying a second (or subsequent) time after the death of or divorce from the first partner. In this text, remarriage is used exclusively to describe marriage to a new partner.

Stepfamilies, Blended Families, and Reconstituted Families   Emily Visher and John Visher (1992), well known for their research on stepfamilies, object to the term **blended family** for a variety of reasons. First and foremost, the label fosters unrealistic expectations that the new family will quickly and easily blend together into a harmonious family. Second, the term assumes a homogeneous unit without previous history or background. On the other hand, the terms **stepfamily** and **stepparent** have suffered from a number of stereotypes, often bringing to mind childhood fairy-tale visions of "wicked stepmothers." But most stepparent/stepchild relationships function relatively well. Other professionals have suggested the term **reconstituted family** rather than stepfamily or blended family.

Growing Family Complexity

The joining together of two families in a second or subsequent marriage adds considerable complexity to a family system. A child of divorced parents who both remarry will have two stepparents; a range of possible combinations of biological siblings, stepsiblings, and half-siblings; up to eight grandparents; and numerous

533

Figure 17.2 Model of the Binuclear Family.
Source: Divorced Families: A Multidisciplinary View, (p. 155) by C. Ahrons and R. Rodgers, 1987, New York: Norton. Copyright 1987 Constance R. Ahrons and Roy H. Rodgers. Reprinted by permission of W. W. Norton and Company.

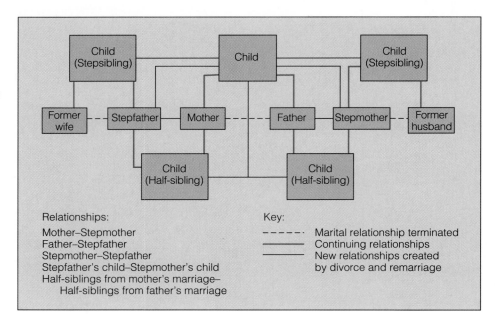

extended relatives of the new spouses (aunts, uncles, cousins, etc.). Figure 17.2 is an example of a binuclear family with a child in the center. This figure is relatively complicated, and yet it shows only the relationships between the child and his or her parents, stepparents, stepsiblings, and half-siblings. If the child's relationships with the rest of the family—siblings, grandparents, and other relatives in the extended family—were added, the figure would become even more complicated. Of course, complexity in a family system is neither good nor bad in itself. Some binuclear families of enormous complexity function quite well. As one 7-year-old girl said, "I love my new family. I now have a whole lot more grandpas and grandmas, and they all give me presents!"

As important new people are added to a family system, the number of potentially positive and negative human relationships increases geometrically. For example, a man from a relatively small family married a woman with a huge extended family. The fellow's mother-in-law has nine brothers and sisters and countless nieces and nephews. His father-in-law has four brothers and sisters, and these folks also have a massive number of progeny. "I have to have a program in hand when I go to a family picnic," the fellow chuckles. "Sometimes there will be more than 200 people at these gatherings. It's almost like going to a soccer game. They should all wear jerseys with numbers."

Differences Between Nuclear Families and Stepfamilies

Many stepfamilies falsely assume that they are like nuclear families. Table 17.1 highlights some of the salient differences between nuclear families and stepfami-

Table 17.1 Differences Between Nuclear Families and Stepfamilies

CHARACTERISTIC	NUCLEAR FAMILY	STEPFAMILY
Role as parent	Two parents Marital dyad are parents May be single parents	Two adults; one is a parent Marital dyad plus previous partner(s) are parents
Biological relationship	Biological family Biological relationship between both parents and children, and between siblings Physical similarity often present	Nonbiological family Biological relationship between one parent and children Children of both parents might be included in family Lower level of physical similarity
Marriage history	Ongoing marriage Often first marriage Parents influence marriage	New marriage partner One or both previously married Parents and previous partner(s) influence marriage
Balancing marriage and parenting	Marriage came before child(ren) Maintaining marriage is goal Parenting often given priority over marriage	Marriage came after child(ren) Developing marriage is goal Marriage often given priority over parenting
Bonding	Bond is primarily to nuclear family and both parents Family rituals and celebrations increase bonding Extended families can support bonding	Bond often greater to one parent Stepparent bond takes time to develop Rituals must be developed and may create conflicts Extended families can create issues and decrease bonding
Loyalty issues	Roots are stable General sense of loyalty and belonging Loyalty to both parents more common	Roots are disrupted; can be rebuilt Loyalty and belonging more difficult to develop Initial loyalty to one parent is common
Parenting issues	Roles and responsibilities tend to develop gradually Child(ren) can play two parents off against each other Parenting roles can be shared and can be conflictual Power hierarchy clear among siblings	Roles and responsibilities disrupted and often must be redefined Child(ren) can play two parents plus stepparents off against each other Parent and stepparent roles often create conflict Grandparents' and stepgrandparents' roles are unclear Power struggles to develop hierarchy among siblings and stepchildren
Financial issues	Parental income to own children No financial support expected from others Financial demands more predictable	Parents' and stepparents' income to own and/or stepchildren Child support payments can create issues More financial demands from new marriage and new family

Source: Adapted from *Treating the Remarried Family* (pp. 23–27), by C. J. Sager, H. S. Brown, H. Crohn, T. Engel, E. Rodstein, and L. Walker, 1983, New York: Brunner/Mazel. Copyright 1983 by Brunner/Mazel. Reprinted by permission.

lies. First of all, there are usually two biological parents in a nuclear family, and the children are clearer about their biological heritage. Because one parent in a stepfamily is not a biological parent, this can increase children's feelings of attachment to their biological parent. In a nuclear family the parents' marriage is ongoing and may have lasted many years, but a stepfamily means there is a change in marriage partner. The new couple have to balance their investment in the new marriage with the handling of parenting and stepparenting issues.

The bonds that children feel with their parents and vice versa are often stronger in nuclear families than in stepfamilies. There are often loyalty issues in stepfamilies, with children, particularly adolescents, feeling greater loyalty to their biological parents than to the stepparent. The differences between nuclear families and stepfamilies create complex and sometimes conflictual dynamics in stepfamilies. Issues regarding grandparents and stepgrandparents add to the complexity. There can also be struggles between stepsiblings when both spouses bring children to the new family. Financial issues can also be complex. When both parents in a stepfamily have children, the financial resources available for child support payments and for meeting the financial demands of all the children can be limited.

One study compared 24 stepfamilies and 24 first-marriage families on the three dimensions of family cohesion, flexibility, and communication from the Family Circumplex Model (Pink & Wampler, 1985). To measure cohesion and flexibility, data were collected using FACES (an acronym for Family Adaptability and Cohesion Evaluation Scales; Olson, Portner, & Bell, 1986). To assess family communication, data were collected using the Parent-Adolescent Communication Scale (Barnes & Olson, 1986). In each stepfamily, the mother, the stepfather, and one or more adolescents completed the questionnaires; in each first-marriage family, the two parents and the adolescents completed the questionnaires.

All stepfamily members indicated lower family cohesion and lower flexibility than did the members of first-marriage families (Figure 17.3). There was also poorer father-adolescent communication in the stepfamilies than in the first-marriage families as rated by the fathers from the two types of families. No differences were found, however, when the adolescents' communication ratings were used. There was no significant difference in mother-adolescent communication between the stepfamilies and the first-marriage families. The reason could be, in part, that the mother was the biological parent in both types of families, whereas that was not the case with the fathers.

Family dynamics in stepfamilies are still unclear to researchers, however. Another team of investigators wanted to test the hypothesis that marital conflict is more frequent in stepfamilies than in biological families. They looked at nationally representative data on 2,655 Black and White married couples with children, comparing the frequency of marital conflict. The researchers found, contrary to their expectations, that remarriage and stepchildren are not necessarily associated with more frequent marital conflict and, in some cases, are associated with less frequent conflict (MacDonald & DeMaris, 1995). More research comparing the two family types is probably necessary, but some observers are skeptical of its usefulness, arguing that the comparison is like one between apples and oranges (K. Pasley, 1995, personal communication).

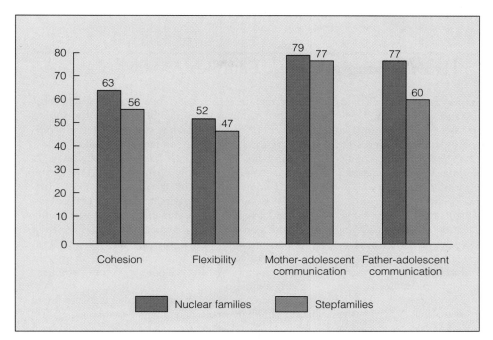

Figure 17.3 Family Cohesion, Flexibility, and Communication in Nuclear Families and Stepfamilies. *Source:* Based on data from "Problem Areas in Stepfamilies: Cohesion, Adaptability, and the Stepfather-Adolescent Relationship" by J. E. T. Pink and K. S. Wampler, 1985, *Family Relations, 34,* p. 331. Copyright 1985 by National Council on Family Relations.

Single-Parent Families

Single-parent households, headed by either a mother or a father, are continuing to increase. In 1970, there were 2.9 million single-parent households headed by mothers in the United States; in 1994, the number was 9.9 million. There were 340,000 single-parent households headed by fathers in 1970; in 1994, there were 1.6 million (U.S. Bureau of the Census, 1995). The percentage of single-parent families headed by fathers increased from 10% of the total in 1970 to 15% of the total in 1994 (U.S. Bureau of the Census, 1995).

Most of the literature on single-parent families since the 1960s has tended to accentuate the negative (Box 17.1, p. 538, discusses some of the reasons). This section identifies the stresses and strains unique to single parents, but it also reports the positive aspects of growing up in a healthy single-parent family.

Most divorced single-parent families fall into one of four categories: (1) mothers with sole custody; (2) fathers with sole custody; (3) split-custody families, in which the father has sole custody of one or more children and the mother has sole custody of one or more children; and (4) joint-custody families, in which both the mother and the father share decision making. These four types of single-parent families were analyzed by John DeFrain, Judy Fricke, and Julie Elmen in their book *On Our Own* (1987). The authors studied 738 single parents in 45 states: 528 mothers with sole custody, 114 fathers with sole custody, 40 mothers and fathers

BOX 17.1

Healthy Single-Parent Families

Since the late 1970s, there has been a resurgence of interest in successful families and a focus on family strengths. Researchers have used different terms to identify this concept of strengths, among them *healthy, balanced, successful, functional,* and *strong.* Today, although many family researchers continue to ask the question "Why do families fail?", a few family researchers are focusing on the question "How do families succeed?"

Shirley M. Hanson (1986) used earlier family strengths research as a foundation for her pioneering efforts in the study of healthy single-parent families. She argued that one reason single-parent families have gotten a "bad press" from researchers over the years is the way researchers have found subject families to study. Researchers, she noted, "have traditionally obtained their samples from clinical populations." By focusing only on the dysfunctional aspects of some single-parent families, researchers have done single-parent families a disservice.

Hanson, instead, recruited single parents for her study through newspaper advertisements and through appearances on radio and television talk shows. The families had to meet two definitions of health. First,

family members themselves had to express the belief that their family was healthy. Second, the descriptions members gave of their families were compared with previous research and theory on family strengths.

Forty-two single-parent families participated in Hanson's research. Family members were interviewed in their homes and also filled out questionnaires. Hanson found that the single parents and their children exhibited fairly high levels of mental and physical health. She also noted that the mental and physical health of both parents and children was related to good communication, social support within and outside the family, socioeconomic status, religiousness, and problem-solving abilities.

Hanson's research is important because she found that "although single-parent families may experience many problems, they are not necessarily less able to manage than the other family configurations." Professionals who work with single-parent families need to know this so that they can help these families identify their strengths and accentuate the positive. This research should help counselors avoid the demoralizing trap of focusing only on problems.

with split custody, and 56 mothers and fathers with joint legal and physical custody. Their findings are summarized below.

Mothers with Custody

Divorced mothers who head single-parent families must cope with many stresses. They also report having many joys.

Stresses   One of the major problems for mothers with sole custody is limited money, often made worse by lack of child support from the father. In a study of 492 court records, K. D. Rettig, D. H. Christensen, and C. M. Dahl (1991) found that the court-ordered awards met only 58% of the children's income needs when measured against poverty-level support. As expected, the parent with whom the children lived spent a much higher proportion of her (or his) income to support the children than the parent with whom the children did not live provided. This

Being a divorced mother with custody of the children has both positive and negative aspects. Money and loneliness are the biggest problems for most single mothers, but the bond between single mothers and their children can be particularly close and rewarding.

is a serious problem nationwide. It is made worse by the fact that only about half (48%) of noncustodial parents make full child support payments, 26% make partial payments, and 26% make no payments at all (Rettig et al., 1991).

Loneliness is a common problem for most single parents. One mother commented, "The only real sorrow we feel about the arrangement [single parenthood] is that her father isn't with us to share in the daily goings on of family life." The other parent is not there to share the child's artwork, the loss of the first tooth, or the birthday parties—in short, the ups and downs of daily childrearing. Some divorced mothers with custody also lamented the loss of positive grandparent relationships. In many families, ties with grandparents are severed by the divorce. "I bleed for my children when I see their loneliness in being away from Dad and former friends. I regret seeking more conversation and support from them in my own loneliness than they can give me," a mother said. Some mothers worry that the day may come when the children will no longer know their father.

For some single parents, battles with the ex-spouse continue for years. Many mothers with custody dread continued contact with the ex-partner. These parents are not the "perfect pals" and "cooperative colleagues" that Ahrons and Rodgers (1987) talked about, but the "angry associates" and "fiery foes" who often square off against each other. In one mother's words, "Because their father sees them as often as he does, they're put in a heavy loyalty dilemma. Consequently, they return home feeling confused by guilt and wanting to blame or hate. This is all happening because their father is trying to get them to live with him. I will never have total peace as long as he's alive!"

Strengths   Stinnett, Stinnett, DeFrain, and DeFrain (1997, in press) believe that strong single-parent families share the same constellation of qualities that strong two-parent families share: appreciation and affection for each of the family members; commitment to the family; open, honest, and straightforward communication patterns; adequate amounts of time together; spiritual well-being; and the ability to cope creatively with stress and crisis. Besides reporting many challenges, mothers with sole custody report a number of specific joys inherent in their situation. These include the freedom to make decisions about their own lives and the lives of their children without interference or harassment from hostile fathers. Also, in many families divorce does not mean the end of meaningful relationships with grandparents. One single mother reported, "My ex-spouse's parents are extremely helpful. They take my preschool daughter some weekends, and the space is wonderful."

For some mothers with custody, the burden of almost total responsibility for the children is nearly unbearable, but others thrive on the responsibility. "The joy that is unique to being a single parent is the all-engulfing satisfaction when things are going well. You not only take all of the responsibility, but you receive all of the joy from the growth and new discovery that the child is experiencing."

Finally, some mothers with sole custody are thankful for fathers who stay involved with their children after the divorce. Former spouses sometimes remain friends, or at least neutral colleagues, in the challenge of rearing children after divorce. This contributes to the health, happiness, and adjustments of the children. Sometimes both parents attend band concerts, Girl Scout meetings, open house at school, and so forth. "The girls are always excited to see Dad. Dad is excited to see the girls. And I'm glad to be alone for a while."

Fathers with Custody

Many family researchers have found that fathers can do a good job raising children after a divorce, just as mothers who formerly were full-time homemakers can successfully work outside the home after a divorce (Grief, 1995; Meyer & Garasky, 1993; Richards & Schmiege, 1993). For example, John DeFrain and Rod Eirick (1981) compared divorced single fathers and divorced single mothers on six major areas of adjustment to divorce: the process of divorce, the stresses of single parenthood, childrearing philosophies and behaviors, children's behaviors, relationships with the ex-spouse, and forming new social relationships. On most of the variables, the researchers found no significant statistical differences between the single-parent fathers and the mothers. Most studies indicate that the answer to the question "Can fathers be good mothers?" is yes. It also appears that the sorrows and joys of solo parenting for fathers are very similar to those related by mothers with custody.

Stresses   Single-parent fathers often feel sorrow over the fact that the family unit has been broken up. Even though the father sees the new single-parent family as a family, it is not, in the eyes of many fathers, a complete family. "I feel sorry for my children because they don't have their mother anymore," one father said.

Many single fathers miss their ex-wives and find the loneliness nearly unbearable. Many also report that both time and money are limited. Single fathers with custody generally make more money than single mothers with custody, but

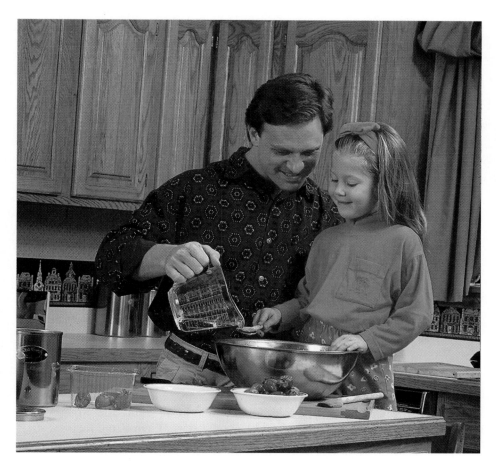

Although fewer men than women have primary custody of the children after a divorce, research shows that single fathers do just as good a job of childrearing as single mothers do, and that they experience the same stresses of loneliness and too little time and money.

time and money pressures are still common complaints among them. "I don't seem to have much time or money to do the things that I would like. It is difficult for me to meet women." Fathers complained that they had no one with whom to share the joys of parenting. Also, fathers reported that the children missed their mother. "It is difficult when she asks, 'Why doesn't my mom call me or want to see me?'"

Strengths   But many single fathers report a considerable number of joys. One is being able to watch the children grow. "To see my son's mind develop" is a great joy. "He is quite intelligent, and his ambitions are much greater with me. The environment around his mother is extremely negative and shameful." Fathers also enjoy the love between their children and themselves. "Now there are only two in our family, and it's much harder on me but well worth it. We have more love and a stronger bond now." Having custody also means having control. Many single fathers had been through lengthy and painful divorce and custody battles with their ex-wives. Now that the battles are over, they feel great relief.

For many fathers, single parenthood has meant becoming closer to their children. One father proudly related how he had become closer to his children after adjusting his priorities in life to put the children before his job and the housework. Fathers with custody have the opportunity to really enjoy their children in a more natural environment. "I get great pleasure from being with my son. This gives me a sense of accomplishment since I do have him and am making it work."

Some fathers do get along with their ex-spouse. One 54-year-old father who was caring for nine children said he was especially pleased that "my ex-wife and I get along. If there is a problem—and we do have some—I get on the phone, and we talk it out and resolve it. That's something we didn't do too well when we were married." Although the marriage is over, ex-spouses can sometimes build a solid partnership for the good of their children (Meyer & Garasky, 1993).

Split Custody

Split custody is a child custody arrangement that involves both divorced parents separately (DeFrain et al., 1987). Each parent has responsibility for at least one of their children and thus has all the stresses and strains of solo parenting.

Split custody is apparently the rarest of all parenting options after divorce, but it works quite well for many. Perhaps the most interesting question about split custody is why parents choose this arrangement. They have a number of answers, including that the child or children wanted it.

A number of fathers said that their sons wanted to live with them, especially during adolescence.

> "My oldest [14] told [my ex-wife] he'd rather live with me," related Edward, a 48-year-old contractor. "I told him it would be all right. She brought him to my house and asked me if I said he could stay. When I told her yes, she said, 'Good, you take him. I can't handle him anymore.' About 6 months later, she wanted him back, but he refused to go."

Mothers told the researchers of "losing" not only sons to their ex-husbands, but daughters. Some "switching" of households may almost be inevitable after divorce; adolescents need to balance their fantasies about life in the other home with the other parent with reality. They may find that the other home is no better than the home in which they currently live.

In many families split custody is a family decision, involving input from all involved. One parent commented, "Ever since the separation we have tried to do the right thing for the children and put aside our own differences. Therefore, the decision on custody was negotiated among the four of us, with no outsider involved."

Joint Custody

In their study of 738 families in 45 states, DeFrain and his colleagues (1987) found that no one particular custody arrangement is best for all families. Rather, each divorce is unique, and what is best for the children has to be decided on the basis of answers to numerous questions, including: (1) Do the children and both parents feel it best that both parents continue contact with the children after the divorce? (2) Are both parents capable of maintaining an adequate home for the children? (3) Can the parents get along with each other well enough to manage a joint-custody arrangement after the divorce? If all members of the family can honestly answer yes to all three questions and can manage the innumerable details that have to be worked out, then joint custody might be a feasible solution.

Parents who have arranged joint custody report less stress than single-custody parents. Joint-custody parents also have more time to pursue their own interests because the ex-spouse assumes a major share of the child care responsibilities.

Studies indicate that joint-custody parents are more likely to come from a burned-out marriage. They are likely to neither love nor hate their ex-spouse but to be able to deal rationally with her or him. Parents who fight for sole custody are more likely to dislike or hate their ex-spouse.

Coping Successfully As a Single Parent

Single parents have developed a number of successful strategies for coping with their unique station in life and offer some suggestions for other single parents:

- Don't rush into a new relationship, where you might just be transferring dependency. Let go of the past and move on. Realistically face what has happened. Learn from it; don't repeat it.

- Don't succumb to feelings of failure and worthlessness. Make the best of the situation and don't blame yourself completely.

- Keep busy with constructive activities. Take up new (or old) activities you always wanted to find time to enjoy.

- Listen to others, but make your own decisions.

- Take one day at a time, setting small goals at first.

- Consider going back to school.

- Be flexible, adaptable, and independent.

Stepfamilies

People whose marriage has unraveled are often quite careful about entering into another marriage. Divorced individuals are likely to be skeptical about the institution of marriage. They are often more open to premarital and marital counseling because they realize that counseling is simply a process of learning. As one remarried man put it, "I take my car in for a tune-up every year, and I know our relationship could use some help at times."

Table 17.2 Stages in the Formation of a Stepfamily

STAGE	PREREQUISITE ATTITUDE	DEVELOPMENTAL ISSUES
1. Entering a new relationship	Recovery from loss of first marriage (adequate "emotional divorce")	Recommitting to marriage and to forming a family, with readiness to deal with the complexity and amount of effort required
2. Conceptualizing and planning the new marriage and family	Accepting one's own fears and those of new spouse and children about remarriage and forming a stepfamily Accepting need for time and patience for adjustment to complexity and ambiguity of: a. Multiple new roles b. Boundaries: space, time, membership, and authority c. Affective issues: guilt, loyalty, conflicts, desire for mutuality, unresolvable past hurts	a. Working on openness in the new relationship to avoid pseudomutuality b. Planning for maintenance of cooperative coparent relationship with ex-spouses c. Planning to help children deal with fears, loyalty conflicts, and membership in two systems d. Realigning relationships with extended family to include new spouse and children e. Planning maintenance of connections for children with extended family of ex-spouse(s)
3. Remarriage and reconstitution of the family	Final resolution of attachment to previous spouse and ideal of "intact" family Acceptance of a different model of family, with permeable boundaries	a. Restructuring family boundaries to allow for inclusion of new spouse/stepparents b. Realigning relationships throughout subsystems to permit interweaving of several systems c. Making room for relationships of all children with biological (noncustodial) parents, grandparents, and other extended family d. Sharing memories and histories to enhance stepfamily integration

Source: "Forming a Remarried Family" (p. 24) by M. McGoldrick and S. Carter. In *The Changing Family Life Cycle: A Framework for Family Therapy*, 2nd ed., edited by S. Carter and M. McGoldrick. Copyright © 1989 by Allyn & Bacon. Reprinted by permission.

Stages in the Formation of a Stepfamily

People go through three stages in the process of forming a new family through remarriage: (1) entering a new relationship, (2) planning the new marriage and family, and (3) remarriage and reconstitution of the family (McGoldrick & Carter, 1989). These stages are summarized in Table 17.2.

Entering a New Relationship   Before beginning this stage, divorced individuals should feel that they have recovered from the loss of the first marriage. A full recovery from a crisis like divorce can take a long time; many people marry again before they have completely recovered from their divorce. If bonding to the second partner is to succeed, however, one must be divorced "emotionally" as well as legally from the first partner.

The major developmental issue during this stage of the process is a recommitment to the institution of marriage itself and to the idea of forming a new partnership and family. Before marrying again, individuals need to decide whether they want a new intimate relationship that requires closeness and personal commitment.

Planning the New Marriage and Family   In the second stage of the process of marrying again, individuals must learn to accept their own fears and the fears of the spouse-to-be and all the children about the new marriage and the formation of a stepfamily. This stage also requires acceptance of the fact that it takes a good deal of time and patience for people to adjust to the complexity and ambiguities of a new family.

One difficulty during this stage is dealing with multiple new roles: that of being a new spouse, a new stepparent, and a new member of a new extended family. Other complexities include adjustments that will need to be made in terms of space, time, membership, and authority. Further complexities and ambiguities that must be dealt with in the affective area include feelings of guilt, loyalty conflicts, the desire for mutuality, and unresolvable past hurts. These feelings can come in a multitude of forms. For example, those planning to marry again often feel guilty because they must spend time and energy developing relationships with members of their soon-to-be family, often at the expense of time spent with the "old" family. One new stepfather acknowledged, "By spending so much time, money, and energy on my new spouse and stepchildren, I am neglecting my biological children."

During this second stage of planning the new marriage and family, a number of developmental issues or tasks must be addressed. All members of the new family need to work to build open, honest, straightforward communication patterns in order to avoid **pseudomutuality,** a false sense of togetherness. Other issues include building and planning to maintain cooperative coparenting relationships with ex-spouses, for the benefit of all parents and the children. It is also necessary to realign relationships with both extended families so that there is a place for the new spouse. If family members can manage to do all these things relatively well, the remarriage will have a better chance of succeeding.

Remarriage and Reconstitution of the Family   In the third stage of the process of forming a new family, the newly married partners need to strengthen their couple relationship so that they can function as coparents. Family members need to see that the new marriage is genuine and that the stepfamily that the couple has begun to build together is a good family.

There are a number of developmental issues or tasks during this third stage of the remarriage process. Family boundaries must be restructured to include the new spouse/stepparent. Relationships throughout the different subsystems of the "old" families may need to change to permit the interweaving of this new family system. In short, there must be room in the family for stepchildren, half-siblings, new sets of grandparents, and extended kin. It is also important to make room for relationships between all the children and their biological (noncustodial) parents, grandparents, and other extended family members. Sharing memories and histories of each side of the new stepfamily can enhance integration.

"Blending" or "reconstituting" or "reorganizing" families with children after divorce and remarriage is very difficult. Stepparents face many challenges in dealing with the offspring of their new spouse (Ahrons & Rodgers, 1987; Burt, 1989; LeMasters & DeFrain, 1989; Visher & Visher, 1988).

Guidelines for Stepfamilies

An excellent set of helpful guidelines for both stepparents and stepfamilies was developed by Emily Visher and John Visher. Called the **Stepping Ahead Program** (E. Visher, 1989), these guidelines can help stepfamilies avoid some common pitfalls and get their new family off to a positive start. This eight-step program, which is explained more fully in Box 17.2, involves:

1. Nurturing the couple relationship so that the new marriage will survive and thrive.

2. Finding personal space and time to relax and unwind from the challenges of a stepfamily.

3. Nurturing family relationships by spending time with each of the new family members.

4. Maintaining a close parent-child relationship.

5. Focusing on the stepparent-stepchild relationship.

6. Building family trust.

7. Strengthening stepfamily ties through a family discussion every week or two.

8. Working at keeping the bridges open to the children's other household so that coparenting can work smoothly.

Stepparents must remember that they are taking on someone else's child and many of the childrearing responsibilities formerly held by a biological parent. Step-

The Stepping Ahead Program

Step 1: Nurturing Your Couple Relationship

- Plan to do something away from your household once a week that you both enjoy doing together.

- Arrange to have 20 minutes of relaxed time alone with each other every day.

- Talk together about the running of your household for at least 30 minutes each week.

Step 2: Finding Personal Space and Time

- Take time to make a special "private" place for each of the adults and children in your household.

- Each take 2 hours a week doing something for yourselves that you would like to do.

Step 3: Nourishing Family Relationships

- Share with family members what you each appreciate about one another.

Step 4: Maintaining Close Parent-Child Relationships

- Parent and child do something fun together for 15–20 minutes once or twice a month.

Step 5: Developing Stepparent-Stepchild Relationships

- Stepparent and stepchild do something fun together for 15–20 minutes once or twice a month.

Step 6: Building Family Trust

- Schedule a family event once a month.

Step 7: Strengthening Stepfamily Ties

- Hold a family discussion once every 2 weeks.

Step 8: Working with the Children's Other Household

- Give the adults in the children's other household positive feedback once a month.

Source: Adapted from "The Stepping Ahead Program" (pp. 58- 89) by E. Visher. In *Stepfamilies Stepping Ahead* edited by M. Burt, 1989, Lincoln, NE: Stepfamilies Press. Copyright 1989 by Stepfamily Association of America. Adapted by permission.

parents can find themselves overidealized by their stepchildren or the victim of displaced hostility.

Not all members of a stepfamily are biologically related. This is an obvious enough fact, and one that should in theory be relatively simple to deal with. But our culture considers biological family ties special. "Blood is thicker than water," the old saying goes. Family bonds are difficult to break, and feelings of being a family run deep.

Many children of divorce keep hoping that Mom and Dad will reunite; the new marriage of one of the parents dashes those hopes. When a stepparent enters the family, children truly know that their mother and father will never get back together. This can cause despair and bitterness toward the stepparent. The stepparent can become the personification of evil in the child's mind: "If only *she* weren't around, Mom and Dad would get back together."

Remarried newlyweds can find it challenging to simultaneously build their relationship and to meet their children's needs. Biological parents need to forestall their children's jealousy toward the new stepparent, and stepparents must remember that their stepchildren's primary loyalty is to their biological parents.

Even though the relationships between biological parent and child are well established, the couple in a stepfamily are newlyweds. It can be very difficult for the couple to balance marital needs and the children's needs. People's loyalties to each other are divided in new and complex ways when a new family member comes on the scene. If a stepparent does not recognize the stepchildren's long-standing bonds with the biological parent and move carefully, the stepparent can end up in a very difficult love triangle.

A common example is a single mother who lives alone with her children for a number of years before marrying again. The mother may have developed strong ties and a comfortable pattern of parenting with her children. If she has an adolescent son or daughter, the mother's relationship with the child may be more like that of a big sister than that of a parent. The adolescent may become very jealous of the new spouse. "She always used to want to talk to me after school. Now she spends all her time with him!"

Girls may develop an almost "wife-like" relationship with their fathers during the single-parent period, according to Geoffrey Grief (1995). Daughters often serve as confidante and household manager for their father, and many enjoy their new status. When the father marries again, the daughter may see the stepmother as a competitor for Dad's time and affection and an intruder on her wife-like roles.

The stepparent must avoid the tendency to try too hard; bonding takes a good deal of time. Newlyweds generally go out of their way to please each other, but when applied to the children of the new spouse, this can create problems for the new stepparent. The stepparent knows that his or her new spouse's children are a major hurdle in establishing a successful marriage and feels that if she or he can only get along with the children, the chances for success in this new marriage are vastly improved. But children do not easily forsake the love of their birth parent for a stepparent. Adolescents, in particular, are often not very open to including an "outsider" in their family.

The stepparent needs to avoid the trap of trying to replace the former parent. In reality the stepparent is not so much a new parent in the family as a new adult in the family. The parent role has to develop slowly. The urge to build a solid new marriage can spur stepparents to play the "superstepmother" or "superstepfather" role, which is neither realistic nor beneficial.

Stepparents also must avoid favoritism in dealing simultaneously with their "real" children and their stepchildren. Children are not always pleasant to be around; they can at times be selfish, whiney, disobedient, and intrusive. It can be difficult to love your own children when they are not acting lovable; trying to love someone else's children can be especially difficult at times. Many stepparents find themselves overcompensating for their tendency to favor their biological children.

Stepparents also need to develop skill in dealing with complex financial realities in their new families. Although people who are marrying again are usually painfully aware of how challenging family money problems can be, few feel comfortable discussing money matters and financial planning before remarriage (Ihinger-Tallman & Pasley, 1987). Some even prefer to avoid talking about minor financial issues until they become more serious problems. In a stepfamily, money problems often become difficult to avoid. For example, a father who remarries is sometimes in the difficult position of sending child support payments to his biological children, supporting his new family, and hoping that his new spouse's former husband will continue to provide financial support for the stepchildren.

Strengths of Stepfamilies

Despite the many unique challenges of the stepparent role, research findings on stepfamilies are generally positive. Many professionals have predicted negative consequences for stepfamilies given the challenges they face, but most stepfamilies do relatively well (LeMasters & DeFrain, 1989).

One review of research on stepfamilies (Coleman & Ganong, 1991) indicates that investigators have often failed to take into account the complexity of stepfamily relationships because of the number of people involved—extra parents, extra siblings, extra grandparents, extra sets of aunts and uncles, and so forth. Some stepfamily studies have also erred by using small samples of stepfamilies and non-random samples. Much of the data has been gathered by self-report questionnaires, rather than through interviews or professional observations. And much of the data has come from only one family member, despite the fact that husbands, wives, children, and grandparents often have very different perceptions of what is going on in a family.

Coleman and Ganong (1991) concluded that there is little documented evidence that children in stepfamilies differ significantly from children in other family structures in terms of self-image, psychosomatic illness, or personality characteristics. Stepchildren are also comparable to children in nuclear families in regard to school grades, academic achievement scores, and IQ. Stepchildren have no more problems in the area of social behavior than children in nuclear families

Figure 17.4 Strengths in Simple Versus Complex Stepfamilies (based on ENRICH). *Source:* Data from "Couple Strengths and Stressors in Complex and Simple Stepfamilies in Australia" by N. C. Shultz, C. L. Schultz, and D. H. Olson, 1991, *Journal of Marriage and the Family, 53*, p. 560. Copyright 1991 by the National Council on Family Relations.

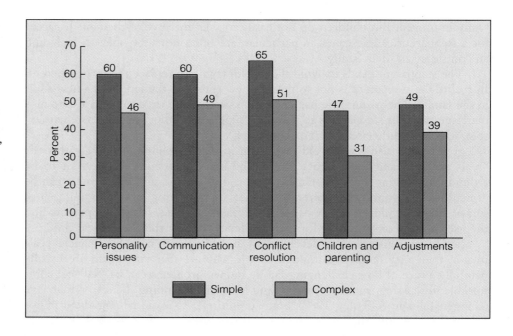

do. Finally, although emotional bonds between stepparents and stepchildren were found, generally, to be less close than bonds between parents and children (Coleman & Ganong, 1991), most stepchildren say that they like their stepparents and get along well with them. Taking everything into account, there is no significant relationship between living in a stepfamily and problem behavior or negative attitudes in stepchildren. An increasing number of family researchers have called for a more objective approach to stepfamilies (Coleman & Ganong, 1991).

The goal of a study by Noel Schultz, Cynthia Schultz, and David Olson (1991) was to identify the major strengths of **simple stepfamilies,** those that include children from only one parent, and compare them with those of **complex stepfamilies,** which include children from both parents. The researchers hypothesized and found that simple stepfamilies have more strengths than complex stepfamilies. It appears that this is because there is less complexity and conflict in simple stepfamilies than in complex stepfamilies, which combine two families. Figure 17.4 summarizes the data, which indicate that simple stepfamilies have more strengths than complex stepfamilies in the areas of personality issues, communication skills, ability to resolve conflict, parenting skills, and adjustment to the process of being a stepfamily.

One of the outcomes of the study by Schultz and his colleagues (1991) is that a new premarital inventory called **PREPARE-MC** (Marriage with Children) was developed to better help couples prepare for a marriage that will create a stepfamily. Like the PREPARE inventory (Olson, Fournier, & Druckman, 1986) discussed in earlier chapters, PREPARE-MC contains 125 questions dealing with 14 important categories in a couple's relationship. The questions in PREPARE-MC were revised so that many of the items focus specifically on issues relevant to stepfamilies. The PREPARE-MC inventory helps people deal with relationship issues before marriage. More people who have been married and divorced are open to preparing for a second marriage than are couples entering their first marriage.

Just because a first marriage ended in divorce does not mean a new marriage will also fail. In fact, the painful process of divorce can be a tremendous learning experience and can help provide the foundation for a successful new marriage and a strong stepfamily.

Summary

- Nearly one third of all U.S. families were headed by a single parent in 1994, most of whom were female.

- Differences between nuclear families and stepfamilies include biological parent-child ties, the nature and length of the couple's marriage, parent-child emotional bonds, loyalty issues, extended-family issues, struggles between children, and the degree of demands on financial resources.

- There are four types of divorced single-parent families, or binuclear families: mothers with sole custody; fathers with sole custody; split-custody families (in which the father has custody of one or more children and the mother has custody of one or more children); and joint-custody families (in which mother and father share decision making and child care responsibilities after the divorce in relatively equal time segments). Researchers have concluded that the type of relationship the ex-spouses have often determines which single-parent family style will work best.

- Divorced single parents face challenges that include loneliness and isolation, money problems, and work overload. Joys of single parenting include freedom to make decisions without interference, the satisfaction of watching the children grow and develop, and increased closeness with the children.

- Single parents advise newly single parents to take time to get to know themselves before rushing into new relationships; to not succumb to feelings of failure, worthlessness, or self-pity; to keep busy with constructive activities; to let the children have as much contact with the other parent as feasible; to try to be flexible; and to remain independent.

- Many divorced individuals with children are extremely cautious about entering a new marriage. Remarriage involves letting go of the old relationship and any pain associated with it; planning for the complexities involved in the new couple and family relationship; and then reconstituting the family to make room for the new spouse, the new spouse's children, one's own children, and all the children's relationships with their biological parents and extended families.

- Stepparenting is challenging because stepparents do not start with a clean slate, may try too hard to establish a successful relationship with their stepchildren, may be resented by or awaken jealousy in their stepchildren, may try to replace the absent biological parent, and must avoid favoring their own children over their stepchildren.

• Research on stepfamilies indicates that the majority have strengths similar to those of other types of families. Stepchildren do not differ significantly from children in nuclear families in terms of self-image, academic achievement, or degree of problem social behavior.

• Steps in building a strong stepfamily include nurturing the couple, family, parent-child, and stepparent-stepchild relationships; building stepfamily trust and ties; keeping bridges open to the children's biological parents; and finding time for oneself.

Key Terms

binuclear family

sole custody

joint custody

split custody

remarriage

blended family

stepfamily

stepparent

reconstituted family

pseudomutuality

Stepping Ahead Program

simple stepfamily

complex stepfamily

PREPARE-MC

Activities

1. Interview a member of a single-parent family. Ask not only about the stresses the family faces, but also about the strengths in the family. How is the family different from a two-parent family? How is it similar? Discuss your findings with other students.

2. Interview a member of a stepfamily, focusing on both the strengths and the stresses in the family. Compare and contrast the family with a nuclear family. Share your findings with other students.

3. Review Table 17.1 and discuss the differences between a nuclear family and a stepfamily. What consequences do these differences have for the parents and the children in each type of family?

Suggested Readings

Ahrons, C. R. (1994). *The good divorce.* New York: Harper/Collins. *A useful, positive perspective on a difficult life event.*

Bernstein, A. C. (1989). *Yours, mine, and ours: How families change when remarried parents have a child together.* New York: Scribner's. *An interesting look at the dynamics of remarriage.*

Burt, M. (Ed.). (1989). *Stepfamilies stepping ahead.* Lincoln, NE: Stepfamilies Press. *A practical publication of the Stepfamily Association of America.*

Clapp, G. (1992). *Divorce and new beginnings: An authoritative guide to recovery and growth, solo parenting, and stepfamilies.* New York: Wiley. *Navigating the difficult straits of loss, growth, and resolution.*

Coleman, M., & Ganong, L. H. (1991). Remarriage and stepfamily research in the 1980s. In A. Booth (Ed.), *Contemporary families: Looking forward, looking back* (pp. 192–207). Minneapolis: National Council on Family Relations. *Insights from researchers at the University of Missouri, Columbia, who have devoted many years to furthering the understanding of stepfamilies.*

DeFrain, J., Fricke, J., & Elmen, J. (1987). *On our own: A single parent's survival guide.* Lexington, MA: Lexington Books/Heath. *How single parents survive and transcend a challenging situation; based on a study of 738 divorced mothers and fathers with sole custody, split custody, or joint custody of their children.*

Folberg, J. (Ed.). (1991). *Joint custody and shared parenting* (2nd ed.). New York: Guilford Press. *Positive outcomes for mothers, fathers, and children sharing parenting responsibilities after divorce.*

Ihinger-Tallman, M., & Pasley, K. (1987). *Remarriage.* Newbury Park, CA: Sage. *Reviews the research on marriage after divorce.*

Kissman, D., & J. A. Allen. (1993). *Single-parent families.* Newbury Park, CA: Sage. *Current research and insights.*

Pasley, K., & Ihinger-Tallman, M. (Eds). (1994). *Stepparenting: Issues in theory, research, and practice.* Westport, CT: Greenwood Press. *A broad selection of current and significant issues and findings.*

Visher, E. B., & Visher, J. S. (1979). *Stepfamilies: A guide to working with stepparents and stepchildren.* New York: Brunner/Mazel.

Visher, E. B., & Visher, J. S. (1988). *Old loyalties: New ties.* New York: Brunner/Mazel.

Visher, E. B., & Visher, J. S. (1992). *How to win as a stepfamily* (2nd ed.). New York: Brunner/Mazel. *Very practical books by two pioneers in the study and understanding of stepfamilies.*

CHAPTER 18

Strengthening Families in the Future

What does the future hold for you and your family? What does it hold for families in the United States? And what does it hold for families all over the world? If we extend the perspective offered by systems theory, we can see that the future of all families on Earth is interconnected. The well-being of every individual and every family is intimately and inextricably linked to the well-being of others.

As emphasized throughout this book, families in this country are wonderfully diverse. The same is true for families around the world. These differences add zest to living. We do not all have to be the same to get along well together. In fact, by having different interests and capabilities, we offer strength to each other as individuals, family members, and citizens of our communities.

There is an apparent paradox here: As individuals and as families, we are all unique and different. Yet, deep down, as human beings, we are all quite similar. This recognition of human commonalities has been voiced by countless people in countless walks of life—novelists, poets, sociologists, anthropologists, singers and songwriters, economists, psychologists, educators (DeFrain, DeFrain, & Lepard, 1994).

For example, novelist James A. Michener, a self-described "citizen of the world," has dedicated a lifetime to understanding people around the world, living in an area for months or years and writing about what he saw and heard. He has concluded that

> We are all brothers [and sisters]. We all face the same problems and find the same satisfactions. We are united in one great band. I am one with all of them, in all lands, in all climates, in all conditions. Since we brothers [and sisters] occupy the entire earth, the world is our home. (Michener, 1991, p. 249)

In the 1930s cultural anthropologists assumed that every culture was unique. Then sociologist George Homans began amassing empirical observations that led him to disagree with the notion of cultural uniqueness. He came to believe instead that certain societal institutions appear in every culture because of the universality of human nature (Homans, 1974).

Anthropologist Colin Turnbull devoted his life to studying the nature of human culture around the world and challenged age-old Western assumptions about the differences between so-called primitive societies and modern societies. In his book *The Human Cycle* (1983) Turnbull examined such disparate cultures as the Mbuti of Zaire, the Hindus of Banaras, and middle-class Western society. He described the human life cycle as it is experienced in each of these cultures and showed that from infancy to old age, the stages of life are identical in meaning in all these cultures. Turnbull believed that the problems of love, work, loneliness, growing up, and growing old are universal; he also argued that these problems may be handled far better by the so-called primitive societies. He concluded that behind all the different rites, customs, and religions, people in various cultures live in the same eternal, immutable human cycle, which is governed by the same laws.

Kenneth Boulding, an economist, philosopher, and general systems theorist, believes that human betterment is the end toward which we individually and collectively should strive. Betterment is a change in some system that is evaluated as "being for the better." It is an increase in the "ultimate good," that which is good

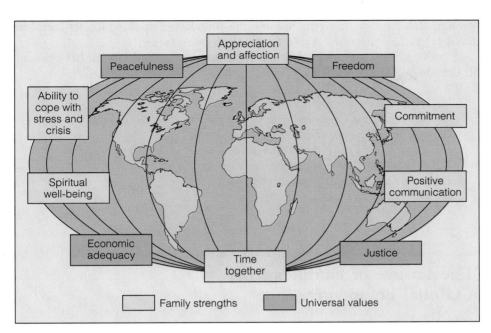

in itself. Four great virtues make up this ultimate good: (1) economic adequacy—"riches" in contrast to poverty; nourishment rather than starvation; adequate housing, clothing, health care, and other essentials of life; (2) justice—in contrast to injustice; equality rather than inequality in access to work, education, and health; (3) freedom—in contrast to coercion and confinement; and (4) peacefulness—in contrast to warfare and strife. Boulding (1985) believes these great virtues may be considered universal values.

Life in families can be a deeply challenging yet fulfilling endeavor—a continuous quest for a sense of spiritual or emotional well-being in a tempestuous environment. Because each family finds itself confronted with life's great challenges as family members pass through the stages of human development, it is not surprising that families who are strong and successful around the world are likely to share similar qualities. These qualities, again, can be categorized as cohesion (a sense of togetherness; a commitment to one another demonstrated by satisfying time spent together); flexibility (the ability to successfully meet the minor and major stressors of life, grounded in a shared set of goals, values, and beliefs that give family members a sense of spiritual well-being); and communication (the capacity to listen and talk effectively with one another and to express appreciation and affection for all family members) (Figure 18.1). In other words, the basic foundation of successful families is remarkably similar from culture to culture. This is a wonderful notion because it gives us, as a family of humankind, something important to share, something we all can understand together.

The family strengths perspective points out that if you look only for problems in families, you will find only problems. If you look for strengths, you will find strengths. A family's strengths become the foundation upon which its members build even more successful ways of relating to one another.

As Peter, Paul, and Mary, folk singers with roots in the 1950s and 1960s, sang in the song "River of Jordan:"

> *We are only one river. We are only one sea.*
> *And it flows through you, and it flows through me.*
> *We are only one people. We are one and the same.*
> *We are all one spirit. We are all one name.*
> *We are the father, mother, daughter and son.*
> *From the dawn of creation, we are one.*
> *We are one.* (Yarrow, 1972)

The Future of Families from a Global Perspective

Perhaps the ultimate general systems theory is the Gaia hypothesis, created by British scientist James E. Lovelock and several colleagues (Lovelock, 1979, 1987). These scientists were inspired by the first photographs of Earth from space, which revealed the planet as a whole. They were stunned to see our planet in a new light: as a living and interconnected entity.

Lovelock argued that ecologists had been rooted in a very down-to-Earth approach to natural history. They had focused on detailed studies of habitats and ecosystems without taking the whole picture into account. He charged that science had, in essence, missed the forest for the trees. He proposed the Gaia hypothesis, which considered Earth to be a planet-sized entity, one with properties that could not be predicted by simply summing its parts.

Lovelock and his colleagues subsequently refined their vision, defining Gaia as "a complex entity involving the Earth's biosphere, atmosphere, oceans, and soil; the totality constituting a feedback or cybernetic system which seeks an optimal physical and chemical environment for life on this planet. The maintenance of relatively constant conditions by active control may be conveniently described by the term from systems theory of homeostasis" (Lovelock, 1987, p. 11).

What does all this have to do with strengthening families? From space, Earth appears to be a single entity, a whole, without political boundaries or cultural divisions. It is apparent that we will all have to work together as a family of humankind to deal successfully with the major problems we face: among them, war, overpopulation, environmental degradation, and ethnic strife.

Family problems also know no boundaries from a global perspective: A tragedy for families in one region affects a whole country; a tragedy in one country affects the world. Individual families sometimes are crushed by events largely out of their control; they simply are not capable of preventing or dealing successfully with catastrophe by themselves.

As one saying tells us, however, we should "think globally and act locally." No

The Earth is alive. This is the essence of the Gaia hypothesis developed by James E. Lovelock after seeing the first photographs of the Earth from space.

individual is in a position to change the world single-handedly. But by keeping attuned to global family concerns, we can act responsibly in our individual worlds. We can unite in groups to find solutions to large-scale problems that affect countless people.

The Future of Your Family

The future of families in the United States and around the world begins with each of us as we create the future in our own family. We asked our students what the future would be like in their families, and we would like to share some of their answers with you. (Their comments were tape-recorded with their consent. Names and identifying details have been changed to preserve anonymity.)

"I think we're a happier family than we were in the past because we laugh a lot," Marta, a 40-year-old divorced mother of three who was completing her college degree, responded. "The children think I'm really a liberated woman, and that's pretty exciting. I'd tell young people to hang in there with your parents and try and understand them, because they love you and they just want the very best for you."

* * * * *

"The future for my family?" 19-year-old-Rachel replied. "I'm not sure. My parents have been divorced for about 15 years, and they're both remarried. My mom's happily remarried. My dad is not so happy. (I can't talk, this is so upsetting.) He always talks about my mom and what she's doing and what they'd be like if they were still together.

"My mom has done a really good job [tears, coughing] of showing us things are okay, even with stressful events. She has raised us very well, I believe. My father . . . he screwed up, and he's realizing it now. And he's telling it to me. . . . [tears] Sorry. And I just don't know what to say to him. Yeah, Dad, you blew it. And I think he's going to get divorced again. For myself, I have the biggest hopes. I know everyone does. But I feel that if I do get divorced, my mom showed me the way to do it right."

* * * * *

"As far as where we're going," 21-year-old Tanya noted, "I think we'll be okay because my partner, Darren, has a strong family. But I don't want my dysfunctional family to overshadow our life because that's something I want to overcome. . . . [tears] Why does everyone cry up here? [laughter] I want to overcome the statistics and have a strong marriage. But, if Darren turns out to be a problem like my dad [laughter], at least I know I can go on because my mom and dad are both very happy now without each other, so at least I know I have an out."

* * * * *

"Now, when it comes to my family, where's it going?" 31-year-old Nina, a graduate student, repeated the question thoughtfully. "I guess I hope that it grows stronger when we get back together, since we're apart now [he's in the military, serving overseas]. We'll be back together in June. Hopefully it will grow stronger, though we'll be a lot closer to our families and their problems. We've been a long way away in the past, and shielded from their problems. I think their problems will be more up front now, and that will either make or break our marriage. We'll either get sucked into the pit of misery they're in, or he'll just figure out that he can't take care of his family. They have to take care of themselves. You're responsible for your own destiny. You can either wallow in your pit or you can carry on in your life, in spite of your past, and be the best that you can be."

* * * * *

"Personally," responded 20-year-old David, "where's my family going in the future? I think we're doing okay. You always knock on wood, because you don't have complete control over your life, no matter how smart you think you are, or how long you've gone to school, or how much you've thought about it, or how many experts you've read, or who you've consulted. You get a real sense of humility, a feeling of humbleness, when you think how difficult life is and how little control you really have. We really don't live in a world where we have a huge amount of control.

* * * * *

"For the future," said 26-year-old Allan, "I want to raise my family differently than my parents did us. I want to be a closer family. There was so much communication that didn't happen in our family. We came home from school, laid our books down, and went into our rooms for the night. I think when I have a family some day I want it to be a very close-knit family, and I want to have open communication and to tell each other every day how much you love one another, because that's one thing our family missed."

* * * * *

"Our child Robbie's birth changed our life and the lives of our parents forever," Diana, a 28-year-old part-time student, responded. "Nothing anyone could have said to Paul or me would have prepared us for the reality of parenthood. Being parents is both the best and the hardest job in the world. It's very rewarding; it can also be very trying, especially when your wonderful 2-month-old son is hungry every 2 hours throughout the day and night and you, the mommy, are the only one in the world who can feed him . . . for obvious reasons.

From the very beginning of my pregnancy, Paul was a very understanding and sensitive husband. He rubbed my back when it hurt, bought me saltine crackers when I was feeling nauseous, and told me to quit my job when I had swollen feet and could barely walk. Paul took great interest in me and what I was going through. He and I read many books together about babies, pregnancy, birth, and parenting. He went to all but one of my doctor's visits, carried our pillows to Lamaze class, and was a very supportive coach in labor. I believe my pregnancy with our son brought me and my husband closer together. There is something amazing about creating a life together. We had no idea about what we were getting ourselves into, but we were doing it together. I am thankful we have such a good marriage, because our strong foundation helped us to build our new family."

In summary, these students provided insights into their life experiences and their thoughts and dreams about their families in the future. Life inevitably brings challenges; the key to life in a strong family is to work together to meet these challenges.

Strengthening Your Marriage and Family Relationships

Fortunately, there are countless sources of support and strength for families in their quest to develop and maintain intimate, satisfying relationships. We discuss several of them in the following sections.

Personal Strategies

In our own studies, we have found that strong families successfully manage life's difficulties in a variety of ways (Stinnett, Stinnett, DeFrain, & DeFrain, 1997). These are some of their strategies:

- *Look for something positive in difficult situations.* Focus on the positive element.

- *Pull together.* Think of the problem not as one family member's difficulty, but as a challenge for the family as a whole.

- *Get help outside the nuclear family.* Call on extended-family members, supportive friends, neighbors, colleagues, church or synagogue members, and community professionals. "It takes a whole village to resolve a crisis."

- *Create open channels of communication.* Challenges are not met when communication shuts down.

- *Keep things in perspective.* "These things, too, shall pass."

- *Adopt new roles in a flexible manner.* Crises often demand that individuals learn new approaches to life and take on different responsibilities.

- *Focus to minimize fragmentation.* Look at the big picture. Focusing on the details rather than the essentials can make people edgy, even hysterical.

- *Give up on worry, or put it in a box.* Worrying itself usually causes us more misery than the event we are worrying about. Sometimes it's best to stuff the worry down or to resolve to worry 10 minutes a day and then forget about it. The mind simply has to rest.

- *Eat well, exercise, love each other, and get adequate sleep.* We often forget that we are biological beings. Like kindergartners, we need a good lunch, and we need to play. We need to have our hair stroked, we need a good hug, and we need a good nap.

- *Create a life full of meaning and purpose.* We all will face severe crises in life. We will not be able to avoid these challenges. Rather, our aim can be to live a useful life of service to our community. This brings a richness and dignity to our lives, in spite of the troubles we endure.

- *Actively meet challenges head-on.* Life's disasters do not go away when we look in another direction. But paradoxically, it can also sometimes help to withdraw and replenish ourselves.

- *Go with the flow to some degree.* Sometimes we are relatively powerless in the face of a crisis. Simply saying to ourselves that things will get better with time can be useful.

- *Be prepared in advance for life's challenges.* Healthy family relationships are like an ample bank balance: If our relational accounts are in order, we will be able to weather life's most difficult storms—together.

Table 18.1 Programs for Couples and Families

	SERVICE	GOAL	PROVIDER
Informal networks	Personal advice	Advice and support	Family and friends
Self-help groups	Focus groups	Insight and support	Lay people concerned with similar issues
Couple education	Functional marriage and family courses	Awareness	High school and college teachers
Couple enrichment	Marriage enrichment	Motivation	Lay couples
Couple counseling	Premarital and marital counseling	Insight and some skills	Clergy, counselors, social workers
Couple skill training	Communication programs	Improved skills	Trained professionals
Couple & family therapy	Marital and family therapy	Insight and change in dynamics	Marital and family therapists, psychologists

- *Learn to laugh and learn to cry.* Expressing both joy and sorrow is essential for maintaining emotional balance.

- *Don't blame others.* Instead, strong families work with others to build a more satisfying world for all.

- *Take life's challenges one day at a time.* In especially tight situations, it may be necessary to take things an hour or even a minute at a time.

- *Realize that suffering can be a catalyst for positive growth.* Crisis, by definition, is a difficult time in life, but it can also plant the seeds for a satisfying future. This lesson is hard to internalize but important to remember.

- *Identify spiritually with the grand procession of life.* Through good times and bad times, individuals come and go, but life itself goes on. Some people find comfort in this thought.

Programs for Couples and Families

Programs and services for couples and families range from informal networks to couple and family therapy (Table 18.1). Program types are listed in order of their therapeutic impact, from least to most intensive, in the table. As couple and family issues become more serious and chronic, a higher level of treatment intensity is recommended. For example, it would be more appropriate for a couple who had been having marital problems for several years and had seriously considered divorce to see a couple therapist rather than to attend a self-help group. Although informal networks and self-help groups can be useful resources for some simple couple and family problems, neither usually has the expertise or the techniques to treat more serious problems.

Couple enrichment and couple skill-training programs can be very useful resources for couples without serious problems. These programs can help couples meet and learn from other couples. The skill-building programs often focus on communication and conflict-resolution skills, which couples can use to improve their relationships and resolve the differences that inevitably arise in any close relationship.

Couple therapy, family therapy, or both are recommended when relationship problems between partners or among family members are chronic and intense. When problems involve the children, family therapy is called for. In families headed by two parents, the parents may also benefit from couple therapy because parenting can put a great deal of stress on the couple relationship. Couple therapy and family therapy are most effective when begun before problems become severe and chronic.

Premarital Counseling

Because of the risk of divorce and the importance of marital happiness, it seems logical that most couples would and should get premarital counseling. In fact, a growing number of couples do seek such counseling. Premarital counseling is especially common when both partners have been married and divorced, presumably because they do not want this remarriage to fail.

There is increasing evidence that a good premarital program can help improve a couple's relationship and reduce their chances of divorce. As discussed in Chapter 11, an effective premarital program has at least three essential components: (1) a premarital inventory with individual feedback for each couple, (2) a skill-building component that focuses on communication and problem solving, and (3) a small group in which couples can discuss their mutual issues. The program should last 6–8 weeks and should be started a year before the marriage so that the couple have time to develop their skills.

Premarital counseling is popular with most clergy. In a national study of 231 clergy from several Protestant denominations, 94% said they thought that all premarital couples should have counseling before marriage, and 100% said they provided premarital counseling to all couples before they would marry them (Jones & Stahman, 1994). About 90–95% provided individual counseling to the partners. About two thirds used some type of premarital inventory and gave the couple materials to read. Group lectures and group couples counseling were used by only about 5% of the clergy.

One of the most popular premarital programs in the United States is the PREPARE Program. As mentioned in Chapter 11, more than 500,000 couples have participated in this program in the past 10 years. The specific goals of the program are to: (1) help the couple explore their relationship strengths and growth areas, (2) help the couple learn to resolve conflict effectively using a 10-step conflict resolution model, (3) help the couple discuss their family of origin and articulate the

Marriage enrichment experiences are increasingly popular both as a means of helping couples deal with marital problems and as a way to deepen already strong relationships. These programs let couples explore issues and feelings in a supportive, relaxing environment, uninterrupted by the distractions of daily life.

characteristics they would like to develop in their own marriage, and (4) motivate the couple to invest time and energy in improving their relationship. The PREPARE Program focuses on 14 important relationship areas, including communication, conflict resolution, financial management, and egalitarian roles. (For a full listing of these areas, see Box 11.4 in Chapter 11.) For more information about premarital counseling, see the entries under "Marriage Preparation and Enrichment" in Resource Section B, "National Directory of Organizations Serving Families.

Marriage Enrichment Programs

There are two types of couple enrichment programs. One type, referred to simply as a couple enrichment program, usually lasts 1 or 2 days and takes place on a weekend. The focus is on motivating the couple to increase the amount of personal information they share with each other. These short-term programs are helpful to some couples who already have a good marriage and want to improve it. However, for couples with more serious relationship issues, such programs can create problems (Doherty, Lester, & Leigh, 1986). One of the unfortunate aspects of enrichment programs is that they can increase expectations without giving the couple the relationship skills to improve their marriage.

The second type of program, the skill-building program, focuses on teaching communication and conflict resolution skills. These programs, which are more effective, usually last about 6 weeks and meet each week for about 2 hours. Skill-building programs that have demonstrated their effectiveness and value to couples include the Couples Communication Program by Sherod Miller, the PREP Program by Howard Markman, Scott Stanley, and Susan Blumberg (1994) and the Relationship Enhancement Program by Bernard Guerney. See the entries under "Marriage Preparation and Enrichment" in the National Directory (Resource Section B) to locate these and other programs.

In a recent study, three couple enrichment programs were compared (Hawley & Olson, 1995). The programs were Preston Dyer and Genie Dyer's Growing Together, Edward Bader's Learning to Live Together, and Don Dinkmeyer and Jon Carlson's Training for Marriage Enrichment (TIME). Seventy-one newlywed couples were assigned to the three programs, and 28 couples were assigned to a control group. All three programs were about 6 weeks long, and all focused on communication, conflict resolution, finances, role relationship, family of origin, and sexuality. Couples met in a small group with about 6 other couples and a trainer on a weekly basis for about 2 hours.

Ninety-eight percent of the couples said they would recommend the program to another couple, and 96% said they would repeat the experience. More than 85% felt the topics were very relevant, and 75% felt their group leader was helpful. There were significant improvements in the couples' scores on communication, conflict resolution, personality issues, financial management, dealing with family and friends, and marital satisfaction on some statistical tests, though not on others. The couples did, however, enjoy the experience and feel it was beneficial.

Marital and Family Therapy

Couples with persistent relationship problems should seek professional help as early as possible. Couples and families who receive help with problems before they become too severe have a much better chance of overcoming the difficulties and building a stronger relationship than do those who wait.

Choosing a Marital and Family Therapist   Therapists who are specifically trained to deal with relationship problems are marital and family therapists and some psychiatrists, psychologists, and social workers. Licensed marital and family therapists are certified by the American Association for Marriage and Family Therapy (AAMFT) and have received specialized training in relationship issues. Psychologists typically have a doctorate or a master's degree in psychology; some have training in working with couples and families, although their initial training tends to emphasize work with individuals. Psychiatrists are medical doctors who have additional training in the field of mental health. Some specialize in working with couples and families. Last, social workers receive some training in working with couples and families. Be sure to check professional credentials and experience when choosing a therapist.

The most highly trained marital and family therapists are certified members of AAMFT or are licensed by the state in which they work. In most localities, the yellow pages of the telephone directory list marital and family therapists under "marital and family counseling." One can also consult a family service agency or the United Way for suggestions. Physicians or clergy may also be able to assist in the search for a qualified professional.

The following are some specific questions one should ask a therapist *before* beginning therapy: What is your professional training and degree? How much specialized training and experience have you had in marital and family therapy? Do you usually see couples and families together or as individuals? What procedure will you use to evaluate our relationship? How much will you charge for that assessment? How frequently will we have sessions? How long will each session be? Can we establish a contract for a specific number of sessions? What does each session cost? Will our insurance cover the cost? Couples who do not feel comfortable with the responses they receive to these questions should feel free to seek another therapist.

How Effective Is Marital and Family Therapy?   In the first national survey of the practice of marital and family therapists, 526 AAMFT therapists from 15 states commented on therapy with 1,422 clients (Doherty & Simmons, 1996). In addition, 492 clients provided outcome data on their satisfaction with their marital and family therapy.

Marital and family therapists spent about half their time working with couples and families and half working with individuals. They spent about 20 hours a week seeing clients in therapy and carried a total caseload of about 24 clients. The common presenting problems were depression (44%), other psychological problems (35%), marital problems (30%), anxiety (21%), parent-child problems (13%), alcohol/drugs (8%), child behavior (8%), and family-of-origin issues (7%). The most frequent DSM-IV diagnostic codes were adjustment disorder (25%), depression (23%), and anxiety disorders (14%).

Marital and family therapy is relatively short term compared with traditional individual therapy provided by psychiatrists and some psychologists. The median number of sessions for the marital and family therapists was 12. The average length of therapy for couples was 11 sessions; for families, 9; and for individuals, 13. Most clients were seen biweekly. Based on the therapists' records, the average cost of therapy was $80 for each one-hour session, for a total of $780. Individual therapy was the most expensive ($845), couple therapy was next ($748), and family therapy was the least expensive ($585).

The outcome of the therapy was usually very successful from the perspective of both the client and the therapist. Overall, 83% of the clients felt the therapeutic goals were achieved, 89% felt their emotional health improved, 78% said their family relationships got better, and 63% felt their relationship with their partner also improved. In addition, most clients were very satisfied with their therapy: 98% rated the service as good to excellent, 97% said they got the kind of help they wanted, 98% said they were able to deal with their problems more effectively, 93% said their needs were met, 94% would return to the same therapist again, and 97% would recommend the therapist to a friend. In summary, it appears that marital and family therapy is a rather cost-effective and efficient approach to dealing with a range of emotional and relationship problems (Doherty & Simmons, 1996) in individuals, couples, and families.

Using the Family Circumplex Model in Family Therapy

The Family Circumplex Model is often used by marital and family therapists working with families with problems. It provides a useful framework for diagnosing and treating several common problems in marital and family systems.

Common Problems in Marital and Family Systems   One frequent problem couples seeking counseling describe is the feeling that they are at opposite extremes on the same dimension of the model. On the cohesion dimension, for example, one partner may want more togetherness whereas the other partner wants more autonomy. Similarly, on the flexibility dimension, one partner may desire more flexibility in the family whereas the partner wants more rules (i.e., rigidity). When couples disagree on the balance of separateness (autonomy) and togetherness in their relationship, this can be negotiated by jointly planning their schedules. When couples disagree on how much flexibility (rules or roles) is appropriate, they can reverse roles at home for a week.

A second common problem for couples occurs when both partners are at the same extreme on one or both model dimensions. Both may be disengaged from the relationship because they are so heavily involved in career or outside interests that they have little time or energy for the marriage. Or both may be enmeshed, so invested in their partner that they have little room to develop personal interests and skills. When couples are too enmeshed, one solution is for them each to develop more separate interests and spend more time apart.

This all may sound quite simple, but difficulties arise because people see their relationships differently and have different expectations about them. For example, the wife and the husband often offer different family descriptions and goals. Add a teenage child, and another description will likely surface.

These differences in perception often increase when a couple or a family is in conflict. For example, a wife might describe her husband as a total monster who is drunk much of the time, went through numerous jobs in 5 years, and beat her and the young children regularly. Her husband might describe himself as a "social drinker" who happened to change jobs occasionally because he had a string of bad luck with a few lousy bosses. Although his wife was a nag and turned his young sons into a "bunch of sissies," he nobly tried to discipline the children.

There is no simple solution to this dilemma of differing family perceptions. If a counselor were to interview only one person in a family, either the husband or the wife, it would be easy. The counselor would get a relatively coherent picture of the family because it would be seen from one person's perspective. But the picture wouldn't represent the family's complexity. The solution lies in getting everyone together, asking countless questions, and dealing with disputes over what is true and what is not true about the family. This approach produces a more valid—and also a more complex—picture of the family's dynamics.

Comparison of Families With and Without Problems   Families with more severe problems tend to fall into the unbalanced types on the Family Circumplex

"If you intend to stay together, you'll have to be apart more."

"The Lockhorns" © 1987 WM Hoest Enterprises
Inc. Distributed by King Features Syndicate.

Model. For example, a study of sex offenders found high levels of unbalanced family types in both their families of origin and their current families (Carnes, 1989). A study of families at risk for destructive parent-child relationships in the adolescent period found the majority of high-risk families to be unbalanced types (Garbarino, Sebes, & Schellenbach, 1984). And a study of families with adolescent juvenile delinquents found only a small percentage to be balanced types and a vast majority to be mid-range or unbalanced types (Rodick, Henggler, & Hanson, 1985). There is strong research support for the notion that balanced families, as defined by the Circumplex Model, are more functional than unbalanced families.

An important qualification of this hypothesis relates to the definition of "problem" families. Generally, problem families are defined as those that are voluntarily or involuntarily involved in some treatment program. There is good clinical evidence that couples or families in treatment programs are often unbalanced on one or both dimensions of the Family Circumplex Model. There are, however, many families who are unbalanced on one or both dimensions who do function well and therefore never seek treatment. There are also families who are unbalanced on these dimensions who have problems but never choose to seek treatment. Because most studies have relied on problem families, those that seek or are placed in treatment, we know very little about families who do not seek help.

Case Study: Diagnosis and Treatment of a Family With Problems   The Davis family has five members: Mary and Don, the parents; 18-year-old Ann; 16-year-old Julie; and 9-year-old Peter. Mary drinks to relieve feelings of inadequacy in a family that is dominated by high achievers: Don and the oldest daughter, Ann. The middle daughter, Julie, also feels inadequate but tries to console her mother and is responsible enough to be a surrogate mother to Peter, the youngest child. The family comes in for therapy shortly after Mary begins treatment for her dependence on alcohol. Ann has left home, angry at Mary for all the problems she has

Although the challenges can be formidable, families are capable of dramatic and positive change. Marital and family therapists can be helpful guides on the journey toward healing.

caused. Julie feels lost because her mother is being "taken care of" by other people and Julie's role as chief counselor has been usurped.

DIAGNOSIS   In terms of cohesion, the Davis family is *enmeshed*. They evidence high emotional bonding as well as high mutual dependency. The mother and the two daughters competed intensely for approval from each other and from Dad. The family's external boundaries were closed. No one felt free to interact with people outside the family, partly because they were afraid Mary would be drunk and embarrass everyone. Friends and relatives were kept at a distance. The only time husband and wife made contact was when one of the children misbehaved. Then the two would team up as parents and support each other; otherwise, they did not interact much. The father-daughter coalitions, especially that between Don and Ann, were strong. In many ways, Don and Ann played the role of parents in the family because Mary's drinking often made her incapable of parenting.

Individual activities were permitted but only within family-approved guidelines. Don and Ann spent a lot of time playing tennis together, but Julie's desire to spend the same amount of time away from the family "partying" with friends was not approved. Close friends, especially males, were not allowed. The family tried desperately to have fun at their cabin on the weekends. Everyone was required to go, and the implicit message was, "You *will* have fun!" The result was that nobody enjoyed the weekends at the cabin. Tending to Peter's needs kept Julie connected to the family after she became adrift when her mother entered the alcohol treatment program.

Much of the conflict in the family seemed to stem from its *rigidity*. The family system and each of its members could seldom think of new ways to solve problems. Also, no one in the family knew how to be appropriately assertive. Rather than making their point firmly but without malice or a loud voice, family members resorted to aggressive behaviors: screaming, throwing things, and occasionally striking each other.

Family roles were stereotypic and rigid. Mary saw herself as in charge of the house, and she saw Don as the boss of the children, the rule enforcer. Mary made many threats, but rarely carried them out. When things got out of hand, Don delivered punishment in a heavy-handed manner. Mary made life difficult for everyone by insisting that each be as compulsive about housekeeping standards as she was. When she felt upset about life, she tended to clean house or drink.

All in all, family leadership, rules, and roles were very rigid. As new situations developed in the family, the members did not have the flexibility to negotiate and create solutions that were reasonable. Ann and Julie could not discuss possible changes in a rational fashion with their parents. The Davises were locked in a dysfunctional family system that was rigidly enmeshed.

TREATMENT   The family therapist sought to focus on those issues in the family on which some movement in a positive direction was already underway. On the dimension of *cohesion*, the goal was to increase the level of individual autonomy in the family—in short, to give each member more space. A related goal was to strengthen the marriage. In terms of *flexibility*, the family therapist taught family members how to negotiate and compromise with each other, rather than alternating between quiet passivity and conflict. Members were taught to see family rules as general guidelines to be discussed and interpreted as new situations arose in day-to-day living. This gave the children a chance to argue their points, and even to change their parents' minds occasionally. When the family as a whole had improved on these dimensions, the focus shifted to the marriage.

Don and Mary continued in marital therapy as a couple. The therapist focused on ways the couple could learn to enjoy each other's company again. They were encouraged to go out on dates without the children and to do things they hadn't felt they had had time to do together for many years. As the marriage improved, the number of disagreements with the children diminished. Why was this? As the marital coalition strengthened and Mary took back her rightful place on the parental team, it was less necessary for Julie and Ann to struggle for a position in coalition with Dad, and Julie no longer felt it necessary to try and fill the vacuum.

The family therapist got a good deal of help from Mary's alcohol counselors and from Alcoholics Anonymous. The chemical dependence specialists were adept at helping Mary maintain sobriety once she had attained it. Al-Anon, which focuses on the family of the alcoholic, gave Don and the children support and ideas in their struggle to live with an alcoholic. As Mary became more secure in her marriage with Don, she was able to be more supportive of Julie in her growth as an individual. The family became more able both to separate from and to connect with each other. Although this may sound easy to those not in a troubled family, it is a long and difficult process, requiring patience, self-discipline, and commitment. Families do change, however, and marital and family therapists can help families who want to deal with their problems.

2001: Recommendations for Strengthening Marriages and Families

The National Council on Family Relations (NCFR) is a nonprofit network of family professionals who work with couples and families through a variety of programs and services, including marriage and family courses, family life education, marriage enrichment, and marital and family therapy. Family professionals work in a variety of settings, including mental health centers, schools, churches, and health care facilities.

An NCFR Presidential Report, *2001: Preparing Families for the Future* (Olson & Kilmer Hanson, 1990), focuses on the future of families in the United States and around the world. Nineteen eminent family scholars contributed to the report, including 13 past presidents of NCFR. This section recounts several key points made in the document.

"Families must be made a national priority if we are to effectively deal with the multitude of problems in our country today," according to David H. Olson, NCFR president in 1988–1989. "Most of the problems with individuals and society either begin or end up in the family" (Olson & Kilmer Hanson, 1990, p. 1). Families must cope with the problems that individual family members face. Yet as a nation we refuse to do much to support families, even though they could be a significant resource for dealing with the most serious problems our society confronts.

American families today are diverse in terms of ethnicity, family dynamics, and type of family structure. The traditional pattern of husband, wife, and children in a nuclear family has changed dramatically, and we see more single-parent families and stepfamilies across all cultural groups. Policies and programs must take family diversity into account, learn from it, and value the strengths it can provide. We must help families of all colors build on their unique strengths.

"In the 21st century, the United States will emerge as a nation with greater ethnic diversity, with a projected distribution of 33 percent of the population being people of color," according to Hamilton S. McCubbin, NCFR president in 1986–1987 (Olson & Kilmer Hanson, 1990, p. 37). McCubbin stresses the critical importance of social policies and programs to address the impact of cultural diversity on the nation as a whole.

According to Paul C. Glick, 1978–1979, NCFR president, "Marriage and child-rearing patterns have become so complex that it is difficult to develop generalities that apply to every type of family. Earlier analyses of the family were made as if only couples in permanent first marriages existed. Because of the increase in divorce and remarriage that scenario is now relevant to only a minority of married couples" (Olson & Kilmer Hanson, 1990, p. 2).

Patricia Voydanoff, director of the Center for the Study of Family Development at the University of Dayton, notes that the family characteristics of the labor force are changing as the number of two-earner families grows, especially among families with babies. Single-parent families are increasing, and the older-adult population in the United States is also growing. Thus, "Many working families are responsible for elder care and child care simultaneously" (Olson & Kilmer

Happy and healthy families are an important foundation for raising children who are also happy and successful. Strong families also help their members cope with their personal problems and crises.

Hanson, 1990, p. 12). These changes increase the need for dependent-care programs.

M. Janice Hogan, NCFR president in 1989–1990, believes that "financial problems are pervasive family concerns. Most family members experience cycles of too many needs with two few resources" (Olson & Kilmer Hanson, 1990, p. 14). These economic challenges often lead to marital and parent-child conflict, home foreclosure, bankruptcy, and other negative consequences. Internal problems within the family and external social forces outside the family both contribute to problems in family economic management.

A big issue for families is health care. Catherine L. Gilliss, associate professor and director of the Family Nurse Practitioner Program at the University of California, San Francisco, notes that the cost of health problems in the United States is absolutely enormous, but education can play an important role in preventing disease: "Health problems represented in these astronomical costs are largely preventable through public health programs for promotion of health, reduction of risk, and services for the poor and underserved. The family's role in health protection and promotion has been overlooked by health planners and providers" (Olson & Kilmer Hanson, 1990, p. 32).

The AIDS epidemic threatens the health of millions of people around the world. Richard N. Needle, coordinator of AIDS research at the National Institute of Mental Health, believes that more effective research on AIDS prevention and on ways to help individuals and families deal with this epidemic is needed. He calls for "a formalized consortium of organizations planning to influence policy, set research agendas, or provide for continuing education of their members" (Olson & Kilmer Hanson, 1990, p. 34).

In a similar vein, James Maddock, past president of the American Association for Sex Education and Counseling, suggests that the term " 'family sexual health' should be a familiar and comfortable concept among policy makers concerned with family well-being." Currently, he sees the threat of AIDS and the prevalence of the sexual abuse of children as problems that leave parents "scared and confused" about how to successfully guide their children's sexual development (Olson & Kilmer Hanson, 1990, p. 22).

Alexis J. Walker, NCFR president in 1995–1996, argues that "the nature and experience of family life today varies considerably by gender." In essence, the world of men and the world of women in families is still quite different, as a result of long-standing beliefs and practices in our culture legitimated by the laws, the courts, and individuals. "Although we are a long way from understanding why gender is related to violence and poverty, solutions can be sought. The goal of social policy should be to achieve a maximum quality of life for women, children, and men in families" (Olson & Kilmer Hanson, 1990, p. 16).

Bert Adams, NCFR president in 1983–1984, and Diane Adams, director of Community Coordinated Child Care (4-C) in Dane County, Wisconsin, write: "Child care is a way of life for millions of children and their families. Families still largely pay for child care on their own, without government support." They point out that the child care infrastructure in this country is large and is growing in a relatively haphazard, unplanned manner, and they caution, "Are we willing to take a risk that an unaccountable 'experiment' is taking place without planning and support for the kind of child care children receive?" (Olson & Kilmer Hanson, 1990, p. 18).

In the words of Elizabeth S. Force, NCFR president in 1968–1969, regarding older family members: "On my 70th birthday I said, 'In my old age I need three things: good health, loads of money, and somebody who gives a damn.' Seventeen years later, at 87, I stand by my list except I've changed the priorities: Somebody who cares has moved to first place." Force believes that the security blanket of caregivers for the elderly is threatened by several factors: diminishing family size, mobility, and the instability of families in America. "Other resources must respond to the need for emotional, financial, housing, and health support" (Olson & Kilmer Hanson, 1990, p. 20).

"Our society has a critical need to learn more about the dynamics underlying healthy family relationships," according to Graham Spanier, 1987–1988 NCFR president and president of Pennsylvania State University (Olson & Kilmer Hanson, 1990, p. 4). Marriage and family strengths are the foundation on which individuals and families build a successful life together, and successful families are the foundation of a strong nation.

Some scholars claim that divorce is a sign that families are in a state of breakdown and decay; others see divorce as an opportunity for growth. Regardless of how one perceives divorce, Sharon J. Price, NCFR president in 1984–1985, argues that "we need to accept the reality of divorce as a viable family transition, to refocus on 'families' rather than a permanent 'family' and to examine both the positive and negative impacts of divorce" (Olson & Kilmer Hanson, 1990, p. 30).

"How can families be the most loving and supportive social institution and also the most violent?" asks Murray A. Straus, NCFR president in 1972–1973. "Over six million children and three million spouses are severely assaulted each year. Physical abuse is a major threat to American families. Those who are not physically injured are often injured psychologically." Straus finds hope, arguing that "shelters and treatment programs have decreased the incidence of spouse and child abuse over the last decade. The trend is slow, and clear national policies and programs are needed" (Olson & Kilmer Hanson, 1990, p. 26).

The abuse of alcohol and other drugs is greatly affecting the family life and the physical, emotional, and economic health of many Americans, according to Robert A. Lewis, professor of family studies at Purdue University. "The growing crime rate is also threatening society as we know it. There is a serious need for family and community involvement, for sweeping changes in attitudes toward the use of addictive substances. An all-out war against the abuse of drugs is necessary to curb the current drug and alcohol epidemic" (Olson & Kilmer Hanson, 1990, p. 28).

In the area of marriage and family enrichment, the late David Mace, NCFR's 1961–1962 president wrote: "I look to the day when we can guide couples continuously from the premarital period, through their first critical year together, right through the life cycle. With this kind of service a vast amount of human misery can be prevented" (Olson & Kilmer Hanson, 1990, p. 6).

"Family life education needs to help individuals develop and maintain mutually satisfying relationships. It also aims to promote skills in getting families to resolve the inevitable conflicts that arise from living with others," according to Richard Hey (NCFR president in 1969–1970) and Gerhard Neubeck (NCFR president in 1977–1978). "Family life education must affect students where they are, whether that is learning how to get along with parents, how to have a successful marriage, or how to enjoy and raise children" (Olson & Kilmer Hanson, 1990, p. 8).

Carlfred Broderick, NCFR president in 1975–1976, argued that "the future of marital and family therapy lies in the replacement of competing therapies with a tested set of broadly accepted principles of systemic intervention having specific components and therapeutic behaviors. This is the time for integration, evaluation, and digestion rather than for bold new paradigms" (Olson & Kilmer Hanson, 1990, p. 10).

"Children are the most valuable and vulnerable resource in our society, and many of them live in high-risk families. These families do not have healthy homes and are not rearing their children in responsible and effective ways," according to Wesley R. Burr, 1981–1982 NCFR president. "Ideally, our children should be reared in families where there is a safe, secure, and helpful environment." Burr believes that children are not just parents' responsibility, but the whole society's responsibility: "We must find ways to adjust national, state, local, industrial, union, commercial, educational, residential, and religious policies and programs to provide a more healthy environment for these families" (Olson & Kilmer Hanson, 1990, p. 24).

With a divorce rate of at least 50% and with high rates of physical, emotional, and sexual abuse, we need to put more time and energy into prevention and education programs that can effectively prepare people to live together in cooperative and loving ways. These programs need to be more family based, beginning as early as the preschool and elementary-school years and continuing through middle school, high school, and college—literally, across all stages of the family life cycle.

One way we can make families a national priority is to develop a family impact statement for every major piece of legislation at the local, state, and national level. This would help us focus on policies that are both more humane and more effective in serving individual and family needs.

Unless we make families a national priority now, as we enter the 21st century there will be more crises that will drain our national resources. During the closing years of the 20th century, one can hope that we will develop more creative family-based programs that will move us toward a more family-oriented society that takes into account diverse family structures and dynamics. Families are our greatest national resource. We must not continue to waste this resource.

Making Every Year the International Year of the Family

Families are the smallest democracy in any society. This idea echoes the theme of the 1994 United Nations International Year of the Family: "building the smallest democracy at the heart of society." UN conference documents extolled the family as:

> the basic unit of society; appreciated for the important socioeconomic functions that it performs. Despite the many changes in society that have altered its role and functions, it continues to provide the natural framework for the emotional, financial, and material support essential to the growth and development of its members, particularly infants and children, and for the care of other dependents, including the elderly, disabled, and the infirm. The family remains a vital means of preserving and transmitting cultural values, and often educates, trains, motivates, and supports its individual members, thereby investing in their future growth and acting as a vital resource for development. (Czaplewski, 1995, p. i)

The 1994 International Year of the Family Conference was held in Malta. The symbol adopted by the conference is shown in Figure 18.2. The conference embodied these seven principles (Czaplewski, 1995, p. i):

- The family constitutes the basic unit of society and therefore warrants special attention. The widest possible protection and assistance should be accorded to all families so that they may assume their responsibilities within the community.

- Families assume diverse forms and functions from one country to another, and within each national society. These forms and functions express the diversity of individual preferences and societal conditions. Consequently, the International Year of the Family encompasses and addresses the needs of all families.

- Activities for the International Year of the Family seek to promote the basic human rights and fundamental freedoms accorded to all individuals by

Figure 18.2 Symbol Adopted by 1994 UN International Year of the Family Conference, Malta

the set of internationally agreed upon instruments formulated under the aegis of the United Nations.

- Policies aim to foster equality between women and men within families and to bring about a fuller sharing of domestic responsibilities and employment opportunities.

- Activities for the International Year should be undertaken at all levels—local, national, regional, and international—but the primary focus is local and national in scope.

- Programs should support families in carrying out their functions, rather than provide substitutes for such functions. They should promote the inherent strengths of families, including their great capacity for self-reliance, and stimulate self-sustaining activities on their behalf. They should give an integrated perspective of families, their members, communities, and society.

- The International Year is intended to constitute an event within a continuing process that will extend far beyond the actual year.

Building on the seven principles, the conference developed six objectives for the International Year of the Family (Czaplewski, 1995, p. ii):

- Increase awareness of family issues among governments and the private sector.

- Encourage national institutions to formulate, implement, and monitor family policies.

- Stimulate responses to problems affecting and affected by the situations of families.

- Enhance the effectiveness of local, regional, and national programs for families by generating new activities and strengthening existing support.

- Improve the collaboration among national and international nongovernmental organizations in support of multisector activities.

- Build upon the results of international activities concerning women, children, youth, older adults, and those with disabilities and other major events of concern to the family and its individual members.

We believe that every year should be the National and International Year of the Family. Families all around the world are tied together in an intimate web of life. If we continue to compete fiercely with one another as individuals and as nations, we will all no doubt continue to suffer the consequences: war, environmental degradation, racism, sexism, poverty, cynicism, and grief on a global scale.

If we learn to work together and share life's joys and sorrows, the people of Mother Earth stand a reasonable chance of surviving and transcending our common human predicament. The challenges are clear. The question is whether we have the intelligence and the goodwill to act.

On a more personal note, we encourage you to keep building positive connections with your family and friends and to become genuinely involved in the life of your community and the family of humankind.

Summary

- Families in the United States and around the world are wonderfully different. Our different interests and capabilities give us the tools to build on each other's strengths to make a more vital society.

- Even though diversity is a fact of life and enhances living, our similarities as human beings and families are often overlooked and may be more important than our differences. Although it seems to be a paradox, all human beings are unique and different and yet, deep down, we are all very similar.

- Families who are strong and successful around the world are likely to share the qualities of cohesion, flexibility, and communication.

- Perhaps the ultimate general systems theory is the Gaia hypothesis, which proposes that the Earth is a living, interconnected entity with no political or cultural boundaries. From a global perspective, families, too, know no boundaries: We are all part of the human family.

- People with couple and family problems can find assistance from a broad range of educational and enrichment programs, self-help groups, skill-building programs, and professional helpers. Unfortunately, most people don't seek help for problems until they are severe.

- The Family Circumplex Model can help identify common types of problems in couple and family dynamics. It can be used by marital and family therapists to provide premarital counseling and to diagnose and treat relationship problems in couples and families.

- Families must be made a national priority if we are to deal effectively with the multitude of problems in our country today. Most individual and social problems either begin or end up in the family. Families must cope with these problems, but we as a nation do little to support them.

- "Building the smallest democracy at the heart of society" was the theme that sparked the 1994 United Nations International Year of the Family. UN documents extolled the family as "the basic unit of society" and argued that because of this status, it warrants special attention.

- To become and remain a healthy individual and a member of a strong family, keep building connections with your family and friends and become genuinely involved in the life of your community and the family of humankind.

Activities

1. In small groups, discuss the Gaia hypothesis, which suggests that the Earth is a living entity. Consider ecological interconnections: how environmental issues affect large areas of our planet. Then consider human interconnections: how challenges individuals and families face in one area of life can affect other areas.

2. What will the future be like in *your* family? What can you do to make it brighter? Write a short essay on this topic, and share it with a small group.

3. What will the future be like for families in the United States and around the world? Discuss this issue in a small group.

4. What can we do as individuals to help other members of the human family? Discuss this issue in a small group.

5. What have you learned about families and about life in this class? Write a short essay on this topic, and share it with a small group.

6. For any or all of the activities above, share the findings of your small group with the class. What differences do you discover? What common themes emerge?

Suggested Readings

Guerney, B., Jr., & Maxson, P. (1991). Marital and family enrichment research. In A. Booth (Ed.), *Contemporary families: Looking forward, looking back*. Minneapolis: National Council on Family Relations (pp. 457–465). *Review of recent advances in marital enrichment techniques, by a team headed by a pioneer in the study of how to enrich relationships.*

Hogan, M. J. (Ed.). 1995. *Initiatives for families: Research, policy, practice, education*. St. Paul, MN: National Council on Family Relations. *NCFR's written contribution to the United Nations International Year of the Family.*

Lovelock, J. E. (1979, 1987). *Gaia: A new look at life on earth*. Oxford, England: Oxford University Press. *Hypothesizes that the Earth, through its atmosphere and oceans, functions effectively as one self-regulated organism.*

Maddock, J. W., Hogan, J., Antonov, A. I., & Matskovsky, M. S. (Eds.). (1994). *Families before and after perestroika: Russian and U.S. perspectives*. New York: Guilford Press. *Illus-*

trates that major differences in political and social orientation do not necessarily go hand in hand with equally major differences in family issues.

McAdoo, H. P. (Ed.). *Family ethnicity: Strength in diversity.* Newbury Park, CA: Sage. *A respectful celebration of ethnic and cultural diversity among families that can prompt discussion at home and in schools.*

Menzel, P. (1995). *Material world: A global family portrait.* San Francisco: Sierra Club Books. *Photographs of families around the world who have placed all their earthly possessions outside, in front of their home; remarkable contrasts among countries and cultures are fascinating.*

Olson, D. H., & Kilmer Hanson, M. (Eds.). (1990). *NCFR Presidential Report. 2001: Preparing families for the future.* St. Paul, MN: National Council on Family Relations. *Nineteen eminent family scholars make recommendations for improving the quality of family life.*

Olson, D. H., McCubbin, H., Barnes, H., Larsen, A., Muxen, M., & Wilson, M. (1989). *Families: What makes them work* (2nd ed.). Newbury Park, CA: Sage. *Summarizes the findings of a study of a national sample of 1,000 healthy families across the life cycle; identifies the major stressors at each stage of the family life cycle; compares the resources of families who coped well with stress with those of families who were less successful.*

Piercy, F. P., & Sprenkle, D. H. (1991). Marriage and family therapy. In A. Booth (Ed.), *Contemporary families: Looking forward, looking back.* Minneapolis: National Council on Family Relations (pp. 446–456). *A comprehensive review of the field of marital and family therapy from 1980 to 1990, a decade in which the field has grown considerably in popularity, influence as a therapeutic approach, and value in helping people with emotional issues.*

Stinnett, N., Stinnett, N., DeFrain, J., & DeFrain, N. (1997, in press). *Good families.* New York: Doubleday. *More empirical evidence for the value of the Family Strengths model; a rich variety of case studies of families illustrates the applicability of the model in this updated edition.*

Weeks, G. R., & Treat, S. (1992). *Couples in treatment: Techniques and approaches for effective practice.* New York: Brunner/Mazel. *A useful, eclectic book for beginning therapists.*

Family Circumplex Scales

An Overview of the Family Circumplex Scales

The Family Circumplex Model can be used to define the way in which a couple or a family interacts—that is, to describe the family system. The Family Circumplex Scales (FCSs) are the tools an interviewer uses to place the couple or family in the Family Circumplex Model. This section provides instructions for use of the scales.

The process consists of six steps:

1. Understanding the dimensions and concepts of the Family Circumplex Model.

2. Interviewing the couple or family.

3. Completing the Coalition Rating Scale.

4. Assigning a scale value for each concept.

5. Assigning a global rating for each dimension.

6. Plotting the global ratings on the Family Circumplex Model.

Step 1: Dimensions and Concepts

There are three primary dimensions in the Family Circumplex Model: family cohesion, family flexibility, and family communication. Each dimension has several concepts that help define and describe it. Before doing an assessment of a couple or a family, the therapist or interviewer reviews all the concepts and their descriptions for each of the three dimensions. Table A.1 (p. 586) lists and describes the concepts for the three dimensions.

Step 2: Interview Questions

To assess a couple or a family, the interviewer must evaluate the family's interactions in terms of each of the concepts for each dimension. In an attempt to elicit this information, a semistructured interview is useful. Although no specific interview format or techniques are recommended, those experienced in using the FCSs find it helpful to encourage the couple or family to discuss with each other the interview questions in Box A.1 (p. 584). The questions focus on the two dimensions of cohesion and flexibility, but not on communication. To assess communication, the interviewer simply observes how the couple or family communicate while they are discussing the interview questions. The interviewer should encourage the couple or the family to talk directly to each other—*not* to the interviewer—so that the interviewer can observe how they interact with each other.

Step 3: The Coalition Rating Scale

After the interview, the interviewer first completes the Coalition Rating Scale, Box A.2, if it applies. It is necessary to use this scale if one or more family members function differently from the rest of the family. For example, it is possible to have a *rigidly enmeshed* family with a *chaotically disengaged* husband. If there is a disengaged member or a coalition, rate these family members separately from the rest of the family system. Complete the Coalition Rating Scale *first* before completing the other scales.

Step 4: Assigning Scale Values

The interviewer next interviews the couple or family (see the next main section) and rates them on each of the concepts that make up the three dimensions, using the scales in Table A.1. Before selecting a value, the interviewer carefully reads the descriptions for each concept and then selects a value from 1 to 8 that most closely represents the couple or family as a unit.

Step 5: Assigning Global Ratings

After assigning a rating for each concept in each of the three dimensions and recording those ratings on Table A.2 (p. 587), the interviewer makes a global rating for each of the three dimensions (cohesion, flexibility, and communication) and records the global ratings on Table A.2. The global rating for each dimension should be based on an overall evaluation rather than on a sum of the subscale (concept) ratings.

Step 6: Plotting Family System Type on the Circumplex Model

Finally, the interviewer plots the couple's or the family's global ratings on cohesion and flexibility on the Family Circumplex Model, Figure A.1 (p. 588). This determines the marital or family system type. If, for example, the interviewer assigns a family a global rating of 5 on the cohesion dimension and 4 on the flexibility dimension, the model will identify the family as *structurally cohesive*, one of the four balanced family types on the Circumplex Model. If the family contains a coalition or a disengaged member, the interviewer also plots the coalition or member on the model.

Interview Questions for Assessing Family Cohesion and Flexibility

Questions for Assessing Family Cohesion

1. *Separateness/Togetherness:* How much do family members go their own way versus spending time with the family?

2. *I-We Balance:* Do family members have a good balance of time apart and together?

3. *Closeness:* Do people feel close to each other?

4. *Loyalty:* Is the family a top priority compared with work or friends?

5. *Activities:* Do people spend much time having fun together?

6. *Dependence/Independence:* Do family members stay in close contact?

Other Useful Questions to Assess Family Cohesion

1. How does your family celebrate birthdays and holidays?

2. Describe your typical dinnertime meal in terms of who is present, who prepares the meal, who cleans up, and the type of family interaction that occurs.

3. What is a typical weekend like in your family?

4. Do you have special times you get together as a family?

Questions for Assessing Family Flexibility

1. *Leadership:* Is leadership shared between parents?

2. *Discipline:* Is (was) discipline strict?

3. *Negotiation:* How do you negotiate differences in your family?

4. *Roles:* Does each spouse do only certain tasks?

5. *Rules:* Do rules change in your family?

6. *Change:* Is change upsetting to your family?

Other Useful Questions to Assess Family Adaptability

1. How open is your family to change?

2. Is your family good at problem solving?

3. Does your family seem disorganized?

4. Who is in charge: the parent(s) or the child(ren)?

The Coalition Rating Scale

Instructions

The functioning of most families can be adequately described based on their assessment as a unit or group. However, some families include individuals or dyadic units (coalitions) whose functioning may be somewhat different from that of the rest of the family. In other words, a subsystem or an individual's functioning may differ markedly from that of the family as a group.

This Coalition Rating Scale provides a way of noting coalitions and disengaged individuals' patterns in family systems. After observing the family's interactions, any coalitions or disengaged individuals should be identified by checking the relevant categories below.

Definitions

Coalition. A coalition is two or more people with a high degree of emotional closeness to one another. During family interaction, the members of a coalition are very connected to one another and may at times exclude other family members. (A husband-wife coalition is considered a positive dyad and is therefore not listed below.)

Disengaged Individual(s). A disengaged individual is emotionally separated from the rest of the family. Disengaged individuals often exhibit a low degree of involvement and interaction with other family members.

Coalitions

____ Mother-Son

____ Mother-Daughter

____ Father-Son

____ Father-Daughter

____ Son-Daughter

____ Same-Sex Siblings

____ Other

Disengaged Individuals

____ Disengaged Mother

____ Disengaged Father

____ Disengaged Child(ren)

____ Other

Levels of Family Cohesion

COHESION							
DISENGAGED (**UNBALANCED**)		**CONNECTED** (**BALANCED**)		**COHESIVE** (**BALANCED**)		**ENMESHED** (**UNBALANCED**)	
SCORE 1	2	3	4	5	6	7	8
Separateness/ Togetherness	High separateness		More separateness than togetherness		More togetherness than separateness		Very high togetherness
I–We balance	Primarily "I"		More "I" than "We"		More "We" than "I"		Primarily "We"
Closeness	Little closeness		Low to moderate closeness		Moderate to high closeness		Very high closeness
Loyalty	Lack of loyalty		Some loyalty		Considerable loyalty		High loyalty
Activities	Mainly separate		More separate than shared		More shared than separate		Mainly shared
Dependence/ Independence	High independence		More independence than dependence		More dependence than independence		High dependence

Levels of Family Flexibility

FLEXIBILITY							
RIGID (**UNBALANCED**)		**STRUCTURED** (**BALANCED**)		**FLEXIBLE** (**BALANCED**)		**CHAOTIC** (**UNBALANCED**)	
SCORE 1	2	3	4	5	6	7	8
Leadership	Authoritarian		Sometimes shared		Often shared		Lack of leadership
Discipline	Strict discipline		Somewhat democratic		Democratic		Erratic/inconsistent
Negotiation	Limited discussion		Organized discussion		Open discussion		Endless discussion
Roles	Roles very stable		Roles stable		Role-sharing		Dramatic role shifts
Rules	Unchanging rules		Few rule changes		Some rule changes		Frequent rule changes
Change	Very little change		Moderate change		Some change		Considerable change

Levels of Family Communication

COMMUNICATION		
POOR	**GOOD**	**VERY GOOD**
SCORE 1 2	3 4	5 6
Listening skills	Poor listening skills	Appears to listen, but feedback is limited	Gives feedback, indicating good listening skills
Speaking skills	Often speaks for others	Speaks for self more than for others	Speaks mainly for self rather than for others
Self-disclosure	Low sharing of feelings	Moderate sharing of feelings	High sharing of feelings
Clarity	Inconsistent messages	Clear messages	Very clear messages
Staying on topic	Seldom stays on topic	Often stays on topic	Mainly stays on topic
Respect and regard	Low to moderate	Moderate to high	High

COHESHION								
	DISENGAGED		CONNECTED		COHESIVE		ENMESHED	
SCORE	1	2	3	4	5	6	7	8
Separateness/ Togetherness	☐	☐	☐	☐	☐	☐	☐	☐
I–We balance	☐	☐	☐	☐	☐	☐	☐	☐
Closeness	☐	☐	☐	☐	☐	☐	☐	☐
Loyalty	☐	☐	☐	☐	☐	☐	☐	☐
Activities	☐	☐	☐	☐	☐	☐	☐	☐
Dependence/ Independence	☐	☐	☐	☐	☐	☐	☐	☐
Global rating	☐	☐	☐	☐	☐	☐	☐	☐

FLEXIBILITY								
	RIGID		STRUCTURED		FLEXIBLE		CHAOTIC	
SCORE	1	2	3	4	5	6	7	8
Leadership	☐	☐	☐	☐	☐	☐	☐	☐
Discipline	☐	☐	☐	☐	☐	☐	☐	☐
Negotiation	☐	☐	☐	☐	☐	☐	☐	☐
Roles	☐	☐	☐	☐	☐	☐	☐	☐
Rules	☐	☐	☐	☐	☐	☐	☐	☐
Change	☐	☐	☐	☐	☐	☐	☐	☐
Global rating	☐	☐	☐	☐	☐	☐	☐	☐

COMMUNICATION						
	POOR		GOOD		VERY GOOD	
SCORE	1	2	3	4	5	6
Listening skills	☐	☐	☐	☐	☐	☐
Speaking skills	☐	☐	☐	☐	☐	☐
Self-disclosure	☐	☐	☐	☐	☐	☐
Clarity	☐	☐	☐	☐	☐	☐
Staying on topic	☐	☐	☐	☐	☐	☐
Respect and regard	☐	☐	☐	☐	☐	☐
Global rating	☐	☐	☐	☐	☐	☐

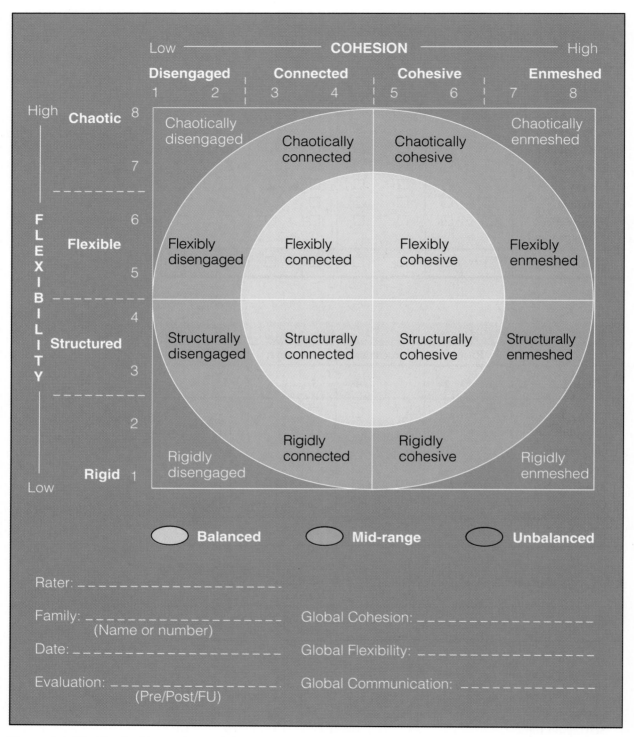

Figure A.1 The Family Circumplex Model

RESOURCE SECTION B

National Directory of Organizations Serving Families

Although the organizations listed here serve families on the national level, many have regional and local offices. Countless other organizations focus on service in the local community and even in neighborhoods. To find out what is available in your own community, look for a special section on human services in your telephone directory.

Abortion

Pro Choice

National Abortion Rights Action League (NARAL)
1424 K St., N.W.
Washington, DC 20005
Phone: 202-828-9300

Pro Life

National Right to Life Committee
419 Seventh St., N.W., Suite 500
Washington, DC 20004
Phone: 202-626-8800

Adoption

Adoptees' Liberty Movement Association
P.O. Box 727
Radio City Station
New York, NY 10101
Phone: 212-581-1568

International Concerns Committee for Children
911 Cypress Dr.
Boulder, CO 80303
Phone: 303-494-8333

OURS, Inc.
3333 Hwy. 100 North
Minneapolis, MN 55422
Phone: 612-535-4829

Alcohol and Drug Abuse Prevention

Al-Anon Family Groups
P.O. Box 862
Midtown Station
New York, NY 10018-0862
Phone: 800-356-9996

Alcoholics Anonymous (AA)
468 Park Ave. South
New York, NY 10016
Phone: 212-870-3400

Cocaine National Treatment and Referral
    Information Service
Phone: 800-262-2463

Drugs Anonymous (DA)
P.O. Box 473
Ansonia Station
New York, NY 10023
Phone: 212-874-0700

Narcotics Anonymous (NA)
19737 Nordhoff St.
Chatsworth, CA 91311
Phone: 818-773-9999

National Clearinghouse for Alcohol and Drug
    Information (NCADI)
11426 Rockville Pike
Rockville, MD 20852
Phone: 301-468-2600

Phoenix House Foundation
164 W. 74th St.
New York, NY 10023
Phone: 212-595-5810

Autism

Autism Society of America
7910 Woodmont Ave.
Bethesda, MD 20814-3015
Phone: 301-657-0881

Birth Alternatives

American College of Nurse-Midwives
818 Connecticut Ave., N.W., Suite 900
Washington, DC 20006
Phone: 202-728-9860

Blindness

National Federation of the Blind
1800 Johnson St.
Baltimore, MD 21230
Phone: 410-659-9314

Breast-Feeding

LaLeche League International, Inc.
P.O. Box 4079
1400 Meacham
Schaumburg, IL 60168-4079
Phone: 847-519-7730; 800-LaLeche

Cancer and Families

National Cancer Institute
Bldg. 31, Rm. 10A24
Bethesda, MD 20892
Phone: 800-4-CANCER

Child Abuse

National Child Abuse Hotline
Phone: 800-422-4453

National Committee for the Prevention of Child
  Abuse
332 South Michigan Ave., Suite 1600
Chicago, IL 60604-4357
Phone: 312-663-3520

National Council on Child Abuse and Family
  Violence
1050 Connecticut Ave., N.W. Suite 300
Washington, DC 20036
Phone: 202-429-6695

Child Custody

Joint Custody Association
10606 Wilkins Ave.
Los Angeles, CA 90024
Phone: 310-475-5352

Women's Legal Defense Fund
Child Custody Project
1875 Connecticut Ave., N.W., Suite 710
Washington, DC 20009
Phone: 202-986-2600

Children's Rights

National Council for Children's Rights
220 I St., N.E.
Washington, DC 20002
Phone: 202-547-6227

Child Stealing

National Center for Missing and Exploited
  Children
2101 Wilson Blvd., Suite 550
Arlington, VA 22201
Phone: 800-843-5678

Child Support

Office for Child Support Enforcement and
  Reference Center
6110 Executive Blvd.
Rockville, MD 20852
Phone: 301-217-7040

Death of Children

The Compassionate Friends, Inc.
P.O. Box 3696
Oak Brook, IL 60522
Phone: 708-990-0010

National Sudden Infant Death Syndrome
  Foundation
1314 Bedford Ave., Suite 210
Baltimore, MD 21208
Phone: 800-221-SIDS (in MD: 301-459-3388)

SHARE (miscarriage/death of a baby)
St. Joseph's Health Center
300 First Capital Dr.
St. Charles, MO 63301-2893
Phone: 800-821-6819

Diabetes

Juvenile Diabetes Foundation
381 Park Ave. South
New York, NY 10016
Phone: 212-689-2860; 800-533-8590

Disabilities

National Information Center for Children and
  Youth with Handicaps
P.O. Box 1492
Washington, DC 20013-1492
Phone: 800-695-0285

Parents Helping Parents
3041 Olcott
Santa Clara, CA 95051
Phone: 408-727-5775

Drug Abuse and Education (*See* Alcohol and Drug Abuse Prevention)

Emotional Problems

Emotions Anonymous
P.O. Box 4245
St. Paul, MN 55104-0245
Phone: 612-647-9712

Epilepsy

Epilepsy Foundation
4351 Garden City Dr.
Landover, MD 20785
Phone: 301-459-3700

Family Studies Graduate Programs

National Council on Family Relations (NCFR)
3989 Central Ave., N.E., Suite 550
Minneapolis, MN 55421
Phone: 612-781-9331

Family Planning

Planned Parenthood Federation of America
1120 Connecticut Ave., N.W., Suite 461
Washington, DC 20036
Phone: 202-785-3351

Public Health Departments
(*See* local telephone directory)

Zero Population Growth (ZPG)
1400 16th St., N.W. Suite 320
Washington, DC 20036
Phone: 202-332-2200

Family Services

Family Service Association of America (FSA)
11700 W. Lake Park Dr.
Milwaukee, WI 53224
Phone: 414-359-1040

Fatherhood

The Fatherhood Project
Bank Street College of Education
610 W. 112th St.
New York, NY 10025-9980
Phone: 212-465-2044

Fertility

American Fertility Society
2140 11th Ave. South, Suite 200
Birmingham, AL 35205
Phone: 205-933-8494

Resolve, Inc.
5 Water St.
Arlington, MA 02174
Phone: 617-643-2424

Gambling

Gamblers Anonymous
P.O. Box 17173
Los Angeles, CA 90017
Phone: 213-386-8789

Gay-Male and Lesbian Resources

National Gay Task Force
2320 17th St., N.W.
Washington, DC 20009-2702
Phone: 202-332-6483

Parents and Friends of Lesbians and Gays
(PFLAG)
1101 14th St., N.W., Suite 1030
Washington, DC 20005
Phone: 202-638-4200

Gender Equality

National Organization for Women (NOW)
1000 16th St., N.W., Suite 700
Washington, DC 20036
Phone: 202-331-0066

Genetic Counseling

National Foundation for Jewish Genetic Disease
45 Sutton Place South
New York, NY 10003
Phone: 212-371-1030

Health Information

Centers for Disease Control and Prevention
(CDCP)
Atlanta, GA 30333
Phone 404-332-4555

National Health Information Center (NHIC)
P.O. Box 1133
Washington, DC 20013-1133
Phone: 800-336-4797

TEL-MED (a medical information audiotape
   system)
952 South Mt. Vernon Ave.
Colton, CA 92324
Phone: 909-825-6034

Healthy Babies

Healthy Mothers–Healthy Babies Coalition
Department of Public Affairs
409 12th St., S.W.
Washington, DC 20024
Phone: 202-638-5577

Incest Prevention

Committee for Children
2203 Airport Way South, Suite 500
Seattle, WA 98134-2027
Phone: 206-343-1223

Learning Disabilities

Association for Children and Adults with Learning
   Disabilities
4156 Library Road
Pittsburgh, PA 15234
Phone: 412-341-1515

Marital and Family Therapy

American Association for Marriage and Family
   Therapy (AAMFT)
1133 15th St., N.W., Suite 300
Washington, DC 20005
Phone: 202-452-0109

American Family Therapy Academy (AFTA)
2020 Pennsylvania Ave., N.W., #273
Washington, DC 20006
Phone: 202-994-2776

National Association of Social Workers (NASW)
750 1st St., N.E., Suite 700
Washington, DC 20002
Phone: 202-408-8600

Marriage Preparation and Enrichment

Association for Couples in Marriage Enrichment
   (ACME)
P.O. Box 10596
Winston-Salem, NC 27108
Phone: 800-634-8325

Couples Communication Program
Interpersonal Communication Programs, Inc.
7201 S. Broadway, Suite 6
Littleton, CO 80122
Phone: 800-328-5099

Institute for Development of Emotional and Life
   Skills (IDEALS)
12500 Blake Road
Silver Spring, MD 20904
Phone: 301-986-1479

PREPARE/ENRICH/Life Innovations, Inc.
Broadway Place West
1300 Godward St., Suite 6850
Minneapolis, MN 55413
Phone: 800-441-1940

National Marriage Encounter
4704 Jamerson Place
Orlando, FL 32803
Phone: 800-828-3351

Prevention and Relationship Enhancement
   Program (PREP)
Center for Marriage and Family Studies
Psychology Department
University of Denver
Denver, CO 80208
Phone: 303-750-8798

Training in Marriage Enrichment (TIME)
American Guidance Services
P.O. Box 99
Circle Pines, MN 55014-1796
Phone: 800-328-2560

Worldwide Marriage Encounter
1908 E. Highland Ave., #A
San Bernardino, CA 92404
Phone: 909-881-3456

Mastectomy

Reach to Recovery
19 W. 56th St.
New York, NY 10019
Phone: 212-586-8700

Mental Illness

National Alliance for the Mentally Ill
200 North Glebe Rd., Suite 1015
Arlington, VA 22203-3754
Phone: 703-524-7600

Recovery, Inc.
802 N. Dearborn St.
Chicago, IL 60610
Phone: 312-337-5661

Mental Retardation

The Arc (formerly Association for Retarded
  Citizens)
500 East Border St., Suite 300
Arlington, TX 76010
Phone: 817-261-6003

Older People

American Association of Retired Persons (AARP)
601 E St., N.W., Suite 200
Washington, DC 20049
Phone: 202-434-2277

Overeating

Overeaters Anonymous
P.O. Box 92870
Los Angeles, CA 90009
Phone: 213-936-4206

Ovum Transfer

Harbor-UCLA Medical Center
1000 W. Carson St.
Torrance, CA 90509
Phone: 310-222-2345

Pensions

Pension Rights Center
918 16th St., N.W., Suite 704
Washington, DC 20006
Phone: 202-296-3778

Psychological and Emotional Problems

American Psychiatric Association (APA)
1400 K St., N.W.
Washington, DC 20005
Phone: 202-682-6000

American Psychological Association (APA)
750 1st St., N.E.
Washington, DC 20002
Phone: 202-336-5500

Runaways

National Runaway Switchboard
Phone: 800-621-4000 (in IL: 800-972-6004)

Self-Help

National Self-Help Clearinghouse
25 W. 43rd St., Room 620
New York, NY 10036
Phone: 212-642-2944

Sex Therapy

American Association of Sex Educators,
    Counselors, and Therapists (AASECT)
P.O. Box 238
Mt. Vernon, IA 52314
Phone: 319-895-8407

Loyola Sexual Dysfunction Clinic
Loyola University Hospital
2160 South First Ave.
Maywood, IL 60153
Phone: 708-216-9000

Masters and Johnson Intensive Day Hospital
1 Campbell Plaza, #4B
St. Louis, MO 63139
Phone: 314-781-1112

Sexual Abuse

Child Help USA
P.O. Box 630
Los Angeles, CA 90028
Phone: 800-422-4453

Sexuality Education

Sexuality Information and Education Council of
    the United States (SIECUS)
130 West 42nd St., Suite 350
New York, NY 10036-7802
Phone: 212-819-9770

Sexually Transmissible Diseases (STDs)

CDC National HIV and AIDS Hotline
Phone: 800-342-AIDS

CDC National STD Hotline
Phone: 800-227-8922

San Francisco AIDS Foundation
10 United Nations Plaza
San Francisco, CA 94102
Phone: 415-487-3000

Single Parenthood

Parents Without Partners International
Phone: 800-637-7974

Single Mothers by Choice
1642 Gracie Square Station
New York, NY 10028
Phone: 212-988-0993

Single Parent Resource Center
31 E. 28th St., Suite 200
New York, NY 10016
Phone: 212-951-7030

Stepfamilies

Stepfamily Association of America
29 Allegheny Ave., Suite 1307
Baltimore, MD 21204

Stepfamily Foundation
333 West End Ave.
New York, NY 10023
Phone: 212-877-3244; 212-799-STEP

Stepfamilies Press
215 Centennial Mall South, Suite 212
Lincoln, NE 68508
Phone: 800-735-0329

Suicide Prevention

The Samaritans
500 Commonwealth Ave.
Boston, MA 02215
Phone: 617-247-0220

Terminal Illness

Hospice Association of America
228 7th St., S.E.
Washington, DC 20003
Phone: 202-546-4759

National Hospice Organization
1901 N. Moore St., Suite 901
Arlington, VA 22209
Phone: 703-243-5900

Widowhood

Widowed Person's Service
American Association of Retired Persons (AARP)
601 E St., N.W., Suite 200
Washington, DC 20049
Phone: 202-434-2277

Youth at Risk

Families Anonymous
P.O. Box 3475
Culver City, CA 90231
Phone: 818-989-7841

RESOURCE SECTION C

Sexual Anatomy and Sexual Response

Sexual Anatomy

Female Sex Organs

Male Sex Organs

Male and Female Arousal

Sources of Sexual Pleasure

Nocturnal Orgasm

Masturbation

Couple Sex

The Influence of Alcohol and Other Drugs on Sex

This resource section briefly explains sexual anatomy—the structure of the male and the female sexual organs—as a basis for understanding human sexual response. Discussions of the mechanics of sexual arousal in both sexes and of various sources of sexual pleasure follow. The section concludes with a look at the influence of alcohol and other drugs on sexual response.

Sexual Anatomy

A baby's sex is determined at the moment of fertilization, but during the first few months of development inside the mother, boys and girls are virtually identical. A small bud develops between the fetus's legs that later becomes the boy's penis or the girl's clitoris. Two swellings emerge, one on either side of the bud. In boys, the swellings develop into a scrotum. In girls, a slit arises between the swellings and develops into a vagina. In the first few months of fetal development, the boy's primitive testicles and the girl's growing ovaries are located deep inside the abdominal cavity.

Although the sex organs of men and women appear different, they develop from the same structures and perform similar functions. Each individual has a pair of **gonads:** Female gonads are called **ovaries** and male gonads are called **testes** (or testicles). Gonads produce germ cells and sex hormones. The female **germ cells** are called **ova** (eggs) and the male germ cells are called **sperm.** Ova and sperm are the basic units of reproduction. Their joining can lead to the development of a new human being (Insel & Roth, 1996).

Female Sex Organs

The external sex organs, or **genitals,** of the female are called the **vulva** ("covering"). The mons pubis is a round body of fatty tissue covering the pubic bone; this area becomes covered with hair during puberty. Below the mons pubis are two pairs of skin folds called labia majora (major lips) and labia minora (minor lips). The labia enclose the clitoris, the opening of the urethra, and the opening of the vagina. The **clitoris** is covered by a prepuce (a fold of skin) called the foreskin or clitoral hood and has a shaft, a glans, and spongy tissue that fills with blood during sexual arousal; in this regard the clitoris and the penis are similar. Because the clitoris is highly sensitive to the touch, it plays an important role in female sexual arousal. The **urethra** is a tube connecting the urinary bladder to its opening, located in the female between the clitoris and the opening of the vagina. In the female, the urethra is independent of the genitals (Insel & Roth, 1996).

The **vagina,** the female organ for sexual intercourse, is a passage that leads to the internal reproductive organs. The opening to the vagina is partially covered by a membrane called the **hymen.** Although some people believe that an intact hymen is the sign of a virgin, this belief is a myth; the hymen can be stretched or torn during athletic activities, as well as by first sexual intercourse. The vagina is the birth canal during childbirth. It has soft, flexible walls that are normally in contact with each other. A cylinder of muscles surrounds the vagina; during sexual excitement, muscle tension increases and the walls of the vagina swell with blood. The vagina leads to the **uterus,** a pear-shaped organ, slanting forward above the bladder, in which a fertilized egg implants itself and grows into an embryo, then a fetus. The neck of the uterus, called the **cervix,** projects into the upper part of the vagina. Two oviducts (or fallopian tubes) lead out from the top of the uterus. The fringed end of each tube surrounds an ovary. Approximately once a month, a mature ovum (egg) bursts from its follicle (sac or cavity) on the surface of one of the ovaries and passes down an oviduct into the uterus. The female sex organs are illustrated in Figure C.1.

Male Sex Organs

The external sex organs of the male are the penis and the scrotum. The **penis** is composed of spongy tissue, which engorges with blood during sexual arousal, causing the organ to enlarge and become erect. The **scrotum** is the pouch containing the man's two testes, in which sperm are produced. The process of sperm production is extremely heat sensitive, and the scrotum helps keep the testes cooler than the rest of the body. When the weather is hot, the scrotum muscles relax and the testes move away from the heat of the body; when it is cold, the scrotum muscles contract and the testes move upward toward the body. These movements help to maintain the temperature differential necessary for sperm production. It has been found that wearing tightly fitting undershorts in the summer can interfere with normal sperm production (Insel & Roth, 1996).

The most sensitive part of the penis and an important source of sexual arousal is the **glans,** the smooth, rounded tip. When a male is born, the **foreskin,** or prepuce, almost completely covers the glans. In 60% of males in the United States (and in an estimated 15% of males worldwide), this retractable fold of skin is surgically removed in a 5-minute procedure called **circumcision.** This surgery, usually performed in infancy, is done for religious and hygienic reasons. The American Academy of Pediatrics has declared itself neutral on the controversial issue of circumcision. Opponents of routine circumcision call it "America's leading unnecessary surgery." In addition to being painful to infants, the process can cause irritation of the penis and there is the risk of complications and surgical errors. Proponents of circumcision argue that the procedure makes it easier to keep the penis clean and that circumcised males are less likely to develop cancer of the penis, a rare disease that occurs almost exclusively in uncircumcised men (the risk of cancer of the penis in uncircumcised men is 1 in 600) (Insel & Roth, 1996).

The male urethra runs the entire length of the penis and carries both urine and **semen** (a mixture of sperm and seminal fluid) to an opening at the tip of the glans. Although urine and semen travel through a common passageway, sphincter muscles control their entry into the urethra and prevent them from passing through the urethra at the same time (Insel & Roth, 1996). Sperm are produced in the testes in tightly packed seminiferous ("sperm-bearing") tubules. These tubules empty into a maze of ducts that flow into a single storage tube, called the epididymis, on the surface of each testis. This tube then leads to the vasa deferentia (singular, vas deferens), two tubes rising into the abdominal cavity and connecting to the prostate gland.

Mons pubis

Labia majora

Prepuce of clitoris

Clitoris (glans)

Labia minora

Urethral opening

Vaginal opening

Anus

Fallopian tube
Ovary

Uterus

Cervix

Bladder
Pubic bone

Rectum

Vagina

Urethra

Clitoris

Urinary opening

Anus

Labia majora

Vaginal opening

Labia minora

Figure C.1 Female Sex Organs. *Source: Core Concepts in Health* (7th ed.— 1996 Update) (p. 102) by P. M. Insel and W. T. Roth, 1996, Mountain View, CA: Mayfield. Copyright 1996 by Mayfield Publishing Co. Reprinted by permission.

Inside the prostate gland the vasa deferentia join the two seminal vesicles, whose secretions provide nutrients to the semen. The **prostate gland** produces some of the fluid in semen that nourishes and transports sperm. The seminal vesicles and the vasa deferentia lead on each side to the ejaculatory duct, which joins the urethra. Cowper's glands, on each side of the urethra, are two small glands that

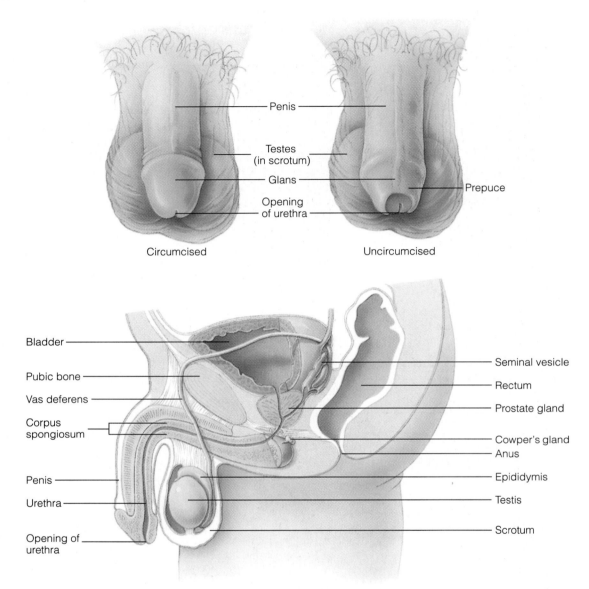

Figure C.2 Male Sex Organs. *Source: Core Concepts in Health* (7th ed.— 1996 Update) (p. 103) by P. M. Insel and W. T. Roth, 1996, Mountain View, CA: Mayfield. Copyright 1996 by Mayfield Publishing Co. Reprinted by permission.

secrete clear, mucuslike fluid during sexual arousal. This fluid appears at the tip of the penis. Although its purpose is not clearly understood, this fluid may contain a few sperm in some men. This is why withdrawal of the penis before ejaculation is not a reliable form of birth control. Figure C.2 shows the male sex organs.

Male and Female Arousal

Erotic stimulation leads to erotic arousal (excitement), and this can culminate for both females and males in **orgasm,** an intensely pleasurable experience. The sense of touch is at the center of the sexual experience. People touch each other with their hands, arms, legs, and faces. The senses of smell, hearing, vision, and taste are also important in sexual arousal. Perhaps just as important, sexual excitement is generated between people on a psychological level. People touch each other, figuratively speaking, with their eyes, their minds, their spirits. Arousal, clearly, is not simply the manipulation of sexual organs in a variety of ways. Sexual intimacy for many people is best when it has become a matter of the heart. Thus, when the sexual aspect of a relationship dies, this can cause great concern for a couple because it just might signify the death of feelings for each other in general (Cohen, 1987).

Researchers studying human sexual response speculate that there are neurological differences between men and women that may trigger a more complex and exciting orgasm in females. As recently as the early 1960s, the conventional wisdom was that men were basically more sexual than women. Sex researchers and therapists William H. Masters and Virginia E. Johnson shattered a number of myths about sexual intercourse, however, in their landmark study *Human Sexual Response* (1966). During a series of studies, subjects were fitted with electrodes to measure heart rate and breathing, sensors to gauge the strength of muscle contractions, and cameras to film the inside of the vagina. Nearly 700 participants were observed during intercourse and masturbation. The researchers tried to study a wide variety of people. Some of the participants were older, some were pregnant, some were homosexual.

To describe what they observed, the researchers developed a four-stage model: excitement, plateau, orgasm, and resolution. These four stages of sexual response involve almost every part of the human body (Figure C.3, p. 604). The excitement phase is a period of gradual buildup—increasing muscle tension, vaginal lubrication, and the engorgement of blood vessels in the penis, the clitoris, and the nipples. Plateau is a sustained period of excitement: heart rate and respiration increase and the skin flushes. Orgasm is the discharge of the built-up tension, marked by muscle contractions throughout the body (particularly in the genital area), disgorgement of the collected blood, ejaculation in the male, and intense pleasure in both sexes. The resolution phase is a period of diminishing tension; the body returns rapidly through the plateau and excitement phases to an unstimulated state.

Masters and Johnson reported several striking similarities between men and women during sex: parallel sensitivities in the penis and the clitoris, flushing of the chest during the plateau phase, and identical rhythmic contractions of the anal sphincter during orgasm. They found at least one critical difference. In men the resolution phase was followed by a complete loss of sexual responsiveness, lasting anywhere from a few minutes in adolescents to a day or more in older men. Women, on the other hand, appeared capable of returning to another orgasmic experience from any point in the resolution phase. Some women experienced one orgasm after another in an uninterrupted succession. It appeared that women were poten-

MALE

Excitement

Vasocongestion of penis results in erection

Partial erection

Unstimulated state

Testes elevate toward perineum

Skin of scrotum tenses, thickens, and elevates

Plateau

Cowper's gland secretion

Color of penile glans deepens

Prostate enlarges

Cowper's gland

Testes increase in size and are fully elevated

Scrotum thickens

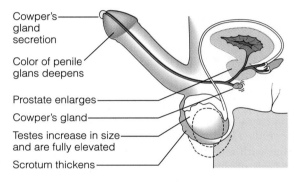

Orgasm

Penile contractions

Sperm and semen expelled by rhythmic contractions of urethra

Vas deferens contracts

Internal sphincter of bladder contracts

Prostate gland contracts

Seminal vesicle contracts

Rectal sphincter contracts

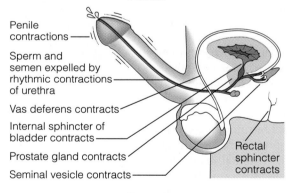

Erection subsides

Unstimulated state

Scrotum thins, folds return

Loss of testicular congestion, testes descend

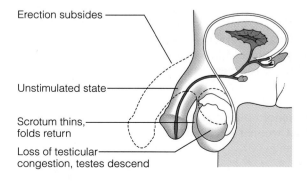

FEMALE

Excitement

Pubic bone

Bladder

Uterus elevates

Vaginal lubrication appears

Clitoris enlarges

Inner labia swell

Outer labia

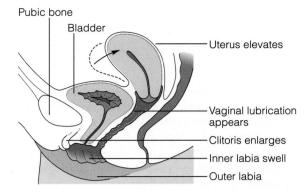

Plateau

Uterus elevates further

Upper part of vagina expands

Vaginal walls swell

Color of labia deepens

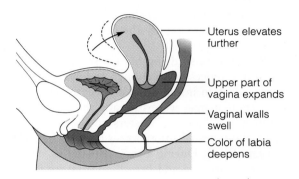

Orgasm

Contractions in uterus

Rhythmic contractions in vagina

Rectal sphincter contracts

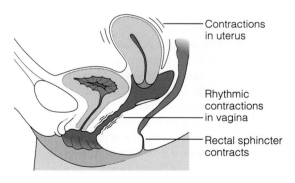

Uterus lowers

Vagina returns to normal

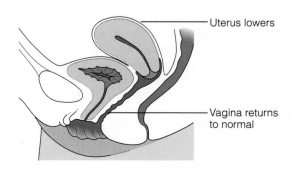

tially more sexually responsive than men. Masters and Johnson's research overturned the Victorian notion of poorer female responsiveness and helped pave the way for a new sort of sexual liberation (Konner, 1988).

Sources of Sexual Pleasure

This section discusses various ways in which men and women achieve sexual satisfaction. It also looks at sexual preferences among members of both sexes.

Nocturnal Orgasm

Nocturnal orgasm is defined as sexual arousal and response that occurs during sleep. Both males and females experience these types of orgasms, which are often accompanied by erotic dreams. The popular term *wet dream* describes male ejaculation during sleep. From both scientific and psychological perspectives, nocturnal orgasms are generally considered enjoyable sexual experiences.

Masturbation

Masturbation, also called *autoeroticism* or *self-stimulation*, is one form of sexual expression. During a major survey of the sexual behavior of 2,765 people of various ages, Janus and Janus (1993) asked subjects about their use of masturbation. About 50–70% of those surveyed reported rarely or never masturbating. About 5–15% reported masturbating monthly, and 10–25% mentioned weekly. About 25% of the men reported masturbating several times a week; this was true for only about 5–10% of the women. In general, across all age groups, men masturbated more frequently than women, and more women rarely or never masturbated than did men.

We describe methods of masturbation in some detail here to help people understand what is stimulating to both women and men. This understanding can foster a more satisfactory sexual relationship.

Women most commonly masturbate by manipulating the clitoris and the inner lips. They may rub themselves up and down or in a circular motion, sometimes lightly or sometimes applying more pressure to the clitoris. Some women prefer rubbing the side of the clitoris, whereas others stimulate the glans of the clitoris directly. The inner lips may also be stroked or tugged. Some men imagine that women masturbate by inserting a finger or some similar-shaped object deep into the vagina. In fact, clitoral and labial manipulation is the most common form of

Figure C.3 The Stages of Sexual Response. *Source: Core Concepts in Health* (7th ed.—1996 Update) (p. 113) by P. M. Insel and W. T. Roth, 1996, Mountain View, CA: Mayfield. Copyright 1996 by Mayfield Publishing Co. Reprinted by permission.

female masturbation. Of those women in the Kinsey study who masturbated, 84% massaged the clitoris and labia, whereas only 20% inserted fingers or other objects into the vagina (Kinsey, Pomeroy, Martin, & Gebhard, 1953).

Almost all men reported masturbating by hand stimulation of the penis; it takes most men only 1–2 minutes to reach orgasm this way (Kinsey, Pomeroy, & Martin, 1948, p. 509). Most men encircle the shaft of the penis with their hand and move the hand up and down to stimulate the shaft and the glans. How tight the man grips the penis, how fast he moves his hand up and down, and how much he stimulates the glans varies from one man to another. Most men increase the speed of the up-and-down movements as they approach orgasm and slow or stop the stimulation at orgasm because further motion is uncomfortable (Masters & Johnson, 1966). At the point of ejaculation, men often grip the shaft tightly. After ejaculation, the tip of the penis is hypersensitive, and men usually avoid further stimulation of the penis for a while.

From both scientific and mental health perspectives, there is little evidence to suggest that masturbation is a problem. Some people worry about "excessive" masturbation, but this is hard to define. If masturbation occurred so often that it precluded other important aspects of life, then it could be termed excessive.

Couple Sex

Couples stimulate each other sexually in a wide variety of ways. Common approaches include mutual masturbation, oral sex, and a variety of coital positions. Mutual orgasm is also discussed in this section.

In terms of sexual pleasure and achieving an orgasm, both men (82%) and women (69%) favored sexual intercourse, according to the Janus survey of 2,765 individuals (Janus & Janus, 1993, p. 98). Surprisingly, 18% of women but only 10% of men preferred oral sex. Only 5% of men and 8% of women preferred masturbation as a way to achieve orgasm.

Mutual masturbation is two partners masturbating each other. It is a pleasurable practice, and the chance of pregnancy or the transmission of sexual diseases is lessened when it is done with care. Mutual masturbation is one of the major techniques gay-male and lesbian couples use during sexual intimacy (Allgeier & Allgeier, 1995).

Attitudes toward **oral sex**—using one's mouth to stimulate the partner's genitals—have become more and more accepting in the past few decades, especially among younger people and the more formally educated. Oral sex is a prelude to sexual intercourse for some couples; others enjoy it without intercourse. Partners can take turns satisfying each other or can simultaneously stimulate each other in the so-called 69 (head-to-foot) position. Couples interested in exploring oral sex should have a relatively positive image of their sexual organs, basic cleanliness, a willingness to try different positions and techniques, and open and honest communication about their likes and dislikes (Francoeur, 1982).

Human beings assume a wide variety of positions when engaging in **sexual intercourse.** Masters and Johnson (1966) found in their research that a woman's sexual response is likely to develop more rapidly and with greater intensity when she is on top of the man in the face-to-face position during sexual intercourse.

The typical coital position used in a culture often depends on the social status of females in that culture (Beigel, 1953). The woman-above position is most popular when sexual satisfaction is just as important for females as it is for men, as in several American Indian tribes and in cultures in the South Pacific. In contrast, Kinsey's research, conducted in the United States, concluded that "nearly all coitus in our English-American culture occurs with the partners lying face to face, with the male above the female. There may be as much as 70 percent of the population which has never attempted to use any other position in intercourse" (Kinsey et al., 1948, p. 578).

Today, this so-called **missionary position** remains popular among Americans, but couples are quite likely to experiment with many different positions. Feminism has changed many aspects of American culture, and it clearly has entered the bedroom. In the face-to-face, man-above position, a woman usually lies on her back, legs apart, knees slightly bent. Advantages of this face-to-face position are that the partners can communicate feelings clearly through erotic kissing, eye contact, and facial expressions. Disadvantages of this position are that when the man's body is a great deal heavier than the woman's body, she is not as free to participate in sexual movements that are pleasurable to her. Also, the man's hands are not as free to stimulate his partner's breasts in this position (Allgeier & Allgeier, 1995).

The advantages of the face-to-face, woman-above position for women are similar to the advantages of the man-above position for men. The woman is free to move in ways pleasurable to her. A further advantage of this position is that the man experiences less sexual intensity. If the woman is slower to respond sexually than the man, which is quite common, this position helps the man prolong the pleasure of his sexual arousal before ejaculation. In short, this position often increases the possibility that both partners will achieve orgasm (Allgeier & Allgeier, 1995).

Side-by-side intercourse offers both partners the chance to control their own body movements simultaneously. In this position, penetration of the penis tends to be somewhat shallow, and movements are not quite as vigorous. But the position does allow for free movement of the hands (Allgeier & Allgeier, 1995). Rear entry, in which the man slides his penis into the female's vagina from behind, is the most common coital position among nonhuman species. Some people find it distasteful for this reason, but it has some advantages for couples. Rear-entry positions can be quite restful, and they work well during the third trimester of pregnancy and during illnesses that do not permit exertion (Allgeier & Allgeier, 1995).

When masturbating, most men slow down or stop manual stimulation of the penis during orgasm. Women masturbating generally prefer continued stimulation of the clitoris or mons during orgasm. During sexual intercourse, men tend to attempt deep vaginal penetration with little further thrusting during orgasm, whereas women prefer continued male thrusting during their orgasm.

This difference in the typical sexual response styles of men and women makes mutual, or simultaneous, orgasm difficult to achieve. Because women can continue coitus indefinitely after an orgasm whereas men tend to lose their erection after ejaculation, a "ladies first" approach to lovemaking often works well for couples. If, for example, the woman finds it easiest to achieve orgasm in the woman-above position or through oral sex, a couple can employ this approach until she reaches orgasm. Then, the couple can try the position that the man considers most stimulating (Allgeier & Allgeier, 1995).

The Influence of Alcohol and Other Drugs on Sex

Sexual intercourse, in an important sense, is an act of relaxation. Sex therapist Terry Mason puts it this way, "In order to 'feel good,' you've got to relax and let some things happen. You can't be afraid or have a lot of anxiety and tension about someone experiencing a part of your body and you experiencing a part of theirs. You can't kiss all tensed up and you can't touch somebody in a very loving sort of way if you're tense or they're tense" (cited in Poinsett, 1988).

Perhaps this is why many people associate sex and alcohol. If a person is nervous about having sex with someone else, he or she might see alcohol as a way of relaxing. Alcohol is a "downer," however, dulling the conscious mind, removing inhibitions, and creating an artificial relaxation. Alcohol may help some people relax and may reduce anxiety and inhibitions and improve sexual responsiveness. However, a large amount of alcohol acts as a depressant and may prevent sexual arousal by reducing sensations (Insel & Roth, 1996). Marijuana is also a downer, having a similar effect on sexual feelings and performance. Cocaine, on the other hand, is an upper but can serve as an anesthetic that prevents an orgasm. "All of these drugs," Mason cautions, "do something that you don't do naturally on your own. The key is to get you to create naturally for yourself by removing all of the hang-ups and inhibitions that you have" (cited in Poinsett, 1988).

Robert Francoeur (1982) concurs:

> Myths and misinformation about the sexual enhancement one can obtain from various drugs can cause serious problems. The stories of "incredible sexual highs" resulting from the use of marijuana, amyl nitrate, Quaaludes, and so forth, are stories with no foundation when the effects are seriously studied by scientific methods. Very often the research has shown that an initial positive enhancement is quickly replaced by sexual dysfunction and the loss of sexual desire or libido when the drug is used for some time. (p. 567)

RESOURCE SECTION D

Pregnancy and Childbirth

This resource section explains the reproductive process, infertility, and pregnancy. It then looks at the birth process and childbirth practices. The section concludes with discussions of the changes a new baby brings to the family and the impact on the family of miscarriage, stillbirth, or infant death.

The Process of Reproduction

Conception is a complicated process. We discuss here how conception occurs, the nature of infertility, and signs of pregnancy.

Conception

The average woman's menstrual cycle is 28 days long. For as long as she is fertile (approximately 35 years, from about age 12 to about age 47), each cycle prepares her body for **conception** and childbearing. The most fertile period occurs about midway through the menstrual cycle, or 14 days before the next **menses** begins. This is the point at which **ovulation** occurs (Figure D.1).

Estimates of women's fertility have ranged from 2 days in a menstrual cycle to 10 or more. Recent research published in the *New England Journal of Medicine* indicates there are 6 days in every menstrual month when a woman can get pregnant ("A Woman's Fertility Window," 1995). Dr. Arthur Wilcox, who teaches at the University of North Carolina, argues that conception is possible if a woman has intercourse on the 5 days before ovulation as well as on the day her ovaries release a new egg. Sex before the 6-day period almost certainly will not result in pregnancy, nor will intercourse just one day after ovulation. The researchers at the National Institute of Environmental Health Sciences in Research Triangle Park, N.C., also found that 94% of pregnancies resulted from sperm that had lingered less than 3 days. There were no pregnancies from sperm more than 5 days old.

The egg, made up of 23 chromosomes, fat droplets, protein substances, and nutrient fluid, travels for 3 or 4 days through an **oviduct** (fallopian tube) into the uterus. The lining of the uterus has already become puffed out, which aids implantation of the fertilized egg, the **zygote.** Unfertilized eggs live about 24 hours; then they disintegrate and are expelled along with the uterine lining during **menstruation.** There are a half-million eggs in the female ovaries at birth. Only 400–500 of them will ripen and be released into the oviducts during a woman's lifetime. Each egg is about the size of a pinpoint ($1/250$ inch in diameter) (Insel & Roth, 1996).

Sperm cells are even smaller than eggs ($1/8,000$ inch in diameter). One average male ejaculation contains approximately 300–400 million sperm. Sperm contain 23 chromosomes and have a tail for mobility. When a male ejaculates during sexual intercourse, the sperm are propelled into the woman's vagina. Unless a sperm reaches and fertilizes an egg, it will die within about 72 hours. Many sperm cells die in the acidic environment of the vagina. The survivors migrate to the cervix, or "neck" of the uterus, where secretions are more alkaline and hospitable to sperm.

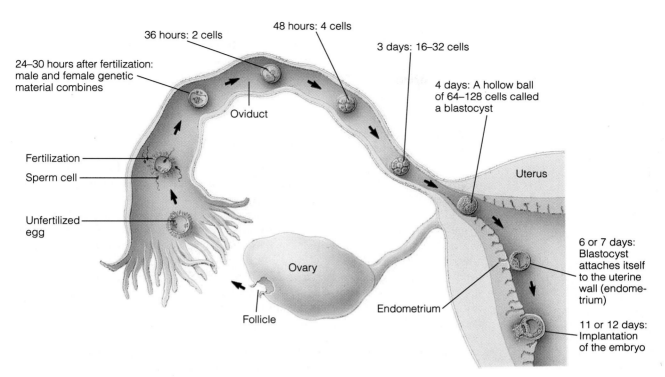

36 hours: 2 cells

48 hours: 4 cells

3 days: 16–32 cells

24–30 hours after fertilization: male and female genetic material combines

4 days: A hollow ball of 64–128 cells called a blastocyst

Oviduct

Fertilization

Sperm cell

Unfertilized egg

Uterus

Ovary

Follicle

Endometrium

6 or 7 days: Blastocyst attaches itself to the uterine wall (endometrium)

11 or 12 days: Implantation of the embryo

Figure D.1 Conception. *Source: Core Concepts in Health* (7th ed.—1996 Update) (p. 189) *by* P. M. Insel and W. T. Roth, 1996, Mountain View, CA: Mayfield. Copyright 1996 by Mayfield Publishing Co. Reprinted by permission.

Once inside the uterus, many sperm fail to reach an oviduct or enter the oviduct that does not contain the egg. If an egg is not present in the oviduct, the sperm swim erratically. If the sperm have found the oviduct with the egg, they swim directly toward it, apparently drawn by chemicals released by the egg. Those sperm that come in contact with the egg must penetrate the tough membrane that encases it.

Each sperm cell that makes contact with the egg deposits an enzyme that helps to dissolve this membrane. About 2,000 sperm manage to make it this far. The first sperm cell that meets a dissolved, bare spot on the egg cell can swim into the cell and merge with the nucleus of the egg. This union is called **fertilization.** The sperm's tail, which has served as a propeller during this journey, gets stuck in the outer membrane and drops off. The head of the sperm cell is implanted inside the egg, and no more sperm can enter, perhaps because on fertilization the egg releases a chemical making it impregnable (Insel & Roth, 1996).

The egg carries the hereditary characteristics of the mother and her ancestors; sperm cells carry the hereditary characteristics of the father and his ancestors. Each parent cell, the egg and the sperm, contains 23 chromosomes, and each chromosome has at least 1,000 genes. These genes are the genetic code of chemical instructions for the design of every part of a new baby. These genes specify that the baby will be a human and whether it will be male or female. The genes also have an influence on whether the baby will tend to be short, tall, fat, or thin, and on hundreds of other characteristics.

Environmental influences also affect the infant's development a great deal during pregnancy. Health authorities urge a prospective mother to eat well; avoid alcohol, drugs, and smoking; get adequate rest and exercise; have medical checkups regularly; build intimate emotional relationships with a network of other people; and generally live a healthy lifestyle (Nilsson, 1990).

Infertility

Infertility is the inability to bear children. An estimated 1 in 13 American couples is unable to have all the children they would like due to a variety of conditions that cause infertility (Insel & Roth, 1996).

There are several causes of infertility in women: failure to ovulate or menstrual cycle irregularities, endometriosis (abnormal tissue in the pelvic cavity, preventing conception), hormonal imbalances, scar tissue in the oviducts, physical abnormalities (an unusually shaped uterus), or an allergic response that kills the partner's sperm. Infertility in men is caused mainly by a low sperm count or by sperm with poor mobility. These problems can often be traced to an injury of the testicles, infection (mumps during adulthood is a common one), exposure to radiation, glandular disorders, birth defects, or exposure of the testicles to high temperatures (such as those produced by hot baths).

Some types of infertility are subject to treatment; others are not. Surgery is sometimes helpful in repairing oviducts, clearing up endometriosis, and correcting anatomical problems. **Artificial insemination**—in which the man's sperm are collected, concentrated, and mechanically introduced into the woman's vagina or uterus—can sometimes aid conception in cases of male fertility problems. Some types of female infertility can be treated through **in vitro fertilization,** in which eggs are removed from the woman's ovary, fertilized in a laboratory dish with her partner's sperm, and implanted in the uterus. The most controversial approach to female infertility is **surrogate motherhood,** in which a fertile woman agrees, for a fee paid by the couple who cannot conceive, to be artificially inseminated by the husband's sperm, carry the baby to term, and give it to the couple at birth. Treatments for infertility are often expensive and emotionally draining, and chances for success are uncertain.

"Am I Pregnant?"

Among the common early indicators of pregnancy are the following:

- A missed menstrual period (although a woman can miss a period for many reasons, including stress, illness, and emotional upset).

- Nausea in the morning, or **morning sickness,** which usually disappears by the 12th week of pregnancy.

- Changes in the shape, coloration, and sensitivity of the breasts. The breasts become fuller; the area around the nipples darkens; veins become more prominent; and the swelling causes tingling, throbbing, or minor pain.

- An increased need to urinate, resulting from pressure from the growing uterus on the bladder and also hormonal changes.

- Fatigue and sleepiness caused by hormonal changes.

- An increase in vaginal secretions, either clear and nonirritating or slightly yellow and itchy.

- Retention of body fluids, including some swelling of the face, hands, and feet.

A woman who wants a more reliable answer to the question "Am I pregnant?" can consult her physician, who can perform a pregnancy test. The woman can also purchase a pregnancy test kit at a pharmacy. To perform the test, the woman simply dips a strip of chemically treated paper in her early-morning urine and observes the color of the paper. If the paper turns red, she is pregnant. The test can determine pregnancy roughly 7–10 days after a missed menstrual period. Home test kits are reliable 95–99% of the time (Allgeier & Allgeier, 1995). Confirmation of the home test, as well as other information and services, can be obtained at a medical clinic.

Pregnancy and Preparation for Birth

Not more than 36 hours after fertilization, the egg has divided in half and then divides a second time. The process of division continues as the egg moves down the oviduct. In 3–4 days the tiny fertilized mass, containing about 100 cells, reaches the uterus. The mass, called a **blastocyst,** is hollow at the center. The outer shell of cells (trophoblast) multiplies faster than the inner cells and eventually grows into the **placenta, umbilical cord,** and **amniotic sac.** The inner cells grow into three distinct layers: the innermost layer (endoderm) becomes the inner body parts; the middle layer (mesoderm) becomes muscle, bone, blood, kidneys, and sex glands; and the outermost layer (ectoderm) eventually grows into the skin, hair, and nervous tissue. Six or seven days after fertilization, the blastocyst begins implanting itself in the wall of the uterus and its cells start to take nourishment from the uterine lining (Cox, 1990). For the stages of fetal development, see Figure D.2, p. 614.

Pregnancy progresses over the course of three **trimesters,** periods of 13 weeks each. During each trimester, important prenatal development milestones occur (Figure D.3, p. 615). During the first trimester, the external appearance of the mother's body changes very little, although she may experience some or all of the common signs of pregnancy listed earlier. In the second trimester, which some women consider the most peaceful part of a pregnancy, the mother gains weight and it becomes clear to others that she is pregnant. Women who are happy about the upcoming birth often report a sense of well-being during the second trimester. The third trimester is often the most difficult part of the pregnancy. The increased demands the growing fetus places on the woman's body may make her lethargic, and she will likely become increasingly impatient to give birth (Insel & Roth, 1996).

Figure D.2 The Fetal Development Process.
Source: Human Development: A Life-Span Approach, 2nd ed., by F. Philip Rice, 1995, p. 53, NJ: Prentice-Hall. Copyright © 1995 by Prentice-Hall, Inc. Reprinted with permission of the publisher.

Third week   Fourth week   Fifth week

Sixth week   Seventh week   Eighth week

The pregnant woman has a great deal of responsibility, because everything that enters or comes in contact with her body can potentially affect the fetus (Insel & Roth, 1996). Her partner, family, and friends also have major responsibilities to support the mother in her efforts to be physically and mentally healthy and, thus, aid in the baby's development. Prenatal care includes appropriate diet, exercise, rest, and the avoidance of alcohol and drugs not prescribed by a physician. Also important are personal mental health and positive relationships with the significant people in her life. There are many things to learn during pregnancy. Medical professionals at clinics and health educators specializing in pregnancy, labor, and delivery can be very helpful.

Although pregnancy and childbirth are clearly "natural" processes, numerous problems can arise, some of them life-threatening to the infant and/or the mother. Because of the potential for problems, women should receive regular medical evaluation and care during pregnancy.

Education for Childbirth

Education is extremely important during this period in a woman's and a couple's life. Expectant couples generally have many questions and sometimes many fears that can be dealt with positively with the help of resources like books, films, and classes. Close and regular medical consultation is also important for the physical health of the infant and the mother.

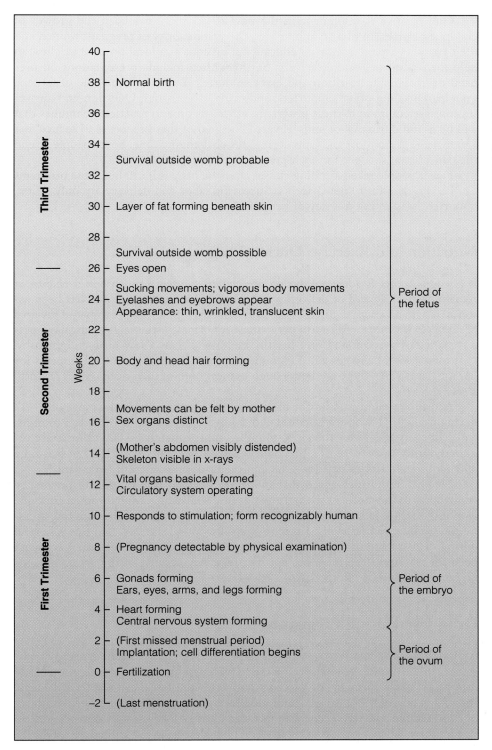

Figure D.3 Milestones of Prenatal Development. *Source: Understanding Children* (2nd ed.) (p. 86) by J. A. Schickedanz, D. I. Schickedanz, K. Hansen, and P. D. Forsyth, 1993, Mountain View, CA: Mayfield. Copyright 1993 by Mayfield Publishing Co. Reprinted by permission.

One positive development in the past 20–25 years has been the growth of childbirth classes. In most communities, the vast majority of pregnant women and their partners attend a series of educational sessions at a local hospital or clinic to help them prepare for the delivery. Sessions often include presentations on prenatal development; nutrition and exercise during pregnancy; the role of fathers, grandparents, and other supporters; and many other issues. Question-and-answer sessions are common in these programs, as well as time to practice techniques that will be useful during labor and delivery. The goal of these classes is to reduce fear and manage discomfort and pain during this challenging time. Some people attend the educational sessions for each pregnancy, as a refresher.

Fewer people take parenting classes after the baby is born, but these programs can be very helpful to new parents. Successful labor and delivery are only a first, important step in the journey of parenthood.

Nutrition and Exercise During Pregnancy

If a woman's diet is adequate during pregnancy, she has a much better chance of remaining healthy and of delivering a healthy baby. Inadequate diet has been associated with a variety of diseases mothers can develop during pregnancy. One goal of diet is to promote a full-term pregnancy: A normal-birth-weight baby has a better chance of survival and of a healthy childhood than a low-birth-weight baby. Not only does a baby get all of its nutrients from its mother, but it competes for her nutrients when there are not enough to meet both of their needs (Insel & Roth, 1996).

A healthy weight gain for the mother during pregnancy is in the range of 24–27 lb (Figure D.4). The average gain is about 1.5–3 lb a month for the first 3 months, and 1 lb every 9 days for the last 6 months. Approximately 80,000 calories are required during the course of a pregnancy. This may sound like a lot, but it is only 300 additional calories per day—the equivalent of one scoop of ice cream.

Medical authorities agree that moderate physical activity during pregnancy contributes to the mother's mental and physical well-being. Many women continue working on their jobs into the final stages of pregnancy, if the job is not too stressful physically or emotionally. Exercise keeps the muscles toned, and this is helpful during delivery and in regaining a nonpregnant shape after childbirth. A woman's need for rest and sleep increases during pregnancy because of the great demands on her body (Insel & Roth, 1996).

Drug Use During Pregnancy

Although the placenta serves as a filter to protect the embryo from dangerous substances in the mother's blood, the so-called placental barrier is not foolproof. Many drugs pass easily through the placenta and enter the fetus, causing fetal damage. Alcohol is one of those drugs. **Fetal alcohol syndrome (FAS)** has been a subject of considerable concern recently. In fact, the Centers for Disease Control and Prevention have labeled it the leading cause of birth defects in the United States (Kelly, 1994). FAS is characterized in children by a small body, facial malformation, and

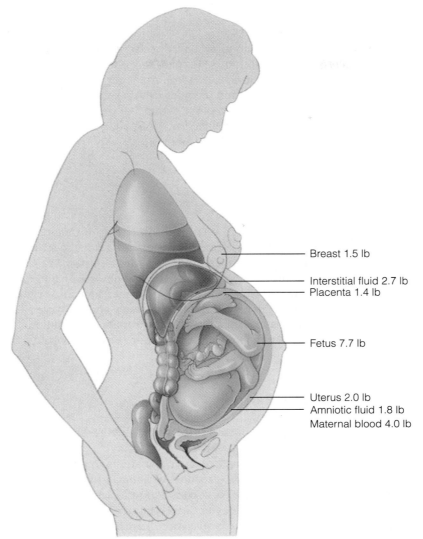

Figure D.4 Weight Gain in Pregnancy. *Source: Sexual Interactions* (4th ed.) (p. 275) by A. R. Allgeier and E. R. Allgeier, 1995, Lexington, MA: Heath. Copyright 1995 by D. C. Heath & Co. Reprinted by permission.

Breast 1.5 lb

Interstitial fluid 2.7 lb
Placenta 1.4 lb

Fetus 7.7 lb

Uterus 2.0 lb
Amniotic fluid 1.8 lb
Maternal blood 4.0 lb

poor mental capabilities. Large-scale surveys indicate that babies of mothers who drink excessively are being exposed to considerable risk of serious malformation during both the early, embryonic stage and the later phases of fetal development. In particular, alcohol easily damages eyes and vision (Nilsson, 1990). Pregnant women can eliminate the possibility of damage to the fetus by not drinking *any* alcohol during pregnancy.

Smoking is also dangerous to the developing fetus. Nicotine and carbon monoxide from smoking pass through the placental barrier into the fetal bloodstream. Babies born to women who smoked heavily during pregnancy almost always weigh less at birth than babies born to women who stopped smoking at the beginning of pregnancy. A smokeless working environment during pregnancy is also important for the mother's and baby's health.

Sex During Pregnancy

Pregnancy generates mixed emotions: joy, discomfort, wonder, fear, insecurity, curiosity, and enthusiastic expectation. Because this is an emotion-filled time, maintaining a healthy sexual relationship is important for pregnant women and their partners. With reasonable caution, couples can make love until the birth process begins. Most couples resume intercourse within 3–6 weeks after the birth of a child (Boston Women's Health Book Collective, 1992; Kelly, 1994).

Labor and Delivery

The first sign of impending birth is **labor,** contractions of the uterus that occur at regular intervals. During labor, the uterine muscles gradually stretch the cervical opening in preparation for birth, and those muscles also push the baby down into the vagina so that it can be born. Signs of the beginning of labor vary from individual to individual. In many mothers it is accompanied by a discharge of the bloody mucus that has plugged the cervix during pregnancy and prevented bacteria from entering the uterus. In approximately 10% of women, the amniotic sac ruptures ("the breaking of the waters") during early labor (Boston Women's Health Book Collective, 1992).

Three Stages of Labor

Medical tradition divides labor into three stages (Figure D.5).

Stage One   During the first stage of labor, the uterus contracts in rhythmic waves and the cervical opening dilates (expands) to about 4 inches in diameter and effaces, or thins out. Early in stage one, contractions occur every 15–20 minutes and last approximately 1 minute. **Contractions**—tightenings of the uterine muscles—are followed by periods of relative relaxation. Later in stage one, the contractions increase in frequency and in length. By the time contractions are about 5 minutes apart, the woman should be in the hospital to begin preparation for the birth. Most women spend all of stage one in a labor room at the hospital. Labor lasts 2–24 hours or more, and during long labors, labor pains may stop and start up again. During a first birth, labor averages about 10 hours. For subsequent babies, labor may average about 8 hours or less, often decreasing with each birth.

Stage Two   The second stage of labor—the **delivery,** or birth, itself—usually takes place in the delivery room and lasts a few minutes to an hour or more. Ninety-nine percent of the time babies enter the world lengthwise, with 96% entering the cervix and traveling through the vagina and into the world head first. Three percent of babies are born buttocks first, called a breech birth. The remaining 1% of babies are in a transverse position, with the back near the cervix. In these cases,

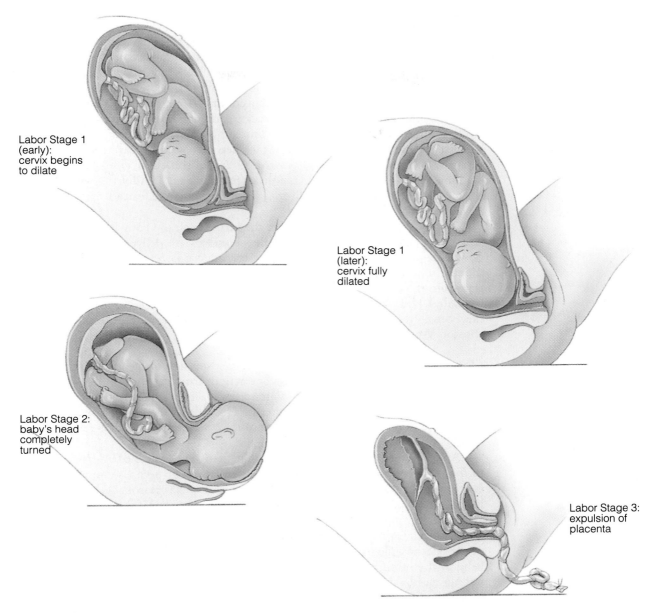

Labor Stage 1 (early): cervix begins to dilate

Labor Stage 1 (later): cervix fully dilated

Labor Stage 2: baby's head completely turned

Labor Stage 3: expulsion of placenta

Figure D.5 The Birth Process. *Source: Core Concepts in Health* (7th ed.—1996 Update) (p. 214) by P. Insel and W. Roth, 1996, Mountain View, CA: Mayfield. Copyright 1996 by Mayfield Publishing Co. Reprinted by permission.

the medical team tries to rotate the baby lengthwise; if they do not succeed, a cesarean section must be performed.

When the baby's head reaches the entrance to the vagina, this is called crowning. The physician or nurse-midwife encourages the mother to "bear down," to help push the child out through the vagina (Boston Women's Health Book Collective, 1992).

The vagina can stretch a great deal to allow the baby to emerge, but the perineum (the tissue between the anus and the vagina) can stretch to the point of tearing. Physicians often prestretch the perineum early in labor to reduce the risk of tearing; extensive tearing makes infection more likely and slows recovery. Some physicians make a minor surgical incision in the perineum—an **episiotomy**—to prevent tearing. After the birth, the episiotomy is repaired with a few surgical stitches and usually heals in about 3 weeks. Although episiotomy has been a relatively routine medical practice in the United States for many years, some controversy surrounds the practice; pregnant women may want to learn more about the pros and cons of the procedure before delivery. In some European countries episiotomies are rarely performed, and many feminists and childbirth groups believe they are unnecessary in most deliveries (Boston Women's Health Book Collective, 1992).

As the baby's head passes through the birth canal, the body rotates somewhat so that the shoulders can exit. After the shoulders are delivered, the rest of the body slips out easily. Shortly after delivery, mucus is removed from the baby's mouth, and the baby begins breathing through its lungs, sometimes after a gentle slap from the physician. The umbilical cord is painlessly cut about 3 inches from the baby's body; the stub dries up and falls off in a few days. In many states, the newborn's eyes are treated against gonorrhea with silver nitrate or an antibiotic (Boston Women's Health Book Collective, 1992).

Stage Three   The third stage of labor is the expulsion of the **afterbirth,** or placenta and fetal membranes, by mild contractions from the uterus. To avoid infection, the physician or the nurses examine the placenta carefully to ascertain that all of it has been expelled from the uterus. This third stage of labor may take only a few minutes or up to an hour. If an episiotomy was performed, it is repaired during this time.

After delivery, the baby is bathed, and in many hospitals the baby is then taken to the recovery room for a visit with mother, father, or perhaps a few other very special people. Mothers are encouraged to be as active as reasonable soon after delivery—to walk around or use the bathroom, for example. (If the mother received anesthesia during delivery, she may not begin to walk around for 12–24 hours.) Some hospitals provide a "rooming-in" option for mothers who want their baby nearby all the time or at least when they are awake. Another option is to bring the baby to the mother every 3–4 hours to be breast- or bottle-fed. If all goes well, mother and baby go home in 1–3 days (Allgeier & Allgeier, 1995). The first major challenge of parenthood has been met.

Cesarean Section

When normal vaginal birth is impossible or undesirable for some reason, a **cesarean section** (C-section), a surgical procedure, is performed to deliver the baby. C-sections are used in a variety of situations: if the baby is too large or the mother's pelvis is too small to allow the baby to move into the vagina; if labor has been very long and hard and the cervix has not dilated or if the mother is near exhaustion; if the umbilical cord has prolapsed (is preceding the baby through the cervix); if there is an Rh (blood factor) incompatibility; if there is excessive bleeding; or if the mother's or baby's condition takes a turn for the worse (Hyde, 1990).

C-sections are performed by making an incision through the mother's abdomen and then through the wall of the uterus. The baby is lifted out, and the uterine and abdominal walls are sewn up. Normal vaginal births are sometimes possible after a woman has delivered by cesarean; other women have two or three cesarean deliveries. The rate of complications related to C-sections is low, but recovery is somewhat longer than for vaginal birth, requiring 5–6 days in the hospital rather than 1–2 (Hyde, 1990).

The number of cesarean deliveries in the United States has risen dramatically in recent years. About 15–25% of U.S. births are C-sections, a considerably higher percentage than in some western European countries. This higher rate may reflect, among other reasons, the availability of sophisticated equipment for detecting fetal distress. A C-section may be performed if, for example, the fetal monitor shows that the baby is receiving inadequate oxygen during labor (Schickedanz, Schickedanz, Hansen, & Forsyth, 1993).

C-sections can be safer for both mother and baby when labor is prolonged and stressful, advocates say. They cite lower rates of maternal and neonatal mortality and of infant brain damage due to trauma during labor and delivery. Critics of the C-section argue that many cesareans are unnecessary, that they are simply more convenient for the physician. They encourage better labor management by medical personnel. The debate is likely to continue on a situation-by-situation basis.

Alternative Approaches to Birth

Childbirth has traditionally been seen as a natural phenomenon requiring little fanfare or special attention. In developed countries, however, beginning about 100 years ago, medical intervention became more and more common. Childbirth came to be viewed more as an illness or a medical emergency. Emphasis on drugs and anesthetics to reduce pain grew, as did the time for recovery from the birth experience. Labor and delivery became mysterious, controlled by physicians and nurses in hospitals. From a feminist perspective, women lost control to medical experts (Kelly, 1994).

Natural Childbirth   In 1932, British physician Grantly Dick-Read published *Childbirth Without Fear*, and women and their partners began to regain some of the control they had formerly held over the birth process. Dick-Read believed that medical intervention generated fear, and fear created more tension and pain. He called his approach natural childbirth, educated women about labor and delivery, and taught them relaxation techniques to reduce tension.

The Lamaze Method   The French obstetrician Fernand Lamaze introduced a similar method in the 1950s, and the Lamaze method of "prepared childbirth" is widespread today. In this method, the baby's father or a friend or relative serves as a coach for the mother. In prenatal classes the mother and her coach learn relaxation and breathing techniques for dealing with the intensity of labor. The woman remains active and alert during the birth of her baby (Kelly, 1994).

The Lamaze approach does not prohibit the use of painkillers during labor but usually reduces the need for them. Routine use of anesthesia during childbirth has been criticized, primarily because drugs can slow the progress of labor and affect the baby's well-being during the first several hours of life (Allgeier & Allgeier, 1995; Boston Women's Health Book Collective, 1992). One rational approach to the controversy over anesthesia and other painkillers is for a pregnant woman to participate in prepared childbirth classes and use the breathing and relaxation techniques of the Lamaze method during labor. If she discovers that she cannot control her pain and wishes an anesthetic, she can request it without guilt. The anesthetic should then be administered with great caution (Hyde, 1990).

Leboyer's "Gentle Birthing"   The French physician Frederick Leboyer (1975) advocated methods for reducing the shock of birth to the baby. Instead of a bright, noisy delivery area, Leboyer recommended a quiet, dimly lit, warm setting. In the Leboyer method, the baby lies on the mother's abdomen for a while before the umbilical cord is cut and then receives a gentle, warm bath.

Home Birth   Because medical complications occur in approximately 1 of 20 births, most professionals recommend delivery in a hospital, where there is access to advanced technology and professional assistance. Some couples choose to have their baby born at home, however. A trained and licensed **midwife** or certified nurse-midwife can assist in the process. It is also recommended that a cooperating physician be on call in case of an emergency (Allgeier & Allgeier, 1995; Kelly, 1994).

Birthing Rooms and Birthing Centers   In response to the desire that birth be a cooperative process between professionals and families and a balance of technology and tenderness, many hospitals have established birthing rooms and birthing centers. Birthing rooms are decorated more like bedrooms than like hospital rooms. Sometimes children and family members are allowed to be present for the birth, as is common in many societies. When a birthing room is used, the mother stays in the same room for labor and delivery. After delivery, the baby is checked for signs of distress, weighed and measured, and kept warm (Kelly, 1994).

Birthing centers humanize the birth process even further. Birthing centers are separate health-care facilities affiliated with hospitals. They have not only birthing rooms but kitchens and other rooms in which visitors and family members can stay. Birthing centers are usually staffed by nurses and nurse-midwives, although physicians are often in attendance for deliveries. They have emergency equipment and arrangements with a hospital if transfer for emergency care is necessary (Allgeier & Allgeier, 1995). Procedures and philosophy vary widely from institution to institution, and prospective parents are advised to consider their options carefully. Parents have clearly gained more control of the process of childbirth in the past few decades.

Physical and Psychological Changes After Birth

After the baby is born, the mother's body undergoes drastic physiological changes. Levels of the hormones estrogen and progesterone have increased during pregnancy. When the placenta is expelled, the levels of these hormones drop sharply, gradually returning to normal over a few weeks to a few months. Other endocrinic changes include a higher level of hormones associated with breast-feeding. During labor and delivery, the woman's body underwent considerable stress; she may feel exhausted. Discomfort from delivery and from the episiotomy, if one was performed, is also common for the first few weeks after childbirth (Hyde, 1990).

For a day or two after birth, the mother often feels elated. In terms of energy expended, mother and baby have indeed been through an ordeal. However, most highs in life have lows connected with them. Within a few days after delivery, many women experience some depression and periods of crying.

Mood swings can range from mild to severe. The "maternity blues" or "baby blues" are the mildest form of depression, with sadness and tears lasting 24–48 hours (Hopkins, Marcues, & Campbell, 1984). It is estimated that 50–80% of mothers experience mild baby blues after delivery. **Postpartum depression,** which affects 20% of mothers and lasts 6–8 weeks, is a bit more serious. It is characterized by depressed mood, insomnia, tearfulness, feelings of inadequacy and the inability to cope, irritability, and fatigue (Hopkins et al., 1984).

A number of factors are thought to contribute to the depression women commonly feel after birth. Being in the hospital is stressful, and when the mother returns home, she faces a new set of stressors. Although her energy level is low, she must care for a newborn, an exhausting task involving almost constant attentiveness. She may get up several times at night to attend to the baby, who may be hungry or sick, may need a diaper change, or may be crying for some unknown reason. Although pregnancy and childbirth are natural processes, the stresses of the associated physiological and physical changes disrupt a woman's life.

More concern and interest has focused on fathers over the past few years. Many fathers are actively involved in the challenging process of parenthood. During pregnancy, labor, and delivery, the father can be a friend, coach, and supporter. The mother, however, is clearly the person who has "run the race." After the birth, fathers have a chance to share in the considerable stresses of parenthood. They can get up at night to feed the baby and can share in other caregiving tasks.

One very positive development in the past two decades has been the increase in support services for new parents. Many services were developed to help so-called at-risk families, those in which there is a potential for abuse or neglect of the baby. Among the risk factors commonly cited are high family stress, a parent who becomes angry easily, a very depressed parent, a parent with little extended-family support, a teenage mother, and alcohol or other drug abuse in the family.

There are also programs for parents who are not at risk for abuse or neglect of their infant but who are simply experiencing the everyday stresses and strains of parenthood. Childbirth and parenting classes are generally available and meet on a regular basis. Typically, a professional gives a short talk on a relevant topic, and there is time for group discussion. Churches, synagogues, and other organizations also sponsor groups where parents can get together socially to share their insights and the challenges they are facing. These programs help parents realize that they are not alone and that they can find ways to cope with this difficult time.

Caring for an Infant

When the infant arrives, a new set of challenges faces the parents. They first need to learn that their baby is more in charge of their life than they are. During the early weeks, the important process of creating a new family begins.

Bonding with the Baby

For most women, the attachment process begins even before the baby is born. During pregnancy, most women develop a sense of the baby as a separate individual and form an emotional attachment to that individual (Leifer, 1980). Many parents-to-be give the fetus a name—some serious, some funny—and mothers and fathers occasionally talk to the baby in the womb, play music for it, massage it. Even before birth, the baby is part of the family. For most parents, bonding develops quickly after birth as they care for this dependent child.

Breast-Feeding

In the early part of the 20th century **breast-feeding** declined in popularity, with many seeing it as somehow "lower class." Bottled formula was considered antiseptic, scientific, sophisticated, and dignified. By the mid-1960s, only about 20% of women breast-fed their babies. A renewed interest in breast-feeding began soon after; by the mid-1980s the percentage had risen to 60%, but the current rate is about 50% (Insel & Roth, 1996).

Breast-fed babies develop a kind of temporary immunity (so-called passive immunity) from antibodies in their mothers' milk; this protects them from a variety of diseases (including respiratory infections, colds, bronchitis, pneumonia, German measles, scarlet fever, and polio) (Olds, London, & Ladewig, 1996). Most studies comparing the benefits of bottle-feeding and breast-feeding conclude that breast-feeding is usually better for the physical well-being of the baby. Human milk is more easily digested than is milk from other animals or from vegetable-based formulas (such as those made from soybeans). Although human milk contains less protein than cow's milk, human infants can utilize almost all of the protein in their mother's milk but only about half the protein in cow's milk. Breast-fed babies are less likely to have diarrhea or to be constipated than are bottle-fed babies; they also tend to have healthier teeth and are less likely to be obese or to get premature atherosclerosis. These apparent advantages led the American Pediatric Society to conclude that breast milk is superior to formula. For those women who simply cannot or prefer not to breast-feed their babies but wish the nutritional advantages of human milk, human milk banks now operate in many large metropolitan areas (Allgeier & Allgeier, 1995).

The average baby ingests about 1,000 calories a day from breast milk, and this can be a great help to a mother who gained more weight than she wished during pregnancy. Mothers generally can lose weight quite steadily without denying themselves food by nursing for 6 months or so (Allgeier & Allgeier, 1995). By about 6 months of age, however, breast milk alone cannot meet the growing baby's needs for calories and protein. It is necessary to introduce solid food as a supplement at that time or even earlier.

Although its advantages are many, breast-feeding causes stress and inconvenience for many women working outside the home. More important than the feeding choice is the quality of the relationship between a mother and her baby: A baby raised in a loving home can grow up to be a healthy, psychologically secure individual whether bottle-fed or breast-fed. Breast-feeding can be a happy experience for both mother and child, but the woman who nurses grudgingly may communicate feelings of resentment and unhappiness to her baby. The infant would be better off with a relaxed, loving, bottle-feeding mother.

Miscarriage, Stillbirth, and Infant Death

Approximately 1% of infants born in the United States die in the first year after birth, and about 1% of babies born each year are stillborn (U.S. Bureau of the Census, 1995). Also, an estimated 14–18% of all known pregnancies end in miscarriage, and one third of all women experience a miscarriage at some time in their reproductive years (Neugebauer et al., 1992; Rosenfeld, 1991).

Miscarriage is defined as the termination of a pregnancy resulting from natural causes before the fetus is viable outside of the mother (that is, during the first or second trimester of pregnancy). Because women may not be aware that they are pregnant, the products of a miscarriage can be mistaken for a menstrual period. For this reason, some authorities have estimated that the true incidence of miscarried pregnancies may be as high as 15–20%. Studies of miscarried fetuses indicate that about 50% showed abnormalities, such as gross chromosomal abnormalities, that were incompatible with life. Psychological and physical trauma, contrary to popular belief, are not common causes of miscarriage. American society tends to define the loss of the fetus as "just a miscarriage," but to most women who experience a miscarriage, the loss is seen as a death—the death of a baby or the death of a dream (Day & Hooks, 1987).

Stillbirth is the death of a so-called viable fetus, a fetus that was mature enough developmentally to have lived outside the womb but for some reason or reasons was born dead. Stillbirths occur in the 7th–9th months of pregnancy (the third trimester). Before this time the event is called a miscarriage. Some causes of stillbirth are known. For example, some babies die of anoxia: the placenta sometimes compresses during delivery through the vagina, cutting off oxygen (Borg & Lasker, 1981). In nearly half of all stillbirths, however, studies indicate that there is no apparent reason for the death. The baby is perfectly formed, but it is born dead (Kirk, 1984).

The chances of an infant dying in this country before its first birthday are about 1%. Some of these deaths are the result of **sudden infant death syndrome (SIDS),** for which the cause is unknown. A common scenario is that the parent or another caretaker puts the seemingly healthy infant in the crib for a nap and comes back a few minutes or hours later to find the baby has died. An autopsy reveals no apparent cause (DeFrain, Ernst, Jakub, & Taylor, 1991).

Although the chance of losing a baby because of miscarriage, stillbirth, or SIDS is relatively small, the loss is a severe crisis in the lives of most families who experience it. When a baby dies, the family begins a long and difficult journey. Many parents and even some grandparents consider suicide after the loss of a baby; the pain and guilt can be overwhelming. Marriages are often strained by the loss, and parental relationships with surviving children sometimes suffer.

Research indicates that family members who have experienced the death of an infant are seriously at risk for major emotional and physical problems. Immediate and effective community support from relatives, friends, and professionals is essential. Most families recover from the death of an infant, but the road back to emotional well-being is long, difficult, and often very lonely. Three to five years of "recovery" is very common among bereaved parents, although as many point out, one never really "recovers" from such a tragedy (DeFrain, 1991).

RESOURCE SECTION E

Contraception

Methods of Contraception

Contraceptives Used in the United States

Contraceptive Methods Used Outside the United States

Making Contraceptive Decisions

In the United States, there are 3.6 million births each year. It has been estimated that half the births result from unintentional pregnancies. Among the other 50%—the intentional conceptions—many are undertaken with little planning (Insel & Roth, 1996). Although parenthood is a challenge that lasts a lifetime, it appears that the majority of pregnancies occur by accident or with little forethought.

Why are unintentional pregnancies so common in our society? In short, because effective contraception takes a good deal of planning and thought, and sex for most people simply does not. Social psychologist Donn Byrne (1983) outlines five steps involved in effective contraception. Our commentary follows each of Byrne's steps:

1. *The individual must acquire and remember accurate information about contraception.* This is no small task.

2. *The individual must acknowledge the likelihood of engaging in sexual intercourse.* Many in our society—in particular, women—receive the message that nonmarital sex is wrong. Preparing for nonmarital sex thus seems doubly wrong.

3. *The individual must obtain the contraceptive.* This involves a visit to a physician, a drugstore, or a clinic. This also involves admitting both to oneself and to others that one is planning to have sex.

4. *The individual must communicate with her or his partner about contraception.* Partners who do not communicate cannot assume the other has taken care of everything. Unfortunately, the likelihood of communication about contraception is relatively low.

5. *The individual must actually use the contraceptive method.* People sometimes resist using contraceptives because they consider some methods to be messy, interruptive, or unromantic.

Byrne's five steps make it clear that there are many barriers to effective understanding and use of contraception. It is little wonder that so many pregnancies are unplanned.

The science of **contraception**—which focuses on the prevention of conception, or pregnancy—has from its very beginnings been an embattled research area. Pressure from religious groups and politicians has impeded progress in this area in the United States.

An ideal contraceptive would be harmless, reliable, free of objectionable side effects, inexpensive, simple, reversible in effect, removed from the sexual act, and protective against sexually transmissible disease. Unfortunately, there is no ideal contraceptive.

Methods of Contraception

Methods of contraception are much the same in developed countries around the world, but some methods not approved for use in the United States are available in other countries. This section looks first at common U.S. contraceptives and then at options available in other countries.

Contraceptives Used in the United States

Birth control methods used by women and men in this county fall into six broad categories: sterilization, oral contraceptives, barrier methods, intrauterine devices (IUDs), spermicides, and Norplant implants (Elmer-DeWitt, 1990; Hatcher et al., 1994; Hyde, 1990; Insel & Roth, 1996; Kelly, 1994). Fertility awareness, a natural method of birth control, is also used by some.

Sterilization **Sterilization** is the contraceptive method of choice for 17% of U.S. women and for 11% of U.S. men (Insel & Roth, 1996). This method is used by men and women who do not wish to have children or who have had all the children they desire. The sterilization procedure for women, called **tubal ligation,** involves tying the woman's fallopian tubes to prevent passage of the ova into the uterus; the procedure is difficult to reverse. The male sterilization procedure, called **vasectomy,** involves surgically severing the vasa deferentia; it is also usually irreversible and should be considered permanent. Sterilization is a more complex procedure in women than in men. In actual practice, sterilization is typically 99.6% effective for women and 98.5% effective for men.

Oral Contraceptives **Oral contraceptives,** or birth control pills, are favored by 32% of U.S. women. Oral contraceptives are 96.3% (the minipill) to 97% (the pill) effective in preventing pregnancy in a given year. The pill, a combination oral contraceptive, contains the hormones **estrogen** and **progestin.** In addition to preventing pregnancy, the pill makes the menstrual cycle more regular, tends to reduce menstrual cramping, and is associated with lower incidences of breast and ovarian cysts and pelvic inflammatory disease (PID). Potential negative side effects of the pill include nausea, weight gain, fluid retention, breast tenderness, headaches, missed menstrual periods, acne, mood changes, depression, anxiety, fatigue, decreased sex drive, and circulatory diseases.

The minipill contains progestin only. Besides reliability, the minipill brings increased regularity to the menstrual cycle, tends to reduce menstrual cramping, and is associated with lower incidence of breast and ovarian cysts and PID.

Barrier Methods **Barrier methods of contraception,** favored by 23% of U.S. women, include condoms, diaphragms, and cervical caps. Failure rates in a given year are 12–28%.

CONDOM   Worn by the male over the penis during intercourse, a **condom,** made of latex rubber, catches semen and prevents it from entering the vagina. Condoms are available without a prescription and offer protection against sexually transmissible diseases. Although condom use is a contraceptive method a man can take responsibility for, one third of all condoms are purchased by women. Condoms can fail for a variety of reasons: breakage; not leaving a space at the tip of the condom to collect the semen; lubrication with petroleum jelly, which weakens latex; seepage of semen around the opening of the condom or the condom slipping off in the vagina after coitus; storing the condom for more than 2 years or storing it at temperature extremes; and not placing the condom on the penis at the beginning of intercourse. Some people are allergic to rubber condoms. (Other "natural" kinds are also available.) Some men complain that condoms reduce sensation on the penis. The failure rate for condoms is about 12%.

DIAPHRAGM A **diaphragm** is a dome-shaped cup of thin rubber stretched over a collapsible metal ring. The diaphragm, which must be used with a spermicidal (sperm-killing) cream or jelly, is inserted into the vagina to cover the mouth of the cervix, blocking sperm from entering the uterus. Inexpensive and reusable, a diaphragm must be fitted by a physician. Common reasons for failure of a diaphragm to prevent pregnancy include improper fitting or insertion of the diaphragm, removal of the diaphragm too soon (sooner than 6–8 hours) after intercourse, not using a sufficient amount of spermicide with the diaphragm, damage to the diaphragm, leakage around the diaphragm, or dislodging of the diaphragm. Some people are allergic to the rubber in diaphragms (plastic diaphragms are also available), and some people are allergic to spermicides. Diaphragm users also have an increased risk of toxic shock syndrome, bladder infection, or vaginal soreness caused by pressure from the rim of the diaphragm. The failure rate for diaphragms is about 18%.

CERVICAL CAP A thimble-shaped rubber or plastic cup, the **cervical cap** fits over the cervix and is held in place by suction. Like the diaphragm, it must be fitted by a clinician and is used with a spermicide; it can, however, be left in place for longer periods of time than the diaphragm. Potential problems that can result in pregnancy include improper fitting, insertion, or placement. Women using cervical caps also have a possible risk of toxic shock syndrome or of an allergic reaction to the rubber or the spermicide. Also, there is a possibility of abrasion or irritation of the vagina or cervix. The failure rate for cervical caps is about 18%.

Intrauterine Devices Most U.S. manufacturers have stopped making **intrauterine devices** (IUDs) because of the fear of costly lawsuits over their safety. Although they are still favored by 2% of women, IUDs have caused pelvic infections, some serious enough to have resulted in the death of about 21 women. Other negative side effects include uterine cramping, abnormal bleeding, and heavy menstrual flow. IUDs come in a variety of shapes. An IUD is inserted through the vagina and cervix into the uterus by a medical professional, where it remains until the woman wishes it to be removed. So that the wearer can be sure the IUD has not been expelled by the uterus, a slender string attached to the IUD protrudes through the cervical opening just far enough into the vagina so that the woman can feel it with her finger. IUD failure rates are typically about 3%, mostly resulting from expulsion of the IUD without the woman's notice. A contraceptive coil, purported to be highly effective, is being marketed in Finland. It is discussed later in this section.

Spermicides Favored by another 3% of women, **spermicides** include foams, creams, jellies, and vaginal inserts (also called vaginal suppositories). They are available without a prescription. Spermicides must be inserted with an applicator into the vagina before intercourse and are only effective for a short time. Failure rates are about 21% in any given year. Sometimes couples do to want to interrupt the sexual act to insert a spermicide. Pregnancy can also result when too little spermicide is used; if the spermicide is placed in the vagina too long before intercourse; if the woman douches within 6–8 hours after intercourse; or in the case of suppositories, if they fail to melt or foam properly. Some people are allergic to the chemicals in spermicides. Some say they taste unpleasant during oral-genital sex.

Hormone Implant   **Norplant** is the trade name of an implant that is placed under the skin on the inside of a woman's upper arm and releases the hormone progestin. It provides 99% protection from pregnancy for up to 5 years. Approved by the U.S. Food and Drug Administration in December 1990, this type of implant represents the first substantially new contraceptive method to become available in the United States in many years (Kelly, 1994). Women who cannot take birth control pills for various medical reasons are cautioned not to consider Norplant. Potential side effects include prolonged or irregular menstrual bleeding, severe headaches, vision loss, nervousness, depression, nausea, dizziness, skin rash, acne, anemia, changes in appetite, breast tenderness, weight gain, ovarian cysts, enlargement of the ovaries or fallopian tubes, and excessive growth of body and facial hair. Side effects may subside after the first year (Cohen, 1995; Goldberg, 1993).

Fertility Awareness   The various contraceptive methods known as **fertility awareness** are based on avoiding intercourse during the fertile phase of a woman's menstrual cycle. The methods differ in the way in which they identify the woman's fertile period.

The effectiveness of one fertility awareness approach, the *calendar method*, depends on careful record keeping for 12 months because few women menstruate on a regular schedule. During this period, another birth control method must be employed. The *temperature method* is based on the knowledge that a woman's body temperature drops slightly before ovulation and rises slightly after ovulation. After about 3 months of daily record keeping, a woman's temperature patterns usually become apparent. A third fertility awareness approach, the *mucus method*, is based on changes in cervical secretions throughout the menstrual cycle. Before ovulation, cervical mucus increases and is clear and slippery. During ovulation, some women can detect a slight change in the texture of the mucus, finding that it can be formed into an elastic thread that can be stretched between thumb and finger. After ovulation, cervical secretions become cloudy and sticky and decrease in quantity. One potential problem with this approach is that vaginal infections and vaginal products or medications can change the composition of the cervical mucus.

Fertility awareness methods of contraception are not recommended for women who have very irregular menstrual cycles (about 15% of all women) and for women for whom pregnancy would be a serious problem. Proponents of fertility awareness methods argue that they are about 90% effective. In practice, however, an estimated 20% of women using these methods become pregnant in any given year.

Ineffective Methods   **Withdrawal** of the penis before ejaculation is a highly un-reliable way to prevent pregnancy. An estimated 18% of women whose partners use this approach will become pregnant in any given year.

Douching—flushing the vagina with some type of liquid—is also an ineffective birth control method. Although it is true that some acidic solutions will kill sperm, it can take sperm only a minute to reach the cervical mucus; once there, they move freely into the uterus, where no douching solution can reach them. The douche itself, in fact, may even push some sperm into the uterus.

Contraceptive Methods Used Outside the United States

Of the nine major firms conducting contraceptive research in the early 1970s in the United States, only one is still doing so today. One reason is that the U.S. Food and Drug Administration can be very slow and cautious in deciding whether new drugs are safe. It can take up to 15 years and $50 million to develop a contraceptive and gain approval for its use in the United States. Conservative opposition to contraception also slows the process (Elmer-DeWitt, 1990; Salholz, 1990).

The following birth control methods are used abroad but are not widely available in the United States:

- **Noristerat,** a 2-month injectable contraceptive that has a 2% failure rate, is approved for use in more than 40 countries.

- **RU-486** is a pill that induces menstruation in a woman whose period is up to 6 weeks late. Opponents of this French-made drug call it an abortion pill. Supporters argue that it is highly effective in dealing with unwanted pregnancies. Because RU-486 induces menses, it is considered an **abortifacient** (an agent that produces abortion) and therefore will be discussed more thoroughly in Resource Section F.

- The **Filshie clip,** a titanium-and-silicone clip that blocks the fallopian tubes without cutting or cauterizing them, has the effect of a tubal ligation but is reversible.

- The **contraceptive coil** is a device that is placed in the uterus and releases synthetic hormones that prevent fertilization. Finnish researchers have documented its effectiveness. The coil is not recommended for young women or for women who have never given birth because these women tend to have ectopic (tubal) pregnancies when using the coil (Elmer-DeWitt, 1990).

The absence of new contraceptive alternatives in the United States has contributed to the abortion rate in this country, which averages about 1.6 million per year. Some authorities estimate that half of all abortions could be prevented by simply developing more options (Elmer-DeWitt, 1990). Many opponents of birth control argue that abstinence is the key to the problem because it is 100% effective in preventing conception.

Making Contraceptive Decisions

In making rational choices about contraceptive methods, individuals and couples should take into account several considerations. First, people need to consider the health risks of each method in terms of personal and family medical history. IUDs are not recommended for young women without children, for example, because they increase the risk of pelvic infection and possible infertility. Oral contraceptives should be used only after an evaluation of a woman's medical history.

Individuals must ask themselves, how important is it to me to avoid pregnancy at this point in life? Oral contraceptives offer by far the best protection against pregnancy, but there are some risks associated with them. Condoms, diaphragms, and cervical caps have fewer related health problems than oral contraceptives, but the risk of pregnancy is greater with these methods. To maximize their effectiveness, they need to be used in combination with a spermicide and used every time a couple has intercourse.

Condom use, preferably with a spermicide, is critically important if there is any possibility of the presence of a sexually transmissible disease. Condoms are especially important for those who are not in an exclusive, long-term relationship. They are also useful for women taking oral contraceptives, because cervical changes that occur during hormone use can increase the likelihood of contracting certain diseases.

Both partners should consider convenience and comfort. Oral contraceptives rank high in both regards, although, again, the possible negative side effects and health risks of the pill need to be factored into the equation. If a woman has difficulty remembering to take her pills, another method might be better.

The type of relationship one is involved in should also be considered. Barrier methods require more motivation than the pill because they generally must be used at or close to the time of intercourse. Both partners must have a well-developed sense of responsibility to ensure the success of these methods. Barrier methods often require cooperation between partners. If one has sexual intercourse only infrequently, barrier methods may make more sense than oral contraceptives.

The ease and cost of obtaining and continuing each method also need to be considered. Oral contraceptives require an annual pelvic exam and periodic medical checkups. Pills are also more expensive than barrier methods. Diaphragms and cervical caps require an initial examination and fitting. Norplant requires implantation by a physician.

Finally, religious and philosophical beliefs should be taken into consideration. Abstinence is the only acceptable approach for some individuals before marriage.

For those who wish to make responsible contraceptive choices, it is important to discuss the options with competent professionals. Both men and women should be knowledgeable in this very important subject area.

RESOURCE SECTION F

Abortion

Abortion Laws

Abortion Procedures

RU-486

Vacuum Curettage

Dilation and Curettage

Induced Labor

Hysterotomy

Methotrexate and Misoprostol

Other Methods

**Physical and Emotional Aspects
of Abortion**

Men and Abortion

Decision Making and Unintended Pregnancy

Preventing Abortion

It has been estimated that approximately one third of all pregnancies in the United States are terminated by abortion (Henshaw, 1990). Nearly 1.6 million abortions are performed each year in this country, 56% on women 24 years of age or younger. About 70% of all the abortions are performed on white women, and 81% on unmarried women (Henshaw, 1987). Of the 1.2 million adolescents who become pregnant each year in this country, 400,000 choose to have an abortion (Kelly, 1994).

Strictly defined, **abortion** is the expulsion of a fetus from the uterus before the fetus has developed sufficiently to survive outside the mother (before viability). In common usage, abortion refers only to artificially induced expulsions, those caused by mechanical means or drugs. Spontaneous abortions, those that occur naturally and are not induced by mechanical means or drugs, are commonly called *miscarriages* (Insel & Roth, 1996).

Abortion Laws

For more than two centuries in early U.S. history (from the 1600s to the early 1900s), abortion was not a crime if it was performed before "quickening" (fetal movement, which begins at approximately 20 weeks). U.S. abortion laws followed English common law during this period. An antiabortion movement began in the early 1800s. It was led by physicians who argued against the validity of the concept of quickening and who opposed untrained people who performed abortions and threatened physician control of medical services. The controversy over abortion attracted minimal attention until the mid-1800s, when newspapers began advertising abortion preparations. Opponents of such medicines argued that women were using them as birth control measures and that women could also hide extramarital affairs through their use. The medicines were seen by some as evidence that immorality and corruption threatened America. By the early 1900s, virtually all states (at the urging of male politicians; women could not vote at the time) had passed antiabortion laws (Insel & Roth, 1996).

Social pressure for the legalization of abortion built in the 1960s. Despite laws against abortion, many illegal abortions were being performed. Women sometimes died due to nonsterile or medically inadequate procedures (Cox, 1990). During this period, courts began to invalidate many of the state laws on the grounds of constitutional vagueness and violation of the right to privacy (Francoeur, 1982; Insel & Roth, 1996).

In the 1973 landmark case *Roe* v. *Wade*, the U.S. Supreme Court made abortion legal by denying the states the right to regulate early abortions. The high court replaced the restrictions most states still imposed at that time with new standards governing abortion decisions. The court conceptualized pregnancy in three parts (trimesters) and gave pregnant women more options in regard to abortion in the first trimester (3 months) than in the second or third trimester. The court ruled that during the first trimester the abortion decision must be left to the judgment of the woman and her physician. The court ruled that during the second trimester, the right to abortion remains, but that a state could regulate certain factors in an effort to protect the health of the woman, such as the type of facility in which an abortion could be performed. The Supreme Court ruled that during the third trimester, the period of pregnancy in which the fetus is viable outside the uterus, a state could regulate and even ban all abortions except in situations in which they are necessary to preserve the mother's life or health (Francoeur, 1982; Hyde, 1990; Insel & Roth, 1996). In addition, in 1976 the Supreme Court decided in *Planned Parenthood* v. *Danforth* that neither the parents of a minor nor the husband of a woman has the right to veto a woman's decision to have an abortion (Francoeur, 1982).

Research indicates that babies born at or before 24 weeks rarely survive, that babies born at 25–26 weeks have a 50% chance of survival, and that a baby's chance of survival increases to 90% at 30 weeks ("Abortion Foes Vow," 1991).

After the Supreme Court's 1973 decision, the number of abortions performed each year rose steadily. The decision did not end the controversy over abortion, however, but in many ways seemed to intensify it (Francoeur, 1982; Insel & Roth, 1996).

Campaigns were begun on the national, state, and local levels by many groups around the country hoping to overturn the decision and restore the ban on abortion. Some favored amending the U.S. Constitution; others worked to weaken the decision by chipping away at its edges in a variety of ways. The Supreme Court, hearing arguments against abortion nearly every year, continued to uphold its 1973 decision. In the original decision the court had voted 7 to 2 in favor of legalizing abortion; by the mid-1980s conservative appointments to the high court had cut the abortion rights majority on the court to an unpredictable 5-to-4 margin (Insel & Roth, 1996).

The controversy boiled over in July 1989, when the Supreme Court handed down its decision in the case of *Webster* v. *Reproductive Health Services*. Although the court did not overturn *Roe* v. *Wade*, it permitted several key abortion restrictions enacted by the Missouri state legislature in 1986 to stand. Two of the most important restrictions to pro-choice advocates upheld in *Webster* v. *Reproductive Health Services* were prohibition of the use of all public facilities, resources, and employees for abortion services and the requirement for costly and time-consuming tests to determine fetal viability if a physician estimated the fetus to be 20 weeks or older.

In the 1989 decision, the majority of the Supreme Court justices also rejected *Roe*'s framework of trimesters, which had been an attempt by the justices in 1973 to balance women's rights and fetal rights. The 1989 decision did not, however, replace the trimester framework with any other standard for balancing these rights. The justices declined to address the preamble of the Missouri law, which stated that "the life of each human being begins at conception," arguing that this was only a "value judgment" and that this value judgment did not "regulate abortion" (Insel & Roth, 1996).

In 1992 tensions mounted again as the nation awaited a Supreme Court decision on *Planned Parenthood* v. *Casey*. Pro-choice activists feared the high court would overturn *Roe* v. *Wade* and make abortion an issue for state regulation. But in a narrow 5-4 decision in early July, the Supreme Court once more upheld the spirit of *Roe* v. *Wade* but once again restricted its reach. States were now free to restrict abortion as long as the restrictions did not place an "undue burden" on women. The Supreme Court held that the state of Pennsylvania could impose a 24-hour waiting period before an abortion, could require doctors to tell women about other options beside abortion, could require women to sign an "informed consent" form before the procedure, could mandate parental notification for minors, and could make doctors provide statistical information about patients. However, the Court also held that the state of Pennsylvania could not force a woman to tell her husband that she was having an abortion (Clift, 1992).

Pro-choice forces expressed some relief after the inauguration of President Clinton in 1993, hoping that the retirement of conservative Supreme Court justices would give Clinton the opportunity to appoint more liberal justices who would vigorously defend abortion rights. The battle for and against abortion rights is now fought on a state-by-state basis. National pro-life groups continue to seek legislation that would make abortion a federal crime; pro-choice groups work to ensure a woman's right to an abortion if she so chooses. Although the outcome of the abortion controversy is unclear, it is unlikely that either side will give up the fight.

Abortion Procedures

About 90% of the abortions in the United States are performed within the first trimester (Kelly, 1994). The type of procedure used generally depends on how far along a woman is in her pregnancy. A variety of abortion procedures are explained below, beginning with those used early in pregnancy and concluding with those employed later in pregnancy.

RU-486

Originally **RU-486** was referred to as a morning-after pill, to be taken after unprotected sexual relations and acting before implantation of the fertilized egg. In actuality, RU-486 can be taken by the 49th day following the last menstrual period and is thus an abortifacient. RU-486 blocks uterine absorption of the hormone progesterone, causing the uterine lining and any fertilized egg to shed. Combined with another drug and under medical supervision, RU-486 has fewer health risks than surgical abortion and is effective 95% of the time. RU-486 is currently being legally marketed or tested in France, China, England, India, Sweden, and the United States (Insel & Roth, 1996; Kelly, 1994).

Both pro-choice activists and pro-life activists see RU-486 as a possible revolutionary development in the abortion controversy. If abortion could be induced simply, safely, effectively, and privately, the nature of the controversy surrounding abortion would change dramatically. Clinics that perform abortions are regularly picketed by antiabortion protesters, making the experience of obtaining a legal abortion difficult for many women. If RU-486 becomes a legal, widely available option for women in the United States, abortion will in essence have become an almost invisible, personal, and relatively private act. RU-486, thus, has great possibilities in the minds of pro-choice activists. Foes of abortion have marshalled their forces in an effort to counter the use of this drug.

Vacuum Curettage

Also called vacuum suction or vacuum aspiration, **vacuum curettage** is a method of abortion that is performed during the first trimester of pregnancy, up to 12 weeks from the beginning of the last menstrual period. It is the most common abortion procedure used during the first trimester in the United States. Vacuum curettage is performed on an outpatient basis using a local or a general anesthetic. It takes about 10–15 minutes, although the woman stays in the doctor's office, clinic, or hospital for a few hours afterward.

Medical professionals prepare the woman for the procedure in a manner similar to preparation for a pelvic examination. An instrument is then inserted into the vagina to dilate the opening of the cervix. The end of a nonflexible tube connected to a suction-producing apparatus is inserted through the cervix into the uterus. The contents of the uterus, including fetal tissue, are then sucked out.

Vacuum curettage is the most common method of early abortion in the United States for two reasons: it is simple, and complications are rare and usually minor. There is a risk of uterine perforation; infection, with fever and chills; hemorrhaging; unsuccessful abortion, in which the fetus continues to grow; and failure to remove all the fetal material. Complications are most likely when the procedure is performed by an unqualified person who lacks professional training. Infection may occur if the woman fails to follow aftercare instructions (Kelly, 1994).

Dilation and Curettage

Dilation and curettage (D & C) is similar to vacuum curettage but must be performed in a hospital under general anesthetic. It is performed at 8–20 weeks after the last menstrual period. By the beginning of the second trimester, the uterus has enlarged and its walls have become thinner. The contents of the uterus cannot be as easily removed by suction, and therefore the D & C procedure is used.

In a D & C, the cervix is dilated and a sharp metal loop attached to the end of a long handle (the curette) is inserted into the uterus and used to scrape out the uterine contents. D & Cs are also performed to treat infertility and menstrual problems.

Vacuum curettage is seen as preferable to a D & C because the former is done on an outpatient basis, eliminating the expense of hospitalization and the risk involved in the use of general anesthetics. A D & C also causes more discomfort than vacuum curettage, and the risks of uterine perforation, infection, and hemorrhaging are greater.

Dilation and evacuation (D & E) is a related procedure used at 13–16 weeks after the last menstrual period. D & E is similar to both a D & C and vacuum curettage, but it is a bit more complicated. It is performed in a hospital or at a clinic (Kelly, 1994).

Induced Labor

Induced labor is a method of abortion performed late in the second trimester, generally in a hospital. In *saline-induced abortion*, the most common type of induced labor, a fine tube is inserted through the abdomen into the amniotic sac, and some amniotic fluid is removed. An equal amount of saline solution is then injected through the tube, causing labor and miscarriage to occur in a few hours. In *prostaglandin-induced abortion*, hormone-like substances called prostaglandins are injected into the amniotic sac, injected intravenously, or inserted by means of vaginal suppository with similar results.

Induced labor is the most common method of abortion for those pregnancies that have progressed late into the second trimester. Induced labor is both more costly and more hazardous than the methods explained earlier. Although serious complications are rare, they can occur. If the technique is done carelessly, saline solution can enter a blood vessel, inducing shock and possibly death. Also, a blood disorder is a possible, although rare, complication from induced labor.

Prostaglandin-induced abortion is preferable to saline-induced abortion because labor begins more quickly and is shorter. But saline-induced abortions do have advantages over prostaglandin-induced abortions: less risk of excessive bleeding, less risk of a retained placenta, less risk of a torn cervix as a result of too-rapid dilation, and less risk of the delivery of a live although nonviable fetus. Nausea, vomiting, and diarrhea are also more common with the prostaglandin method (Hyde, 1990).

Induced labor is physically more uncomfortable than the methods of abortion used earlier in pregnancy. Induced labor is also often more emotionally upsetting for the woman, because she experiences contractions for several hours and then expels a lifeless fetus (Kelly, 1994).

Hysterotomy

A surgical method of abortion, **hysterotomy** is performed at 16–24 weeks after the last menstrual period. A cesarean section is performed, and the fetus is removed. Hysterotomies are relatively rare, but they are useful if the pregnancy has progressed to the late second trimester and the woman's health leads physicians to conclude that neither of the induction methods is appropriate (Hyde, 1990).

Methotrexate and Misoprostol

The number of obstetricians, gynecologists, and hospitals performing abortions has been dropping steadily, but that trend could change as doctors adopt a non-surgical alternative that uses prescription drugs already marketed for other purposes (Brody, 1995; Raeburn, 1995). A study published in the *New England Journal of Medicine* reported that a two-drug combination, **methotrexate and misoprostol,** was effective in inducing abortions at home (Hausknecht, 1995).

The researcher, Dr. Richard U. Hausknecht of the Mount Sinai School of Medicine in New York, said he believes many doctors have already started to prescribe the drugs, and he predicts others will do so in the future. The advantage to doctors is that they can simply tell patients the procedure is available and begin performing abortions without putting "a sign out front." Hausknecht explained that because doctors can do this "very quietly," it is likely to lessen the threats and violence against them by some abortion foes (Raeburn, 1995).

Hausknecht worked with 178 healthy women seeking abortion within the first 63 days of pregnancy. The women received an injection of methotrexate; a week later this was followed by either an oral tablet or a vaginal suppository of misoprostol. If an abortion did not occur after 7 days, the women were given another intravaginal dose of misoprostol. Overall, 171 of the 178 woman had successful abortions after the first or second dose of misoprostol. Seven women needed suction to complete the abortion. None of the women required a blood transfusion, although side effects included swelling of the mouth, brief diarrhea, and nausea. Most women rated their pain at less than 2 on a scale of 0 (low) to 4 (high). The women found this method preferable to surgical abortion (Hausknecht, 1995). Many observers believe this new method of abortion will stir a good deal of further controversy because it can be performed unobtrusively (Brody, 1995; Raeburn, 1995).

Other Methods

There are several other methods of abortion, but they are not widely used in the United States. In Japan, a variety of mechanical methods of stimulating the uterus to induce abortion are used. Though simple and inexpensive to perform, these methods are associated with greater loss of blood and higher risk of infection.

Early abortion, similar to vacuum curettage, is performed as soon as a positive pregnancy test is received, up to 8 weeks after the last menstrual period. A flexible tube is inserted through the cervix without dilating it, and the contents of the uterus are sucked out. This procedure can be performed without an anesthetic. **Menstrual regulation** (also called *endometrial aspiration, preemptive abortion,* and *menstruation extraction*) is similar to early abortion, but the contents of the uterus are sucked out before the woman's menstrual period is due. She then does not know if she was pregnant or not. The procedure takes 2–10 minutes and is simple, inexpensive, and safe (Hyde, 1990).

Physical and Emotional Aspects of Abortion

The chance of dying as a result of a legal abortion in the United States is far lower than the chance of dying during childbirth. Less than one in 100,000 abortions results in the death of a relatively healthy woman. Nearly 20 women die for each 100,000 pregnancies and births (Insel & Roth, 1996).

Infection is a possibility after an abortion, however. Women are advised to consult their physician if they have an elevated temperature, experience severe lower abdominal cramps or pain, experience heavy bleeding (heavier than their normal menstrual period), or if their menstrual period does not begin within 8 weeks after the abortion. Women are also advised to follow directions for prescriptions faithfully, avoid strenuous physical activity, rest as much as possible for several days, and avoid sexual intercourse for 2–3 weeks following an abortion (Boston Women's Health Book Collective, 1992).

Some women experience feelings of guilt after an abortion; others feel great relief that they are no longer pregnant. Still other women are ambivalent: happy not to be pregnant but sad about the abortion. Some of the emotional "highs" and "lows" may be related to hormonal adjustments and cease after the woman's hormone levels return to normal. The intensity of feelings associated with an abortion generally diminishes as time passes, but some women experience anger, frustration, and/or guilt for many years after an abortion (Boston Women's Health Book Collective, 1992; Hyde, 1990; Kelly, 1994).

Those experiencing severe, negative psychological reactions to abortion are rare, according to a review of research findings by a panel commissioned by the American Psychological Association (Adler, David, Major, Roth, Russo, & Wyatt, 1992; Landers, 1989b). The psychologists concluded that there is no such thing as "post-abortion syndrome." They also noted that it is important to keep in mind that "the question is not simply whether abortion has some harmful psychological effects, but whether those effects are demonstrably worse than the psychological consequences of unwanted childbirth" (Landers, 1989a). The investigators argued that abortion is not likely to be followed by severe psychological response but is best understood "within a framework of normal stress and coping rather than a model of psychopathology" (Adler et al. 1992, p. 1194). Many women find it helpful to talk about their experience with sympathetic family members, friends, and professional counselors.

Men and Abortion

Sociologist Arthur Shostak surveyed 1,000 male "abortion veterans" in an effort to identify the effects of abortion on men. Feelings of helplessness were the most common reaction men reported. Most of the men also reported feeling isolated, angry at themselves and their partners, and fearful of emotional and physical damage to the woman. Most of the men tried to hide their stress and to remain outwardly unemotional. Twenty-six percent of the men thought abortion was murder; 81% wondered about what the child would have been like if it had been born. Few of the men reported wanting to be able to overrule the woman's decision, although many wanted to be a part of the decision-making process. Shostak concluded that counseling should be available for male "abortion veterans" (Allgeier & Allgeier, 1995).

Decision Making and Unintended Pregnancy

When one suspects an unintended pregnancy, it is wise first to confirm the pregnancy through a formal laboratory test. A physical examination by a physician will help to establish how long the woman has been pregnant. After pregnancy has been conclusively established, options can be weighed carefully: carrying the child to term and keeping it, carrying the child to term and relinquishing it for adoption, or abortion. This is a decision that can have great effects on an individual's life. It is usually wise to talk with a few people one respects and trusts and who can remain calm and objective during the discussion (Kelly, 1994).

Married couples commonly choose to keep an unplanned baby, though abortion remains an option for many married women, especially those who feel they already have as many children as they can care for properly. Couples who are not married may choose to get married, although many authorities believe that pregnancy is not by itself a sufficient reason for marriage. Some young parents receive help rearing their babies from their own parents and other relatives while they complete their educations and become more capable of assuming parental responsibilities. However, grandparents are often less than excited about becoming "parents" once again.

Currently it is difficult for adoption agencies to find babies for all the couples who wish to adopt. The high rate of abortion has contributed to this situation, along with society's generally negative attitude toward relinquishing babies for adoption. Social attitudes are reflected in the terminology "giving up the child" for adoption. The majority of adolescent mothers who carry their babies to term thus choose to keep them, despite the difficulties young mothers face in this situation. Adoption is seen as a viable alternative by many people, however. Some agencies are making an effort to ease the pain young mothers may feel by allowing them to have continued contact with the child and its adoptive parents.

Many people have strong feelings about the dilemma of unintended pregnancy and are eager to influence the decision in one direction or another. The individual or couple experiencing the dilemma, however, carry the responsibility for the decision. Whatever the decision, an unintended pregnancy is usually a very lonely and stressful time in a woman's life.

Preventing Abortion

The Planned Parenthood Federation of America argues that reducing the number of unintended pregnancies in this country will reduce the number of abortions. Using this line of thought, Planned Parenthood (1985) advocates the following ways to prevent abortion:

- *Make contraceptives more easily available.* Every public dollar spent on family planning saves at least two tax dollars in the next year alone in reduced health and welfare services associated with unintended births.

- *Provide young people with a better teacher than experience.* Support sex education programs instead of hoping that sex will disappear if no one talks about it.

- *Increase the involvement of men.* No woman ever made herself pregnant. Help men recognize equal responsibility in all aspects of sexuality, including obtaining and using contraception.

- *Develop new birth control methods that are temporary, safe, effective, easy to use, and without side effects.* Increase government support for research in this area.

- *Make America friendlier to children.* Research by the Alan Guttmacher Institute indicates that the United States is the only developed country in which teen pregnancy is increasing. Countries with lower rates were found to be more realistic about and accepting of sexuality and to have open access to family planning services.

RESOURCE SECTION G

Sexually Transmissible Diseases

All **sexually transmissible diseases (STDs)** are spread by sexual contact, but some STDs can also be transmitted by other means. There are seven major sexually transmissible diseases: HIV infection, which leads to AIDS; syphilis; gonorrhea; chlamydia; genital herpes (caused by the herpes simplex virus); genital warts (caused by the human papilloma virus); and viral hepatitis. There are also a few other sexually transmissible diseases that are far less serious than the seven just listed; they will not be discussed in this text.

One out of every four Americans may contract an STD in her or his lifetime. Women are the most vulnerable. Two thirds of the 12 million STD cases in the United States each year are among people under age 25 (Centers for Disease Control and Prevention, 1994; Hatcher et al., 1994).

An STD is said to be a "major" disease if on its own it produces serious consequences for the person affected and/or for others, if it causes serious complications if left untreated, and/or if it poses risks to a fetus or a newborn baby. Pelvic inflammatory disease, a common complication of gonorrhea and chlamydia, will also be discussed.

HIV Infection and AIDS

Acquired immune deficiency syndrome (AIDS) is a fatal condition affecting the immune system, the body's natural defense against disease. An otherwise healthy person who has AIDS becomes susceptible to a variety of infections, cancers, and neurological disorders. The condition is caused by a virus called the **human immunodeficiency virus (HIV)** (Hyde, 1990; Insel & Roth, 1996; Kelly, 1994).

A cure for AIDS has not been found, but a number of drugs have been developed that slow the advance of the virus (Insel & Roth, 1996). After a person is infected with HIV, the risk of developing symptoms and eventually AIDS increases with the passage of time. But carrying HIV—being HIV-positive—does not mean one has AIDS. Research indicates that even after 10 years, some people remain free of AIDS symptoms (Kelly, 1994; Lambert, 1990).

HIV lives only within cells and body fluids. The body fluids most commonly involved in the transmission of HIV are blood and blood products (such as plasma), semen, and vaginal secretions (Jackson, 1992). HIV does not live outside the body. It does not live in the air, in swimming pools, on toilet seats, in food, or on objects like knives, forks, or glasses. HIV has been found in saliva, tears, urine, and feces, but there is no direct evidence that the virus has been transmitted through any of these body substances (Jackson, 1992). HIV can, however, be transmitted by people who are infected but who have not developed any symptoms (Kelly, 1994). In essence, people can transmit HIV to others without knowing they are infected themselves.

Transmission most often occurs through sexual activity, when the virus enters the bloodstream by passing through vaginal or rectal membranes, especially if these membranes have been torn during sexual activity. Transmission can also occur through the sharing of needles by injection drug users. If needles or syringes are contaminated with traces of blood, the virus can be transmitted directly into the bloodstream.

All licensed blood banks and plasma centers in the United States are now required to screen for HIV antibodies, to prevent transmission of the virus to those who receive blood. Hemophiliacs who test positive for HIV were probably infected by blood they received before testing began. Individuals who received blood transfusions between 1977 and 1985 and who develop HIV were also probably infected in that way (Insel & Roth, 1996).

HIV first appeared in the United States in 1981. Because the virus has a long **incubation period,** the time during which the virus is multiplying in the body but does not cause any symptoms, people diagnosed with HIV in the early 1980s had actually been infected many years before. By the time there was widespread public awareness of the disease, it was too late for thousands of individuals.

HIV infection is one of the most serious and challenging problems the United States and the world face today. By the year 2000, HIV infection could become the largest epidemic of the 20th century, surpassing the 1918 influenza epidemic that killed 20 million people. The disease continues to spread, and a cure has not been found, in spite of intensive efforts by health professionals worldwide. More than 250,000 Americans had been diagnosed with AIDS by the end of 1992, and more than a million were believed to be infected with HIV. Around the world, it has been estimated that 2 million people have AIDS; and by the turn of the century, 40–120 million people are likely to be HIV-positive (Insel & Roth, 1996).

People with HIV have been identified all over the United States. In the United States, the largest group of HIV-positive people (64%) is homosexual and bisexual males, followed by injection drug users, people who received contaminated blood or blood products between 1977 and 1985, the sex partners of people infected with HIV, children of infected mothers, and a few people with no apparent risk factors. Ninety percent of all HIV cases are male; 10% are female. Early fears that the virus would quickly spread into the non-drug-abusing heterosexual population have not yet been realized, but there is some evidence that this could still occur (Insel & Roth, 1996).

Signs and symptoms associated with HIV infection include unexplained and persistently swollen glands, drenching night sweats, fever, chills, the loss of more than 10 pounds in 2 months (unrelated to illness, dieting, or increased physical activity), and immobilizing fatigue. Some of these symptoms, of course, are also associated with a cold or the flu.

Because HIV weakens the immune system, people with HIV are highly susceptible to both common and uncommon infections. **Pneumocystis carinii pneumonia (PCP),** a protozoan infection, is the largest single cause of death in people with AIDS. **Kaposi's sarcoma,** a rare form of cancer, is the second most common problem. Purple or brownish lesions resembling bruises occur anywhere on the skin and/or inside the mouth, nose, or rectum. The lesions are painless, but they do not heal. HIV infection may also invade the brain, causing progressive neurological disease. People with AIDS have also been diagnosed with unexplained mental deterioration and meningitis (Insel & Roth, 1996; Kelly, 1994).

The most reliable diagnosis of HIV infection is made by detecting the virus in human tissues through laboratory tissue culture procedures. These laboratory techniques are costly and are not available everywhere, so for public health purposes and the screening of blood donations, the HIV antibody test is used instead. A blood sample is drawn from an individual's arm and analyzed to determine whether HIV antibodies are present in the individual's bloodstream; the antibodies are a sign that HIV itself is present in the body. If an individual tests positive for HIV antibodies repeatedly and if this tentative diagnosis is confirmed by follow-up tests, the person is considered to be both infected with HIV and infectious to others (Insel & Roth, 1996).

High-risk sexual behaviors include the following:

- Casual sex with multiple partners who might carry HIV.

- Anal intercourse, with or without a condom, with someone who might carry HIV.

- Vaginal or oral sex without a condom, with someone who might carry HIV.

- Sharing drug needles and syringes. (Insel & Roth, 1996)

HIV and College Students

Many people think of HIV infection as something that happens to somebody else. A survey of 350 students at Syracuse University underscored this point. The researchers (Caron, Bertran, & McMullen, 1987) found that:

- Most students lack knowledge and factual data about HIV.

- Most students fail to see any relevance between ongoing media stories about the growing incidence of HIV and their personal behavior.

- The level of denial among students is high. Although most students agreed that everyone should be concerned about the possibility of contracting HIV, most indicated that they, personally, were not concerned. Some students reported that they were able to "know" which prospective sex partners were "safe." Some students even thought they somehow were personally immune to HIV.

- Students are generally not prepared to deal pragmatically in their relationships with the threat of HIV. Although they could talk with interviewers about the subject, many students found it difficult to talk with their intimate partners about HIV, other STDs, or condoms. Many students reported having had unprotected sex, and "safer sex" was often equated with "not-fun" sex. A few students were unsure of how to bring these delicate subjects up with a partner.

- Some students reported that HIV was changing social attitudes regarding sexual behavior. The "one-night stand" is apparently losing its appeal for some. Some women had become more interested in "virgins," expressing fear of the "guy who has been around" or "the womanizer." Some men also expressed interest in a less experienced partner, but men have traditionally held this view.

Another study conducted by researchers at Brown University also demonstrated that college students have yet to take the HIV crisis in this nation very seriously ("College Sex Habits," 1990). The researchers compared samples of data collected from Brown students in 1975, 1986, and 1989. They found that the use of condoms did increase over the period studied: 12% of the women in 1975 said their partners always used condoms; 21% said this was the case in 1986; and 41%, in 1989. The number of sex partners the women reported having had during their lives did not change significantly from 1975 to 1989, however, nor did the frequency of high-risk sexual behavior. For the most part, students still seemed relatively nonchalant about risky sexual behavior.

Other STDs

This section discusses other major STDs: syphilis, gonorrhea, chlamydia, genital herpes, genital warts, and viral hepatitis.

Syphilis

Syphilis is a bacterial infection that can cause blindness and death. It was once prevalent among gay men, but precautions they have taken to prevent HIV infection have helped combat syphilis as well. This sexually transmissible infection is still common in inner-city areas among crack cocaine addicts (Insel & Roth, 1996). The disease is characterized by sores or lesions known as chancres, which are painless but contain high numbers of bacteria. The chancres usually appear on the genitals, although they can also occur on the mouth, anal area or rectum, fingers, breasts, and inner vaginal wall or cervix. If the disease is not treated, a person can be contagious for up to 18 months. Antibiotics (penicillin, tetracycline, and erythromycin) are effective drugs in treating syphilis, although prevention is the wisest approach (Hyde, 1990; Insel & Roth, 1996; Kelly, 1994; Masters et al., 1992).

Gonorrhea

Gonorrhea, also known as "drip" or "the clap," is a bacterial infection. In men the onset of symptoms usually occurs soon after infection. Symptoms include burning and itching sensations in the urethra, especially during urination, and a thick, pus-like discharge from the urethra, which often shows up on underwear. Although up to 80% of women do not detect gonorrhea in its early stages, the most typical early symptom in women is a greenish or yellowish discharge from the cervical area, accompanied by some vaginal irritation. If gonorrhea is not treated in its early stages, its early symptoms usually disappear on their own, but the bacteria often move on to other organs, where they cause even more serious infections and complications.

Untreated gonorrhea can cause **pelvic inflammatory disease (PID)** in women and **epididymitis,** inflammation of the testicles, in men, either of which can lead to sterility. Gonorrhea can also cause dermatitis, an inflammation of the skin, and a type of arthritis. Babies born to infected mothers can contract gonococcal conjunctivitis, an eye infection that can lead to blindness, as they pass through the birth canal. Diagnosed early, gonorrhea can be treated with penicillin or tetracycline (Hyde, 1990; Insel & Roth, 1996; Kelly, 1994; Masters et al., 1992).

Chlamydia

The bacterial infection **chlamydia** can be particularly insidious because it frequently has no initial symptoms. Serious complications may develop before the infected individual is alerted to the presence of the disease. The Centers for Disease Control and Prevention estimate that there are about 4 million chlamydial infections each year in this country, though some researchers believe the actual number may be closer to 10 million. Symptoms in males include a burning sensation during urination and discharge of pus from the penis; the testicles may also swell and cause discomfort. Early symptoms for females are often mild but can include itching or burning feelings on the vulva, some discharge, and irritation during urination. Later-stage symptoms, all associated with pelvic inflammatory disease, include fever, nausea, abdominal pain, and abnormal patterns of menstruation.

An estimated 45% of sexually active adolescents become infected with chlamydia, and chlamydia infection causes up to 50% of all pelvic inflammatory disease cases. Chlamydia can result in abnormal pregnancies and infertility in women and in problems for newborn babies that include conjunctivitis (which can lead to blindness) and chlamydial pneumonia. Once diagnosed, chlamydia can be treated with certain antibiotics (tetracycline, doxycycline, or erythromycin); the antibiotic penicillin is not effective against it (Cronin & Leviton, 1989; Hyde, 1990; Insel & Roth, 1996; Kelly, 1994; Masters et al., 1992).

Genital Herpes

Although incurable, **genital herpes** is not deadly to adults. It is an infection caused by the herpes simplex virus. Perhaps 20% of sexually active men and women are infected with the virus, but most cases are not reported. The virus lies dormant in the nervous system, and then periodically becomes active, causing painful genital sores. The appearances of the herpes blisters seem related to periods when the individual's resistance is weakened by other illnesses, stress, exhaustion, or inadequate nutrition.

Although there is no cure for herpes, treatments are available that relieve the pain, itching, and burning of the lesions, help prevent secondary infection of the lesions, and prevent the spread of the infection to other parts of the body. The effectiveness of the drug acyclovir in treating genital herpes varies from one individual to another (Cronin & Leviton, 1989; Hyde, 1990; Insel & Roth, 1996; Kelly, 1994; Masters et al., 1992).

Genital Warts

Tiny growths on the sexual organs of men and women, **genital warts** are caused by the human papilloma virus (HPV). They are very contagious, making HPV the most common viral STD in the United States. Women with genital warts apparently have a higher risk of cervical cancer. The warts appear on the penis, vulva, anal area, or urethra. Growth in the urethra can result in difficulty in urinating and can lead to other infections as well. Physicians have a variety of treatment options available. Podophyllin, a toxic agent, can be applied with care directly to the warts. Other approaches include removal by electrocautery, cryosurgery (freezing), surgery, and laser therapy. A drug called alpha-interferon can be injected directly into the lesion and apparently cures the infection, although long-term effects of the treatment are still being assessed (Cronin & Leviton, 1989; Hyde, 1990; Insel & Roth, 1996; Kelly, 1994; Masters et al., 1992).

Viral Hepatitis

Two viruses can cause the liver infection known as **viral hepatitis.** Hepatitis A virus usually enters the body in food contaminated with fecal material and is not generally considered to be an STD. Hepatitis B virus is more common than type A and is frequently transmitted through contaminated food or the sharing of needles during injection drug use. The hepatitis B virus is most likely to be transmitted sexually, however, because it is found in saliva, semen, vaginal secretions, and blood; anal and oral-anal sex are common methods of transmission (Francis et al., 1984; Hyde, 1990; Kelly, 1994; Masters et al., 1992).

People infected with hepatitis may have no symptoms at all or may have complications serious enough to be fatal. Hepatitis A is typically a milder infection than is the B form. Typical symptoms of both viruses include loss of appetite, lethargy, headache, joint achiness, nausea, vomiting, diarrhea, yellowing of the skin (jaundice), darkening of the urine, and some enlargement of the liver. Because hepatitis is a viral infection, there is currently no treatment for it; some medications can provide relief from the symptoms. Hospitalization is usually unnecessary. Bed rest and heavy fluid intake are usually required while the body's immune system gradually conquers the disease. In severe cases, recovery can take several months (Kelly, 1994; Masters et al., 1992; Zuckerman, 1982). A safe and effective vaccination against Hepatitis B is available (Hyde, 1990).

Preventing the Spread of STDs

People who are sexually active can take several proactive measures to reduce their chances of contracting an STD (Allgeier & Allgeier, 1995; Davis & Scott, 1988; Hyde, 1990; Masters et al., 1992):

- Prospective partners should share their medical histories honestly with each other, including the date and findings of their last checkup and whether either has had any recent STD symptoms.

- Prospective partners should share their sexual histories, including whether either is bisexual and whether either has had any partners who were members of a high-risk group.

- Prospective partners should act with integrity: make promises genuine, get all the secrets out on the table, be trustworthy. "Make a physical examination part of your foreplay"—for example, take a shower or a bath together before becoming intimate. This gives each partner an opportunity to check for signs of STDs.

- Prospective partners should trust their feelings. They should listen to their inner voice if it tells then that a potential partner may not be trustworthy, and they should practice caution. Many people, frankly, will say just about anything in order to have sex.

- Partners should use condoms and a spermicide during all sexual acts as protection against STDs. Women must be willing to say "Forget it" to men who refuse to use a condom.

- Partners should not engage in anal sexual contact, because this involves the highest risk of contracting HIV and other STDs.

- Partners should urinate and wash the genitals with warm soapy water after having sex. Urination helps to flush out harmful organisms in the urethra, especially in males.

All of these suggestions are a bit sobering and perhaps take some of the romance out of sexual intimacy. But contracting a sexually transmissible disease takes all the romance out of lovemaking.

Glossary

ABC-X Family Crisis Model A theoretical model of family crisis in which A denotes the stressor, B denotes the family's crisis-meeting resources, C denotes the family's definition of the stressor, and X denotes the crisis.

ability to cope with stress One of the six qualities (commonly found in emotionally healthy families) identified by researchers working within the family strengths framework.

abortifacient Anything used to induce abortion.

abortion Expulsion of a fetus from the uterus before it is sufficiently developed to survive on its own; commonly used to describe only artificially induced terminations of pregnancy. *See also* miscarriage.

accommodating style A style of conflict resolution characterized by nonassertive but cooperative behavior; accommodaters subjugate their own wants and needs to those of others.

acculturation The intermeshing of cultural traits and values with those of the dominant culture.

acquired immune deficiency syndrome (AIDS) A fatal condition caused by the human immunodeficiency virus (HIV), which suppresses the immune system; HIV is transmitted primarily through blood and semen.

afterbirth The placenta and fetal membranes, which are expelled from the uterus during the third stage of labor.

ageism A form of prejudice or discrimination in which one judges an older person negatively based solely on the criterion of age.

aggressive communication A style of interpersonal communication that attempts to hurt or put down the receiver while protecting the aggressor's self-esteem.

agreeing to disagree A negotiating strategy in which two people who cannot reach agreement decide to take neither course of action.

AIDS *See* acquired immune deficiency syndrome.

Al-Anon A self-help group for families of alcoholics.

Alateen A support group for young people with alcoholic parents, based on the Alcoholics Anonymous model.

alcohol abuse A generic term that includes both alcoholism (addiction to alcohol characterized by compulsive drinking) and problem drinking (alcohol consumption that results in functional disability).

Alcoholics Anonymous (AA) A self-help group for alcoholics.

alcoholism Addiction to alcohol characterized by compulsive drinking.

alimony Court-ordered financial support to a spouse or former spouse following separation or divorce.

amniotic sac The membrane that encloses the fetus and holds the amniotic fluid, which insulates the fetus.

androgen Any of the hormones that develop and maintain male secondary sex characteristics.

androgyny A blending of traditionally masculine and traditionally feminine personality characteristics and role behaviors in one person; the absence of sex-typing with regard to roles.

anorgasmia The inability to have an orgasm.

anxiety disorder A mental disorder characterized by attacks of panic that are not occasioned by life-threatening situations or extreme physical exertion.

appreciation and affection One of the six qualities (commonly found in emotionally healthy families) identified by researchers working within the family strengths framework.

arranged marriage *See* parent-arranged marriage.

artificial insemination Induction of semen into the uterus by artificial means in an attempt to cause pregnancy.

assertive communication A style of interpersonal communication in which one makes one's self-interest and wishes known without degrading or putting down the other person.

assimilation Adopting the cultural traits and values of the dominant culture.

attentive listening A style of listening focused on fully understanding the speaker's point of view; characterized by encouragement of rather than direction of the speaker.

authoritarian parenting A parenting style characterized by the demand for absolute obedience to rigid rules and the use of punitive, forceful disciplinary measures.

authoritative parenting A parenting style that establishes the parents' legitimate power to set rules while also recognizing the child's feelings, individuality, and need to develop autonomy; uses positive reinforcement, seldom punishment, to enforce standards. Also called *democratic parenting*.

autonomic power pattern A pattern of sharing power in a relationship in which both partners have about equal authority but in different areas of life; both make decisions in their particular domains independent of each other.

avoidance style A style of conflict resolution characterized by nonassertive and passive behavior; avoiders often withdraw from the conflict or change the subject.

balanced families   Families who fit into the four central categories of the Circumplex Model: families who are flexibly connected, flexibly cohesive, structurally connected, or structurally cohesive. *See also* unbalanced families; midrange families.

bankruptcy   The state of being financially insolvent or unable to pay one's bills.

barrier methods of contraception   Devices that prevent pregnancy by physically blocking the sperm from entering the uterus, including condoms, diaphragms, and cervical caps.

behaviorist   A clinician who, based on learning theories, has developed practical, positive ways of dealing with children's behavior; rather than focusing on punishment, behaviorists encourage "accentuating the positive," the process of *reinforcement.*

belief system   One of the four major components of the sociocultural context in which families live, centering on religious/spiritual/ethical beliefs and other ideas about how to live successfully and happily in the world. *See also* extended family system; family system; social system.

bidirectional effects   Both the effects of the child on the parent and the effects of the parent on the child; child development specialists and family scientists concur that studying these effects is important to an understanding of parent-child dynamics.

bilateral descent   A method of tracing the lineage of children equally through ancestors of both mother and father.

binuclear family   A postdivorce family in which both parents participate in the raising of their children despite living in separate households; the children generally reside with one of the parents.

biopsychosocial approach   An approach to stress management and health care that assumes a connection among a person's physical symptoms, psychological issues, and social context.

bisexual   Sexually oriented toward members of both sexes.

blamer   A person whose style of anger management is characterized by a short temper, emotionally intense responses to stress, and the belief that others are responsible for her or his feelings and problems.

blastocyst   An early stage of the fertilized egg, containing about 100 cells; implants itself in the uterine lining (endometrium).

blended family   A term used to describe a stepfamily. Some researchers object to the term because it creates unrealistic expectations that the new family will quickly and easily "blend" together harmoniously and because it assumes a homogeneous unit, one without previous history or background. *See also* stepfamily.

boomerang kids   Adult children who come back to their parents' home to live as a result of divorce, job loss, or an inability to make it in the "real world."

boundaries   The lines that both separate systems from and connect systems to each other. The notion of a boundary implies a hierarchy of interconnected systems, each larger than the one before it.

boundary ambiguity   Lack of clarity about whether a person is either in or out of the family system; related to family stress levels. The concept includes two variables: physical and psychological presence or absence. High ambiguity (conflicting variables) produces high levels of stress.

brainstorming   Thinking of as many solutions to a problem as possible; a conflict resolution strategy.

breast-feeding   Feeding a baby from the mother's breast rather than from a bottle; usually better than bottle feeding for the physical well-being of the baby.

budgeting   The regular, systematic balancing of income and expenses.

Caring Cluster   One of two groups of characteristics that distinguish romantic relationships from friendships; includes being an advocate for one's partner and giving the utmost. *See also* Passion Cluster.

case study   A detailed description of a person or a family to illustrate a specific idea, concept, or principle.

catharsis conflict   The false belief that venting anger verbally prevents physical violence. Researchers who study family violence have found that verbal and physical violence are related.

centrifugal interaction   Behavior that pushes system components away from one another, decreasing the system's connectedness.

centripetal interaction   Behavior that pulls system components toward one another, resulting in a system's increasing connectedness.

cervical cap   A thimble-shaped contraceptive device that fits snugly over the cervix; must be fitted by a physician and used with a spermicide.

cervix   The narrow lower end of the uterus that adjoins the vagina.

Cesarean section (C-section)   Surgical delivery of the fetus by incising the mother's abdominal and uterine walls.

chaotic family   According to the Family Circumplex Model, a type of family system characterized by a lack of leadership, inconsistent discipline, and changing family roles and rules.

child abuse   The physical or mental injury, sexual abuse, or negligent treatment of a child under the age of 18 by a person who is responsible for the child's welfare.

child-free alternative   The decision by married or cohabiting adults not to have children.

child-to-parent abuse   Violence directed at a parent by a child.

chlamydia   A sexually transmissible disease that causes inflammation of the urinary tract in men and vaginal inflammation in women.

circular causality model   An interpersonal communication model that describes an interaction pattern in which both parties view their behavior as a reaction to the other's behavior rather than as something for which they are each responsible. One person sends out a message that causes a change in and a response from the other person. That response causes a new response in the first person, whose response initiates another response from the second person, and so on. This type of communication cycle can escalate into conflict.

circumcision   The surgical or ritualistic removal of the foreskin of the penis.

Circumplex Model   *See* Family Circumplex Model.

clitoris   An erotically sensitive organ located at the upper end of the female's vulva above the urethral opening; becomes erect during sexual arousal; the counterpart of the male penis.

closed system   A family system that maintains the status quo and avoids change; also called a *morphostatic system.*

closure   Resolution of an issue.

cluttered nest   The presence in the parental home of young-adult children who are unmarried or who have returned to live as a result of divorce or unemployment.

co-culture   A distinct cultural or social group living within a dominant culture but also having membership in another culture, such as gay men and lesbians.

co-dependent   A person, often a spouse, whose actions enable an alcoholic to continue to drink but who is often unaware of the ways in which her or his behavior "enables" the partner's drinking.

cognitive development theory   A model of child development that views growth as the mastery of specific ways of perceiving, thinking, and doing, which occurs at discrete stages.

cohabitation   Two unrelated adults sharing the same living quarters.

cohesion   *See* family cohesion.

collaborative style   A style of conflict resolution characterized by a high degree of assertiveness about reaching one's own goals, coupled with concern for the other person.

commitment   Attachment to another. One of the six qualities (commonly found in emotionally healthy families) identified by researchers working within the family strengths framework; also, the cognitive component of Sternberg's three dimensions of love.

communication   (interaction). The way humans create and share meaning, both verbally and nonverbally; the foundation for developing and maintaining human relationships, especially intimate relationships. *See also* family communication; positive communication.

community divorce   One of Bohannan's six different but overlapping experiences of divorce: changes in friendships and community relationships.

companionate love   A type of love relationship characterized by commitment and intimacy but lacking intense passion; common between partners who have been together for many years.

competitive style   A style of conflict resolution characterized by aggression, lack of cooperation, pursuit of personal concerns at the expense of the other, and the desire to "win" at all costs.

competitive symmetry   A style of communication in which partners attempt to control the situation and the other by escalating the level of hostilities in a competitive manner.

complementary interaction   A style of communication in which the partners adopt two different tactics: One is dominant and one is submissive. *See also* symmetrical interaction.

complementary needs theory   The supposition that people are attracted to partners whose personalities differ from but complement their own. Family researchers have not found much support for this theory.

complex stepfamily   A stepfamily that includes children of both parents. *See also* simple stepfamily.

compromise style   A style of conflict resolution characterized by a willingness to give up something to resolve the issue.

conception   The union of sperm and ovum, which begins the development of the fetus.

conceptual framework   A set of interconnected ideas, concepts, and assumptions that helps organize thinking from a particular perspective. The field of family science includes a variety of major conceptual frameworks: family systems theory (or the family systems framework), the family strengths framework, the family development framework, the symbolic interaction framework, and the feminist framework.

condom   A rubber sheath placed over the penis before intercourse to prevent pregnancy and protect against sexually transmissible diseases.

conjugal family system   A family consisting of husband, wife, and children; also called *nuclear family.*

consanguineal family system   A family system that emphasizes blood ties more than marital ties.

consummate love   A type of love relationship characterized by commitment, intimacy, and passion.

contraception   A deliberate action (use of a device, drug, or technique) taken to prevent conception (pregnancy).

contraceptive coil   A form of intrauterine device, in use in Finland, that releases synthetic hormones to prevent pregnancy.

contractions   Tightenings of the muscles, especially those of the uterus during labor.

control talk A type of communication used to gain agreement or compliance from another person.

convenience A type of cohabiting relationship in which one partner takes and the other gives; a relationship of convenience usually based on sexual, caretaking, economic, or social needs rather than on love.

coparental divorce One of Bohannan's six different but overlapping experiences of divorce: decisions about custody of the children, single-parent homes, and visitation rights for the noncustodial parent.

coparenting A style of parenting in which both parents take on tasks and roles traditionally associated with only the mother or the father.

crisis A drastic change in the course of events; a turning point that affects the trend of future events; an unstable condition of affairs; a time of danger and a time of opportunity.

crisis-loss stage of grief A period of chaotic shock; the first of Brubaker's three stages of the grieving process. *See also* new-life stage of grief; transition stage of grief.

cross-cultural family study A research study focused on how cultural context influences family issues: among them, values and behaviors, courtship and marriage patterns, communication, roles, work and the family, childrearing patterns, and sexuality.

cross-validation A comparison of the results from one study with those from a similar study to see if the findings are replicated.

cultural identity A feeling of belonging that evolves from the shared beliefs, values, and attitudes of a group of people; the structure of the group's marital, sexual, and kinship relationships.

dance of anger Lerner's application of a dance metaphor to describe styles of managing anger and ways in which these styles interact.

dating A form of courtship in which, through a series of appointed meetings for social interaction and activities, an exclusive relationship may evolve between two people. Also called *individual-choice courtship*.

definition of the situation The concept that a situation is based on a person's subjective interpretation; hence, people can have different views of the same situation.

delivery The second stage of labor, lasting from the time the cervix is completely dilated until the fetus is expelled.

devitalized (burned-out) marriage A marriage characterized by a loss of intimacy over the years; possibly the most common reason for divorce.

diaphragm A cup-shaped rubber contraceptive device that is inserted in the vagina before intercourse to cover the cervical opening and block sperm from entering the uterus; must be fitted by a physician and used with a spermicide.

dilation and curettage (D & C) An abortion technique used in the second trimester of pregnancy; performed in a hospital under general anesthetic; after the cervix is dilated (opened), the embryo is removed from the uterus with a sharp instrument (curette).

dilation and evacuation (D & E) An abortion technique used in the second trimester of pregnancy; suction and forceps are used to remove the embryo or fetus.

DINS dilemma DINS stands for double income, no sex; inhibited or hypoactive sexual desire in couples with many demands on their time.

directive listening A style of listening in which the listener attempts to control the direction of the conversation through the use of questions.

disengaged family According to the Family Circumplex Model, a type of family system characterized by lack of emotional closeness and a high degree of separateness among family members.

distancer An individual who wants emotional space when stress is high, values self-reliance, and is private rather than a help-seeker.

distress Feelings of discomfort caused by high levels of stress.

double ABC-X Model A descriptive model of family crisis that recognizes the impact of both hardships resulting from the crisis and unresolved prior crisis on the family's ability to cope; an outgrowth of Hill's ABC-X Family Crisis Model.

double bind A situation in which the message relayed by the speaker calls into question the type of relationship the receiver has with the speaker.

double standard Different standards of appropriate sexual and social behavior for the two sexes; the belief that premarital sex is more acceptable for males than for females.

douching An ineffective form of contraception in which a liquid containing vinegar or another substance is squirted into the vagina.

early abortion Similar to the vacuum curettage method but performed as soon as a positive pregnancy test is received, up to 8 weeks after the last menstrual period; a flexible tube is inserted through the cervix without dilating it, and the contents of the uterus are sucked out.

ecology The study of how all the organisms in a system relate to one another.

economic divorce One of Bohannan's six different but overlapping experiences of divorce: the division of money and property and the establishment of two separate economic units.

egalitarian roles Social equality between the sexes; equal sharing of practical responsibilities and decision making by men and women.

ejaculatory incompetence   The inability of a man to ejaculate in his partner's vagina despite a firm erection and a high level of sexual arousal.

emancipation   A type of cohabiting relationship based on the desire to break free of parental values and influence rather than on love.

emic perspective   The analysis of a society from the inside.

emotional divorce   One of Bohannan's six different but overlapping experiences of divorce: the deterioration of the marriage, the breakdown of bonding and communication, and their replacement with feelings of alienation.

empty love   A type of love relationship involving commitment but no passion or intimacy.

empty nest syndrome   Feelings of malaise, emptiness, and lack of purpose that some parents experience when their last child leaves home. *See also* spacious nest.

enabler   A person, often a spouse, whose actions permit an alcoholic to continue to drink; also called a *co-dependent*.

endogamy   The practice of choosing a mate from within one's own group: ethnic, religious, socioeconomic, and/or general age group.

enmeshed family   According to the Family Circumplex Model, a type of family system characterized by extremely high levels of emotional closeness and togetherness among family members.

ENRICH   A comprehensive marital inventory containing 125 questions in categories that are relevant to married couples and their satisfaction with their relationship. ENRICH is an acronym for **EN**riching **R**elationship **I**ssues, **C**ommunication, and **H**appiness.

epididymitis   Inflammation of the testicles in men, often caused by untreated gonorrhea; can lead to sterility.

episiotomy   A surgical incision from the vagina toward the anus, performed to prevent tearing of the perineum during childbirth.

equalitarian group   Structured on the ideals of democracy, a group believing that the rights and perspectives of both sexes and of all generations ought to be respected. The societal norms of the United States are considered to be equalitarian.

erectile dysfunction   A sexual dysfunction in which a man has difficulty achieving or maintaining penile erection.

estrogen   Although often called the female hormone, any of a group of hormones, produced primarily by the ovaries, that are significant in controlling female physiological functions and directing the development of female secondary sex characteristics at puberty.

ethnic identity   The geographic origin of a minority group within a country or culture; cultural identity transcends ethnic identity.

ethnocentrism   The assumption that one's own culture is the standard by which to judge other cultures.

etic perspective   The analysis of a society from the outside.

eustress   A moderate to high level of stress that is energizing, motivating, positive, and healthy.

exogamy   The practice, discouraged in U.S. society, of choosing a mate from outside one's own group.

expressive role   Caring for the emotional well-being of the family, providing nurturing and comfort; in Parson's model of the modern family, this is the wife-mother's role. *See also* instrumental role.

extended family   A nuclear family and those related to its members by blood, such as aunts, uncles, cousins, and grandparents.

extended family system   One of the four major components of the sociocultural context in which families live; focuses on the degree of importance relatives outside the nuclear family have on the family's life.

family   Two or more people who are committed to each other and who share intimacy, resources, decisions, and values; people who love and care for each other.

Family Circumplex Model   A graphic representation of dynamic relationships within families, containing three central dimensions: cohesion (togetherness), flexibility (ability to change), and communication (a facilitating dimension that helps families move between the extremes on the cohesion and flexibility dimensions). Identifies 16 types of family relationships.

family cohesion   The togetherness or closeness of a family; one of the three dimensions of the Family Circumplex Model.

family communication   Interaction; sharing of thoughts and feelings; the facilitating dimension of the Family Circumplex Model.

family coping   A family's ability to manage stressful events or situations as a unit with minimal or no detrimental effects on any individual members.

family coping resources   Characteristics of a healthy family system on which the family can draw in times of stress; include cohesion, adaptability, and a willingness to adopt nontraditional family roles in the face of changing economic circumstances. *See also* personal coping resources.

family database   An integrated computerized database containing the data from all volumes of the *Inventory of Marriage & Family Literature*, which contains more than 100,000 research articles on families that have been published in English language journals.

family development framework   A conceptual framework that focuses on how family members deal with roles and developmental tasks within the family unit as they move through the stages of the life cycle.

family flexibility   A family's ability to change and adapt in the face of stress or crisis; one of the three dimensions of the Family Circumplex Model.

family hardship   A demand on a family that accompanies a stressor event. For example, the family hardship of reduced income accompanies the stressor event of losing one's job.

family of origin   The family in which a person is raised during childhood.

family power   The ability of one family member to change the behavior of the other family members.

family science   An interdisciplinary field whose primary focus is a better understanding of families, to enhance the quality of family life. Professionals whose main interest is the family tend to call themselves *family scientists;* those who develop educational programs for families sometimes call themselves *family life educators;* those who work clinically with troubled families are called *marriage* (or *marital*) *and family therapists.*

family strengths framework   A conceptual framework proposing that if researchers study only family problems, they will find only problems in families, but that if they are interested in family strengths, they must study strong families. Has identified six qualities that strong families commonly demonstrate: commitment, appreciation and affection, positive communication, time together, spiritual well-being, and the ability to cope with stress and crisis.

family system   This theoretical perspective on the family assumes that all family members are interconnected and that what affects one person affects everyone in the family. Three major dimensions of the family system are family cohesion, family flexibility, and family communication. *See also* belief system; extended family system; social system.

family systems theory (or **family systems framework**) A conceptual framework that views everything that happens to any family member as having an impact on everyone else in the family, because family members are interconnected and operate as a group, or family system.

family therapy   An approach to helping families based on the belief that the roots of an individual's problems may be traced to troubled family dynamics.

fatuous love   A type of love relationship in which commitment is based on passion, but there has not yet been time to develop true intimacy.

fault   Under traditional divorce law, legal blame or responsibility for the end of a marriage. Financial and property determinations depended on a party's "innocence," or lack of fault, leading to heated accusations and counteraccusations between divorcing spouses.

femininity   A gender-linked constellation of personality traits and behavioral patterns traditionally associated with females in a society.

feminist framework   A conceptual framework that emphasizes the value of women's perspectives on society and the family, that recognizes women's subordination, and that promotes change in that status.

feminization of poverty   The statistical fact that the percentage of female single parents in the total percentage of those who are poor in the United States is increasing.

fertility awareness   A variety of contraceptive methods based on predicting a woman's fertile period and avoiding intercourse during that interval (or using an additional method of contraception during that time).

fertilization   The union or joining of an ovum (egg) with a sperm cell; also known as *conception.*

fetal alcohol syndrome (FAS)   Serious malformations (particularly of the facial features and the eyes) seen in children whose mothers drank excessively during their pregnancy.

fight talk   A type of negative control talk focused on getting one's own way; often produces a negative response that generates more negative talk.

Filshie clip   A titanium-and-silicone clip that blocks the fallopian tubes without cutting or cauterizing them, making it a potentially reversible method of sterilization for women; not yet available in the United States.

first order change   Change that occurs on the flexibility dimension within a given family system; a high level of first order change, which leads to ineffective functioning, is found in chaotic (unbalanced) families.

flexibility   *See* family flexibility.

foreskin   In the female, the fold of skin that covers the clitoris (also called the *prepuce* or *clitoral hood*). In the male, the skin that covers the glans (tip) of the penis, removed in most male infants in the United States shortly after birth in the process of circumcision.

gender   The learned characteristics and behaviors associated with biological sex in a particular culture. *See also* sex.

gender identity   A person's internal sense of being female or male, which is expressed in personality and behavior.

gender polarization   The organizing of social life according to male and female gender-role distinctions.

gender role   The traits and behaviors assigned to males or females by a culture.

gender-role stereotype   A rigid, simplistic belief about the distinctive psychological characteristics and behavioral patterns attributable to a man or woman based exclusively on sex.

general systems theory   A set of principles and concepts that can be applied to all types of systems, living and nonliving.

genital herpes   A sexually transmissible disease caused by the herpes simplex virus; lesions similar to cold sores or fever blisters appear on the genitals.

genitals   The external sex or reproductive organs.

genital warts   A sexually transmissible disease caused by the human papilloma virus.

germ cells   Reproductive cells produced by the gonads in both sexes. Female germ cells are called *ova* (eggs), and male germ cells are called *sperm.*

glans   The extremity, or tip, of the male penis and the female clitoris; the most sensitive part of the organ and an important source of sexual arousal.

goals   Specific, achievable objectives or purposes.

gonads   Reproductive glands that secrete sex hormones and produce germ cells; the testes in men and the ovaries in women.

gonorrhea   A sexually transmissible disease that usually remains localized in the genitals and is self-limiting, although if untreated, it can cause serious and permanent damage, including sterility. Symptoms are common in men, but gonorrhea is often asymptomatic, and therefore difficult to detect, in women.

gunnysacking   An alienating ("dirty") fighting tactic in which a person saves up unresolved grievances until he or she explodes and they all come out in a major confrontation.

heterosexual   Sexual orientation toward members of the other sex.

HIV   *See* human immunodeficiency virus.

homogamy   The tendency to marry someone of the same ethnic group, educational level, socioeconomic status, religion, and values.

homophobia   Aversion to homosexuals and homosexuality.

homosexual   Sexual orientation toward members of the same sex.

human immunodeficiency virus (HIV)   The virus that causes AIDS.

husband-dominant power pattern   A pattern of sharing power in a relationship in which the man is the boss.

hymen   A thin membrane that may partially cover the female's vaginal opening before first intercourse.

hypothesis   An assertion subject to verification or proof; a presumed relationship between variables.

hysterotomy   A relatively rare surgical method of abortion, performed in the late second trimester of pregnancy, in which a cesarean section is performed to remove the fetus.

idiographic   Focusing on the study of individuals and individual differences. *See also* nomothetic.

incest   Sexual activity of any kind between members of the same family.

incest taboo   The nearly universal societal prohibition of intercourse between parents and children and between siblings.

incestuous abuse   The sexual exploitation of a child under the age of 18 by a family member.

incongruity humor   Humor that focuses on recognizing things in life that don't fit together logically; a tool for couples and families who want to "fight fair."

incubation period   The time during which a disease-causing organism is multiplying in the body but does not cause any symptoms. HIV, the virus that causes AIDS, has a long incubation period.

induced labor   A method of abortion performed in the late second trimester, generally in a hospital, in which a saline solution or prostaglandins are injected into the amniotic sac to cause the woman's body to expel the fetus.

infatuation   A type of love relationship characterized only by passion, and lacking both intimacy and commitment.

infertility   The inability to conceive a child.

infidelity   Having sex with someone other than one's marriage partner.

insider perspective   How people inside the family describe their relationships. *See also* outsider perspective.

instrumental role   Being the breadwinner, the manager, and the leader of the family; in Parsons's model of the modern family, this is the husband-father's role. *See also* expressive role.

intercultural marriage   Marriage between people from two different cultural or ethnic groups.

interdependence of parts   A characteristic of systems; the parts or elements of a system are interconnected in such a way that if one part is changed, other parts are automatically affected.

intimacy   Sharing intellectually, physically, and/or emotionally with another person; the emotional component of Sternberg's three dimensions of love.

intimacy game   Emotionally manipulating a partner or close friend into doing or giving something while concealing the desired outcome; undermines relationships by destroying closeness and sharing.

intimacy need fulfillment   The satisfaction one receives from having personal needs fulfilled, which leads to greater intimacy; the fourth and final component in Reiss's wheel of love.

intimate experience   An experience in which one feels close to another or shares oneself in one area of life, such as intellectually, socially, emotionally, or sexually.

intimate relationship   A partnership involving an emotional bond between two people, with proven mutual commitment and trust, that provides personal and relationship security and rewards; a relationship in which one shares intimate experiences in several areas of life over time, with expectations that this sharing will continue.

intrauterine device (IUD)   A contraceptive device inserted by a physician into a woman's uterus to prevent conception from occurring.

in vitro fertilization   A method of treating female infertility: Eggs are removed from the woman's ovary, fertilized in a laboratory dish with her partner's sperm, and implanted in the uterus.

joint custody A legal child custody arrangement following a divorce in which children divide their time between the homes of both parents, with both homes having equal importance: "one child, two homes."

Kaposi's sarcoma (KS) A rare form of cancer that causes purple or brownish lesions resembling bruises on the skin and inside the mouth, nose, or rectum; the second most common cause of death in people with AIDS.

kinship The relatedness of certain individuals within a group. Cultures have norms and expectations that structure and govern kin behavior.

labor The stages of delivering a baby, consisting of contractions of the uterine muscles and dilation of the cervix, the birth itself, and the expulsion of the placenta.

learned helplessness theory A theory that a learned passivity develops from giving power over oneself to another; that passivity increases helplessness, reduces problem-solving abilities, and limits options.

learning theories Approaches to understanding human development that focus on how people learn to behave the way they do.

legal divorce One of Bohannan's six different but overlapping experiences of divorce: dissolution of the marriage by the state in the courts.

liking A type of love relationship characterized by intimacy but lacking passion and commitment.

lineage Line of descent, influenced by cultural norms. Lineage determines membership in a kinship group, patterns of inheritance, and kinship obligations or responsibilities. *See also* matrilineal society; patrilineal society.

linear causality model An interpersonal communication model that assumes a direct, or linear, relationship between cause and effect.

Linus blanket A type of cohabiting relationship in which one of the partners is so dependent or insecure that he or she prefers a relationship with anyone to being alone.

longevis marriage A long-term marriage, one that lasts 50 years or more.

looking-glass self The idea that you learn about yourself based on the feedback you receive from others.

male menopause Physical changes in men related to age, similar to those that occur in women during menopause.

managing stress Pauline Boss's alternative to the concept of "coping with" stress; individual family members'

use of their own resources to help their family deal with a stressor or work through a crisis.

marriage An emotional and legal commitment between two people to share emotional and physical intimacy, various tasks, and economic resources.

masculinity A gender-linked constellation of personality traits and behavioral patterns traditionally associated with males in a society.

masturbation Self-stimulation to provide sexual pleasure.

mating gradient The tendency of women to marry men who are better educated or more successful than they are.

matriarchal group A group in which the mother or eldest female is recognized as the head of the family, kinship group, or tribe, and descent is traced through her.

matrilineal society A society in which descent, or lineage, is traced through females.

matrilocal society A society in which the norm is for newly married couples to live with or near the wife's kin, especially her mother's kin group.

medical family therapy A therapeutic framework that uses family systems theory and the biopsychosocial approach in dealing with health problems in family members.

menopause The cessation of ovulation, menstruation, and fertility in women as a result of aging.

menses The menstrual flow, in which the endometrial tissue is discharged.

menstrual regulation A procedure in which the contents of the uterus are sucked out before the woman's menstrual period is due; eliminates knowledge of possible pregnancy. Also called *endometrial aspiration*, *preemptive abortion*, or *menstrual extraction*.

menstruation The discharge from the uterus through the vagina of blood and the unfertilized ovum; occurs about every 28 days in nonpregnant women between puberty and menopause.

metacommunication Communicating about communicating.

methotrexate and misoprostol Two prescription drugs that in combination function as an effective abortifacient.

middle age Generally speaking, the years between the ages of 35 and 65; from the standpoint of the family development conceptual framework, the middle years of the family life cycle are the launching period for young-adult children and the period before the parents' retirement.

midlife crisis A period of questioning one's worth, values, and contributions in life, usually beginning in a person's 40s or early 50s.

mid-range families Families who are extreme on one dimension of the Family Circumplex Model but balanced on the other dimension. There are eight mid-range family types. For example, a family might be structurally enmeshed: extreme on cohesion (enmeshed) but balanced on flexibility (structured). *See also* balanced families; unbalanced families.

midwife   A nonphysician who attends and facilitates birth.

minority group   A social group that differs from the rest of the population in some ways and that often experiences discrimination and prejudice.

miscarriage   The body's spontaneous (unaided) termination of pregnancy.

missionary position   A coital position in which partners lie face to face, with the male above the female.

mixed message   A message in which there is a discrepancy between the verbal and the nonverbal components: The receiver hears one thing but simultaneously feels something else.

monogamy   Being married to one person at a time.

morning sickness   Nausea experienced by many women during the first trimester of pregnancy, often but not exclusively in the morning.

morphogenic system   A system that is open to growth and change; also called an *open system.*

morphostatic system   A system that has the capacity to maintain the status quo, thus avoiding change; also called a *closed system.*

mutual dependency   Two partners wanting and needing each other; the third component in Reiss's wheel of love.

mutual masturbation   A sexual technique in which partners sexually stimulate each other to orgasm without having intercourse.

negative feedback   Information or communication that is intended to minimize change in a system.

neolocal society   A society in which the norm encourages newly married couples to establish their own separate, autonomous residence, independent of either partner's parental kin group.

neutralized symmetry   A style of communication in which partners respect each other, approach each other as equals, and try to avoid exerting control over each other.

new-life stage of grief   The period during which the bereaved establishes a new lifestyle and exhibits to society and self that he or she can live satisfactorily as a single person; the last of Brubaker's three stages of the grieving process. *See also* crisis-loss stage of grief; transition stage of grief.

nocturnal orgasm   Nonvoluntary ejaculation or orgasm occurring during sleep; in men, also called a *wet dream.*

no-fault divorce   Divorce laws that do not place blame (fault) for the divorce on either spouse; one party's assertion that irreconcilable differences exist is sufficient grounds for dissolving the marriage.

nomothetic   Focusing on developing a theory that works for a great number of cases. Researchers using this approach believe it is possible to develop a general family theory. *See also* idiographic.

non-love   A type of love relationship characterized by the absence of commitment, intimacy, and passion.

nonverbal communication   The communication of emotions by means other than words, such as touch, body movement, facial expression, and eye contact.

Noristerat   A 2-month injectable contraceptive that has a 2% failure rate; approved for use in more than 40 countries but not in the United States.

normal-appearing family   A family that looks healthy and functional to outsiders but that can have serious problems, such as incest; the family structure is often traditional, but family members lack nurturing abilities.

Norplant   The trade name of a contraceptive implant placed under the skin on the inside of a woman's upper arm; releases the hormone progestin.

nuclear family   A kinship group in which a husband, a wife, and their children live together in one household; also called *conjugal family system.*

old age   Arbitrarily defined as beginning at age 65, which coincides for most people with retirement.

open system   A family system that is open to growth and change; also called a *morphogenic system.*

oral contraceptives   Birth control pills taken by mouth, containing hormones that suspend ovulation, preventing conception.

oral sex   Stimulation of the partner's genitals with one's tongue or mouth.

organic sexual dysfunction   Impairment of the ordinary physical responses of sexual excitement or orgasm as the result of physical or medical factors, such as illness, injury, or drugs.

organismic theory   Developed by Piaget and expanded by later theorists, a theory of child development emphasizing that children's minds develop through various stages and that children think very differently from adults; sees child-thought as primitive and mystical, with logical reasoning developing slowly into adulthood.

orgasm   The climax of human sexual response, characterized by the release of physical and sexual tensions at the peak of sexual arousal.

outsider perspective   How researchers or therapists perceive a family, in contrast with how family members perceive the family. *See also* insider perspective.

ovaries   The female gonads (sex glands), which produce germ cells called *ova* (eggs) and hormones.

overfunctioner   An individual who not only knows what is best for herself or himself but for everybody else as well;

cannot let others solve their problems themselves.

oviduct In the female reproductive system, a tube through which ova (eggs) travel from an ovary to the uterus. Also called *fallopian tube.*

ovulation The regular monthly release in the female of one or more eggs from an ovary.

ovum (plural, ova) The female reproductive germ cell, or egg.

painful intercourse Intense discomfort during sex, experienced by both women and men and often related to physical problems with the sex organs.

palimony "Equitable relief" (alimony) granted by a court to a cohabiting partner; legal precedent established in *Marvin* v. *Marvin* in 1979.

parent-arranged marriage A practice, common in non-industrialized societies, in which the parents of the bride and groom select the future spouse and arrange the marriage ceremony. Based on the principle that the elders in a community have the wisdom to select an appropriate spouse, this type of marriage generally extends existing family units rather than creating new units.

parent education A lecture-and-discussion approach to learning developed for small or large groups of parents in an effort to help them learn how to raise children successfully.

passion Intense physiological arousal; the motivational component of Sternberg's three dimensions of love.

Passion Cluster One of two groups of characteristics that distinguish romantic relationships from friendships; includes fascination, sexual desire, and exclusiveness. *See also* Caring Cluster.

passive-aggressive behavior Feigning agreement with certain actions or situations but later becoming hostile or aggressive about the same occurrences; an indirect way of expressing anger.

passive communication A style of interpersonal communication characterized by an unwillingness to say what one thinks, feels, or wants.

patriarchal group A group in which the father or eldest male is recognized as the head of the family, kinship group, or tribe, and descent is traced through him.

patrilineal society A society in which descent, or lineage, is traced through males.

patrilocal society A society in which the norm is for newly married couples to live with or near the husband's kin, especially his father's kin group.

pelvic inflammatory disease (PID) A bacterial infection of the oviducts that can spread to the ovaries and uterus; often results from untreated sexually transmissible diseases such as gonorrhea, and can lead to sterility.

penis The male organ of sexual intercourse.

permissive parenting A style of parenting in which the parents permit the child's preferences to dominate and do not require the child to conform to parental standards.

permissiveness The extent to which couples are physically intimate before marriage.

personal coping resources An individual's self-esteem and mastery (confidence in personal abilities); necessary qualities for surviving difficult times. *See also* family coping resources.

personification Believing that everything a partner does is a reflection on oneself; leads to attempts to control the partner's behavior.

persuasive listening A style of listening in which the "listener" is looking only for an opportunity to take over and control the direction of the conversation.

placenta A vascular organ that joins the fetus with the mother's uterus and through which the fetus receives nutrients and discharges wastes; expelled in the final stage of labor, following birth of the baby.

PLISSIT Model Annon's application of four levels of treatment in various sex therapies: permission (P), limited information (LI), specific suggestions (SS), and intensive therapy (IT).

plural marriage A marriage in which a man has more than one wife (polygyny) or a woman has more than one husband (polyandry).

pneumocystis carinii pneumonia (PCP) A life-threatening protozoan infection of the lungs; the major cause of death in AIDS patients.

polyandry A plural marriage in which a woman has more than one husband.

polygamy A marriage in which a man or a woman has more than one mate; a plural marriage.

polygyny A plural marriage in which a man has more than one wife.

positive communication One of the six qualities (commonly found in emotionally healthy families) identified by researchers working within the family strengths framework.

positive feedback Information or communication that is intended to create change in a system.

postpartum depression A feeling of depression after giving birth, characterized by irritability, crying, loss of appetite, and difficulty sleeping; thought to be a result of the many physiological changes that occur after delivery.

post-traumatic stress disorder A severe stress reaction characterized by the reexperiencing of past traumatic events.

power The ability of an individual in a social system through will, influence, or control to change the behavior of other members of the system.

prejudice Negative judgment or opinion having no or limited basis in fact; hostility to a person or a group based on their physical characteristics.

premature ejaculation   A sexual dysfunction in which a man is unable to control his ejaculation reflex voluntarily and reaches orgasm sooner than he or his partner wishes.

PREPARE   A comprehensive premarital inventory that assesses a couple's relationship and determines how idealistic or realistic each person is in regard to marriage, how well the couple communicates, and how well the couple resolves conflicts and financial issues; acronym for **PRE**marital **P**ersonal **A**nd **R**elationship **E**valuation.

PREPARE-MC   A premarital inventory for couples whose marriage will create a stepfamily. Like the PREPARE inventory, PREPARE-MC (**M**arriage with **C**hildren) contains questions dealing with important categories in the couple's relationship, but the questions focus on issues relevant to stepfamilies.

prior strain   Residual effect of family tensions and prior stressor events that may still trouble a family at the time another stressor occurs.

problem drinking   Alcohol consumption that results in functional disability.

progestin   A hormone connected with pregnancy and contained in oral contraceptives.

propinquity   Nearness in time or place; in mate selection, the tendency to choose someone who is geographically nearby.

prostate gland   A gland located near the base of the male urethra that produces some of the fluid in semen that nourishes and transports sperm.

pseudo-kin group   A type of kinship group in which relationships resembling kinship ties develop among "unrelated" individuals.

pseudomutuality   A false sense of togetherness.

psychodynamic theory   Developed by Freud and his followers, a theory of human development that emphasizes the importance of providing a positive emotional environment during early childhood, when the foundation for later life is laid down.

psychological divorce   One of Bohannan's six different but overlapping experiences of divorce: regaining individual autonomy.

psychosocial sexual dysfunction   Impairment of the ordinary physical responses of sexual excitement or orgasm as a result of psychological, developmental, interpersonal, environmental, or cultural factors.

pursuer   An individual who wants a very high degree of togetherness and expression of feelings in a relationship.

quid pro quid   A strategy for negotiating differences in which one agrees to do something the other person requests in exchange for being able to do something one wants to do; "this for this."

quid pro quo   A strategy for negotiating differences in which one agrees to do something in exchange for the other's agreement to do something else of equal value or importance; "this for that."

race   A group of people with similar and distinctive physical characteristics.

racism   Discrimination or prejudice based on the belief that people's physical characteristics determine their human capacities and behaviors and that groups of people with certain characteristics are inferior to others.

rapid orgasm   A sexual dysfunction in which a woman consistently reaches orgasm sooner than she or her partner wishes; the counterpart of premature ejaculation in the male.

rapport   The process of communication in which two people develop understanding and a sense of closeness; the first component in Reiss's wheel of love.

reconstituted family   A term used to describe a stepfamily.

reframing   An internal family coping strategy involving redefining a stressful experience in a positive way so that it can be confronted directly and dealt with successfully.

reinforcement   Rewarding desired behavior to increase the likelihood that it will be repeated.

rejecting parenting   A style of parenting in which parents pay little attention to their children's needs and set few or no expectations for their children's behavior.

remarriage   A marriage in which at least one partner has been married before.

representative sample   A random selection of individuals who accurately reflect the characteristics of a particular group.

research study   An investigation designed to test a specific hypothesis.

resources   Assets that can be used to achieve goals; economic, human, and environmental tools.

resource theory of family power   A theory that the balance of power in a marriage is related to the relative resources (especially money, level of education, and occupational prestige) each spouse has in the relationship.

retarded ejaculation   A sexual dysfunction in which a long and strenuous effort is needed to reach orgasm.

rigid family   According to the Family Circumplex Model, a type of family system characterized by authoritarian leadership, strict discipline, and unchanging roles and rules.

role   The expected behavior of a person or group in a given social category, such as husband, wife, supervisor, or teacher.

role making   The process of creating new roles or revising existing roles.

role taking   The process whereby people learn how to play roles correctly by practicing and getting feedback from others.

romantic love A type of love relationship characterized by intimacy and passion but lacking commitment.

routinization A situation, often encountered in middle age, in which one's job lacks the challenge it once offered and becomes boring.

RU-486 An oral antiprogesterone steroid that acts as an abortifacient if taken within the first 6 weeks of pregnancy; available or being tested in France, China, England, Sweden, India, and the United States.

sandwich generation Parents, usually in their 50s and older, who are simultaneously responsible for childrearing and for caring for their own aging parents; individuals who are "caught in the middle" between two generations.

saver A person whose money-handling style is characterized by compulsive saving, often to the point of having little money free for the essentials.

schizophrenia A mental disorder characterized by bizarre or grandiose delusions; auditory hallucinations; incoherent, illogical thinking; and very grossly disorganized behavior.

scrotum The pouch or sac of skin behind the penis that holds the testes, the two male gonads.

search talk A type of communication used to explore facts and possibilities objectively; its aim is to stop the communication dance, letting the participants step aside for a while and see what is happening.

second order change A change from one family system type to another, often in the face of a crisis.

segregation Isolation of an ethnic group within the dominant culture.

self-disclosure Revealing to another person personal information or feelings that that individual could not otherwise learn.

self-revelation Self-disclosure; the second component in Reiss's wheel of love.

semen The milky fluid containing sperm that is ejaculated from the penis at orgasm.

sex Being biologically male or female; also, sexual activity or behavior. *See also* gender.

sex educator A trained teacher who provides general information and principles about sex and sexuality, generally in a group setting.

sex ratio The relationship between the number of men and the number of women of a given age.

sex therapist A trained individual who teaches and counsels clients individually, in pairs, or in small groups about sex and sexuality.

sex therapy A process of education and counseling designed to help people overcome sexual problems.

sexual dysfunction A state in which one's sexual behavior or lack of it is a source of distress; any malfunction of the human sexual response that inhibits the achievement of orgasm, either alone or with a partner.

sexual intercourse Coitus; the insertion of the male's penis into the female's vagina.

sexual orientation A person's sense of being heterosexual, homosexual, or bisexual.

sexuality The set of beliefs, values, and behaviors by which one defines oneself as a sexual being.

sexually transmissible disease (STD) Any of several highly contagious diseases that may be passed from one individual to another through sexual contact. The seven major STDs are HIV infection (which leads to AIDS), syphilis, gonorrhea, chlamydia, genital herpes, genital warts, and viral hepatitis.

shop talk A type of communication that focuses on work-related matters; its purpose is to establish a connection with another.

sibling abuse Physical violence between siblings; probably the most common form of abuse of children.

SIDS *See* sudden infant death syndrome.

Simple stepfamily A stepfamily that includes children from only one parent. *See also* complex stepfamily.

singlehood The state of being unmarried, divorced, or unattached to another person.

small talk A type of communication intended to build rapport; friendly, conventional, pleasant, and sometimes playful.

social learning theory A psychological theory of development that focuses on learning through observation, imitation, and reinforcement.

social support network An interdependent group of family members, friends, and acquaintances that a person can draw on as a resource.

social system One of the four major components of the sociocultural context in which families live; encompasses the influence of the community, laws, economic resources, educational opportunities, and other external factors on the family.

sole custody A child custody arrangement following a divorce in which only one parent has legal and physical custody of the child or children; the other parent generally has visitation rights.

spacious nest A positive descriptive term for the time in a marriage when the children have left home. *See also* empty nest syndrome.

spender A person whose money-handling style is characterized by enjoyment in purchasing items for himself or herself as well as for others.

sperm The male reproductive cells produced by the testes.

spermicide A contraceptive substance (gel, cream, or foam) that is toxic to sperm; usually used with a barrier device; may protect against certain sexually transmissible diseases.

spiritual well-being One of the six qualities (commonly found in emotionally healthy families) identified by researchers working within the family strengths framework.

spite talk A type of communication that conveys a "poor me" attitude; may reflect low self-esteem; drains the listener's energy and makes the listener want to change the subject or abandon the conversation.

split custody A legal child custody arrangement following a divorce in which each parent has sole custody of one or more of the children.

STD *See* sexually transmissible disease.

stepfamily The family created when one or both partners in a marriage have a child or children from a previous marriage. *See also* blended family; reconstituted family.

stepparent An adult who is married to one's biological parent but who is not one's birth parent.

Stepping Ahead Program An eight-step program designed to build strengths in stepfamilies.

stereotype A standardized, oversimplified view of someone or something.

sterilization Any procedure, but usually a surgical one, by which an individual is made incapable of reproduction.

stillbirth The birth of a dead fetus that was developmentally mature enough to have lived outside the womb; occurs in the 7th–9th months of pregnancy (the third trimester).

straight talk A type of communication that originates from both the head and the heart and attempts to deal completely and congruently with the issue under discussion.

stress The nonspecific response of the body to any demand made upon it.

stressful life event An event that creates a change in the family system.

stressor An external event that causes an emotional and/or a physical response and that can precipitate a crisis.

stress pile-up As described by the Double ABC-X model, the occurrence and after-effects of several stresses within a short period of time, which can strain an individual's or a family's coping abilities.

submissive symmetry A style of communication in which each participant tries to give control of the situation, and responsibility for it, to the other.

subsystem In general systems theory, a small system that is part of a larger suprasystem.

sudden infant death syndrome (SIDS) The sudden, unexpected death of an infant, which cannot be explained by postmortem examination or tests.

suprasystem In general systems theory, a large system that incorporates smaller subsystems.

surrogate motherhood A controversial approach to female infertility in which a fertile woman agrees, for a fee paid by a couple who cannot conceive, to be artificially inseminated by the husband's sperm, carry the baby to term, and give it to the couple at birth.

symbolic interaction framework A conceptual framework that focuses on the internal perceptions of family members and examines how they learn roles and rules in society through interaction and shared meaning.

symmetrical interaction A style of communication in which partners send similar messages designed to control how the relationship is defined. *See also* complementary interaction.

syncratic power pattern A pattern of sharing power in a relationship in which both partners share authority equally and make decisions jointly.

syphilis A sexually transmissible disease transmitted when mucous membranes or broken skin come into contact with an infectious lesion.

system A set of interconnected components that form a whole; what happens to one component affects all the other components.

tender years doctrine The legal presumption under traditional divorce laws that young children would do better with their mother than with their father after a divorce.

testes The male gonads, which produce testosterone and manufacture sperm; also called *testicles*.

testing A type of cohabiting relationship undertaken as a trial in a situation closely resembling marriage.

theory Systematically organized knowledge applicable in a wide variety of circumstances; especially, a system of assumptions, accepted principles, and rules of procedure devised to analyze, predict, or otherwise explain the nature or behavior of a specified set of phenomena.

time together One of the six qualities (commonly found in emotionally healthy families) identified by researchers working within the family strengths framework.

transition stage of grief The period during which the bereaved's grief lessens and he or she begins to recognize that a new life is possible; the second of Brubaker's three stages of the grieving process. *See also* crisis-loss stage of grief; new-life stage of grief.

trimester One of three periods of about 3 months each into which pregnancy is divided.

tubal ligation A female sterilization procedure in which the oviducts (fallopian tubes) are cut or tied and sealed.

umbilical cord A flexible structure that connects the fetus to the placenta and through which nutrients pass to the fetus and waste products are discharged.

unbalanced families Families who fall at the extremes on both the flexibility and the cohesion dimensions of the Family Circumplex Model: chaotically enmeshed, chaotically disengaged, rigidly enmeshed, or rigidly disengaged, families. *See also* balanced families; mid-range families.

uncontested divorce Under traditional divorce law, a divorce in which one party would charge the other party with an infraction that was considered by the court as grounds for granting a divorce and the accused party would agree not to challenge the accuser in court. In many cases parties were forced to collude and to perjure themselves in order to divorce.

underfunctioner   An individual who is disorganized and becomes less competent under stress.

uninvolved parenting   A style of parenting in which parents ignore their children and let them do what they wish unless it interferes with the parents' activities.

urethra   The tubular structure in men and women that carries urine from the bladder to an external opening. In men, semen passes through this duct before ejaculation.

uterus   An organ within the female pelvic cavity in which the fertilized egg develops into the fetus. Also called the *womb*.

vacuum curettage   An abortion method, used during the first trimester of pregnancy, in which the uterine contents are removed by suction.

vagina   The expandable passageway that leads from the uterus to the vulva in the female; acts as the birth canal during childbirth and receives the erect penis during sexual intercourse.

vaginismus   A sexual dysfunction in which a woman's vaginal muscles involuntarily constrict, preventing intercourse.

validity   The accuracy of a measurement.

values   Personal, lasting, deeply held basic beliefs about what is good, desirable, and important.

vasectomy   A male sterilization procedure in which the vasa deferentia are severed and tied.

victimizer   One who victimizes others. Children who grow up with violence often learn the potential for victimizing others as adults.

viral hepatitis   A liver infection caused by either of two viruses: hepatitis A and hepatitis B. The B virus is the more common of the two and is frequently transmitted through contaminated food, the sharing of needles during injection drug use, and during sexual activity because the virus is found in saliva, semen, vaginal secretions, and blood. Hepatitis A is usually transmitted orally.

vulva   The external female genital organs.

wholeness   A characteristic of systems; general systems theorists believe that the whole is more than the sum of its parts.

wife-dominant power pattern   A pattern of sharing power in a relationship in which the woman is the boss.

withdrawal   Removal of the penis from the vagina before ejaculation; an unreliable method of contraception.

zero-sum game   A game in which one side's margin of victory equals the other side's margin of defeat, producing a final sum of zero; what one person wins, the other loses.

zygote   The fertilized ovum (egg).

References

Abbott, D. A., & Meredith, W. H. (1988). Characteristics of strong families: Perceptions of ethnic parents. *Home Economics Research Journal, 17* (2), 140–147.

Abortion foes vow to fight: Maryland's governor OKs abortion-rights law. (1991, February 19). Lincoln [NE] *Journal*, p. 2.

Adler, N. E., David, H. P., Major, B. N., Roth, S. H., Russo, N. F., & Wyatt, G. E. (1992). Psychological factors in abortion: A review. *American Psychologist, 47* (October), 1194–1204.

Agnew, R. (1984). The effect of appearance on personality and behavior: Are the beautiful really good? *Youth and Society, 15* (3), 285–303.

Ahrons, C., & Perlmutter, M. (1982). The relationship between former spouses: A fundamental subsystem in the remarriage family. In J. C. Hansen & L. Messinger (Eds.), *Therapy with remarriage families* (pp. 31–46). Rockville, MD: Aspen.

Ahrons, C., & Rodgers, R. H. (1987). *Divorced families: A multidisciplinary view.* New York: Norton.

Alberti, R. E., & Emmons, M. L. (1983). *Your perfect right: A guide to assertive living.* San Luis Obispo, CA: Impact.

Albrecht, S. L. (1979). Correlates of marital happiness among the remarried. *Journal of Marriage and the Family, 41,* 857–867.

Alcohol impacts four of ten adults. (1991, October 1). Lincoln [NE] *Star*, p. 3.

Aldous, J. (1995). New views of grandparents in intergenerational context. *Journal of Family Issues, 16* (1), 104–122.

Allen, K. R., & Walker, A. J. (1992). Attentive love: A feminist perspective on the care giving of adult daughters. *Family Relations, 41* (July), 284–289.

Allen-Meares, P. (1989). Adolescent sexuality and premature parenthood: Role of the Black church in prevention. *Journal of Social Work and Human Sexuality, 8* (1), 133–142.

Allgeier, A. R., & Allgeier, E. R. (1995). *Sexual interactions* (4th ed.). Lexington, MA: Heath.

Alpern, D. M. (1988, March 14). It scares the hell out of me. *Newsweek*, p. 44.

Altura, J. (1974). Poem. In J. Gillies, *My needs, your needs.* New York: Doubleday.

Amato, P. R. (1993). Children's adjustment to divorce: Theories, hypotheses, and empirical support. *Journal of Marriage and the Family, 55* (February), 23–83.

American Psychiatric Association. (1994). *Diagnostic and statistical manual of mental disorders* (4th ed.). Washington, DC: Author.

Anglin, J. P. (1985). Parent education: Can an old tradition address new needs and new realities? In R. Williams, H. Lingren, G. Rowe, S. Van Zandt, P. Lee, & N. Stinnett (Eds.), *Family strengths 6: Enhancement of interaction* (pp. 203–225). Lincoln, NE: University of Nebraska, Department of Human Development and the Family, Center for Family Strengths.

Annon, J. S. (1994). *The behavioral treatment of sexual problems.* Vol. 1: *Brief therapy.* Vol. 2: *Intensive therapy.* Honolulu: Enabling Systems. New York: Harper & Row.

Aquilino, W. S., & Supple, K. R. (1991). Parent-child relations and parents' satisfaction with living arrangements when adult children live at home. *Journal of Marriage and the Family, 53* (February), 13–27.

Arcus, M. E., Schvaneveldt, J. D., & Moss, J. J. (Eds.). (1993a). *Handbook of family life education: Vol. I. Foundations of family life education.* Newbury Park, CA: Sage.

Arcus, M. E., Schvaneveldt, J. D., & Moss, J. J. (Eds.). (1993b). *Handbook of family life education: Vol. II. The practice of family life education.* Newbury Park, CA: Sage.

Argyle, M. (1988). *Bodily communication.* New York: Methuen.

Arond, M., & Pauker, S. L. (1987). *The first year of marriage.* New York: Warner Books.

Asai, S. (1996). *Gender roles and power allocation in Japanese society and families.* Unpublished manuscript. University of Minnesota, Family Social Science, St. Paul.

Attneave, C. (1982). The role of support systems in building family strengths. In N. Stinnett, J. DeFrain, K. King, H. Lingren, G. Rowe, S. Van Zandt, & R. Williams (Eds.) *Family strengths 4: Positive support systems* (pp. 309–314). Lincoln: University of Nebraska Press.

Azar, S. T., & Rohrbeck, C. A. (1986). Child abuse and unrealistic expectations: Further validation of the parent opinion questionnaire. *Journal of Consulting and Clinical Psychology, 54* (6), 867–868.

Azubike, I. C. (1987). Building strengths within the Black family. In H. G. Lingren, L. Kimmons, P. Lee, G. Rowe, L. Rottmann, L. Schwab, & R. Williams (Eds.), *Family strengths 8–9: Pathways to well-being.* Lincoln: University of Nebraska, Department of Human Development and the Family, Center for Family Strengths.

Baca Zinn, M. (1980). Chicano men and masculinity. *Journal of Ethnic Studies, 10* (2), 29–44.

Bach, G., & Wyden, P. (1969). *The intimate enemy: How to fight fair in love and marriage.* New York: Morrow.

Bader, E., Microys, G., Sinclair, L., Willett, E., & Conway, B. (1980). Do marriage preparation programs really work? A Canadian experiment. *Journal of Marital and Family Therapy, 6,* 171–179.

Bader, E., Riddle, R., & Sinclair, C. (1981). *Family therapy news.* Washington, DC: American Association for Marital and Family Therapy.

Bader, L., DeFrain, J., & Parkhurst, A. (1982). What parents feel when their child divorces. *Family Perspective* (Spring), 93–100.

Baldwin, S. E., & Baranoski, M. V. (1990). Family interactions and sex education in the home. *Adolescence, 25* (Fall), 573–582.

Barkas, J. L. (1980). *Single in America.* New York: Atheneum.

Barnes, H., & Olson, D. H. (1986). Parent-adolescent communication. In D. H. Olson, H. I. McCubbin, H. Barnes, A. Larsen, M. Muxen, & M. Wilson (Eds.), *Family inventories* (pp. 51–57). St. Paul: University of Minnesota, Family Social Service.

Barnhill, L. R. (1979). Healthy family systems. *Family Coordinator, 28,* 94–100.

Bateson, G., Jackson, D. D., Haley, J., & Weakland, J. (1956). Toward a theory of schizophrenia. *Behavioral Science, 1,* 251–264.

Bauer, J. W., & Wollen, B. J. (1990). *Financial management extension consultant program: Young singles and young couples.* St. Paul: Minnesota Extension Service.

Baumrind, D. (1991). The influence of parenting style on adolescent competence and substance abuse. *Journal of Early Adolescence, 11* (1), 56–95.

Baumrind, D. (1994). The social context of child maltreatment. *Family Relations, 43,* 360–368.

Beavers, W. R., & Hampson, R. B. (1990). *Successful families.* New York: Norton.

Becker, L. A. (1989). Family systems and compliance with medical regimen. In C. N. Ramsey (Ed.). *Family systems in medicine* (pp. 416–434). New York: Guilford Press.

Becvar, D. S., & Becvar, R. J. (1993). *Family therapy: A systemic integration* (2nd ed.). Boston: Allyn & Bacon.

Beigel, H. G. (1953). The meaning of coital postures. *International Journal of Sexology, 4,* 136–143.

Bell, R. Q. (1977). *Child effects on adults.* Hillsdale, NJ: Lawrence Erlbaum.

Belsky, J. (1991). Parental and nonparental child care and children's socioemotional development: A decade in review. In A. Booth (Eds.), *Contemporary families: Looking forward, looking back* (pp. 122–140). Minneapolis: National Council on Family Relations.

Bem, S. L. (1993). *The lenses of gender: Transforming the debate on sexual inequality.* New Haven, CT: Yale University Press.

Berger, C. R. (1980). Power and the family. In M. Roloff & G. Miller (Eds.), *Persuasion: New directions in theory and research* (pp. 197–224). Beverly Hills, CA: Sage.

Bernard, J. (1970). Women, marriage, and the future. *Futurist, 4,* 41–43.

Berscheid, E. (1982, January 11). America's obsession with beautiful people: Interview with Ellen Berscheid, psychologist. *U.S. News & World Report,* pp. 60–61.

Bernstein, B. E. (1977). Legal problems of cohabitation. *Family Coordinator* (October), 361–366.

Bierstedt, R. (1950). An analysis of social power. *American Sociological Review, 6,* 7–30.

Billingsley, A. (1986). *Black families in White America.* Englewood Cliffs, NJ: Prentice-Hall.

Blair, S. L., & Lichter, D. T. (1991). Measuring the division of household labor: Gender segregation of housework among American couples. *Journal of Family Issues, 12* (1), 91–113.

Blankenhorn, D. (1990). American family dilemmas. In D. Blankenhorn, S. Bayne, & J. B. Elshtain (Eds.), *Rebuilding the nest.* Milwaukee: Family Service America.

Blankenhorn, D. (1995). *Fatherless America: Confronting our most urgent social problem.* New York: Basic.

Blieszner, R., & Shifflett, P. A. (1990). The effects of Alzheimer's disease on close relationships between patients and caregivers. *Family Relations, 39* (January), 57–62.

Blood, R. O., & Wolfe, D. M. (1960). *Husbands and wives.* Glencoe, IL: Free Press.

Blumstein, P. W., & Schwartz, P. (1983). *American couples.* New York: Morrow.

Bohannan, P. (1970). The six stations of divorce. In P. Bohannan (Ed.), *Divorce and after* (pp. 29–55). New York: Doubleday.

Borcherdt, B. (1989). *Think straight! Feel great! 21 guides to emotional self-control.* Sarasota, FL: Professional Resource Exchange.

Borg, S., & Lasker, J. (1981). *When pregnancy fails: Families coping with miscarriage, stillbirth, and infant death.* Boston: Beacon Press.

Boss, P. (1988). *Family stress management.* Newbury Park, CA: Sage.

Boss, P. (1992). Primacy of perception in family stress theory and measurement. *Journal of Family Psychology, 6* (2), 113–119.

Boston Women's Health Book Collective. (1992). *The new our bodies, ourselves.* New York: Touchstone/Simon & Schuster.

Boulding, K. (1985). *Human betterment.* Beverly Hills, CA: Sage.

Bowker, L. H., Arbitell, M., & McFerron, J. R. (1988). On the relationship between wife beating and child abuse. In K. Yllo & M. Bograd (Eds.), *Feminist perspective on wife abuse* (pp. 158–175). Newbury Park, CA: Sage.

Boyd-Franklin, N. (1989). *Black families in therapy: A multisystems approach.* New York: Guilford.

Bozzi, V. (1985, August). Choose me. *Psychology Today*, pp. 60–61.

Bretschneider, J. G., & McCoy, N. L. (1988). Sexual interest and behavior in healthy 80- to 102-year-olds. *Archives of Sexual Behaviors, 17,* 109–129.

Broderick, C. (1984). *Marriage and the family* (2nd ed.) (pp. 2–4). Englewood Cliffs, NJ: Prentice-Hall.

Brody, J. E. (1995, August 31). Abortion method using two drugs gains in a study. *New York Times*, p. A1.

Browne, A., & Finkelhor, D. (1986). Initial and long-term effects: A review of the research. In D. Finkelhor (Ed.), *Sourcebook on child sexual abuse.* Beverly Hills, CA: Sage.

Browning, R. (1970). Grow old along with me! In I. Jack, (Ed.), *Browning: Poetical works.* Oxford: Oxford University Press. (Original work published 1864)

Brubaker, T. H. (1985). *Later life families.* Beverly Hills, CA: Sage.

Brubaker, T. H. (1991). Families in later life: A burgeoning research area. In A. Booth (Ed.), *Contemporary families: Looking forward, looking back* (pp. 226–248). Minneapolis: National Council on Family Relations.

Brydon, S., & Scott, M. (1997). *Between one and many* (2nd ed.). Mountain View, CA: Mayfield.

Bulcroft, K., & O'Conner-Roden, M. (1986, June). Never too late. *Psychology Today*, pp. 66–69.

Bumiller, E. (1985, December 20). Marriages still arranged but may be vetoed in India. *Washington Post*, p. 8.

Bumpass, L., & Sweet, J. (1989). National estimates of cohabitation: Cohort levels and union stability (NSFH Working Paper No. 2). Madison: University of Wisconsin–Madison, Center for Demography and Ecology.

Burgess, B. J. (1980). Parenting in the Native American community. In M. D. Fantini & R. Cardinas (Eds.), *Parenting in a multicultural society* (pp. 63–73). New York: Longman.

Burgess, E. W., & Wallin, P. (1943). Homogamy in social characteristics. *American Journal of Sociology, 49* (2), 109–124.

Burr, J. (1990). Race/sex comparisons of elderly living arrangements. *Research on Aging, 12* (December), 507–530.

Burr, W. R., Day, R. D., & Bahr, K. S. (1993). *Family science.* Pacific Grove, CA: Brooks/Cole.

Burr, W. R., & Klein, S. R. (1994). *Reexamining family stress.* Thousand Oaks, CA: Sage.

Burt, M. (Ed.). (1989). *Stepfamilies stepping ahead* (3rd ed.). Lincoln, NE: Stepfamilies Press.

Burton, S. (1990, May 14). Straight talk on sex in China. *Time*, p. 82.

Byrne, D. (1983). Sex without contraception. In D. Byrne & W. A. Fisher (Eds.), *Adolescents, sex, and contraception.* Hillsdale, NJ: Lawrence Erlbaum.

Calderone, M. S., & Johnson, E. W. (1989). *The family book about sexuality.* New York: Harper & Row.

Campbell, T. L. (1995). *The effectiveness of family interventions in the treatment of physical illness.* Unpublished manuscript. University of Rochester, Department of Family Medicine, Rochester, NY.

Carnes, P. (1989). *Counseling sexual abusers.* Minneapolis: CompCare Publications.

Caron, S. L., Bertran, R. M., & McMullen, T. (1987). AIDS and the college student: The need for sex education. *SIECUS Report XV* (6, July/August), 6–7.

Carson, D. K., Dail, P. W., Greeley, S., & Kenote, T. (1990). Stresses and strengths of Native American reservation families in poverty. *Family Perspective, 24* (4), 383–400.

Cate, R. M., & Lloyd, S. A. (1991). *Courtship.* Newbury Park, CA: Sage.

Centers for Disease Control and Prevention. (1994, February). *HIV/AIDS surveillance report.* Atlanta, GA: Author.

Cherlin, A. (1993). Personal communication. Baltimore, MD: Johns Hopkins University, Department of Sociology.

Children's Defense Fund. (1988). A children's defense budget: FY 1989. Washington, DC: Author.

Christopher, F. S., & Roosa, M. W. (1990). An evaluation of an adolescent pregnancy prevention program: Is "just say no" enough? *Family Relations, 39,* 68–72.

Clarke, J. (1984). *The family types of schizophrenics, neurotics and "normals."* Unpublished doctoral dissertation. University of Minnesota, Department of Family Social Science, St. Paul.

Clift, E. (1992, July 13). Abortion angst: How the court's ruling will affect women, doctors and activists on both sides. *Newsweek*, pp. 16–19.

Cohen, S. S. (1987). *The magic of touch.* New York: Harper & Row.

Cohen, S. (1995, October 1). 50,000 women plan lawsuits over Norplant contraceptive. Lincoln [NE] *Journal Star*, p. 7A.

Cole, W., Dickerson, J. F., & Smilgis, M. (1994, October 17). Now for the truth about Americans and sex: The first comprehensive survey since Kinsey smashes some of our most intimate myths. *Time*, pp. 62–70.

Coleman, B. C. (1995, September 27). Secondhand smoke threatens workers, new study reveals. Lincoln [NE] *Journal Star*, p. 5A.

Coleman, J. C. (1988). *Intimate relationships, marriage, and family* (2nd ed.). New York: Macmillan.

Coleman, M., & Ganong, L. H. (1991). Remarriage and stepfamily research in the 1980s: Increased interest in an old family form. In A. Booth (Ed.), *Contemporary families: Looking forward, looking back* (pp. 192–207). Minneapolis: National Council on Family Relations.

College sex habits mostly unchanged. (1990, March 22). Lincoln [NE] *Journal*, p. 31.

Cook, E. P. (1985). *Psychological androgyny*. New York: Pergamon.

Corrales, R. (1975). Power and satisfaction in early marriage. In R. E. Cromwell & D. H. Olson (Eds.), *Power in families* (pp. 197–216). New York: Halsted/Wiley.

Courtois, C. A. (1988). *Healing the incest wound*. New York: Norton.

Cowan, A. L. (1989, August 21). Women's gains on the job not without a heavy toll. *New York Times*, pp. I1.

Cowley, G. (1989, March 13). How the mind was designed: Evolutionary theory is yielding rich new insights into everything from cognition to sexual desire. *Newsweek*, pp. 56–58.

Cox, F. D. (1990). *Human intimacy: Marriage, the family and its meaning*. St. Paul, MN: West.

Cox News Service. (1990, September 22). Admitting cheating isn't easy, but some marriages survive. Lincoln [NE] *Sunday Journal and Star*, p. 1J.

Craddock, A. E. (1984). Correlations between marital role expectations and relationship satisfaction among engaged couples. *Australian Journal of Sex, Marriage and the Family, 4*, 33–46.

Cromwell, R. E., & Olson, D. H. (Eds.). (1975). *Power in families*. New York: Halsted/Wiley.

Cronin, M., & Leviton, J. (1989, January 30). The other dangers of close encounters. *Time*, p. 62.

Crosby, J. F. (1991). *Illusion and disillusion*. Belmont, CA: Wadsworth.

Cross, R. J. (1993). What doctors and others need to know: Six facts on human sexuality and aging. *SIECUS Report, 21* (5), 7–9.

Cupach, W. R., & Spitzberg, B. H. (Eds.). (1994). *The dark side of interpersonal communication*. Hillsdale, NJ: Lawrence Erlbaum.

Curran, D. (1983). *Traits of a healthy family*. Minneapolis: Winston Press.

Czaplewski, M. J. (1995). Preface. In M. J. Hogan (Ed.) *Initiatives for families: Research, policy, practice, education* (p. i). St. Paul, MN: National Council on Family Relations.

Dahl, T. (1980). *Model of stress*. Unpublished manuscript. University of Minnesota, Minneapolis.

Daly, M., & Wilson, M. (1985). Child abuse and other risks of not living with both parents. *Ethology and Sociobiology, 6*, 197–210.

Danes, S. (1992). Parental perceptions of children's financial socialization. In R. Imas (Ed.), *Proceedings of the Association for Financial Counseling and Planning Education* (pp. 16–35). Charleston, SC: Assn. for Financial Counseling and Planning Education.

Darnton, N., Springen, K., Wright, L., & Keene-Osborn, S. (1991, October 7). The pain of the last taboo. *Newsweek*, pp. 70–72.

Davis, K. E. (1985, February). Near and dear: Friendship and love compared. *Psychology Today, 19*, pp. 22–30.

Davis, M., & Scott, R. (1988). *Lovers, doctors, and the law*. New York: Perennial/Harper & Row.

Day, A. T. (1991). *Remarkable survivors: Insights into successful aging among women*. Washington, DC: Urban Institute Press.

Day, R. D., Gilbert, K. R., Settles, B. H., & Burr, W. R. (1995). *Research and theory in family science*. Pacific Grove, CA: Brooks/Cole.

Day, R. D., & Hooks, D. (1987). Miscarriage: A special type of family crisis. *Family Relations, 36*, 305–310.

DeFrain, J. (1974, October 26). *A father's guide to parent guides: Review and assessment of the paternal role as conceived in the popular literature*. Paper presented at the annual meeting of the National Council on Family Relations/American Association of Marriage and Family Counselors, St. Louis.

DeFrain, J. (1975). *The nature and meaning of parenthood*. Unpublished doctoral dissertation. University of Wisconsin, Madison.

DeFrain, J. (1979). Androgynous parents outline their needs. *Family Coordinator* (April), 237–243.

DeFrain, J. (1991). Learning about grief from normal families: SIDS, stillbirth, and miscarriage. *Journal of Marital and Family Therapy* (July), 215–323.

DeFrain, J., DeFrain, N., & Lepard, N. (1994). Family strengths and challenges in the South Pacific: An exploratory study. *International Journal of the Sociology of the Family, 24* (2), 25–47.

DeFrain, J., & Eirick, R. (1981). Coping as divorced single parents: A comparative study of fathers and mothers. *Family Relations, 29*, 264–273.

DeFrain, J., Ernst, L., Jakub, D., & Taylor, J. (1991). *Sudden infant death: Enduring the loss*. New York: Lexington Books/Macmillan.

DeFrain, J., Fricke, J., & Elmen, J. (1987). *On our own: A single parent's survival guide*. Lexington, MA: Lexington Books/Heath.

DeFrain, J., Martens, L., Stock, J., & Stork, W. (1986). *Stillborn: The invisible death*. Lexington, MA: Lexington Books/Heath.

DeFrain, J., & Stinnett, N. (1992). Building on the inherent strengths of families: A positive approach for family psychologists and counselors. *Topics in Family Psychology and Counseling, 1* (1, January), 15–26.

Degler, C. N. (1980). *At odds.* New York: Oxford University Press.

DeLuccie, M. (1995). Mothers as gatekeepers: A model of maternal mediators of father involvement. *Journal of Genetic Psychology, 156*(1), 115–131.

DeMaris, A., & Rao, K. V. (1992). Premarital cohabitation and marital stability. *Journal of Marriage and the Family, 54* (February), 178–190.

Denneny, M. (1979). *Lovers: The story of two men.* New York: Avon.

Demo, D. H., & Acock, A. C. (1991). The impact of divorce on children. In A. Booth (Ed.), *Contemporary families: Looking forward, looking back* (pp. 162–191). Minneapolis: National Council on Family Relations.

Detzner, D. F. (1992). Life histories: Conflict in Southeast Asian refugee families. In J. F. Gilgun, K. Daly, & G. Handel (Eds.), *Qualitative methods in family research* (pp. 85–102). Newbury Park, CA: Sage.

Dewit, D. J., Wister, A. V., & Burch, T. K. (1988). Physical distance and social contact between elders and their adult children. *Research on Aging, 10,* 56–80.

Dick-Read, G. (1984). *Childbirth without fear: The original approach to natural childbirth* (5th ed.). New York: Harper & Row.

Dobash, R. E., & Dobash, R. D. (1979). *Violence against wives.* New York: Free Press.

Dobson, J. (1983). *Love must be tough.* Waco, TX: Word Books.

Doherty, W. J. (1992, June). Private lives, public values. *Psychology Today, 25,* pp. 32–37.

Doherty, W. J., & Allen, W. (1994). Family functioning and parental smoking as predictors of adolescent cigarette use: A six-year prospective study. *Journal of Family Psychology, 8* (3), 347–353.

Doherty, W. J., & Baird, M. A. (1983). *Family therapy and family medicine.* New York: Guilford Press.

Doherty, W. J., & Campbell, T. L. (1988). *Families and health.* Newbury Park, CA: Sage.

Doherty, W. J., Kouneski, E. F., & Erickson, M. F. (1996, June). *Responsible fathering: An overview and conceptual framework.* Submitted to Administration for Children and Families, U.S. Department of Health and Human Services.

Doherty, W. J., Lester, M. E., & Leigh, G. (1986). Marriage encounter weekends: Couples who win and couples who lose. *Journal of Marital and Family Therapy, 12,* 49–61.

Doherty, W. J., & Simmons, D. S. (1996). Clinical practice patterns of marriage and family therapists: A national survey of therapists and their clients. *Journal of Marital and Family Therapy, 22,* 9–25.

Doherty, W. J., & Whitehead, D. (1986). The social dynamics of cigarette smoking: A family system perspective. *Family Process, 25,* 453–460.

Doress, P. B., & Siegal, D. L. (1987). *Ourselves, growing older: Women aging with knowledge and power* (pp. 133–136). New York: Simon & Schuster/Touchstone.

Druckman, J. M., Fournier, D. F., Olson, D. H., & Robinson, B. E. (1981). *Effectiveness of various premarital preparation programs.* Unpublished manuscript. University of Minnesota, Department of Family Social Science, St. Paul.

Dubowitz, H., & Egan, H. (1988). The maltreatment of infants. In M. B. Straus (Ed.), *Abuse and victimization across the life span* (pp. 32–53). Baltimore: Johns Hopkins University Press.

Duvall, E. M., & Miller, B. C. (1985). *Marriage and family development* (6th ed.). New York: Harper & Row.

Edwards, P. (1989). Assessment of symptoms in adult survivors of incest: A factor analytic study of the responses to childhood incest questionnaire. *Child Abuse and Neglect, 13,* 101–110.

Ehrlich, H. (1984, December 31). Double duty for moms: Keeping house and a job is a strain. *USA Today,* p. 1.

Einstein, A. (1988). Cosmic religion. In L. D. Eigen and J. P. Siegel (Eds.), *The Macmillan dictionary of political quotations.* New York: Macmillan. (Original work published 1931)

Elias, M. (1985, February 7). Most singles are enjoying life to fullest. *USA Today,* p. D1.

Elmer-DeWitt, P. (1990, February 26). A bitter pill to swallow. *Time,* p. 44.

Epstein, N. B., Bishop, D. S., Ryan, C., Miller, I., & Keitner, G. (1993). The McMaster model of family functioning. In F. Walsh (Ed.), *Normal family processes* (pp. 138–160). New York: Guilford Press.

Erikson, E. H. (1950). *Childhood and society.* New York: Norton.

Erikson, E. H. (1968). Life cycle. In D. L. Sills (Ed.), *International encyclopedia of the social sciences* (p. 9). New York: Free Press/Macmillan.

Family violence top health issue. (1991, October 17). Lincoln [NE] *Star,* p. 3.

Fenell, D. L., & Weinhold, B. K. (1989). *Counseling families: An introduction to marriage and family therapy.* Denver: Love.

Finkelhor, D. (1984). *Child sexual abuse: New theory and research.* New York: Free Press.

Finkelhor, D., & Araji, S. (1986). Explanations of pedophilia: A four-factor model. *Journal of Sex Research, 22,* 145–161.

Fitzpatrick, M. H. (1988). *Between husbands and wives: Communication in marriage.* Beverly Hills, CA: Sage.

Fletcher, W. L., & Hansson, R. O. (1991). Assessing the social components of retirement anxiety. *Psychology and Aging, 6* (March), 76–85.

Fowers, B. J., & Olson, D. H. (1986). Predicting marital success with PREPARE: A predictive validity study. *Journal of Marital and Family Therapy, 12* (4), 403–413.

Fowers, B. J., & Olson, D. H. (1989). ENRICH marital inventory: A discriminate validity study. *Journal of Marital and Family Therapy, 15,* 65–79.

Fox, G. L. (1980). Love match and arranged marriage in a modernizing nation: Mate selection in Ankara, Turkey. *Journal of Marriage and the Family, 42* (4, November), 180–193.

Frahm, L. (1987, November 21). Growing beyond macho attitudes. Lincoln [NE] *Star,* p. 10.

Francis, D., Hadler, S. C., Prendergast, T. J., Peterson, E., Ginsberg, M. M., Lookabaugh, C., Holmes, J. R., & Maynard, J. E. (1984). Occurrences of hepatitis A, B, and non-A, non-B in the United States: CDC Sentinel County hepatitis study. *American Journal of Medicine, 76,* 69–74.

Francoeur, R. T. (1982). *Becoming a sexual person.* New York: Wiley.

Franklin, B. (1980) Poor Richard's almanac (May). In E. M. Beck (Ed.). *Familiar quotations: John Bartlett.* Boston: Little, Brown. (Original work published 1733)

Franklin, C. W., II. (1989). The male sex drive. In L. Richardson & V. Taylor (Eds.), *Feminist frontiers II* (pp. 274–278). New York: Random House.

Fravel, D. L. (1995). *Boundary ambiguity perceptions of adoptive parents experiencing various levels of openness in adoption.* Unpublished doctoral dissertation. University of Minnesota, St. Paul, MN.

Friedan, B. (1963). *The feminine mystique.* New York: Norton.

Friedan, B. (1985, November 3). How to get the women's movement moving again. *New York Times Magazine,* pp. 57–61.

Fromm, E. (1956). *The art of loving.* New York: Harper Bros.

Frost, R. (1946). *The poems of Robert Frost.* New York: Random House.

Furstenburg, F. F., Brooks-Gunn, J., & Morgan, S. P. (1988). *Adolescent mothers in later life.* New York: Cambridge University Press.

Gallup, Inc. (1989). *Love and marriage.* Princeton, NJ: Gallup Organization.

Gallup Poll. (1996). *Gender and society: Status and stereotypes.* Princeton, NJ: Gallup Organization.

Galvin, K. M., & Brommel, B. J. (1986). *Family communication: Cohesion and change* (2nd ed.). Glenview, IL: Scott, Foresman.

Garbarino, J., Sebes, J., & Schellenbach, C. (1984). Families at risk for destructive parent-child relations in adolescence. *Child Development, 55,* 174–183.

Garman, E. T., & Forgue, R. E. (1991). *Personal finance* (3rd ed.). Boston: Houghton Mifflin.

Gary, L. E., Beatty, L. A., & Berry, G. L. (1986). Strong Black families: Models of program development for Black families. In S. Van Zandt, H. Lingren, G. Rowe, P. Zeece, L. Kimmons, P. Lee, D. Shell, & N. Stinnett (Eds.), *Family strengths 7: Vital connections* (pp. 453–468). Lincoln: University of Nebraska, Department of Human Development and the Family, Center for Family Strengths.

Gay, P. (1984). The bourgeois experience: Victoria to Freud. New York: Oxford University Press.

Gelles, R. J. (1972). *The violent home.* Beverly Hills, CA: Sage.

Gelles, R. J., & Cornell, C. P. (1985). *Intimate violence in families.* Beverly Hills, CA: Sage.

Gelles, R. J., & Harrop, J. W. (1989). Violence, battering and psychological distress among women. *Journal of Interpersonal Violence, 4,* 400–420.

Gelles, R. J., & Straus, M. A. (1988). *Intimate violence.* New York: Simon & Schuster.

Gibran, K. (1923/1976). *The Prophet.* New York: Knopf.

Gilewski, M., Faberow, N. L., Gallagher, D. E., & Thompson, L. (1991). Interaction of depression and bereavement on mental health in the elderly. *Psychology and Aging, 6* (1), 67–75.

Glick, P. (1989). Remarried families, stepfamilies, and stepchildren: A brief demographic analysis. *Family Relations, 38,* 24–27.

Glick, P., & Lin, S.-L. (1986). More young adults are living with their parents: Who are they? *Journal of Marriage and the Family, 48* (February), 107–112.

Goldberg, M. S. (1993). Choosing a contraceptive. *FDA Consumer, 27* (7), pp. 18–25.

Goldenberg, I., & Goldenberg, H. (1991). *Family therapy: An overview.* Pacific Grove, CA: Brooks/Cole.

Goldstein, A. P., Keller, H., & Erne, D. (1985). *Changing the abusive parent.* Champaign, IL: Research Press.

Goodman, M. (1986, November). Americans and their money: 1986. *Money,* p. 159.

Gordon, S., & Gordon, J. (1990). *Raising a child conservatively in a sexually permissive world.* New York: Fireside/Simon & Schuster.

Gordon, S., & Snyder, C. (1989). *Personal issues in human sexuality: A guidebook for better sexual health.* Boston: Allyn & Bacon.

Gorman, C. (1991, October 7). Incest comes out of the dark. *Time,* p. 46.

Gould, R. L. (1975, August). Adult life stages: Growth towards self-tolerance. *Psychology Today,* pp. 74–78.

Green, S. K., Buchanan, D. R., & Heuer, S. K. (1984). Winners, losers, and choosers: A field investigation of dating initiation. *Personality and Social Psychology Bulletin, 10* (4), 502–511.

Gregersen, E. (1983). *Sexual practices: The story of human sexuality.* New York: Franklin Watts.

Grief, G. L. (1995). Single fathers with custody following separation and divorce. *Marriage and Family Review, 20* (1/2), 213–232.

Grimes, D. (1994). Teens heed doll's drastic lesson. Sarasota [FL] *Herald-Tribune Syndicate.*

Griswold, R. L. (1993). *Fatherhood in America.* New York: Basic.

Grotevant, H. D., McRoy, R. G., Elde, C., & Fravel, D. L. (1994). Adoptive family system dynamics: Variations by level of openness in the adoption. *Family Process, 33,* 125–146.

Guerney, B., Jr., & Maxson, P. (1991). Marital and family enrichment research. In A. Booth (Ed.), *Contemporary families: Looking forward, looking back* (pp. 457–465). Minneapolis: National Council on Family Relations.

Gurin, J. (1985). From "me" to "we": The us generation. *American Health* (October), 40–41.

Haley, J. (1959). The family of the schizophrenic: A model system. *Journal of Nervous and Mental Disorders, 129,* 357–374.

Haley, J. (1972). *Strategies of psychotherapy.* New York: Bruner & Stratton.

Hall, D. R., & Zhao, J. Z. (1995). Cohabitation and divorce in Canada: Testing the selectivity hypothesis. *Journal of Marriage and the Family, 57,* 421–427.

Hamilton, A., Stiles, W. B., Melowsky, F., & Beal, D. G. (1987). A multilevel comparison of child abusers with nonabusers. *Journal of Family Violence, 2,* 215–225.

Hanline, M. F., & Daley, S. E. (1992). Family coping strategies and strengths in Hispanic, African-American, and Caucasian families of young children. *Topics in Early Childhood Special Education, 12* (3), 351–366.

Hanson, S. M. H. (1986). Healthy single-parent families. *Family Relations, 35,* 125–132.

Hatcher, R. A., Trussell, J., Stewart, F., Stewart, G. K., Kowal, D., Guest, F., Cates, W., & Policar, M.S. (1994). *Contraceptive technology 1992–1994* (16th rev. ed.). New York: Irvington.

Hausknecht, R. U. (1995). Methotrexate and misoprostol to terminate early pregnancy. *New England Journal of Medicine, 333* (9), 537.

Hawkins, W. E., & Duncan, D. F. (1985). Children's illnesses as risk factors for child abuse. *Psychological Reports, 56,* 638.

Hawley, D. R., & Olson, D. H. (1995). Enriching newlyweds: An evaluation of three enrichment programs. *American Journal of Family Therapy, 23,* 129–147.

Hayes, M. P. (1979). Strengthening marriage in the middle years. In N. Stinnett, B. Chesser, & J. DeFrain (Eds.), *Building family strengths: Blueprints for action* (pp. 387–398). Lincoln: University of Nebraska Press.

Hayes, M. P., Stinnett, N., & DeFrain, J. (1980). Learning about marriage from the divorced. *Journal of Divorce, 4* (Fall), 23–30.

Hellmich, N. (1990, April 4). Marriage is no. 1 with men. *USA Today,* p. 1D.

Henshaw, S. (1987). Characteristics of U.S. women having abortions, 1982–1983. *Family Planning Perspectives, 19* (1), 5–9.

Henshaw, S. (1990). Major decline in availability of abortion. *Contemporary Sexuality, 24* (8), 6.

Henton, J., Cate, R., Koval, J., Lloyd, S., & Christopher, S. (1981). Romance and violence in dating relationships. *Journal of Family Issues, 4* (3, September), 467–482.

Herbst, P. G. (1952). The measurement of family relationships. *Human Relations, 5,* 3–35.

Hill, R. (1949). *Families under stress.* New York: Harper.

Hill, R. (1958). Generic features of families under stress. *Social Casework, 49,* 139–150.

Hobfoll, S. E., & Spielberger, C. D. (1992). Family stress: Integrating theory and measurement. *Journal of Family Psychology, 6* (2), 99–112.

Hochschild, A. (1989). *The second shift.* New York: Viking.

Hocker, J. L., & Wilmot, W. W. (1985). *Interpersonal conflict.* Dubuque, IA: William C. Brown.

Hodson, D. S., & Skeen, P. (1994). Sexuality and aging: The hammerlock of myths. *Journal of Applied Gerontology, 13* (3), 219–235.

Hogan, J. M. (1993). Family futures: Possibilities, preferences and probabilities. *Marriage and Family Review, 18,* 255–262.

Holmes, T. H., & Rahe, R. H. (1967). The social readjustment rating scale. *Journal of Psychosomatic Research, 11,* 213–218.

Homans, G. G. (1974). *Social behavior: Its elementary forms* (rev. ed.). New York: Harcourt Brace Jovanovich.

Hopkins, J., Marcues, M., & Campbell, S. B. (1984). Postpartum depression: A critical review. *Psychological Bulletin, 95,* 498–515.

Horn, W. F. (1995). *Father facts.* Lancaster, PA: The National Fatherhood Initiative.

Hunt, B. (1982, June). Six myths about old age. *Reader's Digest,* pp. 113–116.

Hyde, J. S. (1990). *Understanding human sexuality* (4th ed.). New York: McGraw-Hill.

Ihinger-Tallman, M., & Pasley, K. (1987). *Remarriage.* Newbury Park, CA: Sage.

Insel, P. M., & Roth, W. T. (1996). *Core concepts in health* (7th ed.—1996 update). Mountain View, CA: Mayfield.

Jackson, J. K. (1954). The adjustments of the family to the crisis of alcoholism. *Quarterly Journal of Studies on Alcohol, 15*, 562–586.

Jackson, J. K. (1992). *Wellness: AIDS, STD, and other communicable diseases.* Guilford, CT: Dushkin.

Jacob, B. (1986, August 8). Romance flowers in friendship's warmth. *USA Today*, p. 5D.

James, J. (1984, September 23). You. Seattle *Times/Post-Intelligencer*, p. F4.

Janus, S. S., & Janus, C. L. (1993). *The Janus report on sexual behavior.* New York: Wiley.

Johnson, C. K., & Price-Bonham, S. (1980). Women and retirement: A study and implications. *Family Relations, 29* (July), 380–385.

Johnson, V. E. (1973). *I'll quit tomorrow.* New York: Harper & Row.

Jones, E. F., & Stahmann, R. F. (1994). Clergy beliefs, preparation, and practice in premarital counseling. *Journal of Pastoral Care, 48*, 181–186.

Jouriles, E. N., & Norwood, W. D. (1995). Physical aggression toward boys and girls in families characterized by the battering of women. *Journal of Family Psychology, 9*, 69–78.

Kagan, J. (1964). *The nature of the child.* New York: Basic Books.

Kantor, D., & Lehr, W. (1974). *Inside the family.* San Francisco: Jossey-Bass.

Keillor, G. (1994, October 17). It's good old monogamy that's really sexy. *Time*, p. 71.

Kelly, G. F. (1994). *Sexuality today: The human perspective* (4th ed.). Guilford, CT: Dushkin.

Kennedy, J. F. (1990). Inaugural address. In D. B. Baker (Ed.), *Political quotations.* Detroit: Gale Research. (Original work published 1961)

Kerckhoff, A. C., & Davis, K. E. (1962). Value consensus and need complementarity in mate selection. *American Sociological Review, 27*, 295–303.

Kessler, R. C., Turner, J. B., & House, J. S. (1988). Effects of unemployment on health in a community survey. *Journal of Social Issues, 44*, 69–85.

Killorin, E., & Olson, D. H. (1984). The chaotic flippers in treatment. In E. Kaufman (Ed.), *Power to change: Alcoholism.* New York: Gardner Press.

Kilmann, R., & Thomas, K. (1975). Interpersonal conflict: Handling behavior as reflections of Jungian personality dimensions. *Psychological Reports, 37*, 971–980.

Kilpatrick, A. C. (1986). Some correlates of women's childhood sexual experiences: A retrospective study. *Journal of Sex Research, 22*, 221–242.

King, B. M., Camp, J., & Downey, A. M. (1991). *Human sexuality today.* Englewood Cliffs, NJ: Prentice Hall.

Kinsey, A., Pomeroy, W., & Martin, C. (1948). *Sexual behavior in the human male.* Philadelphia: Saunders.

Kinsey, A., Pomeroy, W., Martin, C., & Gebhard, P. (1953). *Sexual behavior in the human female.* Philadelphia: Saunders.

Kirk, E. P. (1984). Psychological effects and management of prenatal loss. *American Journal of Obstetrics and Gynecology, 149*, 46–50.

Kitson, G. C., & Morgan, L. A. (1991). The multiple consequences of divorce: A decade review. In A. Booth (Ed.), *Contemporary families: Looking forward, looking back* (pp. 150–161). Minneapolis: National Council on Family Relations.

Knudsen, D., & Miller, J. L. (Eds.). (1992). *Abused and battered: Social and legal responses to family violence.* New York: Aldine & deGruyter.

Kohlberg, L. (1966). Cognitive stages and preschool education. *Human Development, 9*, 5–17.

Kolb, T. M., & Straus, M. A. (1974). Marital power and marital happiness in relation to problem-solving ability. *Journal of Marriage and the Family, 36*, 756–766.

Kolbe, L. (1992, April 10). Quoted in "Most teens have had sex by 16," says CDC study. *Chicago Tribune*, p. C5.

Konner, M. (1988). Is orgasm essential? *The Sciences* (March/April), 4–7.

Koop, C. E. (1988). *Understanding AIDS: A message from the surgeon general* (Health and Human Services Publication No. [CDC] HHS-88-8404). Washington, DC: U.S. Government Printing Office.

Kottak, C. P. (1989). *Anthropology: The exploration of human diversity* (4th ed.). New York: Random House.

Kouneski, E. F. (1996). Fatherhood today. Unpublished article. St. Paul, MN: University of Minnesota, Family Social Science.

Kouri, K. M., & Lasswell, M. (1993). Black-White marriages: Social change and intergenerational mobility. *Marriage and Family Review, 19*, 241–255.

Krivosha, N. (1983). Transcription of tape-recorded interview with Nebraska Supreme Court Chief Justice Krivosha, conducted by graduate students of the Department of Human Development and the Family, University of Nebraska–Lincoln.

Kroll, J. (1991, June 10). Spiking a fever. *Newsweek*, pp. 44–47.

Krugman, R. D., Lenherr, M., Betz, L., & Fryer, G. E. (1986). The relationship between unemployment and physical abuse of children. *Child Abuse and Neglect, 10*, 415–418.

Kruttschnitt, C., Heath, L., & Ward, D. A. (1986). Family violence, television view habits, and other adolescent experiences related to violent criminal behavior. *Criminology, 24* (2), 235–267.

Krysan, M., Moore, K. A., & Zill, N. (1990). Identifying successful families: An overview of constructs and selected measures. Washington, DC: Child Trends, Inc.

[2100 M St., NW, Suite 610] and the U.S. Department of Health & Human Services, Office of the Assistant Secretary for Planning and Evaluation.

Lambert, B. (1990, July 17). Ten years later, hepatitis study still yields critical data on AIDS. *New York Times*, p. C3.

Landers, A. (1989, January 22). Survey says sex lives fizzle after marriage. Lincoln [NE] *Sunday Journal Star*, p. 4D.

Landers, S. (1989a). Koop will not release abortion effects report. *American Psychological Association Monitor* (March), 1.

LaRossa, R., & Reitzes, D. C. (1993). Symbolic interaction and family studies. In P. G. Boss, W. J. Doherty, R. LaRossa, W. R. Schumm, & S. K. Steinmetz (Eds.), *Sourcebook of family theories and methods* (pp. 135–162). New York: Plenum.

Larsen, A. S., & Olson, D. H. (1989). Predicting marital satisfaction using PREPARE: A replication study. *Journal of Marital and Family Therapy*, 15, 311–322.

Larson, R., & Richards, M. H. (1994). *Divergent realities: The emotional lives of mothers, fathers, and adolescents*. New York: Basic Books.

Lasswell, M., & Lasswell, T. (1991). *Marriage and the family* (3rd ed.). Belmont, CA: Wadsworth, p. 256.

Lauer, J., & Lauer, R. (1985, June). Marriages made to last. *Psychology Today*, 19, pp. 22–26.

Lauer, R. H. (1989). *Social problems and the quality of life* (4th ed.). Dubuque, IA: William C. Brown.

Laumann, E. O., Gagnon, J. H., Michael, R. T., Michaels, S., & Kolata, G. (1995). *Sex in America: A definitive survey*. Boston: Little, Brown.

Leboyer, F. (1975). *Birth without violence*. New York: Knopf.

Lee, G. R., & Stone, L. H. (1980). Mate selection systems and criteria: Variation according to family structure. *Journal of Marriage and the Family*, 42 (2, May), 319–326.

Lee, S. M., & Yamanaka, K. (1990). Patterns of Asian American intermarriage and marital assimilation. *Journal of Comparative Family Studies*, 21, 287–304.

Leifer, M. (1980). *Psychological effects of motherhood: A study of first pregnancy*. New York: Praeger.

LeMasters, E. E. (1957). Parenthood as crisis. *Marriage and Family Living*, 19, 325–355.

LeMasters, E. E., & DeFrain, J. (1989). *Parents in contemporary America: A sympathetic view*. Belmont, CA: Wadsworth.

Leo, J. (1986, November 24). Sex and schools: AIDS and the surgeon general add a new urgency to an old debate. *Time*, pp. 54–60, 63.

Lerner, H. G. (1985). *The dance of anger*. New York: Harper & Row.

Leslie, L. A., Anderson, E. A., & Branson, M. P. (1991). Responsibility for children: The role of gender and employment. *Journal of Family Issues*, 12 (2, June), 197–210.

Levine, J. A., & Pitt, E. W. (1995). *New expectations: Community strategies for responsible fatherhood*. New York: Families and Work Institute.

Levinson, D. (1978). *The seasons of a man's life*. New York: Knopf.

Levinson, M. (1991, November 4). Living on the edge. *Newsweek*, p. 20.

Levy, D. S. (1991, September 16). Why Johnny might grow up violent and sexist. *Time*, pp. 16–19.

Lewis, J. M. (1989). *How's your family?* New York: Brunner/Mazel.

Lewis, R. (1981). Patterns of strengths of American Indian families. In J. R. Red Horse, A. Shattuck, & F. Hoffman (Eds.), *The American Indian family: Stresses and strengths* (pp. 101–106). [Proceedings of the Conference on Research Issues, Phoenix, Arizona, April 1980.] Isleta, NM: American Indian Social Research and Development Associates.

Lewis, R. A., Kozac, E. B., Milardo, R. M., & Grosnick, W. A. (1981). Commitment in same-sex love relationships. *Alternative Lifestyles*, 4 (1), 22–42.

Lewis, R., Spanier, G., Atkinson, V. L. S., & Lehecka, C. F. (1977). Commitment in married and unmarried cohabitation. *Sociological Focus*, 10 (4), 367–374.

Lincoln Family Service Association. (1991). *Violence workshop resources*. Lincoln, NE: Family Service Association.

Lino, M. (1991a). Expenditures on a child by single-parent families. *Family Economics Review*, 4 (1), 2–24.

Lino, M. (1991b). Expenditures on a child by two-parent families. *Family Economics Review*, 4 (1), 25–38.

Litman, T. J. (1974). The family as a basic unit in health and medical care: A social-behavioral overview. *Social Science and Medicine*, 8, 495–519.

Loeber, R., & Dishion, T. J. (1984). Boys who fight at home and school: Family conditions influencing cross-setting consistency. *Journal of Consulting and Clinical Psychology*, 52 (5), 759–768.

LoPiccolo, J., & Stock, W. E. (1986). Treatment of sexual dysfunction. *Journal of Counseling and Clinical Psychology*, 54 (2), 158–167.

Lord, L. (1987, November 30). Coming to grips with alcoholism. *U.S. News & World Report*, pp. 56–62.

Lore, R. K., & Schultz, L. A. (1993). Control of human aggression: A comparative perspective. *American Psychologist*, 48 (January), 16–25.

Lovelock, J. E. (1979, 1987). *Gaia: A new look at life on earth*. Oxford, England: Oxford University Press.

MacDonald, W. L., & DeMaris, A. (1995). Remarriage, stepchildren, and marital conflict. Challenges to the incomplete institutionalization hypothesis. *Journal of Marriage and the Family*, 57 (May), 387–398.

Mace, D. (1982a). Current thinking on marriage and money. *Medical Aspects of Human Sexuality*, 16, 109–118.

Mace, D. (1982b). *Love and anger in marriage.* Grand Rapids, MI: Zondevan Publishing.

Mace, D., & Mace, V. (1980). Enriching marriages: The foundation stone of family strength. In N. Stinnett, B. Chesser, J. DeFrain, & P. Knaub (Eds.), *Family strengths: Positive models for family life.* Lincoln: University of Nebraska Press.

Macklin, E. D. (1980). Nontraditional family forms: A decade of research. *Journal of Marriage and the Family, 42* (November), 905–922.

Madden, M. E. (1987). Perceived control and power in marriage: A study of marital decision making and task performance. *Personality and Social Psychology Bulletin, 13,* 73–82.

Malinowski, B. (1929). *The sexual life of savages.* New York: Harcourt Brace Jovanovich.

Mancini, J. A., & Blieszner, R. (1991). Aging parents and adult children: Research themes in intergenerational relations. In A. Booth (Ed.), *Contemporary families: Looking forward, looking back* (pp. 249–264). Minneapolis: National Council on Family Relations.

Margolin, L., & White, L. (1987). The continuing role of physical attraction in marriage. *Journal of Marriage and the Family, 49,* 21–27.

Markman, H. J., Stanley, S., & Blumberg, S. L. (1994). *Fighting for your marriage: Positive steps for preventing divorce and preserving a lasting love.* San Francisco: Jossey-Bass.

Martin, T. C., & Bumpass, L. L. (1989). Recent trends in marital disruption. *Demography, 26,* 37–51.

Masters, W. H., & Johnson, V. (1966). *Human sexual response.* Boston: Little, Brown.

Masters, W. H., Johnson, V., & Kolodny, R. C. (1988). *Masters & Johnson on sex and human loving.* Boston: Little, Brown.

Masters, W. H., Johnson, V., & Kolodny, R. C. (1992). *Human sexuality.* (4th ed.). New York: HarperCollins.

Masters, W. H., Johnson, V. E., & Kolodny, R. C. (1993). *Biological foundations of human sexuality.* New York: HarperCollins.

May, R. (1969). *Love and will.* New York: Norton

Mayo Foundation for Medical Education and Research. (1993). Sexuality and aging: What it means to be sixty or seventy or eighty in the '90s. *Mayo Clinic Health Letter* (February), pp. 1–8.

McAdoo, H. P. (1993). *Family ethnicity: Strength in diversity.* Thousand Oaks, CA: Sage.

McCaghy, C. (1968). Drinking and deviance disavowal: The case of child molesters. *Social Problems, 16,* 43–49.

McCubbin, H. I., & Patterson, J. (1982). Family adaptation to crises. In H. I. McCubbin, A. Cauble, & J. Patterson (Eds.), *Family stress, coping and social support.* Springfield, IL: Charles C. Thomas.

McDaniel, S. H., Hepworth, J., & Doherty, W. J. (1992). *Medical family therapy: A biopsychosocial approach to families with health problems.* New York: Basic Books.

McGoldrick, M., & Carter, S. (1989). Forming a re-married family. In S. Carter & M. McGoldrick (Eds.), *The family life cycle: A framework for family therapy* (pp. 265–294). New York: Allyn & Bacon.

McGoldrick, M., & Preto, N. G. (1984). Ethnic intermarriage: Implications for therapy. *Family Process, 23,* 347–364.

McIntosh, J. (1991). Middle-age suicide: A literature review and epidemiological study. *Death Studies, 15* (1), 21–38.

McLeod, B. (1986, July). The oriental express. *Psychology Today,* pp. 48–52.

McRoy, R. G., Grotevant, H. D., & Ayers-Lopez, S. (1994). *Changing practices in adoption.* Austin, TX: Hogg Foundation for Mental Health.

Mead, M. (1935). *Sex and temperament in three primitive societies.* New York: Morrow/Quill.

Medicine, B. (1981). American Indian family: Cultural change and adaptive strategies. *Journal of Ethnic Studies, 8* (4), 12–13.

Meier, P. (1991, January 6). War of words: Women talk about how men and women talk. Minneapolis *Star/Tribune, [First Sunday],* p. 8.

Melby, J. N., Conger, R. D., Conger, K. J., & Lorenz, F. O. (1993). Effects of parental behavior on tobacco use by young male adolescents. *Journal of Marriage and the Family, 55* (May), 439–454.

Mendenhall, T. J., Grotevant, H. D., & McRoy, R. G. (1996). Adoptive couples: Communication and changes made in openness levels. *Family Relations 45,* 223–229.

Meredith, W. H., Stinnett, N., & Cacioppo, B. F. (1985). Parent satisfactions: Implications for strengthening families. In R. Williams, H. Lingren, G. Rowe, S. Van Zandt, P. Lee, & N. Stinnett (Eds.), *Family strengths 6: Enhancement of interaction* (p. 147). Lincoln: University of Nebraska, Department of Human Development and the Family, Center for Family Strengths.

Metropolitan Life Insurance Co. (1993). Life expectancy in U.S. at selected ages (1991 estimates). In *World Almanac and Book of Facts* (p. 940). New York: World Almanac.

Meyer, D. R., & Garasky, S. (1993). Custodial fathers: Myths, realities, and child support policy. *Journal of Marriage and the Family, 55* (February), 73–89.

Michener, J. A. (1991). *The world is my home.* New York: Random House.

Miller, B. C., McCoy, J. K., Olson, T. D., & Wallace, C. M. (1986). Parental discipline and control attempts in relation to adolescent sexual attitudes and behavior.

Journal of Marriage and the Family, *48* (August), 503–512.

Miller, B. C., & Moore, K. A. (1991). Adolescent sexual behavior, pregnancy, and parenting: Research through the 1980s. In A. Booth (Ed.), *Contemporary families: Looking forward, looking back* (pp. 307–326). Minneapolis: National Council on Family Relations.

Miller, S., Wackman, D., Nunnally, E., & Miller, P. (1988). *Connecting with self and others.* Littleton, CO: Interpersonal Communication Programs.

Miller, S., Wackman, D., Nunnally, E., & Miller, P. (1989). *Connecting: Skills workbook.* Littleton, CO: Interpersonal Communication Programs

Mindel, C. H., Habenstein, R. W., & Wright, R., Jr. (Eds.). (1988). *Ethnic families in America: Patterns and variations* (3rd ed.). New York: Elsevier.

Mirandé, A. (1977). The Chicano family: A reanalysis of conflicting views. *Journal of Marriage and the Family* (November), 747–756.

Mirandé, A. (1979). A reinterpretation of male dominance in the Chicano family. *Family Coordinator* (October), 473–479.

Montagu, A. (1964). *Man's most dangerous myth: The fallacy of race.* Cleveland: World.

Montaigne, M. E. (1980). *Essays III* (Chapter 1, p. 5). In E. M. Beck (Ed.), *Familiar quotations: John Bartlett.* Boston: Little, Brown. (Original work published 1595)

Murstein, B. I. (1980). Mate selection in the 1970s. *Journal of Marriage and the Family*, *42* (4, November), 52–54.

Murstein, B. I. (1987). A classification and extension of the SVR theory of dyadic pairing. *Journal of Marriage and the Family*, *42*, 777–792.

Mussen, P. H. (1969). Early sex-role development. In D. A. Goslin (Ed.), *Handbook of socialization theory and research.* Chicago: Rand McNally.

Nadelson, C., & Sauzier, M. (1986). Intervention programs for individual victims and their families. In M. Lystad (Ed.), *Violence in the home: Interdisciplinary perspectives.* New York: Brunner/Mazel.

Nakonezny, P. A., Shull, R. D., & Rodgers, J. L. (1995). The effect of no-fault divorce law on the divorce rate across the 50 states and its relation to income, education, and religiosity. *Journal of Marriage and the Family*, *57* (2), 477–488.

National Council on Alcoholism. (1989). Facts about alcohol. New York: Author.

National Council on Alcoholism and Drug Dependence (NCADD). (1995). *If someone you love is an alcoholic.* New York: Author.

Nation's legal drugs may be its worst drugs. (1986, November 23). Lincoln [NE] *Sunday Journal/Star,* pp. 1D, 3D.

Neugarten, B. (1968). The awareness of middle age. In B. Neugarten (Ed.), *Middle age and aging.* Chicago: University of Chicago Press.

Neugebauer, R., Kline, J., O'Connor, P., Shrout, P., Johnson, J., Skodol, A., Wicks, J., & Susser, M. (1992). Determinants of depressive symptoms in the early weeks after miscarriage. *American Journal of Public Health*, *8* (October), 132.

Newman, I. (1990). Technical report 20: Adolescent tobacco use in Nebraska. Lincoln: Nebraska Prevention Center for Alcohol and Drug Abuse, University of Nebraska.

Niebuhr, R. (1988). Serenity prayer. In G. Carruth & E. Ehrlich (Eds.), *Harper book of American quotations.* New York: Harper & Row. (Original work published 1951)

Nilsson, L. (1990). *A child is born.* New York: Delacorte/Seymour Lawrence.

Nock, S. L. (1995). A comparison of marriages and cohabiting relationships. *Journal of Family Issues*, *16*, 53–76.

Norem, R. H., Schaefer, M., Springer, J., & Olson, D. H. (1980). *Effectiveness of premarital education programs: Outcome study and follow-up evaluations.* Unpublished manuscript. University of Minnesota, Department of Family Social Science, St. Paul.

Norton, A. J., & Mooran, J. E. (1987). Current trends in marriage and divorce among American women. *Journal of Marriage and the Family*, *49* (February), 5.

O'Farrell, T. (1992). Families and alcohol problems: An overview of treatment research. *Journal of Family Psychology*, *5* (March/June), 339–359.

O'Farrell, T. J., & Birchler, G. R. (1987). Marital relationships of alcoholic, conflicted, and nonconflicted couples. *Journal of Marital and Family Therapy*, *13*, 259–274.

Okimoto, J. D., & Stegall, P. J. (1987). *Boomerang kids: How to live with adult children who return home.* Boston: Little, Brown.

Olds, L. (1981). *Fully human.* Englewood Cliffs, NJ: Prentice-Hall.

Olds, S. B., London, M. L., & Ladewig, P. W. (1996). *Maternal-newborn nursing* (5th ed.). Redwood City, CA: Addison-Wesley Nursing.

Olson, D. H. (1989). *Alcoholic families and the Circumplex Model.* Unpublished manuscript. University of Minnesota, Family Social Sciences, St. Paul.

Olson, D. H. (1992). Marriage in perspective. In F. D. Fincham & T. N. Bradbury (Eds.), *Psychology of marriage: Basic issues and applications.* (pp. 402–419). New York: Guilford Press.

Olson, D. H. (1993). Circumplex model of marital and family systems: Assessing family functioning. In F.

Walsh (Ed.), *Normal family processes* (2nd ed.) (pp. 104–137). New York: Guilford Press.

Olson, D. H., & Cromwell, R. E. (1975). Power in families. In R. E. Cromwell & D. H. Olson (Eds.), *Power in families* (pp. 3–11). Newbury Park, CA: Sage.

Olson, D. H., & DeRubeis, F. (Eds.). (1987). *Inventory of marriage and the family.* Beverly Hills, CA: Sage.

Olson, D. H., Fournier, D. G., & Druckman, J. M. (1989). *PREPARE, PREPARE-MC and ENRICH inventories* (3rd ed.). Minneapolis: PREPARE/ENRICH.

Olson, D. H., & Kilmer Hanson, M. (Eds.). (1990). *2001: Preparing families for the future.* St. Paul, MN: National Council on Family Relations.

Olson, D. H., McCubbin, H. I., Barnes, H., Larsen, A., Muxen, M., & Wilson, M. (1989). *Families: What makes them work* (2nd ed.). Los Angeles, CA: Sage.

Olson, D. H., Portner, J., & Bell, R. (1986). *FACES II.* St. Paul: University of Minnesota, Family Social Science.

Olson, D. H., Russell, C. S., and Sprenkle, D. H. (1989). *Circumplex Model: Systemic assessment and treatment of families.* New York: Haworth Press.

Olson, J. S., & Wilson, R. (1984). *Native Americans in the twentieth century.* Chicago: University of Illinois Press.

Orr, C., & Van Zandt, S. (1987). The role of grandparenting in building family strengths. In H. G. Lingren, L. Kimmons, P. Lee, G. Rowe, L. Rottmann, L. Schwab, & R. Williams (Eds.). *Family strengths 8–9: Pathways to well-being* (pp. 259–272). Lincoln: University of Nebraska, Department of Human Development and the Family, Center for Family Strengths.

Osmond, M. W., & Thorne, B. (1993). Feminist theories: The social construction of gender in families and society. In P. G. Boss, W. J. Doherty, R. LaRossa, W. R. Schumm, & S. K. Steinmetz (Eds.), *Sourcebook of family theories and methods* (pp. 591–622). New York: Plenum.

Parker Pen Co. (1985). *Do's and taboos around the world.* Elmsford, NY: Benjamin.

Parkerson, G. R., Broadhead, E., & Tse, C. J. (1995). Perceived family stress as a predictor of health-related outcomes. *Archives of Family Medicine, 23,* 357–360.

Parkman, A. M. (1992). *No-fault divorce: What went wrong?* Boulder, CO: Westview Press.

Parsons, T. (1955). The American family: Its relations to personality and the social structure. In T. Parsons & R. F. Bales, *Family socialization and interaction process* (pp. 3–21). Glencoe, IL: Free Press.

Parsons, T. (1965). The normal American family. In S. M. Farber, P. Mustacchi, & R. H. L. Wilson (Eds.), *Man and civilization: The family's search for survival* (pp. 31–50). New York: McGraw-Hill.

Parsons, T., & Bales, R. F. (1955). *Family socialization and interaction process.* Glencoe, IL: Free Press.

Pearce, J. K. (1980). Ethnicity and family therapy. In J. K. Pearce & L. J. Friedman (Eds.), *Family therapy: Combining psychodynamics and family systems approaches.* New York: Grune & Stratton.

Peele, S. (1985). *The meaning of addiction.* Lexington, MA: Lexington Books/Heath.

Pence, E., Duprey, M., Paymar, M., & McDonnell, C. (1989). *The justice system's response to domestic assault cases: A guide for policy development.* Duluth, MN: Domestic Abuse Intervention Project.

Peplau, L. A., & Amaro, H. (1982). Understanding lesbian relationships. In W. Paul, et al. (Eds.), *Homosexuality: Social, psychological, and biological issues.* Beverly Hills, CA: Sage.

Peplau, L. A., Padesky, C., & Hamilton, M. (1981). Satisfaction in lesbian relationships. *Journal of Homosexuality, 8,* 23–35.

Perls, F. (1969). *Gestalt therapy verbatim* (p. 4). Lafayette, CA: Real People Press.

Peters, M. F. (1981). Strengths of Black families. In N. Stinnett, J. DeFrain, K. King, P. Knaub, & G. Rowe (Eds.), *Family strengths 3: Roots of well-being* (pp. 73–91). Lincoln: University of Nebraska Press.

Peters, S., Wyatt, G. E., & Finkelhor, D. (1986). Prevalence. In D. Finkelhor (Ed.), *Sourcebook on child sexual abuse* (pp. 15–59). Beverly Hills, CA: Sage.

Peterson, K. S. (1992a, March 12). Adults should know status of parents. *USA Today,* p. 1D.

Peterson, K. S. (1992b, March 12). Parents hand down financial attitudes. *USA Today,* p. 4D.

Peterson, K. S., & Lee, F. (1985, March). Most find the single life isn't lonely. *USA Today,* p. 1B.

Pink, J. E. T., & Wampler, K. S. (1985). Problem areas in stepfamilies: Cohesion, adaptability, and the stepfather-adolescent relationship. *Family Relations, 34,* 327–335.

Pittman, F. S. (1985). Children of the rich. *Family Process, 24* (December), 461–472.

Pittman, F. (1993a, June). Beyond betrayal: Life after infidelity. *Psychology Today,* 32–38, 78, 80, 82.

Pittman, F. (1993b). *Private lies: Infidelity and the betrayal of intimacy.* New York: Norton.

Planned Parenthood Federation of America. (1985). Five ways to prevent abortion (and one way that won't). In *Family matters* (Spring 1989), p. 2. Lincoln, NE: Planned Parenthood of Lincoln.

Poinsett, A. (1988, April). A crusade against sexual myths. *Ebony,* pp. 108, 110, 112.

Poussaint, A. (1982, August). What every Black woman should know about Black men. *Ebony,* pp. 36–40.

Raeburn, P. (1995, September 23). Drugs may alter drop in abortion availability. Lincoln [NE] *Journal Star,* p. 3A.

Raven, B. H., Centers, R., & Rodrigues, A. (1975). The bases of conjugal power. In R. E. Cromwell & D. H. Olson (Eds.), *Power in families* (pp. 217–232). Newbury Park, CA: Sage.

Reiss, D. (1981). *The family's construction of reality.* Cambridge, MA: Harvard University Press.

Reiss, I. L., & Lee, G. R. (1988). *Family systems in America* (4th ed.). New York: Holt, Rinehart & Winston.

Rempel, J. (1985). Childless elderly: What are they missing? *Journal of Marriage and the Family, 47* (2), 343–348.

Rettig, K. D. (1986). *Social decision making.* St. Paul: Minnesota Extension Service, University of Minnesota.

Rettig, K. D., Christensen, D. H., & Dahl, C. M. (1991). Impact of child support guidelines on the economic well-being of children. *Family Relations, 40,* 167–175.

Rettig, K. D., & Hogan, M. J. (1993). Educating for family resource management. In M. Arcus, J. Schvaneveldt, & J. Moss (Eds.), *Handbook of family life education, Vol. 2* (pp. 115–154). Newbury Park, CA: Sage.

Richards, L. N., & Schmiege, C. J. (1993). Problems and strengths of single-parent families: Implications for practice and policy. *Family Relations, 42* (July), 277–285.

Ridley, C. A., Peterman, D. J., & Avery, A. W. (1978). Cohabitation: Does it make for a better marriage? *Family Coordinator* (April), 129–136.

Risman, B. J., Hill, C. T., Rubin, Z., & Peplau, A. (1981). Living together in college: Implications for courtship. *Journal of Marriage and the Family* (February), 77–83.

Robbins, C. C. (1987, May 25). Expanding power for Indian women. *New York Times,* pp. III, 1.

Robinson, I. E., Ziss, K., Ganza, B., Katz, S., & Robinson, E. (1991). Twenty years of the sexual revolution, 1965–1985: An update. *Journal of Marriage and the Family, 53* (February), 216–220.

Rodgers, R. H., & White, J. M. (1993). Family development theory. In P. G. Boss, W. J. Doherty, R. LaRossa, W. R. Schumm, & S. K. Steinmetz (Eds.), *Sourcebook of family theories and methods* (pp. 99–116). New York: Plenum.

Rodick, J. D., Henggler, S. W., & Hanson, C. L. (1985). An evaluation of Family Adaptability and Cohesion Evaluation Scales (FACES) and the Circumplex Model. *Journal of Abnormal Child Psychology, 14,* 77–87.

Rogler, L. H., & Cooney, R. S. (1984). *Puerto Rican families in New York City: Intergenerational processes.* Maplewood, NJ: Waterfront Press.

Roosa, M. W., Tein, J.-Y., Groppenbacher, N., Michaels, M., & Dumka, L. (1993). Mothers' parenting behavior and child mental health in families with a problem drinking parent. *Journal of Marriage and the Family, 55* (February), 107–118.

Root, M. P. P. (Ed.). (1992). *Racially mixed people in America.* Newbury Park, CA: Sage.

Roscoe, B., & Benaske, N. (1985). Courtship violence experienced by abused wives: Similarities in patterns of abuse. *Family Relations, 34,* 419–424.

Rosenblatt, P. C., Karis, T. A., & Powell, R. D. (1995). *Multiracial couples: Black and White voices.* Thousand Oaks, CA: Sage.

Rosenfeld, J. A. (1991). Bereavement and grieving after spontaneous abortion. *American Family Physician, 6* (May), 1679.

Rosenstein, H. (1973, May). On androgyny. *Ms.,* p. 38.

Ross, C. E., Mirowsky, J., & Goldsteen, K. (1991). The impact of the family on health: The decade in review. In A. Booth (Ed.), *Contemporary families: Looking forward, looking back* (pp. 1059–1078). Minneapolis: National Council on Family Relations.

Rubin, L. B. (1985). *Just friends: The role of friendship in our lives.* New York: Harper & Row.

Rueter, M. A., & Conger, R. D. (1995). Antecedents of parent-adolescent disagreements. *Journal of Marriage and the Family, 57* (May), 435–448.

Russell, D. E. H. (1986). *The secret trauma: Incest in the lives of girls and women.* New York: Basic Books.

Rybash, J. W., Roodin, P. A., & Santrock, J. W. (1991). *Adult development and aging* (2nd ed.). Dubuque, IA: Wm. C. Brown.

Sable, P. (1989). Attachment, anxiety, and loss of a husband. *American Journal of Orthopsychiatry, 59* (October), 550–556.

Safilios-Rothschild, D. (1976). A macro- and micro-examination of family power and love: An exchange model. *Journal of Marriage and the Family, 37* (May), 355–362.

Salholz, E. (1990, February 26). Politics and the pill. *Newsweek,* p. 42.

Schaninger, C. M., & Buss, W. C. (1986). A longitudinal comparison of consumption and finance handling between happily married and divorced couples. *Journal of Marriage and the Family, 48* (February), 129–136.

Schepers, C. J. (1991, November 17). Proof mounting: Passive smoke kills. Lincoln [NE] *Journal/Star,* p. 1J.

Schickedanz, J., Schickedanz, D., Hansen, K., & Forsyth, P. (1993). *Understanding children* (2nd ed.). Mountain View, CA: Mayfield.

Schnaiberg, A., & Goldenberg, S. (1989). From empty nest to crowded nest: The dynamics of incompletely-launched young adults. *Social Problems, 36* (June), 251–269.

Schoen, R. (1992). First unions and the stability of first marriages. *Journal of Marriage and the Family, 54* (May), 281–284.

Schuchardt, J., & Guadagno, M. A. N. (1991). A comparison of lower middle income two-parent and single-mother families. *Family Economics Review, 4* (2), 9–17.

Schultz, N. C., Schultz, C. L., & Olson, D. H. (1991). Couple strengths and stressors in complex and simple stepfamilies in Australia. *Journal of Marriage and the Family, 53,* 555–564.

Schwartz, J., Raine, G., & Robins, K. (1987, May 11). A "superminority" tops out. *Newsweek,* pp. 48–49.

Schwartz, P. (1994, September/October). Peer marriage: What does it take to create a truly egalitarian relationship? *Family Therapy Networker,* 57–61, 92.

Seltzer, J. A. (1991). Relationships between fathers and children who live apart: The father's role after separation. *Journal of Marriage and the Family, 53,* 79–101.

Selye, H. (1974). *The stress of life* (2nd ed.). New York: McGraw-Hill.

Sheehy, G. (1976). *Passages: Predictable crises of adult life.* New York: Dutton.

Sheehy, G. (1992). *The silent passage: Menopause.* New York: Random House.

Shorris, E. (1992). *Latinos: A biography of the people.* New York: Norton.

Shostak, A. (1987). Singlehood. In M. Sussman & S. Steinmetz (Eds.), *Handbook of Marriage and the Family.* New York: Plenum.

Silverstein, L. B. (1995). Fathering is a feminist issue. *Psychology of Women Quarterly, 20,* 3–37.

Simons, R. L., Johnson, C., Beaman, J., & Conger, R. D. (1993). Explaining women's double jeopardy: Factors that mediate the association between harsh treatment as a child and violence by a husband. *Journal of Marriage and the Family, 55* (August), 713–723.

Simpson, J. C. (1989, March 27). Beware of paper tigers. *Time,* pp. 104–105.

Skolnick, A. S., & Skolnick, J. H. (1977). *Family in transition.* Boston: Little, Brown.

Somers, M. S. (1993). A comparison of voluntarily child-free adults and parents. *Journal of Marriage and the Family, 55* (August), 643–650.

Spanier, G. S., & Thompson, L. (1984). *Parting: The aftermath of separation and divorce.* Newbury Park, CA: Sage.

Spitze, G., Logan, J. R., Deane, G., & Zerger, S. (1994). Adult children's divorce and intergenerational relationships. *Journal of Marriage and the Family, 56* (May), 279–293.

Springer, J. S., Fournier, D., & Olson, D. H. (1985). *Commitment and conflict across premarital relationship stages.* Unpublished manuscript. University of Minnesota, Department of Family Social Science, St. Paul.

St. Pierre, T. L., Mark, M. M., Kaltreider, D. L., & Aikin, K. J. (1995). A 27-month evaluation of a sexual activity prevention program in Boys and Girls Clubs across the nation. *Family Relations, 44,* 69–77.

Staples, R., & Mirandé, A. (1980). Racial and cultural variations among American families: A decennial review of the literature on minority families. *Journal of Marriage and the Family, 42,* 887–903.

Stark, E. (1985, June). Androgyny makes better lovers. *Psychology Today,* p. 19.

Stark, E. (1986, October). Young, innocent and pregnant. *Psychology Today,* pp. 28–30, 32–35.

Stark, E., & Flitcraft, A. (1985). Woman-battering, child abuse and social heredity: What is the relationship? *Sociological Review Monograph, 31,* 147–171.

Stauss, J. (1986). The study of American families: Implications for applied research. *Family Perspective, 20* (4), 337–350.

Steinberg, L., Lamborn, S. D., Darling, N., Mounts, N. S., & Dornbusch, S. M. (1994). Over-time changes in adjustment and competence among adolescents from authoritative, authoritarian, indulgent, and neglectful families. *Child Development, 65,* 754–770.

Steinmetz, S. K. (1987). Family violence. In M. B. Sussman & S. K. Steinmetz (Eds.), *Handbook of marriage and the family* (pp. 725–765). New York: Plenum.

Sternberg, D., & Beier, E. G. (1977). Marital communication: Changing patterns of conflict. *Journal of Communications, 27,* 97–99.

Sternberg, R. J. (1986). A triangle theory of love. *Psychological Review, 93,* 119–135.

Sternberg, R., & Barnes, M. (Eds.). (1988). *The psychology of love.* New Haven, CT: Yale University Press.

Stets, J. E., & Henderson, D. A. (1991). Contextual factors surrounding conflict resolution while dating: Results from a national study. *Family Relations, 40,* 29–36.

Stets, J. E., & Straus, M. A. (1989). The marriage as a hitting license: A comparison of assaults in dating, cohabiting, and married couples. In M. A. Pirog-Good & J. E. Stets (Eds.), *Violence in dating relationships* (pp. 33–52). New York: Greenwood Press.

Stewart, K. L. (1988). Stress and adaptation: A multi-system model of individual, couple, family, and work systems. (Doctoral dissertation, University of Minnesota, Family Social Science, St. Paul). *Dissertation Abstracts International, 49,* 8A, p. 2410. (University Microfilms No. 88-23570).

Stewart, K. L., & Olson, D. H. (1990). *Predicting premarital satisfaction on PREPARE using background factors.* Unpublished manuscript. PREPARE/ENRICH, Inc., Minneapolis.

Stierlin, H. (1972). *Separating parents and adolescents: A perspective on running away, schizophrenia, and waywardness.* New York: Quadrangle.

Stinnett, N., & DeFrain, J. (1985). *Secrets of strong families.* Boston: Little, Brown.

Stinnett, N., Sanders, G., & DeFrain, J. (1981). Strong families: A national study. In N. Stinnett, J. DeFrain, K. King, P. Knaub, & G. Rowe (Eds.), *Family strengths 3: Roots of well-being* (pp. 33–42). Lincoln: University of Nebraska Press.

Stinnett, N., Stinnett, N., DeFrain, J., & DeFrain, N. (1997, in press). *Good families.* New York: Doubleday.

Straus, M. A. (1989). *Physical abuse of children and spouses.* Paper presented at the annual meeting of the National Council on Family Relations. Durham: University of New Hampshire, Family Research Laboratory, Family Violence Research Program.

Straus, M. A. (1990). The national family violence surveys. In M. Straus & R. J. Gelles (Eds.). *Physical violence in American families* (pp. 3–16). New Brunswick, NJ: Transaction Books.

Straus, M. A., (1994). *Beating the devil out of them.* New York: Free Press.

Straus, M. A., & Gelles, R. J. (1986). Societal change and change in family violence from 1975 to 1985 as revealed by two national surveys. *Journal of Marriage and the Family, 48,* 465–479.

Straus, M. A., Gelles, R. J., & Steinmetz, S. (1980). *Behind closed doors: Violence in the American family.* Garden City, NY: Doubleday/Anchor Press.

Straus, M., & Sweet, S. (1992). Verbal/symbolic aggression in couples: Incidence rates and relationships to personal characteristics. *Journal of Marriage and the Family, 54* (May), 346–357.

Stroup, A., & Pollock, G. E. (1994). Economic consequences of marital dissolution. *Journal of Divorce and Remarriage, 22* (1/2), 37–54.

Stuart, R. B. (1980). *Helping couples change.* New York: Guilford Press.

Study: 1 of 3 women are abuse victims. (1995, November 15). Lincoln [NE] *Journal Star,* p. 6A.

Stull, D. E., Bowman, K., & Smerglia, V. (1994). Women in the middle: A myth in the making? *Family Relations, 43,* 319–324.

Surra, C. A. (1991). Research and theory on mate selection and premarital relationships. In A. Booth (Ed.), *Contemporary families: Looking forward, looking back* (pp. 54–75). Minneapolis: National Council on Family Relations.

Sweeney, J. (1982, June 21). Taking the long view of marriage: Why do some endure? *Los Angeles Times,* pp. 1, 21–23.

Swift, C. (1986). Preventing family violence: Family-focused programs. In M. Lystad (Ed.), *Violence in the home: Interdisciplinary perspectives.* New York: Brunner/Mazel.

Tannen, D. (1990). *You just don't understand: Women and men in conversation.* New York: Morrow.

Taylor, P. (1988, March 20). It's time to put warnings on alcohol. *New York Times,* p. B2.

Teen moms sexually abused as kids. (1987, September 16). Lincoln [NE] *Star,* p. 40.

Thomas, V., & Olson, D. H. (1993). Problem families and the Circumplex Model: Observational assessment using the clinical rating scale. *Journal of Marital and Family Therapy, 19* (2), 159–175.

Thomson, E., & Colella, U. (1992). Cohabitation and marital stability: Quality or commitment? *Journal of Marriage and the Family, 54* (May), 259–267.

Thorne, B. (1982). Feminist rethinking of the family: An overview. In B. Thorne (Ed.), *Rethinking the family* (pp. 1–24). New York: Longman.

Tiesel, J. W. (1992). *Family system and adolescent development: A meta-analysis.* Unpublished manuscript. University of Minnesota, Family Social Science, St. Paul.

Timberlake, E. M. (1980). The value of grandchildren to grandmothers. *Journal of Gerontological Social Work, 3,* 63–76.

Touliatos, J. (Ed.). (1993). *Inventory of marital and family literature.* Minneapolis: National Council on Family Relations.

Troll, L. E. (1989). Myths of mid-life intergenerational relationships. In S. Hunter & M. Sundel (Eds.), *Mid-life myths: Issues, findings, and practice implications.* Newbury Park, CA: Sage.

Troll, L. E. (1994). Family-embedded vs. family-deprived oldest-old: A study of contrasts. *International Journal of Aging and Human Development, 38* (1), 51–64.

Trotter, R. J. (1986, September). The three faces of love. *Psychology Today,* pp. 46–54.

Turnbull, C. (1983). *The human cycle.* New York: Touchstone/Simon & Schuster.

U.S. Advisory Board on Child Abuse and Neglect. (1990). *Child abuse and neglect: Critical first steps in response to a national emergency.* Washington, DC: U.S. Government Printing Office, p. 1.

U.S. Bureau of the Census. (1989). *Statistical abstract of the United States* (109th ed.). Washington, DC: U.S. Government Printing Office.

U.S. Bureau of the Census. (1991). *Statistical abstract of the United States* (111th ed.). Washington, DC: U.S. Government Printing Office.

U.S. Bureau of the Census. (1994). *Statistical abstract of the United States* (114th ed.). Washington, DC: U.S. Government Printing Office.

U.S. Bureau of the Census. (1995). *Statistical abstract of the United States* (115th ed.). Washington, DC: U.S. Government Printing Office.

U.S. Department of Justice. (1989). *Crime in the United States, 1988* (p. 13). Washington, DC: U.S. Department of Justice, Federal Bureau of Investigation.

Van Zandt, S., Mou, R., & Abbott, D. (1989). Mental and physical health of rural bereaved and nonbereaved elders: A longitudinal study. In D. A. Lund (Ed.), *Older bereaved spouses: Research with practical applications.* New York: Hemisphere.

Veevers, J. (1980). *Childless by choice.* Scarborough, Ontario: Butterworth.

Vega, W. A. (1991). Hispanic families in the 1980s. In A. Booth (Ed.), *Contemporary families: Looking forward, looking back* (pp. 297–306). Minneapolis: National Council on Family Relations.

Vega, W. A. (1995). The study of Latino families. In R. Zambrana (Ed.), *Understanding Latino families* (pp. 3–17). Thousand Oaks, CA: Sage.

Vega, W. A., Patterson, T., Sallis, J., Nader, P., Atkins, C., & Abraham, I. (1986). Cohesion and adaptability in Mexican American and Anglo families. *Journal of Marriage and the Family, 48* (November), 857–867.

Veroff, J., Douvan, E., & Kulka, R. A. (1981). *The inner American: A self portrait from 1957 to 1976.* New York: Basic Books.

Visher, E. B. (1989). The Stepping Ahead Program. In M. Burt (Ed.), *Stepfamilies stepping ahead* (3rd ed.) (pp. 57–89). Lincoln, NE: Stepfamilies Press.

Visher, E. B., & Visher, J. S. (1988). *Old loyalties: New ties.* New York: Brunner/Mazel.

Visher, E. B., & Visher, J. S. (1992). *How to win as a stepfamily* (2nd ed.). New York: Brunner/Mazel.

von Bertalanffy, L. (1968). *General system theory: Foundation, development, applications.* New York: Braziller.

Voydanoff, P. (1991). Economic distress and family relations: A review of the eighties. In A. Booth (Ed.), *Contemporary families: Looking forward, looking back* (pp. 429–445). Minneapolis: National Council on Family Relations.

Voydanoff, P., Donnelly, B. W., & Fine, M. A. (1988). Economic distress, social integration and family satisfaction. *Journal of Family Issues, 9,* 545–564.

Walker, A. J., Pratt, C. C., & Oppy, N. C. (1992). Perceived reciprocity in family caregiving. *Family Relations, 41* (January), 82–85.

Walker, A. J., Shin, H.-Y., & Bird, D. N. (1990). Perceptions of relationship change and caregiver satisfaction. *Family Relations, 39* (April), 147–152.

Walker, A. J., & Thompson, L. (1984). Feminism and family studies. *Journal of Family Issues, 5* (4), 545–570.

Walker, L. (1979). *The battered woman.* New York: Harper & Row.

Waller, W. (1951). *The family* [revised by R. Hill]. New York: Dryden.

Wallerstein, J. S., & Blakeslee, S. (1989). *Second chances: Men, women and children a decade after divorce.* New York: Ticknor & Fields.

Walsh, F., & Olson, D. H. (1989). Utility of the Circumplex Model with severely dysfunctional family systems. In D. H. Olson, C. S. Russell, & D. H. Sprenkle (Eds.), *Circumplex Model: Systemic assessment and treatment of families.* New York: Haworth Press.

Warmbrod, M. T. (1982). Alternative generation in marital problem solving. *Family Relations, 31,* 503–511.

Waters, H. F. (1985, September 2). Cosby's fast track. *Time,* pp. 50–56.

Watson, R. E. L. (1983). Premarital cohabitation vs. traditional courtship: Their effects on subsequent marital adjustment. *Family Relations, 32* (January), 139–147.

Weiss, R. S. (1973). *Loneliness: The experience of emotional isolation.* Cambridge: Massachusetts Institute of Technology.

Weitzman, L. J. (1985). *The divorce revolution: The unexpected social and economic consequences for women and children in America.* New York: Free Press.

Weitzman, L. J., & Dixon, R. B. (1980). The transformation of legal marriage through no-fault divorce. In A. Skolnick & J. H. Skolnick (Eds.), *Family in transition.* Boston: Little, Brown.

West, M. O., & Prinz, R. J. (1987). Parental alcoholism and childhood psychopathology. *Psychology Bulletin, 102,* 204–218.

Whelan, E. (1995, August 31). Some Republicans want more regulations on tobacco. Lincoln [NE] *Journal Star,* p. 4B.

Whitaker, C. (1979). Personal communication [from a teleconference dialogue between Whitaker and graduate students in the Department of Human Development and the Family, University of Nebraska–Lincoln].

Whitam, F. L. (1983). Culturally invariable properties of male homosexuality: Tentative conclusions from cross-cultural research. *Archives of Sexual Behavior, 12,* 207–226.

White, G. L. (1980). Physical attractiveness and courtship progress. *Journal of Personality and Social Psychology, 39,* 660–668.

White, L. K. (1991). Determinants of divorce: A review of research in the eighties. In A. Booth (Ed.), *Contemporary families: Looking forward, looking back* (pp. 141–149). Minneapolis: National Council on Family Relations.

Whitman, C. T. (1995, May 31). Wheaton College commencement address. *Good Morning America.* New York: CBS Television.

Wiener, N. (1956). *I am a mathematician.* New York: Doubleday.

Wilhelm, M. S., & Ridley, C. A. (1988). Unemployment induced adaptations. *Lifestyles, 9,* 5–20.

Willie, C. V. (1988). *A new look at Black families* (3rd ed.). Dix Hills, NH: General Hall.

Winch, R. F. (1958). *Mate selection: A study of complementary needs.* New York: Harper.

Winch, R. F. (1971). *The modern family* (3rd ed.). New York: Holt, Rinehart & Winston.

Winston, M. R. (1994). Dealing with depression and anger: Reactions of family caregivers. *Caring, 13* (8), 52–54.

Woehrer, C. E. (1989). Ethnic families in the Circumplex Model: Integrating nuclear with extended family systems. In D. H. Olson, C. S. Russell, & D. H. Sprenkle (Eds.), *Circumplex Model: Systemic assessment and treatment of families.* New York: Haworth Press.

A woman's fertility window opens six days each month. (1995, December 7). Lincoln [NE] *Journal Star,* pp. 1A, 7A.

Woodman, S. (1986, February). How important is sex? *Self,* pp. 130–131.

Woodward, J. C. (1988). *The solitude of loneliness.* Lexington, MA: Lexington Books/Heath.

Wright, H. N. (1980). *Premarital counseling: A follow-up study.* Unpublished manuscript. Christian Marriage Enrichment, 8000 East Girard, Denver, CO.

Wrobel, G. M., Ayers-Lopez, S., Grotevant, H. D., McRoy, R. G., & Friedrick, S. (1996). Openness in adoption and the level of child participation. *Child Development, 67.*

Wuerffel, J., DeFrain, J., & Stinnett, N. (1990). How strong families use humor. *Family Perspective* (Fall), 129–142.

Wynne, L. (1958). Pseudo-mutuality in the family relations of schizophrenics. *Psychiatry, 21,* 205–222.

Yarrow, P. (1972). River of Jordan. *PP&M Lifelines.* Mary Beth Music, ASCAP. Burbank, CA: Warner Bros. Records.

Yi, S. (1984, October). Women progress. *World Press Review, 31,* 58.

Zigler, E., Rubin, N., & Kaufman, J. (1988, May). Do abused children become abusive parents? *Parents,* pp. 100–104.

Zill, N., Morrison, D. R., & Coiro, M. J. (1993). Longterm effects of parental divorce on parent-child relationships, adjustment, and achievement in young adulthood. *Journal of Family Psychology, 7,* 91–103.

Zuckerman, E. J. (1982). Viral hepatitis. *Practical Gastroenterology, 6* (16), 21–22.

Credits

TEXT CREDITS

Page 8: Copyright © 1996 by Houghton Mifflin Company. Adapted and reprinted by permission from *The American Heritage Dictionary of the English Language*, Third Edition.

Pages 87, 137: From *The Prophet* by Kahlil Gibran. Copyright © 1923 by Kahlil Gibran and renewed 1951 by Administrators C.T.A. of Kahlil Gibran Estate and Mary G. Gibran. Reprinted by permission of Alfred A. Knopf, Inc.

Page 88: "Poem" by Judy Altura. Copyright © 1974 by Judy Altura. From *My Needs, Your Needs, Our Needs* by Jerry Gillies. Used by permission of Doubleday, a division of Bantam Doubleday Dell Publishing Group, Inc.

Page 89: "Gestalt Prayer" by Fritz Perls. Copyright © 1969 by Real People Press. Copyright © 1992 by The Gestalt Journal Press. From *Gestalt Therapy Verbatim* by Fritz Perls. Used with permission of The Gestalt Journal Press.

Page 558: "River of Jordan." Copyright © 1972 Mary Beth Music. All Rights Reserved. Used by permission.

PHOTO CREDITS

Chapter 1 pg. 2, © Bachmann/The Image Works; pg. 6, © Mark Richards/PhotoEdit; pg. 20, © Joel Gordon; pg. 24, © R. Sidney/The Image Works; pg. 27, © David Young-Wolff/PhotoEdit; pg. 32, © Corbis-Bettmann

Chapter 2 pg. 42, © Jeffrey Dunn/Stock Boston; pg. 48, © 1996 Star Tribune/Minneapolis-St. Paul; pg. 49, © Joel Gordon 1987; pg. 50, © Tony Freeman/PhotoEdit; pg. 57, © Bob Daemmrich/The Image Works; pg. 62, © Tony Freeman/PhotoEdit; pg. 64, © Frank Siteman 1989/Jeroboam; pg. 67, © Robert Brenner/PhotoEdit; pg. 75, © David Lee/Motion Picture & Television Photo Archive

Chapter 3 pg. 78, © Bachmann/The Image Works; pg. 88, © Tony Freeman/PhotoEdit; pg. 96, © R. Sidney/The Image Works; pg. 102, © Amy C. Etra/ PhotoEdit; pg. 106, © Elizabeth Crews

Chapter 4 pg. 114, © Joel Gordon; pg. 118L, © H. Gans/The Image Works; pg. 118R, © Suzanne Arms; pg. 124, © 1987 Paramount/Motion Picture & Television Photo Archive; pg. 126, © Robert Brenner/PhotoEdit;

pg. 130, © Joel Gordon 1992; pg. 131, © Tony Freeman/PhotoEdit; pg. 136, © Felicia Martinez/PhotoEdit

Chapter 5 pg. 142, © Wojnarowicz/The Image Works; pg. 146, © M. Granitsas/The Image Works; pg. 149L, © Corbis-Bettmann; pg. 149R, © Topham/The Image Works; pg. 150, © Tony Savino/The Image Works; pg. 155, © Reuters/Susumu Takahashi/Archive Photos; pg. 156, © Gary Conner/PhotoEdit; pg. 161, © Barbara Alper/Stock Boston; pg. 165, © John Boykin/PhotoEdit; pg. 169, © Michael Newman/PhotoEdit; pg. 174, © Roberto Soncin Gerometta/Photo 20-20; pg. 178, © Richard Hutchings/PhotoEdit

Chapter 6 pg. 184, © Michael Newman/PhotoEdit; pg. 188, © Alán Gallegos/AG Photographs; pg. 189L, © Susan Van Etten/PhotoEdit; pg. 189R, © Explorer/Photo Researchers, Inc.; pg. 191, © S. Gazin/The Image Works; pg. 198, © Joel Gordon 1992; pg. 204, © Rhoda Sidney/PhotoEdit; pg. 215, © Suzanne Arms

Chapter 7 pg. 222, © Suzanne Arms; pg. 226, © Robert Brenner/PhotoEdit; pg. 229, © Margaret Miller/Photo Researchers, Inc.; pg. 232, © David Young-Wolff/PhotoEdit; pg. 239, © 1996 James Schnepf; pg. 242, © Bonnie Kamin; pg. 245, © Frozen Images/The Image Works; pg. 251, © Rob Crandall/Stock Boston

Chapter 8 pg. 256, © Joel Gordon 1994; pg. 261, © Gary Conner/PhotoEdit; pg. 264, © Jeff Greenberg/PhotoEdit; pg. 268, © Cynthia Dopkin/Photo Researchers, Inc.; pg. 276, © Robert Brenner/PhotoEdit; pg. 282, © Blair Seitz/Photo Researchers, Inc.

Chapter 9 pg. 286, © Robert Ullmann/Design Conceptions; pg. 289, © D. Littell Greco/Stock Boston; pg. 296, © Richard Hutchings/PhotoEdit; pg. 298, © Jeff Isaac Greenberg/Photo Researchers, Inc.; pg. 303, © Robert Brenner/PhotoEdit; pg. 310, © Fabricius & Taylor/Stock Boston

Chapter 10 pg. 314, © Frank Siteman/Stock Boston; pg. 318, © Bob Daemmrich/The Image Works; pg. 323, © Michael Newman/PhotoEdit; pg. 328, © Joe Sohm/ The Image Works; pg. 329, © Martin A. Levick; pg. 339, © Tony Freeman/PhotoEdit

Chapter 11 pg. 348, © Robert Llewellyn; pg. 351, © Robert Brenner/PhotoEdit; pg. 357, © Phiz Mezey; pg. 360, © Bob Daemmrich/The Image Works; pg. 363, © AP/Wide World Photos/Patrice Picot; pg. 377, © David Young-Wolff/PhotoEdit; pg. 378, © Tim McCarthy/PhotoEdit; pg. 380, © 1995 Strauss/Curtis

Chapter 12 pg. 386, © Elizabeth Crews; pg. 389, © Tony Freeman/PhotoEdit; pg. 391, Everett Collection; pg. 395, © Myrleen Ferguson/PhotoEdit; pg. 400, © Robert Brenner/PhotoEdit; pg. 403, © Myrleen Ferguson/PhotoEdit; pg. 411, © 1996 Steve McCurry/Magnum Photos, Inc.

Chapter 13 pg. 414, © Joel Gordon; pg. 417, © Bob Daemmrich/The Image Works; pg. 419, © David Young-Wolff/PhotoEdit; pg. 425, © Bill Bachmann/Stock Boston; pg. 428, © Joel Gordon 1990; pg. 430, © Rebecca Cooney/Actuality, Inc.; pg. 434, © S. O'Rourke/The Image Works; pg. 435, © Jonathan Nourok/PhotoEdit

Chapter 14 pg. 442, © Dennis MacDonald/PhotoEdit; pg. 449, © Tony Freeman/PhotoEdit; pg. 454, © M. Antman/The Image Works; pg. 455, © Peter Menzel/Stock Boston; pg. 462, © Bob Daemmrich/Stock Boston; pg. 466, © Antman/The Image Works

Chapter 15 pg. 474, © Will & Deni McIntyre/Photo Researchers, Inc.; pg. 480, Courtesy of the Ad Council; pg. 481, © D. Greco/The Image Works; pg. 484, © Dan Habib/Impact Visuals; pg. 489, © Mary Ellen Mark/Library; pg. 493, © Joel Gordon 1984; pg. 501, © David Young-Wolff/PhotoEdit

Chapter 16 pg. 506, © M. Siluk/The Image Works; pg. 511, © James L. Shaffer/PhotoEdit; pg. 515, © Robert Brenner/PhotoEdit; pg. 521, © Steven Ferry/P&F Communications; pg. 522, © Robert Llewellyn; pg. 524, © Tom Prettyman/PhotoEdit

Chapter 17 pg. 528, © Tony Freeman/PhotoEdit; pg. 532, © Tony Freeman/PhotoEdit; pg. 533, © Michael Newman/PhotoEdit; pg. 539, © Skjold Photographs; pg. 541, © Bachmann/The Image Works; pg. 548, © April Saul

Chapter 18 pg. 554, © Bachmann/PhotoEdit, pg. 559, Courtesy NASA; pg. 565, © Michael Newman/PhotoEdit; pg. 570, © F. Pedrick/The Image Works; pg. 573, © Russell Schleipman/Offshoot Stock

Subject Index

Boldface numbers indicate pages on which key terms are defined.